**Blackstone's** Police Manual

# General Police Duties

**Blackstone's**
Police Manual

# General Police Duties

2004

Fraser Sampson

LLB, LLM, MBA, Solicitor

OXFORD
UNIVERSITY PRESS

# OXFORD
**UNIVERSITY PRESS**

Great Clarendon Street, Oxford OX2 6DP

Oxford University Press is a department of the University of Oxford.
It furthers the University's objective of excellence in research, scholarship,
and education by publishing worldwide in

Oxford New York

Auckland Bangkok Buenos Aires Cape Town Chennai
Dar es Salaam Delhi Hong Kong Istanbul Karachi Kolkata
Kuala Lumpur Madrid Melbourne Mexico City Mumbai Nairobi
São Paulo Shanghai Taipei Tokyo Toronto

Oxford is a registered trade mark of Oxford University Press
in the UK and certain other countries

Published in the United States
by Oxford University Press Inc., New York

A Blackstone Press Book

First edition 1998
Second edition 1999
Third edition 2000
Fourth edition 2001
Fifth edition 2002
Sixth edition 2004

The moral rights of the author have been asserted
Database right Oxford University Press (maker)

British Library Cataloguing in Publication Data
Data available

Library of Congress Cataloging in Publication Data
Data available
ISBN 0-19-926247-0

1 3 5 7 9 10 8 6 4 2

Typeset by Newgen Imaging Systems (P) Ltd., Chennai, India
Printed in Great Britain
on acid-free paper by
Ashford Colour Press, Gosport, Hampshire

# Contents

# Preface

The pressure to develop and apply occupational standards continues for the police. In moving towards these standards, the service is having to revisit many of the old debates about the depth and breadth of legal knowledge that can be properly expected of its officers and staff. Police staff of all ranks and position are expected—not unreasonably—by those they serve and by the courts to know the law. However, as the additions to all of the Manuals in this series show, the area that is now becoming recognised as Police Law is being made and implemented at a dizzying pace (no pun intended). By and large, the responsibility for keeping abreast of these legal developments is still left to the individual—and, in trying to keep up, individuals within the police service turn to *Blackstone' Police Manuals* as their first port of call.

The leading reference source on Police Law, and used by officers of all ranks, as well as lawyers, advisers—and even the odd judge—the Manuals have grown considerably in popularity as well as size. Plans to make the Manuals available in electronic format and to supplement them with other operationally focused materials mean that they will become more accessible and comprehensive than ever, providing an invaluable policing tool for the future.

The Manuals are fully indexed and cross-referenced and are published each year to keep them up to date, doing away with the need for inserts or supplements. More importantly for OSPRE candidates, if the law isn't in the latest edition of the Manual, it won't be in the exam.

This Manual addresses both specific areas of police legislation—such as powers of arrest, search and seizure—and also the myriad of other legal areas that affect operational policing. The expansion of the 'police family' and the rapidly changing roles of those, sworn and unsworn, who are tasked with delivering policing services, has brought about a correlative expansion in this Manual, which might be more appropriately titled General *Policing* Duties following the changes introduced by the Police Reform Act 2002. The topics covered touch on some of the most hard-fought and jealously guarded constitutional rights and duties in our legal system. Increased empowerment and education of the police has made maintaining the balance between the exercise of necessarily wide policing powers and the legitimate expectations of those who are subjected to them more tricky and technical than ever. In attempting that daunting feat, the wider policing family would perhaps do well to remember the most important police duty of all—the exercise of discretion. As Lord Scarman observed in his report into the Brixton disorders, that discretion—the art of suiting action to circumstance—is critical to effective and acceptable policing, and forms a police officer's daily task.

While every care has been taken to ensure the accuracy of the contents of this Manual, neither the author nor the publishers can accept any responsibility for any actions taken, or not taken, on the basis of the information contained in this Manual.

The law is stated as at 22 July 2003.

# Acknowledgements

*Blackstone's Police Manuals* are the product, not just of the authors and the editorial team, but also of the wide and varied input of many people—police officers serving and retired, junior and senior, uniformed, detectives and specialists; human resources and support staff; supporters and detractors; lawyers and lecturers; friend and foe.

Thanks in particular to George Cooper of Northamptonshire Police, Paul Murphy of Greater Manchester Police, Mr Paul Stephenson and Detail Technologies. I would also like to thank the Crown Prosecution Service for permission to include the Public Order Charging Standards.

Thanks also go to Heather, Ruth and Mandy, Jane and Marianne and, Alistair MacQueen. Thanks as ever to CC, TA and AC for their support.

# Foreword

In the 21st century, police officers must demonstrate a wide range of knowledge, skills, and abilities—not only if they are to perform effectively in their current role, but also if they are seeking to gain promotion to higher ranks within the service. The knowledge and understanding of relevant law and procedure remains central to the role of any officer, as does the ability to effectively apply this law and procedure in their day-to-day duties.

The *Blackstone's Police Manuals* are presented in four volumes—crime, evidence and procedure, road traffic and general police duties. The manuals have been fully updated to reflect recent changes in legislation, including the 2003 revisions to the PACE Codes of Practice. Oxford University Press work alongside Centrex to ensure that the books are fully accurate and up-to-date, and reflect the content which is required by a police officer in today's service.

The *Blackstone's Police Manuals* are primarily designed to assist candidates preparing for the Sergeants' and Inspectors' OSPRE Part I Police Promotion Examination. In serving this purpose, the books should be used in combination with the official OSPRE Rules & Syllabus document. You may have received a copy of this document when you obtained these manuals. However, additional copies of the Rules & Syllabus can be downloaded from the Employers' Organisation for Local Government website at www.lg-employers.gov.uk.

From a wider perspective, the Manuals are also designed to provide an ongoing reference point for officers seeking to keep their professional knowledge up-to-date. Moreover, the Manuals continue to be widely used by officers seeking a concise explanation of specific aspects of the law they use in their day-to-day duties.

Centrex continues to play a key role within the modern police service through assisting officers in their ongoing professional development. The OSPRE system, developed and delivered by Centrex Examinations & Assessment, not only selects tomorrow's managers and supervisors, but also assists candidates in developing themselves professionally in the knowledge and skills required for these ranks. I believe the Blackstone's Police Manuals continue to play a central role in this process.

If you are using the books to prepare for the OSPRE Promotion Examinations, may I take this opportunity to wish you the best of luck in your studies, and I hope the books will assist you in progressing your career within the service.

Chris Mould
Centrex
Chief Executive

# Table of Cases

# Table of Statutes

# Table of Statutory Instruments

# Police

# 1 | Police

## 1.1 Police legislation

Until recently, the Police Act 1996 has been the principal piece of legislation affecting the maintenance and operation of police services in England and Wales for the past decade. Setting out, among other things, the various police areas (see sch. 1), the requirements for membership of police authorities (schs 2 and 3) and the affirmation to be taken by constables when they are sworn in (sch. 4), the Act imposes requirements for the submission of local policing plans and gives the Secretary of State wide powers in relation to the setting of performance targets, budgetary provisions and alteration of police areas. However, the Act has been extended and revised in a number of key aspects by another significant piece of legislation—the Police Reform Act 2002. During its rocky passage through the parliamentary process, the Police Reform Bill generated considerable debate and was seen by some as altering forever the basis on which policing in England and Wales is delivered. The resultant Police Reform Act 2002, however, represents probably the most significant piece of legislation affecting the way in which policing is controlled and managed across England and Wales in the last 50 years. Amending many pieces of other legislation, including the Police Act 1996, the Police Reform Act 2002 widens the government's ambitious plans for reforming the ways in which policing services are planned, provided and measured, and builds upon some of the recent features that have already been put into place.

The Police Act 1996 continues to set out key offences relating to police officers and is the source of the regulation of efficiency, conduct and complaints for officers of all ranks.

The clear thrust of all this legislation is towards clear and identifiable professional standards, greater flexibility and, above all, greater accountability in the delivery of policing services. As a result, the legislation—both primary and subordinate—is full of targets, performance indicators, measures and plans. What this chapter sets out to do is to unravel some of the legislative provisions that lie beneath the whole complex business of policing in a broader sense, and that will drive policing policy and practice in the future. Those aspects of the Police Reform Act 2002 that affect these issues of planning, provision and measurement are set out in this chapter, while others relating to areas of operational police law have been included throughout the relevant chapters of this and the other Manuals in this series.

### 1.1.1 Policing services and jurisdiction

Home Office police services

Police officers in Home Office services in England and Wales derive their jurisdiction from s. 30 of the Police Act 1996, which states:

> (1) A member of a police force shall have all the powers and privileges of a constable throughout England and Wales and the adjacent United Kingdom waters.

**KEYNOTE**

Section 29 requires that every 'member of a police force' maintained for a police area (as set out in sch. 1) must be attested as a constable by making the appropriate declaration. In its Report on Police Training and Recruitment, the Home Affairs Committee (1999) recommended that probationer constables are not sworn in (or 'attested') until they have completed six months' service. This recommendation was made as a result of evidence received by the Committee to the effect that it was often difficult to deal with newly-appointed officers who showed themselves to be unsuited to or unfit for service. Among the many changes it makes to the constitution of the police service of England and Wales, the Police Reform Act 2002 has removed the nationality bar that formerly prevented non-UK or Commonwealth citizens from joining the police (see s. 82). The Act also alters the wording of the oath that all police constables must take on being attested under the Police Act 1996. The new wording—which is to be found in schedule 4 to the 1996 Act—makes it clear that police officers have a duty to uphold the rights of, and to protect, *all* people in England and Wales (and their property), not simply Her Majesty's subjects as contained in the previous wording. In addition, officers being attested (sworn in) in Welsh forces will have an alternative version of the oath, written in the Welsh language (see the Attestation of Constables (Welsh Language) Order 2002, SI 2002 No. 2312). For further details, see *Preparing for Police Duty* published by Oxford University Press.

Special constables (**see below**) are appointed under s. 27 and are also required to be attested (sworn in) in the same way as members of a police force. Under s. 28, cadets may be appointed by a chief officer to undergo training with a view to their becoming members of that police force.

All regular police officers are required to serve for a probationary period. At the time of writing this period is generally two years but the government has announced plans for this to be revised in line with the changes to the Probationer Training Programme. The statutory instrument providing for the period of probation (the Police Regulations 2003, SI No. 527) allows a chief officer to extend the probationary period (reg. 12). Regulation 13 allows a chief officer to dispense with the services of a police constable during their probationary period at any time if the chief officer considers that the constable is not fitted, physically or mentally, to perform the duties of that office, or that he or she is not likely to become an efficient or well-conducted constable (see reg. 13(1)). The same regulation allows a constable to give notice of his or her retirement to the relevant police authority before being discharged under reg. 13(1) (see reg. 13(3)).

In addition to the general restrictions placed on police officers once attested, the Police Regulations 2003 also require officers to provide a sample of hair or saliva in order to allow a DNA profile to be obtained. These samples are primarily for elimination purposes and are to be stored separately from samples obtained in investigations. For further guidance see Home Office Circular 40/2002.

Occasionally, responsibility for the direction and control of constables in one geographic area is transferred to a chief officer of another Police Service (e.g. under the transitional arrangements for boundary changes within the Metropolitan Police—see the Greater London Authority Act 1999 (Consequential and Transitional Provisions) (Police) Order 1999 (SI 1999 No. 3272)).

Note that the Criminal Justice and Public Order Act 1994 provides for cross-border enforcement of powers of arrest and the execution of warrants; and the Terrorism Act 2000 allows constables to exercise certain powers anywhere in the UK (**see chapter 2**).

The Police Act 1997

The Police Act 1997 was passed in order to:

- make provisions for the National Criminal Intelligence Service and the National Crime Squad;
- make provision for the Police Information Technology Organisation;
- enable the entry on and interference with property and wireless telegraphy in the prevention or detection of serious crime;

- provide for the issue of certificates about criminal records; and
- make administrative provisions for the police.

### National Criminal Intelligence Service

Part I of the Police Act 1997 provides for the continued operation of the National Criminal Intelligence Service (NCIS) under a 'service authority'. The NCIS Service Authority is made up of police service, police authority and independent members, together with a Home Office representative. It has a 'core membership' with the National Crime Squad (**see below**) but, given its very wide geographical and professional boundaries, the Authority also includes representatives of the Secretaries of State for Scotland and Northern Ireland and HM Customs and Excise.

The 1997 Act sets out rules for the administration, organisation and funding of NCIS, together with provisions for the appointment of its Director General.

The statutory functions of NCIS are generally to gather, store and analyse information in order to provide criminal intelligence to police services throughout the UK, as well as to other law enforcement agencies, domestically and internationally. NCIS has a particularly important role in the maintaining of intelligence on football spectators (**see chapter 4**) and sex offenders (**see Crime, chapter 10**).

Many of the statutory conditions relating to police officers as members of their own force (e.g. pensions, membership of the Police Federation, etc.) were extended by the Act to include police officers seconded to NCIS. Officers seconded to central services under s. 97(1)(ca) of the Police Act 1996 (see s. 9(9A)(a) of the Police Act 1997, as amended by the Police Reform Act 2002 and Annex L of the Home Office Guidance on Police Unsatisfactory Performance, Complaints and Misconduct Procedures), although they remain constables in most instances, are not treated as 'members of a police force' and are not subject to the Regulations relating to discipline or conduct. Sections 37 to 40 of the Police Act 1997, however, make provision for discipline and complaints in relation to NCIS members and the relevant Regulations are to be found in the NCIS (Complaints) Regulations 1998 (SI 1998 No. 641), as amended.

The post of Director General of NCIS is no longer restricted to police officers in the rank of chief constable and the Police Reform Act 2002 has opened the role up to suitable qualified and experienced non-police managers. The Act will also enable NCIS to recruit police officers of any rank directly from forces across England and Wales (as well as Scotland, Northern Ireland and a number of non-Home Office forces) rather than simply second them for a limited period (see s. 86). As a result, provision has also been made to allow regulations governing the career paths and human resources structures of permanent NCIS officers (s. 88). The Director General may designate any NCIS employee as an Investigating Officer under s. 38(3) of the Police Reform Act 2002. For the powers that can be given to a designated Investigating Officer **see chapter 2**.

For the Home Secretary's objectives in relation to NCIS, see the National Criminal Intelligence Service (Secretary of State's Objectives) Order 2002 (SI 2002 No. 778).

### National Crime Squad

Part II of the Police Act 1997 created a new concept in British policing: a National Crime Squad (NCS). Like NCIS above, the National Crime Squad also operates under a 'service authority' headed by a Director General. The 1997 Act merged the former Regional Crime Squads into a national investigative body to address major national and international crime and made similar provisions in relation to the constitution of the NCS to those governing NCIS. The NCS Service Authority consists of police service, police authority and independent members, together with a Home Office representative. Although it shares the 'core membership' with NCIS (see above), the NCS authority membership does not extend beyond representatives from England and Wales.

The primary statutory function of the NCS is to prevent and detect serious crime which is of relevance to one or more police areas in England and Wales.

The NCS has previously seconded its sworn constables from the 43 Home Office forces of England and Wales and, in this respect, has been more limited by its available pool of officers than NCIS. The Police Reform Act 2002 amends the Police Act 1997 to allow for the direct recruitment of police officers of any rank into the NCS from the 43 Home Office forces as well as from Scotland, Northern Ireland and a number of non-Home Office forces (s. 87). As with NCIS, regulations governing the career paths and human resources structures of permanent NCS officers are needed and the Police Reform Act 2002 makes provision for this (s. 89).

The Director General may designate any NCS employee as an Investigating Officer under s. 38(3) of the Police Reform Act 2002. For the powers that can be given to a designated Investigating Officer, see chapter 2.

For the Home Secretary's objectives in relation to NCS, see the National Crime Squad (Secretary of State's Objectives) Order 2002 (SI 2002 No. 779).

### Intrusive surveillance

A further measure introduced by the Police Act 1997 also makes provisions for the use of highly specialised and intrusive measures to combat crime. Part III provides for the appointment of a Chief Commissioner and other commissioners to oversee the operation of the powers under this part of the Act. It also identifies 'authorising officers' who may grant the relevant authority with the power to use intrusive surveillance techniques under the strict criteria set out in the Act. The whole area of surveillance and interference with property—particularly to the levels covered by part III—is acutely sensitive in the light of the Human Rights Act 1998. The law regulating the use of surveillance and interception of communications generally is addressed by the Regulation of Investigatory Powers Act 2000 (as to which see Crime, chapter 3).

### Criminal records certificates

Following the former government's White Paper, *On the Record*, together with the report into the murders by Thomas Hamilton (*Report of the Public Inquiry into the Shootings at Dunblane Primary School on 13 March 1996*, Cm 3386), there was a need to create a comprehensive national criminal record collection going beyond that held at New Scotland Yard (the National Identification Service). Part V of the Police Act 1997 (as amended) provides for the creation of a new Criminal Records Bureau which is able to access the data on the Police National Computer and which will issue different types of criminal conviction certificate in response to 'searches' on certain individuals. Requests for such certificates in respect of individuals who have criminal records are not restricted to police officers and are intended to help employers and others 'vet' applications for certain posts or positions, in particular those posts or positions that require contact with children (see Crime, chapter 11). The 1997 Act creates offences in relation to false information and provides for a Code of Practice but again the potential erosion of fundamental freedoms has created some anxiety among commentators.

### Police Information Technology Organisation

The Police Information Technology Organisation (PITO) was set up in 1996 without statutory status. However, the increasingly demanding and diverse requirements of centralised IT support for all police agencies brought about the statutory provisions now to be found in part IV of the Police Act 1997, which makes PITO a non-departmental public body.

In this respect, PITO differs from NCIS and the NCS above. Whereas those two bodies are Service Authorities with special provisions as to their legal capacity and liability, PITO is simply a 'body corporate' (see s. 109(1) of the 1997 Act) carrying out certain limited statutory functions. As PITO's role has developed, however, the need for greater flexibility in altering its constitution, powers and structures has become apparent. The Police Reform Act 2002 introduces (by s. 99) the powers to do just that without having to resort to primary legislation.

Police officers seconded to PITO come under the provisions of s. 97 of the Police Act 1996 but there are no special provisions in relation to their conduct or the handling of complaints. Therefore, where an officer seconded to PITO is the subject of a complaint or the provisions of the Regulations relating to misconduct or efficiency, it would seem that he/she can only be dealt with on his/her return to force (see s. 97(6)).

### Other police services

There are several other full-time police services in Great Britain with statutory policing functions. These include:

- British Transport Police (BTP)—see the British Transport Commission Act 1949 and the Transport Act 1962.
- Ministry of Defence Police (MDP)—see the Ministry of Defence Act 1987.
- UK Atomic Energy Authority Police—see the Atomic Energy Authority Act 1954.
- Ports Police—see, e.g., the Port of London Act 1968 and the Harbour, Docks and Piers Clauses Act 1847.

The jurisdiction of the first two of these forces has been extended over recent years, e.g. by the Anti-terrorism, Crime and Security Act 2001. The Police Reform Act 2002 has made a number of further changes to the jurisdiction of both the BTP and the MDP. As well as opening up the opportunities for officers from these—and other—forces to join and be seconded to NCIS and the NCS, the Act makes many other changes, some of which are summarised below.

### Ministry of Defence Police

Part 5 of the Police Reform Act 2002 is devoted to the MDP and introduces many changes affecting the force, including:

- a new s. 2B in the Ministry of Defence Police Act 1987 extending the jurisdiction of MDP officers when serving under the direction and control of a Home Office force chief officer while on secondment to that force;
- changing the discipline framework to allow it to mirror, as far as possible, that applicable to Home Office forces;
- bringing the MDP within the inspection remit of Her Majesty's Inspector of Constabulary on a statutory basis;
- amending firearms legislation so as to enable MDP recruits/potential recruits to use firearms without the need for a certificate during training or assessment.

### British Transport Police

Other sections of the Police Reform Act 2002 amend various legislative provisions affecting the BTP, including:

- bringing the chief constable into the definition of relevant authorities who can apply for Anti-Social Behaviour Orders (ASBOs—**see chapter 3**) (s. 61);
- providing the Chief Constable with powers to accredit suitable people with limited policing powers under a Railway Safety Accreditation Scheme (**see chapter 13**);

- extending the jurisdiction of officers of or above the rank of superintendent to exercise the powers under s.16 of the Crime and Disorder Act 1998 (removal of truants—**see Evidence & Procedure, chapter 8**);
- extending the relevant provisions of the Road Traffic Offenders Act 1988 relating to fixed penalty regime (as to which **see Road Traffic, chapter 14**), allowing BTP officers to take part in the scheme within their own jurisdiction.

For details of the protocols between non-Home Office forces and other forces see Home Office Circulars 23–25/2002.

### Special constables

The terms under which special constables may be appointed and deployed are also set out in s. 30 of the Police Act 1996. Section 30(2) states:

> (2) A special constable shall have all the powers and privileges of a constable in the police area for which he is appointed and, where the boundary of that area includes the coast, in the adjacent United Kingdom waters.

---

**KEYNOTE**

Special constables have all the powers and privileges of constables in other police areas to which they are sent as part of a mutual aid scheme. They also have jurisdiction in areas contiguous, i.e., next to their own. In the case of special constables in the City of London police, this includes areas contiguous to the Metropolitan Police District. The profile of special constables has increased recently, particularly in light of the concept of the 'extended police family' (**see below and chapter 2**) brought about by the Police Reform Act 2002. Section 35 of the Police Reform Act 2002 effectively allows the Secretary of State to make regulations in relation to the conduct and discipline of special constables.

---

### The extended police family

In addition to introducing the National Policing Plan (**see para. 1.1.3**) and all its other provisions relating to the management and measurement of police services, the Police Reform Act 2002 also brought with it the concept of the 'extended police family'. Some family members, such as the special constabulary (above), have been around for many decades, while other non-sworn members, like street and neighbourhood wardens, are a relatively new thing. However, as well as giving all these contributors to the wider policing service greater publicity, the Police Reform Act 2002 also gave some of them statutory powers—and created a few more family groups at the same time.

The status, powers and restrictions on the newer arrivals to the extended police family are discussed in the next chapter and also in other Manuals in this series. It suffices to say at this stage that the government's reforms in relation to policing are based partly on the premise that policing is far too complicated, important and widespread a business to be left entirely to the police. One of the key distinctions that help make sense of the many new policing roles put in place by the 2002 Act is whether the individual is a sworn constable or not. Full and part-time members of *any* police force who are sworn in as, and have the statutory powers of, a constable are generally unaffected by the fairly complex legislation extending the policing family. So far as these constables are concerned, the key issue remains that of jurisdiction.

## 1.1.2 Vicarious liability of chief officers

Section 88 of the Police Act 1996 originally provided that a chief officer will be vicariously liable for the 'torts' (civil wrongs) of his/her officers committed in the performance (or purported performance) of their duties. This meant that the chief officer was responsible for the payment of any damages arising out of a civil claim in respect of such a tort (for the situation regarding discrimination and other employment matters generally, **see chapter 12**). The extent of this vicarious liability was wider than that imposed on employers generally (see comments of the Court of Appeal in *Weir* v *Chief Constable of Merseyside Police* [2003] EWCA Civ 111).

However, despite the fact that the vicarious liability of chief officers was broader than that of any ordinary employer, its limitation to strictly actionable civil wrongs was felt to have led to some inequities, denying remedies to individuals while failing to impose full accountability on the relevant chief officers. The Police Reform Act 2002 has clarified the position and amends s. 88 to provide that chief officers will be liable for the 'unlawful conduct' (as opposed to purely civil wrongs) of their officers and employees when acting as such (s. 102). Section 88 does not apply in the case of officers seconded to central services such as the NCS or the Central Police Training and Development Authority. However, s. 102 makes parallel amendments to the liability of the relevant Directors General and other individuals in such cases.

### 1.1.3 The national policing plan

Following the passage of the Police Reform Act 2002, the first annual National Policing Plan for England and Wales was introduced to Parliament in November 2002. Section 1 of the Act requires the Home Secretary to prepare an annual National Policing Plan and to publish it by 30 November each year. Before the Plan there was no single document or central system co-ordinating and guiding all the various performance indicators, priorities and development plans of the many policing stakeholders. This situation, whereby the government, police authorities, chief officers and other key groups referred to different sources, focusing on different priorities and working to different timescales in setting out their various plans for the future, was seen as something of a weakness in the overall ability of the police service to plan strategically. The Plan's purpose, therefore, is to set out strategic national priorities for the police service as a whole, along with the indicators against which the service will be judged. So what of local policing plans and the varying needs of individual police forces? The Plan takes account of these local conditions and aims to set out a 'strategic national overview' against which chief officers and police authorities can (and must) prepare their own local three-year policing plans (see s. 92). These three-year strategy plans are themselves a new feature introduced by the Act and are designed to get chief officers and their police authorities to focus on medium and longer-term direction for their forces. In drafting these three-year plans a chief officer must have regard to the views of the public in his or her force area using the procedures already in place under the Police Act 1996. The Secretary of State will issue and revise guidance on the form and content of these plans and will consult relevant organisations and individuals before doing so. Before finalising the three-year plan a police authority must submit it to the Secretary of State who will inform the police authority whether it is inconsistent with the National Policing Plan (see generally s. 6A). The calendar for drafting, submission and implementation of three-year plans is to be set out in regulations.

According to the National Policing Plan, the primary objective for the duration of the three-year plan is:

to deliver improved policing performance and greater public reassurance with particular regard to the following priorities:

- Tackling anti-social behaviour, and disorder.
- Reducing volume crime, street, drug-related and violent and gun crime in line with local and national targets.

- Combating serious and organised crime operating across force boundaries.
- Increasing the number of offences brought to justice.

Each of these four priorities is expanded upon in the Plan which goes on to provide specific guidance to chief officers in the practical steps that they should take. For instance, the Plan provides that the first priority should be supported by the careful use of Crime and Disorder Reduction Partnerships (CDRPs), the deployment of Police Community Support Officers (**see chapter 2**) and other auxiliary staff and the use of tools such as the Anti-Social Behaviour Order (**see chapter 3**).

The National Policing Plan places strong emphasis on the establishment and maintenance of partnerships with local and national agencies and fits within a new framework being introduced by the government for the improved effectiveness and 'professionalisation' of the police. Other features of this framework include the introduction of the Police Standards Unit, the establishment of CENTREX (the Central Police Training and Development Authority which replaced National Police Training after the passage of the Criminal Justice and Police Act 2001) and a National Centre for Policing Excellence.

### Measuring performance and promoting good practice

Central to all of these changes in the way in which the police are managed are the features of performance measurement and the promotion of good practice across the service. These features are apparent in some earlier legislation, such as the Police (Efficiency) Regulations 1999 (SI 1999 No. 732) (**see para. 1.2.1**) and the Best Value requirements under the Local Government Act 1999 (**see para. 1.1.5**) and these earlier provisions still remain as relevant, as indeed are the Police (Efficiency) (Amendment) Regulations 2003 (SI 2003 No. 527). Amendments. In furthering the broader ends of performance enhancement for the police service as a whole, the Police Reform Act 2002 builds upon these existing schemes and introduces a three-tier framework of rules. The first tier consists of regulations. Legally binding, these regulations will tell chief officers, police authorities and others what they are required to do. An example of the regulations will be those made under s. 6 of the Act standardising police equipment, headgear and vehicles. Codes of practice are the second tier and, though not legally binding, chief officers and others will be required to take them into account when tackling the relevant issues. An example of these will be the code of practice to be issued to chief officers concerning the use of Police Community Support Officers and other members of the 'wider police family' (as to which **see chapter 2**). In drafting any codes of practice, the National Centre of Policing Excellence and CENTREX will take the lead role; they will also be consulted in the drafting of any regulations under the first tier. The third tier of governance under the Act is purely guidance which is advisory in nature. Although this tier is entirely advisory, any failure to observe its content may be the subject of comment in litigation arising out of the relevant powers or procedures covered.

The Home Office has also published a series of Public Service Agreements (PSAs) and these are set out at the back of the National Policing Plan. These PSAs cover many of the activities of all criminal justice agencies, not just the police (**see appendix 8**), with PSAs 1 and 2 being the key ones for the police. It can be seen that the PSAs are directly linked to the four policing priorities in the National Policing Plan above.

### Increased accountability

In addition to the measures arising out of s. 1, the Police Reform Act 2002 also contains new powers and procedures aimed at increasing the accountability, efficiency and effectiveness of the police service. The passage of the whole Bill through Parliament was frequently described as 'turbulent' and many aspects of it were indeed vociferously and extensively debated. But the aspects that gave rise to some of the lengthiest and fiercest exchanges were those that follow below as they were viewed by some as an erosion (if not wholesale abandonment) of the operational independence of chief officers. The legislation was eventually passed, having been substantially amended, and it contains a number of procedural safeguards designed to preserve the tripartite structure of policing (chief officers, police authorities and the Home Office) that has been at the heart of policing in England and Wales for over 50 years.

The Police Reform Act 2002 contains new powers for the Secretary of State to order inspections of police forces (and *parts* of police forces), along with inspections of other policing organisations such as NCIS and the NCS. By amending the Police Act 1996, the 2002 Act empowers the Secretary of State to give directions to a police authority where an inspection report by Her Majesty's Inspector of Constabulary (HMIC) is of the opinion that all or part of the force inspected is not efficient or effective, or will cease to be efficient or effective unless remedial measures are taken (see s. 40). In the event of any such report being received from the HMIC, the Secretary of State may direct the police authority to take 'remedial measures'. Any direction to this effect must be made by the Secretary of State in a report laid before Parliament and *only* after the police authority and the chief officer have been given sufficient information about the Secretary of State's grounds and an opportunity to make representations about them. In addition, the police authority must have been given the opportunity to make proposals for any remedial measures that would make any direction by the Secretary of State unnecessary. The Secretary of State must then consider all representations and proposals before he/she has the power to direct any remedial measure to be taken. If the Secretary of State considers that remedial measures are needed, he/she can direct the police authority to submit an action plan, drafted by the chief officer within a matter of weeks. The Secretary of State may make regulations setting out the specific procedure to be followed in these cases (an example of the 'first tier' of measures under the Police Reform Act 2002 discussed above). These provisions are extended to include bodies such as NCIS and the NCS (see the Police Reform Act 2002, sch. 1).

In essence, the statutory procedure gives the chief officer and the relevant police authority notice of those areas highlighted for improvement and the opportunity to put things right before the Home Secretary can intervene. As such, it is anticipated that these new powers will only be used in the rarest of cases—if at all.

### 1.1.4 Crime and disorder strategies

Sections 5 and 6 of the Crime and Disorder Act 1998 placed a statutory responsibility on police services and local authorities to formulate and implement crime and disorder strategies for their respective areas. These sections sought to build upon the work that had already been done in the area of crime prevention before the 1998 Act was passed and follow some of the proposals put forward in the report commissioned by the Home Office Standing Conference on Crime Prevention, 'Safer Communities; The Local Delivery of Crime Prevention through the Partnership Approach 1991' (the Morgan Report). Crime and Disorder Reduction Partnerships were set up under the Crime and Disorder Act 1998 and involved chief officers of police and local authorities formulating and implementing strategies to reduce crime and disorder in their areas. The statutory framework placed a duty on the police to co-operate with a number of other agencies such as the probation service.

A further duty to act in co-operation with other agencies was imposed by the Crime and Disorder Act 1998. Those bodies and agencies, which included:

- schools and educational institutions.
- the Crown Prosecution Service

- youth services, and

- local stakeholder groups

were similarly under an obligation to co-operate with the responsible authorities in exercising these functions.

Section 97 of the Police Reform Act 2002 extends these provisions in several ways. It includes police and fire authorities in the list of responsible authorities required to formulate and implement crime and disorder reduction strategies and adds the appropriate health organisations (Primary Care Trusts in England and the relevant health authority in Wales) to the list. The amended legislation also requires the formulation and implementation of strategies to combat substance misuse, placing the delivery of the National Drugs Strategy on a statutory footing and involving Drug Action Teams (DATs) in the case of England and Drug and Alcohol Action Teams (DAATs) in Wales.

As this legislation is concerned with matters affecting local government, various provisions are made to reflect the different constitutional positions and processes between England and Wales, with the Welsh Assembly being given relevant powers as appropriate.

Crime and Disorder Reduction Partnerships must be submitted to the Secretary of State and must be compiled with regard to any guidance issued by him/her (see ss. 97 and 98).

Before formulating their strategies, the responsible authorities must have carried out a review of the levels and patterns of crime and disorder, taking into account the knowledge and experience of people in the area (s. 6(2)). They must then have published a report of that review and taken account of the views of any bodies and individuals prescribed by the Secretary of State on its contents.

Under s. 6(4) of the 1998 Act the strategy must contain at least:

- objectives to be pursued

- long-term performance targets, and

- short-term performance targets.

The strategy must be published within the relevant area and must be kept under review with a view to monitoring its effectiveness, making any changes that appear necessary or expedient.

## 1.1.5 Best value

Section 3 of the Local Government Act 1999 states:

> (1) A best value authority must make arrangements to secure continuous improvement in the way in which its functions are exercised, having regard to a combination of economy, efficiency and effectiveness.

---

**KEYNOTE**

Section 1 defines what 'best value authorities' are and includes police authorities (s. 1(1)(d)).
'Police authority' for these purposes means—

  (a) a police authority established under section 3 of the Police Act 1996;

  (b) the Common Council of the City of London in its capacity as a police authority;

  (c) the Metropolitan Police Authority.

Therefore, all police authorities in England and Wales are under a statutory duty to comply with the 'best value' requirements imposed by the 1999 Act and by any subsequent regulations.

The key features to note in relation to best value are:

- continuous improvement,
- economy,
- efficiency, and
- effectiveness.

For the purpose of evaluating their functions under s. 3, many services have adopted the Audit Commission's inspection criteria of what are called the four 'C's':

- Challenging—the way in which functions are carried out.
- Consulting—all those people who have an interest in the relevant function.
- Comparing—benchmarking a function against that of other organisations.
- Competing—demonstrating the competitive way in which the function is exercised.

Best value is not about cheapness and cost-cutting; rather it is concerned with achieving the best practicable results with the available resources. It replaces the former requirement for public bodies to engage in compulsory competitive tendering. Section 3 goes on to provide that, for the purpose of deciding how to fulfil the duty arising under subsection (1), an authority must consult:

- representatives of persons liable to pay any tax, precept or levy to or in respect of the authority,
- representatives of persons liable to pay non-domestic rates in respect of any area within which the authority carries out functions,
- representatives of persons who use or are likely to use services provided by the authority, and
- representatives of persons appearing to the authority to have an interest in any area within which the authority carries out functions.

'Representatives' of groups for these purposes means people who appear to the authority to be representative of that group (s. 3(3)).

In deciding who to consult and when, best value authorities must have regard to guidance issued by the Secretary of State (s. 3(4)).

---

### Best value plans and performance indicators

More detailed requirements on the production of best value policies and the conducting of best value reviews are set out in the Local Government (Best Value) Performance Plans and Reviews Order 1999 (SI 1999 No. 3251). Under this Order, best value authorities such as police authorities must conduct their first review of all their functions by 31 March 2005. The Order contains a schedule setting out the areas that police performance indicators must cover, and includes aspects such as answering 999 calls, detecting crime and handling complaints.

In addition, police authorities have their own required performance indicators. The Police Authorities (Best Value) Performance Indicators Order 2003 (SI 2003 No. 1265) sets out a series of categories of indicators within its schedules, which include Citizen Focus, Reducing and Investigating Crime, Promoting Safety and Security, Helping the Public and Resource Usage for Measuring the Performance of an Authority in this area (**see appendix 7**).

Police authorities are also covered by the more general provisions of the Local Government (Best Value) Performance Indicators and Performance Standards Order 2002 (SI 2002 No. 523). Here the relevant indicators are also community safety-related and are set out at sch. 2 (**see appendix 7**).

Specific performance indicators for Wales are set out in the Local Government (Best Value Performance Indicators) (Wales) Order 2002 (SI 2002 No. 757 (W.80))—(**see appendix 7**).

The Local Government Act 1999 extends the remit of HMIC to include reporting on best value requirements.

Policing plans produced under s. 8 of the Police Act 1996 (see above) must also include any action proposed for the purposes of complying with best value requirements. Failure to comply with the best value requirements may result in the Secretary of State exercising any or all of the many powers granted under the 1999 Act and possibly transferring responsibility for exercising the relevant function to another organisation. Most, if not all, police services will have a best value officer and the Home Office can provide detailed advice and guidance on compliance with the duties imposed by s. 3 of the 1999 Act.

1.1.6 **The Police Federation and trade union membership**

Part III of the Police Act 1996 makes provision for the establishment and maintenance of police representative institutions.

Section 59 provides for the continued existence of the Police Federation and specifies that it may represent a police officer in any proceedings brought under Regulations made under s. 50(3) (e.g. efficiency and conduct; see below) or an appeal from such proceedings.

The Secretary of State may make Regulations in relation to matters concerning the Federation (s. 60(1)), e.g. the Police Federation Regulations 1969 (SI 1969 No. 1787), as amended.

Provision is made under s. 61 for a Police Negotiating Board to represent the interests of police authorities and members in relation to:

- hours of duty
- leave
- pay and allowances
- pensions
- clothing, equipment and accoutrements.

Section 64 of the Police Act 1996 states:

(1) Subject to the following provisions of this section, a member of a police force shall not be a member of any trade union, or of any association having for its objects, or one of its objects, to control or influence the pay, pensions or conditions of service of any police force.

---

**KEYNOTE**

Where a person was a member of a trade union before becoming a member of a police service, he/she may, with the consent of the chief officer of police, continue to be a member of that union during the time of his/her service (s. 64(2)).

Whether any body is a trade union or an association to which s. 64 applies will be determined by the chief registrar of friendly societies (s. 64(3)).

---

Section 64(5) states:

(5) Nothing in this section applies to membership of the Police Federations, or of any body recognised by the Secretary of State for the purposes of this section as representing members of police forces who are not members of those Federations.

1.2 **Conduct, complaints and efficiency**

Police officers are not 'employees' for most purposes as they are not employed under contracts as such; they are public office holders (see *Fisher* v *Oldham Corporation* [1930] 2 KB 364; see also *Sheikh* v *Chief Constable of Greater Manchester Police* (1989) ICR 373). For this reason a significant number of the employment rights given to workers in other occupations do not apply to police officers. They cannot bring claims for wrongful dismissal because these are *contractual* claims. Similarly, they are prevented by statute from claiming unfair dismissal and some other protection that is given to ordinary employees by the Employment Rights Act 1996. However, for some purposes (e.g. sex and race discrimination) chief officers are treated *as if they are employers* of their officers. This has caused some technical difficulties in practice (**see chapter 12**). These categories have become blurred even further by recent events. So, for instance, some non-Home Office police officers *do have* a contract for service with their 'employer' (e.g. British Transport Police—see *Spence* v *British Railways Board* [2001] ICR 232). In addition, some of the Police Reform Act 2002 rules allow individuals who are employees in the strict sense to potentially be placed outside the full statutory protection for employees (by the Employment Rights Act 1996, s. 200) because they have the powers and privileges of constables. And for some purposes, statutes refer to the European concept of 'workers' which, being a wider concept than 'employees', often *does* apply to the police. An example of this expression can be found in the Working Time Regulations 1998 (SI 1998 No. 1833). Workers—which include a number of healthcare and emergency personnel—are generally protected under the Public Interest Disclosure Act 1998. At the time of writing, this 'whistleblowers' Act is not applicable to police officers but the Home Office intends to invoke the relevant enabling section of the Police. Reform Act 2002 to extend the protection to the police by April 2004.

So why does any of this matter? Because it explains why the police have had to be given their own statutory framework for dealing with complaints, conduct and efficiency—the subject of the next part of this chapter.

From 1 April 1999 a number of very significant changes were made to the procedures governing the performance and conduct of, and complaints against, police officers. These changes amended some previously existing procedures and process but also introduced some entirely new ones.

Under s. 83 of the Police Act 1996, the Secretary of State may issue guidance to police authorities, chief officers and the members of their police services in respect of the discharge of their functions in matters of performance, conduct and complaints. The Home Office has issued police services with such guidance and its contents are admissible in any proceedings under the various Regulations. More importantly, the guidance specifies that its provisions must be followed unless there is good reasons for departing from them. However, the guidance does not form part of the Regulations and, if it is incompatible with the Regulations in any respect, the Regulations will prevail.

The sources of the changes are to be found mainly within the Police Act 1996 and the various Regulations made under them. What follows is an attempt to steer a path through many of those new pieces of legislation. To this end, this part of the chapter is set out in four sections:

- unsatisfactory performance;
- misconduct;
- complaints; and
- appeals.

Note that there is a general duty for all police officers to obey lawful orders (see reg. 20 of The Police Regulations 2003) (SI 2003 No. 527).

1.2.1    **Unsatisfactory performance**

The Regulations give police managers an objective structure by which to evaluate and address any suspected failures to meet the required standard of performance by their police staff.

Who?

These procedures are generally set out in the Police (Efficiency) Regulations 1999 (SI 1999 No. 732). They do not apply to:

- officers above the rank of chief superintendent;

- probationers;

- cadets; and

- non-warranted (civilian) staff

each of whom has their own specific procedures. For the provisions relating to probationary constables and their dismissal, see regs 12 and 13 of the Police Regulations 2003 (SI 2003 No. 527). For special constables, see s. 27(2) of the Police Act 1996 and the Special Constables Regulations 1965 (SI 1965 No. 536), as amended. Section 35 of the Police Reform Act 2002 allows the Secretary of State to make regulations in relation to the conduct and discipline of special constables (as to which **see para. 1.1.1**). For cadets, see s. 28(2) of the Police Act 1996 and the Police Cadets Regulations 1979 (SI 1979 No. 1727), as amended.

Part 3 of the Police Reform Act 2002 has introduced new measures for the removal, suspension, resignation and disciplining of chief officers. While legislation has provided some extensive measures to deal with officers of up to and including the rank of chief superintendent for many years, the range of options open to police authorities and/or the Secretary of State in relation to chief officers whose conduct or performance has been in question has been very limited. Former legislation meant that chief officers could be required to retire in the interests of effectiveness and efficiency but there are two main reasons why this has not been entirely satisfactory. First is the fact that this is a very restricted option which will not always be appropriate under the circumstances (especially given the cost) and second is the fact that chief officers are being appointed at a younger age than in the past.

In essence, what the new framework set up by the Police Reform Act 2002 does is to provide a system whereby officers of ACPO rank can be suspended or removed by their police authority, either of the authority's own volition or with the intervention of the Secretary of State. This highly controversial change to the constitutional position of chief officers is achieved by amending the Police Act 1996 and making specific regulations thereunder.

Why?

Although there are procedures for dealing with allegations of *misconduct* against police officers (**see para. 1.2.2**), there has been a lack of any formal structure by which police managers can address issues of perceived poor *performance*. The distinction here between conduct and performance is an important one. The complaints system is generally inadequate and often inappropriate in helping police managers tackle issues of performance and it was clear for some time that another, separate mechanism, similar to those used by many other employers, was needed.

Even under the new Code of Conduct (**see para. 1.2.2**) the focus is still on enforcement and punishment and the process follows more of a straight, linear path. In matters of perceived poor performance, however, the process is a cycle. The emphasis needs to be on the early identification of problems followed by discussion and agreement on action and an opportunity to improve. There should then be a monitoring period followed by a review of performance and further agreement and action as appropriate. This notion of providing the under-performing officer with opportunities to improve is a key feature of this new process and can be found right up until after any formal inefficiency hearing has started. In other words, from the point of view of the officer, it is rarely 'too late' to show a sufficient improvement. Clearly there needs to be an end to the process somewhere and that final stage may well involve sanctions but the general tenor of the process is ultimately developmental.

### What?

Unlike several of the other Regulations covered in this chapter, the Police (Efficiency) Regulations 1999 have no equivalent predecessor. Made under s. 50 of the Police Act 1996, the Regulations establish procedures for the management—and ultimately the punishment—of officers whose performance is felt to be unsatisfactory. In the majority of cases, general managerial discretion and appropriate words of guidance will probably suffice. In other cases, however, there may be a need to invoke the formal procedures set out below.

### The Police (Efficiency) Regulations 1999

Regulation 4 states:

(1) Where the reporting officer for a member of a police force is himself a member of that police force and is of the opinion that the performance or the attendance or both of that member is or are un-satisfactory, he may require the member concerned to attend an interview (in these Regulations referred to as a first interview) to discuss the performance or attendance (or both) of the member concerned.

(2) Where the reporting officer for a member of a police force is a person employed under section 15 of the 1996 Act and is of the opinion that the attendance of that member is unsatisfactory, he may require the member concerned to attend an interview (in these Regulations referred to as a first interview) to discuss the attendance of the member concerned.

(3) Where the reporting officer for a member of a police force is a person employed under section 15 of the 1996 Act, any other member of the force who has supervisory responsibility for that first member may, if he is of the opinion that the performance of that member is unsatisfactory, require him to attend an interview (in these Regulations referred to as a first interview) to discuss his performance, and in such a case references in these Regulations to a reporting officer shall be taken to include references to the member with that supervisory responsibility.

---

### KEYNOTE

Throughout the Regulations, the officer whose performance is in question is referred to as the 'member concerned', i.e. the member of a police force in respect of whom proceedings are, or are proposed to be taken (reg. 3(1)). Although not defined in the Regulations or the parent Act 'member of a police force' refers to a sworn police constable. Therefore, even though the reporting officer or countersigning officer (see below) may be a civilian member of staff, the regulations themselves only apply to the performance and attendance of a sworn police officer.

The 'reporting officer' will be the person having immediate supervisory responsibility for the 'member concerned' (reg. 3(1)). In most instances involving constables, the 'reporting officer' will therefore be their sergeant. Where the officer's immediate supervisor is a civilian member of staff (appointed under s. 15 of the Police Act 1996), this person will be the reporting officer for these purposes. However, there is a distinction throughout the newly amended regulations as to when civilian reporting officers and countersigning officers (see below) may act. While reporting officers who are also sworn police officers (e.g. sergeants and inspectors) may implement all the various stages of the procedures in the regulations, *civilian* supervisors and managers may only do so where the relevant police officer's *attendance* (as opposed to performance) is in issue (see reg. 4(2) above).

The Regulations only require that the reporting officer be *of the opinion* that the performance of the member concerned is unsatisfactory. However, single instances of poor performance or attendance would not generally be enough to invoke these Regulations and, as discussed above, the instigation of formal proceedings would not normally happen before day-to-day supervisory discretion had been applied. Although the Regulations do not say so, it would seem fair that, in assessing the performance or attendance of the member concerned, nothing done before April 1999 is taken into account.

The source of the reporting officer's 'opinion' may be from internal observations and reports but it may also arise from members of the public. Although the procedures for performance and attendance improvement and the investigation of complaints (**see para. 1.2.3**) are quite separate, there may be cases where there is an overlap.

### Arranging first interview

Regulation 5 states:

(1) If the reporting officer decides to require a member of a police force to attend a first interview, he shall—
  (a) send a notice in writing to the member concerned—
   (i) requiring him to attend, at a specified time and place, an interview with the reporting officer or, if the member concerned so requests, the countersigning officer;
   (ii) stating the reasons why his performance or attendance is considered unsatisfactory;
   (iii) informing him that he may seek advice from a representative of his staff association and be accompanied at the interview by a member of a police force selected by him; and
  (b) send a copy of the notice to the countersigning officer,
(2) A member of a police force who receives a notice pursuant to paragraph (1) may, not later than 7 days (or such longer period as the reporting officer may permit when sending the notice under paragraph (1)(a)) after the date on which the notice was received by him, request by notice in writing that the interview be conducted by the countersigning officer; and if the member concerned so requests the interview shall be conducted by the countersigning officer.

### KEYNOTE

The 'countersigning officer' will be the person having supervisory responsibility for the reporting officer (as to which, see reg. 4 above). Like the reporting officer, this can be a sworn police officer (in which case he/she must be senior in rank to the reporting officer) or a civilian member of staff. There is no requirement for the countersigning officer to have any direct responsibility for the member concerned.

It is important to note that any superintendent/chief superintendent or Assistant Chief Constable/Commander who attends or *is otherwise involved in* the first interview is barred from appearing on the panel of any later inefficiency hearing involving the member concerned (see below).

The 'first interview' will be with the reporting officer unless the member concerned asks for it to be with the countersigning officer. There is, however, a general time limit on making that request (reg. 5(2)).

Unlike some of the other procedures in this chapter, there does not appear to be any restriction on the timing of the first interview.

The responsibility for sending out the notice containing the details set out at reg. 5(a)(i) to (iii) falls to the reporting officer. The notice, which must be copied to the countersigning officer, must advise the member concerned that he/she may seek advice from the relevant staff association representative *and* that he/she may select another officer, from any police service, to accompany him/her to the interview. This 'friend' is able to advise and assist the member concerned, to speak on the officer's behalf and to produce witnesses and exhibits where appropriate. The notice must also set out the *reasons* why the member's performance is considered to be unsatisfactory.

### Procedure at first interview

Regulation 6 states:

(1) The following provisions of this regulation apply to the procedure to be followed at the first interview.

(2) The interviewing officer shall—
  (a) explain to the member concerned the reasons why the reporting officer is of the opinion that the performance or attendance of that member is unsatisfactory; and
  (b) provide the member concerned, or the member of a police force who has accompanied him to the interview, or both of them, with an opportunity to make representations in response.

(3) If, after considering any representations made in accordance with paragraph (2) (b), the interviewing officer is satisfied that the performance or attendance of the member concerned has been unsatisfactory, he shall—
  (a) inform the member concerned in what respect his performance or attendance is considered unsatisfactory;
  (b) warn the member concerned of any specific action which he is required to take to achieve an improvement in his performance or attendance; and
  (c) warn the member concerned that, if a sufficient improvement is not made within such reasonable period as the interviewing officer shall specify, he may be required to attend a second interview in accordance with regulation 9.

(4) The interviewing officer may, if he considers it appropriate, recommend that the member concerned seek assistance in relation to any matter affecting his health or welfare.

(5) The interviewing officer may adjourn the interview to a specified later time or date if it appears to him necessary or expedient to do so.

---

**KEYNOTE**

The 'interviewing officer' is the person conducting the first interview (reg. 3(1)) and could be either the reporting officer or the countersigning officer (see earlier Keynotes).

Having explained the reasons why the member's performance or attendance is unsatisfactory, the interviewing officer must provide the member, his/her 'friend' *or both*, with an opportunity to make representations in response. A reasonable amount of time must be allowed for the making of such representations.

Those representations must be 'considered' by the interviewing officer, not simply acknowledged or dismissed. The interviewing officer, having so considered the representations made, must carry out the actions set out in reg. 6(3)(a) to (c), provided he/she is 'satisfied' that the member's performance or attendance has been unsatisfactory.

The expression 'warn' at reg. 6(3)(b) seems odd in this context, particularly when the word 'inform' is used at the next stage (see below), but the 'warning' is referred to later in reg. 8. Whatever the terminology, the interviewing officer must tell the member concerned what he/she must do to achieve an improvement in his/her performance or attendance.

Under reg. 6(3)(c) the interviewing officer must specify a 'reasonable period' during which this improvement is to take place. This would appear to be normally no less than three, and probably no more than six months.

Regulation 6 says nothing about what must be done if the interviewing officer is *not* satisfied that the member's performance or attendance was unsatisfactory. Presumably the issue comes to a halt at this stage, although the reporting requirements under reg. 7 (see below) appear to apply irrespective of the outcome of the first interview.

---

### After first interview

Regulation 7 states:

(1) The interviewing officer shall, not later than 7 days after the date of the conclusion of the first interview—
  (a) cause to be prepared a written record of the substance of the matters discussed at the interview; and

(b) send one copy or, where the member concerned was accompanied at the interview by a member of a police force selected by him, two copies of that record to the member concerned together with a notice in writing informing him that he may submit written comments, or indicate that he has no comment to make, not later than 7 days after the date on which the copy is received by him.

(1A) In a case where a member has been required to attend a first interview to discuss his attendance and he has failed to attend the interview, the interviewing officer shall, if he is satisfied that the attendance of the member has been unsatisfactory, not later than 7 days after the date on which the first interview was due to take place—

(a) cause to be prepared a written notice informing and warning the member of the matters mentioned in sub-paragraphs (a) to (c) of regulation 6(3);

(b) send one copy or, where a member of a police force selected by the member concerned attended the interview, two copies of that notice to the member concerned together with a notice in writing informing him that he may submit written comments, or indicate that he has no comments to make, not later than 7 days after the date on which the copy is received by him.

(2) Subject to paragraph (3), the member concerned shall be entitled to submit written comments in relation to the record of the interview to the interviewing officer not later than 7 days after the date on which the copy is received by him.

(3) The interviewing officer may, on the application of the member concerned, extend the period specified in paragraph (2) if he is satisfied that it is appropriate to do so.

---

**KEYNOTE**

The written record need not be a verbatim account of all that took place at the first interview but it must summarise the 'substance' of the matters discussed. If the member concerned does not agree with the record, he/she may raise this in the form of written comments submitted under reg. 7(2).

The requirement under reg. 7(1)(b), to *send* the member and his/her 'friend' a copy of the record suggests that there is no need for personal service. The seven-day period for responding to the service of the documents begins when the copy of the record *is received by the officer*. This would mean that, if the officer were on annual leave or was otherwise unable to receive the posted documents at the place to which they were sent, he/she may not have 'received' them. If so the time limit should not begin until he/she physically receives the documents. If the member concerned applies for the time period to be extended, the interviewing officer may do so if it seems appropriate. The interviewing officer cannot extend the time period of his/her own volition.

The interviewing officer *may* make a recommendation that the member concerned seeks help in relation to his/her health or welfare.

Where the first interview has been required in relation to the officer's *attendance*, and he/she fails to turn up, a further written notice must be issued in accordance with reg. 7 (1A)(a) and (b) above if the interviewing officer is satisfied that the officer's attendance has been unsatisfactory. In effect, this is like having the first interview in the officer's absence.

Any written comments received by the interviewing officer must be retained with the record of interview (reg. 7(5)). Records of any stage of the unsatisfactory performance procedures will be expunged from an officer's personal record after two years have elapsed since the last action was taken (or the last review/appeal was heard (see below)).

---

Other copies

Regulation 7 goes on to state:

(4) The interviewing officer shall send a copy of the record of the interview, and of any written comments of the member concerned, to—

(a) the senior manager;

(b) the personnel officer; and

(c) (i) if the interview was conducted by the reporting officer, the countersigning officer; or

(ii) if the interview was conducted by the countersigning officer, the reporting officer.

**KEYNOTE**

'Senior manager' means the officer who is for the time being the supervisory officer of the countersigning officer (reg. 3(1)(a)). Although the Regulations do not specify that this person must be a police officer, this will generally be a chief inspector or superintendent. Where the member concerned is a superintendent, the 'senior manager' will be his/her supervising officer but again there is no stipulation that this must be a police officer (reg. 3(1)(b)).

'Personnel officer' means a person employed under s. 15 of the Police Act 1996 (a civilian) or a police officer who, in either case, has responsibility for personnel matters relating to members of the force to which the member concerned belongs (reg. 3(1)).

Second interview

Regulation 8 states:

(1) Where the reporting officer is of the opinion that a member of a police force who was warned under regulation 6(3)(b) that he was required to improve his performance has, at the end of the period specified by the interviewing officer under regulation 6(3)(c), failed to make a sufficient improvement in his performance, or, as the case may be, his attendance, he may refer the case to the countersigning officer.

(2) Where a case is referred under paragraph (1) and the countersigning officer is a member of the police force concerned, he may, after consulting with the personnel officer, require the member concerned to attend a further interview (in these Regulations referred to as a second interview) to discuss the performance or the attendance (or both) of the member concerned.

(3) Where a case is referred under paragraph (1) and the countersigning officer is a person employed under section 15 of the 1996 Act, he may, after consulting with the personnel officer, require the member concerned to attend a further interview (in these Regulations referred to as a second interview) to discuss the attendance of the member concerned.

**KEYNOTE**

It is not mandatory for the reporting officer to refer the case back to the countersigning officer if the member concerned has failed to make sufficient improvement. Regulation 8(1) says that he/she *may* do so.

All that is necessary in order to make such a referral is that the reporting officer *is of the opinion* that there has been insufficient improvement in the member's performance or attendance. This broadly drafted requirement gives the reporting officer a considerable degree of latitude but again the importance of general supervisory discretion should perhaps be reinforced here. Such a referral can only be made at the end of the specified period.

As with the procedure for first interviews (see earlier Keynote), the power for a civilian manager to require attendance at a second interview is limited to issues arising out of the officer's attendance.

Although the process is started by the reporting officer, the decision to hold a second interview will be made by the countersigning officer. Once again, there is no requirement to hold such an interview and the wording of reg. 8(2) is permissive rather than mandatory. What is mandatory, however, is that, in reaching his/her decision, the countersigning officer consult with the personnel officer (as defined above).

Note that where an officer has been required to attend a first interview in relation to his/her performance, attendance or both, any second interview can *only* relate to the same category (or categories) of behaviour that was the subject of the first interview (reg. 7(6)).

Regulation 9 states:

If the countersigning officer decides to require a member of a police force to attend second interview, he shall—

(a) send a notice in writing to the member concerned—
  (i) requiring him to attend, at a specified time and place, an interview with the countersigning officer and the personnel officer;

      (ii) stating the reasons why his performance or attendance is considered unsatisfactory and that further action will be considered in the light of the interview; and

      (iii) informing him that he may seek advice from a representative of his staff association and be accompanied at the interview by a member of a police force selected by him; and

  (b) send a copy of the notice to the reporting officer, the senior manager and the personnel officer.

---

### KEYNOTE

Once the decision is reached by the countersigning officer to hold a second interview, the responsibility to comply with the requirements of reg. 9 falls to him/her.

Again the notice must set out the reasons why the member's performance or attendance is considered unsatisfactory and must remind the member of his/her entitlement to consult the relevant staff association and to be accompanied by a 'friend' (police officer).

It is important to note that any superintendent or Assistant Chief Constable/Commander who attends *or is otherwise involved in* the second interview is barred from appearing on the panel of any later inefficiency hearing involving the member concerned (see below).

---

Regulation 10 states:

(1) The following provisions of this Regulation shall apply to the procedure to be followed at a second interview.

(2) The interview shall be conducted by the countersigning officer and the personnel officer.

(3) The countersigning officer shall—

  (a) explain to the member concerned the reasons why the reporting officer is of the opinion that the member concerned has failed to make a sufficient improvement in his performance or attendance or, as the case may be, that his performance or attendance is unsatisfactory and the conditions specified in regulation 8(2) are satisfied; and

  (b) provide the member concerned, or the member of a police force who has accompanied him to the interview, or both of them, with an opportunity to make representations in response.

---

### KEYNOTE

The personnel officer (as defined above) takes part in the second interview although it is clear from reg. 10(3) that the countersigning officer takes the lead in running the proceedings.

The countersigning officer must explain the grounds for the second interview and must provide the opportunity for the member, his/her 'friend' *or both* to make representations in response.

As with the first interview (see above) there will be an option of 'no further action', in which case any note of the procedure followed will be expunged from the member's personal record after two years have elapsed.

---

Regulation 10(4) goes on to state:

(4) If, after considering any representations made under paragraph (3), the countersigning officer is satisfied that the performance or attendance of the member concerned has been unsatisfactory during the period specified by the interviewing officer under regulation 6(3)(c), he shall—

  (a) inform the member concerned in what respect his performance or attendance is considered unsatisfactory;

  (b) warn the member concerned that he is required to improve his performance or attendance in any such respect;

  (c) inform the member concerned of any specific action which he is required to take to achieve such an improvement; and

  (d) warn the member concerned that, if a sufficient improvement is not made within such reasonable period as the countersigning officer shall specify, he may be required to attend an inefficiency hearing at which the officers conducting the hearing will have the power, if appropriate, to require the member concerned to resign from the force or to order reduction in rank.

---

## KEYNOTE

Once again, the representations made under reg. 10(3)(b) must be considered by the countersigning officer (and presumably, though it does not say so, the personnel officer).

The member must be told of any specific action that he/she is required to take to achieve the necessary improvement in performance or attendance. He/she must also be warned at this stage that failure to achieve sufficient improvement by the set date *may* result in a further hearing and that such a hearing would have the power to require the member to resign or to reduce him/her in rank. The warning will also contain a timescale for improvement which, as with the first interview, will not normally be less than three or more than six months from the time of the interview.

The countersigning officer may adjourn the second interview to a later time or a later date if it appears necessary or expedient to do so (reg. 10(5)).

---

### After second interview

Regulation 11 states:

(1) The countersigning officer shall, not later than 7 days after the conclusion of the second interview—
    (a) in consultation with the personnel officer, prepare a written record of the substance of the matters discussed during the interview; and
    (b) send one copy or, where the member concerned was accompanied at the interview by a member of a police force selected by him, two copies of that record to the member concerned together with a notice in writing—
        (i) if a warning was given under regulation 10(4), confirming the terms of that warning; and
        (ii) informing him that he may submit written comments, or indicate that he has no such comments, not later than 7 days after the date on which the copy is received by him.

(1A) In a case where a member has been required to attend a second interview to discuss his attendance and he has failed to attend the interview, the countersigning officer shall, if he is satisfied that the attendance of the member has been unsatisfactory during the period specified by the interviewing officer under regulation 6(3)(c), not later than 7 days after the date on which the second interview was due to take place—
    (i) cause to be prepared a written notice informing and warning the member of the matters mentioned in sub-paragraphs (a) to (d) of regulation 10(4);
    (ii) send one copy or, where a member of a police force selected by the member concerned attended the interview, two copies of that notice to the member concerned together with a notice in writing informing him that he may submit written comments, or indicate that he has no comments to make, not later than 7 days after the date on which the copy is received by him.

(2) Subject to paragraph (3), the member concerned shall be entitled to submit written comments in relation to the record of the interview to the countersigning officer not later than 7 days after the date on which it was received by him.

(3) The countersigning officer may, on the application of the member concerned, extend the period specified in paragraph (2) if he is satisfied that it is appropriate to do so.

(4) If the countersigning officer receives any written comments under paragraph (2), he shall ensure that they are retained with the record of the interview.

(5) The countersigning officer shall send a copy of the record of the interview, and of any written comments by the member concerned, to the reporting officer, the personnel officer and the senior manager.

**KEYNOTE**

The written record must be prepared *in consultation with* the personnel officer. The written record of the interview again appears to be a summary of the substance rather than a verbatim account of what took place. The record must be accompanied by a written notice confirming the 'warning' if one was given under reg. 10(4). As the requirement refers to a singular warning (there are in fact *two* warnings under reg. 10(4)), that warning seems to be the one given in relation to the consequences of failing to improve (i.e. the warning at reg. 10(4)(d)). In practice, such a warning may only be given twice within a period of two years before resulting in a hearing. Once again, as with the first interview, there are requirements relating to the sending of copies to the relevant people concerned, together with the notice of opportunity to submit written comments within seven days. There are also similar requirements in relation to the retention of written responses and the countersigning officer may, on the application of the member concerned, extend the seven-day deadline.

Where the officer's *attendance* is in issue, the process above is, in effect, a repeat performance of the first interview provisions (see reg. 7 above) and the hearing can be determined in his/her absence.

As the earlier provisions, where a member has been required to attend a second interview in relation to his/her performance, attendance or both, any inefficiency hearing can only relate to the category (or categories) of behaviour that formed the subject of the second interview (reg. 11(6)).

## Assessment of performance

Regulation 12 states:

(1) Not later than 14 days after the date on which the period specified under regulation 10(4)(d) ends—
    (a) the countersigning officer shall, in consultation with the reporting officer, assess the performance or attendance of the member concerned during that period; and
    (b) the countersigning officer shall inform the member concerned in writing whether the reporting officer and the countersigning officer are of the opinion that there has been a sufficient improvement in performance or attendance during that period.

(2) If the countersigning officer is of the opinion that there has been an insufficient improvement, the member concerned shall also, within the period of 14 days mentioned in paragraph (1), be informed in writing that he may be required to attend, at a time (being not sooner than 21 days, but not later than 56 days, after the date on which the notification under this paragraph is received by him) to be notified separately, a hearing (in these Regulations referred to as an inefficiency hearing) to consider his performance.

(3) The countersigning officer shall refer any case in which the member concerned has been informed in accordance with paragraph (2) to the senior manager, who shall, if he thinks it appropriate to do so, direct that an inefficiency hearing be arranged under regulation 13.

**KEYNOTE**

The countersigning officer, *in consultation with* the reporting officer must assess the performance or attendance of the member concerned and this must be done no later than 14 days after the period set out in the warning under reg. 10(4)(d). The assessment must relate to the member's performance *during that period*. Following this assessment, the countersigning officer must inform the member in writing whether or not he/she considers that there has been a sufficient improvement in the member's performance or attendance. If there *has* been a sufficient improvement, however, there does not appear to be a specific requirement as to when the member must be so informed. Given the requirement at reg. 12(2)—to inform the member within the 14-day period that he/she may have to attend an inefficiency hearing—it would seem that, if the member has not heard anything from the countersigning officer within 14 days of the assessment period ending, he/she can assume that there must have been sufficient improvement in his/her performance or attendance.

If the countersigning officer feels that there has not been a sufficient improvement, he/she must refer the case to the 'senior manager' (as defined above) who then has the discretion to direct an inefficiency hearing to be held. As with the other stages of the process so far, this element is *discretionary* and there is no compulsion on the senior manager to direct that a hearing be held.

---

### Inefficiency hearing

Regulation 13 states:

(1) The personnel officer shall, not less than 21 days before the date fixed for the hearing, send a notice in writing to the member concerned—
   - (a) requiring him to attend an inefficiency hearing at a specified time and place;
   - (b) stating the reasons why his performance or attendance is considered unsatisfactory;
   - (c) informing him that he may be represented at the hearing—
     - (i)   either by counsel or a solicitor; or
     - (ii) by a member of a police force selected by him; and
   - (d) warning him of the powers under regulation 17 which are available to the officers conducting the inefficiency hearing in the event that they find that the performance or attendance of the member concerned has been unsatisfactory.

(2) If the member concerned wishes to call any witnesses other than the person representing him at the inefficiency hearing, he shall, not later than seven days before the hearing, give notice in writing to the personnel officer of the names and addresses of those witnesses.

(3) In paragraph (2), the reference to the hearing includes a reference to any hearing under regulation 15; and in relation to such a hearing the period within which notice is to be given under that paragraph shall be such period as the chairman of the hearing may direct when he postpones or, as the case may be, adjourns the hearing.

---

### KEYNOTE

The responsibility for sending out the relevant notice here falls to the personnel officer. Such a notice must be *sent*—though not necessarily received—not less than 21 days before the proposed date of the hearing.

The notice will advise the member that he/she may be represented at the hearing by a solicitor/counsel *or* a police officer. This right emanates from s. 84 of the Police Act 1996 which provides that an officer (of the rank of superintendent or below) may not be dismissed, required to resign or reduced in rank as a result of a hearing unless he/she has been given an opportunity to elect to be legally represented.

The requirement under reg. 13(2) is important as only those witnesses that are mentioned in the member's notification are *entitled* (under reg. 14(7)) to give evidence at the hearing (though the chair may admit them under his/her discretion even if they were not specified above). Notification of which witnesses the member wishes to call must be made to the *personnel officer*.

The inefficiency hearing must be conducted by three officers, one of whom will be:

- in the case of a provincial police force—an Assistant Chief Constable
- in the case of the Metropolitan Police—a Commander in that force
- in the case of the City of London Police—a Commander in that force

(reg. 14).

This officer will chair the hearing (reg. 14(1)).

In practice the hearing will comprise any two superintendents/chief superintendents (subject to the rule under reg. 14(2) below) plus the chair.

Where the member concerned is a Metropolitan Police officer, the superintendents/ chief superintendents will be Metropolitan Police officers (reg. 14(3)(b)).

Where the member concerned is a superintendent/chief superintendent, the hearing will comprise two Assistant Chief Constables from outside the member's own force, together with an Assistant Chief Constable from the member's own force who will chair the hearing.

Where the member concerned is a Metropolitan Police superintendent/chief superintendent, the hearing will be chaired by a Commander from the member's own area with two Commanders from another area/other areas.

Where the member concerned is a City of London Police superintendent/chief superintendent, the hearing will be chaired by a City of London Police Commander or the Assistant Commissioner, with two Assistant Chief Constables or Metropolitan Police Commanders.

In any case, the chair and any of the officers assisting him/her must not have attended or otherwise been involved with the first or second interview held in relation to the member concerned (reg. 14(2)).

---

Regulation 14 goes on to state:

(4) As soon as the chief officer of police has appointed the chairman, the personnel officer shall arrange for a copy of any document—
   (a) which was available to the interviewing officer in relation to the first interview;
   (b) which was available to the countersigning officer in relation to the second interview; or
   (c) which was prepared or submitted under regulation 11, 12 or 13,
   to be made available to the chairman; and a copy of any such document shall be sent to the member concerned.

---

**KEYNOTE**

The personnel officer must collate copies of any documents which were available to the interviewing officer and the countersigning officer at the first and second interview respectively and also copies of any document prepared or submitted under regs 11 to 13. The personnel officer must arrange to make these copies available to the chair of the hearing as soon as one has been appointed. These copies must also be sent to the member concerned, though there does not appear to be a specific time limit on this requirement.

Subject to the other provisions in reg. 14, the chair will determine the procedure to be followed at the inefficiency hearing (reg. 14(5)). As such, the chair might decide the 'batting order' for the respective parties and may call witnesses to the proceedings. This apparently wide discretion will, however, also be subject to the general principles of natural justice.

The inefficiency hearing will be held in private but may be in public *if both the chair and the member concerned agree* (reg. 14(6)).

The member concerned must be given the opportunity to make representations in relation to the matters referred to in the notice sent out by the personnel officer under reg. 13 (reg. 14(7)). A further effect of reg. 14(7) is that the member concerned is *entitled* to call any witnesses that he/she named in the notification to the personnel officer under reg. 13(2). There may be good reasons why the member failed to include details of potential witnesses in the reg. 13(2) notification and it would seem that the general discretion given to the chair under reg. 14(5) above would allow for other witnesses not previously named to be called.

Unlike the procedure to be followed at the first and second interview stages, a verbatim record must be made of the proceedings (reg. 14(8)).

---

Postponement and adjournment

In addition to the general power to adjourn the proceedings under reg. 15(7), the chair may adjourn or postpone the hearing in a number of specified circumstances.

*Additional period for assessment*

The chair of the hearing may adjourn the proceedings if, having heard the representations from the member concerned, he/she considers it appropriate to allow a further period for assessment. Therefore, even after the hearing has begun, the member concerned may still be given the opportunity to address his/her shortcomings. Any further period under this regulation must not exceed three months. The time and date for the resumed hearing must be fixed by the chair and, within 14 days of the end of that period, the reporting officer and countersigning officer will prepare a report containing an assessment of the member's performance or attendance over that time (reg. 15(3)).

When the hearing resumes, the member concerned will be allowed to make representations on the matters referred to *in that latest report* and may call any of the original witnesses set out in the notification under reg. 13(2).

Regulation 15(6) makes provision for the situation where the chair of the inefficiency hearing is likely to be absent, incapacitated or suspended from duty when the hearing resumes.

### Non-attendance

If the member concerned does not attend the inefficiency hearing and gives what the chair considers to be a 'good reason' for that non-attendance, the chair *must* postpone or adjourn the hearing (reg. 15(1)). This requirement does not apply where an attendance notice has been sent to the officer under the Regulations (see earlier). This seems to make sense, given that the whole issue of poor attendance is what will have caused the notices to be sent and the hearing convened in the first place. In such cases, however, the chair does not have to adjourn the hearing even where the officer *does have* good reason for not attending.

If the member concerned informs the chair that he/she will be unable to attend the hearing, it must also be postponed or adjourned. A strict reading of the wording of reg. 15(1) suggests that the requirement for a 'good reason' to be given is confined to cases of *non-attendance* rather than a prospective *inability* to attend. The result of such an interpretation, however, would allow for any number of stalling tactics to be used to avoid the hearing and may hold up what is supposed to be a quicker process for dealing with poor performance.

The hearing may proceed in the absence of the member concerned under reg. 14(9) but that option is 'subject to' the provisions of reg. 15(1) above.

Where any of the requirements under regs 14 or 15 cannot be complied with owing to the absence of the member concerned, the case may be proceeded with as if they had been complied with (reg. 14(10)). Again, this is intended to prevent the procedure from being obstructed or held back by the absence of the member concerned.

### Ill health

An officer who is on sick leave may still appear at an inefficiency hearing (see the Police Regulations 2003, reg. 33). Nevertheless, if the state of the officer's health means that he/she is incapacitated to the extent that attendance at the hearing is not possible then, at least in cases where no attendance notice has been sent out, the hearing is likely to be postponed (under reg. 15(1) above).

### The finding

Regulation 16 states:

(1) Subject to paragraph (2), at the conclusion of the inefficiency hearing, the officers conducting the hearing shall reach a decision whether the performance or attendance of the member concerned—
    (a) in the period referred to in regulation 10(4)(d); or
    (b) where the hearing was adjourned under regulation 15(2), over the whole of the period comprising the period referred to in regulation 10(4)(d) and the further period specified by the chairman under regulation 15(3)(a),
    has been satisfactory or not.

(2) The chairman may, at the conclusion of the hearing, defer reaching a decision until a later time or date if it appears necessary or expedient to do so.

(3) The decision of the officers conducting the hearing shall state the finding and, where they have found that the performance or attendance of the member concerned has not been satisfactory, their reasons as well as any sanction which they impose under regulation 17.

(4) The chairman shall record the decision in writing, and shall, not later than three days after the finding is stated under paragraph (3), send a copy of it to—

    (a) the member concerned;

    (b) the senior manager; and

    (c) the personnel officer;

and the copy sent to the member concerned shall be accompanied by a notice in writing informing him of his right to request a review under regulation 19.

---

**KEYNOTE**

Unless the chair decides to defer the decision under reg. 16(2), the officers conducting the hearing must reach a conclusion as to whether the member's performance or attendance in the relevant period has been satisfactory or not. That decision—or a decision under reg. 17 below—need not be unanimous and may be based on a simple majority but this will not be indicated in the finding (reg. 16(5)). This appears to give the officers an equal say in the judgment with no special 'casting' vote being held by the chair.

Their decision must state their finding and, if the member's performance or attendance is found not to have been satisfactory, the decision must give reasons. The decision must also state the relevant sanction to be imposed. Although it is not explicit, there may of course be a finding that the member's performance or attendance has been satisfactory in which case there will be no further action and the relevant records will be removed from the member's personal file.

The record of the decision must be sent to the relevant parties no later than three days *after the finding is stated*. The copy sent to the member must also be accompanied by a notice in relation to the member's right to ask for a review under reg. 19.

---

Sanctions

Regulation 17 states:

(1) If the officers conducting the inefficiency hearing make a finding that the performance of the member concerned during the relevant period has been unsatisfactory, they may—

    (a) require the member concerned to resign from the force either one month after the date on which a copy of the decision sent under regulation 16(4) is received by him or on such later date as may be specified;

    (b) order reduction in his rank with immediate effect and issue a written warning to the member concerned that unless a sufficient improvement in his performance is made within such period as the chairman shall specify, he may, following consideration of his performance during that period in accordance with regulation 18, be required to attend a first interview in respect of that performance; or

    (c) issue such a written warning as is mentioned in sub-paragraph (b).

(2) Where the sanction under paragraph (1)(a) is imposed and where the member concerned has not resigned from the force in accordance with the requirement, then the effect of the decision shall be to dismiss the member concerned from the force as from the time referred to.

(3) If the officers conducting the inefficiency hearing make a finding that the attendance of the member concerned during the relevant period has been unsatisfactory, they may—

    (a) impose the sanction mentioned in paragraph (1)(a);

    (b) in a case where it is established that insufficient support has been given to the member concerned during the relevant period in order to assist him to return to work, specify such measures as must be taken in order to give him sufficient support in order to assist him to return to work;

    (c) issue a written warning to the member concerned that unless a sufficient improvement in his attendance is made within such period as is specified, he may, following consideration of his attendance during that period in accordance with regulation 18A, be required to attend a second inefficiency hearing at which he may be required to resign from the force;

    (d) in a case where it is established that the member's duties within the force contribute directly to his unsatisfactory attendance record, order the member to be redeployed to alternative duties (which may involve a reduction of rank) within the force with immediate effect.

(4) Where the steps under paragraph (3)(b) or (d) are taken, the member concerned shall be issued with a written warning that unless a sufficient improvement in his attendance is made within such period as is specified, he may, following consideration of his attendance during that period in accordance with regulation 18A, be required to attend a first interview, a second interview or an inefficiency hearing, as specified by the officers conducting the inefficiency hearing.

---

**KEYNOTE**

Any requirement for the member to resign cannot take effect before one month after the notice of the finding *was received* by the member. It may take effect at some later date. If the member has not resigned as required by the specified date, he/she will automatically be dismissed as of that date (reg. 17(2)).

Any reduction in rank must take effect 'immediately', an expression which presumably means immediately the finding is made as opposed to it being sent to, or received by, the member concerned. The instant effect of this finding will not be held up or deferred by any review or appeal process. In accordance with the developmental and ongoing nature of this process, a reduction in rank must be accompanied by a warning that a sufficient improvement is still required within a specified period. This indicates that the process is by no means over and that, under reg. 18 below, further reports as to the member's performance will be assessed.

A similar procedure involving a written warning followed by a further report is available as a third sanction without any reduction in rank.

Any sanction imposed under reg. 17 shall be expunged after two years if that period was free from any such sanction (see reg. 15 of the Police Regulations 2003).

In cases arising out of poor *attendance*, the measures in reg. 17(3) may be invoked. These measures include issuing specific written warnings as to the effect of reg. 18A (below) after a further period of assessment. The measures also include a specific provision dealing with cases where the officer's duties have contributed to his/her poor attendance. In such cases, the officer may be redeployed and, if appropriate, reduced in rank in the process.

---

### Further period of assessment

Regulation 18 states:

(1) This regulation applies where the member concerned has been given a written warning under paragraph (1)(b) or (c) of regulation 17.

(2) Not later than 14 days after the end of the period specified in the warning, the reporting officer shall—
   (a) assess the performance of the member concerned during that period
   (b) cause to be prepared a report on the performance; and
   (c) send a copy of the report to the member concerned.

(3) Where the report prepared under paragraph (2)(b) concludes that the performance of the member concerned has been satisfactory during the period specified in the warning, no further action shall be taken in respect of that performance during that period.

(4) Where the report prepared under paragraph (2)(b) concludes that, in the opinion of the reporting officer, the performance of the member concerned has been unsatisfactory during that period, the reporting officer shall request the member concerned to attend a first interview in accordance with regulation 4; and these Regulations shall have effect for the purposes of the performance of the member concerned during that period as if he had been invited to a first interview under regulation 4.

---

**KEYNOTE**

Regulation 18 applies where a written warning under reg. 17(1)(b) or (c) has been issued (performance). Unlike the other stages in the process, this stage makes specific provision for occasions where the member's performance is found to have been satisfactory. In such cases there is to be no further action in respect of *that* performance during *that* period. This does not necessarily mean that there can be no further action in relation to any performance during any other stage of the whole process.

If the 'reporting officer' is of the opinion that the member's performance during this most recent assessment period has been unsatisfactory, the reporting officer *must* request a 'first interview' and the whole cycle begins again. Unlike the original 'first interview' (see above), the wording of reg. 18 does not leave the request of the 'first interview' to the reporting officer's discretion.

Regulation 18A makes very similar provisions for assessing and reporting on the officer's progress in cases of poor attendance (under reg. 17 (3)(c) or (4)). In cases of poor attendance, however, the final report is made by the countersigning officer (not the reporting officer) and if he/she concludes that the officer's attendance has been unsatisfactory or has made insufficient improvement, then:

- if the officer has been given a written warning under reg. 17(3)(c), he/she may be required to attend an inefficiency hearing or
- if the officer has been given a written warning under reg. 17(4), he/she may be required to attend a first interview, second interview or an inefficiency hearing

(see reg 18A).

### The review

Regulation 19 states:

(1) Where the officers conducting the inefficiency hearing have imposed a sanction under regulation 17, the member concerned shall be entitled to request the chief officer of the police force concerned, or where the member concerned is a member of the Metropolitan Police force the Assistant Commissioner, ('the reviewing officer') to review the finding or the sanction imposed, or both the finding and the sanction.

(2) A request for a review must be made to the reviewing officer in writing within 14 days of the date on which a copy of the decision sent under regulation 16(4) is received by the member concerned unless this period is extended by the reviewing officer.

(3) The request for a review shall state the grounds on which the review is requested and whether a meeting is requested.

### KEYNOTE

'Sanction' here would appear to mean any of the three options set out under reg. 17(1)(a) to (c). Therefore, the member concerned may request a review where the hearing only imposes a written warning without any further punishment.

The request will be made to the member's chief officer or, in the case of a Metropolitan police officer, to the Assistant Commissioner for the time being authorised under s. 8 of the Metropolitan Police Act 1856 (see reg. 3(1)). This person is referred to as the 'reviewing officer'.

Regulation 22 makes special provisions for situations where the chief officer or assistant commissioner is an 'interested party' or where there is an assistant chief officer deputising under s. 12 of the Police Act 1996.

For some reason the Regulations do not define 'interested party' but reg. 4 of the Police (Conduct) Regulations 1999 (**see para. 1.2.2**) defines it as 'a witness or any person involved in the conduct which is the subject of the case or who otherwise has a direct interest in the case'. In cases falling under reg. 22, the review will be carried out by the Deputy Chief Constable. Where that Deputy Chief Constable is absent or is an interested party, the review will be carried out by the chief officer of another force.

Where the member concerned is a Metropolitan police officer and the review officer is absent or an interested party, the review will be carried out by the designated Commander. If that Commander is absent or an interested party, the review may be carried out by another Assistant Commissioner (reg. 22(3)).

Where the member concerned is a City of London police officer and the Commissioner is absent or an interested party, the review will be carried out by the chief officer of another force or an Assistant Commissioner in the Metropolitan Police (reg. 22(4)).

The request must be made to the reviewing officer in writing within 14 days of the date on which the member *receives* the notification sent out under reg. 16(4). The period may be extended by the reviewing officer without the need for the member to apply for such an extension.

The purpose of the review can be to consider the finding, the sanction or both. The reviewing officer may confirm the decision of the hearing or he/she may impose a different sanction. However, the reviewing officer may not impose a sanction greater than that imposed at the hearing (reg. 21(2)).

The request must state the grounds on which it is made and whether a meeting is requested. If a meeting is requested, the reviewing officer must hold one (reg. 20(1)). However, a review can be carried out without holding such a meeting. Where a meeting is held, the member may be accompanied by a 'friend' (police officer) and a solicitor/ counsel (reg. 20(2)).

---

### The finding of the review

The member concerned must be informed of the finding of the reviewing officer in writing and within three days of the completion of the review (reg. 21(1)).

The reviewing officer's decision is substituted for that of the hearing and takes effect from the same date (reg. 20(3)). If there is a finding that the performance of the member concerned had not been unsatisfactory the original sanction will be expunged forthwith.

If the reviewing officer's decision results in the member concerned being required to resign or his/her reduction in rank, the member must be notified of the right to appeal to a Police Appeals Tribunal (reg. 20(4)) (**see para. 1.2.4**).

### 1.2.2 **Misconduct**

In addition to performance and attendance management, it is also an important supervisory and managerial function to be alert to the way in which individuals conduct themselves. As with issues of performance and attendance (**see para. 1.2.1**), a great deal of supervisory and managerial discretion is called for in dealing with information concerning the conduct of individual officers. The exercise of supervisory and managerial discretion is generally a matter for local and organisational policy. Any such policy relating to the alleged misconduct of police officers is, however, subject to the legislative provisions discussed in this chapter.

Moreover, the areas that regulate the investigation and determination of alleged police misconduct are the subject of a number of proposals for reform at the time of writing.

It is, however, critical to note at the outset the observations of Lord Donaldson who said that an officer was not to be put in peril in respect of disciplinary proceedings unless there was *substantial compliance* with the regulations (see *Calverley* v *Chief Constable of Merseyside* [1989] 2 WLR 624). This means that even relatively minor departures by investigators and managers from the regularly framework which follows in the rest of this paragraph could result in any subsequent disciplinary proceedings being overturned by a court.

### Who?

The legislative provisions relating to allegations of misconduct can be found in the Police (Conduct) Regulations 1999 (SI 1999 No. 730). These Regulations apply to all police officers other than those above chief superintendent and, subject to the provisions below, revoke the previous Police (Discipline) Regulations 1985 and their respective amendments. As well as setting out the procedures to be followed in cases of alleged misconduct, the 1999 Regulations also introduce a new Code of Conduct which replaces the former Discipline Code (see below).

### When?

The 1999 Regulations came into force on 1 April 1999.

Where a report, complaint or allegation has been received in respect of conduct that occurred or began *before 1 April 1999*, the Regulations will not apply and the former 1985 Regulations will apply (reg. 2(2)).

If the report, complaint or allegation in respect of conduct that occurred or began before 1 April 1999 is *received on or after 1 April 2000*, the conduct will be treated as if it had occurred or begun after 1 April 1999 (reg. 2(3)).

In other words, where the conduct reported or complained of took place before the starting date of these Regulations, the former Regulations will apply unless that report or complaint was itself received on/after 1 April 2000.

### The Code of Conduct

Schedule 1 of the 1999 Regulations states:

1. *Honesty and integrity*
It is of paramount importance that the public has faith in the honesty and integrity of police officers. Officers should therefore be open and truthful in their dealings; avoid being improperly beholden to any person or institution; and discharge their duties with integrity.

2. *Fairness and impartiality*
Police officers have a particular responsibility to act with fairness and impartiality in all their dealings with the public and their colleagues.

3. *Politeness and tolerance*
Officers should treat members of the public and colleagues with courtesy and respect, avoiding abusive or deriding attitudes or behaviour. In particular, officers must avoid: favouritism of an individual or group; all forms of harassment, victimisation or unreasonable discrimination; and overbearing conduct to a colleague, particularly to one junior in rank or service.

4. *Use of force and abuse of authority*
Officers must never knowingly use more force than is reasonable, nor should they abuse their authority.

5. *Performance of duties*
Officers should be conscientious and diligent in the performance of their duties. Officers should attend work promptly when rostered for duty. If absent through sickness or injury, they should avoid activities likely to retard their return to duty.

6. *Lawful orders*
The police service is a disciplined body. Unless there is good and sufficient cause to do otherwise, officers must obey all lawful orders and abide by the provisions of Police Regulations. Officers should support their colleagues in the execution of their lawful duties, and oppose any improper behaviour, reporting it where appropriate.

7. *Confidentiality*
Information which comes into the possession of the police should be treated as confidential. It should not be used for personal benefit and nor should it be divulged to other parties except in the proper course of police duty. Similarly, officers should respect, as confidential, information about force policy and operations unless authorised to disclose it in the course of their duties.

8. *Criminal offences*
Officers must report any proceedings for a criminal offence taken against them. Conviction of a criminal offence may of itself result in further action being taken.

9. *Property*
Officers must exercise reasonable care to prevent loss or damage to property (excluding their own personal property but including police property).

10. *Sobriety*
Whilst on duty officers must be sober. Officers should not consume alcohol when on duty unless specifically authorised to do so or it becomes necessary for the proper discharge of police duty.

11. *Appearance*
Unless on duties which dictate otherwise, officers should always be well turned out, clean and tidy whilst on duty in uniform or in plain clothes.

12. *General conduct*

Whether on or off duty, police officers should not behave in a way which is likely to bring discredit upon the police service.

**Notes**

(a) The primary duties of those who hold the office of constable are the protection of life and property, the preservation of the Queen's peace, and the prevention and detection of criminal offences. To fulfil these duties they are granted extraordinary powers; the public and the police service therefore have the right to expect the highest standards of conduct from them.

(b) This Code sets out the principles which guide police officers' conduct. It does not seek to restrict officers' discretion: rather it aims to define the parameters of conduct within which that discretion should be exercised. However, it is important to note that any breach of the principles in this Code may result in action being taken by the organisation, which, in serious cases, could involve dismissal.

(c) This Code applies to the conduct of police officers in all ranks whilst on duty, or whilst off duty if the conduct is serious enough to indicate that an officer is not fit to be a police officer. It will be applied in a reasonable and objective manner. Due regard will be paid to the degree of negligence or deliberate fault and to the nature and circumstances of an officer's conduct. Where off duty conduct is in question, this will be measured against the generally accepted standards of the day.

---

**KEYNOTE**

Although many of the new paragraphs had a corresponding 'offence' under the former discipline code, there is not an exact overlap. For a table showing what went where, see below. The former offence of being an accessory to a disciplinary offence has gone, but such conduct is probably subsumed under paras 6 and 12. The former protection against double jeopardy has gone (see sch. 9, part II of the Police Act 1996).

The rule (under the now repealed s. 104 of the Police and Criminal Evidence Act 1984) provided that, where an officer had been convicted or acquitted of a criminal offence, he/she would not be liable to be charged with a general disciplinary offence which was in substance the same as the criminal offence.

While the making of an Anti-Social Behaviour Order (ASBO) is a civil matter that does not necessarily arise out of any criminal conduct (**see chapter 2**), it is questionable whether the passing of such an order in respect of a police officer means that he or she has necessarily fallen below the required standard—much would turn on the individual facts and circumstances of each case. It would plainly be wrong to treat every imposition of an ASBO on an officer as conclusive proof that his or her conduct had fallen below the required standard or that this amonunted to proceedings for, or a conviction of a criminal offence per paragraph 8 above.

In relation to 'sobriety' at item 10 above, Home Office guidance suggests that superintendents/chief superintendents will be classed as being 'on duty' while they are formerly 'on call'. They will not be 'on duty' by reason only of their general 24-hour responsibility for their own area of command or department. The guidance further provides that an officer who is *unexpectedly* called out for duty should be able, at no risk of discredit, to say that he/she has had too much to drink. The Home Office has published special guidance on dealing with police officers convicted of drink driving offences (**see Road Traffic**).

---

The Police (Conduct) Regulations 1999

Regulation 5 states:

(1) Where there has been a report, complaint or allegation which indicates that the conduct of a member of a police force does not meet the appropriate standard the chief officer of the force concerned may suspend the member concerned from membership of the force and from his office of constable whether or not the matter has been investigated.

(2) The chief officer concerned may exercise the power to suspend the member concerned under this regulation at any time from the time of the receipt of the report, complaint or allegation until—

(a) the supervising officer decides not to refer the case to a hearing,

(b) the notification of a finding that the conduct of the member concerned did not fail to meet the appropriate standard,

(c) the time limit under regulation 34 for giving notice of intention to seek a review has expired, or

(d) any review under regulation 35 has been completed.

(3) Where the member concerned is suspended under this regulation, he shall be suspended until there occurs any of the events mentioned in paragraph (2)(a) to (d), or until the chief officer decides he shall cease to be suspended, whichever first occurs.

(4) Where the member concerned who is suspended is required to resign under regulation 31, he shall remain suspended during the period of his notice.

(5) The chief officer concerned may delegate his powers under this regulation to an officer of at least the rank of Assistant Chief Constable or, where the member concerned is a member of the City of London or Metropolitan Police force, to an officer of at least the rank of commander.

---

**KEYNOTE**

Many of the terms used within the 1999 Regulations are defined under reg. 4(1).

'Complaint' has the same meaning, as a complaint under s. 65 of the Police Act 1996 (**see para. 1.2.3**). Not every allegation of misconduct will amount to a 'complaint', particularly where the source of the allegation is internal. However, where there has been a 'complaint' so defined, the provisions under the 1996 Act will apply and, as with allegations of unsatisfactory performance (**see para. 1.2.1**), there will be occasions where there is some overlap.

'Appropriate standard' means the standard set out in the Code of Conduct (see above).

'Member concerned' means the officer in relation to whose conduct there has been a report, complaint, or allegation.

The 'supervising officer' is the person appointed under reg. 7 (see below) to supervise the investigation of the case.

For an explanation of regs 34 and 35 which relate to the review procedure, see below.

The power to suspend an officer appears to be very wide and applies whether or not the matter has been investigated (reg. 5(1)). Such a power must, however, be exercised in accordance with the general principles of law and will be subject to judicial review. The power under reg. 5 may be delegated to an Assistant Chief Constable or, in the case of Metropolitan Police or City of London Police officers, to a Commander (reg. 5(5)).

The effect of suspension is that the member continues to be a 'member' of his/her force for the purposes of the Police Regulations 2003 (see reg. 3) but ceases to enjoy the powers and privileges of the office of constable. A further effect is that the officer will not, under the Rules of the Police Promotion Examinations Board, be able to sit the qualifying examination(s) for promotion unless his/her chief officer expressly authorises it.

Generally an officer who is suspended will continue to receive full pay (without any special allowances) unless his/her whereabouts are unknown or where he/she is in custody following conviction (see the Police Regulations 2003, sch. 2).

The power to suspend *may* be exercised at any time from the receipt of the allegation up until any of the circumstances set out at reg. 5(2)(a) to (d) *or* until the chief officer decides otherwise, whichever occurs first. Therefore, although a chief officer may end the member's suspension *before* any of the circumstances set out at reg. 5(2)(a) to (d), he/she may not extend the suspension beyond the time when the first of those things occurs.

When deciding whether to use the power to suspend an officer or not, consideration must be given to the equality of the treatment being applied to all officers under investigation or subject to complaint. Failure to do so can lead to finding that such treatment was discriminatory (see *Virdi* v *Commissioner of Police for the Metropolis* (2000) LTL 5 February).

If a suspended officer is ultimately required to resign under reg. 31 (see below), he/she will remain suspended during his/her period of notice (reg. 5(4)).

---

Outstanding criminal proceedings

Regulation 6 states:

> Where there are criminal proceedings outstanding against the member concerned, proceedings under these Regulations, other than exercise of the power to suspend under regulation 5, shall not take place unless the chief officer concerned believes that in the exceptional circumstances of the case it would be appropriate for them to do so.

---

**KEYNOTE**

Although as a general rule disciplinary proceedings other than suspension will not be brought against an officer while there are any outstanding criminal proceedings against him/her, reg. 6 leaves it open to the chief officer to do so. That discretionary power to institute disciplinary proceedings is limited to 'exceptional circumstances' where the chief officer *believes* it to be appropriate though there is no further requirement for that belief to be a 'reasonable' one.

---

Investigation procedure

*Supervising officer*

Regulation 7 states:

(1) Subject to paragraph (2), where a report, complaint or allegation is received by the chief officer which indicates that the conduct of a member of a police force did not meet the appropriate standard, the case may be referred by him to an officer, who shall satisfy the conditions in paragraph (3), to supervise the investigation of the case.

(2) ...

(3) The supervising officer shall be—
   (a) at least one rank above that of the member concerned;
   (b) of at least the rank of superintendent;
   (c) a member of the same force as the member concerned; and
   (d) not an interested party.

---

**KEYNOTE**

Regulation 7(1) does not apply where the case arises from a complaint the investigation of which *must* be supervised by the Police Complaints Authority (**see para. 1.2.3**).

The supervising officer must meet all of the criteria set out at reg. 7(3)(a) to (d).

The 'supervising officer' is not the same as the 'Investigating Officer' (see below).

An 'interested party' is 'a witness or any person involved in the conduct which is the subject of the case or who otherwise has a direct interest in the case' (reg. 4(1)).

---

*Investigating officer*

Regulation 8 states:

(1) The supervising officer may appoint an investigating officer to investigate the case.

(2) The investigating officer shall be—
   (a) a member of the same police force as the member concerned or, if at the request of the supervising officer the chief officer of some other force agrees to provide an investigating officer, a member of that other force;
   (b) of at least the rank of inspector or, if the member concerned is a superintendent or chief super-intendent, of at least the rank of Assistant Chief Constable or, if the investigating officer is a member of the City of London or Metropolitan Police force, of at least the rank of Commander;
   (c) of at least the same rank as the member concerned; and
   (d) not an interested party.

**KEYNOTE**

The investigating officer must meet all the criteria set out at reg. 8(2)(a) to (d).

He/she may be from a different force from the member concerned and must be at least of inspector rank. If the member concerned is a superintendent/chief superintendent then the Investigating Officer must be of at least Assistant Chief Constable/Commander rank. Although reg. 7 does not specifically require it, it is likely that in cases where the investigating officer is a senior officer, the 'supervising officer' would also be of ACPO rank.

The provisions of reg. 8 are without prejudice to the powers of the Police Complaints Authority (see para. 1.2.3) to make requirements in relation to the appointment of investigating officers (reg. 8(3)).

## *Notice of investigation*

Regulation 9 states:

The investigating officer shall as soon as is practicable (without prejudicing his or any other investigation of the matter) cause the member concerned to be given written notice—

(a) that there is to be an investigation into the case;

(b) of the nature of the report, complaint or allegation;

(c) informing him that he is not obliged to say anything concerning the matter, but that he may, if he so desires, make a written or oral statement concerning the matter to the Investigating Officer or to the chief officer concerned;

(d) informing him that if he makes such a statement it may be used in any subsequent proceedings under these Regulations;

(e) informing him that he has the right to seek advice from his staff association; and

(f) informing him that he has the right to be accompanied by a member of a police force, who shall not be an interested party, to any meeting, interview or hearing.

**KEYNOTE**

The written notice must be given 'as soon as is practicable'. Practicable has been accepted as meaning 'possible to be accomplished with known means or resources' (see *Adsett* v *K & L Steelfounders* [1953] 1 All ER 97). However, the giving of such a notice must not be to the prejudice of the investigation of the matter—whether by the investigating officer or someone else—therefore there may be some justifiable delay in the provision of a reg. 9 notice.

The wording 'cause to be given'—as opposed to 'sent'—suggests that personal service is required.

Although this provision has replaced the troublesome 'reg. 7' wording which caused a lot of legal argument over the years, the effect of failing to serve a correctly-worded notice as soon as practicable should not be underestimated (see *R* v *Chief Constable of Merseyside, ex parte Merrill* [1989] 1 WLR 1077). The purpose of the old reg. 7 notice—and therefore the present notice under reg. 9—is to put the officer on '*very early notice*' that an allegation has been made (see *Calverley* v *Chief Constable of Merseyside* [1989] 2 WLR 624). The whole point of serving a reg. 9 notice is to allow the officer to put forward a denial or explanation and to enable him/her to collect and recollect evidence. Therefore both the issuing of the notice *and the wording contained within it* ought to reflect this (subject to the proviso of prejudicing any investigation).

The making of a statement in response to the receipt of a reg. 9 notice may have significant implications for the member concerned and serious consideration ought to be given to exercising the right to consult with a staff association representative. The Police Reform Act 2002 allows for inferences to be drawn from an officer's silence in similar ways to s. 34 of the Criminal Justice and Public Order Act 1994 (see **Evidence and Procedure, chapter 7**).

## *Investigating officer's report*

Regulation 10 states:

(1) At the end of his investigation the investigating officer shall submit a written report on the case to the supervising officer and, if the Authority are supervising the investigation, also to the Authority.

(2) If at any time during his investigation it appears to the investigating officer that the case is one in respect of which the conditions specified in Part I of Schedule 2 are likely to be satisfied, he shall, whether or not the investigation is at an end, submit to the supervising officer—

   (a) a statement of his belief that the case may be one to which regulation 39 applies and the grounds for that belief, and

   (b) a written report on the case so far as it has then been investigated.

---

**KEYNOTE**

If the investigation is being supervised by the Police Complaints Authority (PCA) (see below), the investigating officer must submit two reports: one to the supervising officer and one to the PCA.

If it appears to the investigating officer that the case is a 'special case' as provided for under reg. 39 (i.e. involving a serious allegation of an imprisonable offence; see below), the investigating officer must submit a report stating his/her belief and setting out the current position of the investigation. Given the seriousness of 'special cases', this report would probably need to be submitted immediately and reg. 10(2) makes it clear that the report does not need to be delayed until the end of the investigation.

It should be noted that as a result of the Police Reform Act 2002 a new organisation will have overall responsibility for the system for complaints against the police from April 2004 onwards, when the Independent Police Complaints Commission will replace the PCA.

---

Regulation 11 states:

(1) Subject to paragraphs (2) and (3), on receipt of the investigating officer's report the supervising officer may refer the case to a hearing.

(2) Where—

   (a) the chief officer has a duty to proceed under section 75(7) or 76(2) or (5) of the 1996 Act; or

   (b) the member concerned has received two written warnings about his conduct within the previous twelve months and has in a statement made under regulation 9 admitted that his conduct failed to meet the appropriate standard,

   the supervising officer shall refer the case to a hearing.

---

**KEYNOTE**

On receiving the report from the investigating officer, the supervising officer *may* refer the case to a hearing. Alternatively, he/she may decide not to refer the case and, where that happens, no reference to the case is to be made on the member's personal record (reg. 11(4)).

If the case comes under reg. 11(2)(a) or (b), the supervising officer *must* refer the case to a hearing (unless it is likely to be a 'special case').

The duties referred to at reg. 11(2)(a) (under s. 75(7) or s. 76(2) or (5) of the Police Act 1996) relate to the notification to, and supervision by, the PCA.

The circumstances at reg. 11(2)(b) require that the member has received two written warnings about his/her conduct in the last 12 months *and* that he/she has made a statement under reg. 9 above that his/her conduct failed to meet the required standard. It would seem that the written warnings must relate to the officer's *conduct* and not simply his/her *performance* (as to which, **see para. 1.2.1**).

If it is the *supervising* officer's opinion that the case is *likely* to satisfy the 'special case' conditions (see below), he/she must refer the case to the 'appropriate' officer.

Under reg. 4(1) 'appropriate officer' means:

- where the member concerned is a member of the Metropolitan Police or the City of London Police, an Assistant Commissioner *in that force*

- in any other case, an Assistant Chief Constable.

The appropriate officer will then need to determine whether the conditions in relation to 'special cases' are satisfied or not. If they are not, he/she must return the case to the supervising officer. If the conditions are satisfied, the appropriate officer must then either certify the case as a 'special case' (under reg. 11(3)(b)(i) ) and refer it to a hearing or, if in his/her opinion it is not appropriate to make such a certification, refer it back to the supervising officer.

Any proceedings resulting from a referral under reg. 11 will be 'disciplinary proceedings' for the purposes of part IV of the Police Act 1996 (reg. 11(5) ).

No sanction may be imposed—under reg. 31 (see below)—unless a case has been referred to a hearing (reg. 14).

---

### Withdrawal

Regulation 12 states:

(1) At any time before the beginning of the hearing the supervising officer may direct that the case be withdrawn, unless the chief officer has a duty to proceed under section 75(7) or 76(2) or (5) of the 1996 Act.

(2) Where a case is withdrawn it shall be treated as if the supervising officer had decided not to refer it to a hearing.

---

### KEYNOTE

For the 'duty to proceed' under the relevant sections of the Police Act 1996, see para. 1.2.3.

The effect of reg. 12(2) is that cases withdrawn before the beginning of a hearing will be treated as if they had never been referred in the first place and therefore no reference to them can be made on the member's personal record (see reg. 11(4) above).

---

### Referral of cases to hearing

Regulation 13(1) states:

(1) The supervising officer shall ensure that, as soon as practicable, the member concerned is given written notice of a decision to refer the case to a hearing and that, not less than 21 days before the date of hearing, the member concerned is supplied with copies of—
(a) any statement he may have made to the investigating officer; and
(b) any relevant statement, document or other material obtained during the course of the investigation.

---

### KEYNOTE

Regulation 13(1) makes two requirements. The first is that the member be given written notice of the decision to refer the case to a hearing *as soon as practicable* (see also reg. 9). As with reg. 9 (see above), the wording suggests that the member must be served personally with the written notice here. This view is further reinforced by the modified wording used in reg. 13 in relation to 'special cases' (see below). This notice must specify the relevant conduct that allegedly failed to meet the appropriate standard, together with the relevant paragraph of the Code of Conduct (as to which, see above) (reg. 13(2) ).

The second requirement is that, not less than 21 days before the date of the hearing, the member concerned be supplied with copies of the documents set out at reg. 13(1)(a) and (b), including a copy of any account or statement given verbally (reg. 13(3) ).

---

### Notice of hearing

Regulation 15 states:

(1) The supervising officer shall ensure that at least 21 days in advance the member concerned is notified of the time, date and place of the hearing.

(2) In a case to which this paragraph applies the hearing may, if the supervising officer considers it appropriate in the circumstances, take place before the expiry of the 21 days referred to in paragraph (1).

(3) Paragraph (2) applies where the member concerned is given a written notice under regulation 13(1) of a decision to refer the case to a hearing and—

   (a) at the time he receives such a notice he is detained in pursuance of the sentence of a court in a prison or other institution to which the Prison Act 1952 applies, or has received a suspended sentence of imprisonment; and

   (b) having been supplied under regulation 13 with the documents therein mentioned he does not elect to be legally represented at the hearing.

---

**KEYNOTE**

Generally the member concerned must be given at least 21 days' notice of the time, date and place of any proposed hearing. However, in the (very unusual) circumstances set out at reg. 15(3)(a) and (b), the supervising officer may allow the hearing to take place earlier if he/she considers it appropriate in the circumstances.

If the supervising officer is of the opinion that the sanctions of

- dismissal

- requirement to resign, or

- reduction in rank

should be available to the hearing, he/she *must* make sure that any member concerned is given written notice that

- they are entitled to elect legal representation at the hearing, and

- that the hearing cannot reduce the member in rank, require them to resign or dismiss them unless they have been given the opportunity to elect such respresentation, and

- that unless they have so elected, they may only be represented at the hearing by a 'friend' (police officer)

(reg. 16).

This further notice must be given at the same time as the reg. 15 notice. Failure to notify the member of this entitlement will mean that the sanctions above will not be available and will also lead to the case being remitted under reg. 29 (see below). Practically, this means that, if the opportunity to be legally represented is not given to the member concerned, the only options open to the hearing are a fine, reprimand or caution (reg. 31(1)).

The member concerned will be 'invited' to state in writing:

- whether or not he/she accepts that his/her conduct did not meet the appropriate standard

- whether he/she wishes to be legally represented (if reg. 16 applies)

- whether he/she proposes to call any witnesses (and if so, their names and addresses so that the supervising officer may secure their attendance)

(reg. 17(1)).

Any such written response must be made within 14 days of the member being 'notified' that the last of the documents under reg. 13(1) have been supplied (reg. 17(1)).

Presumably, the documents must also have *been* supplied otherwise the member will not be in a position to make a full evaluation of the case against him/her.

As with a statement made under reg. 9 (see above), any admission made under reg. 17 may have significant consequences for the member concerned, particularly as an admission can, without more, amount to a finding against him/her (see below).

Any witnesses who are police officers will be ordered to attend the hearing (reg. 17(2)). The member concerned will also be ordered to attend the hearing (reg. 24(1)). If he/she fails to attend the hearing, it may proceed and be concluded in his/her absence (reg. 24(2)) and any requirement under these Regulations that cannot be complied with because the member is absent will be dispensed with (reg. 24(4)). In other words, the hearing does not *have* to be adjourned simply because the member concerned is prevented from attending—either by ill-health or any other cause—and may proceed to conclusion without him/her. If any requirement under the Regulations cannot be complied with because the member concerned has not attended the hearing, that does not mean that the procedure will be delayed; it means that the requirement is dispensed with.

If, however, the member informs the officer presiding over the hearing in advance that he/she is unable to attend as a result of ill-health, *or some other unavoidable reason*, the hearing *may* be adjourned (reg. 24(3)).

The supervising officer must cause any other witnesses to be notified that their attendance is required and to advise them of the time and place of the hearing (reg. 17(2)).

A hearing does not *have* to be adjourned simply because a witness is unable or unwilling to attend (reg. 17(3)). However, the officers conducting a hearing have a discretionary power to do so in the appropriate circumstances.

---

### The hearing

Regulation 18 requires that the hearing be conducted by three officers who are not 'interested parties' (as to which, see above).

Subject to the regulation dealing with 'remission of cases' (see below), the 'presiding officer' at the hearing must be an Assistant Chief Constable or, in the case of a Metropolitan police or City of London police officer, a Commander (reg. 18(2)).

Generally, the other two assisting officers must be at least the rank of superintendent each of whom must be from a force maintained under s. 2 of the Police Act 1996 (reg. 18(3)). However, where the member concerned is a superintendent/chief superintendent, the assisting officers must be assistant chief constables (or Commanders in the case of Metropolitan and City of London officers) in different forces from that of the member concerned (reg. 18(4)).

Where the member concerned accepts, in accordance with reg. 17, that his/her conduct fell short of the 'appropriate standard' (i.e. the Code of Conduct), a summary of the facts of the case will be prepared and a copy supplied to the member at least 14 days before the hearing (reg. 19(1)). If the member disagrees with the summary, he/she may submit a response within seven days *of receiving it* (reg. 19(2)).

If the member has not accepted that his/her conduct fell short of the appropriate standard, there is no need for a summary (reg. 19(3)).

Where a summary of facts has been prepared, a copy of it will be supplied to the officers conducting the hearing in addition to a copy of the reg. 13 notice (reg. 20).

Unless the member has given notice (under reg. 17) that he/she wishes to be legally represented, the *supervising officer* must appoint another police officer to present the case (reg. 21(1)). This would generally be someone of at least inspector rank. Where the member concerned has elected to be legally represented, this regulation leaves it open for the case to be presented by a solicitor/counsel.

The member concerned may conduct his/her own case in person or by another police officer chosen by him/her. If the member has given notice under reg. 17, he/she may then be represented by a solicitor/counsel (reg. 21(2)).

The officers conducting the hearing may adjourn from time to time if it appears to them to be *necessary or expedient for the due hearing of the case* (reg. 22(1)).

Any decision of the officers need only be based on a simple majority but must not indicate whether it was so decided or whether it was reached unanimously (reg. 22(2)). No provision is made for the presiding officer to have any form of 'casting vote' or for his/her view to carry any more weight than the assisting officers.

### Procedure at hearing

The officers conducting the hearing will, subject to the provisions of the Regulations, determine their own procedure (reg. 23(1)). Any question as to whether any evidence is admissible, or whether any question should be put to a witness will also be determined by the officers conducting the hearing (reg. 28(1)). These widely drafted discretionary powers will, however, be subject to general principles of law (e.g. natural justice).

Additionally, the presiding officer may, *with the consent of the member concerned*, allow any document to be adduced in evidence, even though no copy of it was supplied to the member under reg. 13 (reg. 28(2)).

The job of the officers conducting the hearing (set out under reg. 23(2)) is threefold:

- they must first review the facts of the case and decide whether or not the member's?conduct met the 'appropriate standard' (the Code of Conduct);
- if they decide that the member's conduct did not meet that standard, the officers must then decide whether, in all the circumstances, it would be reasonable to impose a sanction and, if so; and
- they must determine which sanction to impose.

Therefore, a finding that the conduct fell short of the required standard does not automatically mean that any sanction must be imposed.

Under reg. 23(3) the officers conducting the hearing can only find that the member's conduct failed to meet the appropriate standard if:

- it is admitted by the member concerned; or
- it is proved by the person presenting the case *on the balance of probabilities*.

Thus, the standard of proof required in such hearings has been reduced to that of an ordinary civil trial (and that required of a defendant where the burden of proof falls on him/her; **see Evidence and Procedure, chapter 11**). Although much attention has been given to this lowering of the standard of proof required, it is a general common law rule that the greater the consequences being faced by the defendant, the greater the degree of evidence that will be required to tip the balance of probabilities against him/her.

A verbatim record of the proceedings must be taken and, if the member concerned lodges notice of appeal (see below) and applies for a copy or transcript of the record within the time limit, it will be supplied to him or her (reg. 30).

### Attendance of others at hearing

Generally, hearings will be conducted in private (reg. 26(1)). However, there are some exceptions:

- The member concerned may be accompanied by another police officer (reg. 26(3)).
- The presiding officer may allow witnesses to be accompanied by a friend or a relative? (reg. 26(4)).

Where there has been a complaint made against the member concerned, whether directly or through the PCA or some other person/body, the person who originated the complaint will generally be allowed to attend parts of the hearing. Regulation 25 provides that the originator of a complaint ('the complainant') will, as a general rule, be allowed to attend the hearing *while witnesses are being examined or cross-examined*. The complainant may also be accompanied by a friend or relative at the discretion of the presiding officer (reg. 25(2)). If the complainant or any accompanying friend/relative is to give evidence, neither will be allowed to attend the hearing before he/she gives evidence (reg. 25(3)).

If the member concerned gives evidence, he/she may be asked questions by the presiding officer on behalf of the complainant after the cross-examination. He/she may also be asked questions *by the complainant* at the presiding officer's discretion (reg. 25(4)).

Notwithstanding these provisions, the complainant and anyone accompanying him/her must not intervene in or interrupt the hearing. If any of these people misconduct themselves or behave in a disorderly or abusive manner, the presiding officer may exclude them from the hearing (reg. 25(5)).

If it appears to the presiding officer that a witness may disclose in evidence information which, in the public interest, ought not to be disclosed to the public, he/she must require any member of the public (including complainants and their accompanying friends) to withdraw while the evidence is given (reg. 27).

The presiding officer has discretion to allow the presence of any solicitor or other person that he/she considers desirable to attend the whole or part of the hearing *subject to the consent of all parties to the hearing* (reg. 26(2)).

Members of the PCA are entitled to attend hearings where there has been a complaint against the member concerned or where the case arose from a matter requiring the mandatory supervision of the investigation by the PCA (**see para. 1.2.3**) (reg. 26(2)). Home Office guidance also advises that members of the PCA be allowed to attend hearings where they have exercised their authority under s. 76 of the Police Act 1996 (recommending or directing that a chief officer bring proceedings against an officer) (note that s. 76 will be repealed shortly by virtue of s. 107(2) of the Police Reform Act 2002).

### Remission of cases

Regulation 29 states:

(1) The hearing of the case—
    (a) shall, in the circumstances mentioned in paragraph (2); or
    (b) may, in the circumstances mentioned in paragraph (5),
    be remitted by the presiding officer concerned to an officer of equivalent rank in the force concerned or to an officer of equivalent rank in another force who, at the presiding officer's request, has agreed to act as the presiding officer in the matter.

(2) A case shall be so remitted if—
    (a) the presiding officer is an interested party otherwise than in his capacity as such; or
    (b) there would not, because the member concerned was not given notice under regulation 16 of the opportunity to elect to be legally represented at the hearing, be available on a finding against him any of the sanctions referred to in that regulation, and it appears to the presiding officer concerned that those sanctions ought to be so available and that accordingly it would be desirable for there to be another hearing at which the member concerned could, if he so wished, be so represented.

---

**KEYNOTE**

Remission of a hearing really means passing it over to another officer of equivalent rank, either in the force concerned or of another force.

The hearing of a case *must* be remitted if:

- the presiding officer is an 'interested party'; or

- if the member was not given the opportunity to elect legal representation under reg. 16 (see above), thereby limiting the sanctions available to the hearing *and* the presiding officer feels that those sanctions ought to be available.

In addition, the hearing of a case *may* be remitted if, either before or during the hearing, the presiding officer considers it appropriate (reg. 29(5)).

If the case is remitted under the second item above, the member must be served in writing with a notice inviting him/her to elect *within 14 days of receipt*, to be legally represented. Further, in such cases, the officer remitting the case must not give any indication of his/her assessment of the case, nor of the sanction that might be imposed to the 'new' officer. This suggests that, in cases where the hearing is remitted under the first item above, or in cases where discretionary remission is adopted, the presiding officer *may* indicate his/her assessment of the case so far and also any sanctions that he/she thinks ought to be imposed.

The sanctions

Regulation 31 states:

(1) Subject to section 84(1) of the 1996 Act, the officers conducting the hearing may impose any of the following sanctions, namely—

(a) dismissal from the force;

(b) requirement to resign from the force as an alternative to dismissal taking effect either forthwith or on such date as may be specified in the decision;

(c) reduction in rank;

(d) fine;

(e) reprimand;

(f) caution.

---

**KEYNOTE**

The reference to s. 84(1) of the Police Act 1996 is to the general prohibition on imposing a reduction in rank, requirement to resign or dismissal without having first given the officer an opportunity to elect legal representation.

Any of the above sanctions *except a requirement to resign*, will have immediate effect (reg. 31(2)). This immediate effect will not be delayed by any appeal procedure.

If a fine is imposed it is subject to a maximum limit (set out under reg. 31(3)). To work out the maximum amount of the fine you must first assume that it is to be recovered from the member concerned by weekly deductions over the next 13 weeks. The overall sum—whether one fine or a number of fines—when spread across these 13 weeks must not exceed one-seventh of the member's weekly pay.

In other words, the fine(s) cannot exceed 13 days' pay—though reg. 31 does not say whether that is gross pay or net pay. Neither does reg. 31 appear to require the fine *to be paid* over the 13-week period following the imposition of the sanctions.

In considering what sanction to impose, the officers conducting the hearing *must* have regard to the member's service record (reg. 32(a)). In doing so, they *may* receive evidence from witnesses if the officers are of the opinion that such evidence would help them (reg. 32(a)).

The member concerned must be given the opportunity to make oral or written representations in respect of any sanction (either in person or through his/her representative) (reg. 32(b)).

At the end of the hearing the member concerned must be informed *orally* of:

- the finding, and

- any sanction imposed.

He/she must also be provided with:

- *written notification*, and

- a *summary of the reasons*

within three days of the end of the hearing (reg. 33).

Chief officers must keep a book recording details of every case brought against a member of their force. The entry in that book must include details of the findings, together with any other decisions reached in proceedings connected with the case.

---

Review

As with the unsatisfactory performance process (**see para. 1.2.1**), the 1999 Regulations provide for a review of any sanction imposed under reg. 31 and for any sanction to be expunged if it is found that the member concerned had not failed to meet the appropriate standard.

The appropriate regulations here are regs 34 to 36. Generally, the provisions relating to a review are the same as those for unsatisfactory performance.

In misconduct cases, the time by which the request for a review must be made to the reviewing officer is 14 days from receipt of the written summary of reasons under reg. 33. The member concerned may be accompanied at any review meeting by a fellow officer but can only be additionally accompanied by a solicitor/counsel where reg. 16 (in relation to the availability of the sanctions of dismissal, requirement to resign or reduction in rank) applies (reg. 35(2)). This is in contrast to a review meeting in relation to unsatisfactory performance where there are no restrictions on the member concerned being accompanied by a solicitor/counsel.

### Special cases

Regulation 39 makes provision for 'special cases' involving allegations of misconduct. There are three elements to qualify as a 'special case':

- the report, complaint or allegation must indicate that the conduct of the member concerned did not meet the appropriate standard
- the conditions set out in part I of sch. 2 are satisfied (see below); and
- the appropriate officer (see above) has issued a certificate under reg. 11(3)(b)(i).

#### The conditions
Part I of sch. 2 states:

(1) The conditions referred to in regulation 39 are—
  (a) the report, complaint or allegation indicates that the conduct of the member concerned is of a serious nature and that an imprisonable offence may have been committed by the member concerned; and
  (b) the conduct is such that, were the case to be referred to a hearing under regulation 11 and the officers conducting that hearing were to find that the conduct failed to meet the appropriate standard, they would in the opinion of the appropriate officer be likely to impose the sanction specified in regulation 31(1)(a) (dismissal from the force); and
  (c) the report, complaint or allegation is supported by written statements, documents or other material which is, in the opinion of the appropriate officer, sufficient without further evidence to establish on the balance of probabilities that the conduct of the member concerned did not meet the appropriate standard; and
  (d) the appropriate officer is of the opinion that it is in the public interest for the member concerned to cease to be a member of a police force without delay.
(2) In this paragraph an 'imprisonable offence' means an offence which is punishable with imprisonment in the case of a person aged 21 or over.

---

**KEYNOTE**

All of the conditions set out under part I must be satisfied before a case can be designated a 'special case'.

The circumstances are such that any 'special case' will be very unusual and will be dealt with under legal advice at a very high organisational level. What constitutes conduct of a 'serious nature' is not clear but there must be an indication that the officer's alleged conduct involves an offence punishable with imprisonment (if commited by a person aged 21 years or over).

A further requirement for a case to be classified as 'special' is that, in the opinion of the appropriate officer, the officers conducting a hearing into the case would be likely to dismiss the member from the force if the case were found proved. 'Special cases' must also be supported by evidence which, again in the appropriate officer's opinion, is enough by itself to establish that the member's conduct did not meet the required standard (on the balance of probabilities).

The final requirement for a case to fall into this category is that, in the appropriate officer's opinion, it is in the public interest that the member concerned ceases to be a police officer without delay.

The times when all these criteria are most likely to be met is when an officer has been caught 'red-handed' in the commission of a serious offence.

---

### Modifications for special cases

The important difference between 'special cases' and other cases involving allegations of misconduct is that the former will be subject to a 'fast track' procedure. That procedure, which is set out at part II of sch. 2, changes a number of the key regulations above. Where a case does meet the special case criteria but is subsequently returned to the supervising officer, the unchanged regulations will then apply once more (reg. 39(3)). A special case may be so returned at any time before the beginning of the hearing.

Generally, the modifications shift many of the administrative responsibilities to the 'appropriate officer'.

Remember that, under reg. 4, 'appropriate officer' means:

- where the member concerned is a member of the Metropolitan Police or the City of London Police, an Assistant Commissioner *in that force*;

- in any other case, an Assistant Chief Constable.

Broadly, the key differences in the regulations under the fast track procedure are:

- the setting of a *maximum* time limit (28 days) as well as a minimum for setting the hearing date;

- the notice informing the member of his/her opportunity to elect legal representation is mandatory in all cases;

- the provisions allowing oral testimony at the hearing are removed;

- the hearing must be heard/reviewed by a chief officer;

- the powers to adjourn the hearing are restricted in their duration and frequency;

- some of the restrictions on the attendance of a complainant at the hearing are removed;

- the time limits on notifying the finding of a hearing and of a review are reduced from three days to 24 hours.

The fast track procedure is designed to be completed within six weeks of the issuing of the relevant notice.

### 1.2.3    Complaints

Part IV of the Police Act 1996 sets out the provisions for the recording and investigation of complaints against police officers. Every police authority and the HMIC is under a statutory duty to 'keep themselves informed' as to the workings of the relevant sections of the Act relating to the recording and investigation of complaints (s. 77). Provisions are also made for the making of regulations in respect of non-Home Office police forces under s. 78 of the 1996 Act.

In the light of a number of perceived shortcomings in the police complaints system—not least of which was the European Court of Human Rights finding that it did not provide an 'adequate remedy' for the purposes of Article 13 of the Convention (as to which, **see chapter 2**) (*Govell* v *United Kingdom* (application 27237/95), 14 January 1998, unreported)—and the Stephen Lawrence Inquiry, the government undertook a wholesale review of the complaints system, its adequacy and, most importantly, its effect on public confidence. As a result of the legal and technical inadequacies of the system, along with the public and professional perceptions canvassed over a long period of consultation and research,

Part 2 of the Police Reform Act 2002 introduces some significant changes in this area. Setting out a new framework for the recording and investigation of police complaints, the Police Reform Act 2002 provisions had not come fully into effect at the time of writing. Some of the foundations for the new framework were brought into effect soon after Royal Assent but the main body of the changes are not expected to come into effect until early 2004.

Section 65 of the Police Act 1996 defines a complaint as:

> . . . a complaint about the conduct of a member of a police force which is submitted—
>
> (a) by a member of the public, or
> (b) on behalf of a member of the public and with his written consent.

---

**KEYNOTE**

Therefore a complaint so defined must emanate from a member of the public and must be made about the conduct of a 'member of a police force'. As special constables and cadets are not members of a police force, the definition—and the attendant procedures—do not apply to them. However, the much broader wording of the Police Reform Act 2002 will bring all people 'serving with the police' within the scope of the complaints system.

The current definition allows for the reporting of complaints by third parties acting on behalf of the member of the public, e.g. MPs, Citizens Advice Bureaux or friends/family. If a complaint is made by another person/organisation, there must be some form of writing that indicates the complainant's willingness for that person/organisation to submit the complaint on their behalf. This would include e-mails and other electronically-generated messages.

Clearly there will be occasions where there may be an overlap in the procedures relating to complaints, conduct and performance. Local advice should be sought in the recording and investigation of such incidents.

There is no requirement for the officer concerned to have been on duty at the time of the conduct complained of and again local guidance should be sought in relation to the recording and investigation of 'complaints' of off-duty police officers.

The definition does not extend to complaints in so far as they relate to the *direction or control* of a police force by the chief officer (s. 67(4)).

Where the conduct complained of is (or has been) wholly or partly the subject of criminal or disciplinary proceedings, none of the provisions relating to the recording and investigation of complaints under chapter 1 of part IV of the 1996 Act applies (s. 67(5)).

The Police Reform Act 2002 provisions will, when in force, extend the recording requirements above to include all conduct matters arising from civil litigation as 'complaints', and introduces a new concept of recordable conduct matters which goes beyond the current definition of a complaint as set out above.

---

### Steps to be taken

Section 67 of the Police Act 1996 states:

(1) Where a complaint is submitted to the chief officer of police for a police area, he shall take any steps that appear to him to be desirable for the purpose of obtaining or preserving evidence relating to the conduct complained of.

(2) After complying with subsection (1), the chief officer shall determine whether he is the appropriate authority in relation to the member of a police force whose conduct is the subject of the complaint.

(3) If the chief officer determines that he is not the appropriate authority, he shall—
   (a) send the complaint or, if it was submitted orally, particulars of it, to the appropriate authority, and
   (b) give notice that he has done so to the person by whom or on whose behalf the complaint was submitted.

**KEYNOTE**

The first duty to fall on a chief officer on receipt of a complaint is to obtain and preserve evidence. This duty is not dependent on the complaint having any *prima facie* foundation, neither is it dependent on the determination as to who is the 'appropriate authority'.

That 'authority' will be:

- in relation to a Metropolitan police officer—the Commissioner
- in relation to an officer above the rank of superintendent from another force—the police authority for that force
- in relation to an officer of superintendent rank or below from another force—the chief officer of that force

(s. 65).

The procedure to be followed in respect of senior officers above the rank of superintendent is set out in s. 68.

If the chief officer receiving the complaint determines that he/she is not the appropriate authority, he/she must follow the requirements set out at s. 67(3)(a) and (b) above.

Once these steps in relation to the preservation of evidence and determination of the appropriate authority have been completed, the complaint must be recorded (s. 69(1)).

The decision as to whether a complaint meets the criteria to be recorded as such rests with chief officers and there is no readily available mechanism for complaints to overturn that decision. This is one area that has generated pressure for change and is addressed in the Police Reform Act 2002, although the responsibility for recording complaints will remain with the chief officer or police authority. A further change is that complainants will be able to complain directly to the Independent Police Complaints Commission (see below).

After recording a complaint, the chief officer must decide whether it is suitable for informal resolution (see below) and may appoint another member of the force to assist (s. 69(2)). If the complaint is suitable for informal resolution, the chief officer must seek to resolve it informally and may appoint another officer from that force to do so (s. 69(4)).

If, after attempts to resolve a complaint informally, it appears to the chief officer that such informal resolution is 'impossible' or that the complaint is, for any other reason, not suitable for informal resolution, he/she must appoint another officer of that, or some other force, to investigate it (s. 69(6)).

A complaint will not be suitable for informal resolution unless:

- the member of the public consents; and
- the chief officer is satisfied that the conduct complained of, even if proved, would not justify criminal *or disciplinary* proceedings

(s. 69(3)).

If the complaint is not suitable for informal resolution, the chief officer must appoint another member of that, or some other force, to investigate it (s. 69(5)).

Any request by a chief officer for the chief officer of another force to provide an officer to investigate a complaint (under ss. 69(5) or (6)) must comply with the request (s. 69(8)).

Any officer who has previously been appointed to resolve a complaint informally may not later investigate the complaint (s. 69(7)).

Unless the investigation of the complaint is supervised by the Police Complaints Authority under s. 72 (see below), the investigating officer must submit any report on the complaint to the chief officer who appointed him/her (s. 69(9)).

Informal resolution

The informal resolution procedures are built on the principles of flexibility and simplicity and they are intended to prevent cases of a minor nature from receiving the full attentions of formal investigation. The current procedure for the informal resolution of complaints is to be found mainly in the Police (Complaints) (Informal Resolution) Regulations 1985 (SI 1985 No. 671), though this will change when the new framework comes into effect.

In addition to the restrictions placed on informal resolution under s. 69(3) of the Police Act 1996 above, a complaint that is supervised by the Police Complaints Authority, under its mandatory or discretionary remit, may not be informally resolved (reg. 3 of the 1985 Regulations).

Informal resolutions are generally felt to be extremely effective in resolving police complaints and this is one of the few areas of the current complaint-handling system about which there is across the board agreement. As a result, the new statutory complaints framework under the Police Reform Act 2002 allows for a similar system for 'local resolution' of certain complaints.

### Appointed officers

If it is decided that informal resolution is appropriate, the officer initially deputed to handle the question may act as the 'appointed officer' (as defined in the 1985 Regulations) and seek an informal resolution. Alternatively, the case might be referred to another officer to undertake the role of appointed officer.

As soon as practicable after the decision to resolve the complaint informally, the appointed officer should seek the views of both the complainant and also the officer whose conduct has been complained of (reg. 4(1)). The officer should be allowed speak to a 'friend' about the matter first if he/she wishes.

At the same time, or thereafter, the appointed officer may take any steps that appear to be appropriate to resolve the complaint.

### Early resolution

Regulation 4(1) of the 1985 Regulations allows a supervisory officer of whatever rank to deal speedily with a complaint if it appears to them that it can be resolved in an informal manner at the time it is made.

Regulation 4 allows a supervisory officer to receive a complaint and, if the officer complained about is both present and willing to explain his/her understanding of the incident giving rise to the complaint, to deal with it at the time. In order to do this, the complainant must accept the explanation given or, if appropriate, any apology as a satisfactory outcome.

There is no requirement imposed on an officer to give an apology and the supervisor cannot do so on the officer's behalf unless he/she agrees that his/her conduct fell below the required standard. However, that does not prevent the supervisor apologising on behalf of the force.

If any explanation or apology is accepted, the supervisory officer should report the matter to the officer who has delegated responsibility for the informal resolution of complaints. If satisfied with the handling of the complaint, that officer may make a record in the complaints register and write to the complainant noting the way in which the complaint was handled and indicating the intention of recording it as having been informally resolved.

Where it appears to the appointed officer that the resolution of a complaint is likely to be assisted by a meeting between the complainant and the officer concerned—or also with any other person considered appropriate—then suitable arrangements may be made.

There will be no obligation on the officer who is the subject of the complaint to attend such a meeting.

A meeting may provide an opportunity for the complainant and the officer to exchange views and for any misunderstandings to be cleared up. It will also allow the officer, where there is an admission to the conduct complained of, to offer an explanation or an apology to the complainant.

If in the course of the informal resolution procedure evidence comes to light of a more serious complaint which might require a formal investigation, the informal procedures should be terminated and the matter reported to the chief officer immediately, whereupon the provisions of part IV of the Act will apply.

Where there has been an attempted or a successful informal resolution of a complaint, no record must be made of it in the personal record of the officer concerned.

Where informal resolution appears to be impossible or it is apparent that the complaint is for any other reason not suitable to be so resolved, arrangements must be made for it to be investigated formally.

A new scheme for the local resolution of complaints under the Police Reform Act 2002 provisions will allow a complainant to appeal to the Independent Police Complaints Commission against the handling of the resolution.

### Admissibility of statements

Generally a statement made for the purpose of an informal resolution of a complaint will not be admissible in any criminal, civil or disciplinary hearing (s. 86(1)). Where an officer makes a voluntary statement—oral or written—to the appointed officer, that officer must be told that this is the case. However, where the statement made consists of, or includes an admission relating to any matter that is not part of that complaint, s. 86(1) will *not* prevent it from being so used (s. 86(2)). Therefore informed consideration should be given by the officer before he/she makes any admissions in relation to the attempted informal resolution of a complaint.

### The Police Complaints Authority

The Police Complaints Authority (PCA) is an independent body set up to oversee, among other things, the investigation of complaints against the police. Replacing the Police Complaints Board, the PCA was originally established under s. 83 of the Police and Criminal Evidence Act 1984. Its role has become increasingly important in ensuring the thorough and impartial investigation and supervision of sensitive and serious matters involving police conduct. However, there have been many criticisms of the way in which the PCA is structured and its lack of investigative powers. The Police Reform Act 2002 contains a number of substantial changes to this area, including the replacement of the PCA by an Independent Police Complaints Commission (IPCC). There will be a transitional period during which both bodies are functioning alongside each other and, at the time of writing, the relevant parts of the Police Reform Act 2002 allowing for the appointment of the IPCC and the making of regulations were already in force. The rules governing the make up of the IPCC, appointment and membership can be found in sch. 2 to the Act.

The PCA is made up of at least eight members plus a chair who is appointed by the Queen. Its constitution can be found in sch. 5 to the Police Act 1996.

Certain complaints made against police officers must be *referred* to the PCA. There are also provisions as to which investigations the PCA either may, or must, *supervise*.

### Referral

Section 70(1)(a) of the Police Act 1996 requires that the following complaints be *referred* to the PCA, i.e. complaints alleging that the conduct complained of resulted in:

- the death of, or serious injury to, some other person
- assault occasioning actual bodily harm, bribery or a serious arrestable offence

(Police (Complaints) (Mandatory Referrals etc.) Regulations 1985 (SI 1985 No. 673)).

Section 70(2) allows the PCA to 'call in' any complaint not referred to them, irrespective of whether it meets the above criteria or not.

Section 71 allows chief officers to refer to the PCA other serious or exceptional matters not arising from a complaint but which indicate that an officer may have committed a criminal offence.

*Supervision*

It appears from the wording of s. 72 of the Police Act 1996 that any complaint involving the conduct set out above must be supervised by the PCA. It must also supervise any other complaint that is not within those criteria but which it determines is in the public interest for it to supervise.

Where the PCA supervise an investigation, it may place certain conditions on the appointment, or continued appointment, of an investigating officer (s. 72(3)). It may also make reasonable requirements in relation to the direction of the investigation and the resources committed to it. However, the PCA may not make any requirement relating to the obtaining and preserving of evidence in connection with a complaint where the possibility of criminal proceedings arises unless it has the consent of the Crown Prosecution Service. It must also seek the views of the relevant chief officer before making a requirement as to the commitment of his/her resources to an investigation.

At the end of a supervised investigation, the investigating officer must submit a report to the PCA as well as sending a copy to the 'appropriate authority' (the chief officer or police authority) (s. 73(1)).

After considering the report, the PCA will send a statement to the appropriate authority and, if it is practicable to do so, send a copy to the officer whose conduct is being investigated and to the complainant. That statement will say whether the investigation has been carried out to the PCA's satisfaction and specify any respect in which it has not been so carried out (s. 73(9)).

Ordinarily, no disciplinary proceedings or criminal proceedings may be brought until the PCA's statement has been submitted (s. 73(6) and (7)) but, in exceptional circumstances, the Director of Public Prosecutions may bring criminal proceedings before the statement has been submitted by the PCA if it is undesirable to wait (s. 73(8)).

*Procedure after investigation*

At the end of any investigation, supervised or not, the chief officer must determine whether the report indicates that a criminal offence may have been committed by the officer. If he/she does conclude that a criminal offence may have been committed, the chief officer must send a copy of the report to the Director of Public Prosecutions (s. 75(2) to (3) to the Police Act 1996).

Once the question of criminal proceedings has been dealt with, the chief officer will send a memorandum to the PCA stating whether or not it is proposed to bring disciplinary proceedings against the officer and if not, why not (s. 75(4)). This memorandum will be accompanied by a copy of the complaint and a copy of the report of the investigation.

Where a memorandum from the chief officer indicates that no disciplinary proceedings are to be brought, the PCA may 'recommend' to him/her that such proceedings *are* brought (s. 76(1)). If, having made such a recommendation and consulted with the chief officer, he/she still does not bring disciplinary proceedings, the PCA may *direct* him/her to do so, giving written reasons (s. 76(3) to (4)).

The chief officer must then:

- comply with this direction unless it is withdrawn (s. 76(5) to (6));

- advise the PCA of any action taken; and

- supply the PCA with such other information as it may reasonably require in discharging its functions

(s. 76(7)).

Under the new Police Reform Act framework, the IPCC will have far greater powers and influence over investigations, including new powers to conduct its own investigation using its own trained investigators, or to 'manage' the police investigation.

*Withdrawn or ill-founded complaints*

Although there is no specific legal remedy available against someone who makes a false complaint against a police officer, there are a number of options open to investigating officers in relation to withdrawn or ill-founded complaints.

If it is apparent from the outset that a complaint cannot or should not be investigated, dispensation from the requirement to investigate may be sought from the PCA (under reg. 3 of the Police (Dispensation from Requirement to Investigate Complaints) Regulations 1985 (SI 1985 No. 672)).

Cases where dispensation is sought will generally come under one or more of the following (D.I.S.P.) categories:

- Delay—where more than 12 months have elapsed between the incident giving rise to the complaint and its being reported *and* either no good reason is given for that delay or it would be unjust to the officer concerned to investigate it.

- Identity—where there is an anonymous complainant who cannot reasonably be contacted or identified.

- Same—in the case of repetitious complaints where the complainant has no fresh allegation/evidence but has made the same complaint before and it has been finalised.

- Practicable—where the investigation is not reasonably practicable (e.g. because of the complainant's own conduct) or where complaint is vexatious, abusive or oppressive.

Even where a complaint falls into one of these categories, it might not receive dispensation, in which case a normal investigation would have to follow.

A complaint may be withdrawn at any time but should only be regarded as withdrawn when a signed statement is received from the complainant (or someone authorised to act on his/her behalf). Withdrawal of a complaint would not necessarily amount to an end to the investigation which might still be pursued under the internal conduct procedures (**see para. 1.2.2**).

In cases where it seems to the investigating officer that the complaint is ill-founded or that it would require a disproportionate amount of effort to investigate it, he/she may submit a report to the appropriate complaints department (or the PCA if supervised) to that effect.

The facility to dispense with the need for an investigation under certain circumstances will be retained under the new Police Reform Act scheme.

## 1.2.4   Appeals

Where an officer has been:

- dismissed
- required to resign, or
- reduced in rank

following a hearing/chief officer's review in relation to unsatisfactory performance or misconduct, that officer has a right of appeal.

### Police Appeals Tribunal

The Police Appeals Tribunal is made up of a number of people drawn by the relevant police authority from a list maintained by the Home Office. The tribunal will comprise:

- a legally-qualified chair person
- a member of the police authority (or, in cases involving Metropolitan Police officers, a member of the Metropolitan Police Committee)

- a serving or former chief officer (not from the appellant's force)
- a retired officer of appropriate rank (i.e. a superintendent/chief superintendent where the appellant was a superintendent, otherwise a chief inspector or below).

A tribunal does not need to have a hearing in all cases (Police Act 1996, sch. 6, para. 6). It may determine an appeal without the formality of a hearing, provided the appellant and respondent are given the opportunity to make representations as to the holding of a hearing and provided also that those representations have been considered.

### The Rules

Section 85 of the Police Act 1996 empowers the Secretary of State to make regulations in respect of appeals from hearings. After consultation with the statutory body that oversees all tribunals, the Council on Tribunals, the Secretary of State made the Police Appeals Tribunals Rules 1999 (SI 1999 No. 818), which came into force on 1 April 1999.

Other than in cases brought under the old Police Discipline Regulations, the 1999 Rules revoke the former Police (Appeals) Rules 1985.

Any expression used in the Rules which also appears in the Police (Conduct) or Police (Efficiency) Regulations 1999 generally has the same meaning as it does in those Regulations (r. (3)).

### Notice of appeal

Rule 5 of the 1999 Rules states:

(1) Subject to rule 7 and paragraph (2), the time within which notice of an appeal under section 85 of the Act shall be given is 21 days from the date on which the decision appealed against was notified to the appellant in pursuance of regulations made in accordance with section 50(3) of the Act.

(2) In a case to which regulation 39 of the Police (Conduct) Regulations 1999 or regulation 25 of the Police (Conduct) (Senior Officers) Regulations 1999 applies where the decision appealed against was given in pursuance of those Regulations as modified by Part II of Schedule 2 or, as the case may be, by Part II of the Schedule to those Regulations, the time within which notice of an appeal under section 85 of the Act shall be given is 28 days from—

(a) the conclusion of any criminal proceedings in which the appellant is charged with an offence in respect of the conduct to which the decision appealed against related; or

(b) a decision that no such criminal proceedings will be instituted or taken over by the Director of Public Prosecutions has been communicated to the appellant.

---

**KEYNOTE**

Notice of the appeal must be given within 21 days of the date *on which the decision appealed against was notified to the member concerned*. It would seem that this means the date on which the member concerned actually received the notification of the decision. This time limit may, however, be extended by the 'relevant police authority' under r. 7(1) (see below). The relevant police authority will be the police authority for the member's force. In the case of Metropolitan Police officers, the authority will be the designated Home Office official of the Metropolitan Police Committee.

In 'special cases' (see para. 1.2.3) under reg. 39 of the Police (Conduct) Regulations 1999—or its equivalent for senior officers—the time limit is 28 days from:

- the end of any related criminal proceedings against the appellant; or

- the date when a decision from the Director of Public Prosecutions not to institute any such proceedings has been communicated to the appellant.

The notice of appeal must be in writing and a copy must be sent to the 'respondent' (r. 5(3)).

The 'respondent' is simply the chief officer of the appellant's force (or, where the appellant is a senior officer, a person designated for that purpose by the relevant police authority) (r. 4).

---

Procedure

Rule 6 states:

(1) As soon as practicable after receipt of a copy of the notice of appeal, the respondent shall provide to the relevant police authority—
(a) a copy of the report of the person who made the decision appealed against;
(b) the transcript of the proceedings at the original hearing; and
(c) any documents which were made available to the person conducting the original hearing.

---

**KEYNOTE**

The 'original hearing' is the conduct or inefficiency hearing which concluded that the appellant failed to meet the appropriate standard or that his/her performance was unsatisfactory (r. 3(1) ).

A copy of the transcript referred to at r. 6(1)(b) must, at the same time, be sent to the appellant (r. 6(2) ). Receiving this transcript provides the trigger for the 28-day time limit for the appellant to submit the various statements and documents under r. 6 (see below).

These copies must be provided/sent 'as soon as practicable' after the notification of appeal has been received.

---

Rule 6 goes on to state:

(3) Subject to rule 7, the appellant shall, within 28 days of the date on which he receives a copy of the transcript mentioned in paragraph (1)(b), submit to the relevant police authority—
(a) a statement of the grounds of appeal;
(b) any supporting documents; and
(c) either—
(i) any written representations which the appellant wishes to make under paragraph 6 of the Schedule 6 to the Act or, as the case may be, any request to make oral representations under that paragraph; or
(ii) a statement that he does not wish to make any such representations as are mentioned in paragraph (i):
Provided that, in a case where the appellant submits a statement under sub-paragraph (c)(ii), nothing in this paragraph shall prevent representations under paragraph 6 of the Schedule 6 to the Act being made by him to the chairman of the tribunal.

---

**KEYNOTE**

The appellant must, within the time limit, submit a statement setting out the grounds of his/her appeal and any supporting documentation to the relevant police authority. This time limit may also be extended by the 'relevant police authority' under r. 7(1) (see below).

He/she must also submit either:

• any written representations or a request to make oral representations (where there is to be no hearing); or

• a negative statement (i.e. that he/she does not wish to make any such representations)

Submission of a negative statement does not, however, prevent an appellant from making representations to the chair of the tribunal where it has been decided to proceed without a hearing (r. 6(3) ).

The documents set out above must also be copied, as soon as practicable, to the members of the tribunal and to the 'respondent' (r. 6(4) ).

---

Rule 6 goes on to state:

(5) The respondent shall, not later than 21 days from the date on which he receives the copy documents sent to him under paragraph (4), submit to the relevant police authority—
(a) a statement of his response to the appeal;
(b) any supporting documents; and

(c) either—

    (i) any written representations which the respondent wishes to make under paragraph 6 of Schedule 6 to the Act or, as the case may be, any request to make oral representations under that paragraph; or

    (ii) a statement that he does not wish to make any such representations as are mentioned in paragraph (i):

Provided that, in a case where the respondent submits a statement under sub-paragraph (c)(ii), nothing in this paragraph shall prevent representations under paragraph 6 of Schedule 6 to the Act being made by him to the chairman of the tribunal.

---

**KEYNOTE**

The respondent must submit similar documents to those required of the appellant under r. 6(3) above and must do so no later than 21 days from the date on which he/she receives the copies of the appellant's documents.

    The documents submitted by the respondent must also be copied to the members of the tribunal (r. 6(7)).

    Only those documents set out in r. 6(5)(a) and (c) must be *copied* to the appellant but a list of any supporting documents must be sent to him/her (r. 6(6)).

    Again, a negative statement in relation to the making of representations will not prevent the respondent from making representations to the chair of the tribunal where it has been decided to proceed without a hearing.

---

### Extension of time limits

Rule 7 allows the police authority to extend the time limits under rr. 5 and 6(3) where:

- the appellant applies for an extension, and
- the authority is satisfied that it is just to grant such an extension
- the special circumstances of the case require it.

Where an appellant makes a request for an extension and that request is turned down, the authority must give him/her written notice setting out the reasons (r. 7(2)). That notice must also advise the appellant of the right of appeal against this decision. The appellant can then appeal, within 14 days of receiving this notice, to the chair of the tribunal against the decision not to grant an extension. The chair may then grant an extension under r. 7.

### Procedure at hearing

Rules 8 to 10 regulate the procedure to be followed at a hearing.

    Under r. 8 the appellant must generally be given at least 28 days' notice of the date of a hearing. However, this may be reduced provided both parties agree (r. 8(1)).

    The provisions of the Local Government Act 1972 (giving powers in relation to local inquiries) are applied where relevant to hearings under these Rules.

    There is no need for the appellant or the respondent to be present at the hearing which may proceed without either of them if it appears just and proper to do so (r. 8(3)).

    The hearing may also be adjourned 'from time to time' as may appear necessary for the due hearing of the case (r. 8(3)).

    Subject to the Rules (and also the general principles of law), the procedure at the hearing will be determined by the tribunal (r. 8(4)).

    The hearing will be in private, though the tribunal has discretion to allow people it considers 'desirable' to attend the whole or part of the hearing (r. 9(1)).

    A complainant (see para. 1.2.3) will be also allowed to attend the hearing where the appeal is not simply against the sanction imposed earlier. In cases where the complainant is allowed to be present, that entitlement only extends to occasions *while witnesses are being examined and cross-examined about the facts alleged* (r. 12). This would not appear to give a complainant any entitlement to be present during the giving of any antecedents, mitigation or extraneous background evidence relating to the appellant. The complainant may be allowed to be accompanied by a friend or relative *who is not going to be called as a witness* where appropriate (r. 12(3) ).

If the complainant is going to give evidence, he/she must not attend before giving that evidence and, if the tribunal feels that a witness is going to give information that ought not to be disclosed to the public, it must require the complainant (and anyone accompanying him/her) to withdraw (r. 12(3) ).

Generally, the respondent will 'open the batting' but the tribunal can determine otherwise (r. 10(1) ). All oral evidence will be given under oath and the tribunal will decide what evidence is admissible or what questions can be put to a witness.

A verbatim record must be made of all evidence given at the hearing and this record must be kept for at least seven years after the end of the hearing (unless the chair asks for a transcript to be made) (r. 10(5) ).

The tribunal may allow evidence to be submitted in a written statement in lieu of admissible oral evidence (r. 11).

### Findings

A Police Appeals Tribunal may make an order which:

- appears to it to be *less* severe than the decision appealed against; and
- which could have been imposed by the person making that decision

(s. 85(2) of the Police Act 1996).

The chair of the tribunal must prepare a written statement of its findings, together with reasons (r. (13(1) ). That statement must be submitted to the relevant police authority (and the Secretary of State where the appellant is a senior officer) 'within a reasonable period' after the determination of the appeal. So too must a record of any order the tribunal makes under its powers under s. 85(2).

The relevant authority must copy the statement and record to the appellant and respondent as soon as practicable (r. 13(3) ).

Where the decision appealed against arose from a complaint, the relevant police authority must also notify the complainant of the outcome of the appeal (r. 13(4) ).

Although the Regulations relating to efficiency and misconduct specify that any decision may be reached by a simple majority (see above), the Appeals Rules make no such provision.

## 1.3 Other regulations

### 1.3.1 Restrictions on private lives

The Police Regulations 2003 (SI 2003 No. 527) impose restrictions on the private lives of officers. Regulation 6 provides that the restrictions contained in sch. 1 shall apply to all members of a police force. It also provides that no restrictions other than those designed to secure the proper exercise of the functions of a constable shall be imposed by the police authority or the chief officer of police on the private lives of members of a police force except such as may temporarily be necessary or such as may be approved by the Secretary of State after consultation with the Police Advisory Board for England and Wales.

Schedule 1

Schedule 1 provides that a member of a police force:

- Shall at all times abstain from any activity which is likely to interfere with the impartial discharge of his/her duties or which is likely to give rise to the impression amongst members of the public that it may so interfere, and in particular a member of a police force shall not take any active part in politics.

- Shall not reside at premises which are not for the time being approved by the chief officer of police.

- Shall not, without the previous consent of the chief officer of police, receive a lodger in a house or quarters with which he/she is provided by the police authority, or sub-let any part of the house or quarters.

- Shall not, unless he/she has previously given written notice to the chief officer of police, receive a lodger in a house in which he/she resides and in respect of which he/she receives an allowance under sch. 3, or sub-let any part of such a house.

- Shall not wilfully refuse or neglect to discharge any lawful debt.

### 1.3.2 Business interests

Source business interests preclude people from applying to be a police constable (reg. 9 of the Police Regulations 2003).

Regulation 7 provides that, if a member of a police force or a relative included in his/her family proposes to have, or has, a 'business interest', the member shall forthwith give written notice of that interest to the chief officer of police unless that business interest was disclosed at the time of the officer's appointment as a member of the force.

On receipt of such a notice, the chief officer shall determine whether or not the interest in question is compatible with the member concerned remaining a member of the force and shall notify the member in writing of his/her decision within 28 days.

Within 10 days of being notified of the chief officer's decision (or within such longer period as the police authority may in all the circumstances allow), the member concerned may appeal to the police authority against that decision by sending written notice to the police authority.

If a business interest is felt to be incompatible, the chief officer may dispense with the member's services after giving them an opportunity to make representations, and subject to any earlier appeal to the Police Authority.

For the purposes of reg. 7, a member of a police force or relative has a business interest if:

- the member holds any office or employment for hire or gain or carries on any business;

- a shop is kept or a like business carried on by the member's spouse (not being separated) at any premises in the area of the police force in question or by any relative living with him/her at the premises where he/she resides; or

- the member, his/her spouse (not being separated) or any relative living with them has a pecuniary interest in any licence or permit granted in relation to liquor licensing, refreshment houses or betting and gaming or regulating places of entertainment in the area of the police force in question.

'Relative' includes a reference to a spouse, parent, son, daughter, brother or sister.

A Police officer must notify their chief officer of any changes in a business interest. The above regulations also apply to chief officer ranks but the relevant authority in such cases is the Police Authority (reg. 8(4)).

## 1.4    **Offences**

OFFENCE:    **Misconduct in a public office—*Common Law***
- Triable on indictment • Imprisonment at large
*(Arrestable offence)*

It is a misdemeanour at common law for the holder of a public office to do anything that amounts to a malfeasance or a 'culpable' misfeasance (*R* v *Wyatt* (1705) 1 Salk 380).

---

**KEYNOTE**

This offence has also been described (somewhat politically, if not constitutionally, incorrectly) thus: 'A man accepting an office of trust concerning the public is answerable criminally to the King for misbehaviour in his office . . . by whomsoever and in whatever way the officer is appointed' (*R* v *Bembridge* (1738) 3 Dougl 327).

Such offences can only be tried on indictment and the court has a power of sentence 'at large', that is, there is no limit on the sentence that can be passed (making this an arrestable offence, **see chapter 2**), The conduct can be separated into occasions of *mal*feasance and *mis*feasance. The first requires some degree of wrongful motive or intention on the part of the officer while the second is more likely to apply where there has been some form of wilful neglect of duty: both are notoriously difficult to prove.

The essence of both is generally an abuse of public power in bad faith (*Thomas* v *Secretary of State for the Home Department* (2000) LTL 7 August). There must at least be some real connection between the alleged misconduct and the public office—for instance where a man employed by a local council as a maintenance manager dishonestly caused his employees to carry out works on his girlfriend's premises (*R* v *Bowden* [1996] 1 WLR 98). Therefore, simply behaving badly while off duty would not of itself make a public office holder (such as a police officer) guilty of this offence (see *Elliot* v *Chief Constable of Wiltshire*, The Times, 5 December 1996—disclosure of previous convictions from PNC to a newspaper capable of amounting to misfeasance). It may, however, make the relevant *chief officer* vicariously liable under other heads of law if the off-duty officer was purporting to rely on his or her status as a constable (for a good example see *Weir* v *Chief Constable of Merseyside* (2003) LTL 29 January). The ingredients of the civil wrong are fully set out in *Three Rivers District Council* v *Governor and Company of the Bank of England (No. 3)* [2000] 2 WLR 1220. Their application, especially in the case of police officers, was discussed at length by the Court of Appeal in reviewing the relevant authorities in *Cornelius* v *London Borough of Hackney* [2002] EWCA Civ 1073. In *Three Rivers* Lord Steyn confirmed that the civil and criminal wrongs bore some resemblance. Although many of the earlier cases involved an element of corruption, this is not a requirement for the offence (*R* v *Dytham* [1979] 2 QB 722). This offence might be committed where a police officer wilfully neglects to prevent a criminal assault (as in *Dytham*), or possibly where a supervisory officer fails to intervene in a situation where one of his/her officers is carrying out an unlawful act.

Any neglect has to be 'wilful' (**see Crime, chapter 1**) and not simply inadvertent; it also has to be done without reasonable excuse or justification. The offence is a very serious one and therefore the conduct must have been sufficiently damaging to the public interest to merit condemnation and criminal punishment. As a result there are very few prosecutions and most of those that are brought seem to be reserved for police officers! From the many authorities (especially the Court of Appeal in *Bowden*) it is arguable that this offence could be extended in appropriate circumstances to misconduct of non-sworn employees such as those designated (or perhaps even those accredited) under the Police Reform Act 2002 (as to which **see chapter 2**).

The Court of Appeal has held recently that, where the police wrote to the registered keepers of vehicles believed to have been stolen in another country, informing those keepers that they may not be the legal owners, the person who imported and sold the vehicles *might* be able to bring a claim for misfeasance—much would depend on the state of mind and intentions of the relevant individual in acting as they did—*R Cruikshank Ltd.* v *Chief Constable of Kent* (2002) LTL 13 December (unreported).

---

OFFENCE:   **Constables on licensed premises—*Licensing Act 1964, s. 178***

> • Triable summarily  • Fine
> *(No specific power of arrest)*

The Licensing Act 1964, s. 178 states:

> If the holder of a justices' licence—
>
> (a) knowingly suffers to remain on the licensed premises any constable during any part of the time appointed for the constable's being on duty, except for the purposes of the execution of the constable's duty, or
>
> (b) supplies any liquor or refreshment, whether by way of gift or sale, to any constable on duty except by authority of a superior officer of the constable, or
>
> (c) bribes or attempts to bribe any constable,
>
> he shall be liable . . .

---

**KEYNOTE**

To prove the offence at s. 178(a), you must show that the licensee committed the offence 'knowingly'. That knowledge must apply both to the fact that the person is a constable *and* that the constable was on duty.

That requirement does not explicitly apply to the other offences (but for state of mind generally, **see Crime, chapter 1**).

---

OFFENCE:   **Impersonating a police officer—*Police Act 1996, s. 90(1)***

> • Triable summarily  • Six months' imprisonment
> *(No specific power of arrest)*

The Police Act 1996, s. 90 states:

> (1) Any person who with intent to deceive impersonates a member of a police force or special constable, or makes any statement or does any act calculated falsely to suggest that he is such a member or constable, shall be guilty of an offence and liable . . .

---

**KEYNOTE**

This is a crime of 'specific intent' (**see Crime, chapter 1**). The intention to deceive must be proved.

---

OFFENCE:   **Wearing or possessing uniform—*Police Act 1996, s. 90(2) and (3)***

> • Triable summarily  • Fine
> *(No specific power of arrest)*

The Police Act 1996, s. 90 states:

> (2) Any person who, not being a constable, wears any article of police uniform in circumstances where it gives him an appearance so nearly resembling that of a member of a police force as to be calculated to deceive shall be guilty of an offence . . .
>
> (3) Any person who, not being a member of a police force or special constable, has in his possession any article of police uniform shall, unless he proves that he obtained possession of that article lawfully and has possession of it for a lawful purpose, be guilty of an offence . . .

---

**KEYNOTE**

'Article of police uniform' means:

- any article of uniform, or

- any distinctive badge or mark, or

- any document of identification

usually issued to members of police forces or special constables (s. 90(4) ).

---

OFFENCE: **Impersonating designated or accredited person—*Police Reform Act 2002, s. 46(3)***

> • Triable summarily • Six months' imprisonment and/or fine

The Police Reform Act 2002, s. 46(3) states:

> Any person who, with intent to deceive—
>
> (a) impersonates a designated person or an accredited person,
> (b) makes any statement or does any act calculated falsely to suggest that he is a designated person or that he is an accredited person, or
> (c) makes any statement or does any act calculated falsely to suggest that he has powers as a designated or accredited person that exceed the powers he actually has,
>
> is guilty of an offence

---

**KEYNOTE**

These offences are based on the corresponding offences for police officers. They are offences of specific intent (see Crime, chapter 1). If the impersonation, deception etc. is done with a view to committing a further offence (e.g. theft or burglary), the relevant offences of going equipped and criminal deception (see Crime, chapter 12) ought to be considered.

---

OFFENCE: **Causing disaffection—*Police Act 1996, s. 91(1)***

> • Triable either way • Two years' imprisonment on indictment; six months' imprisonment and/or a fine summarily
> *(No specific power of arrest)*

The Police Act 1996, s. 91(1) states:

> (1) Any person who causes, or attempts to cause, or does any act calculated to cause, disaffection amongst the members of any police force, or induces or attempts to induce, or does any act calculated to induce, any member of a police force to withhold his services, shall be guilty of an offence . . .

## 1.5 Health and Safety

Because police officers are not 'employees' in the conventional legal sense (they are holders of the office of constable), many of the statutory provisions regulating the workplace do not apply directly to them. The health and safety regime that was set up mainly by the Health and Safety at Work etc. Act 1974 applies principally to 'employees' and therefore did not cover police officers (though it clearly covers their non-sworn support colleagues who *are* employees). However, the Police (Health and Safety) Act 1997 made certain changes to the legislation by treating police officers for certain purposes relating to health and safety as if they were employees. Briefly, these areas include:

• the application of Part 1 of the 1974 Act to the police;

• the right of police officers not to be subjected to a detriment in relation to health and safety issues (e.g. not to be punished for raising appropriate health and safety issues or undertaking duties as health and safety representatives—see s. 49A of the Employment Rights Act 1996);

• the right of police officers not to be unfairly dismissed in relation to health and safety issues—see s. 134A of the Employment Rights Act 1996.

The Police Reform Act 2002 now provides that the police authority (rather than the chief officer as before) will be deemed to be the relevant employer of police officers for the purposes of the applicable health and safety legislation (see s. 95). Similar provision is made for the Service Authorities of NCIS and the NCS. Similarly, it is now the police authority rather than the chief officer who will be treated as the employer of police officers in the case of breaches of a number of health and safety provisions by those officers. The Secretary of State has a power to make regulations in relation to health and safety decisions and to police premises (s. 95(4)).

Note that a new code of practice for chief officers and police authorities will be issued towards the end of 2003.

# 2 Policing powers and human rights

## 2.1 Introduction

In one of the most famous judgments concerning the freedoms enjoyed by people in England and Wales, Sir Robert Megarry pointed out that the UK was not a country 'where everything is forbidden except what is expressly permitted: it is a country where everything is permitted except what is expressly forbidden' (*Malone* v *Metropolitan Police Commissioner (No. 2)* [1979] 2 All ER 620 at 629).

So far as the general public were concerned, this meant that you could do pretty well what you wanted unless there was some rule or law that said you could not. Such a permissive state of affairs was uncontroversial in many respects but there were two key areas in which it was open to criticism. On the one hand there was no mechanism formally expressing and protecting a person's fundamental rights and freedoms, while on the other there was a lack of clarity and certainty in the extent to which the State could interfere with those rights and freedoms. This situation was changed significantly by the Human Rights Act 1998, the history, intentions and effects of which are summarised in this chapter.

Alongside these constitutional developments (which are clearly of the first importance in policing), the complexity of police work in its broadest sense has increased apace. Far-reaching changes in the way police services are organised, resourced and delivered have followed and the very notion of 'policing', with all its attendant roles and functions, has altered significantly over recent years. The arrival of the Police Reform Act 2002 has brought with it the concept of the 'extended police family' embracing a whole range of participants, from sworn constables to accredited employees of businesses. For that reason it is probably more accurate now to refer to *policing* powers (as opposed to police powers) and, against the background of human rights legislation described above, this chapter considers the key issues arising from the existence and use of those powers.

## 2.2 Introducing human rights

The European Convention on Human Rights and the Human Rights Act 1998 have been included in this chapter in some detail because of the effect they have on the use of policing powers. However, this area of law is complex and, to an extent, uncertain, and what follows is only an introduction to some of the key features and principles.

Procedural and constitutional issues affecting the Convention and the Act within the administration of justice system are largely dealt with in **Evidence and Procedure**. Other matters affecting substantive law and the particular effects of the Human Rights Act 1998 on existing legislation have been included throughout the relevant chapters of each Manual in this series.

### 2.2.1 Human rights legislation—why have it?

If England and Wales represent such a permissive society where members of the community are free to do as they please unless some legislation says otherwise, why do we need human rights legislation?

That is a good question—and not everyone in the administration of justice system agrees on the answer. One response is that the traditional freedom of individuals to do anything other than that which is expressly forbidden by law may have resulted in a permissive, democratic society—as described by Sir Robert Megarry above. However, such a system gives no protection from the *misuse* of legal powers by the State. Neither does it provide protection for individuals from the acts or omissions of other public bodies that, although allowed by statute or common law, contravene basic human rights. Both of these shortcomings in our legal system were pointed out by the Lord Chancellor during the second reading of the Human Rights Bill in the House of Lords. Unlike many countries that have a written constitution or a Bill of Rights, our law has made no distinction between a breach of some contractual duty (such as a shopkeeper selling you a faulty TV) and the infringement of a basic human right (such as a breach of your right to meet with friends in public). Until now there has been no 'inalienable right' to meet with others freely any more than there is an inalienable right not to be sold dodgy electrical goods. In either case above, you would have to rely on the prevailing statutory and common law for redress. True, you could, like Mr Malone above, petition the European Court of Human Rights in certain circumstances where you felt that your fundamental rights had been interfered with but the decisions of that Court cannot overrule our domestic laws or overturn national judgments. In addition, the Court is in Strasbourg and applications can take anything up to nine years before being heard!

Incidentally, one of the products of the Human Rights Act 1998 (see below) is that the government began to pass domestic legislation to bolster the rights of individuals generally. As a result, the Regulation of Investigatory Powers Act 2000 would now give Mr Malone a very clear legal framework within which to pursue his claims against the police (**see Crime, chapter 3**).

A final reason for introducing specific human rights legislation is to create a *positive* obligation on public authorities such as the police to protect the rights of others. Such others might be victims of stalking, domestic violence or anti-social behaviour generally. In the spirit of human rights legislation, it is no longer enough for public authorities to say 'we haven't breached anyone's rights ourselves'; police services and others have to consider whether they have taken reasonable and legitimate steps positively to protect the rights of individuals under appropriate circumstances.

### 2.2.2 The European Convention on Human Rights—what is it?

The European Convention for the Protection of Human Rights and Fundamental Freedoms is a Treaty between governments and is by no means 'new'. It was signed in 1950 by the governments of those countries making up the Council of Europe and was intended to give full legal protection to the most fundamental rights and freedoms necessary in democratic societies. At the time the Convention was drawn up, many European countries were trying to come to terms with the total disregard for many of those rights and freedoms in the wake of the Second World War. It is important to bear this in mind when reading the Convention as it was written against the backdrop of a war-ravaged Europe and an emerging Soviet Union. This background explains some of the wording used within the Convention, wording that may sound a little out of place within the modern democratic setting of England and Wales.

The Convention came into force in 1953, has been adopted by a majority of countries throughout Europe—including some former communist States—and has been used as a constitutional template by a great many others.

What *is* relatively new as a concept is the Human Rights Act 1998 (see below) which specifically enshrines most—though not all—of the Convention rights within our domestic legislation for the first time. Even though the Act is fairly new, its preamble reiterates that it is intended to give *further effect* to the rights and freedoms already guaranteed by the Convention.

The Convention is part of *international* law, and consequently creates rights against the State (government) and not against other individuals (however, see below). Since 1966, people in the UK (such as Mr Malone above) have been able to go to Strasbourg and seek the help of the Court or (until November 1998) the European Commission of Human Rights where their civil liberties have been infringed by the State and where no domestic remedy has been available. The Court or the Commission could find that the government had violated the rights of the individual, but there were few practical remedies available even if the applicant was successful.

There have been a number of significant cases affecting the UK that have already appeared before the European Court of Human Rights using this avenue of individual petition. Actions brought via this—and other—domestic routes are important as they have influenced developments in our law within England and Wales. More importantly, they have created a body of case law that will help in gauging how our domestic courts may interpret the Convention in the future. Indeed, under s. 2 of the Human Rights Act 1998 (**see appendix 6**) our courts and tribunals have a duty to take such decisions into account. Less helpfully, those cases do not have to be followed in the same way that cases within the 'domestic' courts of England and Wales do and they may have a limited 'shelf life'. In other words, past results are no guarantee of future performance—as financial advisers might say.

### 2.2.3    What is in it?

The Convention sets out to protect most of what might be seen as the fundamental civil liberties within a democratic society. However, it is a very different concept from an Act of Parliament. There are several key features that need to be understood when considering the Convention and its effects. Those key features include:

- The balancing of competing rights and needs.
- Limitations and restrictions—the 'three tests'.
- The Convention as a 'living' instrument.
- The 'margin of appreciation'.
- Derogations and reservations.

Each of these features will now be considered.

#### Balancing competing rights and needs

Some of the Convention's provisions are *absolute*, that is, they do not permit any infringement under any circumstances. An example would be the right to freedom from torture under Article 3 (**see para. 2.4.2**). Other rights are often limited or restricted in some way, such as the right to liberty under Article 5 (**see para. 2.4.4**). These rights have to be restricted if the 'democratic society' is going to work. If a person is lawfully arrested or detained, his/her right to liberty has been infringed, but the Convention takes account of such situations and imposes limitations on that right. Similarly, there will be times when the freedom of an individual conflicts with the general public interest—the right to freedom of assembly (protected under Article 11) and the need to maintain public order for instance. A perfect example of the balancing act required in a policing context can be seen in the powers to seize and retain a motor vehicle that is being used in an anti-social manner (**see paras. 3.5.4 and 3.6.6**). Here, the owner's rights to enjoy his/her personal possessions have to be balanced with the rights of the general population to enjoy their private and family lives, and the Police Reform Act 2002 creates policing powers to deal with the situation where the two sets of rights collide—the real trick is exercising those powers lawfully, proportionately and sensibly. These categories of rights are generally referred to as 'qualified' rights and the areas of potential conflict they raise are of particular significance to the police and other law enforcement agencies.

In some cases, the rights of individuals may directly compete with one another. An example would be one person's right to freedom of expression (Article 10) and another person's freedom to respect for their private life (Article 8). The potential for such rights to conflict, particularly in the areas of communications (**see chapter 3**) and civil disputes (**see chapter 7**) is painfully clear to most police officers—and will become more so as the Human Rights Act 1998 takes effect.

What the Convention—and the European Court of Human Rights—sets out to do is to *balance* these rights against each other and against the needs of the democratic society within which they exist. For this reason many of the Convention's Articles include any relevant limitations or exceptions. Although each is different, a helpful practical approach when interpreting their extent is to apply the 'three tests'.

### The three tests

Where the Convention gives individuals a particular right, any qualification or limitation on that right will be carefully defined and cautiously applied. Otherwise the effect of the Convention would be diluted by a series of 'get out' clauses or circumstances where the right could be easily overridden. This is particularly the case where the balancing of 'qualified' rights is concerned (see above).

Very generally, any limitations on a Convention right must be:

- prescribed by law
- intended to achieve a legitimate objective
- proportionate to the end that is to be achieved.

Each of these areas has a significant impact on the work of police officers and needs to be examined in turn.

#### Test one—prescribed by law

Any interference with a Convention right must first be traceable to a clear legal source (e.g. the Police and Criminal Evidence Act 1984). A person whose rights have allegedly been infringed is entitled to ask '*where did you get the power to act as you did?*' The public body concerned, whether it is a police service or a local authority or whatever, will have to point to a clear legal source and say '*that's where our authority to act in this way comes from*'. The source of this authority can be statutory or the common law; it can also be contractual (e.g. in matters relating to employment). This is one of the reasons why the need for police officers and anyone exercising policing powers to be able to identify the legal source of any power that they use has become even more important. If no such lawful authority can be identified, the consequent interference with a Convention right will be a violation of the Convention, *irrespective of any other justification*. Therefore if the relevant public authority (see below) cannot point to a legal regulation that allows it to interfere with a Convention right, it will be in breach of its obligations (see e.g. the case involving the tapping of a senior police officer's telephone at work—*Halford* v *United Kingdom* (1997) 24 EHRR 523). The circumstances surrounding this decision and the implications for intercepting communications generally prompted the Regulation of Investigatory Powers Act 2000 (as to which, **see Crime, chapter 3**).

However, it is not enough that such a source of legal authority exists; it must also be readily accessible to the people of the relevant State (see *The Sunday Times* v *United Kingdom* (1979) 2 EHRR 245). This means that the law must be clearly and precisely defined and publicised so that people can make themselves aware of it and regulate their conduct accordingly. Acts of Parliament and statutory instruments would invariably meet this requirement. Our common law (**see Evidence and Procedure**) will probably meet this requirement in most cases (see *The Sunday Times* case above) although it is arguable that there is so much lack of clarity in some areas that all aspects of this requirement are not met by our common law system. A good historical example is in the area of 'lawful chastisement' in relation to punishment of children (as to which, **see Crime, chapter 8**). In a case involving an allegation of assault by a stepfather on his stepson, the European Court of Human Rights held that the United Kingdom was in breach of its obligation to protect individuals from inhuman or degrading punishment (under Article 3) because our law in the area of what was 'reasonable' chastisement was not clear enough (*A* v *United Kingdom* [1998] Crim LR 892).

### Test two—legitimate objective

In addition to being authorised by a clear and accessible legal regulation, restrictions or limitations of qualified Convention rights must generally be directed at achieving a legitimate objective as set out under the Articles themselves. Such an objective might be the prevention of crime, the protection of the public and their property or the upholding of the rights of others. Given the broad nature of these objectives it should be relatively easy for a public authority, *when acting lawfully*, to meet this requirement.

### Test three—proportionality and necessity

The test of proportionality asks '*were the measures you took necessary in a democratic society and in proportion to the ultimate objective?*' It is in this area that the 'balancing' of competing rights and needs takes place. It is also in this area that the use of police powers may be challenged most frequently. Any interference with a Convention right must be shown to have been relevant and proportional to the legitimate aim pursued (*Handyside* v *United Kingdom* (1976) 1 EHRR 737). A good example here would be police actions taken to prevent crime—forcibly entering and searching premises for instance. Clearly the prevention of crime would usually amount to a legitimate objective but *the means employed by the officers would have to be in proportion to the crime that was to be prevented.*

If the manner and extent of an operation were shown to have infringed someone's Convention rights in a way that was out of all proportion to the legitimate aim being pursued, there would almost certainly have been a violation of those rights. As the authors of *Blackstone's Guide to the Human Rights Act 1998* put it 'the State cannot use a sledgehammer to crack a nut'.

It can be seen then that this test has significant implications for those who supervise, manage and carry out law enforcement operations.

Although the decisions of public authorities, such as police services, have been open to the process of judicial review (**see Evidence and Procedure**) for some considerable time, the 'proportionality' test adopted by the European Court of Human Rights represents a much tighter constraint on the activities of public authorities than anything that has gone before. Generally under the judicial review procedure, the courts will not interfere with a decision of a public authority unless it can be shown to meet one of two criteria: unlawful or irrational (in short 'wrong' or 'daft'). Under the *proportionality* test the Court in Strasbourg has taken a different approach and looks for a 'pressing social need' behind the actions complained of. If no such need can be found, the interference may be a violation of the Convention. It is for this reason that legislation in Northern Ireland outlawing consensual buggery between men was held to be an unnecessary interference by the State with an individual's right to privacy (*Dudgeon* v *United Kingdom* (1981) 4 EHRR 149); it is also the reason why a number of new legislative restrictions such as the Anti-Social Behaviour Order (**see chapter 3**) and the Sex Offender Order (**see Crime, chapter 10**) were challenged under the Human Rights Act 1998.

The overall practical result of the three tests means, in short, that the 'ways and means Act' has been repealed once and for all.

### Discrimination

One final, generic test that will be applied to any limitation or restriction on Convention rights is whether the limitation or restriction is discriminatory, i.e. '*did the difference in treatment of the individuals affected have any objective and reasonable justification*' (*Belgian Linguistic Case (No. 1)* (1967) 1 EHRR 241).

### The Convention as a 'living instrument'

As discussed, the Convention is a creature of international law and is therefore different from the Acts of Parliament that appear elsewhere in this book. One difference is that the courts will interpret it in a 'purposive' way, i.e. in a way that gives effect to its central purposes, namely to protect the human rights of individuals and the ideals and values of a democratic society. Any such rights and ideals must not be theoretical, but practical and effective features of the lives of individuals within our democratic society. The Convention is also a 'living' instrument which must be interpreted in the light of present-day conditions (*Tyrer* v *United Kingdom* (1978) 2 EHRR 1). This means that its interpretation will develop alongside society without the need for older cases to be specifically overruled. If the acceptable standards within society become more tolerant (say, of consensual sexual activity or of behaviour in public), then the Convention should be interpreted and applied accordingly. Interestingly, this is the same test that has now been adopted in relation to assessing the appropriateness of a police officer's off-duty conduct under the discipline regulations (**see chapter 1**). Unlike our domestic common law where very old cases become well-established precedents, older case law relating to the Convention will not be followed slavishly by the courts and will therefore need to be considered carefully. This is not particularly helpful to practitioners; it is even less helpful to exam candidates. Nevertheless, it is a significant feature of the Convention.

### What is the 'margin of appreciation'?

As social, economic, political and cultural conditions in the many countries that have signed up to the Convention vary, there must be some latitude in the interpretation of the Convention. As anyone travelling through mainland Europe discovers, behaviour that is socially acceptable in one country may not be so acceptable in another. One country may be more vulnerable to a particular type of threat, e.g. terrorism, and may therefore need to impose restrictions on some freedoms that in another country, where there is no such threat, might be unnecessary. Sensibly, the European Court of Human Rights has accepted that such local distinctions are best made by the relevant governments—albeit under its close supervision. For that reason, the Court will allow governments what is termed a 'margin of appreciation' when deciding to what extent the Convention has been violated by public policy.

An example of how this concept works can be seen in the litigation around transsexuals in the United Kingdom. The government has relied upon its 'margin of appreciation' to avoid changing the law in England and Wales to allow transsexuals to change their gender for certain legal and administrative purposes. The government has declined to change domestic laws in order to recognise the particular status of transsexuals (e.g. in relation to birth record systems and the right to marry). In finally settling the matter, however, the European Court of Human Rights has now said that the government could no longer claim that such matters fell within its margin of appreciation (see *Goodwin* v *UK* [2002] 35 EHRR 18). As a result, the various failures of the UK to provide recognition and protection for transsexuals' rights amounted to breaches of the relevant Convention articles (see below).

As an international law concept, it has been held that the margin of appreciation has no application in domestic proceedings (see *R* v *DPP, ex parte Kebilene* [1999] 3 WLR 972).

### What are derogations and reservations?

Article 15 allows governments to 'derogate' from their obligations under the Convention *in time of war or other public emergency threatening the life of the nation.*

This provision allows governments to restrict the freedoms of individuals under such circumstances but *only to the extent that it is strictly necessary to do so*. Any government availing itself of this provision must inform the Secretary-General of the Council of Europe of any measures it is taking in this regard and must make similar notification once those measures have ceased.

The original derogation that existed at the time when the Human Rights Act 1998 was passed related to the ongoing unrest in Northern Ireland. With the political developments in Northern Ireland, that derogation was removed but, since the events of 11 September 2001, the United Kingdom has passed a further derogation arising out of the Anti-terrorism, Crime and Security Act 2001 and the powers thereunder. As those powers are, on the face of them, incompatible with parts (particularly Article 5) of the Convention (**see para. 2.4.4**), the United Kingdom has passed the Human Rights (Amendment No. 2) Order 2001 (SI 2001 No. 4032). The derogation is set out in part I of sch. 3 to the Human Rights Act 1998 (**see appendix 6**).

The United Kingdom has attached a 'reservation' to its acceptance of one of the protocols to the Convention in relation to education (Protocol 1, Article 2). Article 2 says that no one shall be denied the right to education and the reservation (which has also been registered by several other States) simply adds an amendment about compatibility with domestic provisions and unreasonable public expenditure.

### 2.2.4  Incorporation—international law becomes Our Law

While many of the signatories to the Convention chose to incorporate its provisions directly into their own domestic law, successive governments in the United Kingdom have felt that such incorporation was unnecessary. Many believed (and still do) that the 'permissive' system in England and Wales described above, already provides enough protection for the rights and freedoms of individuals. Although the avenue of individual petition resulted in several cases being brought against the UK government, the Convention itself was never incorporated into the domestic law of England and Wales. However, there were many politicians, lawyers and commentators who felt that there was a need for a specific Bill of Rights for the United Kingdom, going beyond even the direct incorporation of the Convention into our legal system and the issues were debated for years.

Eventually, in December 1996, the Labour Party published a paper entitled *Bringing Rights Home* setting out its own arguments in favour of incorporating the Convention into our domestic law—and including a pledge in its manifesto to do just that. Following victory in the general election of 1997, the Labour government published a White Paper, *Rights Brought Home* (Cm 3782), in which it explained the proposals contained within the Human Rights Bill and the Human Rights Act received Royal Assent in November 1998.

## 2.3  The Human Rights Act 1998

The Human Rights Act 1998 came into force in October 2000. Although there are many academic debates around the niceties of it all, to most intents and purposes the 1998 Act effectively incorporates what are often called an individual's 'Convention rights' into our domestic law. These Convention rights are set out in the various Articles and Protocols of the Convention which appear in sch. 1 to the Act (**see appendix 6**).

2.3.1    **So what?**

The 1998 Act is a very significant piece of legislation—particularly for police officers and the wider 'policing family'. Not only does it give effect to the rights contained within the Convention, the Act also affects the way in which all other legislation will be interpreted and applied. Section 3 requires that, wherever possible, statutory provisions *and the common law* be read and given effect in a way that is compatible with Convention rights (**see Evidence and Procedure, chapter 1**). This requirement, which also applies to new legislation, will have an impact on all courts and tribunals in every jurisdiction, whether criminal or civil, where Convention rights are in issue.

As discussed above, the Convention was aimed at securing rights against the State and public authorities—and the 1998 Act does the same. Although it creates new avenues of redress against 'public authorities' (see below), the Act does not create any new rights in private matters between individuals. Just because someone next to you on the tube infringes your right to a private life by playing dance music on their stereo does not mean that you can now take them to court. Neither can disaffected workers complain that their private sector employers have stifled their freedom of speech by stopping them going to board meetings. However, the definition of 'public authorities' includes the courts (s. 6(3)) and therefore imposes an obligation for a court *in any matter*, criminal or civil, private or public, to give effect to the Act. This is why it is said that there will be occasions where the Act will be of 'indirect effect' as between individuals.

Although it makes changes to the procedures in getting redress locally for human rights infringements, the 1998 Act still allows for occasions where an individual will need to petition the European Court of Human Rights in Strasbourg (**see Evidence and Procedure, chapter 2**).

2.3.2    **Article 13—real and effective remedy**

It should be noted that Article 13—which requires States to ensure that individuals have a 'real and effective remedy' if their Convention rights are violated—has *not* been incorporated into the Human Rights Act 1998. It was the government's view that the introduction of the Act itself is enough to meet these requirements. Nevertheless, because Article 13 is very important in the case decisions of the European Court of Human Rights and s. 2 of the Act requires courts in England and Wales to have regard to those decisions made in Strasbourg, Article 13 will still have some significance in practice.

2.3.3    **Breach of the Act—what can you do about it?**

The Human Rights Act 1998, s. 6 states:

(1) It is unlawful for a public authority to act in a way that is incompatible with a Convention right.

---

**KEYNOTE**

As discussed above, the rights provided by the Convention are intended to be directly enforceable against 'public authorities'. Therefore, if it can be established that a person or organisation is a 'public authority' (as defined below), the Convention rights can be used directly against them in a number of ways. These ways include:

- Bringing proceedings against the public authority, e.g. for false imprisonment.
- Using the public authority's actions as a ground for judicial review (**see Evidence and Procedure, chapter 2**).
- Using the public authority's actions as a defence to any action brought by it, e.g. someone charged with an offence of obstructing a police officer (as to which, **see Crime, chapter 8**).

The first two ways of seeking a remedy are often referred to as using the Convention as a 'sword' while the last can be seen as making use of the Convention as a 'shield'. In using the Convention as a 'shield' in any legal proceedings, the person can do so *whenever the act complained of took place*. This will include citing acts by the public authority that have already taken place before the 1998 Act comes into force. Where a person seeks to rely on their Convention rights as a 'sword', the restrictions and time limits under s. 7 will apply (see para. 2.3.4).

A good example of how the Convention can be used to launch a wide range of attacks on legislation and policing powers can be seen in *R (on the application of Fuller and Secretary of State for the Home Department)* v *Chief Constable of Dorset Police* [2001] 3 All ER 57 (see chapter 9).

In all cases where a person wishes to rely on the relevent Convention right in any proceedings (either as a sword or shield), they must meet the requirements of s. 7 (see para. 2.3.4).

If the person or organisation allegedly violating the individual's Convention rights cannot be shown to be a 'public authority', then there is no *direct* remedy against them (but, see below). An 'act' will include a failure to act under certain circumstances (see below).

### Exceptions

Section 6 goes on to state:

  (2) Subsection (1) does not apply to an act if—
      (a) as the result of one or more provisions of primary legislation, the authority could not have acted differently; or
      (b) in the case of one or more provisions of or made under, primary legislation which cannot be read or given effect in a way which is compatible with the Convention rights, the authority was acting so as to give effect to or enforce those provisions.

### KEYNOTE

The 1998 Act is drafted in such a way as to preserve the concept of parliamentary sovereignty whereby Parliament's expressed intentions cannot be overruled. For this reason, s. 6(2) provides for circumstances where a public authority has acted in a way that is incompatible with a Convention right *but it only did so because it had no choice as a result of other legislation*. This means that if a public authority has a statutory duty to do something and, in so doing, cannot avoid acting in a way that is incompatible with a Convention right, it does not commit a breach of s. 6(1) above. An example might be where there is a statutory requirement to pass on information, as under the Vehicle Excise and Registration Act 1994 (see Road Traffic, chapter 12), and that requirement is enforced by the police or the DVLA. If an individual successfully claimed that such a requirement unnecessarily infringed his/her Convention right to privacy (Article 8), the actions of the police and the DVLA (as 'public authorities') may well be protected by s. 6(2). The proper remedy in such a case would be to seek a declaration from a higher court that the legislation concerned was in fact incompatible with the Convention (see Evidence and Procedure, chapter 1). This represents a key difference between the Human Rights Act 1998 and the legislation of the European Union. If there is a conflict between the domestic law of a member State and the law of the European Union, the latter is able to override the domestic legislation even if it appears in a lawfully enacted Act of Parliament (see s. 2 of the European Communities Act 1972). In such circumstances, the courts in England and Wales are also under an obligation to disapply the inconsistent local legislation and give effect to European Union law (see e.g. *R* v *Secretary of State for Employment, ex parte Equal Opportunities Commission* [1995] 1 AC 1).

The effect of s. 6(2) only extends to *legislation*; it does not therefore appear to exempt the acts of people who are obeying, say, a court order such as a warrant. Moreover, the wording of s. 6(2)(a) suggests that it only applies where the legislation leaves the public authority no choice in the matter. Therefore this would not seem to apply to the exercise of *discretionary* powers such as powers of arrest, search and seizure. The bottom line is that an act or failure to act by a public authority will not be unlawful if:

• it is *not* incompatible with Convention rights,

• the authority could not have acted differently given the relevant primary legislation, or

• the authority acted so as to give effect to, or to enforce provisions made under incompatible primary legislation.

Public authorities

Section 6 goes on to state:

> (3) In this section 'public authority' includes—
>   (a) a court or tribunal, and
>   (b) any person certain of whose functions are functions of a public nature, but does not include either House of Parliament or a person exercising functions in connection with proceedings in Parliament.
>
> (4) In subsection (3) 'Parliament' does not include the House of Lords in its judicial capacity.
>
> (5) In relation to a particular act, a person is not a public authority by virtue only of subsection (3)(b) if the nature of the act is private.
>
> (6) 'An act' includes a failure to act but does not include a failure to—
>   (a) introduce in, or lay before Parliament a proposal for legislation; or
>   (b) make any primary legislation or remedial order.

---

### KEYNOTE

It can be seen from the text above that there is no conclusive definition of what a public authority is; rather there is a descripton of the functions that will make a person/organisation a 'public authority'. It can also be seen that there will be two groups of 'public authorities'—those who are named or who are concerned solely with discharging functions of a public nature ('pure' public authorities) and those who have *some* public functions ('quasi-public' authorities).

In the first category (pure public authorities) would be:

- courts and tribunals (including the House of Lords when sitting as such)

- police, fire and ambulance services

- local authorities and (perhaps) the Police Complaints Authority.

These organisations, and the people working for them, have a duty to conform to the Convention rights of individuals when exercising *any and all* of their functions. Therefore a police service must act in conformity with the Convention in relation to its operational functions (preservation of law and order) and also in relation in its other functions (e.g. as an employee or contractor).

From the definition above it can be seen that, not only are police *organisations* public authorities, but so are individual police officers—whether they are regular officers or special constables-and others who are employed by the police to exercise policing powers. Whether the courts will extend the provisions to cover non-police employees who are designated or accredited with policing powers under the Police Reform Act 2002 (as to which **see para. 2.14.2**) remains to be seen but there is a strong argument for their inclusion in principle.

As courts and tribunals are specified within s. 6(3), judges, magistrates and people chairing tribunals will be under a duty to ensure conformity with the Convention in deciding *any legal issue*—even if the hearing is one of private law between two individuals (e.g. a landlord and tenant dispute or a purely contractual matter).

As the law has not been fully tested in the courts yet, it is difficult to identify accurately all the organisations that would fall into the second category. However, they might include a number of commercial or private organisations charged with some functions of a public nature, e.g.:

- Network Rail

- security companies running prisons/prisoner escort services

- government contractors

- other bodies such as the BBC.

The important thing to establish with such groups is whether they were, at the material time, acting within the scope of their public functions or whether their actions were purely carried out within the ambit of their private functions. It would seem from the wording of s. 6(5) that quasi-public authorities will only be accountable for acting in a way that is incompatible with the Convention *while they are carrying out their public functions*. An example of this distinction might be a surgeon who works both for the NHS and who also has a private practice. While working for the NHS—an organisation having functions of a public nature—the surgeon's acts would probably be caught by s. 6(1). While acting in an entirely private capacity in his/her practice, the surgeon's acts would probably be excluded from the provisions of s. 6(1) by the wording of s. 6(5). This second category of organisations will be important to police services as the growth in public and private partnerships continues. In such cases the police service may be liable for acts committed by private partners in certain circumstances. This distinction will be particularly important where employees of private companies who have no other 'public' functions have been accredited under the Police Reform Act 2002.

### 2.3.4 Who can bring proceedings?

The Human Rights Act 1998, s. 7 states:

(1) A person who claims that a public authority has acted (or proposes to act) in a way which is made unlawful by section 6(1) may—
    (a) bring proceedings against the authority under this Act in the appropriate court or tribunal, or
    (b) rely on the Convention right or rights concerned in any legal proceedings, but only if he is (or would be) a victim of the unlawful act.

(2) ...

(3) If the proceedings are brought on an application for judicial review, the applicant is to be taken to have a sufficient interest in relation to the unlawful act only if he is, or would be, a victim of that act.

---

**KEYNOTE**

Although the application of the 1998 Act is not restricted to natural persons and could include organisations, s. 7 limits the occasions where such 'people' can rely on Convention rights. To so rely on a Convention right, the person must be a 'victim'. The test to see if a person is a 'victim' for these purposes is taken directly from Article 34 of the Convention (which is not included in the Act) (s. 7(7)).

In order to qualify as a 'victim', a person must satisfy the same requirements as they would have to in order to bring a case before the Court in Strasbourg. These requirements are found in the case law from the European Court of Human Rights and principally mean that the person must show that he/she is:

- directly affected or

- at risk of being directly affected

by the act/omission complained of.

There is no need for the person to have actually *been* affected by the act/omission, as long as the person can show a real risk of him/her being directly affected by it in the future. An example can be seen in *Dudgeon* v *United Kingdom* (1981) 4 EHRR 149, where the petitioner was able to challenge the law proscribing consensual homosexual activity even though he had not been prosecuted under that legislation himself.

This limitation on 'victims' means that public interest groups will be excluded from bringing human rights actions directly, as will government organisations and local authorities.

The expression 'victim' is of particular relevance to people who are challenging the lawfulness of their arrest or detention under Article 5 (see below).

The wording of s. 7(3) means that, if an application for judicial review is brought (**see Evidence and Procedure, chapter 2**) on human rights grounds, the applicant will have to meet the requirements of a 'victim' under s. 7 or he/she will not be allowed to bring the case *even though he/she might have sufficient legal standing under the rules governing judicial review generally*.

Whether interest groups such as trade unions and the Police Federation will be held to qualify as 'victims' and therefore allowed to bring human rights actions remains to be seen.

Time limits

Section 7 goes on to state:

> (5) Proceedings under subsection (1)(a) must be brought before the end of—
>
> (a) the period of one year beginning with the date on which the act complained of took place; or
>
> (b) such longer period as the court or tribunal considers equitable having regard to all the circumstances,
>
> but that is subject to any rule imposing a stricter time limit in relation to the procedure in question.

---

**KEYNOTE**

Any proceedings brought against a public authority under s. 7(1)(a) must be brought within one year from the date on which the act complained of took place (subject to the discretion of the relevant court/tribunal).

As the time for judicial review is three months, this stricter time limit will still apply in cases involving allegations of Convention rights infringement.

This time limit does not prevent people from raising the issue of Convention rights as a 'shield' in any other proceedings, neither does it affect the courts' general duty (under s. 3) to give effect to the Convention when interpreting and applying the law.

---

## 2.4 What are the 'Convention rights'?

Having considered some of the key concepts and features of the Convention and the provisions of the Human Rights Act 1998, we can now examine some of the specific rights protected by them. Those rights are also referred to throughout the relevant text of this Manual and the other Manuals in the series.

As Article 1 is simply a statement of the duty of governments signing up to the Convention to secure the relevant rights and freedoms to everyone within their jurisdiction, the starting point for the content of the Convention is Article 2.

### 2.4.1 Article 2—the right to life

Article 2 of the Convention states:

> 1. Everyone's right to life shall be protected by law. No one shall be deprived of his life intentionally save in the execution of a sentence of a court following his conviction of a crime for which this penalty is provided by law.
>
> 2. Deprivation of life shall not be regarded as inflicted in contravention of this Article when it results from the use of force which is no more than absolutely necessary:
>
> (a) in defence of any person from unlawful violence;
>
> (b) in order to effect a lawful arrest or to prevent the escape of a person lawfully detained;
>
> (c) in action lawfully taken for the purpose of quelling a riot or insurrection.

---

**KEYNOTE**

Article 2 provides what must be one of the most important and fundamental rights of individuals, namely the right to life. There are two 'arms' to this Convention right, namely:

- a prohibition on the State from *taking* life, and

- a positive duty placed upon the State to *protect* life

(see *X* v *United Kingdom* (1978) 14 DR 31).

The European Court of Human Rights said of Article 2 that it 'ranks as one of the most fundamental provisions in the Convention—indeed one which in peacetime admits of no derogation under Art. 15. Together with

Art. 3 . . . it also enshrines one of the basic values of the democratic societies making up the Council of Europe . . . as such its provisions must be strictly construed', (*McCann* v *UK* (1995) 21 EHRR 97 at 160).

In a recent case concerning withholding medical treatment, the High Court considered the positive and negative duties under Article 2. The court held that the negative obligation was to refrain from taking a life intentionally. It held that this obligation was not breached by a decision made in the patient's best interests to withdraw life support facilities. The intentional deprivation of life had to involve a deliberate act as opposed to an omission. In relation to the positive obligation, the court held that this required the relevant public authority to take adequate and appropriate steps to safeguard life. Again, the taking of a responsible clinical decision to withhold treatment that was not in the patient's best interests met the State's positive obligation under Article 2 (*NHS Trust A* v *M* [2001] 1 All ER 801). (In this judgment the court reaffirmed the pre-Convention decision (*Airedale NHS Trust* v *Bland* [1993] AC 789) to the same effect.)

### Taking life

It can be seen from the wording of the first paragraph that Article 2 does not prohibit the taking of life by a lawful imposition of the death penalty.

It can be seen that the Article allows for a number of limited exceptions when the taking of life by the State may not be a violation of this Convention right. All of the situations covered by the exceptions are generally concerned with protecting life, preventing crime and preserving order. The exceptions include actions taken in defending another person (not property) from unlawful violence (**see Crime, chapter 4**) and effecting a lawful arrest (**see para. 2.8**). Therefore the Convention acknowledges that there will be occasions where the State is compelled to take the life of an individual, such as where a police officer has to use lethal force to protect the life of another.

However, while limited in themselves, these exceptions will also be subject to very restrictive interpretation by the courts. Given that Article 2 protects one of the most fundamental of all Convention rights, any claimed exceptions to the Article are likely to be very carefully examined by the courts.

When a life is taken under any of the three situations set out at paragraph (a)–(c) above, the force used must be shown to have been *no more than absolutely necessary*—a more stringent test than the general test imposed in our domestic criminal law by s. 3 of the Criminal Law Act 1967 (as to which, **see Crime, chapter 4**). This very strict test was examined by the European Commission of Human Rights in a case where a young boy was killed by a baton round fired by a soldier during an outbreak of serious disorder (*Stewart* v *United Kingdom* (1984) 38 DR 162). There the Commission held that force will be absolutely necessary only if it is strictly proportionate to the legitimate purpose being pursued. In order to meet those criteria, regard must be had to:

- the nature of the aim being pursued
- the inherent dangers to life and limb from the situation
- the degree of risk to life presented by the amount of force employed.

This test applies, not only to cases where there has been an *intentional* taking of life, but also where there has been a permitted use of force that has led to the death of another. The test has been held to be a stricter one than even the general requirement of 'proportionality' that runs throughout the Convention (as to which, **see para. 2.2.3**) (*McCann* v *United Kingdom* (1995) 21 EHRR 97).

This area is of critical importance to police officers in general, but to police supervisors and managers in particular. This is because, not only are the courts concerned with any individual actions that directly lead to the death of another, but also because they will take into account 'other factors' surrounding and leading up to the incident that caused the loss of life.

Such other factors are likely to include:

- the planning and control of the operation,
- the training given to the officers concerned, and
- the briefing/instructions that they received.

Where the use of force by the police results in the deprivation of life, the training, briefing, deployment and overall competence of everyone involved in the relevant operation will potentially come under the scrutiny of the court.

These considerations, which were made very clear by the European Court of Human Rights in the *McCann* case (a case involving the shooting of three terrorists by the SAS in Gibraltar in 1988), were applied by the Court to an incident when police officers shot and killed a gunman and his hostage (*Andronicou* v *Cyprus* (1997) 25 EHRR 491). In that case, the Court found that the police operation had been planned and managed in a way that was intended to minimise the risk to life, even though the officers ultimately made a mistake as to the extent of the gunman's weapons and ammunition when they took the decision to open fire. The Court found that the exceptional requirements of Article 2(2) had been made out and that there had been no violation of Article 2 by the Cyprus police.

### Protecting life

A further area of importance for the police in Article 2 lies in the second arm-that of protecting the lives of others. This area was considered in the case of *Osman* v *United Kingdom* (2000) 29 EHRR 245. In this case a man had been killed by a person who had become fixated with him. The dead man's relatives claimed that they had warned the police about the killer's fixation and tried to sue them for negligence in failing to protect Mr Osman. The High Court dismissed the relatives' action on grounds of public policy and they took their case to the European Court of Human Rights, claiming that the State had violated the second arm of Article 2 by failing to protect the life of Mr Osman. Although the Court held that there had been no such violation on the facts of the case, it went on to examine the positive obligation of the State under Article 2.

The positive obligation on the State to protect life is not an absolute one. In *Osman* the European Commission said that Article 2 must be interpreted as requiring preventative steps to be taken to protect life from *known and avoidable dangers* (emphasis added). The Commission went on to say that the extent of this obligation (which is clearly of the first importance to those tasked with investigating and preventing crime) will vary 'having regard to the source and degree of danger and the means available to combat it' (at 115). The European Court of Human Rights said in *Osman* (at 305) that it will be enough for an applicant to show that the authorities did not do all that could reasonably be expected of them to avoid a *real and immediate risk to life* (emphasis added) of which they have or ought to have knowledge. As such, whether a police officer or police force has failed in this positive obligation to protect life will only be answerable in the light of all the circumstances of a particular case. This requirement is therefore very similar to the test for negligence at civil law in England and Wales.

Under some circumstances, this requirement could make the police power to detain a person suffering from mental illness in a public place (**see para. 2.4.4**) a *duty* to do so.

---

### 2.4.2    Article 3—torture

Article 3 of the Convention states:

> No one shall be subjected to torture or to inhuman or degrading treatment or punishment.

---

**KEYNOTE**

Torture was made a specific criminal offence under s. 134 of the Criminal Justice Act 1988 (**see Crime, chapter 9**) but, whereas that offence has a statutory defence of 'lawful authority, justification or excuse', the prohibition contained in Article 3 is absolute. Irrespective of the prevailing circumstances, there can be no derogation from an individual's absolute right to freedom from torture, inhuman or degrading treatment or punishment.

The European Court of Human Rights has described Article 3 as enshrining one of the basic values of our democratic society and that, as such, its provisions must be strictly construed (see *McCann* v *UK* (1995) 21 EHRR 97 and Article 2 above).

'Degrading treatment' has been held to mean, in the interrogation of suspects, 'ill treatment designed to arouse in victims feelings of fear, anguish and inferiority, capable of humiliating and debasing them (see *Ireland* v *UK* (1978) 2 EHRR 25).

The behaviour envisaged by Article 3 goes far beyond the traditional image of 'torture' and its three features have been identified as having the following broad characteristics:

- torture—deliberate treatment leading to serious or cruel suffering

- inhuman treatment—treatment resulting in intense suffering, both physical and mental

- degrading treatment—treatment giving rise to fear and anguish in the victim, causing feelings of inferiority and humiliation

(see *Ireland* v *United Kingdom* (1978) 2 EHRR 25).

It has been held by the European Commission of Human Rights that causing mental anguish without any physical assault could be a violation of Article 3 (see *Denmark* v *Greece* (1969) 12 YB Eur Conv HR special vol.). Given the advances made in our own common law relating to assault since that date (**see Crime, chapter 8**), it is likely that courts within the United Kingdom would accept that words alone might amount to inhuman or degrading treatment.

As with the preceding Article, Article 3 has two 'arms' to it, namely the duty of the State not to inflict torture etc. upon an individual and the correlative duty to prevent others from doing so.

It can be seen from the various categories of treatment above, Article 3 may be breached, not only by the deliberate application of pain and suffering to an individual, but also by a range of other behaviour. Oppressive interrogation techniques such as sleep deprivation, exposure to continuous loud noise and forcing suspects to adopt uncomfortable postures for prolonged lengths of time have been held to fall within the second and third categories of inhuman and degrading treatment (*Ireland* v *United Kingdom*). In each case, it must be shown that the prohibited behaviour went beyond the 'minimum level of severity. In determining whether the behaviour did go beyond that level, and under which particular category that behaviour falls, the courts will take into account factors such as the age, sex, state of health and general life experience of the victim.

Where an individual was alleged to have been punched and kicked by police officers and pulled along by his hair, the Court found that there had been a violation of Article 3 in the form of inhuman and degrading treatment (*Ribitsch* v *Austria* (1995) 21 EHRR 573). In future, courts may consider the denial of drugs or medical treatment to prisoners under certain circumstances a violation of Article 3, along with the deliberate misuse of CS spray, speed-cuffs or other police equipment.

The government's positive duty to prevent individuals from suffering torture or inhuman and degrading treatment has been raised against proceedings to extradite a murder suspect to the United States where it was argued that he would face a long period awaiting the death penalty (*Soering* v *United Kingdom* (1989) 11 EHRR 439). It has also been used to prevent the deportation of a political activist to India where it was argued that he would be subjected to inhuman treatment by the authorities (*Chahal* v *United Kingdom* (1996) 23 EHRR 413). In each of these cases, the reasonable likelihood of ill-treatment at the hands of the State was held to be capable of giving rise to the positive obligation of the United Kingdom to prevent the extradition/deportation.

---

### 2.4.3 Article 4—slavery and forced labour

Article 4 of the Convention states:

1. No one shall be held in slavery or servitude.

2. No one shall be required to perform forced or compulsory labour.

3. For the purpose of this Article the term 'forced or compulsory labour' shall not include:
   (a) any work required to be done in the ordinary course of detention imposed according to the provisions of Article 5 of this Convention or during conditional release from such detention;
   (b) any service of a military character or, in case of conscientious objectors in countries where they are recognised, service exacted instead of compulsory military service;
   (c) any service exacted in case of an emergency or calamity threatening the life or well-being of the community;
   (d) any work or service which forms part of normal civic obligations.

---

**KEYNOTE**

The prohibition on slavery under Article 4 is another Convention right that cannot be derogated from. Slavery is not defined within the Convention and, at the time of writing, no authoritative reports have been published.

It has been suggested that this Convention right might be used by public sector workers such as police officers who are made to work unreasonably onerous hours under circumstances where they are unprotected by the Working Time Regulations 1998 (SI 1998 No. 1833).

---

2.4.4    **Article 5—the right to liberty and security**

Article 5 of the Convention states:

1. Everyone has the right to liberty and security of person. No one shall be deprived of his liberty save in the following cases and in accordance with a procedure prescribed by law:
   (a) the lawful detention of a person after conviction by a competent court;
   (b) the lawful arrest or detention of a person for non-compliance with the lawful order of a court or in order to secure the fulfilment of any obligation prescribed by law;
   (c) the lawful arrest or detention of a person effected for the purpose of bringing him before the competent legal authority on reasonable suspicion of having committed an offence or when it is reasonably considered necessary to prevent his committing an offence or fleeing after having done so;
   (d) the detention of a minor by lawful order for the purpose of educational supervision or his lawful detention for the purpose of bringing him before the competent legal authority;
   (e) the lawful detention of persons for the prevention of the spreading of infectious diseases, of persons of unsound mind, alcoholics or drug addicts or vagrants;
   (f) the lawful arrest or detention of a person to prevent his effecting an unauthorised entry into the country or of a person against whom action is being taken with a view to deportation or extradition.

---

**KEYNOTE**

This Article is of paramount importance to police officers.

The starting point is the general right to liberty and security of person. Although another fundamental right within a democratic society, this right to liberty is qualified under Article 5 and can be derogated from under Article 15 at certain times (see below). However, a person can only be deprived of his/her general right to liberty under one of the conditions set out on the permitted grounds in Article 5(1)(a)–(f), and even then that deprivation must be carried out in accordance with *a procedure prescribed by law*. As noted at the beginning of this chapter, not only must the 'procedure' be set out in the domestic law of the country; it must also be recorded in such a way that people can appreciate the possible consequences of their actions and adapt their behaviour accordingly. If the legal authority used to deprive a person of his/her liberty is ambiguous or unclear, that may well provide grounds for challenge under Article 5.

Even if a lawful power is sufficiently clear and well established, the list of permitted grounds in Article 5(1)(a)–(f) will have to be construed narrowly by the courts (*Winterwerp v Netherlands* (1979) 2 EHRR 387).

That said, the House of Lords has ruled that, unlike part of Article 5(1)(c), 5(1)(f) does not require that detention has to be *necessary* in order to be justified. As a result, the temporary detention of asylum seekers pending their application to remain in the United Kingdom, is not of itself unlawful (*R (on the application of Shayan Barom & Others) v the Secretary of State for the Home Department* (2002) LTL 31 October).

---

Permitted grounds

Each of the situations envisaged in Article 5(1)(a)–(f) will now be examined. It should be noted at this point that Article 5 does not provide any *power* to arrest or detain; it simply sets out certain circumstances where the general right to liberty may be interfered with *by some existing lawful means.*

### Lawful detention after conviction

This exception allows a person to be detained after their conviction by a 'competent court', i.e. a court having the jurisdiction to try that particular case. Article 6 provides a right to a fair trial (**see para. 2.4.5**). Those people who have been so convicted may be detained in accordance with the order of the court. Clearly if the court does not have the power to pass the relevant order, the exception at Article 5(1)(a) will not apply and any detention will potentially amount to a violation of Article 5.

### Lawful arrest or detention for non-compliance

The exception under Article 5(1)(b) allows for the detention or arrest of a person who has failed to comply with the *lawful* order of a court. Failing to pay a fine or to observe the conditions of an injunction would be examples of such non-compliance. The exception also extends to the arrest or detention in order to secure the fulfilment of any obligation prescribed by law. Such an obligation might include an obligation to provide a roadside breath specimen or to surrender documents relating to a vehicle (as to which, **see Road Traffic**) or an obligation to attend a police station in order to give samples or body impressions (**see Evidence and Procedure, chapter 16**). Once again the circumstances of any arrest or detention will be examined by the courts who will need to consider whether the person was given a reasonable opportunity to comply with the order/obligation. The court will also need to consider whether the arrest or detention was a reasonable way to make sure that the order/obligation was met.

### Lawful arrest/detention in relation to an offence

There are several aspects to the permitted grounds under Article 5(1)(c). The arrest/detention must first be lawful in itself. Any arrest/detention that is later shown to have been *unlawful* cannot be saved under any of the other headings. The implications of Article 5 for custody officers are discussed in **Evidence and Procedure, chapter 15**. Even a lawful arrest/detention will only meet the requirements of Article 5(1)(c) if it can be shown to have been:

- effected for the purpose of bringing the person before the relevant 'competent legal authority' (i.e. a judge or magistrate) on reasonable suspicion that the person had committed an offence; or

- reasonably considered necessary to prevent the person committing an offence or from fleeing afterwards.

Where a person has been lawfully arrested for the purpose of bringing him/her before a competent legal authority, it is not necessary to show that he/she actually *was brought* before that authority (*Brogan* v *United Kingdom* (1988) 11 EHRR 117). It is the *purpose* of the arrest at the time that is relevant as opposed to its ultimate achievement. This interpretation appears to accord with the provisions of s. 30(7) of the Police and Criminal Evidence Act 1984 which require an arrested person to be released if the grounds for detaining him/her cease to exist (**see para. 2.9.3**). Given the statutory status of a custody officer (**see Evidence and Procedure, chapter 15**), he/she would probably not be a 'competent legal authority' for this purpose which seems to be judicial in nature and requiring a degree of independence from the arresting authorities. However, it is hard to see how the expression 'competent legal authority' can be limited to judges and magistrates because Article 5(3) goes on to use a more restrictive expression (*judge or other officer authorised by law to exercise judicial power*) to define just such people (see below). The lack of fit here between the wording and our own police and judicial roles is caused partly by the fact that those roles are different in nature from those in many other European Union countries.

'Reasonable suspicion' here will be assessed objectively and the court will look for 'the existence of facts or information which would satisfy an objective observer that the person may have committed the offence' (see *Fox* v *United Kingdom* (1990) 13 EHRR 157). Other tests applied to powers of arrest will need to be read in conjunction with this provision, as will powers to detain in connection with searches (as to which, **see para. 2.7**).

The permitted grounds set out under the second bullet point appear to accord with those powers that allow the arrest of someone who is *about to commit* an offence (**see para. 2.9**). Article 5(1)(c) does, however, raise some questions in relation to some of the general arrest conditions under the Police and Criminal Evidence Act 1984 (**see para. 2.9.3**). Further, it is now at least debatable as to whether the common law power of arrest relating to a person who is causing a breach of the peace (**see chapter 4**) will continue to exist as a breach of the peace is not 'an offence'. In this, as in all other applications of the 1998 Act, we will just have to wait and see how the courts approach and apply them.

### Lawful detention of minors

This ground refers solely to 'detention' rather than arrest, although Article 5 seems to use the two expressions interchangeably in places (e.g. Article 5(4) below) and there may be occasions where the two are difficult to distinguish anyway. As with Article 5(1)(c) above, the initial detention must be lawful. A minor for these purposes is a person who has not attained the age of 18.

### Lawful detention of others

Article 5(1)(e) also refers to 'detention' of certain people, in this case those who have various physical or mental ailments. It also extends to 'vagrants'. The reasoning behind Article 5(1)(e) is that the people described may need to be detained in their own interests. The permitted grounds set out here appear to allow the detention of people under the Mental Health Act 1983 (as to which, **see Crime, chapter 11**). Although there is a power under s. 34 of the Criminal Justice Act 1972 for a person to be taken after arrest to an approved alcohol treatment centre (**see chapter 10**), it is unlikely that Article 5(1)(e) would apply as there is no further power to *detain* such a person once he/she arrives at the centre. In such cases, the permitted grounds under Article 5(1)(c) above, would be more appropriate.

Whatever its extent, Article 5(1)(e) is likely to be very narrowly applied by the courts and the mere fact that an individual has, for example, an infectious disease, will not of itself justify his/her 'detention'.

### Lawful arrest/detention for deportation or extradition

The House of Lords has ruled that, unlike part of Article 5(1)(c), 5(1)(f) does not require the detention to be *necessary* in order to be justified (*R (on the application of Shayan Barom & others)* v *the Secretary of State for the Home Department* (2002) LTL 31 October). In that case it was held that the temporary detention of asylum seekers pending their application to remain in the United Kingdom, was not unlawful simply by reason of it not being strictly necessary.

Article 5(1)(f) is concerned with the unauthorised entry into the country and also the deportation/extradition of a person from the country. Such cases will invariably be dealt with by the relevant immigration authorities and advice should be sought from the Home Office.

### Procedure

Article 5 goes on to state:

> 2. Everyone who is arrested shall be informed promptly, in a language which he understands, of the reasons for his arrest and of any charge against him.

3. Everyone arrested or detained in accordance with the provisions of paragraph 1(c) of this Article shall be brought promptly before a judge or other officer authorised by law to exercise judicial power and shall be entitled to trial within a reasonable time or to release pending trial. Release may be conditioned by guarantees to appear for trial.

4. Everyone who is deprived of his liberty by arrest or detention shall be entitled to take proceedings by which the lawfulness of his detention shall be decided speedily by a court and his release ordered if the detention is not lawful.

5. Everyone who has been the victim of arrest or detention in contravention of the provisions of this Article shall have an enforceable right to compensation.

---

**KEYNOTE**

The right to be informed of the reason for arrest is already enshrined in our domestic law under s. 28 of the Police and Criminal Evidence Act 1984 (**see para. 2.8.2**). The wording of Article 5(2) strengthens that requirement by specifying that the information must be given in a language that the person understands. For the comparable right (under Article 6) to be given information on being charged with a criminal offence, **see para. 2.4.5**.

The reason for requiring this information to be given would appear to be to allow the arrested person to challenge the arrest and subsequent detention (*X* v *United Kingdom* (1981) 4 EHRR 188). The ability to challenge the lawfulness of that detention (and presumably, the arrest) is itself a Convention right under Article 5(4).

Article 5(3) clearly envisages the extension of bail where appropriate and for a discussion of this, together with the other implications of Article 5(3) and (4), **see Evidence and Procedure, chapters 5 and 15**.

Article 5(5) gives a person who is the 'victim' of an arrest or detention in contravention of the rest of the Article an enforceable right to compensation. This right applies, not only to the people concerned in the arrest/detention itself, but is specifically extended to include the courts (see s. 9 of the Human Rights Act 1998). The expression 'victim' is defined at s. 7(7) of the Act itself (see above).

---

2.4.5 **Article 6—the right to a fair trial**

Article 6 of the Convention states:

1. In the determination of his civil rights and obligations or of any criminal charge against him, everyone is entitled to a fair and public hearing within a reasonable time by an independent and impartial tribunal established by law. Judgment shall be pronounced publicly but the press and public may be excluded from all or part of the trial in the interest of morals, public order or national security in a democratic society, where the interests of juveniles or the protection of the private life of the parties so require, or to the extent strictly necessary in the opinion of the court in special circumstances where publicity would prejudice the interests of justice.

2. Everyone charged with a criminal offence shall be presumed innocent until proved guilty according to law.

---

**KEYNOTE**

Article 6 addresses another fundamental right within a democratic society and can be expected to be given a wide interpretation by the courts. The provisions of Article 6 affect both civil and criminal proceedings, although the Article goes on to provide specific safeguards in relation to criminal matters. For the general effects of these safeguards within the administration of justice in England and Wales, **see Evidence and Procedure**.

The key features of Article 6 are:

- a fair and public hearing
- held within a reasonable time
- by an independent and impartial legal tribunal.

Even a perception that the relevant court or tribunal is partial or biased can result in a breach of Article 6(1), reviving Lord Hewart's famous dictum that it is not enough that justice be done; it must manifestly be *seen* to be done.

Article 6 is restricted, however, to *procedural* issues and not to matters of fairness of the substantive law (see e.g. *R* v *Gemmell and Richards* [2002] Crim LR 926).

It has been held that Article 6 applies to professional disciplinary proceedings (*Wickramsinghe* v *United Kingdom* [1998] EHRLR 338), and there is an argument for its provisions being applied to police disciplinary hearings (**see chapter 1**). However, where an officer is to be interviewed for a *purely disciplinary* matter, he/she has no free standing right to access to a lawyer, even if being interviewed under caution (*Lee* v *United Kingdom* (2000) LTL 22 September).

The Article allows for the right to a public hearing to be restricted under certain circumstances, but requires any judgment to be publicly pronounced.

Article 6 has been interpreted as creating a requirement for 'equality of arms' in any civil or criminal proceedings (*Neumeister* v *Austria* (1968) 1 EHRR 91). Equality of arms requires that both parties be afforded the same opportunities to present their case and to cross-examine the other side. Additionally, both parties should be given the opportunity to be legally represented.

An example of where Article 6 has been used (unsuccessfully) as a 'shield' can be seen in the Scottish case of *Jardine* v *Crowe* 1999 SLT 1023. There the defendant refused to give details of the driver of his vehicle after a relevant offence when required to do so by the police under s. 172 of the Road Traffic Act 1988 (as to which, **see Road Traffic, chapter 2**). He argued that the requirement infringed Article 6 on the grounds that it forced him to incriminate himself. This argument was disposed of in the English and Welsh courts in *DPP* v *Wilson* [2002] RTR 61.

---

### 2.4.6 Article 7—no punishment without crime

Article 7 of the Convention states:

1. No one shall be held guilty of any criminal offence on account of any act or omission which did not constitute a criminal offence under national or international law at the time when it was committed. Nor shall a heavier penalty be imposed than the one that was applicable at the time the criminal offence was committed.

2. This Article shall not prejudice the trial and punishment of any person for any act or omission which, at the time when it was committed, was criminal according to the general principles of law recognised by civilised nations.

---

**KEYNOTE**

The main purpose of Article 7 is to provide a safeguard against retrospective criminal legislation whereby a government passes laws that render previously lawful behaviour unlawful. It also prohibits the imposition of a heavier penalty for a crime than that which was available at the time the crime was committed. Both of these provisions are in accordance with the key principles underpinning the Convention, namely that people should be able to look at the law and to adapt their behaviour in the full knowledge of what may happen to them if they break it.

In one case which illustrates the point, a defendant claimed that the change in the common law relating to marital rape (as to which, **see Crime, chapter 10**) violated Article 7 because he could not have foreseen that the law would be extended to protect wives. The European Court of Human Rights held that this did not amount to a violation of the Article (*SW* v *United Kingdom* (1995) 21 EHRR 363).

Claims that football banning orders (**see chapter 4**) breached this Article have been unsuccessful (see *Gough* v *Chief Constable of Derbyshire Constabulary* [2002] 2 All ER 985).

Article 7(2) is aimed at maintaining the rule *of* law rather than the rule *by* law. It provides for the situation where a person carries out activities that would be classified as 'crimes' according to the general principles of law among civilised nations but which were not necessarily criminal offences under the domestic law of that country (e.g. acts persecuting minority groups carried out with the acquiescence of the government). This very limited exception prevents States from legitimising what would otherwise be criminal acts by passing or repealing criminal laws.

2.4.7    **Article 8—right to private life**

Article 8 of the Convention states:

1.  Everyone has the right to respect for his private and family life, his home and his correspondence.

2.  There shall be no interference by a public authority with the exercise of this right except such as is in accordance with the law and is necessary in a democratic society in the interests of national security, public safety or the economic well being of the country, for the prevention of disorder or crime, for the protection of health or morals, or for the protection of the rights and freedoms of others.

---

**KEYNOTE**

The provisions of Article 8 extend a right to respect for a person's:

- private life,

- family life,

- home, and

- correspondence.

The main aim of the Article is to protect these features of a person's life from the arbitrary interference by 'public authorities' (as to which, see above) (*Kroon* v *Netherlands* (1994) 19 EHRR 263). This is a new concept as there is no statutory 'law of privacy' under the domestic law of England and Wales. However, the Convention does allow for individuals to raise issues of unjustified interference with their private lives and the courts have held that even celebrities have a basic right to privacy which will be protected by Article 8 (see *Campbell* v *Mirror Group Newspapers* [2002] EWHC 499); similar arguments (in a somewhat less genteel context) can be found in *Theakston* v *Mirror Group Newspapers* [2002] EWHC 137. The development of the law in this area has been given far more impetus by changes in the laws on data protection (**see chapter 11**).

Once again this Article is of considerable importance to police officers and managers for a number of reasons. First, the State is under a duty not to interfere with these features of a person's life except in accordance with Article 8(2). Many police activities such as entry onto premises, surveillance and the seizure of property, touch upon the features covered by Article 8. Once it can be shown that they have done so, the police must be able to point to:

- a legal authority allowing the interference,

- a legitimate objective behind their actions, and

- a 'pressing social need' for that interference

(the 'three tests').

An individual's Article 8 rights are among the key reasons behind the introduction of the Regulation of Investigatory Powers Act 2000 (as to which, **see Crime, chapter 3**).

Article 8 was also at the heart of the changes to the Sexual Offences Act 1956 as the European Court of Human Rights found that the law prohibiting consensual sexual acts between more than two men in private (s. 13) was an unjustifiable interference with Article 8 (see *ADT* v *United Kingdom* [2000] Crim LR 1009). For the offences under the 1956 Act generally, **see Crime, chapter 10**.

The Consultancy Service Index maintained by the Secretary of State for the Department of Health providing access to employers' records on people considered to be unsuitable for work with children has been held not to infringe the human rights of those included on it (*R* v *Worcester County Council, ex parte W* [2000] 3 FCR 174). The maintenance of the list was held, by the Divisional Court, to be proportionate to the lawful objective sought (*R* v *Secretary of State for Health, ex parte L(M)* [2001] 1 FLR 406).

A second reason why this Article is of importance to police services is that the State also has a positive obligation to prevent others from interfering with an individual's right to private life (see *Stjerna* v *Finland* (1994) 24 EHRR 194). How far the police would have to go in order to discharge this obligation is unclear, but Article 8 will be relevant in areas such as those set out in **Part 2** of this Manual (community safety), together with other areas such as civil disputes (as to which, **see chapter 7**).

It is here that the notion of balancing the rights and freedoms of individuals against each other and against those of the community at large can be seen most acutely. Article 8—and in particular the requirement for 'proportionality'—provides one of the main arguments that have been raised against the lawfulness of Anti-Social Behaviour Orders (see chapter 3) and Sex Offender Orders (see Crime, chapter 10).

A final reason that Article 8 is so important is that the Article appears to include the right to establish relationships with others, the right to privacy even within an office environment and the right to set up home, all of which have a significant impact on general supervisory and managerial functions. Failing to protect an individual from the unwanted advances of others, searching through an employee's office or directing an employee as to where he/she can and cannot live would all potentially fall within the remit of Article 8.

The European Court of Human Rights has held that there is no justification for barring transsexuals from enjoying rights conferred on others (such as the right to marry—see below) or to recognise their specific status and that to do so is a violation of Article 8 (*Goodwin* v *UK* [2002] 35 EHRR 18).

Article 8 also has implications for the law in relation to data protection and computer misuse (as to which, **see chapter 11**) and the lack of legal regulation governing the use of CCTV cameras has been raised with the European Commission (*R* v *Brentwood Borough Council, ex parte Peck,* The Times, 18 December 1997).

---

2.4.8    **Article 9—freedom of thought**

Article 9 of the Convention states:

1. Everyone has the right to freedom of thought, conscience and religion; this right includes freedom to change his religion or belief and freedom, either alone or in community with others and in public or private, to manifest his religion or belief, in worship, teaching, practice and observance.

2. Freedom to manifest one's religion or beliefs shall be subject only to such limitations as are prescribed by law and are necessary in a democratic society in the interests of public safety, for the protection of public order, health or morals, or for the protection of the rights and freedoms of others.

---

**KEYNOTE**

The freedom of thought, conscience and religion is protected by Article 9 and it is only the freedom to *manifest* one's religion or beliefs that is allowed to be limited under Article 9(2).

An example of the successful use of Article 9 as a defence to a criminal charge (i.e. the 'shield' approach described above) can be found in a Greek case where Jehovah's Witnesses were prosecuted under a domestic law for carrying out door-to-door evangelism. Even though the domestic law was enacted to protect the individual rights of people within their own homes, the Court held that the test of proportionality had not been made out in this case and accordingly held that there had been a violation of the Article (*Kokkinakis* v *Greece* (1993) 17 EHRR 397).

Attempts by employees who have been required to work on holy days of their respective faiths have generally been unsuccessful, but this by no means excludes future claims—particularly by public sector employees—from claiming that such duties are a violation of Article 9, especially if the individuals make their religious beliefs known at the time they enter that employment. The particular needs of religious *organisations* (as opposed to individuals) have also been provided for under s. 13 of the Human Rights Act 1998.

The potential effect of Article 9 on areas of domestic law such as racially-aggravated offences (as to which, **see chapter 3**) and discrimination generally (**see chapter 12**) is not yet clear, but the distinction between 'recognised' and 'unrecognised' religious groups may need to be amended.

The Concept of religion in Article 9 terms is currently far broader than in some other aspects of substantive law—possibly because Article 9 also extends to 'beliefs', clearly a much wider concept. In this respect Druidism has been accepted as a religion for these purposes (see *Pendragon* v *UK* (1999) 27 EHRR CD 179)—a proposal that is unlikely to be accepted under other statutes referring to religion, but you never know . . .

---

2.4.9    **Article 10—freedom of expression**

Article 10 of the Convention states:

1. Everyone has the right to freedom of expression. This right shall include freedom to hold opinions and to receive and impart information and ideas without interference by public authority and regardless of frontiers. This Article shall not prevent States from requiring the licensing of broadcasting, television or cinema enterprises.

2. The exercise of these freedoms, since it carries with it duties and responsibilities, may be subject to such formalities, conditions, restrictions or penalties as are prescribed by law and are necessary in a democratic society, in the interests of national security, territorial integrity or public safety, for the prevention of disorder or crime, for the protection of health or morals, for the protection of the reputation or rights of others, for preventing the disclosure of information received in confidence, or for maintaining the authority and impartiality of the judiciary.

---

**KEYNOTE**

Article 10 protects the freedom:

- of expression
- to hold opinions
- to receive and impart information and ideas

in each case without interference by a public authority.

'Expression' here includes the creation of pictures and images (*Stevens* v *United Kingdom* (1986) 46 DR 245).

Although not providing a general 'right to freedom of information', Article 10 has been used in a number of different settings including the protection of artistic, political and economic expression. It has been used to protect journalists' sources (see *Goodwin* v *United Kingdom* (1996) 22 EHRR 123).

As the right to express freely has to be balanced against the rights of others and the needs of democratic society generally, this area of Convention rights has generated some considerable problems and is often intermingled with issues of freedom of thought, conscience and religion (under Article 9).

In a case where the defendant damaged the perimeter fence of a Trident defence base, the Divisional Court held that her acts could be characterised as an expression of her opinion under Article 10 but that the Convention required the expression of that opinion to be proportionate. There were other ways in which the defendant could have expressed her opinion without committing a crime and therefore her conviction for criminal damage (**see Crime, chapter 14**) was upheld (*Hutchinson* v *DPP, The Independent*, 20 November 2000).

Article 10(1) is drafted to allow for State licensing of broadcasts, television and cinema performances but, as you might expect, the courts will be unlikely to tolerate interference with the freedom of expression without compelling reasons. Once again, the courts will look for a 'pressing social need' and indeed one of the main cases setting out the requirement for proportionality (*Handyside* v *United Kingdom* (1976) 1 EHRR 737) involved an action under Article 10. A good example of how Article 10 can operate is the case in the Republic of Ireland where, although it was shown that injunctions used to prevent women from receiving information about abortion services were issued for a legitimate aim, the overall effect of such legal remedies was found to be disproportionate (*Open Door Counselling and Dublin Well Woman* v *Ireland* (1992) 15 EHRR 244).

Article 10(2) clearly allows for an individual's freedom of expression to be curtailed under a number of circumstances including the prevention of disorder or crime and the protection of morals. Balancing these competing needs is one area where the European Court of Human Rights has allowed a reasonable 'margin of appreciation' (see above). Nevertheless, any restrictions on an individual's freedom of expression will be narrowly construed and closely scrutinised. Demonstrators may be able to rely on Article 10 as a defence to a charge under the Public Order Act 1986 (**see chapter 4**) and hunt saboteurs bound over to keep the peace by magistrates have been able to show that their rights have thereby been unjustifiably restricted (see *Hashman* v *United Kingdom* [2000] Crim LR 185).

The rights under this Article are subject to the restrictions allowed by Article 16 (political activities by aliens, see para. 2.4.15).

---

## 2.4.10 Article 11—freedom of assembly and association

Article 11 of the Convention states:

1. Everyone has the right to freedom of peaceful assembly and to freedom of association with others, including the right to form and to join trade unions for the protection of his interests.

2. No restrictions shall be placed on the exercise of these rights other than such as are prescribed by law and are necessary in a democratic society in the interests of national security or public safety, for the prevention of disorder or crime, for the protection of health or morals or for the protection of the rights and freedoms of others. This Article shall not prevent the imposition of lawful restrictions on the exercise of these rights by members of the armed forces, of the police or of the administration of the State.

### KEYNOTE

Article 11 is closely related to Article 10 and is often raised in conjunction with it, particularly in situations involving the arrest of demonstrators and protestors. In addition to refraining from interference with the individual's right to peaceful assembly, the State is also under a positive duty to prevent others from doing so. The assembly must, however, be *peaceful* and any intention to use violence or to cause disorder may take the individuals actions outside the protection of Article 11.

As with Article 10, there are allowances for reducing rights of assembly etc. under certain conditions including the prevention of disorder and crime and the interests of national security and public safety.

This Article may require changes to the current guidelines on picketing which restrict the number of pickets that may lawfully be allowed to gather at a workplace (see chapter 7).

The right to freedom of association and to join trade unions means, among other things, that trade unions may be victims for the purposes of bringing an action under this Article. The State can impose 'lawful restrictions' on the exercise of these rights by 'members of the police'. It is not clear whether this refers only to attested constables (as under s. 64 of the Police Act 1996) or to all employees of a police service including unsworn civilian staff (see chapter 1). Neither is it clear what would amount to 'lawful restrictions' on officers forming collectives for the protection of their shared interests.

The rights under this Article are subject to the restrictions allowed by Article 16 (political activities by aliens, see para. 2.4.15).

---

## 2.4.11 Article 12—the right to marry

Article 12 of the Convention states:

Men and women of marriageable age have the right to marry and to found a family, according to the national laws governing the exercise of this right.

---

### KEYNOTE

The protection given by Article 12 is fairly narrow in comparison to many of the other Convention rights, and is far more restricted than the right to 'respect for family life' under Article 8 (see para. 2.4.7). So far, Article 12 has only been applied to partnerships of biologically opposite sexes (see e.g. *Cossey* v *United Kingdom* (1990) 13 EHRR 622). Article 12 leaves the regulation of the laws of marriage themselves to each State and provides no list of exceptions to the right to marry and 'found a family'.

Our domestic courts have reiterated this view and have held that a marriage between a man and a woman who was born a man is not a valid marriage for the purposes of Article 12 (see *Bellinger* v *Attorney-General* [2000]

1 FLR 389). The European Court of Human Rights has held, however, that there is no justification for barring transsexuals from enjoying the right to marry and that to do so is a violation of Article 12 (*Goodwin* v *UK* [2002] 35 EHRR 18). Accordingly, the House of Lords has ruled that the statute precluding such marriages is incompatible with Articles 8 and 12 in the light of the *Goodwin* decision (*Bellinger* v *Bellinger & HM Attorney-General (Intervenor)* (2003) LTL 10 April).

---

### 2.4.12    Article 13—the right to an effective remedy

Article 13 of the Convention states:

> Everyone whose rights and freedoms as set forth in this Convention are violated shall have an effective remedy before a national authority notwithstanding that the violation has been committed by persons acting in an official capacity.

**KEYNOTE**

Article 13 is *not* included within sch. 1 to the Human Rights Act 1998. However, it will be of relevance to our courts because it has been so prominent within the case law that has grown up through Convention jurisprudence and, under s. 2 of the 1998 Act, those courts are obliged to take that case law into account.

Article 13 is generally used in conjunction with another Convention right (i.e. the right for which there is allegedly no 'effective remedy'). What Article 13 means is that everyone must have an effective remedy in their national courts to protect their rights irrespective of any official capacity in which the person violating those rights was acting. In one recent case the Commission held that the police complaints procedure (as to which, **see chapter 1**) did not provide an 'effective remedy' for those whose Convention rights has been violated (*Govell* v *United Kingdom* (application 27237/95), 14 January 1998, unreported). It is not clear how far the current avenues of redress for police officers who are the victims of unfounded or malicious complaints and investigations (**see chapter 1**) would meet these requirements. It is interesting to note that the police complaints system generally has been held not to amount to an 'effective remedy' for complaints (*Govell* v *United Kingdom*).

---

### 2.4.13    Article 14—prohibition of discrimination in Convention rights

Article 14 of the Convention states:

> The enjoyment of the rights and freedoms set forth in this Convention shall be secured without discrimination on any ground such as sex, race, colour, language, religion, political or other opinion, national or social origin, association with a national minority, property, birth or other status.

**KEYNOTE**

Article 14 simply provides a guarantee that access to the Convention's other provisions must be enjoyed equally by everyone under the jurisdiction of the particular State. The list set out in the Article is not exhaustive and other categories of people or grounds of discrimination may be added by the courts (and have been added by the European Court of Human Rights). A person claiming a breach of Article 14 must show that his/her own individual circumstances are similar to those of another person who has been treated differently in relation to the enjoyment of Convention rights.

The open-ended wording of Article 14 means that a wide range of categories of people who can be grouped by reference to their status may be protected. That protection certainly extends to a person's sexuality, an area that has generally not been protected in our domestic law (see *Mendoza* v *Ghaidan* [2002] EWCA Civ 1533).

However, it does not make express provision for *indirect* discrimination (as to which **see chapter 12** and the Divisional Court has expressed considerable doubt as to whether Article 14 provides protection against indirect, as opposed to direct, discrimination (see *R (on the application of Barber)* v *Secretary of State for Work and Pensions* [2002] EWHC 1915 (Admin) ).

Some commentators take the view that the partial or uneven application of police powers such as stop and search may amount to a breach of Article 14 (see para. 2.7).

The rights under this Article are subject to the restrictions allowed by Article 16 (political activities by aliens, see para. 2.4.15).

---

### 2.4.14     Article 15—derogation in time of emergency

Article 15 of the Convention states:

1. In time of war or other public emergency threatening the life of the nation any High Contracting Party may take measures derogating from its obligations under this Convention to the extent strictly required by the exigencies of the situation, provided that such measures are not inconsistent with its other obligations under international law.

2. No derogation from Article 2, except in respect of deaths resulting from lawful acts of war, or from Articles 3, 4 (paragraph 1) and 7 shall be made under this provision.

3. Any High Contracting Party availing itself of this right of derogation shall keep the Secretary General of the Council of Europe fully informed of the measures which it has taken and the reasons therefore. It shall also inform the Secretary General of the Council of Europe when such measures have ceased to operate and the provisions of the Convention are again being fully executed.

---

**KEYNOTE**

As discussed above, Article 15 allows a State to derogate from some of its obligations under the Convention during times of war or other public emergency threatening the life of the nation. This is a very narrow restriction and even under those extreme circumstances the derogation may only be made to the extent that is strictly required by the exigencies of the situation.

As also discussed above (see para 2.2.3) the original derogation lodged by the United Kingdom at the time when the Act was passed permitted longer detention of terrorist suspects before charge. That derogation related to the ongoing unrest in Northern Ireland. With political developments in Northern Ireland, that derogation was removed but, since 11 September 2001, the United Kingdom lodged a further derogation under the Anti-terrorism, Crime and Security Act 2001 and the powers thereunder. Because those powers are potentially incompatible with parts of the Convention, Parliament passed the Human Rights (Amendment No. 2) Order 2001 (SI 2001 No. 4032), giving effect to the derogation set out in Part I of sch. 3 to the Human Rights Act 1998 (see appendix 6).

---

### 2.4.15     Article 16—restrictions on political activities of aliens

Article 16 of the Convention states:

Nothing in Articles 10, 11 and 14 shall be regarded as preventing the High Contracting Parties from imposing restrictions on the political activity of aliens.

---

**KEYNOTE**

This apparently widely-drafted Article is felt by many to be slightly out of date. As all nationals of EU member States are 'European citizens' they are unlikely to be classified as aliens and the expression will probably be confined to people whose nationality lies outside the EU. Further, the expression 'political activities' are likely to be very narrowly construed. Nevertheless, if a case meets both expressions, the Convention rights of the person concerned as set out under Articles 10, 11 and 14 may be severely limited.

**2.4.16**   **Articles 17 and 18—protection of convention rights and freedoms**

Article 17 of the Convention states:

> Nothing in this Convention may be interpreted as implying for any State, group or person any right to engage in any activity or perform any act aimed at the destruction of any of the rights and freedoms set forth herein or at their limitation to a greater extent than is provided for in the Convention.

Article 18 of the Convention states:

> The restrictions permitted under this Convention to the said rights and freedoms shall not be applied for any purpose other than those for which they have been prescribed.

---

**KEYNOTE**

These Articles are aimed at protecting the provisions of the Convention. Article 17 is aimed at preventing any of the Convention's provisions from being used oppressively by any 'State, group or person', while Article 18 prevents the permitted restrictions under the Convention rights from being used for a purpose for which they were not intended.

---

**2.4.17**   **Protocol 1, Article 1—protection of property**

Protocol 1, Article 1 to the Convention states:

> Every natural or legal person is entitled to the peaceful enjoyment of his possessions.

> No one shall be deprived of his possessions except in the public interest and subject to the conditions provided for by law and by the general principles of international law.

> The preceding provisions shall not, however, in any way impair the right of a State to enforce such laws as it deems necessary to control the use of property in accordance with the general interest or to secure the payment of taxes or other contributions or penalties.

---

**KEYNOTE**

The Convention itself has been extended by the addition of a number of Protocols, not all of which have been incorporated by the Human Rights Act 1998. Article 1 of the First Protocol sets out the right to peaceful enjoyment of one's possessions. This leaves room for the State to deprive a person of his/her possessions 'in the public interest' (e.g. by nationalisation of an industry) and courts are likely to allow a wide margin of appreciation (see above) in such cases. Broadly, to prove a violation of this part of Protocol 1, it must be shown that the State has:

- interfered with the applicant's peaceful enjoyment of possessions, or
- deprived him/her of those possessions, or
- subjected those possessions to some form of control.

Clear examples of where such State activity can be found is in the seizure of property by HM Customs & Excise and the police. The term 'possessions' is likely to be interpreted very widely and, under European case law, has extended to land, contractual rights and intellectual property. Restrictions on the use of firearms (**see chapter 5**), premises (**chapter 9**) and even animals (**chapter 8**) may provide grounds for alleging a violation of this Convention right.

   A different example of how this right might be used against a public authority can be seen in *AO* v *Italy* (application 22534/93 (2000)). In that case the Italian police were held to have violated the applicant's right to peaceful enjoyment of his property when they continually failed to send any officers to his flat which he was trying to repossess from squatters. Although the action for repossession had been going on for over four years, this case illustrates one way in which private law matters can become issues of liability for public authorities such as police services.

---

2.4.18 **Protocol 1, Article 2—the right to education**

Protocol 1, Article 2 to the Convention states:

> No person shall be denied the right to education. In the exercise of any functions which it assumes in relation to education and to teaching, the State shall respect the right of parents to ensure such education and teaching in conformity with their own religious and philosophical convictions.

**KEYNOTE**

The United Kingdom has lodged a reservation in relation to this Convention provision and accepts the above Article 'only so far as it is compatible with the provision of efficient instruction and training and the avoidance of unreasonable public expenditure'.

The above provision requires the State to have regard to the religious and philosophical convictions of parents in its schools and was at the centre of a successful challenge against corporal punishment in a State school (*Campbell* v *United Kingdom* (1982) 4 EHRR 293). (See now the School Standards and Framework Act 1998 outlawing corporal punishment in all schools.) This Protocol was also successfully used by a Muslim parent against a decision by the local education authority not to allocate the applicant's daughter to a single sex school (*R (on the application of K)* v *Newham London Borough Council* (2002) *The Times*, 28 February). In *K* it was held that the Protocol requires an education authority to recognise religious convictions and to give them due weight when considering admission to a particular school.

2.4.19 **Protocol 1, Article 3—the right to free elections**

Protocol 1, Article 3 to the Convention states:

> The High Contracting Parties undertake to hold free elections at reasonable intervals by secret ballot, under conditions which will ensure the free expression of the opinion of the people in the choice of the legislature.

**KEYNOTE**

This Convention right applies, not only to the *holding* of elections, but also to rights of participation such as the right to vote and the right to stand for election (see *Mathieu-Mohin* v *Belgium* (1987) 10 EHRR 1).

Again, these rights can be restricted by the State and a wide margin of appreciation has been allowed.

The elections concerned must relate to the 'legislature' and it remains to be seen how far the courts will extend that definition. The European Commission has held in the past that the former metropolitan county councils in England were not 'legislatures' (see *Booth-Clibborn* v *United Kingdom* (1985) 43 DR 236).

2.4.20 **Protocol 6—death penalty**

Protocol 6 to the Convention states:

> Article 1 Abolition of the death penalty
> The death penalty shall be abolished. No one shall be condemned to such penalty or executed.

> Article 2 Death penalty in time of war
> A State may make provision in its law for the death penalty in respect of acts committed in time of war or of imminent threat of war; such penalty shall be applied only in the instances laid down in the law and in accordance with its provisions. The State shall communicate to the Secretary General of the Council of Europe the relevant provisions of that law.

**KEYNOTE**

Protocol 6 extends the general right to life (under Article 2, **see para. 2.4.1**). Although a State may make provision for the death penalty under the conditions or threat of war, it does not allow for any general derogations or reservations.

In May 2002 the United Kingdom signed up to a new Protocol (Protocol 13), abolishing the death penalty without *any* exceptions. This goes further than the above Protocol which allows for the penalty under some—albeit very extreme—circumstances.

The death penalty was abolished in England and Wales in 1965 for most crimes and the Crime and Disorder Act 1998 removed its residual application to a few ancient offences such as treason and piracy.

2.4.21　**Remaining Protocols**

There are several other Protocols to the Convention that the United Kingdom has not yet signed. Protocol 7, which addresses issues such as the expulsion of aliens, the rights of review and compensation for people convicted of criminal offences and the equality of private law rights between spouses, is likely to become incorporated into our domestic law in the near future.

2.5　**Policing powers**

Police officers are entrusted with many powers and privileges. The most important of these powers, both practically and constitutionally, are the powers of arrest, search, entry and seizure. All of these powers can be separated into those authorised by warrant and those which can be executed without warrant.

These powers can come from a number of sources and the main authorities are set out below. There are other sources of such powers, for instance those relating to drug trafficking and asset tracing, which are not addressed in this Manual.

As discussed in the introduction to this chapter, some of the powers given to police officers are now being extended to other police and non-police employees as the role of the so-called 'extended police family' grows. While there is still a considerable and significant gap between the legal powers and status of sworn constables and those of their non-sworn counterparts, many of the areas covered in the rest of this part of the Manual are of direct relevance to the policing role of the latter. For a full discussion of the specific powers and regulation of some of these new policing roles **see para. 2.14**.

In addition to the far-reaching effects of the human rights provisions discussed above, using powers improperly can result in officers and their employers being liable, both at civil and criminal law; it can also lead to evidence being excluded and otherwise meritorious prosecutions being dropped. Even where police powers are exercised *lawfully*, the manner or frequency of their use might be perceived by the community as a source of oppression and discrimination, leading to a reduction in confidence in the police and the creation of an atmosphere of distrust. The risk of lawfully employed police powers being perceived in this way was highlighted very clearly in the Stephen Lawrence Inquiry (Cm 4262-I, see para. 46.31 and recommendation 61) (see also PACE Code A).

It is worth noting that where a police officer acts on the authority of a properly sworn warrant issued by a magistrate, he/she is protected against legal action by the Constables Protection Act 1750. This protection does not apply where the warrant has been issued by the High Court.

2.5.1 **Fixed penalty notices**

Although the police have had the power to issue fixed penalty notices as an alternative to conventional prosecution in some road traffic offences for many years (**see Road Traffic, chapter 14**), the Criminal Justice and Police Act 2001 introduced a whole new concept of police powers for fast-track resolution of some lower level criminal offences. The remaining provisions for this new scheme will be implemented across England and Wales by April 2004. The powers in relation to some fixed penalty notices for low level disorder are among those that can be given to Police Community Support Officers designated under sch. 4 to the Police Reform Act 2002 (as to which **see para. 2.14.2**).

The offences which are subject to the fixed penalty scheme are set out in s. 1, along with the relevant penalties which are set in the Penalties for Disorderly Behaviour (Amount of Penalty) Order 2002 (SI 2002 No. 1837) as follows:

(1) For the purposes of this Chapter 'penalty offence' means an offence committed under any of the provisions mentioned in the first column of the following Table and described, in general terms, in the second column:

| Offence creating provision | Description of offence | Penalty |
| --- | --- | --- |
| Section 12 of the Licensing Act 1872 (c. 94) | Being drunk in a highway, other public place or licensed premises | £40 |
| Section 80 of the Explosives Act 1875 (c. 17) | Throwing fireworks in a thoroughfare | £40 |
| Section 31 of the Fire Services Act 1947 (c. 41) | Knowingly giving a false alarm to a fire brigade | £80 |
| Section 55 of the British Transport Commission Act 1949 | Trespassing on a railway | £40 |
| Section 56 of the British Transport Commission Act 1949 | Throwing stones etc. at trains or other things on railways | £40 |
| Section 169C(3) of the Licensing Act 1964 (c. 26) | Buying or attempting to buy alcohol for consumption in a bar in licensed premises by a person under 18 | £40 |
| Section 91 of the Criminal Justice Act 1967 (c. 80) | Disorderly behaviour while drunk in a public place | £40 |
| Section 5(2) of the Criminal Law Act 1967 (c. 58) | Wasting police time or giving false report | £80 |
| Section 43(1)(b) of the Telecommunications Act 1984 (c. 12) | Using public telecommunications system for sending message known to be false in order to cause annoyance | £80 |
| Section 5 of the Public Order Act 1986 (c. 64) | Behaviour likely to cause harassment, alarm or distress | £80 |
| Section 12(4) of the Criminal Justice and Police Act 2001 | Consumption of alcohol in designated public place | £40 |

**KEYNOTE**

Section 1 is in force, along with s. 3 which sets out the form of the fixed penalty notice and the amounts permissible. The Secretary of State may add to this list by statutory instrument and, by July 2002, he had already done so.

The heading to s. 1 in the statute refers to 'on the spot' penalties. This is inaccurate as no payment will be required before 21 days (under s. 5 when in force). While it might be in keeping with the media portrayal of offenders being frog marched to a hole-in-the-wall cash dispenser by a police officer who would then accept payment in return for the offender's release, it is nevertheless misleading.

Just as misleading is the description of the offence under s. 12 of the 2001 Act (described as *'consumption of alcohol in a public place'*); this offence is wider than that (see chapter 10).

The other offences listed above are set out in the relevant parts of this and other Manuals and are indicated in the respective keynotes.

---

Section 3 of the 2001 Act requires any fixed penalty notice to:

- be in the prescribed form (to be set out in future regulations);
- state the alleged offence;
- specify the 'suspended enforcement period' (21 days beginning with the date when the notice was given);
- state the amount of the penalty (which may not be more than a quarter of the maximum fine available for that offence);
- state to whom and where the payment must be made; and
- inform the person of his/her right to be tried and explain how that right might be exercised.

All this information will be set out on any approved form.

The power to issue such notices in respect of the s. 1 offences is set out at s. 2. At the time of writing, this was not in force. Basically, s. 2 allows a police officer in uniform (if away from a police station) or one that has been authorised by their chief officer (if at a police station) to give a person aged 18 or over a fixed penalty notice if he or she has reason to believe that the person has committed a s. 1 offence. A person given a fixed penalty notice will have the option of requesting to be tried in the normal way or of paying the penalty within the suspended enforcement period. The right to request trial is intended as a safeguard of the defendant's right to a fair trial under Article 6 of the European Convention (see para. 2.4.5). If the person fails to pay within that period, a sum of one and a half times the amount of the penalty may be enforced against them as a fine. After the suspended enforcement period ends, proceedings may be brought against the person in the normal way for the relevant offence(s). Full details surrounding the proposed operation of the whole scheme will be made in the form of guidance from the Home Office under s. 6.

This power is among those that can be conferred on a designated person under sch. 4 to the Police Reform Act 2002 (see para. 2.14.2).

## 2.6 Acting ranks

Many of the police powers considered in this—and subsequent—chapters are restricted to officers holding particular ranks. In particular, there are occasions where the Police and Criminal Evidence Act 1984 requires officers of certain ranks to perform roles. The 1984 Act recognises that there may be occasions where officers of the appropriate rank are not readily available and so in limited circumstances allows officers of a lower rank to perform their roles.

Section 107 of the Police and Criminal Evidence Act 1984 sets out occasions where an officer of a lower rank can perform the functions of that required by a higher rank.

Section 107 states:

(1) For the purpose of any provision of this Act or any other Act under which a power in respect of the investigation of offences or the treatment of persons in police custody is exercisable only by or with the authority of a police officer of at least the rank of superintendent, an officer of the rank of chief inspector shall be treated as holding the rank of superintendent if—

(a) he has been authorised by an officer holding a rank above the rank of superintendent to exercise the power or, as the case may be, to give his authority for its exercise, or

(b) he is acting during the absence of an officer holding the rank of superintendent who has authorised him, for the duration of that absence, to exercise the power or, as the case may be, to give his authority for its exercise.

(2) For the purpose of any provision of this Act or any other Act under which such a power is exercisable only by or with the authority of an officer of at least the rank of inspector, an officer of the rank of sergeant shall be treated as holding the rank of inspector if he has been authorised by an officer of at least the rank of superintendent to exercise the power or, as the case may be, to give his authority for its exercise.

---

**KEYNOTE**

Section 107 originally made reference to both superintendents and chief superintendents. This was amended by the Police and Magistrates' Courts Act 1994 to reflect the changes in rank structures within the police service. However, many police services have re-introduced the rank of chief superintendent in spite of the 1994 Act and the Criminal Justice and Police Act 2001 puts it back again. Although that part of the 2001 Act is now in force (see s. 125) and our deputies and chief superintendents have returned, it has not affected the above situation regarding acting ranks.

---

The only mention of officers performing the higher rank of sergeant in the Police and Criminal Evidence Act 1984 is to be found in s. 36. Section 36 states:

(3) No officer may be appointed a custody officer unless he is of at least the rank of sergeant.

(4) An officer of any rank may perform the functions of a custody officer at a designated police station if a custody officer is not readily available to perform them.

However, in *Vince v Chief Constable of Dorset Police* [1993] 1 WLR 415, Steyn LJ (as he was then) made it clear that s. 36(4) should only be an exception:

For my part I would start from the provisional premise that the legislature intended to introduce an effective system for the care and protection of detained suspects by custody officers. And on this basis section 36(4), which allows an independent officer of any rank to perform the function of a custody officer at a designated police station 'if a custody officer is not readily available to perform them', can be viewed as a concession to practicality in the light of the problems which will inevitably occur in a busy police station. In other words, there is much to be said for the view that it was not intended that chief constables would be entitled to arrange matters so that as a matter of routine officers below the rank of sergeant performed the functions of custody officers.

### 2.6.1 Temporary promotion

Regulation 6 of the Police (Promotion) Regulations 1996 (SI 1996 No. 1685) deals with temporary promotion. Regulation 6 states:

A member of a police force who is required to perform the duties of a higher rank may, even if there is no vacancy for that rank, be promoted temporarily to it, but, in the case of promotion to the rank of sergeant or inspector only if he is qualified for the promotion under regulation 3.

## 2.7 Stop and search

There are many specific statutory authorities providing the police (and others) with powers to stop people and vehicles and search them (**see appendix 1**). There is also a general power for police officers to stop and search people and vehicles under the Police and Criminal Evidence Act 1984 (PACE). Both this general power to stop and search and those authorised by most other statutes must be carried out in accordance with Code A of the PACE Codes of Practice. (There are exceptions for certain powers under the Aviation Security Act 1982 and those exercised by statutory undertakers.) Code A has been substantially revised in order to extend its provisions to other areas that were formerly not covered, and to clarify areas of ambiguity. For the full wording of the revised Code **see appendix 1**.

During the course of its amendment, a draft Code A was published for consultation, largely as a response to the report into the murder of Stephen Lawrence, but also as a result of some legislation that came after the Police and Criminal Evidence Act 1984. At one point the revised Code was to apply to all 'stops' of people and vehicles by the police, including everyday road traffic matters. In the end it was felt that further research was needed and several trial schemes were set up within a number of different forces. The results of these will be published in due course, but the government remains committed to implementing recommendation 61 of the Lawrence Report and to phasing-in the recording of all stops by the police (for further details, see the National Policing Plan).

Nevertheless, the provisions of Code A have changed in several significant areas and these are discussed below.

Before considering the specific statutory powers under the Police and Criminal Evidence Act 1984—and then the other main stop and search legislation—it is necessary to consider some general points arising from Code A. It is also worth noting that, as well as applying to these powers of search, Code A applies to some powers that allow the searching of people in the exercise of a power to search *premises*. For instance, the power to enter school premises and conduct searches of people for bladed articles and weapons under s. 139B of the Criminal Justice Act 1988 (as to which **see chapter 6**) will be governed by Code A (**see para. 2.27**). So, too, will the power to search people for controlled drugs under a warrant issued by virtue of s. 23 of the Misuse of Drugs Act 1971 (as to which **see Crime**).

### 2.7.1    Use of stop and search powers

The power to stop and search members of the community is one of the most controversial of all the powers available to the police. Therefore it must be used fairly and responsibly, with respect for the individual and without unlawful discrimination (**see chapter 12**). Paragraph 1 of Code A points out the benefits of properly conducted stop and search practices as an effective policing tool, but emphasises the need for officers to be able to justify using their powers. The primary purpose of stop and search powers is, as Code A reinforces, to enable police officers to allay or confirm suspicions about individuals without exercising their powers of arrest. Code A goes on to point out the potential harm to public confidence in the police that can be brought about by the improper or insensitive use of stop and search powers, as well as setting out a timely reminder that misuse can result in disciplinary action. As discussed in earlier parts of this chapter, the fact that a power is lawfully available does not necessarily mean that its use is appropriate or justified in every case. Parliament has given these discretionary powers to constables (and, on limited occasions, some others who are assisting them) and it is the responsibility of each individual officer to determine, not only whether a power *exists* in the particular circumstances, but also whether its use best serves the overall objectives of his/her police service. Conversely, Code A now specifically provides that, if there is no power to search a person, then an officer must not do so *even where the person being searched consents* (para. 1.5).

A key part of retaining public confidence and ensuring the proper functioning of the stop and search provisions lies in their monitoring and management. Code A imposes clear responsibilities on supervising officers to monitor the use of stop and search powers and, in particular, the possibility that they are being exercised on the basis of stereotyped images or other inappropriate generalisations (para. 5). Code A requires supervising officers to monitor the use of stop and search powers, to examine search records for any trends or patterns giving cause for concern and to take the appropriate action as necessary. This supervision and monitoring must be supported by the compilation of comprehensive statistical records of stops and searches at force, area and local level (para. 5.3). Any apparently disproportionate use of powers by particular officers or groups of officers, or their use in relation to specific sections of the community should be identified and investigated.

In addition to supervisors, Code A places a requirement on senior officers with area or force-wide responsibilities to monitor the 'broader use' of stop and search powers and, where necessary, to take action at the relevant level (para. 5.2). Code A also requires arrangements to be made for stop and search records to be scrutinised by representatives of the community (subject to confidentiality issues—Note 19) and for the use of these powers to be explained to the community at local level (para. 5.4).

### General stop and search powers

The law regulating the general police powers of stop and search is set out under part I of the Police and Criminal Evidence Act 1984 as discussed below. The Act imposes a number of detailed requirements and limits on the availability and use of these powers, while Code A adds further practical detail that officers, their supervisors and managers will need to take into account.

Section 1 of the Police and Criminal Evidence Act 1984 states:

(1) A constable may exercise any power conferred by this section—
   (a) in any place to which at the time when he proposes to exercise the power the public or any section of the public has access, on payment or otherwise, as of right or by virtue of express or implied permission; or
   (b) in any other place to which people have ready access at the time when he proposes to exercise the power but which is not a dwelling.

(2) Subject to subsection (3) to (5) below, a constable—
   (a) may search—
      (i) any person or vehicle;
      (ii) anything which is in or on a vehicle, for stolen or prohibited articles [or any article to which subsection (8A) below applies]; and
   (b) may detain a person or vehicle for the purpose of such a search.

---

### KEYNOTE

The above power applies where the officer has 'reasonable grounds for suspecting' that he/she will find stolen or prohibited articles or articles falling under s. 139 of the Criminal Justice Act 1988 (bladed or sharply pointed articles; **see chapter 6**) (s. 1(3) of the 1984 Act). For a discussion of reasonable grounds, see below.

The power under s. 1 does not authorise the officer to stop a vehicle (s. 2(9)(b) ). For the general power of police officers in uniform to stop vehicles, **see Road Traffic**. Compare this aspect of the stop and search power with that provided by s. 60 of the Criminal Justice and Public Order Act 1994 below.

The power is restricted to those places set out in s. l(l)(a) or (b). This does not mean that the search itself must be carried out there; in fact Code A, paras 3.5 and 3.6 require certain searches to be carried out away from public view.

Code A no longer allows the routine searching of people with their consent and only permits very limited use of the power as a condition of entry (e.g. to a sports ground) (para. 1.5). This means that the practice of conducting 'voluntary' searches in the street or other public places has gone.

### Reasonable grounds

The issue of when an officer has reasonable grounds for suspicion has been developed by the courts for many years. This common law development is now supported by the inclusion of specific guidance on search powers that require reasonable grounds for suspicion (see Code A, paras 2.2–2.4).

Generally, the courts have held that 'suspicion' requires a lower degree of certainty than *belief*. The distinction between the two expressions has been held to be a significant one, intended by Parliament (see *Baker* v *Oxford* [1980] RTR 315). In that particular case—involving road traffic offences—the court held that the statutory requirement for a reasonable *belief* imposed a greater degree of certainty on the officers concerned. Accordingly, police officers using powers that impose such an extra requirement must be prepared to justify their belief. Suspicion, on the other hand, has been described by Lord Devlin as '. . . a state of conjecture or surmise when proof is lacking' (*Shaabin Bin Hussein* v *Chong Fook Kam* [1970] AC 492). That suspicion can be based on any evidence, even if the evidence itself would be inadmissible at trial (e.g. because it is hearsay) (see Evidence and Procedure, chapter 11). In fact Code A provides for occasions where a police officer has reasonable grounds to suspect that a person is in innocent possession of stolen or prohibited articles or other items which give rise to a power to search the person even though there would be no power of arrest, or no offence committed by that person.

Recently the Court of Appeal has reiterated the principle in *Hussein* (above) in the context of an arrest of a person mistakenly thought to have been involved in an offence. The Court went on to say that a state of mind of 'being suspicious but uncertain' would provide reasonable grounds to support an arrest where reasonable suspicion was required (*Parker (Graham Charles)* v *Chief Constable of Hampshire Constabulary* (1999) *The Times*, 25 June; defendant seen in a car used in an earlier shooting incident in another part of the country). Confirmation that the source of reasonable grounds for suspicion can arise from intelligence or other information is supported by the entry in Code A, paras 2.2 and 2.4.

The courts have accepted that reasonable grounds for suspicion can arise from information given to the officer by a colleague, an informant or even anonymously (see *O'Hara* v *Chief Constable of the Royal Ulster Constabulary* [1997] 1 All ER 129).

Whether, in the case of the above powers, there were reasonable grounds for suspecting that the relevant articles would be found during the search is a question of fact that will have to be decided in the light of all the circumstances (see Code A, para. 2.2). The courts have held that it must be shown that any such grounds on which an officer acted would have been enough to give rise to that suspicion in a 'reasonable person' (*Nakkuda Ali* v *Jayaratne* [1951] AC 66).

However, the mere existence of such circumstances or evidence is not enough. The officer must actually *have* a 'reasonable suspicion' that the relevant articles will be found. If, in fact, the officer knows that there is little or no likelihood of finding the articles, the power could not be used (*R* v *Harrison* [1938] 3 All ER 134).

Reasonable suspicion can never be founded on the basis of purely personal factors such as a person's colour, age or appearance (Code A, para. 2.2) and grounds for suspicion cannot be provided retrospectively by questioning a person who the officer had no reason to stop.

However, Code A, para. 2.6 makes provision for the searching of members of gangs or groups who habitually carry:

- knives unlawfully or
- weapons or
- controlled drugs

and wear a distinctive item of clothing or other means of identifying themselves with such a gang or group, but only where there is reliable information or intelligence that members of a group or gang do so.

While there is no power to stop or detain a person in order to *find* grounds for a search (Code A, para. 2.11), in the case of searches under ss. 43 and 44 of the Terrorism Act 2000 (see chapter 4) this general restriction is modified to reflect the whole purpose of such searches. Similarly, Code A recognises that there are many reasons why police officers may be speaking to members of the public and, if during the course of any such non-stop and search encounter reasonable grounds for suspicion arise, the officer may then use his or her powers to search— even though no grounds existed at the beginning of the encounter. In order to make the position absolutely clear, Code A states that if an officer *is* detaining someone for the purpose of a search, he/she should tell the person *as soon as detention begins*.

The whole issue is best summed up at para. 2.5 of Code A which notes that searches are more likely to be more effective, legitimate and secure public confidence when reasonable suspicion is based on a range of factors and that the overall use of such powers is more likely to be effective when up-to-date, accurate intelligence and information is used.

If, in the course of a s. 1 search, the officer does find a stolen, prohibited or 'section 139' article, he/she may seize it (s. 1(6)).

If there are any grounds to suspect that the person has committed any offence, he/she must be cautioned before any questions are put to him/her about his/her involvement in the offence(s) if any answers, *or his/her silence*, are to be used in evidence (Code C). For a full discussion of these provisions, **see Evidence and Procedure, chapter 11.**

For the requirements and restrictions on conducting these searches **see para. 2.7.2.**

Section 1 of the 1984 Act also states:

(7)    An article is prohibited for the purposes of this Part of this Act if it is—
    (a)  an offensive weapon; or
    (b)  an article—
        (i)  made or adapted for use in the course of or in connection with an offence to which this sub-paragraph applies; or
        (ii)  intended by the person having it with him for such use by him or by some other person.

(8)    The offences to which subsection (7)(b)(1) above applies are—
    (a)  burglary;
    (b)  theft;
    (c)  offences under section 12 of the Theft Act 1968 (taking motor vehicle or other conveyance without authority); and
    (d)  offences under section 15 of that Act (obtaining property by deception).

(8A)  This subsection applies to any article in relation to which a person has committed, or is committing or is going to commit an offence under section 139 of the Criminal Justice Act 1988.

(9)    In this Part of this Act 'offensive weapon' means any article-
    (a)  made or adapted for use for causing injury to persons; or
    (b)  intended by the person having it with him for such use by him or by some other person.

**KEYNOTE**

For a full discussion on the law relating to offensive weapons and bladed/sharply pointed articles, **see chapter 6.** For the offences listed at s. 1(8), **see Crime.**

Section 1 of the 1984 Act also states:

(4)  If a person is in a garden or yard occupied with and used for the purposes of a dwelling or on other land so occupied and used, a constable may not search him in the exercise of the power conferred by this section unless the constable has reasonable grounds for believing—
    (a)  that he does not reside in the dwelling; and
    (b)  that he is not in the place in question with the express or implied permission of a person who resides in the dwelling.
(5)  If a vehicle is in a garden or yard occupied with and used for the purposes of a dwelling or on other land so occupied and used, a constable may not search the vehicle or anything in or on it in the exercise of the power conferred by this section unless he has reasonable grounds for believing—
    (a)  that the person in charge of the vehicle does not reside in the dwelling; and
    (b)  that the vehicle is not in the place in question with the express or implied permission of a person who resides in the dwelling.

**KEYNOTE**

If the person to be searched is in a garden, yard or other land occupied with and used as part of a dwelling, the power to search will not apply unless the officer has 'reasonable grounds for believing' that the person does not live there *and* that he/she is not there with the permission (express or implied) of any person who does live there.

If the garden or yard is attached to a house that is not so 'occupied', the restriction at s. 1(4) would not appear to apply.

Similar restrictions are placed on the searching of vehicles found in such places by s. 1(5). For the meaning of 'in charge' of a vehicle, **see Road Traffic, chapter 1**. For these purposes 'vehicle' includes vessels, aircraft and hovercraft (s. 2(10) of the 1984 Act).

---

### 2.7.2 Conducting the search

In keeping with the rest of Code A, the provisions regulating the conduct of searches apply not just to searches under s. 1 of the Police and Criminal Evidence Act 1984, but are of general application. Some of the main provisions of Code A are summarised below but the full text (**see appendix 1**) should always be consulted.

A good starting point is para. 3.1 which states that all stops and searches must be carried out with courtesy, consideration and respect for the person concerned and that every reasonable effort must be made to minimise the embarrassment that the person being searched may experience. In addition, the co-operation of the person being searched must be sought (this is not the same as requiring their *consent*—**see para. 2.7.1**) and forcible searches may be made only if it has been established that the person is unwilling to co-operate or they resist (para. 3.2).

The length of time that a person (or vehicle) is detained should be reasonable and kept to a minimum and the extent and thoroughness of the search must be related to the object of it and the relevant suspicion (para. 3.3). This means that, if you have reasonable suspicion only that the person has something concealed in a particular pocket, the search must be confined to that pocket.

Any search must be carried out *at or near* the place where the person or vehicle was first detained (para. 3.4). The predecessor of this provision in the first Code of Practice caused some confusion and now Note 6 sets the position out more clearly. While the search can take place at a nearby police station or elsewhere, the relevant place should be located within a reasonable travelling distance by car or on foot as appropriate. This applies to *all* such searches, not simply those involving the removal of clothing or which need to be conducted out of public view. If the search amounts to a 'strip search', Code C, Annexe A will apply (**see Evidence and Procedure**).

Generally there is no power to require a person to remove any clothing in public other than an outer coat, jacket or gloves (except under s. 45(3) of the Terrorism Act 2000 which also allows for the removal of headgear and footwear. For further discussion of these powers **see chapter 4**; and under s. 60AA of the Criminal Justice and Public Order Act 1994 which allows for the removal of items used to conceal identity—as to which **see para. 2.7.5**). Code A imposes further restrictions on searches in public (para. 3.6 and Notes 4, 7 and 8). Searches involving the removal of more than outer coats, jackets, gloves, footwear or headwear must not be carried out by, or in the presence of, someone of the opposite sex to the person being searched (para. 3.6). Searches under s. 43(1) of the Terrorism Act 2000 must be carried out by a person of the same sex as the person being searched. Searches involving the exposure of intimate parts must not be routinely carried out simply because nothing was found on the original search and they must not be carried out in public view or in a police vehicle (para. 3.7).

Before carrying out a search, the officer must take reasonable steps to give the person the following information:

- that they are being detained for that purpose
- the officer's name (except terrorism cases or other cases where the officer reasonably believes that this might put him/her in danger—a warrant or identification number must

be given in these cases) and police station. If the officer is not in uniform, he/she must show their warrant cards.

- the legal power that is being used
- a clear explanation of the purpose, any relevant reasonable suspicion that is needed or the relevant authorisation

(see generally Code A, para. 3.8).

Before conducting the search the officer must tell the person (or owner/person in charge of the vehicle) of their entitlement to a copy of the search record (**see para. 2.7.3**). If the person does not appear to understand what is being said, or there is any doubt about their ability to understand English, the officer must take reasonable steps to bring all the relevant information to the person's attention (**see para. 3.11**).

Having summarised the general rules regarding the conduct of searches, the specific requirements of s. 2 of the Police and Criminal Evidence Act 1984 can now be considered.

Section 2 of the Police and Criminal Evidence Act 1984 states:

(1) A constable who detains a person or vehicle in the exercise—
    (a) of the power conferred by section 1 above; or
    (b) of any other power—
        (i) to search a person without first arresting him; or
        (ii) to search a vehicle without making an arrest,
    need not conduct a search if it appears to him subsequently—
        (i) that no search is required; or
        (ii) that a search is impracticable.

(2) If a constable contemplates a search, other than a search of an unattended vehicle, in the exercise-
    (a) of the power conferred by section 1 above; or
    (b) of any other power, except the power conferred by section 6 below and the power conferred by section 27(2) of the Aviation Security Act 1982—
        (i) to search a person without first arresting him; or
        (ii) to search a vehicle without making an arrest,
    it shall be his duty, subject to subsection (4) below, to take reasonable steps before he commences the search to bring to the attention of the appropriate person—
        (i) if the constable is not in uniform, documentary evidence that he is a constable; and
        (ii) whether he is in uniform or not, the matters specified in subsection (3) below;
    and the constable shall not commence the search until he has performed that duty.

(3) The matters referred to in subsection (2)(ii) above are—
    (a) the constable's name and the name of the police station to which he is attached;
    (b) the object of the proposed search;
    (c) the constable's grounds for proposing to make it; and
    (d) the effect of section 3(7) or (8) below, as may be appropriate.

---

### KEYNOTE

As set out above, a person or vehicle may only be detained for such time as is reasonably necessary to permit a search to be carried out either at the place where the person or vehicle was first detained or nearby (s. 2(8)).

Having stopped a person for the purposes of searching them, there is no requirement for the officer to conduct the search if it appears that to do so is not necessary or that it is impracticable (see also Code A, Note 3 and para. 2.10 of Code C).

The officer carrying out the search must *take reasonable steps* to bring the matters at s. 2(3)(a) to (d) to the person's attention *before starting the search*. This information must be given whether it is requested or not. Whether reasonable steps have been taken to communicate information will ultimately be a question of fact for the court to decide and what is 'reasonable' will vary with the particular circumstances of each search (e.g. what is reasonable outside a busy city centre nightclub may well be different from that which is required on a rural public footpath). The requirements for officers to provide details of their names and police stations still apply even though that information is discernible from the officers' uniform; failure to provide the information in such circumstances will make any subsequent search unlawful and will mean that the person being searched may use reasonable force to resist it (*Osman* v *DPP* (1999) *The Times*, 28 September).

In enquiries related to the investigation of terrorism, or where the officer reasonably believes that giving his or her name might put him or her in danger, the requirement for an officer to give his/her name is removed (see Code A, para. 3.8).

The 'effect of section 3(7) or (8)' referred to in s. 2(3)(d) means the person's entitlement to a copy of any search record made.

The 'appropriate person' is the person to be searched or the person in charge of the vehicle to be searched (s. 2(5)).

### 2.7.3 Action after search

Section 3 of the Police and Criminal Evidence Act 1984 and Code A, para. 4 make certain requirements following any search of a person or vehicle (other than one not covered by s. 1 (**see para. 2.7.2**)). The first requirement is that the officer makes a written record of the search. While s. 3(1) makes an exception where it is not practicable to fill out such a record, Code A narrows the exception down to occasions where there are exceptional circumstances making it *wholly impracticable*. This very narrow exception will only be met if there was virtually no chance of the officer being in a position to make the record (e.g. by being called to an emergency immediately after the search). If the exception does apply, the officer must make the record as soon as practicable after the search has been completed (s. 3(2) and Code A, para. 4.1).

Section 3(6) of the Police and Criminal Evidence Act 1984 states:

(6) The record of a search of a person or a vehicle—
  (a) shall state—
    (i) the object of the search;
    (ii) the grounds for making it;
    (iii) the date and time when it was made;
    (iv) the place where it was made;
    (v) whether anything, and if so what, was found;
    (vi) whether any, and if so what, injury to a person or damage to property appears to the constable to have resulted from the search; and
  (b) shall identify the constable making it.

#### KEYNOTE

Where a search record has been made, the person searched, the owner or the person who was in charge of any vehicle that was searched, will be entitled to a copy of the record if he/she requests one within 12 months (s. 3(7), (8) and (9)). Code A requires that a copy of any record made *at the time* must be given immediately to the person who has been searched and the officer must ask for the name, address and date of birth of the person but there is no obligation to provide this information and no power to detain the person if they do not (para. 4.2).

Under the provisions of s. 2(3) (**see para. 2.7.2**), a person must be advised of his/her entitlement to a copy of the relevant search record unless it appears to the officer searching that it will not be practicable to make the record (s. 2(4)).

The requirements of s. 3 will apply to the searches of vehicles, vessels, aircraft and hovercraft (s. 3(10)).

The search record should contain the person's name but, if the officer does not know the name of the person, he/she cannot detain that person simply to find it out (s. 3(3)) and a description should be recorded instead (s. 3(4)). The record must also contain the information set out at Code A, para. 4.3 which includes a note of the person's self-defined ethnic background (see Note 18), the time when the person or vehicle was first detained, the outcome of the search, and the details of any other officer involved in the search (see Note 15). A record of a vehicle search must include a description of the vehicle (s. 3(5)) and the registration number (see Code A, para. 4.3 and Note 16).

A record is required for each person and each vehicle searched. However, if a person is in a vehicle and both are searched *and the object and grounds of the search are the same*, only one search record need be completed (Code A, para. 4.5). If more than one person in a vehicle is searched, separate records for each person must be made. Where a person is detained with a view to a search being carried out but no search is carried out as a result of the grounds being eliminated by questioning, a record must still be completed (para. 4.7).

It has been held that a failure to make a record of a search does not thereby render the search unlawful (*Basher* v *DPP* [1993] COD 372). However, it is not only the lawfulness of a search that is of concern to police officers and the general principles set out in Code A should be borne in mind at all times (**see para. 2.7.1**).

### Unattended vehicles

In the case of unattended vehicles, s. 2 of the Police and Criminal Evidence Act 1984 states:

(6) On completing a search of an unattended vehicle or anything in or on such a vehicle in the exercise of any such power as is mentioned in subsection (2) above a constable shall leave a notice—
(a) stating that he has searched it;
(b) giving the name of the police station to which he is attached;
(c) stating that an application for compensation for any damage caused by the search may be made to that police station; and
(d) stating the effect of section 3(8) below.

(7) The constable shall leave the notice inside the vehicle unless it is not reasonably practicable to do so without damaging the vehicle.

**KEYNOTE**

The requirements in relation to notice on unattended vehicles that are searched are also set out in Code A, para. 4. The requirements apply to the search of anything *on* an unattended vehicle as well as the vehicle itself. The notice must also state the police station where a copy of the search record can be obtained (para. 4.9) and, if practicable, the vehicle must be left secure (para. 4.10).

2.7.4    **Road checks**

The power to stop vehicles generally is provided under s. 163 of the Road Traffic Act 1988 (officers exercising the power must be in uniform; **see Road Traffic, chapter 10**). Having caused a vehicle to stop, there are then certain other powers which may be employed by a police officer (or other authorised people).

Among those powers are the powers set out in the Police and Criminal Evidence Act 1984, s. 4 in relation to 'road checks'.

A road check is where the power under s. 163 of the Road Traffic Act 1988 is used in any locality in such a way as to stop all vehicles or vehicles selected by any criterion (s. 4(2) of the 1984 Act). That general power for uniformed officers to stop vehicles might be used in a particular geographical area to stop all vehicles on the road or all vehicles of a certain make, model or colour, or only those vehicles containing a certain number of adult occupants. In all these cases, there would be a 'road check' for the purposes of s. 4.

The power to carry out road checks following the appropriate authorisation under s. 4 of the Police and Criminal Evidence Act 1984 below is among those that can be conferred on a Police Community Support Officer designated under sch. 4 to the Police Reform Act 2002 (**see chapter 2**). In exercising this power, any such officer may also be given the power of a uniformed constable to stop vehicles (under s. 163 of the Road Traffic Act 1988).

Section 4 of the Police and Criminal Evidence Act 1984 states:

(1) This section shall have effect in relation to the conduct of road checks by police officers for the purpose of ascertaining whether a vehicle is carrying—
  (a) a person who has committed an offence other than a road traffic offence or a vehicle excise offence;
  (b) a person who is a witness to such an offence;
  (c) a person intending to commit such an offence; or
  (d) a person who is unlawfully at large.

(2) ...

(3) Subject to subsection (5) below, there may only be such a road check if a police officer of the rank of superintendent or above authorises it in writing.

(4) An officer may only authorise a road check under subsection (3) above—
  (a) for the purpose specified in subsection (1)(a) above, if he has reasonable grounds—
    (i) for believing that the offence is a serious arrestable offence; and
    (ii) for suspecting that the person is, or is about to be, in the locality in which vehicles would be stopped if the road check were authorised;
  (b) for the purpose specified in subsection (1)(b) above, if he has reasonable grounds for believing that the offence is a serious arrestable offence;
  (c) for the purpose specified in subsection (1)(c) above, if he has reasonable grounds—
    (i) for believing that the offence would be a serious arrestable offence; and
    (ii) for suspecting that the person is, or is about to be, in the locality in which vehicles would be stopped if the road check were authorised;
  (d) for the purpose specified in subsection (1)(d) above, if he has reasonable grounds for suspecting that the person is, or is about to be, in that locality.

---

## KEYNOTE

Road checks may only be authorised for the purposes set out at s. 4(4) and for the duration set out at s. 4(11) (see below). They must, subject to s. 4(5) (see below), be authorised in writing by an officer of superintendent rank or above (s. 4(3)).

For the 'serious arrestable offences', see para. 2.9.1.

The locality in which vehicles are to be stopped must also be specified (s. 4(10)).

If it appears to an officer below the rank of superintendent that a road check is required as a matter of urgency for one of the purposes in s. 4(1), he/she may authorise such a road check (s. 4(5)). What amounts to 'urgency' is not defined, but it would appear to be a somewhat subjective requirement based on the apprehension of the officer concerned. Where such an urgent road check is authorised, the authorising officer must, *as soon as is practicable to do so*, make a written record of the time at which the authorisation is given and must cause an officer of superintendent rank or above to be informed of the authorisation (s. 4(6) and (7)). Where this occurs, the superintendent (or more senior officer) may authorise, *in writing*, that the road check continue (s. 4(8)). If the officer considers that the road check should not continue, he/she must make a written record that it took place as well as the purpose for which it took place (including the relevant 'serious arrestable offence' (s. 4(9) and (14)).

Under s. 4(13), every written authorisation for a road check must include:

* the name of the authorising officer

* the purpose of the road check—including any relevant 'serious arrestable offence'

* the locality in which vehicles are to be stopped.

---

Duration of road check

Section 4 of the 1984 Act goes on to state:

(11) An officer giving an authorisation under this section, other than an authorisation under subsection (5) above—
  (a) shall specify a period, not exceeding seven days, during which the road check may continue; and

(b) may direct that the road check—
(i) shall be continuous; or
(ii) shall be conducted at specified times,
during that period.

(12) If it appears to an officer of the rank of superintendent or above that a road cheek ought to continue beyond the period for which it has been authorised he may, from time to time, in writing specify a further period, not exceeding seven days, during which it may continue.

---

**KEYNOTE**

In recording the purpose for the road check under s. 4(13), the officer must specify a period not exceeding seven days during which the road check is to run.

The road check may run continuously through that specified period or it may be carried out at specific times.

The road check may be extended—in writing—a number of times for further periods up to a total of seven days by a superintendent if it appears to him/her that it 'ought' to continue. There is no restriction of 'reasonableness' or requirement for the existence of particular grounds here and it seems that the judgement may be an entirely subjective one by the superintendent.

Where a vehicle is stopped during a road check, the person in charge of it is entitled to a written statement of the purpose of that road check if he/she applies for one no later than the end of the 12-month period from the day on which the vehicle was stopped (s. 4(15)).

---

### 2.7.5 Criminal Justice and Public Order Act 1994

In addition to the powers above, police officers may stop and search vehicles under the Criminal Justice and Public Order Act 1994.

Section 60 of the 1994 Act states:

(1) If a police officer of or above the rank of inspector reasonably believes—
(a) that incidents involving serious violence may take place in any locality in his area, and that it is expedient to give an authorisation under this section to prevent their occurrence, or
(b) that persons are carrying dangerous instruments or offensive weapons in any locality in his police area without good reason,
he may give an authorisation that the powers conferred by this section shall be exercisable at any place within that locality for a specified period not exceeding 24 hours.

(2) (repealed)

(3) ...

(3A) ...

(4) This section confers on any constable in uniform power—
(a) to stop any pedestrian and search him or anything carried by him for offensive weapons or dangerous instruments;
(b) to stop any vehicle and search the vehicle, its driver and any passenger for offensive weapons or dangerous instruments.

---

**KEYNOTE**

The practical operational aspects of these powers are regulated by the Police and Criminal Evidence Act 1984 Code of Practice (see appendix 1 and para. 2.7). In particular, para. 2.12–2.14 of Code A and Notes 10–13 apply.

Note 10 makes it very clear that the above powers are separate from, and additional to the general stop and search powers discussed earlier in this chapter. The overall purpose of the above powers is to prevent serious violence and the widespread carrying of weapons that might otherwise lead to serious injury, by empowering the police to disarm potential offenders *in circumstances where other powers would not be sufficient*. Therefore these powers should not be used to replace or get round the normal powers for dealing with routine crime problems (Note 10).

Section 60(1)(a) has a generally preventive function in relation to the apprehension of incidents that will involve serious violence. Section 60(1)(b), however, is a much broader provision triggered by the officer's 'reasonable belief' that people are carrying dangerous instruments or offensive weapons. Serious violence is not defined in the 1994 Act but, although violence could relate to property, the whole tenor of the section suggests that it is aimed at tackling violence against people.

'Dangerous instruments' are bladed or sharply pointed instruments, while offensive weapons have the same meaning as that under s. 1(9) of the Police and Criminal Evidence Act 1984 (**seen para. 2.7.1**). For a full discussion of the law relating to weapons generally, **see chapter 6**.

Confusingly, for the purposes of s. 60, 'carrying' will mean 'having in your possession' (s. 60(11A)), a much wider meaning than carrying usually conveys (**see chapter 6 and also Crime, chapter 12**). Why the legislators did not simply use the term 'possession' is not clear.

The person authorising the exercise of the powers under s. 60(1)(a) must reasonably *believe* that it is expedient to do so in order to prevent the occurrence of the incidents involving serious violence. This is a more onerous requirement than reasonable grounds to 'suspect' (**see para. 2.7.1**). The reasonable belief must have an objective basis such as intelligence or a history of antagonism between particular groups or previous incidents of violence connected with certain locations or event (see Note 11). Code A also cites a significant increase in knife-point robberies within an area as being another example of an objective basis for such belief.

The initial period during which the authorisation can last must be no longer than appears to be reasonably necessary to prevent incidents of serious violence or to deal with the problem of carrying dangerous instruments/weapons *and in any event* must not exceed 24 hours (Code A, para. 2.13). Any such authorisation must be in writing and must set out the grounds, locality and period of operation of the authorisation. If an inspector gives an authorisation, he/she must, as soon as practicable, inform an officer of or above the rank of superintendent.

If it appears to an officer of or above the rank of superintendent that:

- having regard to offences that have been, or are reasonably suspected to have been, committed
- in connection with any activity falling within the authorisation and
- it is expedient to do so

he/she may authorise the continuation of the authority to exercise the powers under s. 60(1) for a further period of 24 hours (s. 60(3) and Code A, para. 2.14).

This authorisation must be in writing, signed by the officer giving it, and must specify:

- the grounds on which it is given
- the locality in which it is to operate, and
- the period during which the powers are exercisable

and any direction for the authorisation to continue must also be given in writing at the time or reduced into writing as soon as it is practicable to do so (s. 60(9)). Such a direction for the authorisation to continue may only be given once; thereafter a new authorisation must be sought (Code A, Note 12).

It is for the authorising officer to determine the period of time over which the authorisation will take effect. Not only should the officer set the *minimum* time considered necessary, but he/she should also set the geographical parameters no wider than necessary and it is important that officers taking part in the stop and search exercise are properly briefed as to these limits (see generally Code A, Notes 12–13).

If the power is to be used in response to a threat or incident that straddles police force areas, the relevant authority will have to be given by an officer from each of the forces concerned (Code A, Note 13).

A significant difference between this power and the general powers of stop and search (which are not affected by the granting of this power (s. 60(12)) is that it does not require any grounds at all for the officer to suspect that the person/vehicle is carrying offensive weapons or dangerous instruments (s. 60(5)).

A further difference is that the power under s. 60 authorises officers in uniform to stop vehicles in order to search them and their occupants (but not in relation to the removal and seizure of face coverings; see below).

The power allows the stopping and searching of pedestrians, vehicles (including caravans, aircraft, vessels and hovercraft) and passengers. If a dangerous instrument or anything reasonably suspected to be an 'offensive weapon' (see chapter 6) is found during the search, the officer may seize it (s. 60(6)). There is also provision for the removal and seizure of face coverings (see below). For the disposal of items seized under s. 60 see Police (Retention and Disposal of Items Seized) Regulations 2002 (SI 2002 No. 1372).

Note the general requirements governing searches imposed by Code A (see para. 2.7.2).

Failing to stop (or to stop a vehicle) when required to do so under this power is a summary offence punishable with one month's imprisonment and/or a fine (s. 60(8)(a)). A power of arrest may be available under the legislation dealing with obstruction of a police officer (Police Act 1996, s. 89; see Crime, chapter 8).

Where a vehicle is stopped under s. 60, the *driver* (as opposed to the person 'in charge'; see paras 2.7.1 and 2.7.4) is entitled to a written statement *that the vehicle was so stopped* (as opposed to the 'purpose' for which it was stopped; see para. 2.7.4). That statement must be provided if the driver applies for one no later than the end of the 12-month period from the day on which he/she was stopped (s. 60(10)). A person who is searched under this section is also entitled to a statement stating that he/she was so searched if he/she applies for one no later than the end of the 12-month period from the day on which he/she was stopped (s. 60(10A)). However, note the more stringent recording requirements imposed by Code A, para. 4.

### Powers to require removal of disguises

In a provision that is modelled on the powers in the previous paragraph, the Anti-terrorism, Crime and Security Act 2001 added a further section to the Criminal Justice and Public Order Act 1994. This new section replace the former s. 60(4A). Section 60AA of the Criminal Justice and Public Order Act 1994 states:

(1) Where—
    (a) an authorisation under section 60 is for the time being in force in relation to any locality for any period, or
    (b) an authorisation under subsection (3) that the powers conferred by subsection (2) shall be exercisable at any place in a locality is in force for any period,
    those powers shall be exercisable at any place in that locality at any time in that period.

(2) This subsection confers power on any constable in uniform—
    (a) to require any person to remove any item which the constable reasonably believes that person is wearing wholly or mainly for the purpose of concealing his identity;
    (b) to seize any item which the constable reasonably believes any person intends to wear wholly or mainly for that purpose.

(3) If a police officer of or above the rank of inspector reasonably believes—
    (a) that activities may take place in any locality in his police area that are likely (if they take place) to involve the commission of offences, and
    (b) that it is expedient, in order to prevent or control the activities, to give an authorisation under this subsection,
    he may give an authorisation that the powers conferred by this section shall be exercisable at any place within that locality for a specified period not exceeding twenty-four hours.

### KEYNOTE

These provisions are wider than those under s. 60 in that they are not restricted to anticipated outbreaks of serious violence. The above is not simply a preventative power and can be used where the 'activities' are already underway.

The above powers are governed by Code A of the Police and Criminal Evidence Act 1984 Codes of Practice (see appendix 1) and therefore the general requirements imposed by Code A must be borne in mind (see paras 2.7–2.7.3). More specifically, paras 2.15–2.18 of Code A impose additional requirements on the authorisation and use of these powers. The intention of these powers is to prevent those involved in intimidatory or violent protests using face coverings to conceal identity (Code A, Note 10). Any officer exercising the above powers must reasonably *believe* (not merely 'suspect'—**see para. 2.7.1**) that the person wearing the item is doing so *wholly or mainly for the purpose of concealing his or her identity* (Code A, para. 2.15). Therefore if the person is a cyclist wearing a face mask to prevent the inhalation of traffic fumes, or a motorcyclist wearing a crash helmet, the fact that its *effect* is to conceal their identity will not be enough—concealing their identity has to be the purpose/main purpose of the wearer.

Unlike s. 60, there is no specific power under this section to stop vehicles but, given that this is a power for police officers in uniform, the general power under s. 163 of the Road Traffic Act 1988 (**see Road Traffic, chapter 10**) could be used.

The requirements in relation to the further authority of a superintendent (or above) and the manner and form in which any authority is to be given are broadly similar to those set out in s. 60 (see previous Keynote). The limitations and requirements as to the time and geographical extent of any authorisation are the same (see previous Keynote).

There is no power to *search* for face coverings etc. under this power. The Divisional Court has held that the predecessor to this power (the old s. 60(4A)) neither involved nor required a 'search' and that therefore the provisions of s. 2 of the Police and Criminal Evidence Act 1984 did not apply (*DPP* v *Avery* [2001] EWHC (Admin) 748). The Court went on to hold that, although the power—and its powers of arrest (see below)—mounted to a significant interference with a person's liberty, it was justified by the type of situation envisaged by the legislators whereby the police may need to call upon the law.

Clearly if an item is found during a lawful search for other articles (say under s. 60(4)) which does not require any 'reasonable belief' by the officer, face coverings and masks could then be seized under subsection (b).

The very stringent requirements of Code A in relation to the conduct and recording of searches must be borne in mind (**see paras 2.7–2.7.3**). Further, the specific guidance as to the religious sensitivities that may arise when asking someone (for instance Sikh, Hindu and Muslim men and women) to remove head or face coverings must be considered where appropriate (Code A, Note 4).

The expression 'item' is very wide and would clearly include balaclavas, scarves and crash helmets. It is not specifically restricted to face coverings and would appear to extend to anything that could be worn wholly or mainly for the purpose of concealing identity (e.g. where offenders swap clothing after an offence). Although the purpose of the legislation is primarily to ensure that people are not allowed to commit offences anonymously in situations of public disorder, it is unclear whether other methods that hinder identification—such as face paint—would be caught by this new power as it may be difficult to show that such materials amounted to 'an item' which is capable of being seized.

---

OFFENCE:  **Failing to comply with requirement to remove items—*Criminal Justice and Public Order Act 1994, s. 60AA(7)***

      • Triable summarily  • One month's imprisonment and/or fine.
      *(Arrestable offence)*

Section 60AA(7) of the Criminal Justice and Public Order Act 1994 states:

(7) A person who fails to remove an item worn by him when required to do so by a constable in the exercise of his power under this section shall be liable . . .

---

**KEYNOTE**

The wording of this offence is absolute. There is no requirement that the person failed *without reasonable excuse* or *without good reason* etc.; simply that he/she failed to remove an item worn by him/her. However, it must be shown that:

• the requirement was made (and presumably understood)

• it was made by a police officer in uniform

• in the exercise of powers authorised under s. 60

in the reasonable belief that the person was wearing the item wholly or mainly for the purpose of concealing his/her identity.

This offence is made an arrestable offence by s. 24 and sch. 1A to the Police and Criminal Evidence Act 1984 (see para. 2.9.1).

---

### Retention and disposal of seized items

The procedure to be followed in relation to the retention and disposal of items seized under s. 60 is set out in the Police (Retention and Disposal of Items Seized) Regulations 2002 (SI 2002 No. 1372).

### 2.7.6 Terrorism

In addition to the other general statutory powers discussed above, there are further specific powers given to the police to enable them to stop, search and control the movement of people and vehicles in connection with terrorist investigations. These provisions are now contained in the Terrorism Act 2000 (as to which, **see chapter 4**).

### Cordons

Section 33 of the Terrorism Act 2000 empowers the police to set up cordons if it is considered expedient to do so for the purposes of a terrorist investigation. Under s. 32, 'terrorist investigation' means generally an investigation of:

- the commission, preparation or instigation of acts of terrorism;
- an act which appears to have been done for the purposes of terrorism;
- the resources of a proscribed organisation (**see chapter 4**);
- the commission, preparation or instigation of an offence under the 2000 Act.

Section 34 of the Terrorism Act 2000 states:

(1)  Subject to subsections (1A), (1B) and (2), a designation under section 33 may only be made—
    (a) where the area is outside Northern Ireland and is wholly or partly within a police area, by an officer for the police area who is of at least the rank of superintendent, and
    (b) ...

(1A) A designation under section 33 may be made in relation to an area (outside Northern Ireland) which is in, on or in the vicinity of any policed premises by a member of the British Transport Police Force who is of at least the rank of superintendent.

(1B) A designation under section 33 may be made by a member of the Ministry of Defence Police who is of at least the rank of superintendent in relation to an area outside or in Northern Ireland—
    (a) if it is a place to which subsection (2) of section 2 of the Ministry of Defence Police Act 1987 (c. 4) applies,
    (b) if a request has been made under paragraph (a), (b) or (d) of subsection (3A) of that section in relation to a terrorist investigation and it is a place where he has the powers and privileges of a constable by virtue of that subsection as a result of the request, or
    (c) if a request has been made under paragraph (c) of that subsection in relation to a terrorist investigation and it is a place in, on or in the vicinity of policed premises.

(1C) But a designation under section 33 may not be made by—
    (a) a member of the British Transport Police Force, or
    (b) a member of the Ministry of Defence Police,
    in any other case.

(2)  A constable who is not of the rank required by subsection (1) may make a designation if he considers it necessary by reason of urgency.

**KEYNOTE**

This power is designated to be *investigative* in its nature; contrast the *preventive* powers provided under s. 44 (see below). *The powers to designate under this section were extended to the non-Home Office police forces shown by the Anti-terrorism, Crime and Security Act 2001.*

If the superintendent (or higher-ranking officer) makes the designation orally, he/she must confirm it in writing as soon as reasonably practicable. If the designation is made by another officer under the urgency provisions of s. 34(2) and (3), that officer must, as soon as is reasonably practicable:

- make a written record of the time at which the designation was made, and
- ensure that a police officer of at least the rank of superintendent is informed

(s. 34(3)).

On being so informed, the superintendent must confirm or cancel the designation. If he/she cancels the designation, he/she must make a written record of the cancellation and the reason for it (s. 34(4)).

However, if the designation is made, the person making it must arrange for the demarcation of the cordoned area, so far as is reasonably practicable by means of tape marked with the word 'police', or in such other manner as any police officer considers appropriate (s. 33(4)).

The period of designation begins at the time the order is made (i.e. it cannot be made to begin at some time in the future) and ends on the date specified in the order.

The initial designation cannot extend beyond 14 days from the time the order is made (s. 35(2)). However, the period during which a designation has effect may be extended in writing from time to time by the person who made it, or an officer of at least superintendent rank (s. 35(3)). Any extension must specify the additional period during which the designation is to have effect. Section 35(5) places a limit of 28 days on extended designations; this appears to mean an *overall limit of 28 days* beginning with the day on which the order is made (as opposed to an initial maximum period of 14 days plus a further extension period of 28 days).

Police powers

Specific police powers in relation to terrorist investigations are addressed in sch. 5 to the 2000 Act. Other, more general, police powers appear in the main body of the Act. One such power is under s. 36, which states:

(1) A constable in uniform may—
   (a) order a person in a cordoned area to leave it immediately,
   (b) order a person immediately to leave premises which are wholly or partly in or adjacent to a cordoned area,
   (c) order the driver or person in charge of a vehicle in a cordoned area to move it from the area immediately,
   (d) arrange for the removal of a vehicle from a cordoned area,
   (e) arrange for the movement of a vehicle within a cordoned area,
   (f) prohibit or restrict access to a cordoned area by pedestrians or vehicles.

**KEYNOTE**

The officer giving the order or making the arrangements and prohibitions set out here must be in uniform. Therefore detectives or other plain clothes officers involved in the terrorist investigation will not have these powers available to them.

The powers under s. 36 are among those that can be conferred on a Police Community Support Officer designated under sch. 4 to the Police Reform Act (**see para. 2.14.2**).

Failing to comply with an order, prohibition or restriction under this section is a summary offence punishable by three months' imprisonment and/or a fine (s. 36(2)).

This wording will presumably cover refusal. There is a defence if the person can show that he/she had a reasonable excuse for the failure.

___

### Stop and search authorisations

The Terrorism Act 2000 also gives the police specific powers to authorise stop and search operations under certain conditions.

The exercise of these powers is governed by Code A of the Police and Criminal Evidence Act 1984 Codes of Practice (as to which **see paras 2.7–2.7.3**). Code A (**see appendix 1**) contains specific provisions that relate to the use of these powers, as well as the general guidance that applies to all stops and searches.

Where it appears to any officer of or above the rank of assistant chief constable/commander (in relation to provincial forces and the Metropolitan/City of London police respectively) that it is expedient to do so, in order to prevent acts of terrorism, he/she may authorise the use of stop and search powers in a locality for a period not exceeding 28 days (ss. 44 and 46). An authorisation under s. 44 may be extended by an officer of the specified rank(s). These powers—which replaced those under the former s. 13 of the Prevention of Terrorism (Temporary Provisions) Act 1989—are subject to PACE Code A. Where an officer gives such an authorisation, he/she must take immediate steps to send a copy of the authorisation to the National Joint Unit, Metropolitan Police Special Branch who in turn will forward it to the Secretary of State. If the Secretary of State does not confirm the authorisation within 48 hours of its being given, the authorisation 'runs out' after the 48 hours are up. The unit will inform the force within 48 hours whether the Secretary of State has confirmed, cancelled or reduced the period of the authorisation (Code A, para. 2.23 and Note 14). The authorisation may be given orally but, if so, it must be confirmed in writing as soon as reasonably practicable (s. 44(5)). Similar powers are given to officers of the specified ranks to impose prohibitions or restrictions on parking in a specified area (s. 48). If the driver or person in charge of a vehicle:

- permits it to remain at rest in contravention of any such prohibition or restriction, or
- fails to move the vehicle when ordered to do so by a constable *in uniform*

he/she commits a summary offence (s. 51).

It should be noted that these provisions are *preventive* whereas those relating to the setting up of cordons (see above) are *investigative*. An authorisation under these provisions empowers police officers *in uniform* to stop vehicles and search them and any occupants (s. 44(1)); it also allows such officers to stop and search pedestrians and anything carried by them (s. 44(2)). The authorities under each of these subsections can be combined (Code A, para. 2.19). These searches must be for the purpose of searching for articles of a kind which could be used in connection with terrorism only. The 2000 Act specifically provides that police officers may use reasonable force when exercising these powers (s. 114); however, the general limitations on the use of police powers under the Human Rights Act 1998 must also be borne in mind.

So too must the provisions of Code A. If the authorisation is given orally in the first instance, it must be confirmed in writing by the officer who gave it as soon as reasonably practicable (Code A, para. 2.20). When giving any authorisation under these powers, the officer must specify the geographical limits of the authority as well as the time and date when it will expire (Code A, para. 2.21). It is also important to note that a constable may only exercise the powers under s. 44 for the purpose of searching for articles of a kind that could be used in connection with terrorism but can do so whether or not there are any grounds for suspecting the presence of such articles (Code A, para. 2.24; see also s. 45(1)(b)).

This is very different from the general requirements for reasonable suspicion that apply to most other aspects of Code A (**see para. 2.7.1**). Furthermore, although Code A states that officers must take particular care not to discriminate against members of minority ethnic groups, it acknowledges that there may be circumstances where it is appropriate for officers to take account of a person's ethnic origin in selecting people to be stopped *in response to a specific terrorist threat* (Code A, para. 2.25). The powers must only be used in a way that reflects an objective assessment of a threat posed by various terrorist groups in Great Britain. The requirements for officers to reveal their identities in search records is relaxed slightly when s. 44 powers are used (see code A, para. 4.4) and there is no provision to extend an authorisation after the original one has expired (Note 12).

The powers of a constable in uniform under s. 44 in relation to the stopping and searching of vehicles, passengers and pedestrians, along with the powers of seizure, are among that can be conferred on a Police Community Support Officer (PCSO) designated under sch. 4 to the Police Reform Act (**see para. 2.14.2**). However, a PCSO cannot exercise any power of stop, search or seizure under this provision unless he or she is in the company *and* under the supervision of a constable (the Police Reform Act 2002, sch. 4, para. 15(2)).

People and vehicles may be detained for the purpose of carrying out the search (s. 45(4)). The extent of the search and the entitlement of people to be given a statement to the effect that they were so searched are subject to similar conditions as those under the Criminal Justice and Public Order Act 1994 (**see para. 2.7.5**). Failing to stop when required or wilfully obstructing an officer in the exercise of these powers is a summary offence punishable with six months' imprisonment and/or a fine (s. 47).

For the additional powers to 'seize and sift' under s. 51 of the Criminal Justice and Police Act 2001 **see para. 2.13.9**.

## 2.8 Powers of arrest

An arrest involves depriving a person of his/her liberty to go where he/she pleases (*Lewis* v *Chief Constable of South Wales Constabulary* [1991] 1 All ER 206). In a criminal context an arrest will usually be to answer an alleged charge, but occasionally arrests may be preventive (such as where a person is arrested in connection with a breach of the peace; **see chapter 4**), it may be to take samples or fingerprints (**see Evidence and Procedure, chapter 16**), or it may be to return someone to prison or bring them before a court.

The Football (Disorder) Act 2000 introduced a further concept in police powers; that of a statutory power to detain a person in order to ascertain whether he/she is subject to a football banning order (**see chapter 4**).

Every arrest must be lawful, that is, the person carrying it out must be able to point to some legal authority which allows it; otherwise an arrest will be unlawful and actionable as an assault or a civil wrong (see *Spicer* v *Holt* [1977] AC 987). This position has been significantly reinforced by the Human Rights Act 1998 (see above).

The source of a power of arrest may come from:

- The nature of the offence (i.e. an 'arrestable offence'; **see para. 2.9.1**).
- The conditions at the time (allowing an arrest under the Police and Criminal Evidence Act 1984, s. 25; **see para. 2.9.3**).
- The provisions of the particular Act (e.g. the Public Order Act 1986; **see chapter 4**).
- The provisions of an order (e.g. a court order or a warrant).
- Common law (e.g. breach of the peace; **see chapter 4**).

Merely being told to arrest someone by a more senior officer is *not* a reasonable ground for doing so (see *O'Hara* v *Chief Constable of the Royal Ulster Constabulary* [1997] 1 All ER 129).

Any lawful arrest must be made for a proper purpose. Such a purpose has been held to include an arrest to bring the person to a police station to subject them to the formal atmosphere there (*Holgate-Mohammed* v *Duke* [1984] AC 437) or to obtain a confession even after a complainant has withdrawn his/her initial complaint (*Plange* v *Chief Constable of Humberside* (1992) *The Times*, 23 March). These cases will have to be reviewed in light of the Human Rights Act 1998. Occasionally, officers investigating one offence may find that they have insufficient evidence to arrest for that particular offence, but that the circumstances would allow them to arrest the person for some other offence.

The practice of arresting someone on a 'holding' offence was accepted by the Court of Appeal in *R* v *Chalkley* [1998] 3 WLR 146, *provided the arresting officers had reasonable grounds for suspecting that the person had actually committed that offence*. If that suspicion is present then the fact that the officers making the arrest are doing so with the intention of investigating another, more serious offence does not render the arrest unlawful. If, however, there are no such grounds to suspect that the person had in fact committed the offence, or the officers know at the time of the arrest that there is no possibility of the person actually being charged with it, the arrest will be unlawful.

Section 30(7) of the Police and Criminal Evidence Act 1984 (in keeping with common law) requires that, if the grounds for detaining a person cease to exist before reaching a police station, the person must be released (see below). This is particularly important in relation to arrests made under the 'general' conditions under s. 25 (**see para. 2.9.3**).

Any unlawful arrest will also carry implications for the officer if he/she is assaulted during the course of making it (**see Crime, chapter 8**).

### 2.8.1 Reasonable grounds

Many—though not all—powers of arrest carry some requirement that the arresting officer be acting on 'reasonable suspicion' or has 'reasonable cause' to suspect/believe the existence of certain facts. As those requirements relate to the suspected/believed existence of facts rather than the state of the law, a police officer's mistaken belief that he/she had a power of arrest where in fact he/she did not may make the subsequent arrest unlawful (see e.g. *Todd* v *DPP* [1996] Crim LR 344). An officer's reasonable cause to believe that he/she has a power of arrest is not the same as a reasonable cause to believe that someone has committed an offence which carries a power of arrest.

One of the things about our legislation that make it such fun is the inconsistency in terminology used by Parliament. Enter stage left the latest definition, requiring that a constable has *'reasonable grounds for believing'* certain things before a power to stop and seize motor vehicles is triggered (s. 59 of the Police Reform Act 2002, as to which **see Road Traffic**).

Tests of reasonableness impose an element of objectivity and the courts will consider whether, in the circumstances, a reasonable and sober person might have formed a similar view to that of the officer. Failing to follow up an obvious line of enquiry (e.g. as to the ownership of property found in the possession of the defendant) may well provide grounds for challenging the exercise of a power of arrest (see e.g. *Castorina* v *Chief Constable of Surrey* (1988) 138 NLJ 180). There is no need, however, for the officer to exhaust every possible defence or to obtain conclusive *proof* of the relevant facts or circumstances before effecting an arrest (*Ward* v *Chief Constable of Avon & Somerset Constabulary* (1986) *The Times*, 26 June). However, the test that the courts will apply in assessing the lawfulness of an arrest where an offence is suspected is partly *subjective*. The arresting officer must have formed a genuine suspicion that the person being arrested was guilty of an offence, as well as having reasonable grounds for forming such a suspicion (*Jarrett* v *Chief Constable of the West Midlands Police* (2003) *The Times*, 28 February).

Where information has come from an identifiable informant great care will be needed. The courts have held that the police owe a duty to take reasonable care to avoid unnecessary disclosure to the general public of information which an informant has given to them (*Swinney* v *Chief Constable of Northumbria (No. 2)* (1999) *The Times*, 25 May).

Mistaking an innocent citizen for someone else and then arresting them as a result of that mistaken identity will not necessarily make the arrest unlawful (*Hussein* v *Chong Fook Kam* [1970] AC 942). The lawfulness of an arrest under s. 24(5) will be determined by the reasonable grounds on which an officer's belief was based and being 'suspicious but uncertain' can provide reasonable grounds for a lawful arrest (see the Court of Appeal's decision in *Parker* v *Chief Constable of Hampshire* (1999) *The Times*, 25 June).

An arrest begins at the time when the arresting officer informs the person of it or when his/her words *or actions* suggest that the person is under arrest (*Murray* v *Ministry of Defence* [1988] 1 WLR 692).

Police officers are not under any general duty to arrest without warrant and should always consider the use of the summons procedure where appropriate. (However, see ss. 29 and 31 of the Police and Criminal Evidence Act 1984.)

### 2.8.2    Information to be given on arrest

Whether an arrest is made under the Police and Criminal Evidence Act 1984 or not, s. 28 makes clear provision for the information that *must* be given to a person on arrest. Section 28 states:

(1) Subject to subsection (5) below, where a person is arrested, otherwise than by being informed that he is under arrest, the arrest is not lawful unless the person arrested is informed that he is under arrest as soon as is practicable after his arrest.

(2) Where a person is arrested by a constable, subsection (1) above applies regardless of whether the fact of the arrest is obvious.

(3) Subject to subsection (5) below, no arrest is lawful unless the person arrested is informed of the ground for the arrest at the time of, or as soon as is practicable after, the arrest.

(4) Where a person is arrested by a constable, subsection (3) above applies regardless of whether the ground for the arrest is obvious.

(5) Nothing in this section is to be taken to require a person to be informed—
    (a) that he is under arrest; or
    (b) of the ground for the arrest,

if it was not reasonably practicable for him to be so informed by reason of his having escaped from arrest before the information could be given.

---

**KEYNOTE**

Section 28 clearly makes provision for situations when the person cannot be told or would not be capable of understanding the information. However, as the failure to comply with s. 28 makes any arrest unlawful (see e.g. *Dawes* v *DPP* [1994] Crim LR 604), it is perhaps better to 'err on the side of caution'.

In relation to the requirement at s. 28(2) and (3), particular care should be taken when giving a suspect details of exactly why he/she is being arrested. In a recent case, the Court of Appeal held that it had been unfair—and unlawful—for an arresting officer to withhold facts which had led him to arrest the suspect on suspicion of having committed an offence (*Wilson* v *Chief Constable of Lancashire Constabulary* (2000) LTL 23 November). In that case the court held that an arresting officer's minimum obligation was to give a suspect 'sufficient information as to the nature of an arrest to allow the suspect sufficient opportunity to respond'.

Code C of the Police and Criminal Evidence Act 1984 Codes of Practice also imposes requirements in this area. For instance, para. 10.3 states that when a person is arrested or further arrested, they must be informed at the time or as soon as practicable thereafter that they are under arrest and the grounds for their arrest. Note 10B goes on to say that the arrested person must be given sufficient information to enable them to understand that they have been deprived of their liberty and the reason (e.g. the nature of the offence, when and where it was committed, etc.). If the arrest is made under s. 25 of the Police and Criminal Evidence Act 1984 (as to which **see para. 2.9.3**) the grounds for arrest must include an explanation of the conditions that make the arrest necessary.

Article 5(2) of the European Convention on Human Rights reinforces s. 28 (see above) and also requires that the information be given in a language that the person understands.

The reasons given for the arrest must be the *real* reasons in the officer's mind at the time (see *Christie* v *Leachinsky* [1947] AC 573) and he/she must clearly indicate to the person the fact that he/she is being arrested. This requirement might be met by using a colloquialism, provided that the person is familiar with it and understands its meaning (e.g. 'you're locked up' or 'you're nicked'; see *Christie* v *Leachinsky* above). It does not matter that the words describe more than one offence (e.g. 'burglary' or 'deception'), provided that they adequately describe the offence for which the person has been arrested (*Abbassy* v *Metropolitan Police Commissioner* [1990] 1 WLR 385).

---

### 2.8.3 Caution

The Police and Criminal Evidence Act 1984 Code of Practice, Code C, para. 10.4 (**see Evidence and Procedure**) requires that a person must be cautioned on arrest or further arrest. There is no longer a requirement that the arrest be for an 'offence'. As with the requirements under s. 28 of the 1984 Act, there are exceptions to the requirement to administer the caution and these are:

- where it is impracticable to do so by reason of the person's condition or behaviour at the time; or

- where he/she has already been cautioned immediately before the arrest in accordance with Code C, para. 10.1 (requirement to caution where there are grounds to suspect commission of an offence).

The wording of the general caution is set out at Code C, para. 10.5. Note, however, that there is a different form of words relating to some interviews (Code C, Annexe C) and that the giving of the appropriate caution will determine whether or not adverse inferences can be drawn by a court under the Criminal Justice and Public Order Act 1994. Paragraph 10.7 of Code C provides that minor deviations from the words of *any* caution will not amount to a breach of the Code provided that the sense of the relevant caution is preserved. It goes on to provide that if a person does not appear to understand the caution, the officer who has given it should go on to explain it in his/her own words (Note 10D). For further details of cautioning generally, **see Evidence and Procedure**.

### 2.8.4 Force

Section 117 of the Police and Criminal Evidence Act 1984 allows the use of reasonable force when making an arrest. Section 3 of the Criminal Law Act 1967 also allows the use of such force as is reasonably necessary in the arrest of people and the prevention of crime.

Whether any force used is 'reasonable' will be determined by the court in the light of all the circumstances, including the circumstances as the arresting officer believed them to be at the time. Such force may even be lethal to the defendant. Where serious harm is caused by an arrest, the courts will consider the time that was available to the officer to reflect on his/her actions and whether or not he/she believed that the danger presented to others by failing to arrest the person outweighed the harm caused to the person by the arrest (see *Attorney-General for Northern Ireland's Reference (No. 1 of 1975)* [1977] AC 105). This situation has been reinforced by the European Convention on Human Rights (see above) and the test for justifying the use of force has become more stringent (**see Crime, chapter 8**).

For the general power of search on arrest, **see para. 2.13.2**.

Use of excessive force, while amounting to possible misconduct (**see chapter 1**) and assault (**see Crime, chapter 8**), does not render an otherwise lawful arrest unlawful (*Simpson* v *Chief Constable of South Yorkshire* (1991) *The Times*, 7 March).

## 2.9  Arrest without warrant

As discussed above, there are a number of sources from which a power of arrest can be gained. The main sources of powers of arrest without warrant are ss. 24 and 25 of the Police and Criminal Evidence Act 1984.

### 2.9.1  Arrestable offences

The expression 'arrestable offence' often creates confusion. 'Arrestable offences' should not be confused with those offences *for which a power of arrest exists*, e.g. offences under the Public Order Act 1986 and some drink/driving offences (**see Road Traffic, chapter 5**). '*Arrestable offences*' are a very specific group of offences covered by the provisions of s. 24(1)(c) of the Police and Criminal Evidence Act 1984. Arrestable offences are offences:

- for which the sentence is fixed by law (murder),

- for which a person aged 21 or over (not previously convicted) can be sentenced to five years' imprisonment or more (this age is to be reduced by the Criminal Justice and Court Services Act 2000, s. 74 to '18'—at the time of writing, s. 74 was not in force), or

- listed in Schedule 1A.

Schedule 1A states:

**SCHEDULE 1A**

SPECIFIC OFFENCES WHICH ARE ARRESTABLE OFFENCES

**NOTES**

**Amendment**

Inserted by the Police Reform Act 2002, s. 48(1), (5), Sch. 6.

Date in force: 1 October 2002 (except in relation to offences committed before that date): see SI 2002/2306, art. 2(d)(iv) and the Police Reform Act 2002, s. 48(6).

**1  Customs and Excise Acts**

An offence for which a person may be arrested under the customs and excise Acts (within the meaning of the Customs and Excise Management Act 1979 (c 2)).

**2  Official Secrets Act 1920**

An offence under the Official Secrets Act 1920 (c 75) which is not an arrestable offence by virtue of the term of imprisonment for which a person may be sentenced in respect of them.

**3  Prevention of Crime Act 1953**

An offence under section 1(1) of the Prevention of Crime Act 1953 (c 14) (prohibition of carrying offensive weapons without lawful authority or excuse).

**4  Sexual Offences Act 1956**

An offence under—

   (a) section 22 of the Sexual Offences Act 1956 (c 69) (causing prostitution of women) or
   (b) section 23 of that Act (procuration of girl under 21).

### 5  Obscene Publications Act 1959

An offence under section 2 of the Obscene Publications Act 1959 (c 66) (publication of obscene matter).

### 6  Theft Act 1968

An offence under—

    (a)  section 12(1) of the Theft Act 1968 (c 60) (taking motor vehicle or other conveyance without authority etc.); or

    (b)  section 25(1) of that Act (going equipped for stealing etc.).

### 7  Theft Act 1978

An offence under section 3 of the Theft Act 1978 (c 31) (making off without payment).

### 8  Protection of Children Act 1978

An offence under section 1 of the Protection of Children Act 1978 (c 37) (indecent photographs and pseudo-photographs of children).

### 9  Wildlife and Countryside Act 1981

An offence under section 1 (1) or (2) or 6 of the Wildlife and Countryside Act 1981 (c 69) (taking, possessing, selling etc. of wild birds) in respect of a bird included in Schedule 1 to that Act or any part of, or anything derived from, such a bird.

### 10  An offence under—

    (a)  section 1(5) of the Wildlife and Countryside Act 1981 (disturbance of wild birds);

    (b)  section 9 or 13(1)(a) or (2) of that Act (taking, possessing, selling etc. of wild animals or plants); or

    (c)  section 14 of that Act (introduction of new species etc).

### 11  Civil Aviation Act 1982

An offence under section 39(1) of the Civil Aviation Act 1982 (c 16) (trespass on aerodrome).

### 11A  Aviation (Offences) Act 2003

An offence of contravening a provision of an Order in Council under section 60 of that Act (air navigation order) where the offence relates to—

    (a)  a provision which prohibits specified behaviour by a person in an aircraft towards or in relation to a member of the crew, or

    (b)  a provision which prohibits a person from being drunk in an aircraft, insofar as it applies to passengers.

### 12  Aviation Security Act 1982

An offence under section 21C(1) or 21D(1) of the Aviation Security Act 1982 (c 36) (unauthorised presence in a restricted zone or on an aircraft).

### 13  Sexual Offences Act 1985

An offence under section 1 of the Sexual Offences Act 1985 (c 44) (kerb-crawling).

### 14  Public Order Act 1986

An offence under section 19 of the Public Order Act 1986 (c 64) (publishing etc. material likely to stir up racial or religious hatred).

### 15  Criminal Justice Act 1988

An offence under—

    (a)  section 139(1) of the Criminal Justice Act 1988 (c 33) (offence of having article with a blade or point in public place); or

    (b)  section 139A(1) or (2) of that Act (offence of having article with a blade or point or offensive weapon on school premises).

### 16  Road Traffic Act 1988

An offence under section 103(1)(b) of the Road Traffic Act 1988 (c 52) (driving while disqualified).

### 17

An offence under subsection (4) of section 170 of the Road Traffic Act 1988 (failure to stop and report an accident) in respect of an accident to which that section applies by virtue of subsection (1)(a) of that section (accidents causing personal injury).

**18   Official Secrets Act 1989**

An offence under any provision of the Official Secrets Act 1989 (c 6) other than subsection (1), (4) or (5) of section 8 of that Act.

**19   Football Spectators Act 1989**

An offence under section 14J or 21C of the Football Spectators Act 1989 (c 37) (failing to comply with requirements imposed by or under a banning order or a notice under section 21B).

**20   Football (Offences) Act 1991**

An offence under any provision of the Football (Offences) Act 1991 (c 19).

**21   Criminal Justice and Public Order Act 1994**

An offence under—

(a) section 60AA(7) of the Criminal Justice and Public Order Act 1994 (c 33) (failing to comply with requirement to remove disguise);

(b) section 166 of that Act (sale of tickets by unauthorised persons); or

(c) section 167 of that Act (touting for car hire services).

**22   Police Act 1996**

An offence under section 89(1) of the Police Act 1996 (c 16) (assaulting a police officer in the execution of his duty or a person assisting such an officer).

**23   Protection from Harassment Act 1997**

An offence under section 2 of the Protection from Harassment Act 1997 (c 40) (harassment).

**24   Crime and Disorder Act 1998**

An offence falling within section 32(1)(a) of the Crime and Disorder Act 1998 (c 37) (racially or religiously aggravated harassment).

**25   Criminal Justice and Police Act 2001**

An offence under—

(a) section 12(4) of the Criminal Justice and Police Act 2001 (c 16) (failure to comply with requirements imposed by constable in relation to consumption of alcohol in public place); or

(b) section 46 of that Act (placing of advertisements in relation to prostitution).

---

**KEYNOTE**

For details of the majority of these offences, **see Crime** and the later chapters of this Manual.

The power of arrest (**see para. 2.9.2**) also applies to conspiring or inciting to commit, or aiding, abetting, counselling or procuring the commission of these offences. It also extends to attempts to commit these offences unless they are summary offences (**see s. 24(3)**). For a full discussion of these terms, **see Crime, chapter 3**.

The list above used to be found in s. 24 of the Police and Criminal Evidence Act 1984; now it has moved to sch. 1A to that Act. It is regularly amended and the most recent copy of the 1984 Act should be consulted in cases of doubt. Note that extradition offences (e.g. offences committed abroad which are the subject of an extradition warrant under s. 8 of the Extradition Act 1989) cannot be regarded as 'arrestable offences' within the meaning of s. 24(1) (see *R (on the application of Rottman)* v *Commissioner of Police for the Metropolis* (2001) *The Times*, 26 October),

The commission or suspicion of an arrestable offence brings with it a number of wide powers of entry, search and seizure, some of which are discussed below.

---

A further definition exists for some offences which are classified as 'serious arrestable offences'. This classification generally affects the application of wider powers (e.g. of detention, search and the taking of samples; **see Evidence and Procedure, chapter 16**).

Section 116(2) of the Police and Criminal Evidence Act 1984 provides that the following offences will *always* be 'serious':

(a) an offence (whether at common law or under any enactment) specified in Part I of Schedule 5 to this Act;

(b) an offence under an enactment specified in Part II of that Schedule;

(c) any offence which is specified in paragraph 1 of Schedule 2 to the Proceeds of Crime Act 2002 (drug trafficking offences); and

(d) any offence under section 327, 328 or 329 of that Act (certain money laundering offences).

Schedule 5 specifies the serious arrestable offences:

PART I OFFENCES MENTIONED IN SECTION 116(2)(A)

1. Treason.
2. Murder.
3. Manslaughter.
4. Rape.
5. Kidnapping.
6. Incest with a girl under the age of 13.
7. Buggery with a person under the age of 16.
8. Indecent assault which constitutes an act of gross indecency.
9. An offence under section 170 of the Customs and Excise Management Act 1979 (c 2) of being knowingly concerned, in relation to any goods, in any fraudulent evasion or attempt at evasion of a prohibition in force with respect to the goods under section 42 of the Customs Consolidation Act 1876 (c 36) (prohibition on importing indecent or obscene articles).

PART II OFFENCES MENTIONED IN SECTION 116(2)(B)

Explosive Substances Act 1883 (c 3)
1. Section 2 (causing explosion likely to endanger life or property).

Sexual Offences Act 1956 (c 69)
2. Section 5 (intercourse with a girl under the age of 13).

Firearms Act 1968 (c 27)
3. Section 16 (possession of firearms with intent to injure).
4. Section 17(1) (use of firearms and imitation firearms to resist arrest).
5. Section 18 (carrying firearms with criminal intent).

Taking of Hostages Act 1982 (c 28)
7. Section 1 (hostage-taking).

Aviation Security Act 1982 (c 36)
8. Section 1 (hi-jacking).

Criminal Justice Act 1988 (c 33)
9. Section 134 (torture).

Road Traffic Act 1988 (c 52)
10. Section 1 (causing death by dangerous driving).
10A. Section 3A (causing death by careless driving when under the influence of drink or drugs).

Aviation and Maritime Security Act 1990 (c 31)
11. Section 1 (endangering safety at aerodromes).
12. Section 9 (hijacking of ships).
13. Section 10 (seizing or exercising control of fixed platforms).

Channel Tunnel (Security) Order 1994 No. 570
14. Article 4 (hijacking of Channel Tunnel trains).
15. Article 5 (seizing or exercising control of the tunnel system).

Protection of Children Act 1978 (c 37)
14. Section 1 (indecent photographs and pseudo-photographs of children).

Obscene Publications Act 1959 (c 66)
15. Section 2 (publication of obscene matter).

Section 116(6) goes on to provides that *any other arrestable offence* will be serious if its commission would lead to, or it is intended or likely to lead to:

(a) serious harm to the security of the State or to public order;
(b) serious interference with the administration of justice or with the investigation of offences or of a particular offence;
(c) the death of any person;

(d) serious injury to any person;

(e) substantial financial gain to any person; and

(f) serious financial loss to any person.

---

**KEYNOTE**

These consequences or intended consequences should be borne in mind when considering arrestable offences that do not fall under s. 116(2) above. They may also bring the relevant activity within the new definition of terrorism (see chapter 4).

'Loss' is serious if, having regard to all the circumstances, it is serious for the person who suffers it (s. 116(7))—therefore the test is a *subjective* one based on the victim's circumstances.

'Injury' includes any disease and any impairment of a person's physical or mental condition (s. 116(8)).

---

### 2.9.2  Power of arrest: arrestable offences

Section 24 of the Police and Criminal Evidence Act 1984 goes on to state:

(4) Any person may arrest without a warrant—

  (a) anyone who is in the act of committing an arrestable offence;

  (b) anyone whom he has reasonable grounds for suspecting to be committing such an offence.

(5) Where an arrestable offence has been committed, any person may arrest without a warrant—

  (a) anyone who is guilty of the offence;

  (b) anyone whom he has reasonable grounds for suspecting to be guilty of it.

(6) Where a constable has reasonable grounds for suspecting that an arrestable offence has been committed, he may arrest without a warrant anyone whom he has reasonable grounds for suspecting to be guilty of the offence.

(7) A constable may arrest without a warrant—

  (a) anyone who is about to commit an arrestable offence;

  (b) anyone whom he has reasonable grounds for suspecting to be about to commit an arrestable offence.

---

**KEYNOTE**

The first two powers (s. 24(4) and (5)) are exercisable under the appropriate conditions by anyone and are the powers most likely to be used by store detectives and security staff. They will also be available to people who have been designated or accredited with policing powers under the Police Reform Act 2002. The requirement for an arrestable offence to have been committed can cause problems as it applies retrospectively. Thus, if a person involved in an alleged incident of say, theft, was arrested under s. 24(5) and later acquitted, no arrestable offence would have *been committed*. Therefore the arrest would be unlawful but the person making it would not find this out until many months later when the case (or often the appeal) was decided (*R* v *Self* [1992] 3 All ER 476).

For these subsections it is not enough that the person making the arrest *suspects* that an arrestable offence has been committed, however strong that suspicion may be. For that reason, s. 24(6) specifically provides police officers with a power of arrest under those circumstances. Provided there are reasonable grounds to suspect that an arrestable offence has been committed, the power will apply—but only to police officers acting within their jurisdiction (see chapter 1).

The final power (s. 24(7)), again limited to police officers, provides for occasions where a person is *about* to commit an arrestable offence.

'Reasonable grounds for suspicion' are not defined but the police officer must be able to demonstrate what those grounds were. The source of those grounds may be information passed on by another officer or by a PNC operator; they may even come from an anonymous call (*DPP* v *Wilson* [1991] RTR 284) or an informant (*James* v *Chief Constable of South Wales* [1991] 6 CL 80).

The power of arrest (see para. 2.9.2) also applies to conspiring to commit, or inciting, aiding, abetting, counselling or procuring the commission of these offences. It also extends to attempts to commit these offences but *not* where the offence is a summary offence (see s. 24 (3) ).

Note the power to enter premises in order to arrest a person for an arrestable offence (see para. 2.13.2).

---

2.9.3   **General arrest power: Police and Criminal Evidence Act 1984, s. 25**

Section 25 of the Police and Criminal Evidence Act 1984 states:

(1)  Where a constable has reasonable grounds for suspecting that any offence which is not an arrestable offence has been committed or attempted, or is being committed or attempted, he may arrest the relevant person if it appears to him that service of a summons is impracticable or inappropriate because any of the general arrest conditions is satisfied.

(2)  In this section 'the relevant person' means any person whom the constable has reasonable grounds to suspect of having committed or having attempted to commit the offence or of being in the course of committing or attempting to commit it.

---

**KEYNOTE**

There are three main elements to the power under s. 25.

The first element is the presence of:

- reasonable grounds for suspecting

- that *any* offence—other than an 'arrestable offence' above—however minor

- *has been* committed/attempted, or

- *is being* committed/attempted.

Although the power relates to any non-arrestable offence, some difficulty arises when dealing with 'attempts' to commit summary offences. As summary offences cannot be 'attempted' under the provisions of the Criminal Attempts Act 1981 (see Crime, chapter 3), there could be no likelihood of charging/summonsing a person with *attempting* to commit a summary offence at the time of any arrest. This would, on the basis of some authorities on 'arrest' (e.g. *Holgate-Mohammed* v *Duke* [1984] AC 437; *R* v *Chalkley* [1998] 1 WLR 146; see para. 2.8) make such an arrest unlawful unless some other *preventive* power could be found.

The second element is the 'relevant person'. This is *any* person whom the officer has reasonable grounds to suspect of:

- having committed/attempted to commit the offence, or

- being in the course of committing/attempting to commit the offence.

Therefore the power will not be available in relation to people who are reasonably suspected of being *about* to commit a non-arrestable offence, nor those reasonably suspected of conspiring, inciting or aiding another to do so.

The third element is the appearance to the officer that the service of a summons is:

- impracticable, or

- inappropriate

- *because any of the general arrest conditions are satisfied*.

The wording of s. 25 makes a presumption that the summons procedure will generally be used and it is only in the circumstances set out at s. 25(3)—the 'general arrest conditions'—(see below) that a person can be arrested under this section.

---

Section 25 of the 1984 Act goes on to state:

(3) The general arrest conditions are—
- (a) that the name of the relevant person is unknown to, and cannot be readily ascertained by, the constable;
- (b) that the constable has reasonable grounds for doubting whether a name furnished by the relevant person as his name is his real name;
- (c) that—
  - (i) the relevant person has failed to furnish a satisfactory address for service; or
  - (ii) the constable has reasonable grounds for doubting whether an address furnished by the relevant person is a satisfactory address for service;
- (d) that the constable has reasonable grounds for believing that arrest is necessary to prevent the relevant person—
  - (i) causing physical injury to himself or any other person;
  - (ii) suffering physical injury;
  - (iii) causing loss of or damage to property;
  - (iv) committing an offence against public decency; or
  - (v) causing an unlawful obstruction of the highway;
- (e) that the constable has reasonable grounds for believing that arrest is necessary to protect a child or other vulnerable person from the relevant person.

(4) For the purposes of subsection (3) above an address is a satisfactory address for service if it appears to the constable—
- (a) that the relevant person will be at it for a sufficiently long period for it to be possible to serve him with a summons; or
- (b) that some other person specified by the relevant person will accept service of a summons for the relevant person at it.

(5) Nothing in subsection (3)(d) above authorises the arrest of a person under sub-paragraph (iv) of that paragraph except where members of the public going about their normal business cannot reasonably be expected to avoid the person to be arrested.

(6) This section shall not prejudice any power of arrest conferred apart from this section.

---

### KEYNOTE

If a person refuses to give his/her details the conditions under s. 25(3)(a) and (b) do not amount to an offence themselves. This is in contract with some provision under the road traffic legislation (see Road Traffic, chapters 4 and 11) and also the specific offence under the Police Reforms Act 2002, s. 50 (see chapter 3). Refusing or failing to give correct details here simply creates a potential power to arrest.

The *reason* for the arrest is not that the person has failed to give his/her details or has given dubious details; *it is the person's suspected involvement in the original offence*, together with that fact. If the officer knows the persons from previous dealings, or knows his/her address, these conditions would not be satisfied. Where life does get interesting is where the offence itself is that under s. 50 of the Police Reform Act 2002 because the overlap with the general arrest condition is almost exact.

When using the general arrest conditions it is important that officers tell the person:

- what the offence is; and

- that one of the general arrest conditions applies.

Code C of the Police and Criminal Evidence Act 1984 Codes of Practice requires an arresting officer using the s. 25 power to include an explanation of the condition that make the arrest necessary (Note 10B).

It is not necessary for officers to use the exact wording from s. 25 describing the particular arrest conditions, neither is it necessary for the courts to apply an overly lawyerly test when assessing the arresting officers' conduct. The decision to arrest when one of the conditions is present is a *subjective* one made by an officer in the light of the prevailing circumstances, which might include the attitude and behaviour of the defendant (see *Abdul Ghafar* v *Chief Constable of West Midlands Police* (2000) *The Times*, 12 May).

The requirement under s. 25(3)(b) and (3)(c)(ii) for the officer to have 'reasonable grounds for doubting', is on the face of it a very wide expression. This, together with the expression 'reasonable grounds for suspecting' (as to which, see para. 2.7.1) should be contrasted with the further general arrest conditions set out under s. 25(3)(d) and (e). The expression used there is a narrower one requiring the officer to have reasonable grounds to *believe* that the arrest is *necessary*—as opposed to simply desirable—in order to prevent the person from bringing about the consequences set out in those subsections.

If the grounds for detaining the arrested person cease to exist before he/she reaches a police station and there are no further grounds for detaining him/her, the officer must release the person (s. 30(7); **see para. 2.12**).

The condition as to a satisfactory address under s. 25(3)(c) does not necessarily mean the person's own address; any reasonable address would suffice. It is up to the officer to justify why he/she thought the address was not satisfactory and there is no specific power to detain a person while an address is being checked.

In relation to the other conditions, there must still have been an offence or an attempted offence; simply to present a danger to oneself or to be *likely* to commit an offence against public decency is not enough. For the law governing the areas of assault, indecency, children/vulnerable persons and damage, **see Crime**; for obstruction of the highway, **see Road Traffic**. The circumstances set out at s. 25 are also referred to in relation to the power of arrest for offences involving importuning by men under s. 32 of the Sexual Offences Act 1956 (**see Crime, chapter 10**).

For the general offences and powers in relation to the obstruction of the highway, **see Road Traffic, chapter 8**).

### 2.9.4 Preserved powers of arrest

Section 26 of the Police and Criminal Evidence Act 1984 states:

(1) Subject to subsection (2) below, so much of any Act (including a local Act) passed before this Act as enables a constable—
   (a) to arrest a person for an offence without a warrant; or
   (b) to arrest a person otherwise than for an offence without a warrant or an order of a court, shall cease to have effect.

(2) Nothing in subsection (1) above affects the enactments specified in Schedule 2 to this Act.

Schedule 2 specifies the preserved powers of arrest:

| | |
|---|---|
| 1892 c 43 | Section 17(2) of the Military Lands Act 1892. |
| 1911 c 27 | Section 12(1) of the Protection of Animals Act 1911. |
| 1920 c 55 | Section 2 of the Emergency Powers Act 1920. |
| 1936 c 6 | Section 7(3) of the Public Order Act 1936. |
| 1952 c 52 | Section 49 of the Prison Act 1952. |
| 1952 c 67 | Section 13 of the Visiting Forces Act 1952. |
| 1955 c 18 | Sections 186 and 190B of the Army Act 1955. |
| 1955 c 19 | Sections 186 and 190B of the Air Force Act 1955. |
| 1957 c 53 | Sections 104 and 105 of the Naval Discipline Act 1957. |
| 1959 c 37 | Section 1(3) of the Street Offences Act 1959. |
| 1969 c 54 | Section 32 of the Children and Young Persons Act 1969. |
| 1971 c 77 | Section 24(2) of the Immigration Act 1971 and paragraphs 17, 24 and 33 of Schedule 2 and paragraph 7 of Schedule 3 to that Act. |
| 1976 c 63 | Section 7 of the Bail Act 1976. |
| 1977 c 45 | Sections 6(6), 7(11), 8(4), 9(7) and 10(5) of the Criminal Law Act 1977. |
| 1981 c 22 | Sections 60(5) and 61(1) of the Animal Health Act 1981. |
| 1983 c 2 | Rule 36 in Schedule 1 to the Representation of the People Act 1983. |
| 1983 c 20 | Sections 18, 35(10), 36(8), 38(7), 136(1) and 138 of the Mental Health Act 1983. |
| 1984 c 47 | Section 5(5) of the Repatriation of Prisoners Act 1984. |

**KEYNOTE**

The effect of s. 26 is to repeal all other police powers of arrest without warrant which existed before the 1984 Act, except those listed in sch. 2. It does not repeal statutory powers of arrest for people other than police officers, such as railway ticket inspectors (*Moberly* v *Alsop* (1991) 156 JP 154). Although the reference to s. 24(2) of the Immigration Act 1971 still appears in this Schedule, that section was removed by the Immigration and Asylum Act 1999, sch. 14 and a new statutory power of arrest was created in its place (**see Crime, chapter 15**). There has been some uncertainty in relation to statutes which provide powers of arrest for 'any person' (e.g. the offence of being disorderly whilst drunk in a public place; **see chapter 4**). Such powers are not generally preserved under sch. 2 above, and there is Home Office guidance to the effect that police officers should revert to their general arrest powers under s. 25 (see Home Office Circular 88/85). However, in two cases it has been made clear that the expression 'any person' in relation to a power of arrest includes polices officers. The first case, *DPP* v *Kitching* (1989) 154 JP 293, related to the offence of being disorderly whilst drunk in a public place under s. 91 of the Criminal Justice Act 1967, while the second, *Gapper* v *Chief Constable of Avon & Somerset* [1998] 4 All ER 248, concerned the general power of arrest attached to the Vagrancy Act 1824. In both cases it was held that the Police and Criminal Evidence Act 1984 had not removed the powers of arrest in respect of police officers and that such powers were therefore still available to the police.

A remaining oddity can be found in the offence of 'going equipped' under s. 25 of the Theft Act 1968 (**see Crime, chapter 12**) which is both an arrestable offence under s. 24 and sch. 1A to the Police and Criminal Evidence Act 1984 and also carries a power of arrest without warrant by 'any person' under certain circumstances (s. 25(4)).

The reference to s. 7 (11) of the Criminal Law Act 1977 appears to be an error in the Act as the power of arrest is to be found under s. 7(6) (**see chapter 9**).

### Absentees and deserters

Section 186 of the Army Act 1955 and the Air Force Act 1955 provide a power of arrest without warrant where a constable has reasonable cause to suspect a person has deserted or is absent without leave. The Acts also make provision for the issuing of arrest warrants in respect of absentees/deserters, and give a power of arrest to forces personnel in respect of absentees/deserters where no constable is available.

Similar provisions for arresting Royal Navy personnel exist under s. 105 of the Naval Discipline Act 1957.

Where suspected absentees or deserters have been arrested, they must be taken directly to a magistrates' court and the appropriate service authority should be informed. Magistrates' courts may remand absentees or deserters until they can be collected by a service escort. If the escort is likely to be provided soon after the person's appearance at court, the magistrates may remand that person to a police station and must issue a certificate which must be given to the service escort. Most police services have local arrangements in respect of military personnel who surrender themselves to police stations as being absent without leave.

### 2.9.5 Fingerprinting

For the power of arrest under s. 27 of the Police and Criminal Evidence Act 1984 to take a person's fingerprints, **see Evidence and Procedure, chapter 16**.

### 2.9.6 Failure to answer police bail

Section 46A of the Police and Criminal Evidence Act 1984 states:

(1) A constable may arrest without a warrant any person who, having been released on bail under this Part of this Act subject to a duty to attend at a police station, fails to attend at that police station at the time appointed for him to do so.

(2) A person who is arrested under this section shall be taken to the police station appointed as the place at which he is to surrender to custody as soon as practicable after the arrest.

(3) For the purposes of—
   (a) section 30 above (subject to the obligation in subsection (2) above), and
   (b) section 31 above,

an arrest under this section shall be treated as an arrest for an offence.

---

**KEYNOTE**

The offence will be treated as if the person had been arrested for the original offence for which bail was granted. For a detailed discussion on bail, see Evidence and Procedure, chapter 5.

---

### 2.9.7   Arrest to take samples

Section 63A of the Police and Criminal Evidence Act 1984 provides a power of arrest without warrant in respect of people:

- who have been charged with/reported for a recordable offence and who have not had a sample taken or the sample was unsuitable/insufficient for analysis;

- who have been convicted of a recordable offence and have not had a sample taken since conviction;

- who have been so convicted and have had a sample taken before or since conviction but the sample was unsuitable/insufficient for analysis.

This is simply a summary of s. 63A and reference should be made to the 1984 Act for the exact wording. For further detail, **see Evidence and Procedure, chapter 16.**

### 2.9.8   Cross-border arrest without warrant

The Criminal Justice and Public Order Act 1994 (ss. 136 to 140) makes provision for officers from one part of the UK to go into another part of the UK to arrest someone there in connection with an offence committed within their jurisdiction and powers to search on arrest.

Under the 1994 Act an officer from a police service in England and Wales may arrest a person in Scotland where the offence committed within their jurisdiction is an 'arrestable offence' or where it would be impracticable to serve a summons for the same reasons which would justify an arrest in England and Wales.

A Scottish officer may arrest someone suspected of committing an offence in Scotland who is found in England, Wales or Northern Ireland if it would have been lawful to arrest that person had he/she been found in Scotland. In such a case the officer must take the person to a designated police station in Scotland or to the nearest designated police station in England or Wales (see s. 137(7)).

The 1994 Act sets out where a person arrested outside the relevant country should be taken on arrest (see s. 137(7)). The Act also provides wide powers of search in connection with arrests (see s. 139).

### 2.9.9   Mentally disordered people

There is a power to remove a person who is apparently suffering from a mental disorder from a public place to a place of safety (**see Crime, chapter 11**). This power is aimed at protecting the person's best interests rather than bringing them before a court to answer a charge.

2.10    **Arrest under warrant**

Arrest warrants may be issued by magistrates (generally under s. 1 of the Magistrates' Courts Act 1980) and the Crown Court (under the Supreme Court Act 1981, s. 80(2)) where the statute in question, together with the powers of the court allow. Warrants of arrest may also be issued to secure the attendance of witnesses (see s. 97 of the Magistrates' Courts Act 1980 and s. 4 of the Criminal Procedure (Attendance of Witnesses) Act 1965).

Magistrates' courts may generally only issue an arrest warrant for offences that are imprisonable or indictable or where the person's address is not sufficient for the service of a summons. They can only issue a warrant for failing to appear at court where the offence is imprisonable or where they intend to impose a disqualification from holding a licence having convicted the defendant. The police owe defendants a duty of care when drawing up and enforcing the contents of warrants. Therefore, where officers put the wrong date on an arrest warrant issued by a magistrates' court and, as a result, the defendant was not released by the Prison Service when he should have been, the police were liable in damages for the defendant's unlawful imprisonment (*Clarke* v *Chief Constable of Northamptonshire Police* (1999) *The Times*, 14 June).

Warrants issued in relation to an offence may be backed for bail in which case the person is then granted bail in accordance with the conditions on the warrant. If not backed for bail, the warrant will specify where the person is to be brought (i.e. before the next sitting of the court).

For bail generally, **see Evidence and Procedure, chapter 5**.

Warrants issued in England, Wales, Scotland or Northern Ireland may be executed by officers from the country where they are issued or in the country where the person is arrested (see s. 136 of the Criminal Justice and Public Order Act 1994).

Warrants from the Republic of Ireland (provided they are not issued for political offences) may be executed in England and Wales if so endorsed (s. 125 of the Magistrates' Courts Act 1980), as indeed may warrants issued in the Isle of Man or the Channel Islands if so endorsed (s. 13 of the Indictable Offences Act 1848).

Warrants issued in connection with 'an offence' (or for some purposes concerning the armed forces and domestic proceedings; see s. 33 of the Police and Criminal Evidence Act 1984) do not need to be in the possession of the officer executing them at the time (s. 125 of the Magistrates' Courts Act 1980).

The requirement under s. 28 of the Police and Criminal Evidence Act 1984 to tell a person why they are being arrested applies to arrests under warrant.

For the law relating to warrants generally, **see Evidence and Procedure, chapter 4**.

The long awaited arrival of a European Arrest Warrant is expected to come into effect on 1 January 2004 (see Council Framework Decision 2002/584). The detail of this new procedure is outside the scope of this Manual.

2.11    **Voluntary attendance at a police station**

Section 29 of the Police and Criminal Evidence Act 1984 states:

> Where for the purpose of assisting with an investigation a person attends voluntarily at a police station or at any other place where a constable is present or accompanies a constable to a police station or any such other place without having been arrested—
>
> (a) he shall be entitled to leave at will unless he is placed under arrest;
> (b) he shall be informed at once that he is under arrest if a decision is taken by a constable to prevent him from leaving at will.

---

**KEYNOTE**

The person's attendance at a police station or other place must be for the purpose of 'assisting with an investigation', which would, on a strict interpretation, encompass witnesses and victims. The main principle behind s. 29 (and see also Code C, para. 3.25) is to avoid the situation where people find themselves at a police station (or any other place where there is a police officer present) and feel compelled to remain there but without the attendant procedural protection that follows a formal arrest. Section 29(b) is unusual in that it (along with s. 31 below) imposes an obligation on a police officer to make an arrest, an activity that is usually entirely within his/her discretion.

If such a person is cautioned (under PACE Code C, para. 10), they must also be told that they are free to leave the police station. Although not in police detention (see s. 118), voluntary attenders should be given the opportunity to seek legal advice if they wish and should be given the appropriate notice (see Code C).

---

Section 31 of the 1984 Act goes on to state:

> Where—
> (a) a person—
>   (i) has been arrested for an offence; and
>   (ii) is at a police station in consequence of that arrest; and
> (b) it appears to a constable that, if he were released from that arrest, he would be liable to arrest for some other offence,
>
> he shall be arrested for that other offence.

---

**KEYNOTE**

Like s. 29 above, this section also imposes an obligation to make an arrest under certain circumstances. In *R v Samuel* (1988) 87 Cr App R 232, the Court of Appeal said that the purpose of the s. 31 requirement was to prevent the release and immediate re-arrest of an offender—therefore, the Court noted, s. 31 did not prevent any further arrest from being delayed until the release of the prisoner for the initial arrest was imminent. This decision would now have to be considered in the light of the Human Rights Act 1998.

The power (though not, on the strict wording, the *obligation*) to arrest a person at a police station for a further offence under s. 31 is among those that can be conferred on an Investigating Officer designated under sch. 4 to the Police Reform Act 2002 (**see para. 2.14.2**). Where this power is exercised by a designated Investigating Officer, the provisions of s. 36 of the Criminal Justice and Public Order Act 1994 (failing to account for objects etc.—see **Evidence and Procedure**) will apply.

Where a person is re-arrested under this provision, the power of search under s. 18 of the Police and Criminal Evidence Act 1984 apply (**see para. 2.13.2**).

---

## 2.12 After arrest

Section 30 of the Police and Criminal Evidence Act 1984 provides for the procedure to be adopted after a person has been arrested. Section 30 states:

(1) Subject to the following provisions of this section, where a person—
  (a) is arrested by a constable for an offence; or
  (b) is taken into custody by a constable after being arrested for an offence by a person other than a constable,
  at any place other than a police station, he shall be taken to a police station by a constable as soon as practicable after the arrest.

(2) Subject to subsections (3) and (5) below, the police station to which an arrested person is taken under subsection (1) above shall be a designated police station.

(3) A constable to whom this subsection applies may take an arrested person to any police station unless it appears to the constable that it may be necessary to keep the arrested person in police detention for more than six hours.

(4) Subsection (3) above applies—

    (a) to a constable who is working in a locality covered by a police station which is not a designated police station; and

    (b) to a constable belonging to a body of constables maintained by an authority other than a police authority.

(5) Any constable may take an arrested person to any police station if—

    (a) either of the following conditions is satisfied—

        (i) the constable has arrested him without the assistance of any other constable and no other constable is available to assist him;

        (ii) the constable has taken him into custody from a person other than a constable without the assistance of any other constable and no other constable is available to assist him; and

    (b) it appears to the constable that he will be unable to take the arrested person to a designated police station without the arrested person injuring himself, the constable or some other person.

(6) If the first police station to which an arrested person is taken after his arrest is not a designated police station, he shall be taken to a designated police station not more than six hours after his arrival at the first police station unless he is released previously.

---

## KEYNOTE

When arrested at a place other than a police station, the person must be taken to a designated police station unless the conditions under s. 30(5) and (6) apply.

As discussed above (**see para. 2.9.3**), under s. 30(7), the officer *must* de-arrest a person if he/she is satisfied, before reaching the police station, that there are no grounds for detaining that person. This may happen where the person has been arrested under one of the general arrest conditions and the particular condition has ceased to apply (e.g. the person gives a suitable name and address having originally failed to do so). An officer who releases a prisoner under s. 30(7) must record the fact that he/she has done so and must make that record as soon as practicable after the release (s. 30(8) and (9)).

Section 30(10) allows the officer to delay taking the arrested person to a police station where his/her presence elsewhere is *necessary in order to carry out such investigations as it is reasonable to carry out immediately*. Where there is such a delay, the reasons for it must be recorded when the person first arrives at the police station (s. 30(11)).

Escort Officers designated under sch. 4 to the Police Reform Act 2002 may be authorised to take people who have been arrested by a constable in the relevant police area to a police station under the provisions of s. 30(1) above. The provisions for taking a prisoner to a non-designated police station (see s. 30(3) and 4(a)), and also the provisions allowing a delay in taking the prisoner to a police station (s. 30(10)) will also apply to any exercise of the powers by a designated Escort Officer (see the Police Reform Act 2002, sch. 4, Part 4). Escort Officers are subject to a number of further provisions in relation to the transfer and detention of people in police detention (**see Evidence and Procedure, chapter 15**). For a general discussion of the powers and roles of Escort Officers and other designated staff, **see para. 2.14.2**.

Other exceptions in the application of subsection 1 to terrorism and immigration are made by s. 30(12).

The delay permitted under s. 30(10) and (11) will only apply if the matter requires *immediate* investigation; if it can wait, the exception will not apply and the person must be taken straight to a police station (*R* v *Kerrawalla* [1991] Crim LR 451).

Taking an arrested person to check out an alibi before going to a police station may be justified in some circumstances (see *Dallison* v *Caffery* [1965] 1 QB 348).

## 2.13 Entry, search and seizure

Police powers to enter premises, search them and seize evidence and property are governed mainly by the Police and Criminal Evidence Act 1984 and Code B (**see appendix 2**). The 1984 Act covers entry, search and seizure both with and without a warrant.

Code B applies to searches of premises by the police for the purposes of an investigation into an alleged offence with the occupier's consent other than those set out at para. 2.3 (e.g. routine crime scene searches, activation of fire or burglar alarms, insecure premises and bomb threats). Code B also applies to searches with consent. While these are generally treated in the same way as any other relevant premises search (see para. 5), this feature distinguishes them from searches of *individuals* under Code A (**see para. 2.7**).

Note that the Criminal Justice and Police Act 2001 has introduced new provisions extending police powers of seizure under certain circumstances (e.g. where there is a large volume of material involved or where evidential material is mixed in with other documents/data)—**see para. 2.13.9**.

As Code B points out, the right to privacy and respect for personal property are key principles of the Human Rights Act 1998. Therefore police powers of entry, search and seizure must be clearly justified before being used and officers should consider whether or not their objectives can be met by using less intrusive means (para. 1.3). In all cases, officers should exercise their powers courteously and with respect for people and their property, using only reasonable and proportionate force where necessary (para. 1.4).

Where a *person* is searched during a search of premises without being arrested, that search should take place in accordance with Code A (**see para. 2.7**).

Whenever premises are to be searched under the provisions of Code B, one officer must be appointed to act as the officer in charge of the search (para. 2.10). The duties of this officer (who will normally, but not always, be the most senior officer present—see Note 2F) are set out throughout the Code. Searches carried out by employees designated under the Police Reform Act 2002 (**see para. 2.14**) are also subject to the provision of Code B (para. 211).

Any person claiming property seized by the police generally may make an application to the magistrates' court under the Police Property Act 1897 and should be advised of this procedure (Code B, Note 7A). There are special provisions where the property has been seized under the extended powers of the Criminal Justice and Police Act 2001 (**see para. 2.13.9**).

Throughout the 1984 Act some evidence is described as 'material' and certain categories are subject to particular safeguards in the search procedure (**see para. 2.13.8**). If anything found during a search is to be used as evidence, it is critical that the officers conducting the search can point to the relevant authority under which they were acting at the time. If they cannot justify the search then, in addition to the risk of possible civil liability, there is a strong likelihood that any evidence found will be excluded under the relevant provisions available to the courts (**see Evidence and Procedure, chapter 13**).

### 2.13.1 Powers of search and seizure under warrant

There are many statutes which make provision for a court to issue a search warrant to police officers and other investigators, many of which are covered within this Manual under the relevant headings. Some non-police investigators enjoy specific powers based upon amended versions of the following provisions (see e.g. the Police and Criminal Evidence Act 1984 (Department of Trade and Industry Investigators) Order 2002 (SI 2002 No. 2326)).

The application for and execution of all such warrants is governed by the 1984 Act and the Codes of Practice. However, the Code does not affect any directions in a search warrant or order requiring seized items to be handed over to the police or other authority (Code B, para. 2.6). (For a fuller discussion of summonses and warrants, **see Evidence and Procedure, chapter 4**.)

Section 15 of the Police and Criminal Evidence Act 1984 states:

(1) This section and section 16 below have effect in relation to the issue to constables under any enactment, including an enactment contained in an Act passed after this Act, of warrants to enter and search premises; and an entry on or search of premises under a warrant is unlawful unless it complies with this section and section 16 below.

(2) Where a constable applies for any such warrant, it shall be his duty—
    (a) to state—
        (i)   the ground on which he makes the application; and
        (ii)  the enactment under which the warrant would be issued;
    (b) to specify the premises which it is desired to enter and search; and
    (c) to identify, so far as is practicable, the articles or persons to be sought.

(3) An application for such a warrant shall be made ex parte and supported by an information in writing.

(4) The constable shall answer on oath any question that the justice of the peace or judge hearing the application asks him.

(5) A warrant shall authorise an entry on one occasion only.

(6) A warrant—
    (a) shall specify—
        (i)   the name of the person who applies for it;
        (ii)  the date on which it is issued;
        (iii) the enactment under which it is issued; and
        (iv)  the premises to be searched; and
    (b) shall identify, so far as is practicable, the articles or persons to be sought.

(7) Two copies shall be made of a warrant.

(8) The copies shall be clearly certified as copies.

---

**KEYNOTE**

Sections 15 and 16 (see below) apply to *all* warrants to enter and search premises. 'Premises' include vehicles, vessels and hovercraft (see s. 23), including those issued to and executed by an Investigating Officer designated under sch. 4 to the Police Reform Act 2002 (as to which **see para. 2.14.2**).

If the provisions of these sections are not complied with, any entry and search made under a warrant will be unlawful. Although the officers executing the warrant may have some protection from personal liability where there has been a defect in the *procedure* by which the warrant was issued, failure to follow the requirements of ss. 15 and 16 may result in the exclusion of any evidence obtained under the warrant (see **Evidence and Procedure, chapter 13**). The details of the extent of the proposed search should be made clear in the application and the officer swearing the warrant out must be prepared to answer *any* questions put to him/her on oath under s. 15(4). Many courts will go into background detail about the particular premises, or part of the premises, and who is likely to be present on the premises at the time the warrant is executed (e.g. children). The action to be taken in relation to the swearing out of a warrant is set out in PACE Code B, para. 3.

Applications for all search warrants must be made with the written authority of an officer of at least the rank of inspector (Code B, para. 3.4). However, in cases of urgency where no such officer is 'readily available', the senior officer on duty may authorise the application.

If an application for a warrant is refused, no further application can be made unless it is supported by additional grounds.

Details of the information needed in applying for a warrant are set out at Code B, para. 3.6. This paragraph makes provision for the warrant to authorise other people to be present during the search (para. 3.6 (f) ) but such a person has no authority to force entry, to search for or seize property (Note 3C).

Section 16 of the Police and Criminal Evidence Act 1984 states:

(1) A warrant to enter and search premises may be executed by any constable.

(2) Such a warrant may authorise persons to accompany any constable who is executing it.

(3) Entry and search under a warrant must be within one month from the date of its issue.

(4) Entry and search under a warrant must be at a reasonable hour unless it appears to the constable executing it that the purpose of a search may be frustrated on an entry at a reasonable hour.

(5) Where the occupier of premises which are to be entered and searched is present at the time when a constable seeks to execute a warrant to enter and search them, the constable—

    (a) shall identify himself to the occupier and, if not in uniform, shall produce to him documentary evidence that he is a constable;

    (b) shall produce the warrant to him; and

    (c) shall supply him with a copy of it.

(6) Where—

    (a) the occupier of such premises is not present at the time when a constable seeks to execute such a warrant; but

    (b) some other person who appears to the constable to be in charge of the premises is present, subsection (5) above shall have effect as if any reference to the occupier were a reference to that other person.

(7) If there is no person present who appears to the constable to be in charge of the premises, he shall leave a copy of the warrant in a prominent place on the premises.

(8) A search under a warrant may only be a search to the extent required for the purpose for which the warrant was issued.

(9) A constable executing warrant shall make an endorsement on it stating—

    (a) whether the articles or persons sought were found; and

    (b) whether any articles were seized, other than articles which were sought.

---

**KEYNOTE**

Although s. 16 allows for other people to be included in the warrant, authorising them to accompany the officer, some warrants *require* the presence of other people when a warrant is executed (e.g. under s. 135 of the Mental Health Act 1983; see Crime, chapter 11).

Failure to comply with the requirements under s. 16 will make the entry and subsequent seizure of property unlawful. Therefore, where officers failed to provide the occupier of the searched premises with a copy of the warrant (under s. 16(5)(c)), they were obliged to return the property seized during the search (*R* v *Chief Constable of Lancashire, ex parte Parker* [1993] Crim LR 204).

Very minor departures from the letter of the warrant, however, will not render any search unlawful (see *Attorney-General of Jamaica* v *Williams* [1998] AC 351).

If the execution of the warrant is likely to have an adverse effect on community relations, the community liaison officer must be informed unless the case is urgent, in which case that officer must be advised as soon as practicable after the search—see Code B, paras 3–5.

Code B goes on to make further provisions for the execution of the warrant.

If a warrant itself is invalid for some reason, any entry and subsequent seizure made under it are unlawful (*R* v *Central Criminal Court and British Railways Board, ex parte AJD Holdings Ltd* [1992] Crim LR 669). After a warrant has been executed, or if it has not been used within one month from its date of issue, it must be returned to the chief executive to the justices or the court officer as appropriate (s. 16(10)). These returned warrants must then be kept by the respective people for a period of 12 months in order that the occupiers of the named premises may inspect them (s. 16(11) and (12)).

Search warrants for serious arrestable offences

Section 8 of the Police and Criminal Evidence Act 1984 states:

(1) If on an application made by a constable a justice of the peace is satisfied that there are reasonable grounds for believing—
  (a) that a serious arrestable offence has been committed; and
  (b) that there is material on premises specified in the application which is likely to be of substantial value (whether by itself or together with other material) to the investigation of the offence; and
  (c) that the material is likely to be relevant evidence; and
  (d) that it does not consist of or include items subject to legal privilege, excluded material or special procedure material; and
  (e) that any of the conditions specified in subsection (3) below applies, he may issue a warrant authorising a constable to enter and search the premises.

(2) A constable may seize and retain anything for which a search has been authorised under subsection (1) above.

(3) The conditions mentioned in subsection (1)(e) above are—
  (a) that it is not practicable to communicate with any person entitled to grant entry to the premises;
  (b) that it is practicable to communicate with a person entitled to grant entry to the premises but it is not practicable to communicate with any person entitled to grant access to the evidence;
  (c) that entry to the premises will not be granted unless a warrant is produced;
  (d) that the purpose of a search may be frustrated or seriously prejudiced unless a constable arriving at the premises can secure immediate entry to them.

(4) In this Act 'relevant evidence', in relation to an offence, means anything that would be admissible in evidence at a trial for the offence.

(5) The power to issue a warrant conferred by this section is in addition to any such power otherwise conferred.

---

**KEYNOTE**

For 'serious' arrestable offences, see para. 2.9.1. The officer applying for a warrant under s. 8 must have reasonable grounds for believing that material which is *likely to be of substantial value to the investigation of the offence* is on the premises specified. Therefore, when executing such a warrant, the officer must be able to show that any material seized thereunder fell within that description (*R* v *Chief Constable of the Warwickshire Constabulary, ex parte Fitzpatrick* [1998] 1 All ER 65). Possession of a warrant under s. 8 does not authorise police officers to seize all material found on the relevant premises to be taken away and 'sifted' somewhere else (*R* v *Chesterfield Justices, ex parte Bramley* [2000] 2 WLR 409). This means that material which is solely of value for *intelligence* purposes may not be seized under a s. 8 warrant. The limits imposed by this decision on the extent of authority granted by a s. 8 Warrant is the reason behind the extended powers of sift and seizure introduced by the Criminal Justice and Police Act 2001 (see para. 2.13.9).

The power to apply for and execute a warrant under s. 8 and to carry out the actions under s. 8(2) are among those powers that can be conferred on a person designated as an Investigating Officer under sch. 4 to the Police Reform Act 2002 (see para. 2.14.2).

The conditions set out under s. 8(1)(e) are part of the *application* process, not part of the general execution process (which is set out at s. 16 above). Therefore the officer swearing out a s. 8 warrant will have to satisfy the court that any of those conditions apply.

Where the search includes information contained in a computer, the provisions of s. 20 apply (see para. 2.13.7).

The power to issue a warrant under s. 8 also applies to certain offences under s. 4 of the Immigration Act 1971, offences which include illegal entry, obtaining leave to remain in the country by deception and staying beyond the time allowed (see s. 73 of the Asylum and Immigration Act 1996).

2.13.2    **Powers without warrant**

Apart from a general power of entry to prevent a breach of the peace (**see chapter 4**), all common law police powers of entry were abolished by the Police and Criminal Evidence Act 1984. The Act introduced wide powers of entry, search and seizure particularly when made in connection with an arrest. Note the importance of the general principles and specific content of Code B in relation to these searches (**see appendix 1**).

Arrestable offences

Section 18 of the Police and Criminal Evidence Act 1984 states:

(1) Subject to the following provisions of this section, a constable may enter and search any premises occupied or controlled by a person who is under arrest for an arrestable offence, if he has reasonable grounds for suspecting that there is on the premises evidence, other than items subject to legal privilege, that relates—
(a) to that offence; or
(b) to some other arrestable offence which is connected with or similar to that offence.

(2) A constable may seize and retain anything for which he may search under subsection (1) above.

(3) The power to search conferred by subsection (1) above is only a power to search to the extent that is reasonably required for the purpose of discovering such evidence.

(4) Subject to subsection (5) below, the powers conferred by this section may not be exercised unless an officer of the rank of inspector or above has authorised them in writing.

(5) A constable may conduct a search under subsection (1) above—
(a) before the person is taken to a police station; and
(b) without obtaining an authorisation under subsection (4) above,

if the presence of that person at a place other than a police station is necessary for the effective investigation of the offence.

(6) If a constable conducts a search by virtue of subsection (5) above, he shall inform an officer of the rank of inspector or above that he has made the search as soon as practicable after he has made it.

(7) An officer who—
(a) authorises a search; or
(b) is informed of a search under subsection (6) above, shall make a record in writing—
(i) of the grounds for the search; and
(ii) of the nature of the evidence that was sought.

(8) If the person who was in occupation or control of the premises at the time of the search is in police detention at the time the record is to be made, the officer shall make the record as part of his custody record.

---

**KEYNOTE**

This power only applies where a person has been arrested for an 'arrestable offence' (**see para. 2.9.1**); it does not apply where the person has been arrested under the general arrest conditions (**see para. 2.9.3**).

For items that relate to legal privilege, **see para. 2.13.8**.

The premises must be occupied or controlled by the arrested person. This expression is not defined but it is a *factual* requirement, i.e. it is not enough that the officer suspects or believes that the premises are occupied or controlled by that person.

The search is limited to evidence relating to the arrestable offence for which the person has been arrested or another arrestable offence which is similar or connected; it does not authorise a general search for anything that might be of use for other purposes (e.g. for intelligence reports). The extent of the search is limited by s. 18(3). If you are looking for a stolen fridge-freezer, you would not be empowered to search through drawers or small cupboards. You would be able to, however, if you were looking for packaging, receipts or other documents relating to the fridge-freezer.

The search authority must be given in writing and only by an officer of or above the rank of inspector (Code B, para. 4.3). The authorising officer must be satisfied that the necessary grounds exist. If possible he/she should record the authority on the Notice of Powers and Rights given to the occupier, while a record of the grounds for the search and the nature of evidence sought should be made in the custody record (if there is one); otherwise in the officer's pocket book or the search record. That authority is for a search which is lawful *in all other respects*, that is, the other conditions imposed by s. 18 must be met. An inspector cannot make an otherwise unlawful entry and search lawful simply by authorising it (*Krohn* v *DPP* [1997] COD 345).

In addition to the general conditions of Code B above, where officers carry out a search under s. 18 they must, so far as is possible under the circumstances, explain to the occupier(s) the reason for it. If officers attempt to carry out an authorised search under s. 18 without attempting to explain to an occupier the reason, it may mean that the officers are not acting in the execution of their duty and their entry may be lawfully resisted (*Lineham* v *DPP, The Independent*, 22 November 1999).

The provision under s. 18(5) relates to cases where the presence of the person *is in fact necessary* for the effective investigation of the offence. This is a more stringent requirement than merely reasonable suspicion or grounds to believe on the part of the officer concerned. If such a search is made, the searching officer must inform an inspector (or above) as soon as practicable after the search.

If the person is in police detention after the arrest, the facts concerning the search must be recorded in the custody record. Where a person is re-arrested under s. 31 (**see para. 2.11**) for an arrestable offence, the powers to search under s. 18 begin again, that is, a new power to search is created in respect of each arrestable offence. Where the search includes information contained in a computer, the provisions of s. 20 apply (**see para. 2.13.7**).

---

### Powers to search after arrest for other offences

Where a person is arrested for any other offence, s. 32 of the Police and Criminal Evidence Act 1984 provides a number of general powers of entry, search and seizure.

Section 32 states:

(1) A constable may search an arrested person, in any case where the person to be searched has been arrested at a place other than a police station, if the constable has reasonable grounds for believing that the arrested person may present a danger to himself or others.

(2) Subject to subsections (3) to (5) below, a constable shall also have power in any such case-

   (a) to search the arrested person for anything—

      (i) which he might use to assist him to escape from lawful custody; or

      (ii) which might be evidence relating to an offence; and

   (b) . . .

(3) The power to search conferred by subsection (2) above is only a power to search to the extent that is reasonably required for the purpose of discovering any such thing or any such evidence.

(4) The powers conferred by this section to search a person are not to be construed as authorising a constable to require a person to remove any of his clothing in public other than an outer coat, jacket or gloves but they do authorise a search of a person's mouth.

(5) A constable may not search a person in the exercise of the power conferred by subsection (2)(a) above unless he has reasonable grounds for believing that the person to be searched may have concealed on him anything for which a search is permitted under that paragraph.

---

### KEYNOTE

The power to search the arrested person under s. 32(1) is a general one relating to safety. For the power to search at a police station, **see Evidence and Procedure, chapter 15.**

Section 32(2)(a) then goes on to provide a power to search the person in relation to anything that the arrested person might use to escape from lawful custody and anything that 'might be' evidence relating to *an offence*. There are restrictions placed on the extent and circumstances of the search (s. 32(3) and (4)) and the officer must have reasonable grounds to *believe* (as opposed to mere suspicion) that the person may have such things concealed on him/her (s. 32(5)). Nevertheless, this is still a very wide power. Some years ago the House of Lords confirmed that the police have a common law power to search for and seize property after a lawful arrest (*R* v *Governor of Pentonville Prison, ex parte Osman* [1990] 1 WLR 277). This decision was confirmed recently by the House of Lords in *R (on the application of Rottman)* v *Commissioner of Police of the Metropolis* [2002] 2 AC 692. In *Rottman* their Lordships held that it was a well-established principle of the common law that an arresting officer had the power to search a room in which a person had been arrested (*per Ghani* v *Jones* [1970] 1 QB 693). This extended power is not limited to purely 'domestic' offences, but also applies to cases involving extradition offences.

---

Section 32(9) states:

(9) A constable searching a person in the exercise of the power conferred by subsection (2)(a) above may seize and retain anything he finds, other than an item subject to legal privilege, if he has reasonable grounds for believing—
   (a) that he might use it to assist him to escape from lawful custody; or
   (b) that it is evidence of an offence or has been obtained in consequence of the commission of an offence.

### Search of premises after arrest

Section 32 also provides that a constable shall have the power in such a case to enter and search any premises in which the person was when arrested or immediately before being arrested (s. 32(2)(b)). The search may be conducted for the purpose of finding evidence relating to the offence for which the person was arrested.

Section 32 goes on to state:

(6) A constable may not search premises in the exercise of the power conferred by subsection (2)(b) above unless he has reasonable grounds for believing that there is evidence for which a search is permitted under that paragraph on the premises.

(7) In so far as the power of search conferred by subsection (2)(b) above relates to premises consisting of two or more separate dwellings, it is limited to a power to search—
   (a) any dwelling in which the arrest took place or in which the person arrested was immediately before his arrest; and
   (b) any parts of the premises which the occupier of any such dwelling uses in common with the occupiers of any other dwellings comprised in the premises.

(8) A constable searching a person in the exercise of the power conferred by subsection (1) above may seize and retain anything he finds, if he has reasonable grounds for believing that the person searched might use it to cause physical injury to himself or to any other person.

(a) . . .

(10) Nothing in this section shall be taken to affect the power conferred by section 43 of the Terrorism Act 2000.

---

**KEYNOTE**

Both 'reasonable grounds' and 'immediately' are questions of fact for a court to determine. It has been held that the power under s. 32(2)(b) is one for use at the time of arrest and should not be used to return to the relevant premises some time after the arrest in the way that s. 18 (see above) may be used (*R* v *Badham* [1987] Crim LR 202).

Officers exercising their power to enter and search under s. 32 must have a genuine belief (i.e. more than mere suspicion) that there is evidence on the premises; it is not a licence for a general fishing expedition (*R* v *Beckford* [1991] Crim LR 918).

---

Code B sets out the procedure to be followed after searches have been carried out (paras 8 and 9).

### 2.13.3    Other powers of entry without warrant

Just as there are many statutes which provide the police (and others) with powers to apply for warrants, there are as many statutes which provide a power of entry without warrant (an example would be s. 6 of the Scrap Metal Dealers Act 1964 which allows a constable entry at all reasonable times, onto a scrap metal dealer's premises to inspect the register and any scrap metal). Other examples are the power to enter:

- any land other than a dwelling house in order to search for crossbows (under the Crossbows Act 1987) (**see chapter 6**);
- *any place* for the purpose of carrying out a search under s. 47 of the Firearms Act1968 (**see chapter 5**);
- school premises in connection with weapons under the Criminal Justice Act 1988 (**see chapter 6**); and
- relevant premises in connection with a direction to leave and remove vehicles etc. under the Criminal Justice and Public Order Act 1994 (**see chapter 9**).

The only common law power of entry without warrant is for dealing with a breach of the peace (**see chapter 4**). This power is preserved by s. 17(6) and only applies where officers have a genuine and reasonable belief that a breach of the peace is happening or is about to happen in the immediate future (*McLeod* v *Commissioner of Police for theMetropolis* [1994] 4 All ER 553).

Where police officers enter premises *lawfully* (including where they are there by invitation), they are on the premises for *all lawful purposes* (see *Foster* v *Attard* [1986] Crim LR 627). This means that they can carry out any lawful functions while on the premises, even if that was not the original purpose for entry. For instance, if officers entered under a lawful power provided by the Misuse of Drugs Act 1971 (**see Crime, chapter 6**), they may carry out other lawful functions such as enforcing the provisions of the Gaming Act 1968.

If officers are invited onto premises by someone entitled to do so they are lawfully there unless and until that invitation is withdrawn. Once the invitation is withdrawn, the officers will become trespassers unless they have a power to be there and the person may remove them by force (*Robson* v *Hallett* [1967] 2 QB 939). If that invitation is terminated, the person needs to communicate that clearly to the officer; it has been held that merely telling officers to 'fuck off' is not necessarily sufficient (*Snook* v *Mannion* [1982] RTR 321 (**see Road Traffic, chapter 5**).

Once officers are lawfully on premises they may exercise the powers of seizure under s. 19 of the Police and Criminal Evidence Act 1984 (**see para. 2.13.7**).

### 2.13.4    Power of entry: Police and Criminal Evidence Act 1984, s. 17

Section 17 of the Police and Criminal Evidence Act 1984 states:

(1) Subject to the following provisions of this section, and without prejudice to any other enactment, a constable may enter and search any premises for the purpose—
  (a) of executing—
    (i)  a warrant of arrest issued in connection with or arising out of criminal proceedings; or
    (ii) a warrant of commitment issued under section 76 of the Magistrates' Courts Act 1980;
  (b) of arresting a person for an arrestable offence;
  (c) of arresting a person for an offence under—
    (i)   section 1 (prohibition of uniforms in connection with political objects) . . . of the Public Order Act 1936;
    (ii)  any enactment contained in sections 6 to 8 or 10 of the Criminal Law Act 1977 (offences relating to entering and remaining on property);
    (iii) section 4 of the Public Order Act 1986 (fear or provocation of violence);
    (iiia) section 163 of the Road Traffic Act 1988 (c 52) (failure to stop when required to do so by a constable in uniform);

<ul>
<li>(iv) section 76 of the Criminal Justice and Public Order Act 1994 (failure to comply with interim possession order);</li>
</ul>

(ca) of arresting, in pursuance of section 32(1A) of the Children and Young Persons Act 1969, any child or young person who has been remanded or committed to local authority accommodation under section 23(1) of that Act;

(cb) of recapturing any person who is, or is deemed for any purpose to be, unlawfully at large while liable to be detained—

<ul>
<li>(i) in a prison, remand centre, young offender institution or secure training centre, or</li>
<li>(ii) in pursuance of section 92 of the Powers of Criminal Courts (Sentencing) Act 2000 (dealing with children and young persons guilty of grave crimes), in any other place;</li>
</ul>

(d) of recapturing any person whatever who is unlawfully at large and whom he is pursuing; or

(e) of saving life or limb or preventing serious damage to property.

(2) Except for the purpose specified in paragraph (e) of subsection (1) above, the powers of entry and search conferred by this section—

(a) are only exercisable if the constable has reasonable grounds for believing that the person whom he is seeking is on the premises; and

(b) are limited, in relation to premises consisting of two or more separate dwellings, to powers to enter and search—

<ul>
<li>(i) any parts of the premises which the occupiers of any dwelling comprised in the premises use in common with the occupiers of any other such dwelling; and</li>
<li>(ii) any such dwelling in which the constable has reasonable grounds for believing that the person whom he is seeking may be.</li>
</ul>

(3) The powers of entry and search conferred by this section are only exercisable for the purposes specified in subsection (1)(c)(ii) or (iv) above by a constable in uniform.

(4) The power of search conferred by this section is only a power to search to the extent that is reasonably required for the purpose for which the power of entry is exercised.

(5) Subject to subsection (6) below, all the rules of common law under which a constable has power to enter premises without a warrant are hereby abolished.

(6) Nothing in subsection (5) above affects any power of entry to deal with or prevent a breach of the peace.

---

### KEYNOTE

The warrants under the Magistrates' Courts Act 1980 are warrants in connection with failing to pay fines or compensation orders (**see para. 2.10**) or maintenance orders.

For the offences listed at s. 17(1)(c), **see chapters 4 and 9**.

In a recent case where police had been called to an address by an abandoned 999 call, the officers had to move a man away from the front door in order to gain entry under s. 17. The Queen's Bench Divisional Court held that the officers had the power to use reasonable force in order to do so (*Smith (Peter John)* v *DPP* [2001] Crim LR 735). The source of the power to use force here is s. 117 of the Police and Criminal Evidence Act 1984 (as to which, **see para. 2.8.4**).

For a discussion of s. 163 of the Road Traffic Act 1988 referred to at s. 17(1)(c)(iiia) above see **Road Traffic, chapter 10**.

'Unlawfully at large' does not have a particular statutory meaning; it can apply to someone who is subject to an order under the Mental Health Act 1983, or someone who has escaped from custody (however, 'escaping' is an arrestable offence anyway, **see Crime, chapter 15**). The pursuit of the person must be 'fresh', that is, the power will only be available while the officer is actually 'pursuing' the person concerned (*D'Souza* v *DPP* (1993) 96 Cr App 278). Force may be used in exercising the power of entry where it is necessary to do so. Generally, the officer should first attempt to communicate with the occupier of the premises, explaining by what authority and for what purpose entry is to be made, before making a forcible entry. Clearly though, there will be occasions where such communication is impossible, impracticable or even unnecessary; in those cases there is no need for the officer to enter into such an explanation (*O'Loughlin* v *Chief Constable of Essex* [1998] 1 WLR 374).

The officer must have reasonable grounds to *believe* that the person is on the premises in all cases except saving life and limb at s. 17(1)(e). This expression is narrower than 'reasonable cause to suspect' and you must be able to justify that belief before using this power (although see *Kynaston* v *DPP* (1987) *The Times*, 4 November where the court accepted reasonable cause to *suspect*).

Note the requirement for an officer to be in uniform for the purposes of s. 17(1)(c)(ii) and (iv), and the restrictions on the power of *search* under s. 17(4) (i.e. that any such search is limited to the extent that is reasonably required *for the purpose for which you entered the premises in the first place*).

Code B regulates the way in which these powers of entry will be executed.

Again this section contains restrictions on the extent of any searches made (see para. 2.7).

The power to enter and search any premises in the relevant police area for the purpose of saving life or limb or preventing serious damage to property above is among those that can be conferred on a designated person under sch. 4 to the Police Reform Act 2002 (see para. 2.14.2).

---

## 2.13.5 Fire

Section 30(1) of the Fire Services Act 1947 provides that, among others, a constable may enter and if necessary break into:

- any premises or place
- in which a fire has or is reasonably believed to have broken out.

The constable may also break into or enter:

- any premises or place
- which it is necessary to enter for the purposes of extinguishing a fire
- or of protecting the premises from acts done for firefighting purposes

and may do all such things as he/she deems necessary for extinguishing the fire or for protecting from fire any such premises or place, or for rescuing any person or property therein.

This is clearly a very wide power which extends to adjacent premises or other places in need of protection from the fire *or* from the effects of firefighting.

The reasonable belief that a fire has broken out does not appear to have to be the *officer's* belief and the wording of s. 30 appears to suggest that *anyone* holding such a belief may trigger the power.

OFFENCE: **False alarms of fire—*Fire Services Act 1947, s. 31***
> • Triable summarily • Three months' imprisonment and/or a fine
> *(No specific power of arrest)*

The Fire Services Act 1947, s. 31 states:

> (1) Any person who knowingly gives or causes to be given a false alarm of fire to any fire brigade maintained in pursuance of this Act or to any member of such a brigade shall be liable . . .

---

**KEYNOTE**

This offence is a 'penalty offence' for the purposes of s. 1 of the Criminal Justice and Police Act 2001 (see para. 2.5.1).

---

## 2.13.6 Powers of seizure under the Police and Criminal Evidence Act 1984

The Police and Criminal Evidence Act 1984 provides many powers for the seizure of property. These include property:

- discovered during a stop/search (s. 1(6)), **see para. 2.7.1;**
- discovered when executing a search warrant issued by a magistrates' court in connection with a serious arrestable offence (s. 8(2)), **see para. 2.13.1;**

- discovered when executing a warrant issued by a circuit judge under sch. 1, **see para. 2.13.8**;

- discovered during a search in connection with an arrestable offence (s. 18(2)), **see para. 2.13.2**;

- discovered while lawfully on premises (s. 19), **see para. 2.13.7**;

- discovered after a person's arrest at a place other than a police station (s. 32), **see para. 2.13.2**;

- discovered during a search at a police station/while in police detention (ss. 54(3) and 55(12)), **see Evidence and Procedure, chapter 15**.

For the extended powers of seizure under the Criminal Justice and Police Act 2001, **see para. 2.13.9**.

### 2.13.7 General powers of seizure under the Police and Criminal Evidence Act 1984

Section 19 of the Police and Criminal Evidence Act 1984 states:

(1) The powers conferred by subsections (2), (3) and (4) below are exercisable by a constable who is lawfully on any premises.

(2) The constable may seize anything which is on the premises if he has reasonable grounds for believing—
  (a) that it has been obtained in consequence of the commission of an offence; and
  (b) that it is necessary to seize it in order to prevent it being concealed, lost, damaged, altered or destroyed.

(3) The constable may seize anything which is on the premises if he has reasonable grounds for believing—
  (a) that it is evidence in relation to an offence which he is investigating or any other offence; and
  (b) that it is necessary to seize it in order to prevent the evidence being concealed, lost, altered or destroyed.

(4) The constable may require any information which is stored in any electronic form and is accessible from the premises to be produced in a form in which it can be taken away and in which it is visible and legible or from which it can readily be produced in a visible and legible form if he has reasonable grounds for believing—
  (a) that—
    (i) it is evidence in relation to an offence which he is investigating or any other offence; or
    (ii) it has been obtained in consequence of the commission of an offence; and
  (b) that it is necessary to do so in order to prevent it being concealed, lost, or destroyed.

(5) The powers conferred by this section are in addition to any power otherwise conferred.

(6) No power of seizure conferred on a constable under any enactment (including an enactment contained in an Act passed after this Act) is to be taken to authorise the seizure of an item which the constable exercising the power has reasonable grounds for believing to be subject to legal privilege.

---

**KEYNOTE**

For this very wide power to apply, the officer concerned must be on the premises lawfully (see para. 2.13.2 and also PACE Code B). If the officers are on the premises only with the consent of the occupier, they become trespassers once that consent has been withdrawn (see para. 2.13.3). Once the officers are told to leave, they are no longer 'lawfully' on the premises—even though they must be given a reasonable opportunity to leave—and cannot then seize any property that they may find. For this reason, it is far safer to exercise a power where one exists, albeit that the *co-operation* of the relevant person should be sought.

The power of seizure only applies where the officer has 'reasonable grounds for believing' that:

- the property has been obtained in consequence of the commission of an offence, or

- the property is *evidence* in relation to an offence, *and*

in each case, that its seizure is *necessary* to prevent the property being concealed, lost or destroyed.

Where the 'premises' searched is a vehicle (see s. 23), the vehicle can itself be seized (*Cowan* v *Commissioner of Police for the Metropolis* [2000] 1 WLR 254). In *Cowan* it was argued that the powers given by ss. 18 (as to which, **see para. 2.13.2**) and 19 authorise the seizure of anything in or on the premises but not the *premises* themselves. The Court of Appeal disagreed, holding that the power to seize 'premises', where it was appropriate and practical to do so, was embodied in both ss. 18 and 19 and also at common law and the defendant's claim for damages following the seizure of his vehicle after his arrest for serious sexual offences was dismissed. This decision is now acknowledged in Code B, Note 7B.

Unless the elements above are satisfied, the power under s. 19 will not apply. Therefore, the power does not authorise the seizure of property purely for intelligence purposes (**see also para. 2.13.1**).

Section 19(5) expressly preserves any common law power of search and seizure; however, in *R (on the application of Rottman)* v *Commissioner of Police for the Metropolis* [2002] 2 AC 692, the House of Lords held that s. 19 was confined to 'domestic' offences (e.g. and did not extend to extradition offences). The same applies to powers under s. 18 of the Police and Criminal Evidence Act 1984 (**see para. 2.13.2**).

If the warrant under which entry or seizure was made is invalid, the officers will not be on the premises lawfully (**see para. 2.13**).

The power of seizure under s. 19(1), along with the power to require information stored in any electronic form to be made accessible under s. 19(4), are among those that can be conferred on an Investigating Officer designated under sch. 4 to the Police Reform Act 2002 (**see chapter 2**). The safeguards provided by s. 19(6) in relation to privileged material also apply to the exercise of these powers by designated Investigating Officers.

---

Section 20(1) states:

(1) Every power of seizure which is conferred by an enactment to which this section applies on a constable who has entered premises in the exercise of a power conferred by an enactment shall be construed as including a power to require any information stored in any electronic form and accessible from the premises to be produced in a form in which it can be taken away and in which it is visible and legible or from which it can readily be produced in a visible and legible form.

(2) This section applies—
   (a) to any enactment contained in an Act passed before this Act;
   (b) to sections 8 and 18 above;
   (c) to paragraph 13 of Schedule 1 to this Act; and
   (d) to any enactment contained in an Act passed after this Act.

---

**KEYNOTE**

This provision applies to:

- powers conferred under pre-PACE statutes;
- powers exercised under a s. 8 warrant (for 'serious arrestable offences');
- powers exercised under s. 18 (following arrest for an arrestable offence);
- powers under sch. 1 ('excluded' or 'special procedure material');
- powers exercised under s. 19 (officers lawfully on premises);
- powers of seizure exercised by Investigating Officers designated under sch. 4 to the Police Reform Act 2002 (as to which **see para. 2.14.2**).

See also PACE Code B, para. 7.6 which reinforces the power to require electronically stored information to be produced in a visible and legible form that can be taken away or reproduced (**appendix 2**).

As the legitimate use of information technology increases, so too does its unlawful application. The increased use of electronic media to facilitate criminal activity has meant that more conventional police powers of search and seizure have not been adequate for the needs of the police and other investigatory agencies. This is particularly true where data or information that may be of evidential value in a criminal enquiry has been 'encrypted'— that is, where some form of code or password has been used to prevent access to it. Part III of the Regulation of Investigatory Powers Act 2000 addresses these problems by providing a power to serve written notices requiring the holders of 'protected information' to disclose either the information in an intelligible format or, if relevant, the 'key' to it. Protected information in this context is generally electronic data that cannot be accessed readily or put into an intelligible form without a key (s. 56). The power to serve a notice (given by s. 49) generally applies to protected information that has been obtained or seized by some lawful means, for example where a computer has been taken under the authority of a warrant or voluntarily handed in to the police. At the time of writing, this part of the Act had not been brought into force.

Which person will have appropriate permission under the 2000 Act to issue the relevant s. 49 notice will depend largely on how the protected information was come by. Broadly, sch. 2 to the Act lists the people who may issue such notices and, just as importantly, appropriate circumstances under which they may do so. A circuit judge in England and Wales will have appropriate permission to grant police applications in all cases. Others included in the Schedule are the Secretary of State and chief officers of police (under the appropriate circumstances). As with other areas of the 2000 Act (**see Crime, chapter 3**), the power to issue s. 49 notices will be restricted to occasions where its use is both necessary and proportionate to the interests of national security, the prevention or detection of crime and the economic well-being of the United Kingdom. In addition, a s. 49 notice cannot be issued unless it is not reasonably practicable for the person with appropriate permission to obtain the protected information in an intelligible form in any other way. Part III of the Act imposes certain requirements for reporting the use of the s. 49 powers to the Chief Surveillance Commissioner and creates safeguards for the storage and use of any keys and data obtained thereby. Knowingly failing to comply with a s. 49 notice will be, under appropriate circumstances, an offence triable either way and attracting an unlimited fine in the Crown Court (s. 53). There is also to be a more serious offence of 'tipping off' another person where a s. 49 notice has been authorised and that notice contains an express requirement for secrecy. This offence (under s. 54) will also be triable either way but carrying a maximum sentence of five years' imprisonment making it an 'arrestable offence' for the purposes of s. 24 of the Police and Criminal Evidence Act 1984 (**see para. 2.9.1**).

This discussion is merely a summary of the key aspects of this new power. To find the full extent of the powers and duties under this Part of the 2000 Act, the statutory text should be used along with the relevant code of practice in force at the time.

For other powers and offences involving data and information, **see chapter 11**.

Section 21 of the 1984 Act makes provision for the supplying of copies of records of seizure to certain people after property has been seized. If requested by the person who had custody or control of the seized property immediately before it was seized, the officer in charge of the investigation must allow that person access to it under police supervision. The officer must also make provisions to allow for the property be to photographed or copied by that person or to supply the person with photographs/copies of it within a reasonable time. Such a request need not be complied with if there are reasonable grounds to believe that to do so would prejudice any related investigation or criminal proceedings (s. 21(8)).

Section 22 of the 1984 Act makes provision for the retention of seized property. Section 22(1) provides that anything seized may be retained for as long as necessary in all the circumstances. However, s. 22(2) allows for property to be retained for use as evidence in a trial, forensic examination or further investigation *unless a photograph or copy would suffice*. This is reinforced generally by PACE Code B, para. 75. Seized property may be retained in order to establish its lawful owner (s. 22(2)(b)). Once this power to retain property is exhausted, a person claiming it can rely on his/her right to possession at the time the property was seized as giving sufficient title to recover the property from the police. This situation was confirmed by the Court of Appeal in a case where the purchaser of a stolen car was allowed to rely upon his possession of the car at the time it was seized. As it could not be established that anyone else was entitled to the vehicle, the Court allowed the claimant's action for return of the car to him (*Costello* v *Chief Constable of Derbyshire Constabulary* [2001] 1 WLR 1437). Clearly any claim based on previous possession where it would be unlawful for the police to return the property (e.g. a controlled drug) could not be enforced. Provisions amending this area of legislation are now contained in the Criminal Justice and Police Act 2001. There is no specific provision under s. 22 for the retention of property for purely intelligence purposes.

The provisions for accessing and copying of seized material as set out in ss. 21 and 22 of the Police and Criminal Evidence Act 1984 also apply to powers of seizure exercised by Investigating Officers designated under sch. 4 to the Police Reform Act 2002 (as to which **see para. 2.14.2**).

Property seized simply to prevent an arrested person from using it to escape or to cause injury, damage etc. cannot be retained for those purposes once the person has been released (s. 22(3)). This includes car keys belonging to someone who is released from police detention having been detained under the relevant drink driving legislation (see Road Traffic, chapter 5).

Information gained as a result of a lawful search may be passed on to other individuals and organisations for purposes of investigation and prosecution. It must not be used for private purposes (*Marcel* v *Commissioner of Police for the Metropolis* [1992] Ch 225; also see chapter 1 for the requirements as to confidentiality in the Code of Conduct for police officers).

For the provisions regarding the disposal of property in police possession, see the Police (Property) Act 1897.

There are powers of seizure—although not a specific power of *search*-under the Confiscation of Alcohol (Young Persons) Act 1997 and the Criminal Justice and Police Act 2001, together with a power of arrest for failing to comply (see chapter 10).

There is also a power of seizure for any radio scanning or other equipment under the Telecommunications Act 1984, s. 79(1)(ba) (see chapter 3).

In addition, there is also a *duty* of seizure for a constable (and a park keeper!) in uniform in respect of people under 16 years old who have tobacco and cigarette papers in a public place (s. 7(3) of the Children and Young Persons Act 1933) (see Crime, chapter 11).

---

### 2.13.8    Protected material

Some material cannot be seized, either under the Police and Criminal Evidence Act 1984 or any other enactment; certain other material can only be seized under special circumstances set out in the Act (and the extended 'Sift and Seize' powers under the Criminal Justice and Police Act 2001—see para. 2.13.9).

Legally privileged material

Material which falls within the definition at s. 10(1) of the 1984 Act is subject to legal privilege which means that it cannot be searched for or seized.

Section 10(1) states:

(1) Subject to subsection (2) below, in this Act 'items subject to legal privilege' means—
 (a) communications between a professional legal adviser and his client or any person representing his client made in connection with the giving of legal advice to the client;
 (b) communications between a professional legal adviser and his client or any person representing his client or between such an adviser or his client or any such representative and any other person made in connection with or in contemplation of legal proceedings and for the purposes of such proceedings; and
 (c) items enclosed with or referred to in such communications and made-
  (i) in connection with the giving of legal advice; or
  (ii) in connection with or in contemplation of legal proceedings and for the purposes of such proceedings,
when they are in the possession of a person who is entitled to possession of them.

---

**KEYNOTE**

Items held with the intention of furthering a criminal purpose are no longer subject to this privilege (s. 10(2)). However, when making an application for a warrant to search for and seize such material the procedure under sch. 1 should be used. Occasions where this will happen are very rare and would include instances where a solicitor's firm is the subject of a criminal investigation (see *R* v *Leeds Crown Court, ex parte Switalski* [1991] Crim LR 559). However, it may be possible during a search to ascertain which material is subject to legal privilege and which might be lawfully seized under the warrant being executed. Therefore, although a warrant cannot authorise a search for legally privileged material, the fact that such material is inadvertently seized in the course of a search authorised by a proper warrant does not render the search unlawful (*HM Customs & Excise, ex parte Popely* [2000] Crim LR 388). For further discussion in relation to the extent of legal privilege, see Evidence and Procedure, chapter 10.

---

Excluded material

Access to 'excluded material' can generally only be gained by applying to a judge for a production order under the procedure set out in s. 9 of, and sch. 1 to the 1984 Act and PACE Code B. That strict statutory procedure also applies to the application for and execution of warrants by Investigating Officers designated under sch. 4 to the Police Reform Act 2002 (as to which **see para. 2.14.2**).

Section 11 of the 1984 Act states:

(1) Subject to the following provisions of this section, in this Act 'excluded material' means—
  (a) personal records which a person has acquired or created in the course of any trade, business, profession or other occupation or for the purposes of any paid or unpaid office and which he holds in confidence;
  (b) human tissue or tissue fluid which has been taken for the purposes of diagnosis or medical treatment and which a person holds in confidence;
  (c) journalistic material which a person holds in confidence and which consists—
    (i) of documents; or
    (ii) of records other than documents.

(2) A person holds material other than journalistic material in confidence for the purposes of this section if he holds it subject—
  (a) to an express or implied undertaking to hold it in confidence; or
  (b) to a restriction on disclosure or an obligation of secrecy contained in any enactment, including an enactment contained in an Act passed after this Act.

(3) A person holds journalistic material in confidence for the purposes of this section if—
  (a) he holds it subject to such an undertaking, restriction or obligation; and
  (b) it has been continuously held (by one or more persons) subject to such an undertaking, restriction or obligation since it was first acquired or created for the purposes of journalism.

---

**KEYNOTE**

Medical records and dental records would fall into this category, as might records made by priests or religious advisers.

'Personal records' are defined under s. 12 of the 1984 Act and include records relating to the physical or mental health, counselling or assistance given to an individual who can be identified by those records.

'Journalistic material' is defined under s. 13 as material acquired or created for the purposes of journalism.

---

Special procedure material

Special procedure material can be gained by applying for a search warrant or a production order under sch. 1 to the 1984 Act.

Section 14 of the 1984 Act states:

(1) In this Act 'special procedure material' means—
  (a) material to which subsection (2) below applies; and
  (b) journalistic material, other than excluded material.

(2) Subject to the following provisions of this section, this subsection applies to material, other than items subject to legal privilege and excluded material, in the possession of a person who—
  (a) acquired or created it in the course of any trade, business, profession or other occupation or for the purpose of any paid or unpaid office; and

    (b) holds it subject—

        (i) to an express or implied undertaking to hold it in confidence; or

        (ii) to a restriction or obligation such as is mentioned in section 11(2)(b) above.

---

**KEYNOTE**

For items subject to 'legal privilege' and 'excluded material', see the Keynote above.

The person believed to be in possession of the material must have come by it under the circumstances set out at s. 14(2)(a) *and* must hold it under the undertakings or obligations set out at s. 14(2)(b).

---

## 2.13.9 Seize and sift powers

One of the practical problems faced by operational officers when seizing certain types of material is that of sorting the 'wheat from the chaff'—sifting out those documents or computer-stored data that are pertinent to the case from the general mass of material within which they are found. As discussed above (**see para. 2.13.1**), if officers executing a search warrant under s. 8 of the Police and Criminal Evidence Act 1984 take away material from the named premises to sift through it at another location and some of the seized material is later found to fall outside the scope of the warrant, those officers' actions are not covered by the warrant (*R* v *Chesterfield Justices and Chief Constable of Derbyshire, ex parte Bramley* [2001] 1 All ER 411). Although the Divisional Court recognised the common sense of allowing police officers under certain circumstances to remove large amounts of papers, data or other potential evidence from premises and then sort through it elsewhere, there were at the time of the *Bramley* case no specific provisions allowing them to do this. As a result, part 2 of the Criminal Justice and Police Act 2001 now provides the police with specific powers to 'seize and sift' under strict conditions and subject to a number of rigid procedural safeguards. One such safeguard is the specific application of Code B of the Police and Criminal Evidence Act 1984 Codes of Practice (**see appendix 1**).

### Extended powers

The first point to note about these seize and sift powers is that they will be rarely used and, even then, those using them will have to be able to show that it was *essential* (rather than simply convenient or preferable) to do so (Code B, para. 7.7). The second thing to note about these powers is that they only extend the scope of *some other existing power*. In other words, they do not provide free-standing powers to seize property—rather they supplement other powers of search and seizure where the relevant conditions and circumstances apply. The full list of these powers is set out in sch. 1 to the Act and includes all the relevant powers under the Police and Criminal Evidence Act 1984, along with those under other key statutes such as the Firearms Act 1968 and the Misuse of Drugs Act 1971. If there is no existing power of seizure other than the Criminal Justice and Police Act 2001, then there is no power.

The Criminal Justice and Police Act 2001 powers allow officers to remove materials from the premises being searched where there are real practical difficulties in not doing so— e.g. because there will be insufficient time to examine all the material properly, where special equipment is needed to examine it or where the material is stored on a computer.

In summary, s. 50 of the Act provides the extended powers to seize material where it is not reasonably practicable to sort through it at the scene of the search. The factors that can be taken into account in considering whether or not it is reasonably practicable for something to be determined, or for relevant material to be separated from other materials, are set out in s. 50 (3); these include the length of time and number of people that would be required to carry out the determination or separation on those premises within a reasonable period, whether that would involve damage to property, any apparatus or equipment that would be needed and (in the case of separation of materials) whether the separation would be likely to prejudice the use of some or all of the separated seizable property. Section 50 also allows for the seizure of material that is reasonably believed to be legally privileged (**see para. 2.13.8**) where it is not reasonably practicable to separate it. In some cases, the power to 'seize' will be read as a power to take copies (see s. 63).

Section 52 provides for extended seizure of materials in the same vein as above but where the material is found on people who are being lawfully searched.

One of the main purposes behind this legislative framework is to balance the competing needs of the criminal justice system with the individual rights of the person owning the property (see Code B, para. 7.7–7.8). Seizing large volumes of material and removing them from the owner's premises can have considerable consequences, particularly where they are taken from business premises. Therefore there are many strict requirements imposed on the police, not only in seizing the property in the first place, but also after the property has been lawfully seized by virtue of the new powers. The first of these is the duty to carry out an initial examination.

### Initial examination

Where any property has been seized under ss. 50 or 51, the officer in possession of it is under a duty to make sure that a number of things are done (s. 53). These include ensuring that an initial examination of the property is carried out *as soon as reasonably practicable* after the seizure. In determining the earliest practicable time to carry out an initial examination of the seized property, due regard must be had to the desirability of allowing the person from whom it was seized (or a person with an interest in it) an opportunity of being present, or of being represented, at the examination (s. 53(4)).

The officer must also ensure that any such examination is confined to whatever is *necessary* for determining how much of the property:

- is property for which the person seizing it had power to search when making the seizure but is not property that has to be returned (by s. 54—see below)
- is property authorised to be retained (by s. 56—see below) or
- is something which, in all the circumstances, it will not be reasonably practicable, following the examination, to separate from the property above

(see generally s. 53(3)).

The officer must ensure that anything found not to fall within the categories above is separated from the rest of the seized property and *is returned as soon as reasonably practicable* after the examination of all the seized property. That officer is also under a duty to ensure that, until the initial examination of all the seized property has been completed and anything which does not fall within the categories above has been returned, the seized property is kept separate from anything seized under any other power. There are special provisions where the property is inextricably linked to relevant material (e.g. where the 'innocent' material is completely mixed up with or inseparable from the material that is properly the subject of the investigation). However, those provisions place very strict limits on what use can be made of this inextricably linked material (see s. 62).

While there are great sensitivities over the use of widespread powers of seizure such as these in any event, those sensitivities are increased even further where legally privileged or special procedure material is involved (as to which **see para. 2.13.8**). Accordingly the Act imposes specific duties on the police in relation to these materials.

### Protected material

If, at any time, after a seizure of anything has been made in exercise of *any statutory power of seizure*, it appears that the property is subject to legal privilege (or it has such an item comprised in it), s. 54 imposes a general duty on the officer in possession of the property to ensure that the item is returned as soon as reasonably practicable after the seizure. This general duty is subject to some exceptions (e.g. where in all the circumstances it is not reasonably practicable for that item to be separated from the rest of that property without prejudicing the use of the rest of that property—see s. 54(2)) but is otherwise very wide-ranging and absolutely clear. A similar duty is generally imposed in relation to property that appears to be excluded material or special procedure material (as to which **see para. 2.13.8**)—s. 55.

### Retention of property

The Act authorises the retention of certain seized property by the police. In order to be retained, the property must have been seized on any premises by a constable who was lawfully on the premises, by a person authorised under a relevant statute (see s. 56(5)) who was on the premises accompanied by a constable, or by a constable carrying out a lawful search of any person (s. 56). Generally property so seized will fall within these categories if there are reasonable grounds for believing—

- that it is property obtained in consequence of the commission of an offence or
- that it is evidence in relation to any offence *and* (in either case)
- that it is necessary for it to be retained in order to prevent its being concealed, lost, altered or destroyed

(for full details see s. 56(2) and (3)). Note, so far as s. 56(2) is concerned, property may be retained if it is necessary to prevent its being 'damaged', in addition to the other factors listed.

These are fairly wide provisions and, if the property fits the above description, it may be retained even if it was not being searched for. Section 57 goes on to make certain provisions for the retention of property under other statutes including s. 22 of the Theft Act 1968 (**see Crime**) and s. 5(4) of the Knives Act 1997 (**see Chapter 6**). Further guidance on retention of property is set out in Code B, para. 7.14–7.15.

### Notice

Where a person exercises a power of seizure conferred by ss. 50 or 51, that person will be under a duty, on doing so, to give the occupier or person from whom property is seized a written notice (s. 52). That notice will specify:

- what has been seized and the grounds on which the powers have been exercised
- the effect of the safeguards and rights to apply to a judicial authority for the return of the property (see below)
- the name and address of the person to whom notice of an application to a judge and an application to be allowed to attend the initial examination should be sent.

Where it appears to the officer exercising a power of seizure under s. 50 that the occupier of the premises is not present at the time of the exercise of the power, but there is some other person present who is in charge of the premises, the officer may give the notice to that other person (s. 52(2)). Where it appears that there is no one present on the premises to whom a notice can be given, the officer must, before leaving the premises, attach a notice in a prominent place to the premises (s. 53 (3)).

There are specific obligations on the police to return property seized under these powers—particularly where the property includes legally privileged, excluded or special procedure material. The general rule is that any extraneous property initially seized under these provisions must be returned—usually—to the person from whom it was seized unless the investigating officer considers that someone else has a better claim to it (see ss. 53–58).

Any person with a relevant interest in the seized property may apply to the appropriate judicial authority, on one or more of the grounds in s. 59 (3) for the return of the whole or a part of the seized property. Generally those grounds are that there was no power to make the seizure or that the seized property did not fall into one of the permitted categories (see s. 59). Where a person makes such an application, the police must secure the property in accordance with s. 6l (e.g. in a way that prevents investigators from looking at or copying it until the matter has been considered by a judge). There are other occasions where protected material is involved that will give rise to the duty to secure the property under s. 61 too. What will amount to 'securing' will vary depending on the type of property and the circumstances and may involve 'bagging up' property and controlling access to it in many cases (see Code A, Note 7F). The 'judicial authority' (at least a crown court judge) will be able to make a number of wide-ranging orders in relation to the treatment of the seized property, including its return or examination by a third party. Failure to comply with any such order will amount to a contempt of court (s. 59(9)).

For further detail on the extent and use of these powers, see Home Office Circular 19/2003.

## 2.14 Extending the policing family

A further highly controversial feature of the Police Reform Act 2002 (**see chapter 1**) lies in what has been called the 'extended police family'. Given the nature of the roles that the legislation creates, it is perhaps more accurate to refer (if you have to) to an extended *policing* family as some of the people endowed with powers of enforcement and regulation under the Act will not be employed by the police at all, though they will have policing responsibilities. The idea behind the introduction of these is broadly twofold. On the one hand, there has been a recognition within and outside the police service that police officers spend too much time tied up by administrative or non-core tasks. On the other hand, civilian support staff employed to help with these and some front-line functions do not have the powers to carry out their roles effectively. For example, the processing of police prisoners can often involve a number of police officers for many hours, documenting, fingerprinting, interviewing, escorting and transporting. Creating specific roles of detention and escort officers, and giving them relevant powers to let them carry out their jobs, has the potential to free up police officers to concentrate on the core policing tasks that require the full range of powers and training that they offer. Similarly, training people (not just police staff, but also employees in shopping malls, clubs and retail parks) and giving them the relevant powers to deal with low-level disorder and anti-social behaviour, as well as for those occasions where it is a case of 'all hands to the pumps' (such as cordoning off areas following terrorist acts), can spread the policing burden and increase their capacity. This then is the rationale that lies behind some of the provisions set out in part 4 of the Police Reform Act 2002. (For more detail see Home Office Circular 67/2002.)

### 2.14.1 New policing powers

Part 4 of the Police Reform Act 2002 introduces some novel developments in the law regulating policing powers by potentially extending some of those powers to a whole range of non-police individuals. These individuals will be designated in a particular role(s) or accredited with certain powers. They will be given a number of different titles, including the titles specifically used in the legislation (such as Investigating Officers and Detention Officers). Some forces refer to these individuals collectively as police auxiliaries. The particular title applied to each of these individuals is largely irrelevant—what matters is the extent of the designation or accreditation conferred on the person by the chief officer. The whole system works by allowing the relevant chief officer—to confer certain powers on different groups of people by designating or accrediting them. The chief officer does not *have* to confer any powers on any such groups and he or she can decide to confer only a reduced number of powers or to place further limitations on those powers: the Act simply gives the chief officer the freedom and flexibility to do so.

The legislation has been drafted in a fairly complex way and the whole framework that it puts in place can seem a little daunting on first reading. When approaching these new powers and their applicability to different individuals, however, a good starting point is to consider who the relevant person's employer is. Some roles created under the Act (such as Police Community Support Officers and Investigating Officers) can only be carried out by police employees; if you do not work directly for the police, you cannot have these powers or perform these roles. In other roles (Detention Officers and Escort Officers), the person does not necessarily have to be employed by the police. If the person is not employed by the force, then their employer must have a contract with the relevant police authority. These people will have their powers contained in a 'designation' from the relevant chief officer. Another group of people who can have powers conferred on them by a chief officer are not employees of either the police or a police authority contractor. These people are 'accredited' with powers that can only come from their accreditation under a statutory Community Safety Accreditation Scheme. And in order to perform *any* of the roles and exercise *any* of the powers under part 4 of the Act, an individual must be employed by somebody because it is through the person's employer that the chief officer or the relevant police authority can exercise a degree of control over those auxiliary staff who are not directly employed by the police. Therefore, if you are unemployed or self-employed, the legislation will not allow you to have these new powers or to carry out any of the relevant functions.

Another feature to note at the outset is that there is a sort of 'chain of control' linking the auxiliary or individual to a chief officer or police authority. The further along the chain a person is, the less control a chief officer or police authority has over them—and therefore the fewer powers they can be given under the Act. In the case of staff directly employed by a particular police force, they will have a contract of employment with their own force as will any member of non-sworn civilian staff. Moving down the chain of control, you find individuals who are not police employees but are employed by an outside organisation which itself has a contract with a police authority. Examples would be security companies providing prisoner escort services. These employees can be given more limited powers and roles under the Act. Further still along the chain of control are people employed by entirely independent non-police organisations. These people could be working for any number of local businesses or organisations within a police area and the Act allows a chief officer to accredit their employees with limited policing powers.

### 2.14.2 Designated police employees

The first group of people who can be empowered under part 4 of the Police Reform Act 2002 are people employed by the police authority maintaining that force and under the direction and control of their chief officer. These police employees can be 'designated' under s. 38 by their chief officer as *one or more* of the following:

- Police Community Support Officers (PCSOs)
- Investigating Officers

- Detention Officers
- Escort Officers.

For a full discussion of Detention Officers and Escort Officers, **see Evidence and Procedure**.

Designations as Investigating Officers can also be made by the Directors General of NCIS and the NCS of their own staff (see s. 38(3)).

No one may be designated in these roles unless the chief officer (or Director General) is satisfied that they are a suitable person to carry out the designated functions, are capable of carrying out those functions effectively and that they have received adequate training. Adequate training is not defined but it would have to cover the exercise and performance of the relevant powers and duties to be conferred on the person (see s. 38(4)). Considerable weight was given to these safeguards—and the restrictions on any use of force (**see below**)—during the passage of the Police Reform Bill through Parliament and the provision of effective training was seen as an essential measure to the proper functioning of this new framework.

Because these designated staff are employees of the relevant force, the chief officer is responsible for dealing with reports of misconduct and complaints against them in the normal way. However, once the Independent Police Complaints Commission (IPCC) is fully operative under the Police Reform Act 2002, that body will have jurisdiction over any such allegations or complaints.

### Powers conferred on designated police employees

The specific powers that can be conferred by the chief officer on these designated employees depend on which designated role(s) they are given. The powers are set out in sch. 4 to the Act. Schedule 4 is itself divided into further parts, 1–4, with each part containing a number of statutory powers. Helpfully the parts of sch. 4 correspond to the four roles set out in the list above so that the respective powers under parts 1–4 and the relative designated employee roles look like this:

| Person | Powers |
| --- | --- |
| PCSO | Part 1 |
| Investigating Officer | Part 2 |
| Detention Officer | Part 3 |
| Escort Officer | Part 4 |

The powers set out in sch. 4 are many and various but they do follow a degree of common sense when you consider the practical requirements of the roles they cover. For example, it makes sense for an Investigating Officer to be given investigative powers such as powers of entry, search and seizure, along with powers to arrest suspects during an interview where further offences are revealed. Similarly, Detention Officers need powers to fingerprint and search prisoners. People already employed by the police in certain roles can be designated under this Part of the Act (e.g. scenes of crime officers can be given powers of entry and search).

The full list of powers available is summarised below. Where appropriate, references have also been included alongside the relevant text in this and the other Manuals in this series.

The schedule works by taking existing powers under various pieces of legislation and adapting them so that they apply to the relevant person (PCSO etc.). For a fuller discussion of the powers under this schedule, see Home Office Circular 67/2002.

Part 1 of Schedule 4 to the Police Reform Act 2002—Police Community Support Officers

Each of the following paragraphs will only apply if the designation specifically applies it to the Police Community Support Officer (PCSO) concerned.

### Power to issue fixed penalty notices—paragraph 1

The powers below may be conferred on a PCSO in relation to any individual who the PCSO has reason to believe has committed a relevant fixed penalty offence at a place within the relevant police area. Those powers are:

(a) the powers of a constable in uniform and of an authorised constable to give a penalty notice under Chapter 1 of Part 1 of the Criminal Justice and Police Act 2001 (fixed penalty notices in respect of offences of disorder—**see para. 2.5.1**);

(b) the power of a constable in uniform to give a person a fixed penalty notice under s. 54 of the Road Traffic Offenders Act 1988 (fixed penalty notices—**see para. 2.5.1**) in respect of an offence under s. 72 of the Highway Act 1835 (riding on a footway—**see chapter 3**) committed by cycling;

(c) the power of an authorised officer of a local authority to give a notice under s. 4 of the Dogs (Fouling of Land) Act 1996 (fixed penalty notices in respect of dog fouling—**see chapter 3**); and

(d) the power of an authorised officer of a litter authority to give a notice under s. 88 of the Environmental Protection Act 1990 (fixed penalty notices in respect of litter—**see chapter 3**)

(para. 1(2) ).

  'Relevant fixed penalty offence' = an offence which—

• is an offence by reference to which a notice may be given to a person in exercise of any of the powers mentioned in 1(2)(a) to (d) above and

• is specified or described in the PCSO's designation as an offence he/she has been designated to enforce (para. 1(3) ).

### Power to detain—paragraph 2

Where the PCSO has reason to believe that another has committed a relevant offence in the relevant police area, the PCSO may require that other person to give him/her their name *and* address (para. 2(2) ).

  [Where a person has been required to give their name and address as above and

(a) they fail to comply with the requirement, or

(b) the PCSO who imposed the requirement has reasonable grounds for suspecting that the other person has given a name or address that is false or inaccurate,

*the PCSO who imposed the requirement* may require the other person to wait with him/her, for a period not exceeding thirty minutes, for the arrival of a constable (para. 2(3) ) and may, if so designated, use reasonable force in order to prevent the person from making off (para. 4).]

  [A person who has been required to wait with a PCSO as above may, if requested to do so, choose to accompany the PCSO imposing the requirement to a police station in the relevant police area instead of waiting (para. 2(4) ) and the PCSO may, if so designated, use reasonable force in order to prevent the person from making off (para 4).]

  The powers in square brackets have been brought into force only in a limited number of police areas—Devon & Cornwall, Gwent, Lancashire, Northamptonshire, West Yorkshire and the Metropolitan Police District.

  'Relevant offence' = any offence which is—

• a relevant fixed penalty offence for the purposes of the application of paragraph 1 above; or

• an offence the commission of which appears to the PCSO to have caused—

i)   injury, alarm or distress to any other person; or

ii)  the loss of, or any damage to, any other person's property;

(para 2(6) ).

  Note that a designation applying this paragraph to a PCSO may provide that an offence is not to be treated as a 'relevant offence' unless some other specified conditions are satisfied.

### Power to require name and address of person acting in an anti-social manner—paragraph 3

Under this paragraph a PCSO will, in the relevant police area, have the powers of a constable in uniform under s. 50 to require a person whom he/she has reason to believe to have been acting, or to be acting, in an anti-social manner (within the meaning of s. 1 of the Crime and Disorder Act 1998—anti-social behaviour orders) to give his/her name *and* address (para. 3(1)).

The powers (currently limited to the six police force areas above) to require the person to remain with the PCSO or to accompany the PCSO to a police station as set out above also apply here (para. 3(2), as does the power, if so designated, to use reasonable force in order to prevent the person from making off (para. 4)). For the use of force generally **see para. 2.13**.

### Powers relating to alcohol consumption in designated public places—paragraph 5

Under this paragraph a PCSO will have the powers of a constable under s. 12 of the Criminal Justice and Police Act 2001 (alcohol consumption in public places—**see chapter 10**) in the relevant police area—

(a) to impose a requirement under subsection (2) of that section; and

(b) to dispose under subsection (3) of that section of anything surrendered to him/her;

and that section will have effect in relation to the exercise of those powers by that PCSO as if the references to a constable in subsections (1) and (5) were references to the PCSO.

### Power to confiscate alcohol—paragraph 6

Under this paragraph a PCSO will have the powers of a constable under s. 1 of the Confiscation of Alcohol (Young Persons) Act 1997 (confiscation of intoxicating liquor—**see chapter 10**) in the relevant police area—

(a) to impose a requirement under subsection (1) of that section; and

(b) to dispose under subsection (2) of that section of anything surrendered to him/her;

and that section shall have effect in relation to the exercise of those powers by that PCSO as if the references to a constable in subsections (1) and (4) (but not the reference in subsection (5) (power of arrest)) were references to the PCSO.

### Power to confiscate tobacco—paragraph 7

Under this paragraph a PCSO will have within the relevant police area—

(a) the power to seize anything that a constable in uniform has a duty to seize under subsection (3) of s. 7 of the Children and Young Persons Act 1933 (seizure of tobacco etc. from young persons—**see Crime**); and

(b) the power to dispose of anything that a constable may dispose of under that subsection;

and the power to dispose of anything shall be a power to dispose of it in such manner as the police authority may direct.

### Power of entry to save life or limb or prevent serious damage to property—paragraph 8

Under this paragraph a PCSO will have the powers of a constable under s. 17 of the Police and Criminal Evidence Act 1984 (**see para. 2.13.6**) to enter and search any premises in the relevant police area for the purpose of saving life or limb or preventing serious damage to property.

### Power to seize vehicles used to cause alarm—paragraph 9

Under this paragraph a PCSO—

• will have all the powers of a constable in uniform under s. 59(3) of this Act (**see Road Traffic**) within the relevant police area; and

• references in that section to a constable, in relation to the exercise of any of those powers by that PCSO, are references to the PCSO

(para. 9(1)).

*A PCSO can not enter any premises in exercise of the power conferred by section 59(3)(c) except in the company, and under the supervision, of a constable*

(para. 9(2)).

Powers to deal with abandoned vehicles—paragraph 10

Under this paragraph a PCSO will have any such powers in the relevant police area as are conferred on people designated under that section by regulations under s. 99 of the Road Traffic Regulation Act 1984 (removal of abandoned vehicles—**see Road Traffic**).

Power to stop vehicles for testing—paragraph 11

Under this paragraph a PCSO will have the power of a constable in uniform to stop a vehicle under subsection (3) of s. 67 of the Road Traffic Act 1988 (**see Road Traffic**) within the relevant police area for the purposes of a test under subsection (1) of that section.

Power to control traffic for purposes of escorting a load of exceptional dimensions—paragraph 12

Under this paragraph a PCSO will have, for the purpose of escorting a vehicle or trailer carrying a load of exceptional dimensions either to or from the relevant police area, the power of a constable engaged in the regulation of traffic in a road—

(a) direct a vehicle to stop;

(b) to make a vehicle proceed in, or keep to, a particular line of traffic; and

(c) to direct pedestrians to stop

(para. 12(1) ).

Sections 35 and 37 of the Road Traffic Act 1988 (offences of failing to comply with directions of constable engaged in regulation of traffic in a road—**see Road Traffic**) will have effect in relation to the exercise of those powers by a designated PCSO as if the references to a constable engaged in regulation of traffic in a road were references to that PCSO (para. 12(2) ) and will have effect in any police area in England and Wales (para. 12 (3) ).

'Vehicle or trailer carrying a load of exceptional dimensions' = a vehicle or trailer the use of which is authorised by an order made by the Secretary of State under s. 44(1)(d) of the Road Traffic Act 1988 (para. 12(4) ).

Carrying out of road checks—paragraph 13

Where a designation applies this paragraph to a PCSO, that PCSO will have the following powers in the relevant police area—

(a) The power to carry out any road check authorised under s. 4 of the Police and Criminal Evidence Act 1984 (**see para. 2.13**); and

(b) for the purpose of exercising that power, the power conferred by s. 163 of the Road Traffic Act 1988 (power of police to stop vehicles—**see Road Traffic**) on a constable in uniform to stop a vehicle.

Cordoned areas—paragraph 14

Under this paragraph a PCSO will, in relation to any cordoned area in the relevant police area, have all the powers of a constable in uniform under s. 36 of the Terrorism Act 2000 (enforcement of cordoned area—**see chapter 4**) to give orders, make arrangements or impose prohibitions or restrictions.

Power to stop and search in authorised areas—paragraph 15

Under this paragraph a PCSO—

• will, in any authorised area within the relevant police area, have all the powers of a constable in uniform by virtue of ss. 44(1)(a) and (d) and (2)(b) and 45(2) of the Terrorism Act 2000 (powers of stop and search—**see chapter 4**)—

(i) to stop and search vehicles;

(ii) to search anything in or on a vehicle or anything carried by the driver of a vehicle or any passenger in a vehicle;

(iii) to search anything carried by a pedestrian; and

(iv) to seize and retain any article discovered in the course of a search carried out by him or by a constable by virtue of any provision of s. 44(1) or (2) of that Act;

(para. 15(1)(a) ).

References to a constable in subsections (1) and (4) of s. 45 of that Act (which relate to the exercise of those powers) will have effect in relation to the exercise of any of those powers by that PCSO as references to that PCSO (para. 15(1)(b)).

*A PCSO can not exercise any power of stop, search or seizure by virtue of this paragraph except in the company, and under the supervision, of a constable*

(para. 15(2)).

OFFENCE: **Failing to comply with requirements-*Police Reform Act 2002, Sch. 4, paras 2(5) and 3(2)***

  • Triable summarily • Fine

The Police Reform Act 2002, Sch. 4, para. 2(5) states

  (5) A person who—
    (a) fails to comply with a requirement under sub-paragraph (2),
    (b) makes off while subject to a requirement under sub-paragraph (3), or
    (c) makes off while accompanying a person to a police station in accordance with an election under sub-paragraph (4),
  is guilty of an offence.

---

### KEYNOTE

Failing here must include 'refusing' otherwise this controversial piece of legislation is rendered pretty well useless. The offences created by para. 2(5) also apply in the case of para. 3(1) (requirement to give name and address when acting in an anti-social manner). Therefore failing to comply with such a requirement is an offence along the same lines as the above (see para. 3(2)).

It will be critical that the designated person produces their authority and that, if relevant, they are in the correct uniform and wearing the proper badge etc.

The requirements referred to at (b) and (c) relate to the use of powers currently in force only in a limited number of police areas, namely Devon & Cornwall, Gwent, Lancashire, Northamptonshire, West Yorkshire and the Metropolitan Police District, for a pilot period.

---

Part 2 of sch. 4 to the Police Reform Act 2002—Investigating Officers

Each of the following paragraphs will only apply if the designation specifically applies it to the Investigating Officer concerned.

Search warrants—paragraph 16

Under this paragraph, an Investigating Officer—

• may apply as if he/she were a constable for a warrant for entry and search under s. 8 of the Police and Criminal Evidence Act 1984 (**see paras 2.13.6–8**) in respect of any premises in the relevant police area (para. 16(a));

• will have the power of a constable to seize and retain things under s. 8(2) of that Act in any premises in the relevant police area, and the relevant safeguards under s. 15 of that Act will have effect in relation to the issue of such a warrant to the Investigating Officer as they have in relation to a constable (para. 16(b) and (c));

The following sections of the Police and Criminal Evidence Act 1984 will also have effect in relation to the execution of such warrants and attendant powers by Investigating Officers:

• Section 19(6) (protection for legally privileged material from seizure)

• Section 20 (extension of powers of seizure to computerised information)

• Section 21(1) and (2) (provision of record of seizure) and

• Sections 21(3) to (8) and 22 (access, copying and retention)

(para. 16(e)–(i)).

Access to excluded and special procedure material—paragraph 17

Under this paragraph, an Investigating Officer—

- will have the powers of a constable under s. 9(1) of the Police and Criminal Evidence Act 1984 (special provisions for access) to obtain access, in accordance with sch. 1 to that Act.

Further provision is made in respect of excluded material and special procedure material (**see paras 2.13.6–8**) to ensure that Investigating Officers are under the same obligations and controls as sworn police constables.

In particular, the following sections of the Police and Criminal Evidence Act 1984 will apply, with appropriate amendments, to Investigating Officers:

- Section 19(6) (protection for legally privileged material from seizure)
- Section 20 (extension of powers of seizure to computerised information)
- Section 21(1) and (2) (provision of record of seizure) and
- Sections 21(3) to (8) and 22 (access, copying and retention)

(para. 17(b)–(f) ).

Entry and search after arrest—paragraph 18

Under this paragraph, an Investigating Officer will have the powers of a constable under s. 18 of the Police and Criminal Evidence Act 1984 (entry and search after arrest—**see para. 2.13.2**) to enter and search any premises in the relevant police area and to seize and retain anything for which he/she may search under that section.

The power to carry out a search before an arrested person is taken to police station and the duty to inform an officer of the rank of inspector or above (**see para. 2.13.2**) will have effect in relation to any exercise by the Investigating Officer as if the references in the relevant subsections ( (5) and (6) ) to a constable were references to the Investigating Officer (para. 18(b) ).

The various sections (19 to 22) of the Police and Criminal Evidence Act 1984 as set out under paragraph 17 above will also apply to any powers of entry and search made by Investigating Officers here.

General power of seizure—paragraph 19

Under this paragraph, an Investigating Officer—

- will, when lawfully on any premises in the relevant police area, have the same powers as a constable under s. 19 of the Police and Criminal Evidence Act 1984 (general powers of seizure—**see para. 2.13.6**) to seize things and
- will have the powers of a constable to impose a requirement by virtue of s. 19 (4) in relation to information accessible from such premises

(para. 19(a) and (b) ).

In keeping with the last two paragraphs, various sections (19(6), 21 and 22) of the Police and Criminal Evidence Act 1984 will also apply in amended form where appropriate to any powers of seizure used under this paragraph to ensure that Investigating Officers are under the same obligations and controls as sworn police constables.

Access and copying in the case of things seized by constables—paragraph 20

Under this paragraph, an Investigating Officer will be subject to the same duties and obligations as a constable under s. 21(3), (4) and (5) of the Police and Criminal Evidence Act 1984 (supervision of access and photographing of seized items—**see para. 2.13.7**).

Power to arrest at a police station for another offence—paragraph 21

Under this paragraph, an Investigating Officer will have the power to make an arrest at any police station in the relevant police area in any case where an arrest is required to be made under s. 31 of the Police and Criminal Evidence Act 1984 (arrest for a further offence of a person who is already at a police station—**see para. 2.11**).

Section 36 of the Criminal Justice and Public Order Act 1994 (consequences of failure by an arrested person to account for any objects, marks, etc.—see below) will apply in the case of a person arrested by an Investigating Officer under this power (para. 21(2) ).

Power to transfer prisoners into custody of Investigating Officers—paragraph 22

Under this paragraph, the custody officer for a designated police station in the relevant police area may transfer or permit the transfer to that Investigating Officer of a person in police detention for an offence which is being investigated by the Investigating Officer.

An Investigating Officer into whose custody another person is so transferred will be—

- treated for all purposes as having that person in his/her lawful custody

- under a duty to prevent his/her escape and

- entitled to use reasonable force to keep that person in his/her custody

(para. 22(2)).

Where a person is transferred into the custody of an Investigating Officer under this paragraph, the provisions of s. 39(2) and (3) of the Police and Criminal Evidence Act 1984 relating to custody officers and the safeguarding of the independence of that role (see **Evidence and Procedure, chapter 15**) will have effect as if references to the 'police officer investigating an offence' referred to the Investigating Officer.

Power to require arrested person to account for certain matters—paragraph 23

Under this paragraph, an Investigating Officer will have the powers of a constable under ss. 36(1)(c) and 37(1)(c) of the Criminal Justice and Public Order Act 1994 (see **Evidence and Procedure, chapter 11**) to request a person who—

(i) has been arrested by a constable, or any person arrested by an Investigating Officer under paragraph 21 above and

(ii) is detained at any place in the relevant police area,

to account for the presence of an object, substance or mark, or for the presence of the arrested person at a particular place.

References to 'a constable' in ss. 36(1)(b) and (c) and (4) and 37(1)(b) and (c) and (3) of that Act will have effect as including references to the Investigating Officer.

Extended powers of seizure—paragraph 24

Under this paragraph, an Investigating Officer will have the same extended powers of seizure that are provided to constables under Part 2 of the Criminal Justice and Police Act 2001. Similarly, s. 56 of that Act (retention of property seized by a constable) will have effect as if the property referred to included property seized by the Investigating Officer.

### 2.14.3 Employees of contracted-out businesses

Moving another link along the chain of control from a chief officer and the relevant employee you come across the next group of people who can be granted powers under sch. 4 to the Police Reform Act 2002. Although their employee status is the source of control over these employees' activities and performance, the first thing to note is that they are *not* employed by the police force. Where a police authority has entered into a contract for the provision of services relating to the detention or escorting of people in custody, s. 39 allows the chief officer to designate employees *of the contractor* as either Detention Officers or Escort Officers or both. As such these people may be given some or all of the powers of those roles set out in parts 3 and 4 of sch. 4 to the Act (see above). These contracted-out personnel cannot be given the powers of PCSOs and Investigating Officers as they are not police employees—they are employees of the contractor. This slightly unconventional arrangement raises some interesting questions as to whether or not they are performing a public role such that they would come within the parameters of the Human Rights Act 1998 (**see para. 2.3.3**).

Before designating anyone under this part of the Act, a chief officer must be satisfied that the person:

- is a suitable person to carry out the functions for which he/she is to be designated;

- is capable of effectively carrying out those functions; and

- has received adequate training in the carrying out of those functions and in the exercise of those powers and duties to be conferred on him/her

(s. 39(4)).

As with the police employees given powers under parts 1–4 of sch. 4, a great deal of emphasis was placed on these safeguards in securing the passage of the Police Reform Bill through Parliament and, in particular, the provision of effective training was seen as an essential measure to the proper functioning of the new measures. Further weight was given to the reassurances provided by the restrictions on the use of force (see below).

If an employee stops being an employee of the contractor, or the contract between the employer and the police authority comes to an end, any designation ceases to have effect (s. 39(13)). Section 39 also allows for regulations to be made regarding the handling of complaints and misconduct issues arising out of the functions of designated employees.

### 2.14.4 Accredited employees

Moving further still along the chain of control linking the force with the employee brings you to those people who are simply employed by local businesses and employers in the relevant police area. Those businesses do not have to have an existing contract with the police authority and their employees only gain their accreditation from powers conferred under a Community Safety Accreditation Scheme (CSAS).

A CSAS is a scheme set up and maintained by a chief officer for the purposes of:

- contributing to community safety and security

- combating crime and disorder, public nuisance and other forms of anti-social behaviour.

For the law specifically relating to Railway Safety Accreditation Schemes, **see chapter 13**.

#### Community Safety Accreditation Schemes

Before establishing a CSAS, a chief officer must consult with the police authority and every local authority any part of whose area lies within his/her force (s. 40(4)). In the case of the Metropolitan Police Force the commissioner must also consult with the Mayor of London. Any CSAS must also appear in the policing plan of any force (as to which **see chapter 1**). A CSAS must contain provisions for making arrangements with local employers carrying on business (including those carrying out statutory functions) for the supervision of any of their employees who become accredited under the scheme (s. 40(8)). In addition, it is the duty of the chief officer to ensure that the employers of the persons on whom powers are conferred have established and maintain satisfactory arrangements for handling complaints relating to the carrying out of functions under the scheme (s. 40(9)). This is all the more important as the accredited employees will have no formal individual link with the force, either directly (as in the case of designated police employees under parts 1–4 of sch. 4 above) or indirectly (as with employees of contracted-out businesses whose employees are designated under parts 3–4 of the schedule).

Under a CSAS, s. 40 of the Police Reform Act 2002 allows a chief officer to accredit people with certain policing powers. These powers are set out in sch. 5 to the Act.

Schedule 5 to the Police Reform Act 2002—accredited employees

Each of the following paragraphs will only apply if the designation specifically applies it to the employee accredited under an authorised Community Safety Accreditation Scheme, established and maintained under s. 40.

Power to issue fixed penalty notices—paragraph 1

The powers below may be conferred on an Accredited Employee in relation to any individual who the employee has reason to believe has committed a relevant fixed penalty offence at a place within the relevant police area. Those powers are:

(a) the power of a constable in uniform to give a person a fixed penalty notice under s. 54 of the Road Traffic Offenders Act 1988 (fixed penalty notices—**see para. 2.5.1**) in respect of an offence under s. 72 of the Highway Act 1835 (riding on a footway—**see chapter 3**) committed by cycling;

(b) the power of an authorised officer of a local authority to give a notice under s. 4 of the Dogs (Fouling of Land) Act 1996 (fixed penalty notices in respect of dog fouling—**see chapter 3**); and

(c) the power of an authorised officer of a litter authority to give a notice under s. 88 of the Environmental Protection Act 1990 (fixed penalty notices in respect of litter—**see chapter 3**)

(para. 1(2)).
'Relevant fixed penalty offence' = an offence which—

• is an offence by reference to which a notice may be given to a person in exercise of any of the powers mentioned in (a) to (c) above and

• is specified or described in the Accredited Employee's accreditation as an offence he/she has been designated to enforce

(para. 1(3)).

Power to require giving of name and address—paragraph 2

Under this paragraph, where an Accredited Employee has reason to believe that another person has committed a relevant offence in the relevant police area, he/she may require that other person to give his/her name and address. 'Relevant offence' = any offence which is—

• a relevant fixed penalty offence for the purposes of the application of paragraph 1 above; or

• an offence the commission of which appears to the Accredited Employee to have caused—

i) injury, alarm or distress to any other person; or

ii) the loss of, or any damage to, any other person's property

(para. 2(3)).
Note that an accreditation applying this paragraph to an Accredited Employee may provide that an offence is not to be treated as a 'relevant offence' unless some other specified conditions are satisfied.

Power to require name and address of person acting in an anti-social manner—paragraph 3

Under this paragraph an Accredited Employee will, in the relevant police area, have the powers of a constable in uniform under s. 50 to require a person whom he/she has reason to believe to have been acting, or to be acting, in an anti-social manner (within the meaning of s. 1 of the Crime and Disorder Act 1998—anti-social behaviour orders—**see chapter 3**) to give his/her name *and* address (para. 3(1)).

Powers relating to alcohol consumption in designated public places—paragraph 4

Under this paragraph an Accredited Employee will have the powers of a constable under s. 12 of the Criminal Justice and Police Act 2001 (alcohol consumption in public places—**see**) in the relevant police area—

(a) to impose a requirement under subsection (2) of that section; and

(b) to dispose under subsection (3) of that section of anything surrendered to him/her;

and that section will have effect in relation to the exercise of those powers by that Accredited Employee as if the references to a constable in subsections (1) and (5) were references to the Accredited Employee.

Power to confiscate alcohol—paragraph 5

Under this paragraph an Accredited Employee will have the powers of a constable under s. 1 of the Confiscation of Alcohol (Young Persons) Act 1997 (confiscation of intoxicating liquor—**see chapter 11**) in the relevant police area—

(a)  to impose a requirement under subsection (1) of that section; and

(b)  to dispose under subsection (2) of that section of anything surrendered to him/her;

and that section shall have effect in relation to the exercise of those powers by that Accredited Employee as if the references to a constable in subsections (1) and (4) (but not the reference in subsection (5) (power of arrest)) were references to the Accredited Employee.

Power to confiscate tobacco—paragraph 6

Under this paragraph an Accredited Employee will have within the relevant police area—

(a)  the power to seize anything that a constable in uniform has a duty to seize under subsection (3) of s. 7 of the Children and Young Persons Act 1933 (seizure of tobacco etc. from young persons-**see Crime**); and

(b)  the power to dispose of anything that a constable may dispose of under that subsection;

and the power to dispose of anything shall be a power to dispose of it in such manner as the Accredited Employee's employer may direct.

Powers to deal with abandoned vehicles—paragraph 7

Under this paragraph an Accredited Employee will have all such powers in the relevant police area as are conferred on people accredited under that section by regulations under s. 99 of the Road Traffic Regulation Act 1984 (removal of abandoned vehicles—**see Road Traffic**).

Power to stop vehicles for testing—paragraph 8

Under this paragraph an Accredited Employee will have the power of a constable in uniform to stop a vehicle under s. 67(3) the Road Traffic Act 1988 (**see Road Traffic**) within the relevant police area for the purposes of a test under s. 67(1) of that section.

Power to control traffic for purposes of escorting a load of exceptional dimensions—paragraph 9

Under this paragraph an Accredited Employee will have, for the purpose of escorting a vehicle or trailer carrying a load of exceptional dimensions either to or from the relevant police area, the power of a constable engaged in the regulation of traffic in a road—

(a)  to direct a vehicle to stop;

(b)  to make a vehicle proceed in, or keep to, a particular line of traffic; and

(c)  to direct pedestrians to stop

(para. 9(1)).

Sections 35 and 37 of the Road Traffic Act 1988 (offences of failing to comply with directions of constable engaged in regulation of traffic in a road—**see Road Traffic**) will have effect in relation to the exercise of those powers by an Accredited Employee as if the references to a constable engaged in regulation of traffic in a road were references to that Accredited Employee (para. 9(2)) and will have effect in any police area in England and Wales (para. 9(3)).

'Vehicle or trailer carrying a load of exceptional dimensions' = a vehicle or trailer the use of which is authorised by an order made by the Secretary of State under s. 44(1)(d) of the Road Traffic Act 1988 (para. 9(4)).

---

OFFENCE: **Failing to comply with requirements—*Police Reform Act 2002, Schedule 5, para. 2(2)***

• Triable summarily  •  Fine

The Police Reform Act 2002, sch. 5, para. 2(2) states

(2)  A person who fails to comply with a requirement under sub-paragraph (1) is guilty of an offence.

---

**KEYNOTE**

This offence is similar to those created by sch. 4 (**see para. 2.14.2**) In making the requirement it will be critical that the accredited person produces their authority and that, if relevant they are in the correct uniform and wearing the proper badge etc.

---

2.14.5 **General considerations for designated or accredited employees**

A designated or accredited employee empowered under the Police Reform Act 2002 exercising any powers granted thereunder in relation to any person must produce their authority to that person if requested to do so (s. 42(1)). Their powers are only exercisable if the employee is wearing the relevant uniform as determined or approved by the chief officer and identified or described in the designation/accreditation (s. 42(2)). Any designation or accreditation will specify the extent, nature and duration of the powers conferred by it and also any uniform that the employee is required to wear. In the case of an accredited employee (i.e. acting under the authority of sch. 5 of the Act) he or she must also be wearing an appropriate badge as specified by the Secretary of State in the manner or place specified (s. 42(2)).

A chief officer of police may modify or withdraw an employee's designation or accreditation *at any time* simply by giving the employee notice (s. 42(3)). This power of revocation or amendment is absolute and there is no requirement for any misconduct or poor performance on the part of the employee. The same power applies to the Directors General of NCIS and the NCS (s. 42(4)). If a designation or accreditation is modified of withdrawn, the chief officer (or Director General) must send a copy of the notice to the relevant employer (see s. 42(5)–(6)).

Any liability for civil wrongs (torts) arising out of conduct in the course of an employee's designation or accreditation will be apportioned jointly between the police authority (or Service Authority in the case of NCIS and the NCS), the employer and the individual (see s. 42). This should make life interesting, particularly in the areas of remedies and the application of the Human Rights Act 1998.

2.14.6 **Use of force**

The use of force by police officers is a contentious area that has kept—and will no doubt continue to keep—the courts, litigants and their representatives busy for decades. The use of force by non—sworn personnel carrying out policing functions (the 'extended police family' members) is likely to be at least as contentious, if not more so. There are two main sources of a designated employee's power to use reasonable force. The first source is the specific power granted under sch. 4 to the Police Reform Act 2002 as set out earlier. The second source is to be found in s. 38(6) of the Act. This provides that if a designated employee has a power which, if exercised by a constable, would have a further power to use reasonable force then the designated employee will also have the same entitlement to use reasonable force. For instance, where a constable is exercising powers under the Police and Criminal Evidence Act 1984 where the consent of another person other than a police officer is not needed (e.g. most powers of arrest, search and seizure), s. 117 gives the officer a power to use reasonable force if necessary (**see para. 2.8.4**). If an Investigating Officer designated under part 2 of sch. 4 to the Police Reform Act 2002 uses a power to enter premises following an arrest (per sch. 4, para. 18), he or she will be entitled to use reasonable force if necessary because a constable using the same power to enter and search would also have the power to use reasonable force. However, given the sensitivities around the use of force by the police and other agents of the State, there are further restrictions on the use of force by a designated employee. If, as in the above example, the designated employee uses force to enter premises, that power can *only* be used:

- in the company *and* under the supervision of a constable or
- for the purpose of saving life or limb or preventing serious damage to property

(s. 38(9)).

The accompanying constable in such circumstances can expect to be closely questioned over the extent and effectiveness of their 'supervision' in the event that the matter comes to trial or is investigated following a complaint, report or allegation of misconduct. It is unlikely that the requirements of s. 38(9) would be satisfied by a merely passive physical presence by a constable at a time when the power is exercised and the legislation envisages some form of active and effective supervision by the constable. Similarly, any designated employee using these powers will need to be able to show how the various criteria were met by the particular circumstances at the time.

The general rules and restrictions on the use of force will apply in these cases (**see para. 2.8.4**) and any use of force by a designated employee will come under close scrutiny—particularly where that person is a Detention Officer or Escort Officer employed by a contracted-out business under s. 39.

# PART TWO

# Community Safety

# 3 | Harassment, hostility and anti-social behaviour

## 3.1  Introduction

In addition to the generic policing powers considered in chapter 2, there is a growing list of measures available to police staff and the wider police family to help them preserve safety and quality of life within the community. Driven mainly by the government's efforts in the direction of community safety, effective crime and disorder strategies and, latterly, the assault upon 'yob culture', the legislation affecting policing in this area has grown significantly over the last five years.

This chapter, and the rest of **Part II**, aims to set out the key areas of statutory and common law legislation that are available to address public and individual anxiety, threats to personal safety and anti-social behaviour.

## 3.2  Racially and religiously aggravated offences

Since the offence of inciting racial hatred was created by the Race Relations Act in 1965, various governments have tried to install an effective method by which the criminal law can address offending that is actuated by racism. That, and the many provisions which followed, were found to present a number of practical problems, many relating to the actual or perceived difficulties of proving the various elements of the offences. In addition to the racial hatred offences, there have been other attempts to single out criminal conduct that has an overtly racist element (for example the offences of 'racialist' chanting under the Football (Offences) Act 1991 (**see chapter 4**)).

For whatever reasons, the various measures introduced since 1965 had not succeeded in preventing a rise in the number of reported 'racial incidents' (as defined by ACPO). Although the Home Affairs Select Committee recommended the creation of a new offence of racially motivated violence, the most immediate response was the amendment of the Public Order Act 1986 (under s. 154 of the Criminal Justice and Public Order Act 1994), inserting a new s. 4A. This created a summary offence of intentionally causing harassment, alarm or distress (**see chapter 4**). Again there has been some dissatisfaction as to the extent to which this additional offence (s. 4A) has addressed the behaviour that it was aimed at curbing. More recently, the Stephen Lawrence inquiry focused a great deal of attention on the many potential sources of racism—particularly those that are not immediately apparent on the surface. The inquiry observed (at para. 45.17) that:

> We believe that the use of the words 'racial' and 'racially motivated' are in themselves inaccurate because we all belong to one human race, regardless of our colour, culture or ethnic origin . . .

Consequently, the inquiry recommended (para. 45.17) a new definition of a *racist incident* namely 'any incident which is perceived to be racist by the victim or any other person'.

That definition does not yet appear in any legislation. However, the Crime and Disorder Act 1998 (passed before the report of the Stephen Lawrence inquiry) re-visited the whole issue of racially aggravated crime. Although adopting the use of the expression 'racially aggravated', the Act sought to address many of the issues of criminal law arising from the Stephen Lawrence inquiry. It sets out certain conditions under which specified offences will be deemed to be 'racially aggravated' and increases the powers available to the courts in the punishment of racist offenders.

The 1998 Act was itself amended to incorporate religiously aggravated offending in the aftermath of the terrorist attacks on the United States in 2001.

The Powers of Criminal Courts (Sentencing) Act 2000 allows the courts to take account of any element of racial or religious aggravation in an offence coming before them. Although that section formalises an earlier sentencing decision (*R v Ribbans* (1995) 12 Cr App R(S) 698) in requiring a court to take any element of racial or religious aggravation into account when passing sentence, the new statutory requirement means that the court must also state openly that racial or religious aggravation features of the offence have been taken into consideration.

The requirement under s. 153 applies to *any offence other than the new racially or religiously aggravated offences* created by the Act. It was felt by the legislators that, even though some offences carried a high enough maximum penalty under the existing legislation (examples of which might be arson (**see Crime, chapter 14**) or wounding with intent (**see Crime, chapter 8**), s. 153 would make the courts take account of, and draw attention to, any racial or religious aggravation when determining the appropriate sentence in any particular case.

### 3.2.1   **The offences**

Sections 28–33 of the Crime and Disorder Act 1998 did not so much create *new* offences, but rather took *existing* offences and set out circumstances under which those offences will be deemed to be 'aggravated'. Those offences are:

- wounding or grievous bodily harm—Offences Against the Person Act 1861, s. 20
- causing actual bodily harm—Offences Against the Person Act 1861, s. 47
- common assault—Criminal Justice Act 1988, s. 39

(s. 29; **see Crime, chapter 8**)

- 'simple' criminal damage—Criminal Damage Act 1971, s. 1(1)

(s. 30; **see Crime, chapter 14**)

- causing fear or provocation of violence—Public Order Act 1986, s. 4
- intentional harassment, alarm or distress—Public Order Act 1986, s. 4A
- causing harassment, alarm or distress—Public Order Act 1986, s. 5

(s. 31; **see chapter 4**)

- harassment—Protection from Harassment Act 1997, s. 2
- putting in fear of violence—Protection from Harassment Act 1997, s. 4

(s. 32; **see para. 3.4**).

This area of the law was changed once again after the terrorist attacks of 11 September 2001 by the Anti-terrorism, Crime and Security Act 2001. Part 5 of that Act amended the

Crime and Disorder Act 1998, extending the provisions of what were 'racially aggravated' offences to include 'racially *or religiously* aggravated' offences (as to which, see below).

In order to prove these offences there must be proof of the relevant, substantive offence (e.g. common assault) together with further proof of the aggravating circumstances. Once both conditions have been made out, the offences attract greater maximum penalties and powers. For that reason the specific effects of this legislation are dealt with under the relevant chapters in this Manual.

For a useful discussion of some of the relevant issues here, **see chapter 4**.

### 3.2.2   'Racially or religiously aggravated'

The test for racial or religious aggravation is set out at s. 28 of the Crime and Disorder Act 1998 (s. 28 added by the Anti-Terrorism, Crime and Security Act 2001, s. 39(4)):

(1) An offence is racially or religiously aggravated for the purposes of sections 29 to 32 . . . if—
   (a) at the time of committing the offence, or immediately before or after doing so, the offender demonstrates towards the victim of the offence hostility based on the victim's membership (or presumed membership) of a racial or religious group; or
   (b) the offence is motivated (wholly or partly) by hostility towards members of a racial or religious group based on their membership of that group.

(2) In subsection (1)(a) above—
   'membership', in relation to a racial or religious group, includes association with members of that group; 'presumed' means presumed by the offender.

(3) It is immaterial for the purposes of paragraph (a) or (b) of subsection (1) above whether or not the offender's hostility is also based, to any extent, on any other factor not mentioned in that paragraph.

(4) In this section 'racial group' means a group of persons defined by reference to race, colour, nationality (including citizenship) or ethnic or national origins.

(5) In this section 'religious group' means a group of persons defined by reference to religious belief or lack of religious belief.

---

### KEYNOTE

The aggravating factors for the purposes of s. 28 can be divided into:

- *demonstration* of hostility by the defendant
- *motivation* by hostility of the defendant.

The second type of situation, where the defendant is *motivated* by racial or religious hostility, is the type at which the government's policies to tackle racism are aimed; it is also by far the harder of the two to prove, even though the relevant offence need only be *partly* motivated by racial or religious hostility.

The revised wording of s. 28 (amended after the events of 11 September 2001) now includes 'religious groups'. These will include groups of people defined, not only by their religious belief, but also their *lack* of any such belief.

In a case involving abuse and assault of a doorman, the Administrative Court held that a racial insult uttered a few moments before an assault was enough to make the offence racially aggravated for the purposes of s. 29 of the Crime and Disorder Act 1998. The Court also held that the victim's own perception of the words used was irrelevant, as was the fact that he was not personally upset by the situation. Similarly, the fact that the defendant might have been motivated to utter the words merely by frustration rather than racism was also irrelevant (*DPP* v *Woods* [2002] EWHC Admin 85).

---

### Hostility

Common to both factors under s. 28(1)(a) and (b) is the notion of hostility.

Hostility is not defined. However, in comparison to the problematic expression of 'racial hatred' used in the Public Order Act 1986 (**see para. 3.3**), hostility may well be much easier to identify and prove. The *Oxford English Dictionary* defines 'hostile' as 'of the nature or disposition of an enemy; unfriendly, antagonistic'. It would seem relatively straightforward to show that someone's behaviour in committing the relevant offences was 'unfriendly or antagonistic'. The difficult bit will come when trying to show that the hostility was *based on* the relevant person's membership of a racial or religious group.

### Racial groups

In each case the hostility must be based on the relevant person's membership of a racial group, i.e. membership of a group of people defined by reference to:

- race
- colour
- nationality (including citizenship)
- ethnic origins
- national origins

(s 28(4)).

This definition is the same as that used in the Public Order Act 1986 (see below). It is also very similar to that used in the Race Relations Act 1976. In determining whether or not a group is defined by *ethnic origins*, the courts will have regard to the judgment in the House of Lords in *Mandla* v *Dowell Lee* [1983] 2 AC 548. In that case their Lordships decided that Sikhs were such a group (for the purposes of the Race Relations Act 1976) after considering whether they as a group had:

- a long shared *history*;
- a *cultural tradition* of their own, including family and social customs and manners, often, but not necessarily, associated with religious observance;
- either a *common geographical origin* or descent from a small number of *common ancestors*;
- a *common language*, not necessarily peculiar to that group;
- a *common literature* peculiar to that group;
- a *common religion* different from that of neighbouring groups or the general community surrounding the group; and
- the characteristic of being a *minority* or an *oppressed* or a *dominant* group within a larger community.

Lord Fraser's *dictum* suggests that the first two characteristics above are essential in defining an 'ethnic group', while the others are at least relevant. His Lordship also approved a decision from New Zealand to the effect that Jews are a group with common ethnic origins (*Kings-Ansell* v *Police* [1979] 2 NZLR 531).

### Religion

Lord Fraser's sixth point above refers to religion as a possible defining characteristic of an ethnic group. Although this was a notable omission from the ambit of *racial groups* as defined under the original s. 28(4) of the Crime and Disorder Act 1998, religious groups have now been included as a result of the Anti-terrorsim, Crime and Security Act 2001. This means that the former case law (mostly arising in an employment context) over whether religious groups could also be regarded as racial groups is largely irrelevant. The change means that a purely religious group such as Rastafarians (who have been held not to be members of an ethnic group *per se* (*Dawkins* v *Crown Suppliers (Property Services Agency)* (1993) *The Times*, 4 February; [1993] ICR 517) are now covered by the aggravated forms of offences. In reality, a number of racial groups will overlap with religious groups in any event—Rastafarians would be a good example. An attack on a Rastafarian might be a racially aggravated offence under s 28 because it was based on the defendant's hostility towards a *racial group* (e.g. African-Caribbeans) into which many Rastafarians fall. Alternatively, an attack might be made on a white Rastafarian based on the victim's religious beliefs (or lack of religious beliefs), i.e. his 'membership of a religious group'. Muslims have also been held not to be a racial group (*J.H. Walker* v *Hussain* [1996] ICR 291) but Muslims are clearly members of a religious group and, as such, are now covered by the Act.

Note that there is some disparity here between the recognition of religion for these specific purposes and those that appear under Article 9 of the European Convention on Human Rights (as to which **see chapter 2**).

Although the offences that were made 'racially aggravated' by the Crime and Disorder Act 1998 now include religiously aggravated features as well, the proposal to create a specific offence of incitement to religious hatred by the government was withdrawn. At the time of writing the House of Lords announced a select committee to investigate this area of law more fully. Similarly, the civil legislation outlawing discrimination (as to which **see chapter 12**) against will come into force at the end of this year religious groups.

### Other racial groups

Traditional 'gypsies' (as opposed to travellers) are capable of being a racial group on the basis of ethnic origin (*Commission for Racial Equality* v *Dutton* [1989] QB 783). English and Scottish people have been held to constitute groups defined by reference to national origins and thus as members of 'racial groups' in the broad sense as defined and protected from discrimination under the Race Relations Act 1976 (*Northern Joint Police Board* v *Power* [1997] IRLR 610). This decision ought logically to extend to Irish and Welsh people.

### Membership

An important extension of 'racial or religious groups' lies in the inclusion of people who associate with members of that group. 'Membership' *for the purposes of s. 28(1)(a)* will include *association* with members of that group (a slightly circular definition) (s 28(2)). This means that a white man who has a black female partner would potentially fall within the category of a 'member' of her racial group—and vice versa. Moreover, people who work within certain racial or religious groups within the community could also be regarded as members of those groups for these purposes.

*For the purposes of s. 28(1)(a)*, 'membership' will also include anyone *presumed by the defendant* to be a member of a racial or religious group. Therefore, if a defendant wrongly presumed that a person was a member of a racial or religious group, say a Pakistani Muslim, and assaulted them as a result, the defendant's *presumption* would be enough to make his/her behaviour 'racially or religiously aggravated', even though the victim was in fact an Indian Hindu.

Such a presumption would not extend to the aggravating factors under s. 28(1)(b). The only apparent reason for this would seem to be that the s. 28(1)(a) offence requires hostility to be demonstrated towards a particular person ('the victim') while the offence under

s. 28(1)(b) envisages hostility towards members of a racial or religious group generally and does not require a specific victim.

Section 28(3) goes on to provide that it is immaterial whether the defendant's hostility (in either case under s. 28(1)) is also based to any extent on *any other factor*.

This concession in s. 28(3) only prevents the defendant pointing to another *factor* in order to explain his/her behaviour in committing the relevant offence (assault, criminal damage, etc.). Although it removes the opportunity for a defendant to argue that his/her behaviour was as a result of other factors (e.g. arising out of a domestic dispute), the subsection does not remove the burden on the prosecution to show that the defendant either demonstrated racial or religious hostility or was motivated by it.

### Demonstration of Hostility

Under s. 28(1)(a) it must be shown that the defendant *demonstrated* the required hostility:

- at the time of the offence
- immediately before, or
- immediately after committing the offence.

No guidance is given as to how *immediately* will be interpreted. It is submitted that whether a defendant's demonstration of hostility came immediately before or after the relevant offence will be a question of fact to be decided in light of all the circumstances.

In deciding the issue of immediacy the courts will have to consider the degree of proximity between the defendant's demonstration of racial or religious hostility and the relevant offence itself. It is submitted that the degree of proximity will have to be very high before the defendant's hostility could be shown to have been *immediately* before or after the *actus reus* of the offence. This might cause problems with offences that are said to be 'continuing' or 'ongoing'.

In the context of the offence under s. 4 of the Public Order Act 1986 (**see para. 4.8.1**) the Divisional Court held that, where a court finds that the defendant has committed an offence under s 4 and used racist, threatening and abusive words, it is immaterial for the purposes of s. 28(1)(a) of the 1998 Act that the defendant might have had additional reasons for using that language (*DPP* v *McFarlane* [2002] EWHC 485).

It is also necessary, for the purposes of s. 28(1)(a), to show that the defendant demonstrated his/her hostility *towards the victim of the offence*. Again this may be problematic in relation to certain offences, e.g. criminal damage (**see Crime, chapter 14**).

Racially or religiously aggravated offences can be committed where the aggravating behaviour is directed at or towards a police officer and police officers are entitled to the protection offered by this offence in the same way as any other person (see *R* v *Jacobs* (2000) *The Times*, 28 December).

## 3.3 Other offences involving racism: racial hatred

In addition to the racially or religiously aggravated offences discussed above—and elsewhere in this Manual—there are still several former offences under earlier legislation. Few prosecutions took place under these headings before the passing of the Crime and Disorder Act 1998. However, the Anti-terrorism, Crime and Security Act 2001 has focused greater attention on this area of law: what follows is a summary of the offences.

The Public Order Act 1986 introduced several offences aimed at addressing incidents specifically motivated by racial hatred.

For these purposes 'racial hatred' means hatred against a group of persons defined by reference to colour, race, nationality (including citizenship) or ethnic or national origins (s. 17). This area of criminal law was not specifically extended to cover religious groups.

### 3.3.1 Use of words, behaviour or display of written material

OFFENCE: **Use of words or behaviour or display of written material—*Public Order Act 1986, s. 18***

- Triable either way • Seven years' imprisonment and/or a fine on indictment; six months' imprisonment and/or a fine summarily

*(Arrestable offence)*

The Public Order Act 1986, s. 18 states:

(1) A person who uses threatening, abusive or insulting words or behaviour, or displays any written material which is threatening, abusive or insulting, is guilty of an offence if—
   (a) he intends thereby to stir up racial hatred, or
   (b) having regard to all the circumstances racial hatred is likely to be stirred up thereby.

(2) An offence under this section may be committed in a public or a private place, except that no offence is committed where the words or behaviour are used, or the written material is displayed, by a person inside a dwelling and are not heard or seen except by other persons in that or another dwelling.

---

**KEYNOTE**

This, and the other offences under this part of the Act, may not be prosecuted without the consent of the Attorney-General (or Solicitor-General).

Generally, in order to prove these offences, you must show that a defendant:

- *intended* to stir up racial hatred; or

- that he/she *intended* the relevant words, behaviour or material to be threatening, abusive or insulting; or

- that he/she *was aware* that the relevant words/behaviour/material might be threatening, abusive or insulting.

This offence does not apply to broadcasts in a programme (but see below) and there are exemptions in the case of fair and accurate reports of parliamentary or court proceedings.

Although recently mode on arrestable offence by virtue of its sentence, this offence at the time of writing also had a specific power of arrest for constables (see s. 18(3) ).

---

### Defence

The Public Order Act 1986, s. 18 states:

(4) In proceedings for an offence under this section it is a defence for the accused to prove that he was inside a dwelling and had no reason to believe that the words or behaviour used, or the written material displayed, would be heard or seen by a person outside that or any other dwelling.

### Power of arrest

The Public Order Act 1986, s 18 states:

(3) A constable may arrest without warrant anyone he reasonably suspects is committing an offence under this section.

3.3.2 **Publishing or distributing written material**

OFFENCE: **Publishing or distributing written material—*Public Order Act 1986, s. 19***
- Triable either way • Seven years' imprisonment and/or a fine on indictment; six months' imprisonment and/or a fine summarily.
*(Arrestable offence)*

The Public Order Act 1986, s. 19 states:

(1) A person who publishes or distributes written material which is threatening, abusive or insulting is guilty of an offence if—
(a) he intends thereby to stir up racial hatred, or
(b) having regard to all the circumstances racial hatred is likely to be stirred up thereby.

(2) . . .

(3) References in this Part to the publication or distribution of written material are to its publication or distribution to the public or a section of the public.

---

**KEYNOTE**

This offence has attracted more prominence in the last 12 months and its penalty was increased, along with those for other offences under this part of the Act, by the Anti-terrorism, Crime and Security Act 2001.

Prosecution of this offence needs the consent of the Attorney-General (or Solicitor-General).

---

Defence

The Public Order Act 1986, s. 19 states:

(2) In proceedings for an offence under this section it is a defence for an accused who is not shown to have intended to stir up racial hatred to prove that he was not aware of the content of the material and did not suspect, and had no reason to suspect, that it was threatening, abusive or insulting.

3.3.3 **Other offences under part III**

Other Public Order Act 1986 offences involving activities intended or likely to stir up racial hatred are:

- presenting or directing a public performance of a play—s. 20
- distributing, showing or playing recordings—s. 21
- providing, producing, directing or appearing in a programme service—s. 22
- possessing written material or recordings with a view to displaying, publishing, distributing and playing in a programme service—s. 23.

Each of these offences is triable either way, carries seven years' imprisonment and has its own specific statutory defence.

3.4 **Protection from harassment**

The Protection from Harassment Act 1997 was introduced after a number of highly-publicised cases of stalking. Although intended for such situations, the Act's extensive provisions have been applied—and interpreted—widely. In passing the legislation set out below, the government anticipated prosecutions under the 1997 Act to be only several hundred; in fact, many thousands of prosecutions have been brought and the following legislation can be a useful and potent tool for the police.

Some of the 1997 Act's most sweeping provisions have been brought into force by the Crime and Disorder Act 1998.

### 3.4.1 The offences

OFFENCE: **Harassment—*Protection from Harassment Act 1997, ss. 1 and 2***
- Triable summarily • Six months' imprisonment and/or a fine

*(Arrestable offence)*

OFFENCE: **Racially or religiously aggravated harrassment—*Crime and Disorder Act 1998, s. 32(1)(a)***
- Triable either way • Two years' imprisonment and/or a fine on indictment; six months' imprisonment and/or a fine summarily

*(Arrestable offence)*

The Protection from Harassment Act 1997, ss. 1 and 2 state:

1.—(1) A person must not pursue a course of conduct—
    (a) which amounts to harassment of another, and
    (b) which he knows or ought to know amounts to harassment of the other.

2.—(1) A person who pursues a course of conduct in breach of section 1 is guilty of an offence.

---

**KEYNOTE**

This offence is made an 'arrestable offence' (see chapter 2) by s. 2(3).

The racially or religiously aggravated offence is made an arrestable offence by s. 32(2) of the Crime and Disorder Act 1998 which adds it to those offences listed under s. 24(2) of the Police and Criminal Evidence Act 1984 (see chapter 2).

Unlike some of the other racially or religiously aggravated offences (see below and **Crime, chapters 8 and 14**), provisions are specifically made for alternative verdicts in relation to harassment (see s. 32(5) ).

For a full explanation of the meaning of 'racially or religiously aggravated', **see para. 3.2.**

'Harassment' includes alarming the person or causing them distress (s. 7(1) of the 1997 Act).

The inclusion of alarm or distress is significant as it has been held by the Divisional Court that a person—in this case, a police officer—can be alarmed for the safety of another (*Lodge* v *DPP [1989] COS 179*).

The deceptively simple wording of the definition for a 'course of conduct' has caused a surprising number of problems for the courts—and defendants. 'Course of conduct' must involve conduct on at least two occasions but it can involve speech (s. 7(3) and (4) ). The issue of whether two acts of harassment against two different victims would suffice for an offence under s 2 was raised in *DPP* v *Williams (Michael)*, [1998] CLY 954. In that case the defendant had reached in through an open bathroom window while one woman was taking a shower and had then climbed onto a roof to see the woman and a friend through a bedroom window. Unfortunately, the Divisional Court held that there was no need to construe the wording of the Act as one of the women had been involved in both incidents. It is arguable that, under the terms of s. 6 of the Interpretation Act 1978, the requirements of the offence could be met where there are two separate victims. However, this issue was considered again by the Divisional Court in *Lau* v *DPP* [2000] Crim LR 580. In that case the 'course of conduct' involved a battery (slapping across the face) against the complainant on one occasion, followed some time later by a threat being made to the complainant's boyfriend in her presence. In *Lau* the court held that the evidence of a 'course of conduct' by the defendant was insufficient to convict. The court also said that, in determining whether such a course of conduct had been made out, regard should be had to the number of incidents and the relative times when they took place—the fewer the incidents and the further apart in time that they took place, the less likely it was that a court would find that harassment had taken place. What the court did decide in *Williams,* however, was that the offence was not restricted to acts of 'stalking'.

In *King* v *DPP* (2000) *The Independent*, 31 July, the Divisional Court considered the situation where a number of incidents had taken place and it was alleged that they amounted to a 'course of conduct'. The court held that, although some individual incidents may not amount to harassment in themselves, they could form a background against which further events were to be viewed. In the particular case the defendant had approached the victim to strike up conversations and had sent her a gift. The court accepted that, *on their particular facts*, these incidents were not enough to constitute harassment or a course of conduct amounting to harassment. They did, however, provide a background against which the defendant's later behaviour—covertly filming the victim and rummaging through her rubbish—and his state of mind could be considered. The court went on to say that the defendant's filming the victim (even though she had not been aware of it) and rummaging through her rubbish were acts that were capable of amounting to harassment or part of a course of conduct amounting to harassment.

On occasions the courts have accepted that two instances of behaviour by the defendant several months apart will suffice. So, where a defendant wrote two threatening letters to a member of the Benefits Agency staff, he was convicted of harassment even though there had been four and a half months' interval between the two letters. In that case the Divisional Court also refused to endorse the view that people in such public service posts were expected to be more robust and therefore less likely to be distressed or frightened by the content of such personal communications (*Baron* v *Crown Prosecution Service*, 13 June 2000, unreported).

But what of the opposite type of conduct, where the acts complained of are so close together that they are alleged to be one continuing act? What if a defendant makes several calls to the victim's mobile phone in the space of five minutes—is this a 'course of conduct'? According to the High Court in *R* v *Kelly* [2002] EWHC Admin 1428, magistrates were entitled to find that it was. But what if, instead of answering the phone as the calls were made, the victim later listened to the abusive and threatening messages left by the defendant on her voicemail facility, replaying each message one after the other? Again, these were the facts in *Kelly* above and the magistrates were entitled to find that this still amounted to a course of conduct. In addition, the Court held that it was enough that the victim was alarmed or distressed by the course of conduct as a whole rather than by each act making up the course of conduct. This is a different requirement from the more serious offence under s. 4 (see below) where the victim must be caused to fear violence on at least two occasions.

*There is no specific requirement that the activity making up the course of conduct be of the same nature. Therefore two distinctly different types of behaviour by the defendant (e.g. making a telephone call on one occasion and damaging the victim's property on another) may suffice. In a case involving the racially or religiously aggravated offence, the aggravating element will need to be proved in relation to both instances of the defendant's conduct.*

Some behaviour will be sufficiently disturbing or alarming for two instances alone to suffice' (e.g. the making of overt threats). If sufficiently alarming or distressing, the behaviour may also amount to an offence in itself under some other legislation (**see Crime chapter 8**). Other behaviour, however, may not be sufficient to establish 'harassment' after only two occasions (e.g. the sending of flowers and gifts) and may require more than the bare statutory minimum of two occasions.

Although it may be helpful in terms of proving the occurrence of two or more acts amounting to 'a course of conduct', the practice in some police areas of issuing warnings and maintaining a register of the same (particularly in relation to their own officers) is not a specific requirement of the Act and may raise some issues of procedural fairness.

A limited company cannot be the 'victim' of harassment, although an individual employee or a clearly defined group of individuals could be—*DPP* v *Dziurzynski* [2002] EWHC 1380.

The definition of harassment in s. 7 of the Protection from Harassment Act 1997 is an inclusive but not exhaustive list. Although the words used in s. 7 are 'alarm *and* distress', the Divisional Court has held that they should be taken disjunctively and not conjunctively, that is, the court need only be satisfied that the behaviour involved one or the other; alarm *or* distress (*DPP* v *Ramsdale* [2001] EWHC Admin 106).

All in all this has turned out to be a very prosecution-friendly piece of legislation extending to behaviour far beyond that which was probably envisaged by its authors.

The repeated commission of other offences (say, public order offences or offences against property) involving the same victim may also amount to harassment. In such cases the advice of the Crown Prosecution Service should be sought as to which *charge(s) to prefer*.

In short, in order to prove this offence you must show that:

- the defendant pursued a 'course of conduct',

- the course of conduct amounted to harassment as defined in s. 7(1), and

- the defendant knew, or ought to have known, that his/her conduct amounted to harassment.

To avoid the practical difficulties of proving the subjective *intention* of the defendant, the offence focuses on an objective test.

---

In addition, s. 1(2) states:

(2)  For the purposes of this section, the person whose course of conduct is in question ought to know that it amounts to harassment of another if a reasonable person in possession of the same information would think the course of conduct amounted to harassment of the other.

---

**KEYNOTE**

Section 1(2) requires the jury/court to consider whether the defendant ought to have known that his/her conduct amounted to harassment by the objective test of what a 'reasonable person' would think. Section 1(3)(c) also imposes an objective test as to whether that conduct was reasonable in the judgment of the jury/court. As a result, the Court of Appeal has held that no characteristics of the defendant can be attached to the word 'reasonable' (*R* v *Colohan* [2001] Crim LR 845).

Although the defendant's mental illness may be relevant to sentence, the protective and preventative nature of the Act together with the objective nature of the tests above means that such illness does not provide a defence. (Contrast the relevance of a defendant's personal characteristics in the defences of duress and provocation—**see Crime, chapter 4.**)

---

Aiding and abetting

As a result of incidents against the directors and staff of life science research companies, the Protection from Harassment Act 1997 was amended (see the Criminal Justice and Police Act 2001, s. 44). Those changes mean that if someone aids, abets, counsels or procures another to commit an offence under the 1997 Act, the conduct of the 'primary' defendant will be taken to be the conduct of the aider, abettor, counsellor or procurer of the offence. This does not prevent the primary defendant's conduct from being relevant; what it does is to make the aider, abettor, etc. of the offence liable for the conduct which he/she has facilitated. The 2001 Act also makes provision for determining the knowledge and intention of aiders, abettors, etc. Although the Act refers to this area as 'collective harassment', it overlaps with the whole concept of incomplete offences (**see Crime, chapter 3**) and the advice of the Crown Prosecution Service should be sought in formulating appropriate charges.

If the person concerned in the course of conduct can show that he/she did so:

- for the purpose of preventing or detecting crime, or

- under any enactment or rule of law to comply with a particular requirement, or

- in circumstances whereby the course of conduct was reasonable

the offence under s. 1(1) will not apply (s. 1(3) ).

The burden of proving any of these features or circumstances lies with the defendant (on the balance of probabilities, **see Evidence and Procedure, chapter 11**).

Examples might be police or DSS surveillance teams, or court officers serving summonses. (See also the defence under s. 12 below.)

Whether a course of conduct is 'reasonable' will be a question of fact for a court to decide in the light of all the circumstances. The wording of s. 1(2) suggests that such a test might be an *objective* one (i.e. as a reasonable bystander) and not one based upon the particular belief or perception of the defendant—otherwise the main effect of the 1997 Act would be considerably diluted.

For the powers of a court to issue a restraining order or injunction in relation to this offence, see below.

Under s. 3(1) conduct or apprehended conduct falling within s. 1 may be the subject of a civil claim by the victim/intended victim. This creates a 'statutory tort' of harassment in addition to the criminal offence.

OFFENCE: **Putting people in fear of violence—*Protection from Harassment Act 1997, s. 4***
- Triable either way • Five years' imprisonment and/or a fine on indictment; six months' imprisonment and/or a fine summarily
*(Arrestable offence)*

OFFENCE: **Racially or religiously aggravated—*Crime and Disorder Act 1998, s. 32(1)(b)***
- Triable either way • Seven years' imprisonment and/or a fine on indictment; six months' imprisonment and/or a fine summarily
*(Arrestable offence)*

The Protection from Harassment Act 1997, s. 4 states:

(1) A person whose course of conduct causes another to fear, on at least two occasions, that violence will be used against him is guilty of an offence if he knows or ought to know that his course of conduct will cause the other so to fear on each of those occasions.

---

**KEYNOTE**

'Course of conduct' is discussed above.

The defendant's course of conduct must cause the victim to fear that violence *will* (rather than might) be used against him or her. This is quite a strict requirement and showing that the conduct caused the victim to be seriously frightened of what might happen in the future is not enough (*R* v *Henley* [2002] Crim LR 582).

You must show that the defendant knew, or ought to have known that their conduct would cause the other person to fear violence. This may be shown by any previous conversations or communications between the defendant and the victim, together with the victim's response to the defendant's earlier behaviour (e.g. running away, calling the police, etc.).

The fear of violence being used against the victim must be present on both occasions. If it is present on one occasion but not the other, the offence under s. 2 above may be appropriate.

The course of conduct for the purpose of s. 4 has to cause a person to fear, on at least two occasions, that violence would be used against *him/her* rather than against a member of their family (*Mohammed Ali Caurti* v *DPP* [2002] Crim LR 131).

For a full explanation of the meaning of 'racially or religiously aggravated', **see para. 3.2.**

Unlike some of the other racially or religiously aggravated offences (**see Crime, chapters 8 and 14**), provisions are specifically made for alternative verdicts in relation to harassment (see s. 32(6)). Where the racially or religiously aggravated form of the offence is charged, the aggravating element of the defendant's conduct must be shown in relation to both instances.

As with the s. 2 offence, a single instance of behaviour may be enough to support a charge for another offence (e.g. assault, **see Crime, chapter 8**, or threats to kill, see below).

Again, this offence is not one of *intent* but one which is subject to a test of reasonableness against the standard of an ordinary person in possession of the same information as the defendant.

For the powers of a court to issue a restraining order or injunction in relation to this offence, see below.

For the police power to give directions in relation to the behaviour of people in the vicinity of dwellings, see chapter 4.

---

Section 4 goes on to state:

(2) For the purposes of this section, the person whose course of conduct is in question ought to know that it will cause another to fear that violence will be used against him on any occasion if a reasonable person in possession of the same information would think the course of conduct would cause the other so to fear on that occasion.

### Defence

Section 4(3) states:

(3) It is a defence for a person charged with an offence under this section to show that—
  (a) his course of conduct was pursued for the purpose of preventing or detecting crime,
  (b) his course of conduct was pursued under any enactment or rule of law or to comply with any condition or requirement imposed by any person under any enactment, or
  (c) the pursuit of his course of conduct was reasonable for the protection of himself or another or for the protection of his or another's property.

---

**KEYNOTE**

There is a slight difference in the wording of the defence when compared to that under s. 1(3) above. There, the defendant may show that his/her conduct was reasonable in the particular circumstances. In relation to the more serious offence under s. 4, the defendant must show that his/her conduct was reasonable *for the protection of themselves, another person or their own/another's property*. These are the only grounds on which the defendant may argue reasonableness in answer to a charge under s. 4. He/she could not therefore argue, say, that the pursuit of the course of conduct was 'reasonable' in order to enforce a debt or to communicate with the victim.

In addition, s. 12 allows for the Secretary of State to certify that the conduct was carried out by a 'specified person' on a 'specified occasion' related to:

- national security,
- the economic well-being of the UK, or
- the prevention or detection of serious crime

on behalf of the Crown. If such a certification is made, the conduct of the specified person will not be an offence under the 1997 Act.

---

3.4.2    **Injunctions**

Under s. 3(1) of the Protection from Harassment Act 1997, the High Court or a county court may issue an injunction in respect of civil proceedings brought in respect of an actual or apprehended breach of s. 1. The effect of this is that a defendant may be made the subject of an injunction even though his/her behaviour has not amounted to an offence under the 1997 Act.

Section 3(3) states:

(3) Where—
  (a) in such proceedings the High Court or a county court grants an injunction for the purpose of restraining the defendant from pursuing any conduct which amounts to harassment, and
  (b) the plaintiff considers that the defendant has done anything which he is prohibited from doing by the injunction,

the plaintiff may apply for the issue of a warrant for the arrest of the defendant.

N.B.: Amendment not yet in force.

**KEYNOTE**

Anyone arrested under such a warrant may be dealt with by the court at the time of his/her appearance. Alternatively, the court may adjourn the proceedings and release the defendant, dealing with him/her within 14 days of his/her arrest provided the defendant is given not less than two days' notice of the adjourned hearing (see the Rules of the Supreme Court (Amendment) 1998 (SI 1998 No. 1898) and the County Court (Amendment) Rules 1998 (SI 1998 No. 1899)).

This is in contrast to some other injunctions (e.g. under the Family Law Act 1996 (**see chapter 7**) and the Housing Act 1996 (**see chapter 9**)). In a case involving an injunction restraining the actions of an anti-vivisection group, the Divisional Court held that the 1997 Act was not a means of preventing individuals from exercising their right to protest over issues of public interest. Eady J said that such an extension of the law had clearly not been Parliament's intention and that the courts would resist any attempts to interpret the Act widely (*Huntingdon Life Sciences Ltd* v *Curtin*, The Times, 11 December 1997).

Of far greater significance is the offence created by s. 3(6) of the Protection from Harassment Act 1997.

OFFENCE: **Breach of Injunction—*Protection from Harassment Act 1997, s. 3(6)***
       • Triable either way • Five years' imprisonment and/or a fine on indictment;
        six months' imprisonment and/or a fine summarily
       *(Arrestable offence)*

The Protection from Harassment Act 1997, s. 3(6) states:

(6) Where—
    (a) the High Court or a county court grants an injunction for the purpose mentioned in subsection (3)(a), and
    (b) without reasonable excuse the defendant does anything which he is prohibited from doing by the injunction, he is guilty of an offence.

**KEYNOTE**

Civil injunctions generally will only involve the police where a power of an arrest has been attached (e.g. under s. 3(3) above). In these cases the role of the police will be to bring the defendant before the court in order that he/she can explain his/her behaviour. There is therefore no investigative or prosecuting function on the part of the officers. Section 3(6), however, creates a specific offence of breaching the terms of an injunction. Like the Anti-Social Behaviour Order (ASBO) (see below) and Sex Offender Order (SOO) (**see Crime, chapter 10**) this marked a new concept in the criminal law.

If a defendant breaches an injunction and commits the offence under s. 3(6) above, he/she will be dealt with in the way of any other prisoner brought into police detention and will face a prison sentence of five years.

It is important to distinguish the offence under s. 3(6), breaching an injunction, from the provisions of s. 5 which deal with restraining orders.

### 3.4.3 Restraining orders

Section 5 of the Protection from Harassment Act 1997 provides that a court dealing with a person convicted of an offence under s. 2 or 4 may make an order (a restraining order). Such an order can only be made after a defendant's conviction for an offence under s. 2 or 4 of the 1997 Act. It is therefore much more limited than the injunction discussed above.

Section 5(2) goes on to state:

(2) The order may, for the purpose of protecting the victim of the offence, or any other person mentioned in the order, from further conduct which—

(a) amounts to harassment, or

(b) will cause a fear of violence, prohibit the defendant from doing anything described in the order.

---

**KEYNOTE**

The purpose behind these orders is to empower the courts to restrain the conduct of offenders following their conviction—an area that was previously seen as one of particular weakness in the criminal justice system.

Unlike the injunction under s. 3(3), restraining orders can be made in a criminal court.

The order may be made for the protection of the victim or anyone else mentioned and it may run for a specified period or until a further order. Any order must identify by name the parties it is intended to protect (*R* v *Mann* (2000) 97(14) LS Gaz 4).

In a case arising out of protests against fur retailers, the Divisional Court held that restraining orders under the 1997 Act did not generally breach the right to freedom of speech and association as protected by Articles 10 and 11 of the European Convention (as to which, **see chapter 2**) (*Silverton* v *Gravett* (2001) LTL 31 October).

The prosecutor, the defendant or anyone else mentioned in the order may apply to the court that made it to have the order varied or discharged (s. 5(4)).

---

OFFENCE:   **Breach of restraining order—*Protection from Harassment Act 1997, s. 5(5)***

- Triable either way • Five years' imprisonment and/or a fine on indictment;
  six months' imprisonment and/or a fine summarily
  *(Arrestable offence)*

The Protection from Harassment Act 1997, s. 5(5) states:

(5) If without reasonable excuse the defendant does anything which he is prohibited from doing by an order under this section, he is guilty of an offence.

---

**KEYNOTE**

The fact that restraining orders can only be made after a conviction for one of the offences under s. 2 or 4 may affect decisions when selecting appropriate charges arising out of an incident. Substituting or failing to include a charge under s. 2 or 4, removes the court's powers to make a restraining order which may be the main remedy sought by a victim. In any cases of doubt the guidance of the Crown Prosecution Service should be sought.

---

## 3.5   **Anti-social behaviour**

In aiming to create communities which are safer and which feel safer, the government introduced a new form of restraint that can be imposed on the behaviour of some members of those communities—the Anti-Social Behaviour Order (ASBO) and the Sex Offenders Order (SOO); **see Crime, chapter 10.** (See also the remedies under the Protection from Harassment Act 1997, **para. 3.4.**)

In light of several practical shortcomings in the ASBO system as originally introduced, various changes to it have been made by the Police Reform Act 2002. Some of these changes were not in force at the time of writing and the amended statutory text should be referred to where necessary. The government's commitment to tackling anti-social behaviour in its broadest sense was further affirmed when, in November 2002, the Home Secretary announced the creation of a new Anti-Social Behaviour Unit.

A significant feature of ASBOs lies in the fact that they are civil complaints, made under the procedure set out in the Magistrates' Courts Act 1980. This point was confirmed by the Court of Appeal in a recent case where it was held that the purpose behind ASBOs was the protection of an identified section of the community, not 'crime and punishment' and that this purpose had to be borne in mind when determining the compatibility of ASBO proceedings with the Human Rights Act 1998 (*R (on the application of M (a child))* v *Manchester Crown Court* [2001] EWCA Civ 281). In a case involving a SOO the Divisional Court reiterated that these proceedings are *civil* in nature for the purposes of Article 6 of the European Convention (**see chapter 2**) (see *B* v *Chief Constable of Avon & Somerset Constabulary* [2001] 1 WLR 340 and *R (on the application of McCann)* v *Manchester Crown Court* [2002] UKHL 39). This means that the civil standard of proof applies (i.e. on the balance of probabilities) (**see Evidence and Procedure, chapter 11**). It also means that the procedural requirements of Article 6(2) and (3) of the European Convention do not apply. While any proceedings have to be 'fair' in accordance with Article 6(1) and any restriction on the defendant's liberty in an order is an 'interference' with their private life (under Article 8), the whole point of such proceedings is to try and predict how far past behaviour gives reasonable cause to believe that an order is necessary under the circumstances to curb future misconduct (*Jones (Peter)* v *Greater Manchester Police Authority* [2001] EWHC Admin 189).

In *S* v *Dorset Borough Council* (2001) LTL 12 February, a juvenile, who was the subject of an ASBO application, had already been convicted of several offences under the Education Act 1996. He objected to the same material being used from his criminal trial to support the application for an ASBO, arguing that the use of the ASBO had been intended as an alternative to criminal prosecution. Hearing the appeal by way of case stated, the Divisional Court held that it was 'perfectly proper' to use the same material in this way and that the ASBO is akin to an injunction.

### 3.5.1 The Anti-Social Behaviour Order (ASBO)

The Anti-Social Behaviour Order (ASBO) is a central feature of the government's community safety strategy. At the time of writing, there were plans to extend its effects and simplify the application process.

The Crime and Disorder Act 1998, s. 1 states:

(1) An application for an order under this section may be made by a relevant authority if it appears to the authority that the following conditions are fulfilled with respect to any person aged 10 or over, namely—

    (a) that the person has acted, since the commencement date, in an anti-social manner, that is to say, in a manner that caused or was likely to cause harassment, alarm or distress to one or more persons not of the same household as himself, and

    (b) that such an order is necessary to protect relevant persons from further anti-social acts by him.

. . .

(1A) In this section and sections 1B and 1E 'relevant authority' means—

    (a) the council for a local government area;

    (b) the chief officer of police of any police force maintained for a police area;

    (c) the chief constable of the British Transport Police Force; or

    (d) any person registered under section 1 of the Housing Act 1996 (c 52) as a social landlord who provides or manages any houses or hostel in a local government area.

(1B) In this section 'relevant persons' means—

    (a) in relation to a relevant authority falling within paragraph (a) of subsection (1A), persons within the local government area of that council;

    (b) in relation to a relevant authority falling within paragraph (b) of that subsection, persons within the police area;

    (c) in relation to a relevant authority falling within paragraph (c) of that subsection—

        (i) persons who are on or likely to be on policed premises in a local government area; or

        (ii) persons who are in the vicinity of or likely to be in the vicinity of such premises;

(d) in relation to a relevant authority falling within paragraph (d) of that subsection—

    (i) persons who are residing in or who are otherwise on or likely to be on premises provided or managed by that authority; or

    (ii) persons who are in the vicinity of or likely to be in the vicinity of such premises

(2) ...

(3) Such an application shall be made by complaint to the magistrates' court whose commission area includes the local government area or police area concerned.

(4) If, on such an application, it is proved that the conditions mentioned in subsection (1) above are fulfilled, the magistrates' court may make an order under this section (an 'anti-social behaviour order') which prohibits the defendant from doing anything described in the order.

---

## KEYNOTE

In order to apply for an ASBO it must appear to the relevant authority that:

- a relevant person acted in a manner that caused, or was likely to cause harassment, alarm or distress to one or more people who are not of the same household as the relevant person, and

- that such an order is necessary to protect people from further anti-social acts by that person. The 'relevant authority' for the purposes of an ASBO is the local authority or the chief officer of police, any part of whose police area lies within the area of that local authority. However, the chief constable of the British Transport Police may also apply for an ASBO to protect people from anti-social behaviour within the force's jurisdiction and 'registered social landlords' (under the Housing Act 1996, s. 1) may apply for orders in relation to such behaviour on or in the vicinity of premises owned by them. The Secretary of State may also add to this list of relevant authorities (see s. 1A).

A requirement for local authorities and chief officers to consult before applying for an ASBO is now imposed by s. 1E, meaning that, in practice, both of these sources of authority will have to work together in bringing any application for an ASBO. Applications by other relevant authorities must be made in consultation with the local chief officer and the local council in the area in which the person lives or appears to live. This imposition of multiple responsibility, which effectively enforces a collaborative approach between the police and local authorities, is another key feature of the 1998 Act (see also ss. 5 and 6, chapter 1).

For these purposes, the relevant local government areas are:

- in relation to England, a district or London borough, the City of London, the Isle of Wight and the Isles of Scilly;

- in relation to Wales, a county or county borough

(s. 1(12)).

In these circumstances it is the relevant authority who makes the application for an ASBO, thereby removing from the 'victim' of the conduct the burden of seeking a remedy themselves (contrast this with the new remedy using an injunction in cases of harassment; see para. 3.4.2).

The proviso at s. 1 (1)(a)—which excludes people from the same household—shows that the ASBO is not intended as a remedy for domestic disputes (as to which, see chapter 7).

Chief constables can delegate or devolve the functions set out in s. 1(1) and (2) of the Act to any officer(s) judged suitable by them—*R (on the Application of Chief Constable of West Midlands Police) v Birmingham Magistrates' Court* [2002] EWHC Admin 1087.

An application may be made in respect of the behaviour of any person aged 10 or over. This is another significant departure from the earlier law and, together with the abolition of the presumption of *doli incapax* (see Crime, chapter 4), is consistent with the government's expressed intention to impose criminal responsibility on older children.

Local councils and chief officers may now make applications to protect people in their respective areas whether or not the original anti-social behaviour occurred in that area or elsewhere.

Criminal courts can also make an ASBO in respect of a defendant where he or she has been convicted of an offence after the coming into force of s. 1C. The court can make such an order of its own volition, irrespective of whether any specific application has been made but it can only be made *in addition* to any sentence or conditional discharge (s. 1C(4)). This illustrates that the order is, as under the other methods of application, a preventive measure rather than a punishment. If the defendant is detained in legal custody (e.g. given a custodial sentence or remanded into police custody), the order may be suspended until he or she is released (see s. 1C(5)).

### ASBOs in county court proceedings

A newly inserted s. 1B of the Crime and Disorder Act 1998 allows relevant authorities to apply to a county court where then are, or have become, a party to the proceedings and similar conditions apply to such orders as those made by magistrates' courts.

### Interim orders

Either the magistrates' or the county court may make an interim ASBO under the provisions of s. 1D if it considers that it is just to do so. Interim orders can be made in this way pending the determination of the main application and any such order must be for a fixed period; it can be varied, renewed or discharged and ceases to have effect once the main application has been determined (e.g. once a full ASBO has been made or the application refused (s. 1D(4)).

Section 1(6) (amended by Police Reform Act 2002, s. 61) goes on to state:

(6) The prohibitions that may be imposed by an anti-social behaviour order are those necessary for the purpose of protecting persons (whether relevant persons or persons elsewhere in England and Wales) from further anti-social acts by the defendant.

Section 1(5) states:

(5) For the purpose of determining whether the condition mentioned in subsection (1)(a) above is fulfilled, the court shall disregard any act of the defendant which he shows was reasonable in the circumstances.

---

**KEYNOTE**

This requirement clearly places the burden of showing the reasonableness of his/her behaviour on the defendant.

---

### 3.5.2    **Duration of Anti-Social Behaviour Order**

An ASBO has a minimum period of two years' duration (s. 1(7)).

For the duration of interim orders **see para. 3.5.1.**

Under s. 1(8) of the 1998 Act, either the applicant or the defendant may apply to have the order varied or discharged but, under s. 1(9), no ASBO shall be discharged before the end of two years except with the consent of both parties.

OFFENCE:    **Breaching an Anti-Social Behaviour Order—*Crime and Disorder Act 1998, s. 1(10)***

• Triable either way • Five years' imprisonment and/or a fine on indictment; six months' imprisonment and/or a fine summarily
*(Arrestable offence)*

The Crime and Disorder Act 1998, s. 1(10) (amended by Police Reform Act 2002, s. 61) states:

(10) If without reasonable excuse a person does anything which he is prohibited from doing by an anti-social behaviour order, he is guilty of an offence and liable—

(a) on summary conviction, to imprisonment for a term not exceeding six months or to a fine not exceeding the statutory maximum, or to both; or

(b) on conviction on indictment, to imprisonment for a term not exceeding five years or to a fine, or to both.

---

**KEYNOTE**

The above offence applies to all ASBOs including interim orders and those made by the county court.

As the punishment provided by a conditional discharge (under the Powers of Criminal Courts (Sentencing) Act 2000) has the same general effect as an ASBO, a court cannot impose a conditional discharge on a defendant found guilty of committing an offence under s. 1(10) above (s. 1(11)).

Given the breadth of an ASBO, which may restrain a defendant from communicating with a particular person or from creating noise or nuisance, the behaviour required to commit this offence could be relatively minor. The advice of the Crown Prosecution Service may need to be sought in cases involving what appear to be innocuous but technical breaches of such an order.

It appears from the wording of the 1998 Act that a person might have an ASBO made against him/her in his/her absence. Although a magistrates' court has the power to issue a summons and then a warrant (under the Magistrates' Courts Act 1980) in order to compel the person to come to court when an application for an ASBO is being heard, it does seem that the court can go on to make an ASBO *ex parte* (in the absence of the other party). Again, if this is the case, there are serious human rights implications which may allow the procedure to be challenged.

---

### 3.5.3 Appeal

The Crime and Disorder Act 1998, s. 4 (amended by Police Reform Act 2002, s. 68) states:

(1) An appeal shall lie to the Crown Court against the making by a magistrates' court of an anti-social behaviour order, an order under section 1D above, a sex offender or an order under section 2A above ...

(2) On such an appeal the Crown Court—
   (a) may make such orders as may be necessary to give effect to its determination of the appeal; and
   (b) may also make such incidental or consequential orders as appear to it to be just.

---

**KEYNOTE**

The right of appeal process above applies to both full ASBOs and interim orders made by a magistrates' court; it does not apply to ASBOs made by the county court in civil proceedings under s. 1B.

There is no right of appeal open to the local authority or chief officer against a decision of a court not to make an order. That would not preclude the applicant from requiring the court to 'state a case' for consideration by the Divisional Court in appropriate circumstances.

---

### 3.5.4 People acting in anti-social manner

In addition to the ASBO system above, the police have other specific powers to deal with anti-social behaviour. If a constable in uniform has reason to believe that a person has been, or is, acting in an anti-social manner (within the meaning of s. 1 of the Crime and Disorder Act 1998—**see para. 3.5.1**), the constable may require the person to give their name and address (Police Reform Act 2002, s. 50). This power is among those that can be conferred on a Community Support Officer designated under sch. 4 to the Police Reform Act 2002 and a person accredited under sch. 5 to that Act (**see chapter 2**).

Where motor vehicles are involved, there are further specific powers to stop the vehicle and to seize it (**see Road Traffic**).

OFFENCE: **Failing to comply with requirement to give name and address—*Police Reform Act 2002, s. 50(2)***

> • Triable summarily • Fine
> *(No specific power of arrest)*

The Police Reform Act 2002, s. 50(2) states:

> (2) Any person who—
>     (a) fails to give his name and address when required to do so under subsection (1), or
>     (b) gives a false or inaccurate name or address in response to a requirement under that subsection,
>         is guilty of an offence . . .

---

**KEYNOTE**

This new provision creates a specific offence of failing to give a name and address under the circumstances outlined. This should not be confused with the general arrest condition under s. 25 of the Police and Criminal Evidence Act 1984 (**see chapter 2**). However, although there is no specific statutory power of arrest accompanying this offence, the arrest condition at s. 25(3) of the Police and Criminal Evidence Act 1984—and especially s. 25(3)(b)—means that such a power will almost always be available.

The wording of the offence suggests that it will be complete if either the name *or* address given is false or inaccurate, not both. As with all such powers, you will need to show that the person both heard and understood the requirement—and that you both heard and noted the response. Just how 'inaccurate' the details given would need to be before the offence is committed remains to be seen.

---

## 3.6 Nuisance

There are many forms of behaviour which, although not falling within some of the more 'serious' offences discussed elsewhere in this Manual, are nevertheless a source of annoyance or disquiet to the community. Some of these activities are usefully classified as 'nuisances'.

### 3.6.1 Public nuisance

Although many of the activities dealt with in this chapter are described as 'nuisances', there is a specific offence of creating or being responsible for a public nuisance, an offence that overlaps with some other aspects of criminal behaviour.

The common law concept of nuisance is separated into public and private nuisance. Private nuisance is dealt with under civil law as a *tort* ('wrong'). Public nuisance, however, can also be dealt with under criminal law.

A public nuisance is an unlawful act or an omission to discharge a duty which, in either case, obstructs or causes inconvenience or damage to the public in the exercise of their common rights (see *Attorney-General* v *PYA Quarries Ltd* [1957] 2 QB 169).

Although there is no 'magic number' of people who must suffer from the annoyance or obstruction in order for it to amount to a *public nuisance*, you must show that the act or omission affected the public in general as opposed to a small group of people (such as the employees of a firm). Therefore, in *R* v *Madden* [1975] 1 WLR 1379, where a person made a hoax bomb call (**see para. 3.7.1**) to an organisation it was held that such behaviour could in theory amount to a public nuisance, although in *Madden* it did not as the annoyance/obstruction was limited in its effect.

People who entered school premises for the purpose of glue sniffing were held to have committed a public nuisance by unduly interfering with the comfortable and convenient enjoyment of the land, even though the school was empty (*Sykes* v *Holmes* [1985] Crim LR 791). (For offences and powers in relation to educational premises specifically, **see chapter 9.**)

Given that the courts have unlimited sentencing power in relation to this offence, there may well be advantages in considering its application to cases where the only other offences disclosed would be summary offences. An example is the case of *R* v *Johnson* [1997] 1 WLR 367 where the defendant made several hundred obscene telephone calls to women across a county over a period of five years. As the only other available offence (before the offences of harassment were available) appeared to be the summary offence under the Telecommunications Act 1984 (as to which, **see para. 3.7**), the availability of the offence of public nuisance gave the courts and the investigating officers far wider powers in dealing with the defendant.

OFFENCE: **Public nuisance—*Common Law***

> • Triable either way • Unlimited powers of sentence on indictment; statutory maxima apply summarily
> *(Arrestable offence)*

It is an offence at common law for a person to cause a public nuisance.

---

**KEYNOTE**

As this offence is a common law 'misdemeanour', a court may pass sentence at its discretion on indictment, that is, its sentencing powers are unlimited.

The behaviour of the defendant must interfere with the material rights enjoyed by a class of Her Majesty's subjects (*R* v *Johnson* [1997] 1 WLR 367).

It is not necessary to prove that every member within a class of people in the community has been affected by the defendant's behaviour; simply that a representative cross-section has been so affected (*Attorney-General* v *PYA Quarries Ltd*, The Times, 4 May 1961). Such a cross-section might include members of a housing estate or users of a public transport facility such as a main-line railway station.

In Lord Denning's view (also in the *PYA* case), a nuisance would need to be 'so widespread in its range or so indiscriminate in its effect' that it would not be reasonable to expect one person to bring proceedings on his/her own to put a stop to it.

There is no need to show that the defendant intended his/her actions or omission to cause a public nuisance and, as with the offence of harassment (**see para. 3.4**) it will be enough that he/she knew or ought to have known that the conduct would bring about a public nuisance (*R* v *Shorrock* [1994] QB 279).

A good practical example of how the law of public nuisance can be used in a policing context can be seen in *R* v *Harvey* [2003] EWCA Crim 112. In that case the defendant was convicted of causing a public nuisance after following different groups of children in his car, sounding the horn and smiling at them. Evidence was adduced to show that he presented a real threat to children with the possibility of his luring them into his car for unlawful purposes. Although the defendant was originally sentenced to life imprisonment, that was later reduced in the absence of features of sex or violence, to three years.

Other examples of criminal public nuisances have included:

• Allowing a rave to take place in a field (*R* v *Shorrock*).

• Making hundreds of nuisance telephone calls to at least 13 women (*R* v *Johnson*).

• Contaminating 30 houses with dust and noise from a quarry (*Attorney-General* v *PYA Quarries Ltd*).

• Selling meat which was unfit for consumption (*R* v *Stephens* (1866) LR 1 QB 702).

In addition, the Environmental Protection Act 1990, s. 79 sets out a list of 'statutory nuisances', any of which would potentially be capable of amounting to a criminal offence if they met the relevant conditions.

### Defence

Statutory authorisation for a person's conduct (e.g. building a road or a railway), will be a defence provided the behaviour is specifically permitted by that statute (*Hammersmith and City Railway Co.* v *Brand and Louisa* (1868) LR 4 QB 171).

### Enforcement

In addition to providing powers of arrest and sentencing for tackling public nuisance through the criminal process, there is always the preventive measure of a court injunction available. Historically, the Attorney-General has sought injunctions on behalf of the public at large. However, local authorities have the power to apply for a public nuisance injunction under the Local Government Act 1972 (see *Stoke-on-Trent City Council* v *B & Q (Retail) Ltd* [1984] AC 754) and there appears to be no reason why chief officers should not do the same.

### 3.6.2 Fireworks

Restrictions on the sale of gunpowder, including fireworks (s. 39), are imposed by s. 30 of the Explosives Act 1875.

Section 31 of the 1875 Act provides a summary offence in respect of anyone selling gunpowder to a person who appears to be under 16 years old.

There are also restrictions on fireworks in the Fireworks (Safety) Regulations 1997 (SI 1997 No. 2294). Made under s. 11 of the Consumer Protection Act 1987, the Regulations describe virtually every conceivable type of firework and go on to place a number of restrictions on the supply of such items. As you would expect, the Regulations also make a number of concessions and exceptions, allowing the supply of certain fireworks by certain people under certain conditions.

Regulation 6(1) of the 1997 Regulations creates a summary offence of supplying any firework—or assembly that includes a firework—to any person apparently under the age of 18. The offence is charged under s. 12 of the Consumer Protection Act 1987 and is punishable with six months' imprisonment and/or a fine. The offence does not apply to the supply of any cap, cracker snap, novelty match, party popper, 'serpent' or 'throw down' (as defined in reg. 2) (reg. 6(2)).

Regulation 7 goes on to create a number of other summary offences—again chargeable under s. 12—in relation to the supply of certain fireworks and in particular makes it an offence to supply a sparkler unless it is in a packet marked with the words, 'Warning: not to be given to children under 5 years of age'.

Regulation 8 creates a similar offence for any person who carries on a retail business involving, to whatever extent, the sale of fireworks, to supply a firework that has been removed from a 'primary' pack or selection pack.

For offences involving fireworks on highways and related offences, **see Road Traffic, chapter 8.**

OFFENCE: **Throwing fireworks into highway or street—*Explosives Act 1875, s. 80* (amended by Consumer Protection Act 1987)**

> • Triable summarily • Fine
> *(No specific power of arrest)*

The Explosives Act 1875, s. 80 states:

> If any person throw, cast, or fire any fireworks in or into any highway, street, thoroughfare, or public place, he [shall be guilty of an offence and liable] . . .

**KEYNOTE**

This offence is a 'penalty offence' for the purposes of s. 1 of the Criminal Justice and Police Act 2001 (see para. 2.5.1).

For other offences involving explosives, see chapter 4.

---

### 3.6.3 Post boxes

The Post Office Act 1957 formerly contained a number of criminal offences involving the postal service. Several of these offences have been replaced by the Postal Services Act 2000 (**see para. 3.7.2**). The old legislation also contained offences involving post boxes. These too have been replaced by the Postal Services Act 2000 by a series of summary offences, punishable by a fine. These offences relate to property owned or used by 'universal service providers'. These are organisations who are empowered under the 2000 Act to carry on many of the services that were formerly provided by the Post Office. Briefly, the offences are:

- affixing advertisements or other things to post boxes or other property belonging to or used by a 'universal service provider'(s. 86(1))

- painting or disfiguring such a post box without due authority (s. 86(2)—consider also the offences under the Criminal Damage Act 1971 (**see Crime, chapter 14**)

- placing or maintaining misleading descriptions on houses, doors, boxes, vehicles, etc. in a way that implies to the public that it is a universal service provider's post box or post office (s. 87(1)).

### 3.6.4 Noise

The Noise Act 1996 provides powers to allow local authorities to tackle the problems of noise within their community. Sections 2 and 3 of the 1996 Act allow for the serving of warning notices in relation to 'excessive noise' emanating from one house which can be heard in another at night. Night is defined as being between 11 pm and 7 am (s. 2(6)).

The noise level must be measured using an 'approved device' (s. 6). Any warning must be served on the person who appears to be responsible for the noise or by leaving the warning notice at the 'offending dwelling' (s. 3(3)).

There is no requirement for evidence of acoustic measurements in the Environmental Protection Act 1990 and a court may convict on other evidence (e.g. evidence from an environmental enforcement officer of excessively loud music being played) (*Lewisham Borough Council* v *Hall* [2002] EWHC 960).

For police powers to close premises in relation to disturbances emanating therefrom, **see chapter 10**).

OFFENCE: **Exceeding noise level after service of notice—*Noise Act 1996, s. 4(1)***
- Triable summarily • Fine
*(No specific power of arrest)*

The Noise Act 1996, s. 4 states:

(1) If a warning notice has been served in respect of noise emitted from a dwelling, any person who is responsible for noise which—
   (a) is emitted from the dwelling in the period specified in the notice, and
   (b) exceeds the permitted level, as measured from within the complainant's dwelling,
   is guilty of an offence.

(2) It is a defence for a person charged with an offence under this section to show that there was a reasonable excuse for the act, default or sufferance in question.

The 'permitted level' may be set or varied under regulations made by the Secretary of State (s. 5).

Sections 8 and 9 provide for the local authority to implement a 'fixed penalty procedure' whereby liability to prosecution under s. 4 above can be avoided by paying the fee (currently £100) within the prescribed period.

Section 10 provides powers of entry to local authority officers where a warning notice has been served in respect of a dwelling and excessive noise is still measured as having come therefrom. There is also a power to seize any sound equipment involved, together with a power to apply for a warrant for local authority officers to enter premises.

Obstruction of anyone exercising these powers is a summary offence (s. 10(8) ) and the provisions for the seizure and disposal of any equipment are set out in the schedule to the 1996 Act.

## 3.6.5 Litter

The law regulating the roles of local authorities in controlling litter can be found in the Litter Act 1983. The 1983 Act makes allowances for actions by 'litter authorities' (i.e. local councils and park boards, see s. 10) to discourage the dropping of litter and for the provision of litter bins.

Removing or interfering with local authority litter bins or litter notices is a summary offence under s. 5(9).

The remainder of the provisions regulating the dropping of litter are in the Environmental Protection Act 1990.

OFFENCE: **Leaving litter—*Environmental Protection Act 1990, s. 87(1)***
　　　　　　　• Triable summarily • Fine
　　　　　　　*(No specific power of arrest)*

The Environmental Protection Act 1990, s. 87 states:

(1) If any person throws down, drops or otherwise deposits in, into or from any place to which this section applies, and leaves, any thing whatsoever in such circumstances as to cause, or contribute to, or tend to lead to, the defacement by litter of any place to which this section applies, he shall, subject to subsection (2) below, be guilty of an offence.

...

(4) In this section 'public open place' means a place in the open air to which the public are entitled or permitted to have access without payment; and any covered place open to the air on at least one side and available for public use shall be treated as a public open place.

Under s. 87(3), the offence can be committed in any 'open space' and also relevant land belonging to:

• the principal litter authority (i.e. local council etc.)

• the Crown

• a designated statutory undertaker (e.g. a railway, tramway or dock company)

• a designated educational institution.

A telephone kiosk enclosed on all sides with a six inch gap around the bottom was held not to be a 'public open place' in *Felix* v *DPP* [1998] EHCR Dig 278.

'Litter' can include animal droppings for this purpose (Litter (Animal Droppings) Order 1991 (SI 1991 No. 961) ). Note also the powers given to local authorities to designate areas which must be kept free from dogs under the Dogs (Fouling of Land) Act 1996.

Section 4 of that Act allows authorised officers to issue a fixed penalty notice in respect of dogs fouling public land. Similarly, s. 88 of the Environmental Protection Act 1990 makes provision for the issuing of fixed penalty notices in respect of the general litter offence above. Section 88 provides that, where a notice setting out the prescribed details is given to an offender, by an authorised officer of a litter authority, no proceedings can be instituted against that person for 14 days. Payment of the fixed penalty will prevent the person's prosecution for that offence. Where the offender pays by posting the required amount properly to the relevant address, payment will be regarded as having been made at the time of the expected *delivery* (not the time the letter is posted) in the normal course of post (s. 88(4)).

The power to issue fixed penalty notices in relation to the Dogs (Fouling of Land) Act and the Environmental Protection Act are among those that can be conferred on a Community Support Officer designated under sch. 4 to the Police Reform Act 2002 and a person accredited under sch. 5 to that Act, along with the relevant power to require the person to give their name and address (for a full discussion of these and related powers **see chapter 2**).

Under s. 91 of the 1990 Act, a magistrates' court may act on a complaint of anyone who is aggrieved by the defacement by litter or refuse of any relevant road, highway or land occupied by relevant statutory undertakers or educational institutions. Before doing so, the court must notify the occupier of the complaint. The court may then issue a litter abatement order requiring the relevant person to remedy the situation and failure to comply with such an order is a summary offence under s. 91(9).

Section 99 and sch. 4 to the 1990 Act give local authorities powers to deal with problems involving the abandonment of shopping trolleys and luggage trolleys. Schedule 4 allows local authorities (after abiding by the procedure in s. 99) to seize, retain and ultimately dispose of such trolleys.

---

Section 87(2) states:

(2) No offence is committed under this section where the depositing and leaving of the thing was—
    (a) authorised by law, or
    (b) done with the consent of the owner, occupier or other person or authority having control of the place in or into which that thing was deposited.

### 3.6.6 Vehicles used for causing harassment etc.

Section 59 of the Police Reform Act 2002 gives a constable in uniform powers in relation to motor vehicles that he or she has reasonable grounds for believing are being, or have been, used in a manner which—

- contravenes s. 3 or 34 of the Road Traffic Act 1988 (careless and inconsiderate driving and prohibition of off-road driving), *and*

- is causing, or is likely to cause, alarm, distress or annoyance to members of the public.

Those powers include the power to order the person driving it to stop the vehicle, to seize and remove the motor vehicle and to enter any premises on which he or she has reasonable grounds for believing the motor vehicle to be. However, the powers are subject to a system of warnings and limitations. For a full discussion of these provisions **see Road Traffic, chapter 2**.

## 3.7 Offences involving communications

As with many areas of criminal law and policing, the terrorist attacks on and after 11 September 2001 dramatically increased the relevance of the offence below. The making of direct threats to people's lives or their property is covered by a number of statutes. There are, however, specific offences which deal with the making of general threats and other communications which are intended to cause alarm or anxiety among people receiving them.

3.7.1 **Threats and hoaxes**

The fear and disquiet that can be generated by a single telephone call is considerable, as is the potential economic loss to businesses within the community. Similarly, the panic and disruption that can ensue from sending packages and substances to carefully chosen target addresses is all too evident after the anthrax letters and other threats that terrorised the international community during 2001. The following offences are designed to deal with the whole spectrum of such behaviour.

OFFENCE: **Placing or sending substances—*The Anti-terrorism, Crime and Security Act 2001, s. 114***
- Triable either way • Seven years' imprisonment on indictment; six months' imprisonment and/or a fine summarily
*(Arrestable offence)*

The Anti-terrorism, Crime and Security Act 2001, s. 114 states:

(1) A person is guilty of an offence if he—
  (a) places any substance or other thing in any place; or
  (b) sends any substance or other thing from one place to another (by post, rail or any other means whatever);
  with the intention of inducing in a person anywhere in the world a belief that it is likely to be (or contain) a noxious substance or other noxious thing and thereby endanger human life or create a serious risk to human health.

OFFENCE: **Placing or sending articles—*Criminal Law Act 1977, s. 51(1)***
- Triable either way • Seven years' imprisonment on indictment; six months' imprisonment and/or a fine summarily
*(Arrestable offence)*

The Criminal Law Act 1977, s. 51 states:

(1) A person who—
  (a) places any article in any place whatever; or
  (b) dispatches any article by post, rail or any other means whatever of sending things from one place to another,
  with the intention (in either case) of inducing in some other person a belief that it is likely to explode or ignite and thereby cause personal injury or damage to property is guilty of an offence. In this subsection 'article' includes substance.

---

**KEYNOTE**

The definitions above are very wide. The Criminal Law Act 1977 offence relates specifically to bomb threats while the 2001 offence (which is modelled on the earlier offence) is far broader and applies to creating a belief in someone anywhere in the world. For the purposes of the Anti-terrorism, Crime and Security Act 2001, 'substance' here includes any biological agent and any other natural or artificial substance (whatever its form, origin or method of production (s. 115(1))). The 'article' concerned in s. 51(1) can also be anything at all.

It is the inducing of a relevant belief in someone else that is the key element to the first offence not any actual endangering of life or risk to human health. You do not have to show that the defendant had any particular person in mind in whom he/she intended to induce the belief in question (see the Anti-terrorism, Crime and Security Act 2001, s. 115 and the Criminal Law Act 1977, s. 51(3)).

Both offences are offences of 'specific intent', **see Crime, chapter 1**.

The Home Office guidance to the Anti-terrorism, Crime and Security Act 2001 offence gives examples of acts which, though at one time would not have been seen as threatening, would now amount to an offence under this section—examples such as scattering white powder in a public place or spraying water droplets around in an underground train, in each case with the requisite intent.

---

OFFENCE: **Threats involving noxious substances or things—*The Anti-terrorism, Crime and Security Act 2001, s. 114***
- • Triable either way • Seven years' imprisonment on indictment; six months' imprisonment and/or a fine summarily

*(Arrestable offence)*

The Anti-terrorism, Crime and Security Act 2001, s. 114 states:

> (2) A person is guilty of an offence if he communicates any information which he knows or believes to be false with the intention of inducing in a person anywhere in the world a belief that a noxious substance or other noxious thing is likely to be present (whether at the time the information is communicated or later) in any place and thereby endanger human life or create a serious risk to human health.

OFFENCE: **Communicating false information—*Criminal Law Act 1977, s. 51(2)***
- • Triable either way • Seven years' imprisonment on indictment; six months' imprisonment and/or a fine summarily

*(Arrestable offence)*

The Criminal Law Act 1977, s. 51 states:

> (2) A person who communicates any information which he knows or believes to be false to another person with the intention of inducing in him or any other person a false belief that a bomb or other thing liable to explode or ignite is present in any place or location whatever is guilty of an offence.

---

**KEYNOTE**

The essence of these offences is the communication of information which the defendant knows or believes to be false. Again, the 1977 Act offence relates specifically to bomb hoaxes while the 2001 Act offence is far wider and applies to creating a belief in someone anywhere in the world. The meaning of 'substance' for the 2001 Act offence is the same as in the Keynote above and, in neither case is there a need to show that the defendant had any particular person in mind. Under the Criminal Law Act 1977 it has been held that while the information communicated need not be specific, a message saying that there is a bomb somewhere has been held to be enough, even though no location was given (*R* v *Webb* (1995) 92(27) LS Gaz 31.

The wording of the 1977 Act offence is in the *present* tense which suggests that a message threatening to place a bomb etc. sometime in the *future* would not suffice, while the 2001 Act specifically allows for such a situation.

The use of some form of code word is not a prerequisite of the offence but it does go towards proving the defendant's intention that the threat etc. be taken seriously; it may also be taken into account when passing sentence.

The 'communication' can be in any form (including, it would seem, on the Internet) and can be direct (e.g. to a railway station or department store where the bomb or device is alleged to be) or indirect (to a radio station switchboard).

There is no need for the person making the communication to have any particular person in mind at the time (s. 51(3)).

Both offences are offences of 'specific intent', see Crime, chapter 1.

### 3.7.2   Misuse and obstruction of postal services

OFFENCE:   **Interfering with mail—*Postal Services Act 2000, s. 84***
  • Triable summarily • Six months' imprisonment and/or fine
  *(No specific power of arrest)*

The Postal Services Act 2000, s. 84 states:

(1) A person commits an offence if, without reasonable excuse, he—
  (a) intentionally delays or opens a postal packet in the course of its transmission by post, or
  (b) intentionally opens a mail-bag

(2) . . .

(3) A person commits an offence if, intending to act to a person's detriment and without reasonable excuse, he opens a postal packet which he knows or reasonably suspects has been incorrectly delivered to him.

---

**KEYNOTE**

The Postal Services Act 2000 was introduced to make the extensive changes in the law that were required by the 'privatisation' of the Post Office and its functions.

The Act creates two offences in relation to interfering with the mail, along with a further offence of opening someone else's mail that has been incorrectly delivered.

The first general offence, under s. 84(1) above, applies to anyone. There is a second offence (under s. 83) which specifically applies to postal workers and which is triable either way, carrying a maximum of two years' imprisonment. Under the second, more specific, offence, you have to prove the same elements as the above offence but also need to show that the person was engaged in the business of a postal operator and that he/she was acting contrary to his/her duty.

To prove the above offence you must show that the defendant acted without any reasonable excuse and that he/she also acted intentionally (as to which **see Crime, chapter 1**). The offence does not apply where the actions were carried out under a lawful warrant or statutory provision (e.g. the Regulation of Investigatory Powers Act 2000—**see Crime, chapter 3**). Similarly, any action carried out in accordance with the terms and conditions of postage will not attract criminal liability here. Delays (but not the opening of mail) caused by industrial action also fall outside this offence.

The offence under s. 84(3) above looks simple enough but requires proof of a number of elements. First, it must be shown that the defendant opened a postal packet (as opposed to delaying it under s. 84(1)). It must also be shown that he/she did so intending 'to act to another person's detriment'—this can be any other person's detriment, not simply the addressee, but it is nevertheless a key feature of the offence. It must also be shown that the defendant knew or reasonably suspected that the postal packet had been incorrectly delivered to him/her. This means that the packet must have been 'delivered'; it would be difficult to show that someone reasonably suspected a packet that is still in transit to have been 'incorrectly delivered' to him/her. As with the general offence under s. 84(1), any opening of postal packets that is done properly in pursuance of a warrant, statutory authority or under the conditions of postage will not be an offence under s. 84(3).

For the further offences of intercepting communications **see Crime, chapter 3**.

---

OFFENCE:   **Sending prohibited article by post—*Postal Services Act 2000, s. 85***
  • Triable either way • Twelve months' imprisonment on indictment; a fine summarily.
  *(No specific power of arrest)*

The Postal Services Act 2000, s. 85 states:

(1) A person commits an offence if he sends by post a postal packet which encloses any creature, article or thing of any kind which is likely to injure other postal packets in course of their transmission by post or any person engaged in the business of a postal operator.

(2) Subsection (1) does not apply to postal packets which enclose anything permitted (whether generally or specifically) by the postal operator concerned.

(3) A person commits an offence if he sends by post a postal packet which encloses—

(a) any indecent or obscene print, painting, photograph, lithograph, engraving, cinematograph film or other record of a picture or pictures, book, card or written communication, or

(b) any other indecent or obscene article (whether or not of a similar kind to those mentioned in paragraph (a)).

(4) A person commits an offence if he sends by post a postal packet which has on the packet, or on the cover of the packet, any words, marks or designs which are of an indecent or obscene character.

---

**KEYNOTE**

Section 85 creates a number of offences, all concerned with the sending of postal packets via the newly-created postal infrastructure. The first offence addresses the sending of things that are likely to harm either other postal packets or postal workers. Evidence that any article is in the course of transmission by post, or has been accepted by a postal operator for transmission by post, will be enough to prove that it is in fact a 'postal packet' (s. 109). This offence will not apply to the sending of things that are permitted by the relevant postal operator.

The other offences under s. 85 apply irrespective of whether the offending packets are permitted by the postal operator and include indecent or obscene contents or packaging.

Whether an article is obscene etc. is a question of fact for the court to determine in each case. That test will not look at the particular views or frailties of the recipient but will be an objective test based on a reasonable bystander (*Kosmos Publications Ltd* v *DPP* [1975] Crim LR 345).

As causing severe shock can amount to an assault, the relevant offences against the person may be considered (**see Crime, chapter 8**).

For specific offences of harassment, **see para. 3.4.**

---

OFFENCES: **Obstruction—*Postal Services Act 2000, s. 88***

• Triable summarily • Fine
*(No specific power of arrest)*

The Postal Services Act 2000, s. 88 states:

(1) A person commits an offence if, without reasonable excuse, he—

(a) obstructs a person engaged in the business of a universal service provider in the execution of his duty in connection with the provision of a universal postal service, or

(b) obstructs, while in any universal postal service post office or related premises, the course of business of a universal service provider.

(2) ...

(3) A person commits an offence if without reasonable excuse, he fails to leave a universal postal service post office or related premises when required to do so by a person who—

(a) is engaged in the business of a universal service provider, and

(b) reasonably suspects him of committing an offence under subsection (1).

(4) A person who commits an offence under subsection (3)—

(a) ...

(b) may be removed by any person engaged in the business of a universal service provider.

---

**KEYNOTE**

Section 88 creates two offences relating to obstruction. The first offence involves the general obstruction, without reasonable excuse, of someone engaged in the business of a 'universal service provider'. These providers are broadly organisations empowered under the 2000 Act to carry on many of the services that were formerly provided by the Post Office.

The second offence relates to conduct in a post office or related premises. Such conduct must be shown to have obstructed, without reasonable excuse, *the course of business* of a universal service provider. Therefore, it is not a member of staff who has to be obstructed here, but rather the postal business itself.

Subsection (3) is of more immediate relevance to police officers. This offence is committed if a person fails without reasonable excuse to leave a post office or related premises when required to do so by someone engaged in the provider's business who reasonably suspects the other person of committing one of the obstruction offences under s. 88(1). Anyone failing to leave when properly required to do so under subsection (3) may be removed by the post office staff but also, subsection (5) provides that '*any constable shall on demand remove, or assist in removing, any such person*'. This places a clear duty on—as opposed to just granting a power to—individual police officers to help in removing offenders under these circumstances. It is similar to the powers and obligation placed on police officers in relation to licensed premises (as to which **see chapter 10**).

'Related premises' are any premises belonging to a universal postal service post office or used together with any such post office (s. 88(6)).

### 3.7.3   Malicious communications

OFFENCE:   **Malicious communications—*Malicious Communications Act 1988, s. 1(1)***
> • Triable summarily  • Six months' imprisonment and/or a fine
> *(No specific power of arrest)*

The Malicious Communications Act 1988, s. 1 states:

(1) Any person who sends to another person—
   (a) a letter, electronic communication or article of any description which conveys—
      (i)   a message which is indecent or grossly offensive;
      (ii)  a threat; or
      (iii) information which is false and known or believed to be false by the sender; or
   (b) any article or electronic communication which is, in whole or part, of an indecent or grossly offensive nature,
   is guilty of an offence if his purpose, or one of his purposes, in sending it is that it should, so far as falling within paragraph (a) or (b) above, cause distress or anxiety to the recipient or to any other person to whom he intends that it or its contents or nature should be communicated.

**KEYNOTE**

The offence is not restricted to threatening or indecent communications and can include giving false information provided that *one* of the sender's purposes in so doing is to cause distress or anxiety. 'Purposes' appears simply to be another way of stating intention in which case this an offence of 'specific intent' (**see Crime, chapter 1**).

The wording of the offence was changed—and broadened—by the Criminal Justice and Police Act 2001 to include electronic communications and to cover *any* article. 'Electronic communication' includes any oral communication by means of a telecommunication system and any other communication in electronic form (e-mails, text messages, pager messages, etc.) (s 2A). The 2001 Act also increases the penalty for this offence which can now attract a term of imprisonment.

'Sending' will include transmitting.

The relevant distress or anxiety may be intended towards the recipient *or* any other person.

It is clear from s. 1(3) that the offence can be committed by using someone else to send, deliver or transmit a message. This would include occasions where a person falsely reports that someone has been a victim of a crime in order to cause anxiety or distress by the arrival of the police. (For wasting police time, **see Crime, chapter 15.**)

Section 1(1)(b) covers occasions where the article itself is indecent or grossly offensive (such as putting dog faeces through someone's letter box).

Defence

Section 1(2) of the 1988 Act states:

A person is not guilty of an offence by virtue of subsection (1)(a)(ii) above if he shows—

(a) that the threat was used to reinforce a demand made by him on reasonable grounds; and

(b) that he believed, and had reasonable grounds for believing, that the use of the threat was a proper means of reinforcing the demand.

---

**KEYNOTE**

The wording of the statutory defence has been changed (by the Criminal Justice and Police Act 2001) to make the relevant test objective. It will no longer be enough that the person claiming the defence under s. 1(2) believed that he/she had reasonable grounds; the defendant will have to show:

- that there were in fact reasonable grounds for making the demand;

- that he/she believed that the accompanying threat was a proper means of enforcing the demand; and

- that reasonable grounds existed for that belief.

Given the decisions of the courts in similarly-worded defences under the Theft Act 1968 (blackmail; see **Crime, chapter 12**), it is unlikely that any demand could be reasonable where agreement to it would amount to a crime.

The defence is intended to cover financial institutions and other commercial concerns who often need to send forceful letters to customers. However, for the offence of unlawfully harassing debtors, see s. 40 of the Administration of Justice Act 1970.

---

3.7.4  **Threats to kill**

OFFENCE:  **Making a threat to kill—*Offences Against the Person Act 1861, s. 16***
- Triable either way • Ten years' imprisonment on indictment; six months' imprisonment and/or a fine summarily
*(Arrestable offence)*

The Offences Against the Person Act 1861, s. 16 (amended by Criminal Law Act 1977; s. 65 sch. 12) states:

A person who without lawful excuse makes to another a threat, intending that that other would fear it would be carried out, to kill that other or a third person shall be guilty of an offence...

---

**KEYNOTE**

The proviso that the threat must be made 'without lawful excuse' means that a person acting in self-defence or in the course of his/her duty in protecting life (e.g. an armed police officer) would not commit this offence (provided that his/her behaviour was 'lawful'; see **Crime, chapter 4**).

You must show that the threat was made (or implied (*R* v *Solanke* [1970] 1 WLR 1)) with the intention that the person receiving it would fear that it would be carried out. It is the intention of the person who makes the threat which is important in this offence. It does not matter whether the person to whom the threat is made *does* fear that the threat would be carried out, or that the person whose life is threatened so fears (unless that person is the same person to whom the threat is made). The threat may be to kill another person at some time in the future or it may be an immediate threat, but the threatened action must be directly linked with the defendant. Simply passing on a threat on behalf of a third person would probably be insufficient for this offence.

3.7.5    **Telephone calls**

OFFENCE:    **Improper use of public telecommunication systems—*Telecommunications Act 1984, s. 43***

> • Triable summarily • Six months' imprisonment and/or a fine
> *(No specific power of arrest)*

The Telecommunications Act 1984, s. 43 states:

> (1) A person who—
>    (a) sends, by means of a public telecommunication system, a message or other matter that is grossly offensive or of an indecent, obscene or menacing character; or
>    (b) sends by those means, for the purpose of causing annoyance, inconvenience or needless anxiety to another, a message that he knows to be false or persistently makes use for that purpose of a public telecommunication system,
>    shall be guilty of an offence . . .

---

**KEYNOTE**

This offence is designed to deal with 'nuisance' calls. It only applies to 'public' telecommunication systems which are those systems designated by the Secretary of State as such (s. 9(1)) and would therefore not include internal calls in a work place. It appears from the wording that this offence may apply to the sending of messages via the Internet (provided the system used comes within the definition under s. 9(1)).

Again this offence applies to calls which convey false information.

The wording of the offence suggests that there is no need to show a particular 'purpose' (intention) in the case of behaviour falling under s. 43(1)(a) and the offence is complete if the defendant sends the relevant message or other matter that is, as a matter of fact, indecent, obscene or menacing.

The s. 43(1)(b) offence is a 'penalty offence' for the purposes of s. 1 of the Criminal Justice and Police Act 2001 (see para. 2.5.1); the other offence is *not*.

In the case of a charge under s. 43(1)(b) there is a need to prove that the defendant acted *for the purpose* of causing annoyance, inconvenience or needless anxiety to another.

Unlike the offence under s. 51(2) of the Criminal Law Act 1977 (see para. 3.7.1), there is no need for any information passed to be 'false'.

Where a number of calls have been made to several different people within the community, the offence of public nuisance may also be considered (see para. 3.6.1).

---

3.7.6    **Unsolicited publications**

It is a summary offence to send unsolicited material or advertising material which describes or illustrates human sexual techniques (s. 4 of the Unsolicited Goods and Services Act 1971). This offence cannot be prosecuted without the consent of the Director of Public Prosecutions.

3.7.7    **Interception of messages**

The whole area of communications interception has been substantially revised by the Regulation of Investigatory Powers Act 2000.

For the relevant police powers and the consequences on police operations, **see Crime, chapter 3.**

# 4 Public disorder and terrorism

## 4.1 Introduction

Threats to public order or the 'normal state of society' can arise in many forms, from intimidating and anti-social behaviour to full scale riot and acts of terrorism. The role of the police in maintaining the normal state of society is both extremely important but also increasingly challenging. It is one thing to provide police officers and auxiliary staff with statutory and common law powers to tackle disorder in all its many forms and, perhaps more importantly, to prevent anticipated disorder in advance; it is quite another to use those powers in a way that is sensitive to the competing needs and expectations of people and the communities in which they live. Although such powers help the police in their efforts to preserve a peaceful state of society, their use is frequently controversial and often confrontational. This area of constitutional law involves balancing the opposing rights of individuals with one another against the wider entitlements and requirements of society— a task that, in practical terms, can seem like trying to satisfy the insatiable.

The Human Rights Act 1998 has brought further challenges to this aspect of police work. (For a full discussion of the Act and its potential effect on the law in this area, **see chapter 2**.) For the purposes of the laws as addressed in this chapter, the most significant rights under the European Convention on Human Rights are Articles 8 (respect for private life), 9 (freedom of thought, conscience and religion), 10 (freedom of expression) and 11 (freedom of assembly and association).

When reading this chapter, regard should be had to the CPS Public Order Offences Charging Standard (**see appendix** 3).

## 4.2 Breach of the peace

The lowest level of threat to public order is probably represented in the common law 'complaint' of a breach of the peace. Defined specifically in *R v Howell* [1982] QB 416, a breach of the peace generally occurs when an act is done, or threatened to be done:

- which harms a person or, in his/her presence, his/her property; or

- which is likely to cause such harm; or

- which puts someone in fear of such harm.

A breach of the peace is not an offence (*R v County of London Quarter Sessions Appeals Committee, ex parte Metropolitan Police Commissioner* [1948] 1 KB 670). This situation was recently confirmed by the Court of Appeal who decided that the position had not been altered by the Human Rights Act or Article 3 of the European Convention on Human Rights (as to which **see chapter 2**)—*Williamson v Chief Constable of the West Midlands Police* [2003] EWCA Civ 337. As a result, someone who is arrested for a breach of the peace is not, strictly speaking, in police detention per s. 118 of the Police and Criminal Evidence Act 1984 (**see Evidence and Procedure, chapter 15**) and cannot be granted bail. They may, however, be detained and placed before the next available sitting of a court or held until the likelihood of a recurrence of the breach of the peace has gone and it is a matter of good practice to treat people so arrested and detained as though the provisions of the Police and Criminal Evidence Act 1984 applied (see *Williams* above). In a different case the Court of Appeal held that the power of detention to prevent a further breach of the peace should be limited to *real* (as opposed to fanciful) apprehensions that a further breach of the peace would occur if the defendant were released. These apprehensions should be based on all the circumstances and an honest belief based on objective, reasonable grounds that further detention is *necessary* in order to prevent a breach of the peace (*Chief Constable of Cleveland Police* v *Grogan* [2002] EWCA Civ 86). In such circumstances, the defendant's continued detention needs to be constantly reviewed.

A breach of the peace may take place on private premises as well as in public places (*R* v *Chief Constable of Devon and Cornwall, ex parte Central Electricity Generating Board* [1982] QB 458). The police are entitled to enter premises to prevent a breach of the peace and to remain there in order to do so (*Thomas* v *Sawkins* [1935] 2 KB 249). This power has not been affected by the general powers of entry provided by the Police and Criminal Evidence Act 1984 (**see chapter 2** and s. 17(6) of the 1984 Act).

Where a breach of the peace takes place on private property, there is no requirement to show that the resulting disturbance affected members of the public outside that property—*McQuade* v *Chief Constable of Humberside Police* [2001] EWCA Civ 1330. The presence of a member (or members) of the public is, however, a highly relevant factor when dealing with a breach of the peace (see *McConnell & Anor* v *Chief Constable of Greater Manchester Police* [1990] IWLR 364 CA).

Although the police have a general duty to preserve the Queen's peace and enjoy common law powers to carry out that duty, they also have a wide discretion as to how they go about that function. The common law powers of the police allow them, where appropriate, to prevent people from travelling to certain locations (e.g. striking miners heading for a working coalfield where their presence would give reasonable grounds to apprehend a breach of the peace (*Moss* v *McLachlan* [1985] IRLR 76)). Such an 'anticipatory' power is, however, exceptional (*Foulkes* v *Chief Constable of Merseyside Police* [1998] 3 All ER 705) (see below). Where the exercise of conflicting interests—such as the right to engage in lawful trade and a right to protest—threaten a breach of the peace, chief officers are required to balance the competing needs of the parties and the other policing needs of the community at large. There is no rule that prevents the police from restraining lawful activity where to do so is the only realistic way of preventing a breach of the peace. In deciding what strategy to adopt in order to avoid a breach of the peace, not only are chief officers able to consider restraining lawful activities of others, they are also entitled to consider the financial resources available to them, together with the rights of others in their police area and the risk of injury to all concerned. Consequently, there is no absolute requirement for a chief officer to deploy his/her resources in order to protect a person's right to trade, even where the disruption of that trade is caused by unlawful conduct and under circumstances in which other chief officers had acted differently in the past (*R* v *Chief Constable of Sussex, ex parte International Trader's Ferry Ltd* [1999] 2 AC 418).

However, when exercising discretionary powers to prevent disorder, police officers will in future be expected to focus their attention on those who are likely to present the actual threat of violence or disorder. This is the approach first taken by the Divisional Court in a case where people preaching on the steps of a church were warned by police that they were antagonising passers by. Despite the warning, the preachers continued and, as there was an imminent likelihood of a recently-gathered crowd attacking them, the preachers were arrested (see below) (*Redmond-Bate* v *DPP* [1999] Crim LR 998). The Divisional Court felt that the approach taken by the police was incompatible with Article 10 of the European Convention on Human Rights and that the officers' attention should have been directed at the crowd from whom the threat to the 'peace' was emanating. The individuals preaching were simply exercising their right to freedom of expression. It was the crowd who, in the court's view, ought to have received the warning and who should have been arrested in the event of their continuing to represent a threat to public order. In the most recent and authoritative case, the Court of Appeal reiterated that this power of arrest was wholly exceptional and set out the conditions that must be met before this power should be used. Those conditions are:

- there must be the clearest of circumstances and a real and present threat to the peace to justify the arrest,
- the threat must be coming from the person who is ultimately arrested,
- his/her conduct must be clearly interfering with the rights of another, and
- that conduct must be unreasonable

(*Bibby* v *Chief Constable of Essex Police* (2000) 164 JP 297). These cases have resurrected an age-old common law question of how far the lawful activities of one person can be restrained because they will cause others to act unlawfully. Despite many notable contradictions since, the view of Fielding J in *Beatty* v *Gillbanks* (1882) 9 QBD 308, was that there was no legal authority for such a proposition; it may be that the Human Rights Act 1998 will bring a return to that approach by the courts.

### 4.2.1 Power of arrest

A constable or any other person may arrest without warrant any person:

- who is committing a breach of the peace;
- who he/she reasonably believes will commit a breach of the peace in the immediate future; or
- who has committed a breach of the peace, where it is reasonably believed that a recurrence of the breach of the peace is threatened.

This power of arrest may be exercised on private premises, even where there is no other member of the public present (*McConnell* v *Chief Constable of Greater Manchester Police* above), and it is not affected by the Public Order Act 1986 (see s. 40(4)).

In one case, police officers were called to an electricity board showroom by staff who were having difficulty in removing a customer from their premises. When the officers, at the request of the staff, tried to remove the customer, she resisted and was arrested for a breach of the peace. It was held that the customer's continued presence in the showroom, having been asked to leave by the occupier, amounted to a civil trespass (as to which, **see chapter 9**) and that the officers were acting lawfully in assisting the occupier to remove her. Once the customer's behaviour created an imminent likelihood of a breach of the peace, the officers were empowered to arrest her (*Porter* v *Commissioner of Police for the Metropolis*, The Times, 20 October 1999).

Even if exercising the power under circumstances where a breach of the peace has not yet occurred, it is enough that a constable uses the wording 'I am arresting you for a breach of the peace' when arresting the person (*R* v *Howell* [1982] QB 416).

## 4.3 **Drunk and disorderly**

OFFENCE: **Drunk and disorderly—*Criminal Justice Act 1967, s 91(1)***
- Triable summarily • Fine
*(Statutory power of arrest)*

The Criminal Justice Act 1967, s. 91 (amended by CJA 1972, s. 4 and CJA 1982, s. 38) states:

(1) Any person who in any public place is guilty, while drunk, of disorderly behaviour may be arrested without warrant by any person and shall be liable . . .

---

**KEYNOTE**

To prove this offence you must show that the defendant was both drunk and disorderly. The drunkenness must be as a result of excessive consumption of *alcohol*; if the person's state is caused by some other intoxicant (e.g. glue solvents), the offence is not made out (*Neale* v *R. M. J. E. (a minor)* (1984) 80 Cr App R 20). The same ruling applies to a person 'found drunk' in a public place (*Lanham* v *Rickwood* (1984) 148 JP 737 (**see** chapter 10). This can be contrasted with the situation in relation to drink/driving cases (**see** Road Traffic, chapter 5) where unfitness to drive can arise from drugs as well as alcohol.

'Drunkenness' here means where the defendant has taken intoxicating liquor to an extent that affects his/her steady self-control (per Goff LJ in *Neale*).

Where there are *several* causes of a person's incapacitated state, one of which is alcohol, a court can find that the person was in fact 'drunk', even though some additional intoxicant had an exacerbating effect on his/her loss of 'steady self-control'.

This offence is a 'penalty offence' for the purposes of s. 1 of the Criminal Justice and Police Act 2001 (**see** para. 2.5.1).

For further offences and powers relating to the sale and consumption of alcohol on premises and public places, **see** chapter 10.

Despite the effects of s. 26(1) of the Police and Criminal Evidence Act 1984 (**see** chapter 2), the Divisional Court has held that the statutory power of arrest still applies to constables (*DPP* v *Kitching* [1990] Crim LR 394). Nevertheless, the general power of arrest under the 1984 Act may well be available (see Home Office Circular 88/1985).

When a person is arrested for this offence by a constable, he/she may be taken to an approved treatment centre for alcoholism (a 'detoxification' centre) and he/she will be treated as being in lawful custody for the purposes of that journey (see s. 34(1) of the Criminal Justice Act 1972).

The conduct of passengers who are drunk on an aircraft has a potential impact on the safety of the aircraft and the people therein, therefore they can be dealt with under s. 61 of the Civil Aviation Act 1982 as the relevant regulators made thereunder (see e.g. *R* v *Tagg* [2001] EWCA Crim 1230 SI 1995 No. 1970 made under Civil Aviation Act 1982 and the Airports Act 1986).

---

### 4.3.1 **Found drunk**

OFFENCE: **Being found drunk—*Licensing Act 1872, s. 12***
- Triable summarily • Fine
*(Statutory power of arrest)*

The Licensing Act 1872, s. 12 states:

Every person found drunk in any highway or other public place, whether a building or not, or on any licensed premises, shall be liable . . .

**KEYNOTE**

This offence is committed if a person is on the highway or public place and shown to be drunk. It does not matter that the person is only there briefly or of his/her own volition.

'Other public place' will include all places to which the public have access (whether on payment or otherwise).

The offence has held to apply to the licensee when found drunk on the licensed premises, even when those premises were not open to the public (see *Evans* v *Fletcher* (1926) 135 LT 153).

The drunkenness must be as a result of excessive consumption of *alcohol*; if the person's state is caused by some other intoxicant, e.g. glue solvents, the offence is not made out (*Lanham* v *Rickwood* (1984) 148 JP 737). The same ruling applies to a person who is disorderly whilst drunk.

This offence is a 'penalty offence' for the purposes of s. 1 of the Criminal Justice and Police Act 2001 (see Chapter 2).

Under s. 1 of the Licensing Act 1902 a person found drunk in a highway or public place is liable to arrest if he/she is incapable of taking care of himself/herself. The power is not restricted to police officers and may be used where there is an honest belief based on reasonable grounds that the person is committing this offence (see *Trebeck* v *Croudace* [1918] 1 KB 158).

On arresting a person for this offence, a police officer may, if he/she thinks fit, take the person to an approved treatment centre under s. 34 of the Criminal Justice Act 1972. During the journey to such a treatment centre the person will be deemed to be in lawful custody. Section 34 does not allow a person to be detained at the centre and does not preclude any charge being brought in relation to the offence.

For the offence of being drunk in charge of a carriage (under s. 12 of the Licensing Act 1872), see Road Traffic, chapter 5.

## 4.4   The Public Order Acts

Many of the most common offences regulating public disorder and threats to public order were formerly contained in the Public Order Act 1936. This left several key offences, such as riot and affray to the common law. These provisions were felt to be inadequate and the Public Order Act 1986 was passed in an attempt to codify the law in this area.

## 4.5   Riot

OFFENCE:   **Riot—*Public Order Act 1986, s. 1***
   • Triable on indictment • Ten years' imprisonment
   *(Arrestable offence)*

The Public Order Act 1986, s. 1 states:

(1) Where 12 or more persons who are present together use or threaten unlawful violence for a common purpose and the conduct of them (taken together) is such as would cause a person of reasonable firmness present at the scene to fear for his personal safety, each of the persons using unlawful violence for the common purpose is guilty of riot.

(2) It is immaterial whether or not the 12 or more use or threaten unlawful violence simultaneously.

(3) The common purpose may be inferred from conduct.

(4) No person of reasonable firmness need actually be, or be likely to be, present at the scene.

(5) Riot may be committed in private as well as in public places.

**KEYNOTE**

This offence requires the consent of the Director of Public Prosecutions before a prosecution can be brought. Although there may be occasions where 12 or more people behave in the way proscribed by s. 1, it still very rare for a charge of riot to be brought. This may have something to do with the provisions of the Riot Damages Act 1886 which enables people who have suffered loss or damage during a riot to claim compensation from the local police budget (s. 2) irrespective of whether there has been any proven negligence on the part of the police. This provision attracted a great deal of criticism following the disturbances in Bradford, Oldham and Burnley in 2001 and, in the same year, the lodging of civil claims following disorder at the Yarl's Wood detention centre.

It is not necessary that all 12 people concerned use or threaten unlawful violence at the same time. However, the courts have held that each defendant must be shown to have *used* unlawful violence and not merely threatened to do so (*R v Jefferson* [1994] 1 All ER 270). A defendant must be shown to have *intended* to use/threaten violence or to have *been aware* that his/her conduct may have been violent (s. 6(1)).

The offence may be committed in private as well as in a public place. There is no need to prove that a person of reasonable firmness was actually caused to fear for his/her safety; merely that such a person would be caused so to fear (although clearly one way to prove that element would be by the testimony of those witnessing the behaviour).

Although there must be a common purpose, this need not be part of a pre-determined plan, nor be unlawful in itself. A common purpose to get into a rock concert or even the January sales at a high street store could therefore be enough, provided all other elements are present.

### 4.5.1 Violence

Section 8 of the Public Order Act 1986 provides guidance on when conduct will amount to 'violence':

'violence' means any violent conduct, so that—
  (a) except in the context of affray, it includes violent conduct towards property as well as violent conduct towards persons, and
  (b) it is not restricted to conduct causing or intended to cause injury or damage but includes any other violent conduct (for example, throwing at or towards a person a missile of a kind capable of causing injury which does not hit or falls short).

**KEYNOTE**

It has been held that the use of the term 'unlawful' in the 1986 Act has been included to allow for the general defences—such as self-defence (see **Crime, chapter 4**)—to be applicable (see *R v Rothwell* [1993] Crim LR 626).

### 4.5.2 Drunkenness

The effect of drunkenness on criminal liability generally is discussed in **Crime, chapter 4**. However, Parliament has specifically catered for self-induced intoxication, not just for the offence of riot, but in relation to other offences under the 1986 Act by s. 6 which states:

  (5) For the purposes of this section a person whose awareness is impaired by intoxication shall be taken to be aware of that of which he would be aware if not intoxicated, unless he shows either that his intoxication was not self-induced or that it was caused solely by the taking or administration of a substance in the course of medical treatment.

  (6) In subsection (5) 'intoxication' means any intoxication, whether caused by drink, drugs or other means, or by a combination of means.

## 4.6    Violent disorder

OFFENCE:    **Violent disorder—*Public Order Act 1986, s. 2***
- Triable either way • Five years' imprisonment and/or a fine on indictment;
  six months' imprisonment and/or a fine summarily
  *(Arrestable offence)*

The Public Order Act 1986, s. 2 states:

(1)  Where 3 or more persons who are present together use or threaten unlawful violence and the conduct of them (taken together) is such as would cause a person of reasonable firmness present at the scene to fear for his personal safety, each of the persons using or threatening unlawful violence is guilty of violent disorder.

(2)  It is immaterial whether or not the 3 or more use or threaten unlawful violence simultaneously.

(3)  No person of reasonable firmness need actually be, or be likely to be, present at the scene.

(4)  Violent disorder may be committed in private as well as in public places.

---

### KEYNOTE

In order to convict any defendant of this offence, you must show that there were three or more people using or threatening violence. If this is not proved then the court should acquit each defendant (*R* v *McGuigan* [1991] Crim LR 719). Ordinarily this will mean that, if there are only three defendants, the acquittal of one will mean the acquittal of all, unless you prove that there were others taking part in the disorder who were not charged (*R* v *Worton* ((1990) JP 201) 154 JP 201).

The requirements as to the hypothetical effects on an equally hypothetical person of reasonable firmness are the same as for the offence of riot. However, there is no requirement to prove a common purpose.

Again, a defendant must be shown to have *intended* to use/threaten violence or to have *been aware* that his/her conduct may have been violent (s. 6(2)) and the offence may be committed in private as well as in a public place. 'Violence' for these purposes can include violent conduct towards property (s. 8).

---

## 4.7    Affray

OFFENCE:    **Affray—*Public Order Act 1986, s. 3***
- Triable either way • Three years' imprisonment and/or a fine on indictment;
  six months' imprisonment and/or a fine summarily
  *(Statutory power of arrest)*

The Public Order Act 1986, s. 3 states:

(1)  A person is guilty of affray if he uses or threatens unlawful violence towards another and his conduct is such as would cause a person of reasonable firmness present at the scene to fear for his personal safety.

(2)  Where 2 or more persons use or threaten the unlawful violence, it is the conduct of them taken together that must be considered for the purposes of subsection (1).

(3)  For the purposes of this section a threat cannot be made by the use of words alone.

(4)  No person of reasonable firmness need actually be, or be likely to be, present at the scene.

(5)  Affray may be committed in private as well as in public places.

---

### KEYNOTE

Formerly an offence requiring more than one person, this offence may now be committed by a single defendant although, if he/she acts with another, the conduct of them taken together will be the relevant factor in determining their criminal conduct (s. 3(2)).

The House of Lords has held that, in order to prove the offence of affray, the threat of unlawful violence has to be towards a person(s) present at the scene (*I* v *DPP* [2001] UKHL 10). Once this element has been proved, it will be necessary to prove the second element, namely whether the defendant's conduct would have caused a hypothetical person present at the scene to fear for his/her personal safety (*R* v *Sanchez* (1996) 160 JP 321).

The threat cannot be made by words alone (s. 3(3)), therefore there must be some action by the defendant—even if that 'action' consists of utilising something else such as a dog to threaten the violence (*R* v *Dixon* [1993] Crim LR 579).

Although violence is 'not restricted to conduct causing or intended to cause injury or damage but includes any other violent conduct' (s. 8), the expression does not include conduct towards property as it does with the offences under ss. 1 and 2.

Once more, a defendant must be shown to have *intended* to use/threaten violence or to have *been aware* that his/her conduct may have been violent (s. 6).

### 4.7.1 Power of arrest

The Public Order Act 1986, s. 3 states:

> (6) A constable may arrest without warrant anyone he reasonably suspects is committing affray.

**KEYNOTE**

The power of arrest here is limited to the present tense, that is, to someone who is reasonably suspected of being in the process of committing an affray. This is the same as the power provided for offences under ss 4 and 4A (see below). A preventive power can be found under the common law provisions in respect of an apprehended breach of the peace (see para. 4.2). Other powers may be available in relation to assaults or threats to cause damage (see Crime, chapters 8 and 14).

## 4.8 Fear or provocation of violence

OFFENCE: **Fear or provocation of violence—*Public Order Act 1986, s. 4***
  • Triable summarily • Six months' imprisonment and/or a fine
  *(Statutory power of arrest)*

OFFENCE: **Racially or religiously aggravated—*Crime and Disorder Act 1998, s. 31(1)(a)***
  • Triable either way • Two years' imprisonment and/or a fine on indictment;
    six months' imprisonment and/or a fine summarily
  *(Statutory power of arrest)*

The Public Order Act 1986, s. 4 states:

> (1) A person is guilty of an offence if he—
>   (a) uses towards another person threatening, abusive or insulting words or behaviour, or
>   (b) distributes or displays to another person any writing, sign or other visible representation which is threatening, abusive or insulting,
>   with intent to cause that person to believe that immediate unlawful violence will be used against him or another by any person, or to provoke the immediate use of unlawful violence by that person or another, or whereby that person is likely to believe that such violence will be used or it is likely that such violence will be provoked.
>
> (2) An offence under this section may be committed in a public or a private place, except that no offence is committed where the words or behaviour are used, or the writing, sign or other visible representation is distributed or displayed, by a person inside a dwelling and the other person is also inside that or another dwelling.

**KEYNOTE**

The term 'threatening, abusive or insulting' is not defined but it was interpreted by the courts under the Public Order Act 1936. Whether words or behaviour are threatening, abusive or insulting will be a question of fact for the magistrate(s) to decide in each case (see *Brutus* v *Cozens* [1973] AC 854).

As with many of the other public order offences that follow in this chapter, the effect that an individual's rights (such as the right to freedom of expression under Article 10 of the European Convention on Human Rights) will have here is not yet clear. The problems of balancing such freedom of expression with the expectations and sensibilities of ordinary members of society can be seen in other countries where these individual rights have been specifically protected by a written constitution. To paraphrase one American judge in a case involving the use of obscene language by an anti-Vietnam protester, 'it is often true that one person's vulgarity is another person's lyric' (see *Cohen* v *State of California* 403 US 15 (1971) 25).

It is not enough that conduct is 'offensive' but it has been held that masturbation towards a police officer in a public lavatory is capable of being insulting (*Parkin* v *Norman* [1983] QB 82).

'Immediate' unlawful violence does not have to be instantaneous but it must be shown that the defendant's conduct was likely to lead to more than some form of violence at some later date. Therefore publication and sale of material by the author Salman Rushdie, however insulting it may have been to some people, was not enough on its facts to support a charge against the publishers under s 4 (*R* v *Horseferry Road Metropolitan Stipendiary Magistrate, ex parte Siadatan* [1991] 1 QB 260). 'Immediate' here requires some close proximity between the acts of the defendant and the apprehended violence, with no intervening occurrence.

In this, and the s 4A offence (below), the victim of the racially or religiously aggravated behaviour can be a police officer and the courts have held that police officers are entitled to the same protection under the legislation as anyone else (see *R* v *Jacobs* [2001] 2 Cr App R(s) 38).

There are a number of ways in which this offence can be committed (see below). In all of these, however, there must be the use of threatening/abusive/insulting words or behaviour (or distribution/display of writing, signs, etc.). This must be carried out with the requisite state of mind set out at s. 6(3) which states:

> (3) A person is guilty of an offence under section 4 only if he intends his words or behaviour, or the writing, sign or other visible representation, to be threatening, abusive or insulting, or is aware that it may be threatening, abusive or insulting.

In addition, it must be shown that the person further *intended* to bring about the consequences set out below (at (a) and (b)) or that the consequences (at (c) and (d)) were likely.

The offence was broken down into four component parts in *Winn* v *DPP* (1992) 156 JP 881. For each of these parts it must be shown:

(a) that the defendant:

- intended the person against whom the conduct was directed

- to believe

- that immediate unlawful violence would be used

- either against him/her or against anyone else

- by the defendant or anyone else; *or*

(b) that he/she:

- intended to provoke the immediate use of unlawful violence

- by that person or anyone else; *or*

(c) that:

- the person against whom the words or behaviour (or distribution/display of writing etc.) were directed
- was likely to believe
- that immediate unlawful violence would be used; *or*

(d) that:

- it was likely that immediate unlawful violence would be provoked.

In the case at (a) above, it does not have to be shown that the other person *actually believed* that immediate violence would be used; it has to be shown that the defendant *intended to cause* him/her to believe it (*Swanston* v *DPP* (1997) 161 JP 203).

The person in whom the defendant intends to create that belief must be the same person at whom the conduct is directed (*Loade* v *DPP* [1990] 1 QB 1052). Therefore, if the defendant uses threatening behaviour towards person A, intending that this will cause person B to believe that immediate unlawful violence will be used, the offence under s. 4 is not, without more, made out.

The inclusion of this offence within the provisions of the Crime and Disorder Act 1998 attracts a higher maximum sentence (under s. 31(4) of the 1998 Act) where the offence is racially or religiously aggravated.

For a full explanation of the meaning of 'racially or religiously aggravated', **see chapter 3**).

Unlike some of the other racially or religiously aggravated offences (**see Crime, chapters 8 and 14**), provisions are specifically made for alternative verdicts in relation to the above public order offence (see s. 31(6) of the 1998 Act).

---

Under the Public Order Act 1986, s. 8, dwelling is defined as:

> . . . any structure or part of a structure occupied as a person's home or as other living accommodation (whether the occupation is separate or shared with others) but does not include any part not so occupied, and for this purpose 'structure' includes a tent, caravan, vehicle, vessel or other temporary or movable structure.

---

**KEYNOTE**

Given that the offence at s. 4 can be committed in private (under the restrictions in relation to dwellings by s. 4(2) above), it appears that the offence could be committed by a person sending out e-mails or other forms of communication from his/her house to other non-dwellings or from his/her place of work to people's houses.

Communal landings which form access routes to separate dwellings have been held not to constitute part of a dwelling even though they could only be entered by way of an entry phone system (*Rukwira* v *DPP* [1993] Crim LR 882).

---

### 4.8.1 Power of arrest

The Public Order Act 1986, s. 4 states:

> (3) A constable may arrest without warrant anyone he reasonably suspects is committing an offence under this section.

---

**KEYNOTE**

For the effect of this and alternative powers of arrest, **see para. 4.7.1.**

Section 31(2) of the Crime and Disorder Act 1998 provides a constable with a power of arrest without warrant in respect of anyone whom he/she reasonably suspects to be committing an offence under this section which is racially or religiously aggravated.

## 4.9    **Intentional harassment, alarm or distress**

OFFENCE:    **Intentionally causing harassment, alarm or distress—*Public***
            ***Order Act 1986, s. 4A***
   • Triable summarily  • Six months' imprisonment and/or a fine
   *(Statutory power of arrest)*

OFFENCE:    **Racially or religiously aggravated—*Crime and Disorder Act 1998, s. 31(1)(b)***
   • Triable either way  • Two years' imprisonment and/or fine on indictment;
     six months' imprisonment and/or fine summarily
   *(Statutory power of arrest)*

The Public Order Act 1986, s. 4A (added by Criminal Justice and Public Order Act 1994, s. 54) states:

> (1)  A person is guilty of an offence if, with intent to cause a person harassment, alarm or distress, he—
>   (a)  uses threatening, abusive or insulting words or behaviour, or disorderly behaviour, or
>   (b)  displays any writing, sign or other visible representation which is threatening, abusive or insulting,
>
>   thereby causing that or another person harassment, alarm or distress.

---

### KEYNOTE

The inclusion of this offence within the provisions of the Crime and Disorder Act 1998 attracts a higher maximum sentence (under s. 31(4) of the 1998 Act) where the offence is racially or religiously aggravated.

For a full explanation of the meaning of 'racially or religiously aggravated', see chapter 3.

For the purpose of the racially or religiously aggravated form of causing fear or provocation of violence, any words used by the defendant have to be construed within the meaning that they are given in England and Wales. In construing those words, the courts should not have any regard to the *defendant's* own racial, national or ethnic origins—or presumably their religious beliefs or lack of such (*R v White (Anthony Delroy)* [2001] EWCA Crim 216). In *White* the defendant had been challenged by a bus conductor who believed she had seen him reaching into someone's handbag. The defendant called the bus conductor a 'stupid African bitch' and, on his arrest, an 'African cunt'. The defendant had been born in the West Indies and regarded himself as 'African'. He appealed against his conviction on (among other things) the grounds that:

- the expression he had used, however unpleasant, did not involve an imputation of membership of a racial or ethnic group, or of a particular colour;

- Parliament could not have intended to criminalise his conduct because he was of the same racial group as the bus conductor;

- evidence of his conduct when arrested by the police was not covered by the statute and should not have been admitted.

The Court of Appeal held that:

- the defendant's words had to be construed as they were generally used in England and Wales. The court did not have to stick to any precise dictionary definition (*Mandla v Dowell Lee* [1983] 2 AC 548). On that basis, the word 'African' described a racial group defined by reference to race because, although capable of including other groups (such as Egyptians and white South Africans), the word was not generally used to describe such other groups. The word 'Asians' had been similarly recognised (see *DPP v Rishan Kqumar Pal* [2000] Crim LR 756).

- There was no basis in law for the second ground. Although it may make it more difficult to establish hostility of racial, national or ethnic origin where a defendant is of the same racial, national or ethnic group as a victim, it is still possible to do so.

- The defendant's remarks about the bus conductor made upon arrest did not amount to racial aggravation under s. 31 of the 1998 Act because it was not conduct '*at the time of committing the offence or immediately after doing so*'. Nevertheless, admission in evidence of those remarks did not render the trial unfair in these circumstances because the jury was entitled to know the complete sequence of events.

Unlike some of the other racially or religiously aggravated offences (see Crime, chapters 8 and 14), provisions are specifically made for alternative verdicts in relation to the above public order offence (see s. 31(6) of the 1998 Act).

In order to prove this offence you must show that the defendant *intended* to cause harassment, alarm or distress and, it seems, that by so doing, the defendant actually caused some harassment, alarm or distress.

Harassment, alarm or distress are not defined and it would appear that they are to be given their ordinary everyday meaning. A police officer can be caused such harassment, alarm or distress (*DPP* v *Orum* [1989] 1 WLR 88); and can also be the victim of the racially aggravated form of the offence (see *R* v *Jacobs* [2001] Cr App R(s) 38); and he/she can feel that harassment, alarm or distress for someone else present (e.g. a child—see *Lodge* v *DPP,* The Times, 26 October 1988).

Whether the use of a particular phrase, in the context and circumstances in which it was used, was intended to cause harassment, alarm or distress for the offences above is a question of fact for the relevant magistrate/jury to decide (see *DPP* v *Weeks,* The Independent, 17 July 2000). Consequently, in that case where the defendant was alleged to have called the victim a 'black bastard' during a heated argument over a business transaction, the magistrates were still entitled to find him not guilty of the aggravated s. 4A offence if they were satisfied that the relevant intention was not present.

Posting a threatening, abusive or insulting letter through someone's letter box is not an offence under this section (*Chappell* v *DPP* (1988) 89 Cr App R 82). It may, however, amount to an offence under the Malicious Communications Act 1988 (see chapter 3).

---

Section 4A (added by Criminal Justice and Public Order Act 1994, s. 154) states:

> (2) An offence under this section may be committed in a public place or a private place, except that no offence is committed where the words or behaviour are used, or the writing, sign or other visible representation is displayed, by a person inside a dwelling and the person who is harassed, alarmed or distressed is also inside that or another dwelling.

---

**KEYNOTE**

For 'dwelling' see para. 4.8.

---

4.9.1 **Defence**

The Public Order Act 1986, s. 4A provides a specific defence:

> (3) It is a defence for the accused to prove—
> (a) that he was inside a dwelling and had no reason to believe that the words or behaviour used, or the writing, sign or other visible representation displayed, would be heard or seen by a person outside that or any other dwelling, or
> (b) that his conduct was reasonable.

---

**KEYNOTE**

If is for the defendant to prove that one of the elements existed at the time of the offence. The standard of proof here will be that of the balance of probabilities, i.e. that it was more likely than not.

---

4.9.2 **Power of arrest**

The Public Order Act 1986, s. 4A states:

(4) A constable may arrest without warrant anyone he reasonably suspects is committing an offence under this section.

**KEYNOTE**

For the effect of this and alternative powers of arrest, see para. 4.7.1.

Section 31(2) of the Crime and Disorder Act 1998 provides a constable with a power of arrest without warrant in respect of anyone whom he/she reasonably suspects to be committing an offence under this section which is racially or religiously aggravated.

## 4.10 Harassment, alarm or distress

OFFENCE: **Harassment, alarm or distress—*Public Order Act 1986, s. 5***
• Triable summarily • Fine
*(Statutory power of arrest)*

OFFENCE: **Racially or religiously aggravated—*Crime and Disorder Act 1998, s. 31(1)(c)***
• Triable summarily • Fine
*(Statutory power of arrest)*

The Public Order Act 1986, s. 5 states:

(1) A person is guilty of an offence if he—
(a) uses threatening, abusive or insulting words or behaviour, or disorderly behaviour, or
(b) displays any writing, sign or other visible representation which is threatening, abusive or insulting,
within the hearing or sight of a person likely to be caused harassment, alarm or distress thereby.

**KEYNOTE**

Unlike the other racially or religiously aggravated forms of public order offences, the offence under s. 5 remains triable summarily, even if aggravated by the conditions set out in s. 28 of the Crime and Disorder Act 1998 (s. 31(5)). (For a full explanation of the meaning of 'racially or religiously aggravated', see chapter 3.)

The racially or religiously aggravated circumstances set out at s. 28(1)(a) of the Crime and Disorder Act 1998 deal with situations where the defendant demonstrates racial or religious hostility at the time of (or immediately before or after) commiting the offence, towards the *victim*. To clarify such situations in relation to the racially or religiously aggravated form of the above offence, s. 31(7) provides that the person 'likely to be caused harassment, alarm or distress' will be treated as the 'victim'. This appears to be a more useful provision than its counterpart in relation to the Criminal Damage Act 1971 (see Crime, chapter 14).

Note that 'disorderly' is not defined and ought to be given its ordinary everyday meaning. It need not be shown that the disorderly behaviour is itself threatening, abusive or insulting, nor that it brought about any feelings of apprehension in the person to whom it was directed (*Chambers* v *DPP* [1995] Crim LR 896). The wording of s. 5 is not limited to rowdy behaviour and will extend to any behaviour that could be construed as threatening, abusive or insulting. 'Insulting' has been held by the Divisional Court to include the actions of a market trader who installed a hidden video camera to film women trying on swimwear (*Vigon* v *DPP* (1998) 162 JP 115).

The discussion above (see para. 4.9) in relation to intentional harassment, alarm or distress also applies to this offence, except here there needs to be a person within whose sight or hearing the conduct takes place.

Quashing a conviction under s. 5, the Administrative Court has held that there is a presumption that a defendant's conduct was protected by Article 10 unless and until it is established that a restriction on their freedom of expression was strictly necessary (*Percy* v *DPP* [2001] EWHC Admin 1125). That case involved the defendant defacing an American flag as part of a political protest at a US air base. The Court held that ss. 5 and 6 of the Act contained the necessary balance between the right of individual freedom of expression and the right of others not to be insulted and/or distressed. However, on the facts of the case itself, the issues of proportionality had not been properly considered and therefore the defendant's conviction was quashed.

This offence is a 'penalty offence' for the purposes of s. 1 of the Criminal Justice and Police Act 2001 (see para. 2.5.1).

Section 5 states:

(2) An offence under this section may be committed in a public or a private place, except that no offence is committed where the words or behaviour are used, or the writing, sign or other visible representation is displayed, by a person inside a dwelling and the other person is also inside that or another dwelling.

**KEYNOTE**

For 'dwelling', see para. 4.8.

### 4.10.1 State of mind

The Public Order Act 1986, s. 6 states:

(4) A person is guilty of an offence under section 5 only if he intends his words or behaviour, or the writing, sign or other visible representation, to be threatening, abusive or insulting, or is aware that it may be threatening, abusive or insulting or (as the case may be) he intends his behaviour to be or is aware that it may be disorderly.

### 4.10.2 Defence

The Public Order Act 1986, s. 5 provides a specific defence:

(3) It is a defence for the accused to prove—
(a) that he had no reason to believe that there was any person within hearing or sight who was likely to be caused harassment, alarm or distress, or
(b) that he was inside a dwelling and had no reason to believe that the words or behaviour used, or the writing sign or other visible representation displayed, would be heard or seen by a person outside that or any other dwelling, or
(c) that his conduct was reasonable.

**KEYNOTE**

It is for the defendant to prove that one of the elements existed at the time of the offence. The standard of proof here will be that of the balance of probabilities, i.e. that it was more likely than not.

In deciding whether a defendant's conduct was reasonable under s. 5(3)(c) an objective test will be applied (*DPP* v *Clarke* (1991) 94 Cr App R 359).

### 4.10.3 Power of arrest

The Public Order Act 1986, s. 5(4)(a) (amended by Public Order (Amendment) Act 1996, s. 1) states:

(4) A constable may arrest a person without warrant if—
(a) he engages in offensive conduct which a constable warns him to stop, and
(b) he engages in further offensive conduct immediately or shortly after the warning.

The Crime and Disorder Act 1998, s. 31(3) states:

> (3) A constable may arrest a person without warrant if—
> - (a) he engages in conduct which a constable reasonably suspects to constitute an offence falling within subsection (1)(c) above;
> - (b) he is warned by that constable to stop; and
> - (c) he engages in further such conduct immediately or shortly after the warning.
>
> The conduct mentioned in paragraph (a) above and the further conduct need not be of the same nature.

---

**KEYNOTE**

It is no longer necessary that the warning be given by the same officer who later arrests the defendant (s. 1 of the Public Order (Amendment) Act 1996). For a warning to be sufficient, the words must convey to the defendant that to continue with his/her conduct will amount to an offence (*Groom* v *DPP* [1991] Crim LR 713).

The second power of arrest applies to suspected offences which are racially or religiously aggravated.

---

4.10.4     **Police direction to prevent harassment**

In response to a number of campaigns against individuals believed to be involved in animal experiments, the Criminal Justice and Police Act 2001 gives the police specific powers to prevent the intimidation or harassment of people in their own or others' homes. Situations envisaged by the legislation typically arise where protestors gather outside a house where a particular individual is believed to be. Under such circumstances s. 42 provides the most senior ranking police officer at the scene with discretionary powers to give directions to people in the vicinity. The power arises where:

- the person is outside (or in the vicinity of) any premises that are used by any individual as his/her dwelling, and
- the constable believes, on reasonable grounds, that the person is there for the purpose of representing or persuading the resident (or anyone else)
- that they should not do something they are entitled or required to do or
- that they should do something that they are under no obligation to do, and
- the constable also believes, on reasonable grounds, that the person's presence amounts to or is likely to result in, the harassment of the resident or is likely to cause alarm or distress to the resident.

Although the premises involved may be in use by any 'individual' (e.g. *not* a company) and the purpose may be to persuade that or any other 'individual', the officer must believe that the ultimate effect will be harassment, alarm or distress of the *resident*. The requirement for 'belief' by the police officer here is greater than mere concern or suspicion. The requirement for reasonable grounds means that their existence or otherwise will be judged objectively and not simply from the personal standpoint of the officer using the power. Nevertheless, the officer is given a great deal of individual discretion in using this power. Given the discretion and the potential impact on the competing rights of all involved, the use and extent of this power must be carefully considered in the light of the principles of the Human Rights Act 1998 (**see chapter 2**).

A direction given under s. 42 requires the person(s) to do all such things as the officer specifies as being *necessary* to prevent the harassment, alarm or distress of the resident, including a requirement to leave the vicinity either immediately or after a specified time (s. 42(2) and (4)). The officer may decide that people can remain within a certain distance from the relevant premises and may limit the number or identity of people who can remain in the vicinity (s. 42(5)).

The direction may be given orally and, where appropriate, may be given to a group of people together (s. 42(3)). There is no requirement that the officer giving the direction be in uniform (however, see the power of arrest for contravention of such an order below).

The power under s. 42 cannot be used to direct someone to refrain from conduct made lawful under the Trade Union and Labour Relations (Consolidation) Act 1992, s. 220 (peaceful picketing, **see chapter 7**).

OFFENCE: **Knowingly contravening a s. 42 direction—*Criminal Justice and Police Act 2001, s. 42(7)***

• Triable summarily • Three months' imprisonment and/or a fine
*(Statutory power of arrest)*

The Criminal Justice and Police Act 2001, s. 42 states:

(7) Any person who knowingly contravenes a direction given to him under this section shall be guilty of an offence.

---

**KEYNOTE**

The wording of this offence means that you will have to prove a number of key aspects. First, you will need to show that the person acted 'knowingly' in contravening the direction and secondly that it was 'given to them'. Generally the best proof of this will be to show that the person had received the direction (and the detail of its extent) personally and that they understood it. Therefore, although the section allows for directions to be given to groups, there may be practical benefits in giving personal directions where circumstances allow.

---

Power of arrest

The Criminal Justice and Police Act 2001, s. 42(8) states:

A constable in uniform may arrest without warrant any person he reasonably suspects is committing an offence under this section.

---

**KEYNOTE**

This power is restricted to officers in uniform (though it may be appropriate under the circumstances to use another power such as the common law power to prevent an imminent breach of the peace (**see para. 4.2**)). The power is also limited to those people who are reasonably suspected to be in the act of committing the offence, as opposed to those who may *have committed* the offence. For a discussion of 'reasonable suspicion', **see chapter 2**.

---

The Criminal Justice and Police Act 2001 also makes specific provision for protecting the directors (and those who live with them) of certain companies involved in sensitive and emotive operations from harassment in their homes or private lives. Under the 2001 Act (see s. 45), an individual who is (or proposes to be) a director, secretary or permanent representative of a relevant company can apply to the Secretary of State for a 'confidentiality order', exempting the individual's personal details from many of the public records that have to be maintained under the Companies Act 1985. This provision is designed to prevent activists who are opposed to the operations of certain research organisations from gaining access to the personal details of the company's officers through public registers.

4.11    **Wearing of political uniforms in public places**

Section 1 of the Public Order Act 1936 prohibits the wearing of uniforms signifying association with any political organisation in a public place or at a public meeting and creates a
summary offence to that effect. A chief officer of police may, with the consent of the
Secretary of State, permit the wearing of such uniforms under certain circumstances.

Care will need to be taken in enforcing and prosecuting this particular offence given
the strong protection that is accorded to freedom of political expression under Article 10
of the European Convention on Human Rights (see e.g. *Bowman* v *United Kingdom* (1998)
26 EHRR 1).

Section 2 of the 1936 Act outlaws quasi-military organisations which are trained or
organised to usurp the functions of the police or the armed forces, or to display physical force
in promoting any political object. Note that there is a specific offence under the Terrorism Act
2000 of providing or receiving instructions or training in the use of firearms (s. 54).

Although the 1936 Act (s. 7(3)) creates a power of arrest without warrant by a constable in
relation to any person he/she reasonably suspects to be committing an offence under s 1, no
prosecution can be brought under either s. 1 or 2 without the consent of the Attorney-
General (or Solicitor-General).

## 4.12    Public processions and assemblies

### 4.12.1    Procession organiser

The Public Order Act 1986 places certain obligations on the organisers of public processions
that are intended:

- to demonstrate support for, or opposition to, the views or actions of any person or body
- to publicise a cause or campaign, or
- to mark or commemorate an event.

If a public procession is to be held for any of these purposes, the organisers must give written
notice—by delivering it to a police station in the relevant police area—unless it is not
reasonably practicable to do so (s. 11(1) and (4)).

In the case of a procession that is to begin in Scotland but will cross over into England,
the notice must be delivered to a police station in the first police area in England on the
proposed route (s. 11(4)(b)).

Under s. 11(3), the notice must specify:

- the date and time of the proposed procession
- the proposed route, and
- the name and address of the person(s) proposing to organise it.

If such a procession is held without compliance with these requirements, or if a procession
takes place on a different date, time or route, each of the people organising it commits
a summary offence (s. 11(7)).

As with the offences in relation to the wearing of political uniforms (at **para. 4.11** above),
particular care will need to be taken in utilising the powers under this legislation in light of
the protection that is given, both by the European Convention on Human Rights, and the
courts, to freedom of speech and assembly.

Defence

The Public Order Act 1986, s. 11 states:

(8) It is a defence for the accused to prove that he did not know of, and neither suspected nor had reason to suspect, the failure to satisfy the requirements or (as the case may be) the difference of date, time or route.

(9) To the extent that an alleged offence turns on a difference of date, time or route, it is a defence for the accused to prove that the difference arose from circumstances beyond his control or from something done with the agreement of a police officer or by his direction.

### 4.12.2 Imposing

Section 12 of the Public Order Act 1986 allows for conditions to be imposed on public processions. These conditions may be imposed by 'the senior police officer' in each case. For the purposes of s. 12, the 'senior police officer' is:

- in relation to a procession being held or intended to be held where people are assembling to take part in it, *the most senior rank present at the scene*;
- in relation to any other intended procession, the chief officer of police.

Therefore, where advance notice of a procession is given, the chief of police may impose conditions on it as set out below. Where the procession has already begun, or where people are gathering to take part in it, the most senior officer present at the scene may impose those conditions.

The chief officer's directions must be in writing (s. 12(3)); the directions of other officers may be given orally, though it will be far easier to prove the relevant offences of failing to comply with those directions if there is some permanent and reliable record of them.

If the senior police officer, having regard to:

- the time or place of the procession *and*
- the conditions in which it is to be held *and*
- its route/proposed route

'reasonably believes' (**see chapter 2**) that it may result in:

- serious public disorder
- serious damage to property *or*
- serious disruption to the life of the community

he/she may give directions imposing such conditions as appear to him/her to be necessary to prevent such disorder, damage or disruption on the organisers or the people taking part (s. 12(1)).

The senior police officer (as defined above) may also give those directions where he/she reasonably believes that the purpose of the person(s) organising the procession is the intimidation of others with a view to compelling them either:

- not to do an act they have a right to do *or*
- to do an act they have a right not to do.

In any of the cases above, the directions may include directions as to the route of the procession or a prohibition on it entering certain public places (s. 12(1)).

Offences

There are three summary offences created in relation to these directions under s. 12(4), (5) and (6).

The first two are:

- organising or
- taking part in

a public procession and, in doing so, *knowingly* (**see Crime, chapter 1**) failing to comply with a condition imposed under s. 12. In either case it is a defence for the person to show that the circumstances were beyond their control.

The third offence is inciting another (**see Crime, chapter 3**) to take part in a public procession in a way which the person incited knows is failing to comply with an imposed condition.

Power of arrest

The Public Order Act 1986, s. 12 states:

> (7) A constable in uniform may arrest without warrant anyone he reasonably suspects is committing an offence under subsection (4), (5) or (6).

---

**KEYNOTE**

This power of arrest, limited to a constable in uniform, is drafted in the present tense, that is, it will only apply where there is a reasonable suspicion that the person is in the act of committing one of the relevant offences. For a further general power of arrest relating to obstructing a police officer, see Crime, chapter 8.

For a discussion of 'reasonable suspicion', see chapter 2.

---

4.12.3    **Prohibited processions**

Section 13 of the Public Order Act 1986 allows for a public procession to be prohibited, either by the district council on application from the chief constable (outside the City of London or the Metropolitan Police District) or the Commissioner with approval of the Secretary of State.

As with the conditions imposed under s. 12 above, there are three summary offences created in relation to prohibited public processions. The first two offences are committed by people who either organise a public procession which they *know* has been prohibited under s. 13 or who take part in such a procession *knowing* that it has been so prohibited (s. 13(7) and (8)). There is also an offence of a person inciting another to take part in a procession which he/she knows has been prohibited (s. 13(9)).

Power of arrest

The Public Order Act 1986, s. 13 states:

> (10) A constable in uniform may arrest without warrant anyone he reasonably suspects is committing an offence under subsection (7), (8) or (9).

---

**KEYNOTE**

This power of arrest is limited to officers in uniform. It is drafted in the present tense, that is, it will only apply where there is a reasonable suspicion that the person is in the act of committing one of the relevant offences.

For a discussion of 'reasonable suspicion', see chapter 2.

---

### 4.12.4 Public assemblies

Section 14 of the Public Order Act 1986 allows for the 'senior police officer' (as defined above) to impose conditions on public assemblies in the same way as public processions.

A public assembly is an assembly of 20 or more people in a public place that is wholly or partly open to the air (s. 16).

The circumstances under which such conditions may be imposed are the same as for public processions with the added provision that the officer may direct:

- the maximum duration or

- the maximum number of people

as appears necessary to him/her in order to avoid disorder, damage, disruption or intimidation (s. 14(1)).

The chief officer's directions must be given in writing but, as with the offences relating to public processions, it will be easier to prove the offences under s. 14 if there is a reliable record of any directions given by the senior officer.

Summary offences are again created in relation to the organising, taking part or inciting others to take part in a public assembly in each case where the person knowingly fails to comply with a condition imposed under s. 14 (s. 14(4), (5) and (6)). In the cases of people organising or taking part in such an assembly, there is a statutory defence available if the defendant can prove that the failure to comply with the relevant condition arose from circumstances beyond his/her control.

It is important to note that situations envisaged by s. 14 are different from those envisaged by s. 12. One envisages public processions, the other public assemblies. The relevance to police officers of this distinction lies in the conditions that may be imposed under each section. This distinction was considered at length in *DPP* v *Jones* [2002] EWHC 110 by the Administrative Court where demonstrators against the Huntingdon Life Sciences centre were prosecuted for failing to comply with a condition set out in a police notice issued under s. 14. It was held on appeal that some of the conditions imposed were more properly concerned with a public procession and therefore were beyond the police powers under s. 14. Although in *Jones* the offending parts of the police notice were 'severed', leaving the enforceable bits intact, it may be safer to issue two separate notices in appropriate circumstances, one relating to the conditions to be observed by participants in the 'procession' element of an operation and the other imposing conditions on the 'assembly' element.

Power of arrest

The Public Order Act 1986, s. 14 states:

> (7) A constable in uniform may arrest without warrant anyone he reasonably suspects is committing an offence under subsection (4), (5) or (6).

---

**KEYNOTE**

See Keynote above.

---

### 4.12.5 Trespassory assemblies

The provisions of s. 14 above apply to public assemblies. However, occasions have arisen where the assembly has been *trespassory*, that is, on land which is either private or where there is only a limited right of public access and the permission of the relevant landowner has not been granted. In such instances, s. 14A of the Public Order Act 1986 provides the police with certain powers.

Section 14A allows a chief officer of police (including the Commissioners of the City of London and Metropolitan Police) to apply to the relevant district council for an order prohibiting the holding of trespassory assemblies.

The conditions under which a chief officer may make such an application are where he/she reasonably believes that an assembly is to be held in any district at a place on land to which the public has no right/limited rights of access and that the assembly:

- is likely to be held without the permission of the occupier of the land *or*
- to conduct itself in such a way as to exceed the limits of the public's right of access

and that the assembly may result:

- in serious disruption to the life of the community or
- where the land (or a building/monument on it) is of historical, architectural, archaeological or scientific importance, significant damage to the land, building or monument.

The classic example of such a situation can be found at sites such as Stonehenge.

On receiving the application, the council may—*with the consent of the Secretary of State*—make an order either in the terms of the application or with such modifications as may be approved by the Secretary of State (s. 14A(2)(a)). The order must be in writing or reduced into writing as soon as practicable after being made (s. 14A(8)).

If such an order is made it must not last for more than four days nor must it apply to an area beyond a radius of five miles from a specified centre (s. 14A(6)).

As with a 'public' assembly, an assembly for these purposes means 20 or more people; 'land' means land in the open air; and 'public' includes a section of the public (s. 14A(9)).

### Offences

There are three summary offences in relation to trespassory assemblies in respect of which an order has been passed. These offences, under s. 14B(1), (2) and (3) apply to people who:

- organise or
- take part in

an assembly that they *know* is prohibited by an order under s. 14A *or*

- who incite another to take part in such an assembly.

Even where an order has been passed, there will be a need to show that the assembly was obstructive of the highway or at least that it exceeded the public's general right of access (*DPP* v *Jones* [1999] 2 AC 240).

### Power of arrest

The Public Order Act 1986, s. 14B (added by Criminal Justice and Public Order Act 1994, s. 70) states:

> (4) A constable in uniform may arrest without a warrant anyone he reasonably suspects to be committing an offence under this section.

---

**KEYNOTE**

This power of arrest, which is restricted to officers in uniform, is drafted in the present tense, that is, it will only apply where there is a reasonable suspicion that the person is in the act of committing one of the relevant offences. For a further general power of arrest relating to obstructing a police officer, see **Crime, chapter 8**.

For a discussion of 'reasonable suspicion', see **chapter 2**.

---

Police powers

Section 14C of the 1986 Act (added by Criminal Justice and Public Order Act 1994, s. 71) states:

(1) If a constable in uniform reasonably believes that a person is on his way to an assembly within the area to which an order under section 14A applies which the constable reasonably believes is likely to be an assembly which is prohibited by that order, he may, subject to subsection (2) below—
    (a) stop that person, and
    (b) direct him not to proceed in the direction of the assembly.

(2) The power conferred by subsection (1) may only be exercised within the area to which the order applies.

(3) A person who fails to comply with a direction under subsection (1) which he knows has been given to him is guilty of an offence.

(4) A constable in uniform may arrest without a warrant anyone he reasonably suspects to be committing an offence under this section.

---

**KEYNOTE**

This power allows officers to stop people, though not, it would seem, vehicles (in which case the general power under the Road Traffic Act 1988 must be used; **see Road Traffic, chapter 10**). This is the type of non-Police and Criminal Evidence Act 1984 power that may be required to be recorded in the same way as general stop and search powers in accordance with Recommendation 61 of the Lawrence Report. For more detail on these general powers to stop people and vehicles and the recording requirements, **see chapter 2**. As with the other powers of arrest in relation to processions and assemblies, this power applies only to someone reasonably suspected of being in the act of committing an offence under this section. There seems to be no requirement that the officer exercising the power of arrest is the same officer as the officer who issued the direction not to proceed (which would dilute the efficacy of the power).

---

4.12.6    **Public meetings**

It is an offence to attempt to break up a public meeting.

OFFENCE:    **Trying to break up a public meeting—*Public Meeting Act 1908, s. 1***
            • Triable summarily  •  Six months' imprisonment and/or a fine
            *(No specific power of arrest)*

The Public Meeting Act 1908, s. 1 (amended by Representation of the People Act 1949 sch. 9, Criminal Justice Act 1982, s. 46 and Criminal Law Act 1977, sch. 1) states:

(1) Any person who at a lawful public meeting acts in a disorderly manner for the purpose of preventing the transaction of the business for which the meeting was called together shall be guilty of an offence and shall on summary conviction be liable to imprisonment for a term not exceeding six months or to a fine not exceeding level 5 on the standard scale or to both . . . .

(2) Any person who incites others to commit an offence under this section shall be guilty of a like offence.

---

**KEYNOTE**

If a constable reasonably suspects any person of committing this offence, he/she may, *if requested by the person chairing the meeting*, require the offender to declare his/her name and address immediately. Failing to comply with such a request or giving false details is a summary offence (s. 1(3) ).

'Public meeting' is not defined in the 1908 Act. There appears to be no requirement for the meeting to be lawfully assembled.

This offence does not apply to meetings held in relation to the Representation of the People Act 1983, s. 97 (meetings concerned with public elections) (s. 1(4)). In the case of people acting or inciting others to act in a disorderly way at such meetings, there is a specific summary offence under s. 97(1) of the 1983 Act.

## 4.13    Sporting events

In addition to the more general offences regulating public order, there are several offences and statutory measures which are specifically aimed at tackling disorder and anti-social behaviour at sporting events. There are several immediate problems with this legislation, both practically and when trying to study it for examination purposes. These primarily arise from the fact that it has been developed piecemeal over the last 15 years, bringing the words 'dogs' and 'breakfast' to mind. The relevant legislation is therefore sprinkled across a number of different Acts, some of which are cross-referenced to each other and all of which are affected by different statutory instruments.

Despite several opportunities to consolidate all this legislation into one Act—particularly in the run up to the 2002 World Cup—we acquired another couple of pieces to add to the legislative jigsaw, the latest of which was the Football Disorder (Amendment) Act 2002. The sorry state of the legislation (set out more fully in earlier editions of this Manual) makes this probably the most confusing and confused set of statutory provisions in our criminal law.

One of the more important pieces of recent football legislation, the Football (Disorder) Act 2000, significantly altered the powers of courts and police in football-related matters. In short, the 2000 Act:

- combined the international and domestic banning orders;
- introduced 'regulated football matches' (association football matches which are prescribed matches or matches of a prescribed description) and 'external tournaments' (football competitions which include regulated football matches outside England and Wales); and
- introduced 'control periods' in relation to regulated matches or external tournaments (generally a period beginning five days before the day of the match or the first match in a tournament and ending when the match or last match is finished or cancelled).

More importantly, the 2000 Act contained specific police powers, including:

- the power for a chief officer to apply for a banning order by way of complaint to a magistrates' court;
- the power for police officers in uniform to detain British citizens for short periods of time during 'control periods' while enquiries are made into their background in relation to violence and disorder; and
- the power for police officers to issue written notices during 'control periods' requiring the person to appear before a magistrates' court, not to leave England and Wales, to surrender their passport and a power to arrest the person if necessary to secure compliance.

These wide police powers, which were rushed through Parliament at an alarming rate, were operative during an 'initial period'. That period was one year from the time the relevant sections came into force but was extended by statutory instrument. A further extension has now been made by the Football Disorder (Amendment) Act 2002.

These areas are discussed in more detail below.

4.13.1 **Offences under the Football (Offences) Act 1991**

OFFENCE: **Misbehaviour at designated football match—*Football (Offences) Act 1991, ss. 2, 3 and 4***

- Triable summarily • Fine

*(Arrestable offence)*

The Football (Offences) Act 1991, ss. 2, 3 and 4 state:

2. It is an offence for a person at a designated football match to throw anything at or towards—
   (a) the playing area, or any area adjacent to the playing area to which spectators are not generally admitted, or
   (b) any area in which spectators or other persons are or may be present, without lawful authority or lawful excuse (which shall be for him to prove).

3.—(1) It is an offence to engage or take part in chanting of an indecent or racialist nature at a designated football match.
   (2) For this purpose—
   (a) 'chanting' means the repeated uttering of any words or sounds (whether alone or in concert with one or more others); and
   (b) 'of racialist nature means consisting of or including matter which is threatening, abusive or insulting to a person by reason of his colour, race, nationality (including citizenship) or ethnic or national origins.

4. It is an offence for a person at a designated football match to go onto the playing area, or any area adjacent to the playing area to which spectators are not generally admitted, without lawful authority or lawful excuse (which shall be for him to prove).

---

**KEYNOTE**

A 'designated' match for these purposes is the same as a 'regulated' match under the Football Spectators Act 1989 (see below).

These offences can be separated into those affecting the playing area and adjacent parts of the ground (ss. 2 and 4) and the offence of indecent or 'racialist' chanting (s. 3).

They are 'arrestable' offences by virtue of s. 24(2) of and sch. 1A to the Police and Criminal Evidence Act 1984 (see para. 2.9.1) and can usefully be remembered by abbreviating the statute's title (the Football Offences Act).

In the case of the first offence (s. 2), throwing anything at or towards the playing area etc., there is a defence of having lawful authority or lawful excuse (which presumably would cover returning the ball to the field of play). Generally there seem to be few occasions on which a defendant would have lawful authority/reasonable excuse for the behaviour prohibited by s. 2.

Section 4 makes the same savings in relation to lawful authority/reasonable excuse and, in both cases, the burden of proof falls on the defendant. (The *standard* of proof will be that of the balance of probabilities; see Evidence and Procedure, chapter 11.)

For the offence under s. 3, the defendant must be shown to have *repeated* the words or sounds before it can be classed as 'chanting'. The definition under subsection (2) was amended by the Football (Offences and Disorder) Act 1999 to cater for occasions where the offence is committed by one person acting alone.

'Indecent' is not defined and will be a question of fact for the court to decide in all the circumstances.

'Racialist' is a slightly outdated term. The wording of s. 3(2)(b) requires that the chanting *is* rather than might potentially be, threatening, abusive or insulting (compare with the wording under the other general public order offences above). Therefore, although there is no express requirement for a 'victim' of the offence under this section, the best way to prove that element of the offence would be to find someone who was so threatened, abused or insulted by the behaviour.

For a recent example where the Administrative Court held that shouting 'you're just a town full of Pakis' at supporters from Oldham fell squarely within the definition, see *DPP* v *Stoke on Trent Magistrates Court* [2003] EWHC 1593.

As with the racially or religiously aggravated offences created by the Crime and Disorder Act 1998, religion is not included in the definition. For a full discussion on racist behaviour generally, see chapter 3.

---

### Designated and regulated football matches

Many of the offences and powers relating to football fixtures relate to 'designated' or 'regulated' football matches. These expressions have now been standardised to a great extent (see the Football (Offences) (Designation of Football Matches) Order 2000 (SI 2000 No. 2329 made under Football (Offenses) Act 1991, s. 1)) and mean (under r. 3 and the schedule to the Order):

> An association football match—
> (a) in which one or both of the participating teams represents a club which is for the time being a member (whether a full or associate member) of the Football League, the Football Association Premier League or the Football Conference, or represents a club from outside England and Wales, or represents a country or territory; and
> (b) which is played—
> (i) at a sports ground which is designated by order under section 1(1) of the Safety of Sports Grounds Act 1975, or registered with the Football League or the Football Association Premier League as the home ground of a club which is a member of the Football League or the Football Association Premier League at the time the match is played; or
> (ii) in the Football Association cup (other than in a preliminary or qualifying round).

### 4.13.2    Banning orders and detention

Under earlier statutes, a distinction was made between international banning orders and domestic banning orders. The two have been replaced by a generic banning order under the Football (Disorder) Act 2000. Banning orders can be made in two ways. The first way is on conviction for a relevant offence (under s. 14A of the Football Spectators Act 1989). The relevant offences are set out at sch. 1 to the 1989 Act (see appendix 4). They include offences relating to drunkenness, violence or threats of violence or public order offences committed on journeys to or from regulated matches or during the period of such a match.

Rather than simply having the power to make such orders, courts are under a statutory duty to pass such orders if they are satisfied that there are reasonable grounds to believe that the orders would help prevent violence or disorder at/in connection with a 'regulated football match' (see above). Violence here includes violence towards property and disorder includes stirring up racial hatred (s. 14C of the 1989 Act). If the court does not pass an order, it must state in open court its reasons for not doing so.

A banning order may only be made in addition to a sentence imposed by the court but can be passed even if the originating offence is dealt with by way of a conditional or absolute discharge.

The second, more contentious, way of getting a banning order is by way of complaint by a chief officer of police for the area in which a person resides (s. 14B of the 1989 Act). On such an application a magistrates' court can make an order if the person has at any time caused or contributed to any violence or disorder in the United Kingdom or elsewhere. This provision (which was inserted by the Football Disorder Act 2000) was given a restricted 'shelf life' when the 2000 Act was passed (see para. 4.13) but this has been extended by the Football Disorder (Amendment) Act 2002.

The court may impose conditions on banning orders and, under the provisions of the Football Disorder Act 2000, *must* require the surrender of the person's passport in connection with regulated football matches outside the United Kingdom unless there are exceptional circumstances (s. 14E(3) of the 1989 Act). If there are such exceptional circumstances, the court must state them in open court.

The effect of a banning order is that the person initially has to report to the police station specified in it within five days of the day on which the order is made (s. 14E(2)). This requirement is suspended in the case of a person detained in legal custody.

Banning orders made under s. 14A of the 1989 Act (on conviction of a relevant offence) in addition to an immediate sentence of imprisonment will have a minimum of six and a maximum of ten years' duration (s. 14F(3)). Other banning orders made under s. 14A (i.e. where they do not accompany a sentence of immediate imprisonment) have a minimum of three and a maximum of five years' duration (s. 14F(4)). Banning orders made under s. 14B (on complaint by a chief officer of police) have a minimum of two and a maximum of three years' duration (s. 14F(5)). If a banning order has been in effect for at least two-thirds of its period, the person subject to it can apply to the court which passed the order for its termination. The National Criminal Intelligence Service (NCIS) (**see chapter 1**) have responsibility for monitoring the movement of football spectators and collating relevant intelligence. The Football Banning Orders Authority is the 'designated authority' for the purposes of the 1989 Act. Under the Football Disorder Act 2000, NCIS are empowered to disclose information for the purposes of the 1989 Act.

International banning orders do not contravene either the general European law on the free movement of people within the European Union, nor the European Convention on Human Rights (*Gough* v *Chief Constable of Derbyshire* [2002] EWCA Civ 354).

In *Gough*, the Court of Appeal held that there was no absolute right to leave one's country. As banning orders were to be imposed only where there were strong grounds for concluding that the person had a propensity to take part in football hooliganism, the court held that it was appropriate that such people should be subject to a scheme that restricted their ability to indulge in that hooliganism. Like Sex Offender Orders (**see Crime, chapter 10**) and Anti-Social Behaviour Orders (**see chapter 3**), banning orders are not criminal charges, nor are the proceedings in applying for them 'criminal' proceedings (*Gough*). However, although the standard of proof is the civil standard in applying for banning orders, that standard is flexible and has to reflect the consequences that would follow if the case for a banning order were made out. In reality, this means that magistrates should apply a standard of proof which is hard to distinguish from the criminal one. If properly made, any interference with an individual's Article 8 rights by a banning order will be justified (under Article 8(2)) as the order is necessary for the prevention of disorder.

Given the current state of the legislation within this area, the advice of NCIS should be sought when exercising any of the statutory provisions specifically relating to football matches and the behaviour of supporters.

OFFENCE: **Failing to comply with banning order—*Football Spectators Act 1989, s. 14J***
    • Triable summarily • Six months' imprisonment and/or a fine
    *(Arrestable offence)*

(1) A person subject to a banning order who fails to comply with—
    (a) any requirement imposed by the order, or
    (b) any requirement imposed under section 19(2B) or (2C) below is guilty of an offence.

---

**KEYNOTE**

The offence of failing to comply with a banning order is an arrestable offence under s. 24 of the Police and Criminal Evidence Act 1984 (**see chapter 2**). The reference to s. 19(2B) and (2C) is to the power for the enforcing authority to issue written notices requiring individuals to report to police stations and, where relevant, to surrender their passports, in advance of certain matches outside England and Wales.

A number of exemptions are provided for under s. 20. These allow, among other things, for the person on whom an order has been passed to apply for exemption from the duties of the order under special circumstances.

### Power of detention

The Football Spectators Act 1989, s. 21A states:

(1) This section and section 21B below apply during any control period in relation to a regulated football match outside England and Wales or an external tournament if a constable in uniform—

    (a) has reasonable grounds for suspecting that the condition in section 14B(2) above is met in the case of a person present before him, and

    (b) has reasonable grounds to believe that making a banning order in his case would help to prevent violence or disorder at or in connection with any regulated football matches.

(2) The constable may detain the person in his custody (whether there or elsewhere) until he has decided whether or not to issue a notice under section 21B below, and shall give the person his reasons for detaining him in writing.

    This is without prejudice to any power of the constable apart from this section to arrest the person.

(3) A person may not be detained under subsection (2) above for more than four hours or, with the authority of an officer of at least the rank of inspector, six hours.

### KEYNOTE

The power under s. 21A requires the police officer to be in uniform and may be exercised only in relation to a person who is a British citizen (see s. 21C(1)).

The initial period of detention allowed is a *maximum* of four hours, extendable to a further *maximum* of six hours by an inspector. There is no requirement under this section that the inspector be either present or in uniform. The purpose of the detention is for the officer to decide whether or not to issue a notice (see below).

The condition under s. 14B(2) referred to is that the person has at any time caused or contributed to any violence or disorder in the United Kingdom or elsewhere.

'Control period' means, in relation to a regulated football match outside England and Wales, the period:

(a) beginning five days before the day of the match, and

(b) ending when the match is finished or cancelled

and in relation to an external tournament, means any period described in an order made by the Secretary of State:

(a) beginning five days before the day of the first football match outside England and Wales which is included in the tournament, and

(b) ending when the last football match outside England and Wales which is included in the tournament is finished or cancelled,

but, for the purposes of paragraph (a), any football match included in the qualifying or pre-qualifying stages of the tournament is to be ignored (see s. 14(5) and (6)).

References to football matches include matches intended to be played (s. 14(7)). A person who has been detained under subsection (2) above may only be further detained under that subsection in the same control period in reliance on information which was not available to the constable who previously detained him/her; and a person on whom a notice has been served under s. 21B(2) may not be detained under subsection (2) above in the same control period (s. 21A(4)).

---

### Service of notice

The Football Spectators Act 1989, s. 21B states:

(1) A constable in uniform may exercise the power in subsection (2) below if authorised to do so by an officer of at least the rank of inspector.

(2) The constable may give the person a notice in writing requiring him—
    (a) to appear before a magistrates' court at a time, or between the times, specified in the notice,
    (b) not to leave England and Wales before that time (or the later of those times), and
    (c) if the control period relates to a regulated football match outside the United Kingdom or to an external tournament which includes such matches, to surrender his passport to the constable, and stating the grounds referred to in section 21A(1) above.

(3) The times for appearance before the magistrates' court must be within the period of 24 hours beginning with—
    (a) the giving of the notice, or
    (b) the person's detention under section 21A(2) above,
whichever is the earlier.

---

### KEYNOTE

The power above requires the police officer to be in uniform and the authority of an inspector or above. It applies during any control period in relation to a regulated football match outside England and Wales or an external tournament (as to which, see the Keynote above).

A constable may arrest a person to whom he/she is giving a notice if he/she has reasonable grounds to believe that it is *necessary* to do so in order to secure that the person complies with the notice (s. 21B(5)).

For the purposes of s. 14B, the notice is to be treated as an application for a banning order made by complaint (s. 21B(4)).

As with the provision for detention under s. 21A, the powers conferred above may be exercised only in relation to a person who is a British citizen (s. 21C(1)).

---

OFFENCE: **Failing to comply with notice—*Football Spectators Act 1989, s. 21C***

    • Triable summarily • Six months' imprisonment and/or a fine
    *(Arrestable offence)*

The Football Spectators Act 1989, s. 21C states:

(2) A person who fails to comply with a notice given to him under section 21B above is guilty of an offence ...

---

### KEYNOTE

The notice must have been lawfully given in order to attract liability for this offence. Where a person who has been given a notice appears before a magistrates' court as required by the notice (whether under arrest or not), the court may remand him/her and the court may require the person not to leave England and Wales as a condition of bail (s. 21C(3) and (4)). Also, if the control period relates to a regulated football match outside the United Kingdom or to an external tournament which includes such matches, the court can order the person to surrender his/her passport to a police constable, if he/she has not already done so.

---

4.13.3 **Offences under the Sporting Events (Control of Alcohol etc.) Act 1985**

OFFENCE: **Alcohol on coaches and trains—*Sporting Events (Control of Alcohol etc.) Act 1985, s. 1***
  • Triable summarily • Three months' imprisonment and/or a fine (s. 1(3));
    fine (s. 1(2) and (4))
  *(Statutory power of arrest)*

The Sporting Events (Control of Alcohol etc.) Act 1985, s. 1 states:

(1) This section applies to a vehicle which—
    (a) is a public service vehicle or railway passenger vehicle, and
    (b) is being used for the principal purpose of carrying passengers for the whole or part of a journey to or from a designated sporting event.

(2) A person who knowingly causes or permits intoxicating liquor to be carried on a vehicle to which the section applies is guilty of an offence—
    (a) if the vehicle is a public service vehicle and he is the operator of the vehicle or the servant or agent of the operator, or
    (b) if the vehicle is a hired vehicle and he is the person to whom it is hired or the servant or agent of that person.

(3) A person who has intoxicating liquor in his possession while on a vehicle to which this section applies is guilty of an offence.

(4) A person who is drunk on a vehicle to which this section applies is guilty of an offence.

**KEYNOTE**

Section 1 creates a number of offences in relation to public service vehicles and trains being used principally (though not exclusively) to carry passengers for the whole or part of a journey, to or from a designated sporting event.

The offences can be committed by the vehicle operator/hirer or his/her servant or agent provided there is evidence of *knowingly* causing or permitting the carrying of intoxicating liquor (for 'cause and permit', see **Road Traffic, chapter 1**).

The other offences are committed by people who have intoxicating liquor in their 'possession' (as to which, see **Crime, chapter 6**) and by people who are drunk on a relevant vehicle. Generally, any mature and competent witness may give evidence as to drunkenness (see **Evidence and Procedure, chapter 11**).

Section 7(3) provides a power for a police officer to stop a public service vehicle in order to search it where he/she has reasonable grounds to suspect an offence under this section *is being or has been committed* in respect of that vehicle. It also provides a power to search a railway carriage (though not to stop the train) under the same circumstances. The power to search people in those vehicles comes from s. 7(2).

OFFENCE: **Alcohol on other vehicles—*Sporting Events (Control of Alcohol etc.) Act 1985, s. 1A***
  • Triable summarily • Three months' imprisonment and/or a fine (s. 1A(3));
    fine (s. 1A(2) and (4))
  *(Statutory power of arrest)*

The Sporting Events (Control of Alcohol etc.) Act 1985, s. 1A states:

(1) This section applies to a motor vehicle which—
    (a) is not a public service vehicle but is adapted to carry more than 8 passengers, and
    (b) is being used for the principal purpose of carrying two or more passengers for the whole or part of a journey to or from a designated sporting event.

(2) A person who knowingly causes or permits intoxicating liquor to be carried on a motor vehicle to which this section applies is guilty of an offence—

    (a) if he is its driver, or

    (b) if he is not its driver but is its keeper, the servant or agent of its keeper, a person to whom it is made available (by hire, loan or otherwise) by its keeper or the keeper's servant or agent, or the servant or agent of a person to whom it is so made available.

(3) A person who has intoxicating liquor in his possession while on a motor vehicle to which this section applies is guilty of an offence.

(4) A person who is drunk on a motor vehicle to which this section applies is guilty of an offence.

---

**KEYNOTE**

This section creates similar offences to those set out under s. 1 but these relate to mechanically propelled vehicles that are intended or adapted for use on roads and that are adapted to carry more than eight passengers (not being PSVs). For an explanation of each of these terms, **see Road Traffic, chapter 1**.

For the purposes of the above offences, a vehicle's 'keeper' is the person having the duty to take out a vehicle excise licence for it (**see Road Traffic, chapter 12**) (s. 1A(5)).

The power to stop and search vehicles and their occupants under s. 7(3) above also applies to an offence under this section.

---

Designated sporting event

A 'designated' sporting event means an event or proposed event which has been designated or is part of a class designated by order made by the Secretary of State. It also includes events designated under comparable Scottish legislation. Events which are to be held outside Great Britain can also be designated.

Power of arrest

Section 7(2) provides that a constable may search a person he/she has reasonable grounds to suspect is committing or has committed an offence under the 1985 Act, and may arrest such a person.

OFFENCE:   **Alcohol at sports grounds—*Sporting Events (Control of Alcohol etc.) Act 1985, s. 2***

    • Triable summarily • Three months' imprisonment and/or a fine (s. 2(1)); fine (s. 2(2))

    *(Statutory power of arrest)*

The Sporting Events (Control of Alcohol etc.) Act 1985, s. 2 states:

(1) A person who has intoxicating liquor or an article to which this section applies in his possession—

    (a) at any time during the period of a designated sporting event when he is in any area of a designated sports ground from which the event may be directly viewed, or

    (b) while entering or trying to enter a designated sports ground at any time during the period of a designated sporting event at that ground, is guilty of an offence.

(1A) Subsection (1)(a) above has effect subject to section 5A(1) of this Act.

(2) A person who is drunk in a designated sports ground at any time during the period of a designated sporting event at that ground or is drunk while entering or trying to enter such a ground at any time during the period of a designated sporting event at that ground is guilty of an offence.

**KEYNOTE**

The articles to which s. 2 applies are:

- articles capable of causing injury to a person struck by them, being
- bottles, cans or other portable containers (including ones that are crushed or broken), which
- are for holding any drink, and
- are of a kind which are normally discarded or returned to/left to be recovered by the supplier when empty

and include parts of those articles. Any such article that is for holding any medicinal product (within the meaning of the Medicines Act 1968) is excluded from this definition (s. 2(3)).

Section 7(1) provides a power for a constable to enter any part of a ground during a designated sporting event for the purpose of enforcing the provisions of the Act.

---

OFFENCE:   **Having fireworks, flares etc.—*Sporting Events (Control of Alcohol etc.) Act 1985, s. 2A***
- Triable summarily • Three months' imprisonment and/or a fine
*(Statutory power of arrest)*

The Sporting Events (Control of Alcohol etc.) Act 1985, s. 2A states:

(1) A person is guilty of an offence if he has an article or substance to which this section applies in his possession—
  (a) at any time during the period of a designated sporting event when he is in any area of a designated sports ground from which the event may be directly viewed, or
  (b) while entering or trying to enter a designated sports ground at any time during the period of a designated sporting event at the ground.

(2) ...

(3) This section applies to any article or substance whose main purpose is the emission of a flare for purposes of illuminating or signalling (as opposed to igniting or heating) or the emission of smoke or a visible gas; and in particular it applies to distress flares, fog signals, and pellets and capsules intended to be used as fumigators or for testing pipes, but not to matches, cigarette lighters or heaters.

(4) This section also applies to any article which is a firework.

---

**KEYNOTE**

There is a defence under s. 2A(2) for the person to prove that he/she had possession of the article with lawful authority. 'Possession' is quite a broad concept going beyond 'carrying' (see Crime, chapter 6).

For other offences involving fireworks, see chapter 3, and for explosives offences generally, see below.

As with all other offences under the 1985 Act, the powers of entry, search and arrest under s. 7 apply to this offence.

---

### Designated sports ground

Under s. 9 of the 1985 Act, a 'designated sports ground' means:

(2) ...any place—
  (a) used (wholly or partly) for sporting events where accommodation is provided for spectators, and
  (b) for the time being designated, or of a class designated, by order made by the Secretary of State, and an order under this subsection may include provision for determining for the purposes of this Act the outer limit of any designated sports ground.

The period of a 'designated sporting event' is also covered by s. 9:

(4) The period of a designated sporting event is the period beginning two hours before the start of the event or (if earlier) two hours before the time at which it is advertised to start and ending one hour after the end of the event, but—

(a) where an event advertised to start at a particular time on a particular day is postponed to a later day, the period includes the period in the day on which it is advertised to take place beginning two hours before and ending one hour after that time, and

(b) where an event advertised to start at a particular time on a particular day does not take place, the period is the period referred to in paragraph (a) above.

### 4.13.4 Ticket touts

OFFENCE: **Ticket touts—*Criminal Justice and Public Order Act 1994, s. 166***
- Triable summarily. • Fine
*(Arrestable offence)*

The Criminal Justice and Public Order Act 1994, s. 166 states:

(1) It is an offence for an unauthorised person to sell, or offer or expose for sale, a ticket for a designated football match in any public place or place to which the public has access or, in the course of a trade or business, in any other place.

---

**KEYNOTE**

Unless a person has written authorisation from the home club or by the match organisers, he/she is 'unauthorised'.

'Ticket' will include anything which purports to be a ticket (s. 166(2)).

A 'designated' football match has the same meaning as under I or II of the Football Spectators Act 1989 (as to which, see above).

This offence is split into two categories, the first being capable of commission by anyone who sells, offers/exposes for sale a ticket in any public place or place to which the public has access. The second category applies to people who are selling, offering or exposing for sale any ticket in the course of a trade or business. In such cases, there is no restriction of the place of sale/offering for sale. There appears to be no need for the trade or business to be the defendant's own and selling tickets on behalf of someone else's business would appear to meet the requirements of the second part of this offence.

This offence was classified as an arrestable offence under s. 24 of and sch. 1A to the Police and Criminal Evidence Act 1984.

The power to search on arrest under s. 32 of the 1984 Act (**see chapter 2**) extends to vehicles that it is believed are being used by ticket touts.

---

## 4.14 Terrorism

For many years the legislation addressing terrorism within England and Wales had two key features. First, it was temporary in its nature, having to be re-enacted before it lapsed. Second, the main thrust of the legislation was towards terrorist activity connected with the affairs of Northern Ireland. Although extended in more recent years to tackle some aspects of international terrorism, the legislation did not apply to terrorism connected with UK affairs—what has become known as 'domestic terrorism'. Both of these features were then rectified by the Terrorism Act 2000 which extended earlier law and powers so that they encompassed all forms of terrorism, both in England and Wales and elsewhere; it also redefined 'terrorism'. Even at that point, terrorist offences and activities remained a highly unusual area of criminal law. Political changes in Northern Ireland meant that the United Kingdom's derogation under the Human Rights Act 1998 allowing for the connected detention and questioning of terrorist suspects was withdrawn. Then, in September 2001, came the attacks on the World Trade Centre in New York and other targets in the United States and terrorism became a very prominent feature of our everyday lives. Since then the threat posed by terrorist activity has become much more prominent and the laws addressing that threat have changed significantly.

### 4.14.1    Terrorism Act 2000

The Terrorism Act 2000 (as amended) is set out in eight parts. Broadly, these are as follows:

- part I—the definition of terrorism, the repeal of the Prevention of Terrorism (Temporary Provisions) Act 1989 and making of transitional arrangements;
- part II—proscribed organisations and the associated offences;
- part III—terrorist property, fund raising and financial matters;
- parts IV and V—terrorist investigations and police powers;
- part VI—miscellaneous offences;
- part VII—provisions relating to Northern Ireland;
- part VIII—technical provisions.

Given the specialist nature of terrorist investigations and the extent of the revised legislation, it is not appropriate to cover all aspects of counter-terrorist law here. What follows is a summary of some of the key areas of the legislation in so far as they might be encountered by operational police officers in general.

### 4.14.2    Terrorism

Terrorism is defined in s. 1 of the 2000 Act as:

(1) . . . the use or threat of action where—
   (a) the action falls within subsection (2),
   (b) the use or threat is designed to influence the government or to intimidate the public or a section of the public, and
   (c) the use or threat is made for the purpose of advancing a political, religious or ideological cause.

(2) Action falls within this subsection if it—
   (a) involves serious violence against a person,
   (b) involves serious damage to property,
   (c) endangers a person's life, other than that of the person committing the action,
   (d) creates a serious risk to the health or safety of the public or a section of the public, or
   (e) is designed seriously to interfere with or seriously to disrupt an electronic system.

(3) The use or threat of action falling within subsection (2) which involves the use of firearms or explosives is terrorism whether or not subsection (1)(b) is satisfied.

---

**KEYNOTE**

As discussed above, this new definition extends far beyond the original boundaries of terrorism defined under the former Prevention of Terrorism (Temporary Provisions) Act 1989 and will now include domestic terrorism. The definition is now so broad that it should be considered when dealing with other, more familiar offences such as blackmail, contamination of goods and threats to kill (as to which, **see Crime**). In fact it is so wide that it technically covers some threats of industrial action (though it would be extraordinary to contemplate using the legislation in that context).

The above definition recognises that terrorist activity may be motivated by religious or ideological reasons rather than simply political ones. The definition also encompasses broad activities (including threats) which, though potentially devastating in their impact on society, may not be overtly violent. Examples of such activity might be interference with domestic water and power supplies or serious disruption of computer networks. For the specific offence of deliberately infecting animals **see chapter 8**.

The provision at s. 1(3) means that, where the relevant criminal activity involves the use of firearms or explosives, there is no further need to show that the behaviour was designed to influence the government or to intimidate the public or a section of the public. An example of such activity might be the shooting of a senior military or political figure. A 'firearm' for this purpose includes air weapons (s. 121); it is not clear whether the definition includes imitation firearms (as to which, **see chapter 5**).

The reference to 'action' here includes action outside the UK. Similarly, references to people, property, the public and governments apply to all those features whether in the UK or elsewhere (s. 1(4)).

### 4.14.3   Proscribed organisations

Part II of the 2000 Act allows the Secretary of State to proscribe specific organisations This power existed in the former legislation but in a greatly restricted way. The most recent list of proscribed organisations contains, not only those organisations connected with the affairs of Northern Ireland, but also some of the most active and widely-known terrorist groups across the world including al-Qaeda (see sch. 2 to the Act). The main purpose of proscription is that there are many specific offences in relation to proscribed organisations In summary, these are:

- belonging or professing to belong to a proscribed organisation (s. 11(1));
- inviting support for a proscribed organisation (s. 12(1));
- arranging or managing (or assisting in doing so) a meeting of three or more people (in public or private) which the defendant knows is—
  - to support a proscribed organisation,
  - to further the activities of a proscribed organisation, or
  - to be addressed by a person who belongs or professes to belong to a proscribed organisation (s. 12(2)) *or* addressing a meeting to encourage support for a proscribed organisation or to further its activities (s. 12(3)).

All of the above offences are punishable by ten years' imprisonment on indictment and are therefore 'arrestable' offences (**see chapter 2**).

There is a further, summary, offence of wearing an item of clothing, or wearing, carrying or displaying an article in such a way or in such circumstances as to arouse reasonable suspicion that the defendant is a member or supporter of a proscribed organisation (s. 13).

The 2000 Act makes detailed provision for organisations to appeal against their proscribed status and sets up the Proscribed Organisations Appeal Commission (see sch. 3).

### 4.14.4   Terrorist offences

The Terrorism Act 2000 contains a large number of other offences, the vast majority of which are also punishable with long terms of imprisonment and which, therefore, are also 'arrestable'. Given their nature and object, such offences will invariably meet the definition of 'serious arrestable offences' (**see chapter 2**). The 2000 Act also re-enacts many of the offences that existed under the Prevention of Terrorism (Temporary Provisions) Act 1989, as well as setting out a number of specific statutory defences.

As a general summary, the main offences include:

- *inviting* another to provide money or other property;
- *providing* money or other property;
- *receiving* money or other property;

- *possessing* money or other property;

- *arranging* for money or other property to be made available;

in each case intending, or having reasonable cause to suspect that it may be used, for the purposes of terrorism (ss. 15, 16(2) and 17):

- *using* money or other property for the purposes of terrorism (s. 16(1) );

- *concealing, moving or transferring* any terrorist property (s. 18).

Each of these offences is punishable by a maximum of 14 years' imprisonment on indictment (s. 22).

In addition, under s. 19, where a person:

- believes or suspects that another person has committed an offence under any of ss. 15 to 18

- and bases that belief or suspicion on information which comes to his/her attention in the course of a trade, profession, business or employment

he/she must disclose to a constable as soon as is reasonably practicable that belief or suspicion, and the information on which it is based, otherwise he/she commits an offence punishable with five years' imprisonment.

This offence imposes a duty on banks and other businesses to inform the police without delay where they have suspicions over the activities of individuals with whom they come into contact. The s. 19 offence applies only where the suspicion has arisen in the course of the defendant's *work*. The former offence that tried to impose a similar duty on people who became suspicious in their general day-to-day life has not been replicated in the 2000 Act. There are several provisos and qualifications to the obligations imposed by s. 19.

### Disclosure of information

Section 38B of the Terrorism Act 2000 introduces an offence for failing to disclose information about acts of terrorism to an appropriate authority.

OFFENCE:   **Information about acts of terrorism—*Terrorism Act 2000, s. 38B***
- Triable either way • Five years' imprisonment on indictment, six months' imprisonment and/or fine summarily
*(Arrestable offence)*

The Terrorism Act 2000, s. 38B (added by Anti-terrorism Crime and Security Act 2001, s. 117) states:

(1) This section applies where a person has information which he knows or believes might be of material assistance—
   (a) in preventing the commission by another person of an act of terrorism, or
   (b) in securing the apprehension, prosecution or conviction of another person, in the United Kingdom, for an offence involving the commission, preparation or instigation of an act of terrorism.

(2) The person commits an offence if he does not disclose the information as soon as reasonably practicable in accordance with subsection (3).

(3) Disclosure is in accordance with this subsection if it is made—
   (a) in England and Wales, to a constable,
   (b) in Scotland, to a constable, or
   (c) in Northern Ireland, to a constable or a member of Her Majesty's forces.

(4) ...

(5) ...

(6) Proceedings for an offence under this section may be taken, and the offence may for the purposes of those proceedings be treated as having been committed, in any place where the person to be charged is or has at any time been since he first knew or believed that the information might be of material assistance as mentioned in subsection (1).

---

**KEYNOTE**

This offence was added by the Anti-terrorism, Crime and Security Act 2001, along with other provisions relating to the monitoring of bank accounts (see s. 38A). Unlike some of the Act's other provisions, this offence relates to *any* person who has information which he/she knows or believes might help prevent an act of terrorism or help bring terrorists to justice.

In England and Wales the disclosure must be made to a police officer.

The provisions of s. 38B(6) mean that a person resident in the UK could be charged with the offence even if he/she was outside the country when he/she became aware of the information.

It is a defence for a person charged with an offence under subsection (2) to prove that he/she had a reasonable excuse for not making the disclosure (s. 38B(4)).

---

The 2000 Act also provides for two offences designed to prevent 'tipping off', both of which are punishable on indictment with five years' imprisonment. The first such offence generally prohibits:

- the disclosure of anything which is likely to prejudice an investigation resulting from s. 19 above, or

- interference with material which is likely to be relevant to such an investigation

(s. 39(4)). An example of this offence would be where a bank advises the police of some suspicious activity by one of its customers (under its s. 19 duty) and an employee of the bank tips the customer off.

The second offence is more general and applies where a person knows or has reasonable cause to suspect that a police officer is conducting (or proposes to conduct) a terrorist investigation. In such circumstances, under s. 39(2), the person commits an offence if he/she:

- discloses to another anything which is likely to prejudice the investigation, or

- interferes with material which is likely to be relevant to the investigation.

For the definition of a 'terrorist investigation', **see chapter 2**. There are specific statutory defences available for both of the above offences.

### 4.14.5 Police powers

The Terrorism Act 2000 provides the police with many wide-ranging powers. These powers specifically exist *in addition* to any more general powers that the police may have and reasonable force may be used in their exercise (s. 114). Nevertheless, given the nature and extent of these powers, the application of the relevant principles under the Human Rights Act 1998 must be adhered to. In relation to the general police powers, it is worth noting that most offences connected with terrorist activity will be arrestable under s. 24 of the Police and Criminal Evidence Act 1984 (**see chapter 2**). An important additional power, however, is provided by s. 41 of the Terrorism Act 2000. This section gives a constable a power to arrest without a warrant a person whom he/she reasonably suspects to be 'a terrorist'. The definition of 'a terrorist' here is broadly a person who:

- has committed one of the main terrorism offences under the Act (including ss. 11, 12 and 15 to 18); or

- is or has been concerned in the commission, preparation or instigation of acts of terrorism.

(For the full definition see s. 40.)

Where a person is arrested under this power, special provisions apply in relation to their detention and treatment (**see Evidence and Procedure, chapter 15**).

One of the benefits of this power is the requirement that the officer reasonably suspects the person of being 'a terrorist' rather than suspecting his/her involvement in a specific offence. A further benefit to the police is that a person who has the powers of a constable in one part of the UK may exercise the power of arrest anywhere in the UK (s. 41(9)). Similarly, s. 43 gives a constable the power to:

- stop and search a person whom he/she reasonably suspects to be a terrorist to discover whether they have in their possession anything which may constitute evidence that they are a terrorist—note the applicability of the PACE Codes of Practice to these powers (**see Chapter 2**); and

- seize and retain anything which he/she discovers in the course of the search which he/she reasonably suspects may constitute evidence that the person is a terrorist and a person who has the powers of a constable in one part of the UK may exercise these powers (in addition to the powers of arrest above) anywhere in the UK (s. 43(5)).

### 4.14.6    Other terrorist offences under the 2000 Act

The Terrorism Act 2000 goes on to create a number of further offences in relation to terrorism. In summary, the key offences are:

- *Directing* the activities of an organisation which is concerned in the commission of acts of terrorism (s. 56). This offence (which is often easier to prove than some of the better known offences) carries a maximum sentence of life imprisonment.

- *Providing or receiving instruction or training* in the making or use of firearms or explosives (s. 54).

- *Possessing articles* in circumstances which give rise to a reasonable suspicion that the possession is for a purpose connected with the commission, preparation or instigation of an act of terrorism (s. 57).

- *Collecting or making a record* of information (including photographs and electronic records) of a kind likely to be useful to a person committing or preparing an act of terrorism, or possessing a document or record containing information of that kind (s. 58).

- *Inciting* another person to commit an act of terrorism wholly or partly outside the UK (s. 59).

All of these are arrestable offences.

### 4.14.7    Explosives

OFFENCE:    **Causing explosion likely to endanger life or property—*Explosive Substances Act 1883, s. 2***
- Triable on indictment • Life imprisonment
*(Serious arrestable offence)*

The Explosive Substances Act 1883, s. 2 states:

A person who in the United Kingdom or (being a citizen of the United Kingdom and Colonies) in the Republic of Ireland unlawfully and maliciously causes by any explosive substance an explosion of a nature likely to endanger life or to cause serious injury to property shall, whether any injury to person or property has been actually caused or not, be guilty of an offence...

**KEYNOTE**

The consent of the Attorney-General (or Solicitor-General) is required before prosecuting this offence (s. 7(1) of the 1883 Act).

'Explosive substance' includes any materials for making any explosive substance; any implement or apparatus used, or intended or adapted to be used for causing or aiding any explosion (s. 9(1)).

The definition of 'explosive' under the Explosives Act 1875 (see chapter 3) also applies to this offence (see *R* v *Wheatley* [1979] 1 WLR 144). Therefore fireworks and petrol bombs will be covered (*R* v *Bouch* [1983] QB 246). For offences involving fireworks generally, **see chapter 3**; for offences involving fireworks at sporting events, see above.

Other articles which have been held to amount to 'explosive substances' include:

- shotguns (*R* v *Downey* [1971] NI 224);
- electronic timers (*R* v *Berry (No. 3)* [1995] 1 WLR 7);
- gelignite with a fuse and detonator (*R* v *McCarthy* [1964] 1 WLR 196).

You must prove that the act was carried out 'maliciously' (see **Crime, chapter 1**).

Sections 73 to 75 of the Explosives Act 1875 provide powers to search for explosives in connection with the above offence.

---

OFFENCE:  **Attempting to cause explosion or keeping explosive with intent—*Explosive Substances Act 1883, s. 3***
   - Triable on indictment • Life imprisonment
   *(Arrestable offence)*

The Explosive Substances Act 1883, s. 3 states:

(1) A person who in the United Kingdom or a dependency or (being a citizen of the United Kingdom and Colonies) elsewhere unlawfully and maliciously—

   (a) does any act with intent to cause, or conspires to cause, by an an explosive substance an explosion of a nature likely to endanger life, or cause serious injury to property, whether in the United Kingdom or the Republic of Ireland, or

   (b) makes or has in his possession or under his control an explosive substance with intent by means thereof to endanger life, or cause serious injury to property, whether in the United Kingdom or the Republic of Ireland, or to enable any other person so to do, shall, whether any explosion does or does not take place, and whether any injury to person or property is actually caused or not, be guilty of an offence . . .

OFFENCE:  **Making or possessing explosive under suspicious circumstances—*Explosive Substances Act 1883, s. 4***
   - Triable on indictment • Fourteen years' imprisonment
   *(Arrestable offence)*

The Explosive Substances Act 1883, s. 4 states:

(1) Any person who makes or knowingly has in his possession or under his control any explosive substance under such circumstances as to give rise to a reasonable suspicion that he is not making it or does not have it in his possession or under his control for a lawful object, shall, unless he can show that he made it or had it in his possession or under his control for a lawful object, be guilty of felony . . .

---

**KEYNOTE**

The offence under s. 3 is one of specific intent (see **Crime, chapter 1**).

Both of the above offences require the consent of the Attorney-General (or Solicitor-General) before a prosecution can be brought.

It would seem that the wording of these offences requires the prosecution—in cases of 'possession'—to prove that a defendant *had* the relevant article in his/her possession and that he/she *knew* the nature of it (see *R v Hallam* [1957] 1 QB 569). This should be contrasted with the usual approach to offences involving 'possession' where the second part (knowledge of the 'quality' of an item) does not need to be shown; see Crime, chapter 6.

'Reasonable suspicion' in this case will be assessed *objectively*, that is, you must prove that the circumstances of the possession or making of the explosive substance would give rise to suspicion in a reasonable and objective bystander (*R v Fegan* (1971) 78 Cr App R 189).

Whether a person's purpose in having the items prohibited by these offences is a 'lawful object' will need to be determined in each case (*Fegan*).

Sections 73 to 75 of the Explosives Act 1875 provide powers to search for explosives in connection with the above offence.

---

### Gunpowder

Sections 28 to 30 of the Offences Against the Person Act 1861 create arrestable offences of exploding gunpowder to cause bodily injury; throwing or placing gunpowder or corrosive fluid with intent to cause bodily harm; and placing gunpowder or explosives near buildings or vessels with intent to cause bodily injury. The 1861 Act also creates an offence of possessing or making gunpowder or explosives (or other noxious things) with intent to enable any other person to commit an offence under the Act (s. 64). This offence is triable on indictment and carries two years' imprisonment.

### 4.14.8   Other Offences connected with terrorism

Other terrorist activity may be covered by one or more of the offences listed below, all of which carry life imprisonment:

- Hijacking of aircraft (Aviation Security Act 1982, s. 1)—serious arrestable offence.
- Destroying, damaging or endangering aircraft (Aviation Security Act 1982, ss. 2 and 3)—arrestable offence.
- Endangering safety at aerodromes (Aviation and Maritime Security Act 1990, s. 1)— serious arrestable offence.
- Hijacking of ships (Aviation and Maritime Security Act 1990, s. 9)—serious arrestable offence.
- Hostage taking (Taking of Hostages Act 1982, s. 1)—serious arrestable offence (**see Crime, chapter 9**).
- Kidnapping (common law)—serious arrestable offence (**see Crime, chapter 9**).
- Endangering safety on railways (Offences Against the Person Act 1861)—arrestable offence (**see chapter 13**).
- Hijacking channel tunnel trains or seizing control of the tunnel system (Channel Tunnel (Security) Order 1994)—serious arrestable offence.
- Contamination of goods (Public Order Act 1986)—arrestable offence (**see Crime, chapter 14**);
- Using noxious substances to cause harm or intimidation (Anti-terrorism, Crime and Security Act 2001, s. 113) (**see Crime, chapter 9**).

For offences involving weapons and firearms respectively, **see also chapters 5 and 6**.

# 5 Firearms

## 5.1 Introduction

The law regulating the possession, transfer and use of firearms remained largely unchanged between the passing of the main Firearms Act in 1968 and the introduction of the Firearms (Amendment) Act in 1988. During 1997, however, the law underwent significant amendment and what were already fairly stringent controls were reinforced by further restrictions on the ownership and use of firearms generally.

In addition to the primary legislation, s. 53 of the Firearms Act 1968 allows the Secretary of State to make rules in relation to the 1968 Act's implementation (see e.g. the Firearms Rules 1989 (SI 1989 No. 854), as amended. The Home Office has also issued guidance to chief officers on the control and licensing of firearms.

In considering the legislation that follows in this chapter, it is worth bearing in mind the provisions of the Terrorism Act 2000 and, in particular, the offences of providing or receiving instruction in the use of firearms and some other weapons (**see chapter 4**). The leading authority giving guidance in relation to sentencing for offences involving firearms is *R* v *Avis* [1998] 1 Cr App R 420. There it was held that there were four questions a sentencing court had to ask itself when assessing the seriousness of a firearms offence:

- what sort of weapon was involved;
- what use had been made of the weapon;
- with what intention did the defendant possess or use the firearm; and
- what was the defendant's record.

All of these issues should arguably be borne in mind when gathering and presenting evidence in firearms cases. It is also worth noting that, following a report from the National Criminal Intelligence Service (NCIS), a firearms database containing details of all licensed firearm and shotgun holders in Great Britain is being set up. Further amendments to some of the penalties (**see appendix 5**) were proposed at the time of writing.

## 5.2 The 'this' checklist

When considering any situation involving firearms legislation, whether practically or for the purposes of study, it is useful to apply the 'this' checklist.

The 'this' checklist, which is also useful in other areas of law (**see Road Traffic**), means asking whether:

- **this** certificate/exemption
- covers **this** person
- for **this** activity

- involving **this** firearm/ammunition
- for **this** purpose.

### 5.2.1    This certificate/exemption

The Firearms Act 1968 provides for people to be authorised by certificate to hold, transfer or buy firearms under specified conditions.

The 1968 Act—and the amending legislation—also contains many exemptions, some generally applicable and others very specific.

In each case, whether considering a certificate or other authority, or a possible exemption, it is critical that you establish what conditions apply.

### 5.2.2    This person

Certificates will authorise the *holder* to do certain things (e.g. to buy firearms); other authorities will allow a wider group of people to do things (e.g. borrow the rifle of a certificate holder). In considering offences it is important to establish exactly which person is authorised or is exempt from any liability.

### 5.2.3    This activity

Certificates and exemptions never grant unlimited authority to undertake any activity with every firearm or ammunition. Certificates will usually specify whether the holder can have a firearm in his/her '*possession*'; which firearms or ammunition he/she can possess; and whether he/she can *sell* or *transfer* firearms *or* ammunition. Exemptions are the same in that they will not apply to everyone in respect of all activities.

### 5.2.4    This firearm/ammunition

In addition to the restrictions on the activity, certificates and exemptions will only apply to particular firearms and/or ammunition. A person authorised to possess a shotgun is not thereby permitted to have an automatic rifle. Similarly, a person who runs a mini rifle range is not thereby given authority to possess mortar shells!

### 5.2.5    This purpose

Certificates and exemptions will specify the precise purposes for which they apply. For instance, if a certificate allows a person to possess a firearm for slaughtering animals while at the slaughterhouse, that does not permit the possession of the firearm by the slaughterer while at home or travelling to work.

Similarly, some of the general exemptions apply only to the people concerned while they are involved in *the ordinary course of their business*, whether they are registered firearms dealers or members of the armed forces; possession or use of a firearm outside the particular circumstances will not be covered.

## 5.3    Firearms generally

Section 57 of the Firearms Act 1968 states:

(1) In this Act, the expression 'firearm' means a lethal barrelled weapon of any description from which any shot, bullet or other missile can be discharged, and includes—
   (a) any prohibited weapon, whether it is such a lethal weapon as aforesaid or not; and

    (b) any component part of such a lethal or prohibited weapon; and

    (c) any accessory to any such weapon designed or adapted to diminish the noise or flash caused by firing the weapon.

---

**KEYNOTE**

'Lethal barrelled weapon' is not defined under the 1968 Act.

The way in which the courts have determined whether or not something amounts to such a weapon is by asking:

- Can any shot, bullet or other missile be discharged from the weapon?, or

- Could the weapon be adapted so that any shot, bullet or other missile can be discharged?

- If so, is the weapon a 'lethal barrelled' weapon?

(See *Grace* v *DPP* (1989) 153 JP 491.)

A weapon is a lethal barrelled weapon if it is capable of causing injury, irrespective of the intentions of its maker (*Read* v *Donovan* [1947] KB 326). In determining whether a firearm is in fact a lethal barrelled weapon from which missiles can be discharged a court need not consider any specific evidence of someone who has seen the effects of it being fired. Therefore, where magistrates had heard evidence from a gun shop assistant that an air rifle was in working order, they were entitled to conclude that it fell within the definition even though no evidence was given as to the actual effects of the gun being fired (*Castle* v *DPP* The Times, 3 April 1998).

Air pistols (*R* v *Thorpe* [1987] 1 WLR 383), imitation revolvers (*Cafferata* v *Wilson* [1936] 3 All ER 149) and signalling pistols (*Read* v *Donovan*, above) have all been held to be lethal barrelled weapons. That is not to say, however, that they will always be so and each case must be determined in the light of the evidence available.

Component parts, such as triggers or barrels, are also included in the definition, as are silencers and accessories to hide the muzzle flash of a weapon. If a defendant is found in possession of a silencer which has been manufactured for a weapon that is also in the defendant's possession, that will be enough to bring it under s. 57(1). If, however, the silencer is made for a different weapon, it may still come under the s. 57 definition but the prosecution will have to show that it could be used with the defendant's weapon and that he/she had it for that purpose. This slightly odd result is the result of the Court of Appeal's decision in *R* v *Buckfield* [1998] Crim LR 673. Following that reasoning, a silencer or accessory on its own does not appear to be a firearm for the purposes of s. 57(1). Section 57(1) does not include telescopic sights.

---

A weapon may cease to be a firearm if it is de-activated in line with the provisions of the Firearms (Amendment) Act 1988, s. 8 which states:

> For the purposes of the principal Act and this Act it shall be presumed, unless the contrary is shown, that a firearm has been rendered incapable of discharging any shot, bullet or other missile, and has consequently ceased to be a firearm within the meaning of those Acts, if—
>
>     (a) it bears a mark which has been approved by the Secretary of State for denoting that fact and which has been made either by one of the two companies mentioned in section 58(1) of the principal Act or by such other person as may be approved by the Secretary of State for the purposes of this section; and
>
>     (b) that company or person has certified in writing that work has been carried out on the firearm in a manner approved by the Secretary of State for rendering it incapable of discharging any shot, bullet or other missile.

---

**KEYNOTE**

For the 'two companies' referred to, **see para. 5.4.2.**

---

## 5.4    **Definitions**

The law regulating firearms classifies weapons into several categories, each of which is specifically defined. As with offences under road traffic legislation (**see Road Traffic, chapter 1**), it is critical that the relevant definition is considered before deciding upon a particular charge or offence.

### 5.4.1    **Prohibited weapon**

A prohibited weapon is defined under the Firearms Act 1968, s. 5. The definition formerly covered the more powerful or potentially destructive firearms—and their ammunition—such as automatic weapons and specialist ammunition.

Since the Firearms (Amendment) Acts of 1997, however, s. 5 also covers many small firearms which were formerly covered by other parts of the 1968 Act.

The test as to whether a weapon is a 'prohibited' weapon is a purely objective one and is not affected by the intentions of the defendant. Therefore, where a firearm was capable of successively discharging two or more missiles without repeated pressure on the trigger, that weapon was 'prohibited' irrespective of the intentions of the firearms dealer who was in possession of it (*R* v *Law* [1999] Crim LR 837).

Whereas a firearms certificate is usually needed in order to possess, buy or acquire firearms and ammunition, the authority of the Secretary of State is needed if the firearm or ammunition is a 'prohibited weapon'.

The full list of prohibited weapons and ammunition under s. 5 of the Firearms Act 1968 is as follows:

(1) ...

    (a) any firearm which is so designed or adapted that two or more missiles can be successively discharged without repeated pressure on the trigger;

    (ab) any self-loading or pump-action rifled gun other than one which is chambered for 0.22 rim-fire cartridges;

    (aba) any firearm which either has a barrel less than 30 centimetres in length or is less than 60 centimetres in length overall, other than an air weapon, a muzzle-loading gun or a firearm designed as signalling apparatus;

    (ac) any self-loading or pump-action smooth-bore gun which is not an air weapon or chambered for 0.22 rim-fire cartridges and either has a barrel less than 24 inches in length or is less than 40 inches in length overall;

    (ad) any smooth-bore revolver gun other than one which is chambered for 9mm rimfire cartridges or a muzzle-loading gun;

    (ae) any rocket launcher, or any mortar, for projecting a stabilised missile, other than a launcher or mortar designed for line-throwing or pyrotechnic purposes or as signalling apparatus;

    (b) any weapon of whatever description designed or adapted for the discharge of any noxious liquid, gas or other thing;

    (c) any cartridge with a bullet designed to explode on or immediately before impact, any ammunition containing or designed or adapted to contain any such noxious thing as is mentioned in paragraph (b) above and, if capable of being used with a firearm of any description, any grenade, bomb (or other like missile), or rocket or shell designed to explode as aforesaid.

(1A) ...

    (a) any firearm which is disguised as another object;

    (b) any rocket or ammunition not falling within paragraph (c) of subsection (1) of this section which consists in or incorporates a missile designed to explode on or immediately before impact and is for military use;

(c) any launcher or other projecting apparatus not falling within paragraph (ae) of that subsection which is designed to be used with any rocket or ammunition falling within paragraph (b) above or with ammunition which would fall within that paragraph but for its being ammunition falling within paragraph (c) of that subsection;

(d) any ammunition for military use which consists in or incorporates a missile designed so that a substance contained in the missile will ignite on or immediately before impact;

(e) any ammunition for military use which consists in or incorporates a missile designed, on account of its having a jacket and hard-core, to penetrate armour plating, armour screening or body armour;

(f) any ammunition which incorporates a missile designed or adapted to expand on impact;

(g) anything which is designed to be projected as a missile from any weapon and is designed to be, or has been, incorporated in—

(i) any ammunition falling within any of the preceding paragraphs; or

(ii) any ammunition which would fall within any of those paragraphs but for its being specified in subsection (1) of this section.

---

**KEYNOTE**

Therefore the firearms which will require the authority of the Secretary of State before they can be possessed, acquired, bought, sold or transferred will include:

- automatic weapons

- most self-loading or pump-action weapons

- any firearm which is less than 60 cms long *or* which has a barrel less than 30 cms long (other than an air weapon or signalling apparatus)

- most smooth-bore revolvers

- any weapon—of whatever description—designed or adapted for the discharge of any noxious liquid, gas or other thing

- military weapons and ammunition including grenades and mortars.

Taking empty washing-up liquid bottles and filling them with a noxious fluid such as hydrochloric acid does not amount to 'adapting' them, neither is such a thing a 'weapon' for the purposes of s. 5(2) (*R* v *Formosa* [1991] 2 QB 1).

An electric 'stun gun' has been held to be a prohibited weapon as it discharges an electric current (*Flack* v *Baldry* [1988] 1 WLR 393) and it continues to be such even if it is not working (*R* v *Brown*, The Times, 27 March 1992).

The Secretary of State may amend the list above.

Note that s. 5A of the Firearms Act 1968 creates exemptions under the European Council Directive 91/477/EEC on control of the acquisition and possession of weapons [1991] OJL 256/51 which allows people from Member States to possess some prohibited weapons under certain circumstances (**see para. 5.7.1**).

---

5.4.2 **Shotguns**

A shotgun is defined under s. 1(3)(a) of the Firearms Act 1968. Section 1 (amended by Firearms (Amendment) Act 1988 s. 2) states:

(3) ...

(a) a shotgun within the meaning of this Act, that is to say a smooth-bore gun (not being an airgun) which—

(i) has a barrel not less than 24 inches in length and does not have any barrel with a bore exceeding 2 inches in diameter;

(ii) either has no magazine or has a non-detachable magazine incapable of holding more than two cartridges; and

(iii) is not a revolver gun....

(3A) A gun which has been adapted to have such a magazine as is mentioned in subsection (3)(a)(ii) above shall not be regarded as falling within that provision unless the magazine bears a mark approved by the Secretary of State for denoting that fact and that mark has been made, and the adaptation has been certified in writing as having been carried out in a manner approved by him, either by one of the two companies mentioned in section 58(1) of this Act or by such other person as may be approved by him for that purpose.

---

**KEYNOTE**

A barrel's length is measured from the muzzle to the point at which the charge is exploded on firing the weapon (s. 57(6)(a) of the 1968 Act).

The 'two companies' referred to are the Society of the Mystery of Gunmakers of the City of London and the Birmingham proof house.

---

### 5.4.3  Air weapons

Air weapons are defined under s. 1(3)(b) of the Firearms Act 1968 as being 'an air rifle, airgun or air pistol', including a rifle, pistol or gun powered by compressed carbon dioxide (see s. 48 of the Firearms (Amendment) Act 1997).

Some air weapons are deemed to be specially dangerous and therefore subject to stricter control than conventional air weapons. Those which are subject to this stricter control are those declared to be so by the Secretary of State. Listed in r. 2 of the Firearms (Dangerous Air Weapons) Rules 1969 (SI 1969 No. 47 made under Firearms Act 1968 ss. 1 and 53), they include:

(1) [any] air rifle, air gun or air pistol—
    (a) which is capable of discharging a missile so that the missile has, on being discharged from the muzzle of the weapon, kinetic energy in excess, in the case of an air pistol of 6 ft lb or, in the case of an air weapon other than an air pistol, of 12 ft lb. [other than one designed for use when submerged in water, or]
    (b) which is disguised as another object.

### 5.4.4  Section 1 firearm

There is a group of firearms which, although not a category defined in the 1968 Act, are subject to a number of offences including s. 1 (see below). Firearms which fall into this group are often referred to as 'section 1 firearms' and include all firearms except shotguns (**see para. 5.4.2**) and conventional air weapons (**see para. 5.4.3**). Shotguns which have been 'sawn off' (i.e. had their barrels shortened) are section 1 firearms, as are air weapons declared to be 'specially dangerous'.

Section 1 ammunition includes any ammunition for a firearm except:

- cartridges containing five or more shot, none of which is bigger than 0.36 inch in diameter;

- ammunition for an airgun, air rifle or air pistol; and

- blank cartridges not more than one inch in diameter

(s. 1(4)).

### 5.4.5  Conversion

Some weapons which began their life as section 1 firearms or prohibited weapons will remain so even after their conversion to a shotgun, air weapon or other type of firearm (see s. 7 of the Firearms (Amendment) Act 1988).

5.4.6 **Imitation firearms**

Some, though not all, offences which regulate the use of firearms will also apply to *imitation* firearms. Whether they do so can be found either in the specific wording of the offence, or by virtue of the Firearms Act 1982.

Put simply there are two types of imitation firearms:

- general imitations—those which have the appearance of firearms (which are covered by s. 57 of the Firearms Act 1968); and

- imitations of section 1 firearms—those which both have the appearance of a *section 1 firearm* and which can be readily converted into such a firearm (which are covered by ss. 1 and 2 of the Firearms Act 1982).

Where 'imitation firearms' are referred to *in the wording of the offence*, that offence will apply to the first category above, that is, 'anything which has the appearance of being a firearm'. Note that this category does not include anything which resembles a prohibited weapon *under s. 5(1)(b)*. Prohibited weapons under s. 5(1)(b) are those which are designed or adapted to discharge noxious liquid etc. (**see para. 5.4.1**).

In some other offences, *the definition of the 1982 Act is applicable*. These offences are all offences which involve section 1 firearms, except those under ss. 4(3) and (4), 16 to 20 and 47 of the 1968 Act.

If an offence does not come within either of the circumstances above, it will not apply to an imitation firearm.

Whether or not something has the appearance of being a firearm will be a question of fact for the jury/magistrate(s) to decide in each case.

## 5.5 Possessing etc. firearm or ammunition without certificate

OFFENCE: **Possessing etc. firearm or ammunition without certificate—*Firearms Act, 1968 s. 1***

- Triable either way • Sentence: see sch. 6, appendix 5
*(Arrestable offence)*

The Firearms Act 1968, s. 1 states:

(1) Subject to any exemption under this Act, it is an offence for a person—
   (a) to have in his possession, or to purchase or acquire, a firearm to which this section applies without holding a firearm certificate in force at the time, or otherwise than as authorised by such a certificate;
   (b) to have in his possession, or to purchase or acquire, any ammunition to which this section applies without holding a firearm certificate in force at the time, or otherwise than as authorised by such a certificate, or in quantities in excess of those so authorised.

---

**KEYNOTE**

This offence relates to those firearms described above as section 1 firearms.

If the firearm involved is a sawn-off shotgun, the offence becomes 'aggravated' (under s. 4(4)) and attracts a maximum penalty of seven years' imprisonment (see sch. 6 at **appendix 5**).

The Firearms Act 1982 applies to this section and therefore the second definition of 'imitation firearms' at **para. 5.4.6** above applies here.

The certificate referred to is issued by the chief officer of police under s. 26. Such certificates may carry significant restrictions on the types of firearms which the holder is allowed, together with the circumstances under which he/she may have them (see s. 44(1) of the Firearms (Amendment) Act 1997).

The purpose of the legislation regulating the licensing of firearms is to provide certainty and consistency in the effective control of such weapons. Therefore the issue of whether a certificate covers a particular category of weapon is a matter of law for the judge to decide and cannot be affected by the intentions or misunderstanding of the defendant (*R v Paul (Benjamin)* (1998) 95(32) LS Gaz 30).

For the forms to be used in relation to the grant of certificates and permits, see the Firearms Rules 1998 (SI 1998 No. 1941 made under Firearms Act 1968).

A person may hold a European firearms pass or similar document, in which case he/she will be governed by the provision of ss. 32A to 32C of the Firearms Act 1968.

If a person has such a certificate which allows the possession etc. of the firearm in question and under the particular circumstances encountered, no offence is committed.

---

### 5.5.1 Possession

As in other areas of criminal law (**see Crime, chapter 6**), the meaning of possession is wider here than actual physical custody of the firearm in question. A person can remain in possession of a firearm even if someone else has custody of it (*Sullivan* v *Earl of Caithness* [1976] QB 966).

Possession for the purposes of this offence does not require any specific knowledge on the part of the defendant. For example, if X knows he is in possession of *something* (e.g. a box), then X is in possession of its contents, *even though X does not know what those contents are* (*R* v *Hussain* [1981] 1 WLR 416).

Therefore there is no need to prove that the defendant knew the nature of the thing which he/she possessed in order to prove this offence (and the offence under s. 19, **see para. 5.8.7**). If a defendant is carrying a rucksack and that rucksack turns out to contain ammunition for a section 1 firearm, the defendant is 'in possession' of that ammunition irrespective of his/her knowledge—or ignorance—of its presence in the rucksack (see *R* v *Waller* [1991] Crim LR 381). (For a discussion of the situation in respect of drugs, **see Crime, chapter 6**.)

### 5.5.2 Acquire

Acquire will include hiring, accepting as a gift and borrowing (s. 57(4) of the Firearms Act 1968).

### 5.5.3 Exemptions

The offence specifies that it is subject to any exemptions under the 1968 Act. There are three main categories of exemption under the firearms legislation:

- General exemptions—listed below.
- European exemptions—these are made under s. 5A to reflect the European Weapons Directive (**see para. 5.7.1**).
- Special exemptions—which apply to the provisions affecting prohibited weapons under s. 5 (**see para. 5.7.1**).

Many of the exemptions overlap as they follow a fairly common sense approach to the necessary possession and use of firearms/ammunition in the course of work and leisure.

### 5.5.4 General exemptions

The general exemptions, which apply to the provisions of ss. 1 to 5 of the Firearms Act 1968 are mainly concerned with the various occupations of people whom you might expect to be in contact with firearms in one form or another. They include:

### Police permit holders

Under s. 7(1) of the 1968 Act, the chief officer of police may grant a permit authorising the possession of firearms or ammunition under the conditions specified in the permit.

### Clubs, athletics and sporting purposes

Section 11 of the 1968 Act provides exemptions for a person:

- borrowing the firearm/ammunition from a certificate holder *for sporting purposes only* (s. 11(1));
- possessing a firearm at an athletic meeting for the purposes of starting races (s. 11(2));
- in charge of a miniature rifle range buying, acquiring or possessing miniature rifles and ammunition, and using them at such a rifle range (s. 11(4));
- who is a member of an approved rifle club, miniature rifle club or pistol club to possess a firearm or ammunition *when engaged as a club member in target practice* (s. 15(1) of the Firearms (Amendment) Act 1988);
- borrowing a shotgun from the occupier of private premises and using it on those premises in the occupier's presence (s. 11(5) of the 1968 Act);
- using a shotgun at a time and place approved by the chief officer of police for shooting at artificial targets (s. 11(6)).

### Borrowed rifle on private premises

Section 16 of the Firearms (Amendment) Act 1988 allows a person to borrow a rifle from the occupier of private premises, provided the person is on those premises and in the presence of the occupier (or his/her servant), as long as the occupier holds a certificate and that the borrowing of the rifle complies with that certificate. The person borrowing the rifle may buy or acquire ammunition for it in accordance with the certificate's conditions.

### Visitors' permits

Section 17 of the Firearms (Amendment) Act 1988 provides for issuing of a visitors' permit by a chief officer of police and for the possession of firearms and ammunition by the holder of such a permit.

Visitors' permits will not be issued to anyone without a European firearms pass. It is a summary offence (punishable with six months' imprisonment) to make a false statement in order to get a visitors' permit, and it is a similar offence to fail to comply with any conditions within such a permit (see s. 17(10)).

### Antiques as ornaments or curiosities

Section 58(2) of the 1968 Act allows for the sale, buying, transfer, acquisition or possession of antique firearms *as curiosities or ornaments*. Whether a firearm is such an antique will be a question of fact to be determined by the court in each case. Mere belief in the fact that a firearm is an antique will not be enough (*R v Howells* [1977] QB 614).

### Authorised firearms dealers

Section 8(1) of the 1968 Act provides for registered firearms dealers (or their employees) to possess, acquire or buy firearms or ammunition in the ordinary course of their business without a certificate. If the possession etc. is not in the ordinary course of their business, the exemption will not apply.

### Auctioneers, carriers or warehouse staff

Section 9(1) of the 1968 Act allows auctioneers, carriers, warehousemen or their employees to possess firearms and ammunition in the ordinary course of their business without a certificate.

Section 14(1) of the Firearms (Amendment) Act 1988 makes it a summary offence (punishable by six months' imprisonment) for such people to fail to take reasonable precautions for the safe custody of the firearms and ammunition in their possession, or to fail to report the theft of those firearms and ammunition.

Again, if the possession of the firearm or ammunition is in circumstances which do not fall within the ordinary course of their business, the exemption will not apply.

### Licensed slaughterers

Section 10 of the 1968 Act allows licensed slaughterers to have in their possession a slaughtering instrument (or ammunition for it) in any *slaughterhouse* or knackers' yard in which they are employed.

The exemption will only apply to slaughtering instruments and ammunition while in the places specified. If these conditions are not met, the exemption will not apply.

### Theatrical performers

Section 12 of the 1968 Act allows people taking part in theatrical performances or films to possess firearms without a certificate, *during, and for the purpose of*, the performance, rehearsal or production. If performers do anything which falls outside this strict definition, they will not be exempt.

### Ships or aircraft equipment

Section 13(1) of the 1968 Act provides for the possession of signalling equipment and firearms/ammunition for that purpose when on board ships or at aerodromes, or when removing the equipment from such places.

Section 13(1)(c) provides for the removal of firearms or signalling apparatus from ships, aircraft and aerodromes where authorised by a police permit to do so. The removal to or from such a place must only be done under the authority of police permit and must only be for the purpose specified therein (e.g. to get the firearm or signalling apparatus repaired).

### Crown servants

The effect of s. 54(1) of the 1968 Act is to exclude Crown servants from some of the provisions of the Act relating to possession. This general exemption applies to police officers, members of Her Majesty's armed forces (including cadet corps) and visiting forces from other countries. The exemptions are restricted to certain conditions and again only operate where the relevant person is acting in his/her official capacity.

This exemption extends to people employed by a police authority under the direction and control of a chief officer (e.g. civilian crime scene examiners) and also to members of NCIS and the National Crime Squad (**see chapter 1**).

People on service premises may possess a firearm or ammunition if they are supervised by a member of HM armed forces (s. 16A(1) of the Firearms (Amendment) Act 1988). This provision does not include civilian guards who are engaged in the protection of service premises.

### Proof houses

Under s. 58(1) of the 1968 Act, members of the Mystery of Gunmakers of the City of London and the guardians of the Birmingham proof house and the Small Heath range at Birmingham have certain statutory duties involving firearms (**see, e.g., para. 5.4.2**). They are therefore exempt from those provisions of the Act which interfere with their statutory functions.

Museums Licence

Section 19 of the Firearms (Amendment) Act 1988 provides for people involved in the management of certain museums to hold a museums firearms licence which allows them to possess, buy or acquire firearms and ammunition under certain circumstances.

There are several summary offences involved in the fraudulent application for such licences and the failure to comply with their conditions (see para. 4 to the schedule to the 1988 Act).

## 5.6 Shotgun offences

OFFENCE: **Possessing shotgun without certificate—*Firearms Act 1968, s. 2(1)***
  • Triable either way • Sentence: see sch. 6, appendix 5
  *(Arrestable offence)*

The Firearms Act 1968, s. 2 states:

(1) Subject to any exemption under this Act, it is an offence for a person to have in his possession, or to purchase or acquire, a shotgun without holding a certificate under this Act authorising him to possess shot guns.

---

**KEYNOTE**

For the definition of 'shotgun', see para. 5.4.2.

The relevant exemptions above will also apply to shotguns.

A shotgun certificate is granted by a chief officer of police under s 26 of the 1968 Act and will have certain conditions attached to it. A person failing to comply with those conditions commits the following offence:

---

OFFENCE: **Failing to comply with conditions of shot gun certificate—*Firearms Act 1968, s. 2(2)***
  • Triable summarily • Sentence: see sch. 6, appendix 5.
  *(No specific power of arrest)*

The Firearms Act 1968, s. 2 states:

(2) It is an offence for a person to fail to comply with a condition subject to which a shot gun certificate is held by him.

## 5.7 Possessing or distributing prohibited weapons or ammunition

OFFENCE: **Possessing or distributing prohibited weapons or ammunition—*Firearms Act 1968, s. 5***
  • Triable either way • Sentence: see sch. 6, appendix 5
  *(Arrestable offence)*

The Firearms Act 1968, s. 5 states:

(1) A person commits an offence if, without the authority of the Secretary of State or the Scottish Ministers, he has in his possession, or purchases, or acquires, or manufactures, sells or transfers [a prohibited weapon or ammunition] . . .

---

**KEYNOTE**

See para. 5.4.1 for prohibited weapons. For 'possession', see para. 5.5.1.

'Self-loading' and 'pump-action' mean designed or adapted so that the weapon is either automatically reloaded, or is reloaded by manual operation of the fore-end or forestock (s. 57 of the 1968 Act).

Section 5(7) provides guidance in determining whether certain arms and ammunition will fall within the descriptions in s. 5, including the fact that any folding or detachable butt-stock of a firearm will not count when measuring the weapon's overall length.

---

5.7.1　**Exemptions**

The first set of exemptions were discussed in relation to the offence under s. 1 (**see para. 5.5.3**); the second and third set are relevant to the offences under s. 5. Those remaining exemptions are:

- European exemptions—exemptions to conform with the European weapons directive.

- Special exemptions.

### European Weapons Directive

The European Weapons Directive (91/477/EEC) was brought into effect in order to adjust our domestic legislation in line with the expansion of the European internal market. Its effect is to create certain additional savings and exemptions in relation to the possession of, or some transactions in, specified firearms and ammunition by people who have the relevant certificates or who are recognised as collectors under the law of another country.

To this end, s. 5A of the Firearms Act 1968 provides for a number of occasions where the authority of the Secretary of State will not be required to possess or deal with certain weapons under certain conditions.

The main areas covered by s. 5A are:

- authorised collectors and firearms dealers possessing or being involved in transactions of weapons and ammunition;

- authorised people being involved in transactions of particular ammunition used for lawful shooting and slaughtering of animals, the management of an estate or the protection of other animals and humans.

Section 57(4A) of the Firearms Act 1968 makes other provisions in relation to the European directive as an authority for certain uses of firearms.

### Special exemptions

The list of general exemptions to the offences involving firearms under s. 5(1)(aba) focuses largely on people in jobs where they will need to come into contact with firearms mainly in connection with animals or leisure activities.

The exemptions include:

- **Slaughterers**—A slaughterer, if entitled under s. 10 of the 1968 Act (**see para. 5.5.4**), may possess a slaughtering instrument. In addition, persons authorised by certificate to possess, buy, acquire, sell or transfer slaughtering instruments are exempt from the provisions of s. 5 (s. 2 of the Firearms (Amendment) Act 1997). This is the most common exemption.

- **Humane killing of animals**—A person authorised by certificate to possess, buy or acquire a firearm solely for use in connection with the humane killing of animals may possess, buy, acquire, sell or transfer such a firearm (s. 3 of the Firearms (Amendment) Act 1997).

When determining whether a firearm falls within the meaning of a 'humane killer', the definition of a 'slaughtering instrument' under s 57(4) may be referred to (*R* v *Paul (Benjamin)* (1998) 95(32) LS Gaz 30).

- **Shot pistols for vermin**—A person authorised by certificate to possess, buy or acquire a 'shot pistol' solely for the shooting of vermin, may possess, buy, acquire, sell or transfer such a pistol (s. 41 of the Firearms (Amendment) Act 1997). A 'shot pistol' is a smooth-bored gun chambered for .410 cartridges or 9mm rim-fire cartridges (s 4(2)).

- **Treatment of animals**—A person authorised by certificate to possess, buy or acquire a firearm for use in connection with the treatment of animals may possess, buy, acquire, sell or transfer any firearm or ammunition designed or adapted for the purpose of tranquillising or treating any animal (s. 8 of the Firearms (Amendment) Act 1997). This exemption also applies to offences involving firearms under s. 5(1)(b) and (c) (**see para. 5.4.1**).

- **Races at athletic meetings**—A person may possess a firearm at an athletic meeting for the purpose of starting races at that meeting (s. 5(1) of the Firearms (Amendment) Act 1997). Similarly, a person authorised by certificate to possess, buy or acquire a firearm solely for the purposes of starting such races may possess, buy, acquire, sell or transfer a firearm for such a purpose (s. 5(2)).

- **Trophies of war**—A person authorised by certificate to do so may possess a firearm which was acquired as a trophy before 1 January 1946 (s. 6 of the Firearms (Amendment) Act 1997).

- **Firearms of historic interest**—Some firearms are felt to be of particular historical, aesthetic or technical interest. Section 7(4) of the Firearms (Amendment) Act 1997 makes detailed provision for the exemption of such firearms, exemptions which exist in addition to the general exemptions under s. 58 of the Firearms Act 1968 (**see para. 5.5.4**). These provisions are set out in the Firearms (Amendment) Act 1997 (Firearms of Historic Interest) Order 1997 (SI 1997 No. 1537) and the Firearms (Amendment) Act 1997 (Transitional Provisions and Savings) Regulations 1997 (SI 1997 No. 1538).

## 5.8    Further offences

### 5.8.1    Possession with intent to endanger life

OFFENCE:    **Possession with Intent to Endanger Life—*Firearms Act 1968, s. 16***
- Triable on indictment • Sentence: see sch. 6, appendix 5
*(Serious arrestable offence)*

The Firearms Act 1968, s. 16 states:

> It is an offence for a person to have in his possession any firearm or ammunition with intent by means thereof to endanger life or cause serious injury to property, or to enable another person by means thereof to endanger life or cause serious injury to property, whether any injury has been caused or not.

---

**KEYNOTE**

There is no reference to imitation firearms in the wording of the offence, neither does the 1982 Act apply, therefore this offence cannot be committed by possessing an imitation firearm (**see para. 5.4.6**).

The offence involves 'possession' (**see para. 5.5.1**); there is no need for the firearm to be produced or shown to another.

This is a crime of 'specific intent' (**see Crime, chapter 1**). You will have to show an intention by the defendant to behave in a way that he/she knows will in fact endanger the life of another (*R* v *Brown* [1995] Crim LR 328).

That intent does not have to be an immediate one and it may be conditional (e.g. an intent to shoot someone if they do not do as they are asked) (*R* v *Bentham* [1973] QB 357).

The life endangered must be the life of 'another', not the defendant's (*R* v *Norton* [1977] Crim LR 478) but that other person may be outside the UK (*R* v *El-Hakkoui* [1975] 1 WLR 396).

The firearm must provide the means by which life is endangered; it is not enough to have a firearm at the time when life is endangered by some other means (e.g. by dangerous driving).

There may be occasions where self-defence can be raised in answer to a charge under s. 16 of the 1968 Act but these circumstances will be very unusual (see *R* v *Georgiades* [1989] 1 WLR 759).

### 5.8.2   Possession with intent to cause fear of violence

OFFENCE:   **Possession with intent to cause fear of violence—*Firearms Act 1968, s. 16A***
> • Triable on indictment  •  Sentence: see sch. 6, appendix 5
> *(Arrestable offence)*

The Firearms Act 1968, s. 16A (added by Firearms (Amendment) Act 1994, s. 1) states:

> It is an offence for a person to have in his possession any firearm or imitation firearm with intent—
>
> (a)  by means thereof to cause, or
>
> (b)  to enable another person by means thereof to cause,
>
> any person to believe that unlawful violence will be used against him or another person.

**KEYNOTE**

This offence includes imitation firearms in the general sense (**see para. 5.4.6**).

This is a crime of 'specific intent' (**see Crime, chapter 1**).

As with the offence under s. 16, the offence is committed by possession, accompanied by the required intent; there is no need for the firearm to be produced or shown to anyone. The firearm must provide the 'means' for the threat; possession of a firearm while making a general threat to someone who does not know of its presence is unlikely to fall within this section.

### 5.8.3   Using firearm to resist arrest

OFFENCE:   **Using firearm to resist arrest—*Firearms Act 1968, s. 17(1)***
> • Triable on indictment  •  Sentence: see sch. 6, appendix 5
> *(Serious arrestable offence)*

The Firearms Act 1968, s. 17 states:

> (1)  It is an offence for a person to make or attempt to make any use whatsoever of a firearm or imitation firearm with intent to resist or prevent the lawful arrest or detention of himself or another person.

**KEYNOTE**

If the defendant has the firearm or imitation firearm with them at the time of resisting or preventing an arrest, they commit the offence under s. 18 (**see para. 5.8.6**).

The 'firearm' to which s. 17 refers is that defined at **para. 5.3**, *except* component parts and silencers/flash diminishers (s. 17(4)).

This offence includes imitation firearms in the general sense (**see para. 5.4.6**) but not imitation component parts, etc.

This is a crime of 'specific intent' (**see Crime, chapter 1**). It requires proof, not of possession, but of evidence that the defendant made some actual use of the firearm and did so intending to resist/prevent the arrest of themselves or someone else. Any arrest which the defendant intended to prevent/resist must have been 'lawful'.

### 5.8.4 Possessing firearm while committing a schedule 1 offence

OFFENCE: **Possessing firearm while committing or being arrested for schedule 1 offence—*Firearms Act 1968, s. 17(2)***

- Triable on indictment • Sentence: see sch. 6, appendix 5
*(Arrestable offence)*

The Firearms Act 1968, s. 17 states:

(2) If a person, at the time of his committing or being arrested for an offence specified in schedule 1 to this Act, has in his possession a firearm or imitation firearm, he shall be guilty of an offence under this subsection unless he shows that he had it in his possession for a lawful object.

**KEYNOTE**

This offence may be committed in two ways; either by being in possession of the weapon at the time of committing the sch. 1 offence or by being in possession of it *at the time of being arrested* for such an offence. Clearly in the second case, there may be some time between actually committing the sch. 1 offence and being arrested for it.

Nevertheless, if the defendant is in possession of the firearm at the time of his/her arrest, the offence is committed (unless he/she can show that it was for a lawful purpose).

For this offence, you need to prove that the person *was in possession* of the firearm but not that they actually *had it with them*. This fine but important distinction was recently reviewed by the Court of Appeal where it was reiterated that the two expressions have different meanings throughout the Act, with possession being a deliberately wider concept than the expression 'has with him' (*R v North* [2001] EWCA Crim 544).

There is no need for the defendant to be subsequently *convicted* of the sch. 1 offence, nor even to prove the elements of it; all that is needed is to show that the defendant, at the time of his/her arrest for a sch. 1 offence, had a firearm/imitation firearm in his/her possession (*R v Nelson (Damien)* [2001] QB 55 CA).

It is for the defendant to prove that the firearm was in his/her possession for a lawful purpose, presumably on the balance of probabilities (**see Evidence and Procedure, chapter 11**).

This offence includes imitation firearms in the general sense (**see para. 5.4.6**).

Schedule 1 Offences

The *main* offences listed in sch. 1 are:

- Damage—s. 1 of the Criminal Damage Act 1971.
- Assaults and woundings—ss. 20 and 47 of the Offences Against the Person Act 1861, assault police (s. 89 of the Police Act 1996) and civilian custody officers (s. 90(1) of the Criminal Justice Act 1991 and s. 13(1) of the Criminal Justice and Public Order Act 1994).
- Rape and 'taking out of possession'—ss. 1, 17, 18 and 20 of the Sexual Offences Act 1956. Part I of the Child Abduction Act 1984.
- Theft, robbery, burglary, blackmail and taking a conveyance—Theft Act 1968.

(**D.A.R.T.**)

Although covering several types of assault, sch. 1 does not extend to wounding/causing grievous bodily harm with intent. Schedule 1 also covers the aiding, abetting or attempting to commit such offences.

### 5.8.5   Trespassing with firearms

OFFENCE:   **Trespassing with firearm in building—*Firearms Act 1968, s. 20(1)***
   - Triable either way (unless imitation firearm or air weapon)
   - Sentence: see sch. 6, appendix 5
   *(Arrestable offence unless imitation firearm or air weapon)*

The Firearms Act 1968, s. 20 states:

(1) A person commits an offence if, while he has a firearm or imitation firearm with him, he enters or is in any building or part of a building as a trespasser and without reasonable excuse (the proof whereof lies on him).

---

**KEYNOTE**

This offence includes a specific reference to imitation firearms (see para. 5.4.6).

If the relevant firearm is an imitation or an air weapon, the offence is triable summarily (see appendix 5).

This offence can be committed either by entering a building/part of a building or simply by *being* in such a place, in each case as a trespasser while having the firearm. As there is no need for the defendant to have 'entered' the building as a trespasser in every case, the offence might be committed after the occupier has withdrawn any permission for the defendant to be there. (Contrast the offence of trespassing with a weapon of offence; see chapter 6.)

For a discussion of the elements of entering a building/part of a building as a trespasser, see Crime, chapter 12. For the interpretation of 'has with him', see para. 5.8.6.

It will be for the defendant to prove that he/she had reasonable excuse and the standard of that proof will be judged against the balance of probabilities.

The power of entry and search under s. 47 of the 1968 Act applies to this offence (see para. 5.10).

---

OFFENCE:   **Trespassing with firearm on land—*Firearms Act 1968, s. 20(2)***
   - Triable summarily  •  Sentence: see sch. 6, appendix 5
   *(No specific power of arrest)*

The Firearms Act 1968, s. 20 states:

(2) A person commits an offence if, while he has a firearm or imitation firearm with him, he enters or is on any land as a trespasser and without reasonable excuse (the proof whereof lies on him).

---

**KEYNOTE**

The elements of this offence are generally the same as those for the s. 20(1) offence above.

As with the s. 20(1) offence, there is no requirement that the defendant had the firearm/imitation firearm with him/her when entering onto the land (compare with the offence of aggravated burglary under the Theft Act 1968; see Crime, chapter 12).

'Land' for these purposes will include land covered by water (s. 20(3)).

Although this section does not have a specific power of arrest, there is a power of arrest for a police officer in uniform in relation to a person reasonably suspected of trespassing with a weapon of offence which may be appropriate (see chapter 6).

---

5.8.6 **Having firearm with intent to commit indictable offence or resist arrest**

OFFENCE: **Having firearm with intent to commit an indictable offence or resist arrest—*Firearms Act 1968, s. 18(1)***
- Triable on indictment • Sentence: see sch. 6, appendix 5
*(Serious arrestable offence)*

The Firearms Act 1968, s. 18 states:

(1) It is an offence for a person to have with him a firearm or imitation firearm with intent to commit an indictable offence, or to resist arrest or prevent the arrest of another, in either case while he has a firearm or imitation firearm with him.

---

**KEYNOTE**

This offence, which overlaps with that under s. 17(1) (**see para. 5.8.3**), requires the defendant to have the firearm 'with him'. This is a more restrictive expression than 'possession' (as to which, **see para. 5.5.1**), and requires that the firearm is 'readily accessible' to the defendant (e.g. in a car nearby) (*R* v *Pawlicki* [1992] 1 WLR 827).

Despite this narrower meaning, the defendant does not have to be shown to have been 'carrying' the firearm (*R* v *Kelt* [1977] 1 WLR 1365), a decision which now conflicts with the situation relating to identical statutory expressions under the Theft Act 1968 (**see Crime, chapter 12**) and also under the legislation relating to weapons (**see chapter 6**).

This is a crime of 'specific intent' (**see Crime, chapter 1**) and, in proving that intent, s. 18(2) states:

(2) In proceedings for an offence under this section proof that the accused had a firearm or imitation firearm with him and intended to commit an offence, or to resist or prevent arrest, is evidence that he intended to have it with him while doing so.

It is not necessary to show that the defendant intended to *use* the firearm to commit the indictable offence or to prevent/resist the arrest (*R* v *Duhaney* [1998] 2 Cr App R 25). (Contrast the offence under s 17(1); **see para. 5.8.3**.)

An indictable offence includes an offence triable either way (Interpretation Act 1978).

Section 18 does not appear to require that any arrest be 'lawful' and it may be that Parliament intended for this offence to be broader in that respect than the offence under s. 17.

This offence includes imitation firearms in the general sense (**see para. 5.4.6**).

The power of entry and search under s. 47 of the 1968 Act applies to this offence (**see para. 5.10**).

5.8.7 **Having loaded firearm in public place**

OFFENCE: **Having loaded firearm in public place—*Firearms Act 1968, s. 19***
- Triable either way • Sentence: see sch. 6, appendix 5
*(Arrestable offence unless air weapon)*

The Firearms Act 1968, s. 19 states:

A person commits an offence if, without lawful authority or reasonable excuse (the proof whereof lies on him), he has with him in a public place a loaded shot gun or loaded air weapon, or any other firearm (whether loaded or not) together with ammunition suitable for use in that firearm.

---

**KEYNOTE**

Public place includes any highway and any other premises or place to which the public have access at the material time, or to which the public are permitted access at the material time whether on payment or otherwise (see s. 57(4) of the 1968 Act).

'Loaded' here means if there is ammunition in the chamber or barrel (or in any magazine or other device) whereby the ammunition can be fed into the chamber or barrel by the manual or automatic operation of some part of the weapon (see s. 57(6)(b) ).

If the weapon is a firearm other than an air weapon or a shotgun, the offence is committed by having suitable ammunition with it; there is no requirement for it to be loaded.

If the weapon is an air weapon the offence is only triable summarily (**see appendix** 5).

The Firearms Act 1982 does not apply here, neither is there any mention of imitation firearms in the wording of the section. Therefore the offence does not apply to imitation firearms.

For the meaning of 'has with him', **see para. 5.8.6.**

This offence is an 'absolute' offence like s 1 (**see para. 5.5**). Therefore, if you can show that the defendant (X) knew he had something with him and that the 'something' was a loaded shotgun/air weapon (or other firearm with ammunition), the offence is complete (*R* v *Vann* [1996] Crim LR 52).

It is for the defendant to show lawful authority or reasonable excuse; possession of a valid certificate does not of itself provide lawful authority for having the firearm/ammunication in a public place (*Ross* v *Collins* [1982] Crim LR 368).

## 5.9    **Possession or acquisition of firearms by certain people**

Sections 21 to 24 of the Firearms Act 1968 place further restrictions on the people who can possess, acquire, receive or otherwise have involvement with firearms. Section 21 deals with people who have been convicted of certain offences while ss. 22 to 24 set out minimum ages in respect of certain firearms and transactions.

Section 21 generally provides that any person who has been sentenced to:

- custody for life, or
- to preventive detention, imprisonment, corrective training, youth custody or detention in a young offender institution for three years or more

must not, *at any time*, have a firearm or ammunition in his/her possession.

Section 21 goes on to provide that any person who has been sentenced to imprisonment, youth custody detention in a young offender institution or a secure training order for three months or more, *but less than three years*, must not have a firearm or ammunition in his/her possession at any time before the end of a five-year period beginning on the date of his/her release.

Date of release means, for a sentence partly served and partly suspended, the date on which the offender completes the part to be served and, in the case of a person subject to a secure training order, the date on which he/she is released from detention (under the various relevant statutes) or the date halfway through the total specified by the court making the order, whichever is the latest (s. 21(2A) ).

A person holding a licence under the Children and Young Persons Act 1933 or a person subject to a recognisance to keep the peace or be of good behaviour with a condition relating to the possession of firearms, must not, *at any time during the licence or the recognisance*, have a firearm or ammunition in his/her possession (s. 21(3) ).

Where sentences or court orders are mentioned, their Scottish equivalents will also apply and a person prohibited in Northern Ireland from possessing a firearm/ammunition will also be prohibited in Great Britain (s. 21(3A) ).

Section 21 does not apply to imitation firearms as there is no express reference to them in the section and because the reference in the Firearms Act 1982 does not apply (see para. 5.4.6).

If the person who has been sentenced as set out in s. 21 contravenes the provisions above (e.g. by possessing etc. any firearm), he/she commits an either way offence punishable with a maximum of five years' imprisonment (thereby making it an arrestable offence).

### 5.9.1 Supplying firearm to person prohibited by section 21

OFFENCE: **Selling or transferring firearm to person prohibited by section 21—** *Firearms Act 1968, s. 21(5)*

• Triable either way • Sentence: sch. 6, appendix 5
*(Arrestable offence)*

The Firearms Act 1968, s. 21 states:

(5) It is an offence for a person to sell or transfer a firearm or ammunition to, or to repair, test or prove a firearm or ammunition for, a person whom he knows or has reasonable ground for believing to be prohibited by this section from having a firearm or ammunition in his possession.

---

**KEYNOTE**

Given that all people are presumed to know the law once it is published, it would seem that the knowledge or belief by the defendant would apply to the *convictions of* the other person, not the fact that possession by that person was an offence.

What you must show is knowledge by the defendant or at least *reasonable ground for believing*; this latter requirement is stronger than mere cause to *suspect* (see chapter 2).

---

### 5.9.2 Other restrictions on possession or acquisition

In addition to the general provisions relating to possession, acquisition etc., ss. 22 to 24 create a number of summary offences restricting the involvement of people of various ages in their dealings with firearms and ammunition. The table opposite provides a brief summary of some of those provisions. For the full extent of these restrictions and their exemptions, reference should be made to the 1968 Act.

It is a summary offence (punishable by one month's imprisonment and/or a fine) to be in possession of *any* loaded firearm when drunk (s. 12 of the Licensing Act 1872). There is no requirement that the person be in a public place. This offence carries a power of arrest in relation to any person found committing it. Given the decisions in other cases where similar powers of arrest remain applicable (**see, e.g., chapter 4 and Crime, chapter 10**), that power would appear to be available to police officers.

## 5.10 Police powers

Section 47 of the Firearms Act 1968 states:

(1) A constable may require any person whom he has reasonable cause to suspect—
    (a) of having a firearm, with or without ammunition, with him in a public place; or
    (b) to be committing or about to commit, elsewhere than in a public place, an offence relevant for the purposes of this section,
    to hand over the firearm or any ammunition for examination by the constable.

**KEYNOTE**

This power has two distinct elements. The first applies where the officer has reasonable cause to suspect that a person has a firearm with him/her in a public place. The second relates to a situation where the officer has reasonable cause to suspect that the person is committing or is about to commit an offence relevant to this section anywhere else.

An 'offence relevant to this section' appears to be an offence under s. 18(1) and s. 20 (see s. 47(6) ).

It is a summary offence to fail to hand over a firearm when required under this section (s. 47(2) ).

In order to exercise this power, a police officer may search the person and may detain him/her for that purpose (s. 47(3) ). The officer may also enter *any place* (s. 47(4) ).

If the officer has reasonable cause to suspect that:

- there is a firearm in a vehicle in a public place, or

- that a vehicle is being/about to be used in connection with the commission of an 'offence relevant to this section' (see above)

he/she may search the vehicle and, for that purpose, may require the person driving or in control of the vehicle to stop it (s. 47(4) ).

The provisions of the PACE Codes of Practice, Code A, will apply to the exercise of these powers of stop and search (**see appendix 1**).

For powers of stop and search generally, **see chapter 2.**

| Age | Restrictions | Applies to imitation? |
|---|---|---|
| Under 14 years | • Having with them air weapon or ammunition for one (s. 22(4) subject to exception*†). | No |
| | • Possessing any s. 1 firearm or ammunition without lawful authority (except as permitted or sports and shooting clubs etc.). | Yes |
| | • Giving or lending s. 1 firearm or ammunition or parting with possession to such a person except as permitted (for sports and shooting clubs etc.) (s. 24(2) ). | Yes |
| | • Giving or parting with possession of air weapon to such a person (unless under permitted circumstances*) (s. 24(4) ). | Yes |
| Under 15 years | • Having with them assembled shotgun unless supervised by person aged at least 21 or while shotgun is securely covered (s. 22(3) ). | No |
| | • Giving shotgun or ammunition for one to such a person (s. 24(3) ). | No |
| Under 17 years | • Buying or hiring any firearm or ammunition (s. 22(1) ). | No |
| | • Having with them air weapon in public place except airgun or air rifle, in each case securely covered† (s. 22(5) ). | No |
| | • Selling or letting on hire to such a person any firearm or ammunition (s. 24(1) ). | No |
| Under 18 years | • Holder of certificate using firearm for purpose not authorised by European Weapons Directive (s. 22(1A) ). | No |

*Section 23 provides that no offence is committed if the person is under the supervision of another who is at least 21 years old. The person under 14 must not use the air weapon for firing missiles beyond the relevant premises and the supervising person must not allow the air weapon to be so used.

†Section 23 goes on to provide that no offence is committed where a person who is a member of an approved rifle club (or miniature rifle club) has with them an air weapon or ammunition while engaged in target shooting as such, nor where he/she is using the weapon at a shooting gallery where the air weapons or miniature rifles being used do not exceed .23 inch calibre.

Note that s. 24 makes a number of defences where the person giving, lending etc. is mistaken about the true age of the other person concerned.

Section 48 states:

(1) A constable may demand, from any person whom he believes to be in possession of a firearm or ammunition to which section 1 of this Act applies, or of a shot gun, the production of his firearm certificate or, as the case may be, his shot gun certificate.

---

**KEYNOTE**

The demand for the relevant documentation may be made where the police officer 'believes' that a person is in possession of a section 1 firearm or ammunition or a shotgun. There is no requirement that the officer's belief be reasonable.

Where the person fails to:

- produce the relevant certificate or

- show that he/she is not entitled to be issued with such a certificate or

- show that he/she is in possession of the firearm exclusively in connection with recognised purposes (collecting/historical/cultural) under the law of another EU member State

the officer may demand the production of the relevant valid documentation issued in another member State under any corresponding provisions (s. 48(1A)).

Failing to produce any of the required documents *and* to let the officer read it, or failing to show an entitlement to possess the firearm or ammunition triggers (!) the power of seizure under s. 48(2). It also gives the officer the power to demand the person's name and address. This requirement is similar to the provision under s. 170 of the Road Traffic Act 1988 (duty to give details after an accident; **see Road Traffic, chapter 4**) where it has been held that the name and address of the person's solicitor would suffice (*DPP* v *McCarthy* [1999] RTR 323). That decision was based on the purpose behind the Road Traffic Act requirement, namely to allow the respective parties to the accident to get in touch with each other in the future. It is suggested that the purpose of the Firearms Act power is a very different one of regulating the possession of weapons and that the furnishing of details of some convenient administrative location for correspondence would not be enough to satisfy the requirements of this section.

If the person refuses to give his/her name or address or gives a false name and address, he/she commits a summary offence (s. 48(3)).

A person from another Member State who is in possession of a firearm and who fails to comply with a demand under s. 48(1A) also commits a separate summary offence (s. 48(4)).

---

## 5.11 Shortening and conversion of firearms

OFFENCE: **Shortening barrel of shotgun to less than 24 inches—*Firearms Act 1968, s. 4(1)***
- Triable either way • Sentence: see sch. 6, appendix 5
*(Arrestable offence)*

The Firearms Act 1968, s. 4 states:

(1) Subject to this section, it is an offence to shorten the barrel of a shot gun to a length less than 24 inches.

OFFENCE: **Shortening barrel of other smooth-bore section 1 firearm to less than 24 inches—*Firearms (Amendment) Act 1988 s. 6(1)***
- Triable either way • Five years' imprisonment and/or a fine on indictment; six months' imprisonment and/or a fine summarily
*(Arrestable offence)*

The Firearms (Amendment) Act 1988, s. 6 states:

(1) Subject to subsection (2) below, it is an offence to shorten to a length less than 24 inches the barrel of any smooth-bore gun to which section 1 of the principal Act applies other than one which has a barrel with a bore exceeding 2 inches in diameter; . . .

OFFENCE:    **Converting imitation firearm—*Firearms Act 1968, s. 4(3)***
    • Triable either way • Sentence: see sch. 6, appendix 5
    *(Arrestable offence)*

The Firearms Act 1968, s. 4 states:

(3) It is an offence for a person other than a registered firearms dealer to convert into a firearm anything which, though having the appearance of being a firearm, is so constructed as to be incapable of discharging any missile through its barrel.

---

**KEYNOTE**

The relevant definitions are considered at **para. 5.4**.

The first two offences are concerned with the shortening of barrels while the third involves conversion of anything which has the appearance of a firearm so that it can be fired. Registered firearms dealers (**see para. 5.5.4**) are excluded from the wording of the conversion offence. They are also exempted by ss. 4(2) and 6(2) from the relevant offences involving shortening barrels provided the shortening is done *for the sole purpose* of replacing a defective part of the barrel *so as to produce a new barrel having an overall length of at least 24 inches*.

The length of the barrel of a weapon will be measured from its muzzle to the point at which the charge is exploded (s. 57(6)(a) of the 1968 Act).

Once the shortening or conversion has taken place, the nature of the firearm will have changed (e.g. from a shotgun into a section 1 firearm or from an imitation into a real firearm), in which case the person will also commit the relevant possession offences unless he/she has the appropriate authorisation.

---

## 5.12    Restrictions on transfer of firearms

The Firearms (Amendment) Act 1997 created a number of offences concerned with the transfer, lending, hiring etc. of firearms and ammunition.

In brief, a person 'transferring' (that is, selling, letting on hire, lending or giving) a section 1 firearm or ammunition to another must:

• produce a certificate or permit entitling him/her to do so (s. 32(2)(a) ),

• he/she must comply with all the conditions of that certificate or permit (s. 32(2)(b) ), and

• the transferor must personally hand the firearm or ammunition over to the receiver

(s. 32(2)(c) ).

The 1997 Act also requires any person who is the holder of a certificate or permit who is involved in such a transfer (which includes a lending of the firearm/ammunition for a period exceeding 72 hours) to give notice to the chief officer of police who granted the certificate or permit (s. 33(2) ).

Notice is also required of certificate or permit holders where a firearm is lost, de-activated or destroyed or where ammunition is lost, or where firearms are sold outside Great Britain (see ss. 34 and 35).

OFFENCE:    **Failing to comply with requirements—*Firearms (Amendment) Act 1997, ss. 32–35***
    • Section 1 firearm/ammunition: triable either way • Five years' imprisonment and/or fine on indictment; six months' imprisonment and/or fine summarily
    *(Arrestable offence)*

• Shotguns: triable summarily • Six months' imprisonment and/or a fine
*(No specific power of arrest)*

OFFENCE: **Trade transactions by person not registered as firearms dealer—**
**Firearms Act 1968, s. 3(1)**
• Triable either way • Sentence: see sch. 6, appendix 5
*(Arrestable offence)*

The Firearms Act 1968, s. 3 states:

(1) A person commits an offence if, by way of trade or business, he—
(a) manufactures, sells, transfers, repairs, tests or proves any firearm or ammunition to which section 1 of this Act applies, or a shot gun; or
(b) exposes for sale or transfer, or has in his possession for sale, transfer, repair, test or proof any such firearm or ammunition, or a shot gun,
without being registered under this Act as a firearms dealer.

---

**KEYNOTE**

The various definitions are considered above. A registered firearms dealer is a person who, by way of trade or business, manufactures, sells, transfers, repairs, tests or proofs firearms or ammunition to which s. 1 applies, or shotguns (s. 57(4) of the 1968 Act).

If the person undertakes the repair, proofing etc. of a s. 1 firearm or ammunition or a shotgun otherwise than as a trade or business, he/she commits an offence (carrying the same punishment as the s. 3(1) offence above) under s. 3(3) unless he/she can point to some authorisation under the Act allowing him/her to do so.

Section 3 goes on to create further either way offences of selling or transferring a firearm or ammunition to someone other than a registered firearms dealer or someone otherwise authorised under the Act to buy or acquire them and of falsifying certificates with a view to acquiring firearms. These offences also carry the same punishment as the s. 3(1) offence above.

Registration is under s. 33 of the 1968 Act.

'Transferring' is also defined under s. 57(4) and includes letting on hire, giving, lending and parting with possession.

Section 9(2) of the 1968 Act exempts auctioneers from the restrictions on selling and possessing for the purposes of sale of firearms and ammunition where the auctioneer has a permit from the chief officer of police. There are further defences provided by s. 9 (for carriers and warehouse staff) and also under s. 8 (transfer to people authorised to possess firearms without certificate).

---

## 5.13 Other offences under the Firearms (Amendment) Act 1988

There are two offences under the Firearms (Amendment) Act 1988 introduced to ensure compliance with the European Weapons Directive; ss. 18(6) and 18A(6). Both are summary offences punishable with three months' imprisonment and/or a fine.

Other summary offences under the 1968 Act include:

• A firearms dealer failing to send the required notification within 48 hours to the chief officer of police, after selling a firearm or shotgun (s. 18(5)).

• The transferor of a shotgun to another failing to notify police of the details of that transfer as required by s. 4 (s. 4(5)).

• Selling certain ammunition to a person who is not a registered firearms dealer and is not permitted to have the relevant weapon for the ammunition (s. 5(2)).

- A pawnbroker taking a s. 1 firearm or ammunition as a pawn (s. 3(6)).

- Any person selling or transferring any firearm or ammunition or carrying out repairs or tests on such for another person who is drunk or of unsound mind (s. 25).

## 5.14   **Documentation**

The enforcement of the firearms legislation depends heavily on the possession and production of the relevant documents and ss. 30A to 30D of the Firearms Act 1968 allow for the revocation or partial revocation of certificates by chief officers of police. There are therefore many offences which deal with the application for and obtaining of documents, the falsification of records and documents and the failure to maintain proper records. The offences under the Firearms Act 1968 are under ss. 26(5), 29(3), 30(4), 38(8), 39(1) to (3), 40(5) and 52(2)(c), see sch. 6, **appendix 5**.

There is also an offence under s. 12(2) of the Firearms (Amendment) Act 1988 of failing to comply with a notice from the chief officer of police for the surrender of a certificate. This is a summary offence punishable with three months' imprisonment and/or a fine.

There are further summary offences which were created to ensure compliance with the European Weapons Directive (see, ss. 32B(5), 32C(6), 42A(3) and 48A(4) of the Firearms Act 1968).

# 6 | Weapons

## 6.1 Introduction

The carrying of weapons has become an issue of considerable concern over recent years. The law has developed in a slightly untidy fashion and, in considering the different offences and restrictions, it is important to look at the *particular weapons* covered by each piece of legislation, together with the *particular activity* which Parliament has sought to control.

Although it is convenient to refer to the *possession* of offensive weapons, that word has a wide meaning which goes beyond the expressions used in most offences involving the carrying of weapons.

When considering this area, it is important to remember that the carrying of weapons is a very different thing from the use of weapons. This is why simply picking up a handy object and clouting someone with it will not usually amount to an offence under the relevant legislation dealing with carrying of weapons.

It is also useful to bear in mind the differences between offensive weapons and *weapons of offence*. The latter are specifically concerned with the entry onto premises as a trespasser and are slightly wider in their definition than offensive weapons.

## 6.2 Offensive weapons

OFFENCE: **Having offensive weapon in public place—*Prevention of Crime Act 1953, s. 1(1)***
- Triable either way • Four years' imprisonment and/or a fine on indictment; six months' imprisonment and/or a fine summarily
(*Arrestable offence*)

The Prevention of Crime Act 1953, s. 1 states:

(1) Any person who without lawful authority or reasonable excuse, the proof whereof shall lie on him, has with him in any public place any offensive weapon shall be guilty of an offence.

---

**KEYNOTE**

'Lawful authority' means those occasions where people from time to time are required to carry weapons as a matter of duty, such as police officers or members of the armed forces (*Bryan* v *Mott* (1976) 62 Cr App R 71). Security guards carrying truncheons, even if required to do so by their contracts of employment, are not covered (*R* v *Spanner* [1973] Crim LR 704). If someone does not fall into this—very limited—group, he/she may still have a 'reasonable excuse' for having the weapon with him/her.

'Reasonable excuse' may arise from a number of circumstances. People having tools with them in the course of their trade (e.g. craft knives for fitting carpets or hammers for carpentry) may have a 'reasonable excuse' (see

*Ohlson* v *Hylton* [1975] 1 WLR 724). If a person passing the scene of a recent disturbance sees a weapon lying on the ground and he/she picks it up and puts it in his/her car intending to take it to the nearest police station, those circumstances would amount to a reasonable excuse for having the weapon with him/her.

The issues arising our of reasonable excuses under this offence overlap greatly with those of 'good reason' under the Criminal Justice Act 1988 offence below (**see para 6.3.1**) and the two should be read together to make any sense of the many decisions. Along with harassment (**see chapter 3**) and the breathalyser laws (**see Road Traffic**), this area of criminal legislation has provided some of the most litigation in recent years, to the point that most arguments open to even the most creative defendants have been tried. By way of summary:

- Not being aware that you have an offensive weapon with you is *not* a reasonable excuse in itself (*R* v *Densu* [1998] 1 Cr App R 400).
- Neither is forgetting that you have a weapon with you (*R* v *Lorimer* [2003] EWCA Crim 72) generally, or forgetting that there is one in the car you are driving (*R* v *McCalla* (1988) 87 Cr App 372).
- However, where a taxi driver was found with a piece of wood and a cosh in the back of his cab where they had been left by passengers earlier in the week, the Court of Appeal held that his forgetting to remove the weapons might have been accepted as a reasonable excuse and the question should have been left for the jury (*R* v *Glidewell* (1999) 163 JP 557).
- Under the Criminal Justice Act offence below, however, there can be circumstances where forgetfulness could be relevant to the defence of 'good reason' (e.g. where it results from illness or medication)—*Bayliss* v *DPP* (2003) LTL 6 February.

Some of these decisions are more evidential niceties surrounding matters for summing up than policing issues but they might at least explain to bewildered officers/victims the odd acquittal when it happens.

It is not reasonable to have a weapon with you as a *general precaution* in case you are attacked (*Evans* v *Hughes* [1972] 1 WLR 1452). It may, however, be reasonable to have a weapon if you have good grounds to anticipate an unprovoked or unlawful attack (e.g. for a person guarding cash transits—see *Malnik* v *DPP* [1989] Crim LR 451).

Having a weapon for some other reason may amount to a reasonable excuse and whether or not it does so is a matter of fact for the court/jury to decide (see e.g. *Houghton* v *Chief Constable of Greater Manchester Police* (1986) 84 Cr App R 319 where the defendant was in 'fancy dress' costume as a police officer and had a truncheon with him as part of the costume—held to amount to 'reasonable excuse').

The burden of proving the reasonable excuse or lawful authority rests with the defendant, but only when the prosecution have established that the defendant had an offensive weapon with him/her at the time. That burden of proof will be judged against the balance of probabilities and not 'beyond a reasonable doubt' (**see Evidence and Procedure, chapter 11**).

Note that there is a specific offence relating to the carrying of weapons on school premises (**see para. 6.3.2**).

---

### 6.2.1  'Has with him'

This expression (which is also discussed in relation to firearms, **see chapter 5**), shows that the offence is designed to prevent the carrying of weapons; it is not an offence of *intention* and the reported decisions of the courts have consistently reflected that fact.

This is most apparent where an 'innocent' article is used offensively. In *Ohlson* v *Hylton* [1975] 1 WLR 724 the defendant had a bag of tools with him in the course of his trade. He produced a hammer from the bag and used it to hit someone. The court held that, as he had formed the intention to use the hammer *after* it came into his possession, the offence was not made out. Although the court accepted that there might be times where a later intention to use an innocent article offensively would amount to an offence under the 1953 Act, the main purpose of the law was to prevent people from arming themselves with weapons.

Similar decisions have been reached in relation to picking up a discarded knife during a fight (*Bates* v *Bulman* [1979] 1 WLR 1190), brandishing a jack taken from a car (*R* v *Dayle* [1974] 1 WLR 181) and using a penknife—which the defendant happened to be carrying—to stab someone who attacked him (*R* v *Humphreys* [1977] Crim LR 225).

Some confusion has been caused in this area by the different interpretations of the expression 'has with him' in relation to firearms offences (**see chapter 5**).

The fact that the offence is not one of intention is supported by the decisions on 'reasonable excuse' above; the reasonable excuse must relate to the *carrying* of the weapon or article and not the *intention* of the person carrying it (*R* v *Jura* [1954] 1 QB 503).

It is possible for more than one person to have the same weapon 'with them', provided you can show that they knew of its existence in the hands of another at the time (*R* v *Edmonds* [1963] 2 QB 142).

You must show that the defendant knew that he/she had *something* with him/her and that the 'something' was, in fact, an offensive weapon (*R* v *Cugullere* [1961] 1 WLR 858). For a similar situation regarding 'possession' of drugs, **see Crime, chapter 6**.

### 6.2.2 Public place

Section 1(4) of the 1953 Act states:

> (4) In this section 'public place' includes any highway and any other premises or place to which at the material time the public have or are permitted to have access, whether on payment or otherwise...

### 6.2.3 Offensive weapon

Section 1(4) of the 1953 Act also states:

> (4) ...'offensive weapon' means any article made or adapted for use for causing injury to the person, or intended by the person having it with him for such use by him or by some other person.

---

**KEYNOTE**

Offensive weapons fall into three categories for the purposes of this offence, namely articles:

- **made** for causing injury (offensive weapons *per se*);
- **adapted** for causing injury; and
- **intended** by the person who has it, for causing injury.

(For the definition of a 'weapon of offence' used in aggravated burglary, **see para. 6.4** and **Crime, chapter 12**.)

Offensive weapons *per se* are those which have been manufactured for use for causing injury and include truncheons, PR-24 batons and bayonets. A swordstick has been held to be such a weapon (*R* v *Butler* [1988] Crim LR 695) as have flick-knives (*R* v *Simpson* [1983] 1 WLR 1494) and butterfly knives (*DPP* v *Hynde* [1998] 1 WLR 1222). In *Hynde* the court took notice of the fact that butterfly knives were outlawed under the Criminal Justice Act 1988 (**see para. 6.5**) in deciding that such knives were clearly 'made' for causing injury.

Once it has been shown that the article in question was in fact an offensive weapon, there is no need for the prosecution to show any intention to use it for causing injury (*Davis* v *Alexander* (1970) 54 Cr App R 398).

Weapons *adapted* for causing injury can include virtually anything. Whether something has in fact been so adapted is a question of fact for the court/jury to decide in each case. Bottles or glasses which have been broken in order to create a jagged edge have been held to be 'adapted' (*R* v *Simpson* [1983] 1 WLR 1494), so too has a potato with razor blades protruding from it (*R* v *Williamson* (1978) 67 Cr App R 35). If the article itself has not been altered in any physical way (such as by putting ammonia in a 'Jif' lemon to squirt in people's eyes—*R* v *Formosa* [1991] 2 QB 1), it has not been adapted.

It is still unclear whether the adaptation has to be to cause injury to *another* person or whether its capacity for self-inflicted injury (as in a suicide attempt) is enough. It is submitted that, as it is the *adaptation* of the article which is relevant, and not the *intention* of the person carrying it, the ultimate 'victim' is irrelevant (see *Bryan* v *Mott* (1975) 62 Cr App R 71).

Weapons *intended* to be used for causing injury can also include virtually anything. Here the intention of the person carrying it *is relevant* and you must prove an intention to cause injury (as to intention generally, **see Crime, chapter 1**). An intention to cause shock can be enough to satisfy this condition (see the memorably named *R* v *Rapier* (1979) 70 Cr App R 17) but simply using the article to scare potential attackers away will not (see the less menacingly named *R* v *Snooks* [1997] Crim LR 230). To an extent this overlaps with the issues of 'reasonable excuse' and 'has with him' discussed above. In a recent case, a woman walking her dog put the dog over a wall when approached by police officers but kept the metal dog lead which she went on to swing at the officers. The Divisional Court held that it was necessary to examine how closely the adoption of the relevant object and the intention to use it occurred, along with the circumstances in which the offence took place—*C* v *DPP* [2002] Crim LR 322. These issues are more matters for the prosecutor to consider but are clearly relevant when collecting and presenting evidence.

## 6.3   **Other offences involving the carrying of weapons**

### 6.3.1   **Having bladed or pointed article in public place**

OFFENCE:   **Having bladed or sharply pointed article in public place—*Criminal Justice Act 1988, s. 139(1)***

- Triable either way • Two years' imprisonment and/or a fine on indictment;
  six months' imprisonment and/or a fine summarily
  *(Arrestable offence)*

The Criminal Justice Act 1988, s. 139 states:

(1) Subject to subsections (4) and (5) below, any person who has an article to which this section applies with him in a public place shall be guilty of an offence.

---

**KEYNOTE**

This offence applies to any sharply pointed article or article having a blade. Folding pocket knives are excluded unless the cutting edge of the blade exceeds three inches (7.62 cms). If the knife is a lock-knife, it will be covered by this offence, irrespective of whether the blade is actually locked open at the time (*Harris* v *DPP* [1993] 1 WLR 82).

Whether an article falls within the parameters of s. 139 is a question of law for the judge/magistrate(s) to determine (*R* v *Deegan* [1998] 2 Cr App R 121—a case that concerned the carrying of a folding pocket-knife that *was* locked open). In *R* v *Davis* [1998] Crim LR 564 the Court of Appeal reiterated that the question of whether an article was 'bladed' or not was a matter of law for the judge to decide. In that case the defendant had been carrying a screwdriver which, the prosecution contended, was a 'bladed' article capable of causing injury. The court decided that the test to be applied in such cases was not whether the 'bladed' article was capable of caus-ing injury, but whether it had a cutting edge. Deciding whether or not an article was caught by the provisions of s. 139 was not a matter of interpreting the ordinary English word 'blade', but required the straightforward construction of the statute. This decision does not mean that a screwdriver can *never* fall within the type of article outlawed under s. 139 and if the screwdriver is pointed or it has been sharpened, it may still be caught by the above offence.

The fact that an article prohibited under s. 139 is part of something that has other innocuous features (e.g. a utility tool or 'Swiss army knife'), does not save it from falling under this offence if the other ingredients are present (see *R* v *Giles* [2003] EWCA Crim 1287).

'Has with him' is discussed above (**see para. 6.2.1**). The need to prove that the defendant was aware that he/she had the weapon with them for this offence was re-affirmed by the Court of Appeal in *R* v *Daubney* (2000) 164 JP 519.

'Public place' is similar to that under the Prevention of Crime Act 1953 (**see para. 6.2.2**).

Note that there is a specific offence relating to the carrying of weapons on school premises (**see para. 6.3.2**).

### Defences

The defendant may show that he/she had 'good reason' or 'lawful authority' for having the article in a public place (s. 139(4) and (5)). Lawful authority is discussed above; good reason is similar to reasonable excuse (**see para. 6.2**), also discussed above. This approach was confirmed by the Court of Appeal in *R* v *Emmanuel* [1998] Crim LR 347 where it accepted that 'good reason' could include self-defence. Again it will be for the defendant to prove this authority or reason on the balance of probabilities and, again, forgetting that you have the article with you is not a general defence (*DPP* v *Gregson* (1992) 96 Cr App R 240).

Under s. 139 of the Criminal Justice Act 1988 there is a 'strong public interest' in bladed articles not being carried in public without good reason. The Divisional Court so held, finding that the requirement on the defendant to prove a good reason for having the relevant article is not an infringement of human rights legislation—*Lynch* v *DPP* [2002] 2 All ER 854. The Court of Appeal went on to consider the relevant issues here in *R* v *Matthews* (2003) LTL 27 March. There it was held that the plain and ordinary meaning of s. 139 (4) and (5) was that these provisions imposed a persuasive burden on the defendant, not merely an evidential burden (**see Evidence and Procedure**). As such, the defence made an inroad into Article 6 (2) but, because the defendant is the only person who knows why he or she has a bladed article in a public place, there is an objective justification for this burden being imposed on a defendant. Such a measure was proportionate and struck a fair balance between the general interest of the community and the individual's rights.

A defendant may also show that he/she has the article:

- For use at work, e.g. joiners, chefs, gardeners etc.

- For religious reasons, e.g. members of the Sikh religion having a *kirpan*.

- As part of any national costume—such as someone in Highland Dress with a *skean dhu*.

In *Mohammed* v *Chief Constable of South Yorkshire* [2002] EWHC 406 the defendant was stopped by police while driving a van. The officers found a meat cleaver under the driver's seat, which the defendant admitted having put there the previous evening. The defendant used the meat cleaver to chop up meat in the course of his business—a takeaway—and he claimed to have had it with him to take it to be sharpened the following day. In answer to a charge under s. 139, he argued that he had the cleaver with him for 'good reason' (per s. 139(4)) or, in the alternative, that he had it with him for use at work (per s. 139(5)). On conviction, the defendant appealed by way of case stated to the Administrative Court who held that it was not a 'good reason' to show that the ultimate use of an article would be lawful unless there was a sufficient connection in time between having the article and that ultimate purpose. Basically, the 'ultimate lawful purpose' as claimed here had been too far distant from the time when the defendant was caught with the article. The Court also held that the defendant did not have the knife for use at work; he had it for the purpose of *rendering it possible* to use it at work. He had taken the cleaver on a Saturday night intending, he claimed, to have it sharpened on the following Monday. The Court held that there was no reason for him not to have taken the cleaver on the Monday, taking it directly to be sharpened.

Strangely, whether or not an article is for the uses or reasons set out above appears to be a question of *fact* (see *R* v *Manning* [1998] Crim LR 198).

6.3.2   **Weapons on school premises**

OFFENCE:   **Having bladed or sharply pointed article on school premises—*Criminal Justice Act 1988, s. 139A(1)***

- Triable either way • Two years' imprisonment and/or a fine on indictment;
  six months' imprisonment and/or a fine summarily
  *(Arrestable offence)*

The Criminal Justice Act 1988, s. 139A states:

(1)  Any person who has an article to which section 139 of this Act applies with him on school premises shall be guilty of an offence.

---

**KEYNOTE**

'Has with him' is much narrower than 'possession', **see chapter 5** and also **Crime, chapter 6**.

'School premises' means land used for the purposes of a school *excluding any land occupied solely as a dwelling by a person employed at the school*. This means that the provisions would not apply to someone found in the garden of a caretaker's house if that house was occupied solely as a dwelling by the school caretaker.

'School' under the Education Act 1996, s. 4, means:

(1)  . . . an educational institution which is outside the further education sector and the higher education sector and is an institution for providing—
  (a)  primary education;
  (b)  secondary education, or
  (c)  both primary and secondary education,
  whether or not the institution also provides part-time education suitable to the requirements of junior pupils or further education.

This offence applies to the same articles as those covered under s. 139(1), **see para. 6.3.1.**

---

Defence

The defences are the same as for s. 139(1), **see para. 6.3.1.**

OFFENCE:   **Having offensive weapon on school premises—*Criminal Justice Act 1988, s. 139A(2)***

- Triable either way • Four years' imprisonment and/or a fine on indictment;
  six months' imprisonment and/or a fine summarily
  *(Arrestable offence)*

The Criminal Justice Act 1988, s. 139A states:

(2)  Any person who has an offensive weapon within the meaning of section 1 of the Prevention of Crime Act 1953 with him on school premises shall be guilty of an offence.

---

**KEYNOTE**

For the purposes of this offence, 'offensive weapons' fall into the three categories discussed at **para. 6.2.3.**

'Has with him', 'school premises' and 'school' are all discussed above.

---

Power of entry

The Criminal Justice Act 1988, s. 139B (added by Offensive Weapons Act 1996, s. 4) states:

(1) A constable may enter school premises and search those premises and any person on those premises for—
   (a) any article to which section 139 of this Act applies, or
   (b) any offensive weapon within the meaning of section 1 of the Prevention of Crime Act 1953, if he has reasonable grounds for believing that an offence under section 139A of this Act is being, or has been, committed.

(2) If in the course of a search under this section a constable discovers an article or weapon which he has reasonable grounds for suspecting to be an article or weapon of a kind described in subsection (1) above, he may seize and retain it.

(3) The constable may use reasonable force, if necessary, in the exercise of the power of entry conferred by this section.

---

**KEYNOTE**

The power of search under this provision is covered by the Police and Criminal Evidence Act 1984 Codes of Practice (see chapter 2).

---

## 6.4 Trespassing with weapon of offence

As a further complication, there is another offence relating to weapons, namely that under the Criminal Law Act 1977. As opposed to the carrying of weapons in public, or the carrying of them on school premises, this offence is concerned with preventing people *trespassing* with weapons in much the same way as aggravated burglary.

OFFENCE: **Trespassing with weapon of offence—*Criminal Law Act 1977, s. 8(1)***
   • Triable summarily • Six months' imprisonment and/or a fine
   *(Statutory power of arrest)*

The Criminal Law Act 1977, s. 8 states:

(1) A person who is on any premises as a trespasser, after having entered as such, is guilty of an offence if, without lawful authority or reasonable excuse, he has with him on the premises any weapon of offence.

---

**KEYNOTE**

The definition of 'weapon of offence' is the same as that for aggravated burglary (see Crime, chapter 12), namely any article made or adapted for use for causing injury to or incapacitating a person, or intended by the person having it with him/her for that use (s. 8(2)).

This offence is restricted to a person who has entered the relevant premises as a trespasser. It does not therefore extend to a person who, having entered lawfully, then becomes a trespasser for whatever reason (e.g. because the occupier has told him/her to leave).

'Premises' for this purpose means:

• any building or

• any part of a building under separate occupation

• any land adjacent to and used/intended for use in connection with a building

• the site comprising any building(s) together with ancillary land

- any fixed structure

- any movable structure, vehicle or vessel designed or adapted for residential purposes

(s. 12 of the 1977 Act).

There are specific offences of trespassing on land or in buildings with firearms (**see** chapter 5).

For a further discussion of the meaning of 'has with him', 'trespasser' and 'made, adapted or intended', **see Crime, chapter 12.**

---

### Power of arrest

Section 8(4) states:

> (4) A constable in uniform may arrest without warrant anyone who is, or whom he with reasonable cause suspects to be, in the act of committing an offence under this section.

---

**KEYNOTE**

This power of arrest is a 'preserved' power under s. 26 and sch. 2 of the Police and Criminal Evidence Act 1984. It is limited to officers in uniform and is drafted in the present tense, that is, it will only apply where there is a reasonable suspicion that the person is in the act of committing this offence.

For a discussion of 'reasonable cause to suspect', **see** chapter 2.

---

## 6.5 Manufacture and sale of weapons

In addition to the controls on the carrying of weapons, there are also restrictions on the sale, manufacture, hire and buying of some weapons. The legislation is aimed at restricting the supply of such weapons and their availability in England and Wales. As such, they are mainly concerned with manufacture, sale, offering for sale etc. and should not be confused with offences of *carrying* such weapons (which are dealt with above).

Some of the offences relate to *possession* for the purpose of sale, hire etc.; this is a much wider term than that used in the carrying offences ('has with him') and is discussed in greater detail in the context of drugs (**see Crime, chapter 6**) and firearms (**see chapter 5 above**).

OFFENCE: **Manufacture, sale or hire of weapons—*Restriction of Offensive Weapons Act 1959, s. 1***
- Triable summarily • Six months' imprisonment and/or a fine
*(No specific power of arrest)*

The Restriction of Offensive Weapons Act 1959, s. 1 states:

> (1) Any person who manufactures, sells or hires or offers for sale or hire or exposes or has in his possession for the purpose of sale or hire, or lends or gives to any other person—
> (a) any knife which has a blade which opens automatically by hand pressure applied to a button, spring or other device in or attached to the handle of the knife, sometimes known as a 'flick knife' or 'flick gun'; or
> (b) any knife which has a blade which is released from the handle or sheath thereof by the force of gravity or the application of centrifugal force and which, when released, is locked in place by means of a button, spring, lever, or other device, sometimes known as a 'gravity knife', shall be guilty of an offence...

OFFENCE: **Manufacture, sale and hire of offensive weapons—*Criminal Justice Act 1988, s. 141***

> • Triable summarily • Six months' imprisonment and/or a fine
> *(No specific power of arrest)*

The Criminal Justice Act 1988, s. 141 states:

> (1) Any person who manufactures, sells or hires or offers for sale or hire, exposes or has in his possession for the purpose of sale or hire, or lends or gives to any other person, a weapon to which this section applies shall be guilty of an offence

---

**KEYNOTE**

The importation of the weapons described in these offences is also prohibited (under s. 141(2) and (4) respectively.

---

The weapons to which the 1988 Act offence applies are set out in the schedule to the Criminal Justice Act 1988 (Offensive Weapons) Order 1988 (SI 1988 No. 2019 made under Criminal Justice Act 1988, s. 141). The weapons listed include knuckledusters, swordsticks, some telescopic truncheons, butterfly knives and a whole range of martial arts weapons. The complete list is as follows:

> …
>
> (a) a knuckleduster that is, a band of metal or other hard material worn on one or more fingers, and designed to cause injury, and any weapon incorporating a knuckleduster;
> (b) a swordstick, that is, a hollow walking-stick or cane containing a blade which may be used as a sword;
> (c) the weapon sometimes known as a 'handclaw', being a band of metal or other hard material from which a number of sharp spikes protrude, and worn around the hand;
> (d) the weapon sometimes known as a 'belt buckle knife', being a buckle which incorporates or conceals a knife;
> (e) the weapon sometimes known as a 'push dagger', being a knife the handle of which fits within a clenched fist and the blade of which protrudes from between two fingers;
> (f) the weapon sometimes known as a 'hollow kubotan', being a cylindrical container containing a number of sharp spikes;
> (g) the weapon sometimes known as a 'footclaw', being a bar of metal or other hard material from which a number of sharp spikes protrude, and worn strapped to the foot;
> (h) the weapon sometimes known as a 'shuriken', 'shaken' or 'death star', being a hard non-flexible plate having three or more sharp radiating points and designed to be thrown;
> (i) the weapon sometimes known as a 'balisong' or 'butterfly knife', being a blade enclosed by its handle, which is designed to split down the middle, without the operation of a spring or other mechanical means, to reveal the blade;
> (j) the weapon sometimes known as a 'telescopic truncheon', being a truncheon which extends automatically by hand pressure applied to a button, spring or other device in or attached to its handle;
> (k) the weapon sometimes known as a 'blowpipe' or 'blow gun' being a hollow tube out of which hard pellets or darts are shot by the use of breath;
> (l) the weapon sometimes known as a 'kusari gama', being a length of rope, cord, wire or chain fastened at one end to a sickle;
> (m) the weapon sometimes known as a 'kyoketsu shoge', being a length of rope, cord, wire or chain fastened at one end to a hooked knife;
> (n) the weapon sometimes known as a 'manrikigusari' or 'kusari', being a length of rope, cord, wire or chain fastened at each end to a hard weight or hand grip;
> (o) a disguised knife, that is any knife which has a concealed blade or concealed sharp point and is designed to appear to be an everyday object of a kind commonly carried on the person or in a handbag, briefcase, or other hand luggage (such as a comb, brush, writing instrument, cigarette lighter, key, lipstick or telephone).

For the purposes of the schedule, a weapon is an antique if it was manufactured more than 100 years before the date of any offence alleged to have been committed in respect of the weapon.

**KEYNOTE**

The courts will take notice of the fact that a weapon has been outlawed under this legislation in deciding whether or not it is 'made' for causing injury under the Prevention of Crime Act 1953 (see para. 6.2.3). The articles set out at paragraph (o) were added in response to the hijacking of American airliners in September 2001.

### Defences

There are a number of defences which include Crown servants and visiting forces (s. 141(5) to (7)) and transactions made by or to museumsand galleries (s. 141(8) to (11)).

## 6.6    Knives

Although some knives will fall into the categories of offence covered above, there are further restrictions which apply to knives generally.

### 6.6.1    Sale of knives etc. to persons under 16

OFFENCE: **Selling, knives and articles to under 16's—*Criminal Justice Act 1988, s. 141A***

> • Triable summarily  • Six months' imprisonment and/or a fine
> *(No specific power of arrest)*

The Criminal Justice Act 1988, s. 141A states:

(1) Any person who sells to a person under the age of sixteen years an article to which this section applies shall be guilty of an offence . . .

(2) Subject to subsection (3) below, this section applies to—
    (a) any knife, knife blade or razor blade,
    (b) any axe, and
    (c) any other article which has a blade or which is sharply pointed and which is made or adapted for use for causing injury to the person.

(3) This section does not apply to any article described in—
    (a) section 1 of the Restriction of Offensive Weapons Act 1959,
    (b) an order made under section 141(2) of this Act, or
    (c) an order made by the Secretary of State under this section.

**KEYNOTE**

This offence does not apply to folding pocket knives with a cutting edge not exceeding three inches (7.62 cms), neither does it apply to certain types of razor blade in a cartridge where not more than 2 mm of blade is exposed (Criminal Justice Act 1988 (Offensive Weapons) (Exemptions) Order 1996 (SI 1996 No. 3064).

### Defence

Section 141A of the 1988 Act states:

(4) It shall be a defence for a person charged with an offence under subsection (1) above to prove that he took all reasonable precautions and exercised all due diligence to avoid the commission of the offence.

6.6.2    **Unlawful marketing of knives**

OFFENCE:    **Unlawful marketing of knives—*Knives Act 1997, s. 1***
- Triable either way  • Two years' imprisonment and/or a fine on indictment; six months' imprisonment and/or a fine summarily
*(No specific power of arrest)*

The Knives Act 1997, s. 1 states:

(1) A person is guilty of an offence if he markets a knife in a way which—
  (a) indicates, or suggests, that it is suitable for combat; or
  (b) is otherwise likely to stimulate or encourage violent behaviour involving the use of the knife as a weapon.

---

**KEYNOTE**

'Knife' for this purpose means any instrument which has a blade *or* which is sharply pointed (s. 10 of the 1997 Act).

Marketing will include selling, hiring, offering or exposing for sale or hire and possessing it for those purposes (s. 1(4)).

'Indicates or suggests' is a very loose concept requiring no *mens rea* on the part of the defendant (however, see defences below).

'Suitable for combat' means suitable for use as a weapon for inflicting injury to anyone *or causing them to fear injury*, and 'violent behaviour' means an unlawful act inflicting injury *or causing a person to fear injury* (s. 10). The elements in italics (author's emphasis) show that the legislation is intended to address the fear of the use of knives as well as their actual use.

The suggestion that knives are suitable for combat may be express or it may be implied by the name given to a product (e.g. 'commando') or by the packaging or advertisement relating to it (s. 1(3)). Therefore such packaging or advertising material, together with any surrounding advertisements, can be produced in evidence.

---

Defences

The Knives Act 1997, ss. 3 and 4 state:

3.—(1) It is a defence for a person charged with an offence under section 1 to prove that—
  (a) the knife was marketed—
    (i)   for use by the armed forces of any country;
    (ii)  as an antique or curio; or
    (iii) as falling within such other category (if any) as may be prescribed;
  (b) it was reasonable for the knife to be marketed in that way; and
  (c) there were no reasonable grounds for suspecting that a person into whose possession the knife might come in consequence of the way in which it was marketed would use it for an unlawful purpose.
(2) It is a defence for a person charged with an offence under section 2 to prove that—
  (a) the material was published in connection with marketing a knife—
    (i)   for use by the armed forces of any country;
    (ii)  as an antique or curio; or
    (iii) as falling within such other category (if any) as may be prescribed;
  (b) it was reasonable for the knife to be marketed in that way; and
  (c) there were no reasonable grounds for suspecting that a person into whose possession the knife might come in consequence of the publishing of the material would use it for an unlawful purpose.

4.—(1) It is a defence for a person charged with an offence under section 1 to prove that he did not know or suspect, and had no reasonable grounds for suspecting, that the way in which the knife was marketed—

(a) amounted to an indication or suggestion that the knife was suitable for combat; or

(b) was likely to stimulate or encourage violent behaviour involving the use of the knife as a weapon.

(2) It is a defence for a person charged with an offence under section 2 to prove that he did not know or suspect, and had no reasonable grounds for suspecting, that the material—

(a) amounted to an indication or suggestion that the knife was suitable for combat; or

(b) was likely to stimulate or encourage violent behaviour involving the use of the knife as a weapon.

(3) It is a defence for a person charged with an offence under section 1 or 2 to prove that he took all reasonable precautions and exercised all due diligence to avoid committing the offence.

---

**KEYNOTE**

The defences at s. 3 require the person to show that the knife was marketed/the material published:

- for one of the uses at s. 3(1)(a)(i)–(iii) and s. 3(2)(a)(i)–(iii) *and*

- that it was reasonable to market it in that way *and*

- that there were no reasonable grounds for suspecting that a person would use the knife for an unlawful purpose.

The defences at s. 4 require the person to show that he/she:

- did not know or suspect, or

- *have any reasonable grounds to suspect*

- that the marketing/the marketing material amounted to an indication or even a *suggestion* that the knife was suitable for combat *or*

- was likely to stimulate or encourage violent behaviour involving the use of the knife as a weapon.

There is also the general defence under s. 4(3) for the person to show that he/she took *all* reasonable precautions and exercised *all* due diligence to avoid committing the offence.

In each of these cases, the standard of proof will be against the balance of probabilities (**see Evidence and Procedure, chapter 11**).

---

Section 5 allows a court to issue a warrant for the entry onto premises and for the search, seizure and removal of knives (or materials where as offence under s. 6 in involved—**see para. 6.6.3**). Any knives or publications which have been seized and removed by a constable under a warrant issued under this section may be retained until the conclusion of proceedings against the suspect (s. 5(4)).

6.6.3    **Publications relating to knives**

OFFENCE:    **Publications relating to knives—*Knives Act 1997, s. 2***
- Triable either way • Two years' imprisonment and/or a fine on indictment; six months' imprisonment and/or a fine summarily
*(No specific power of arrest)*

The Knives Act 1997, s. 2 states:

(1) A person is guilty of an offence if he publishes any written, pictorial or other material in connection with the marketing of any knife and that material—

(a) indicates, or suggests, that the knife is suitable for combat; or

(b) is otherwise likely to stimulate or encourage violent behaviour involving the use of the knife as a weapon.

---

**KEYNOTE**

This offence is aimed at the publishers of advertisements rather than those who are involved in the sale and marketing of knives. The defences are shown above.

A search warrant may be issued under s. 5 for relevant publications (see earlier Keynote).

---

## 6.7 Crossbows

Even though they might fit into some of the other offences discussed above, crossbows are also subject to specific legislation.

OFFENCE:  **Person under 17 having crossbow—*Crossbows Act 1987, s. 3***
  • Triable summarily • Fine
  *(No specific power of arrest)*

The Crossbows Act 1987, s. 3 states:

A person under the age of seventeen who has with him—
(a) a crossbow which is capable of discharging a missile, or
(b) parts of a crossbow which together (and without any other parts) can be assembled to form a crossbow capable of discharging a missile,
is guilty of an offence, unless he is under the supervision of a person who is twenty-one years of age or older.

OFFENCE: **Selling or letting on hire crossbow to person under 17—*Crossbows Act 1987, s. 1***
  • Triable summarily • Six months' imprisonment and/or a fine
  *(No specific power of arrest)*

The Crossbows Act 1987, s. 1 states:

A person who sells or lets on hire a crossbow or a part of a crossbow to a person under the age of seventeen is guilty of an offence, unless he believes him to be seventeen years of age or older and has reasonable ground for the belief.

OFFENCE:  **Purchase or hire of crossbow by person under 17—*Crossbows Act 1987, s. 2***
  • Triable summarily • Fine
  *(No specific power of arrest)*

The Crossbows Act 1987, s. 2 states:

A person under the age of seventeen who buys or hires a crossbow or a part of a crossbow is guilty of an offence.

---

**KEYNOTE**

The offence under s. 3 again relates to a person 'having with him' (see para. 6.2.1) and it only applies to a crossbow which is capable of firing a missile or the parts of one which can be assembled to do so. If the crossbow has a 'draw weight' (the force required to pull back the cord to load it) of less than 1.4 kg, the provisions of the Act do not apply.

In each of the above cases the court may order forfeiture of the crossbow or parts of a crossbow.

---

Power of search and seizure

The Crossbows Act 1987, s. 4 states:

(1) If a constable suspects with reasonable cause that a person is committing or has committed an offence under section 3, the constable may—
    (a) search that person for a crossbow or part of a crossbow;
    (b) search any vehicle, or anything in or on any vehicle, in or on which the constable suspects with reasonable cause there is a crossbow, or part of a crossbow, connected with the offence.

---

**KEYNOTE**

This power of search is governed by PACE Codes of Practice, Code A (**see appendix 1**). For a full discussion of police powers to stop and search, **see chapter 2**.

A police officer may detain a person or vehicle for the purpose of a search under this power (s. 4(2)).

Anything that appears to be a crossbow or part of a crossbow to the officer found during the search may be seized (s. 4(3)).

For the purposes of exercising the powers above, a police officer may enter any land other than a dwelling house (s. 4(4)).

---

# PART THREE

# General Police Duties

# 7 | Civil disputes

## 7.1 Introduction

Although most civil disputes, by definition, do not involve the core functions of the police, there are occasions when the involvement of the police is necessary. The most common are 'domestic' disputes (usually involving close friends, partners and relatives) and trade disputes. The effects of the Human Rights Act 1998 and the increased focus on the State's positive duty to protect some of the competing rights of individuals (**see chapter 2**) has meant that the police are increasingly being brought into what appear to be essentially private disputes. Other common sources of civil dispute are addressed under **chapters 3 and 9**.

## 7.2 Domestic disputes

A 'domestic' dispute may involve a whole range of infringements of the criminal law, from a breach of the peace (**see chapter 4**), to serious assault and homicide (**see Crime, chapters 8 and 5** respectively).

Each of these is dealt with in other areas of this work, together with any attendant powers of entry and arrest (**see chapter 2**).

There are also occasions where police officers become involved in enforcing what are in effect civil matters in relation to *matrimonial* or *family* domestic disputes. Generally these occasions will come about where one party is subject to a court order preventing them from doing certain acts, acts which they nevertheless go on to carry out.

Home Office Circular 19/2000 provides guidance to police officers on the issues arising from domestic violence and also sets out agreed definitions for the purposes of reporting incidents to Her Majesty's Inspector of Constabulary and for identifying Best Value performance indicators (**see chapter 1**).

### 7.2.1 Court orders

Any court having jurisdiction over family law matters can make an order under the Family Law Act 1996.

#### The Family Law Act 1996

The Family Law Act 1996 consolidated many aspects of the law regulating family proceedings. Part IV of the Act makes provisions for family homes and for dealing with domestic violence.

Non-molestation orders

Section 42 of the 1996 Act provides for 'non-molestation' orders. Section 42 states:

(1) In this Part a 'non-molestation order' means an order containing either or both of the following provisions—

(a) provision prohibiting a person ('the respondent') from molesting another person who is associated with the respondent;

(b) provision prohibiting the respondent from molesting a relevant child.

(2) The court may make a non-molestation order—

(a) if an application for the order has been made (whether in other family proceedings or without any other family proceedings being instituted) by a person who is associated with the respondent; or

(b) if in any family proceedings to which the respondent is a party the court considers that the order should be made for the benefit of any other party to the proceedings or any relevant child even though no such application has been made.

---

**KEYNOTE**

Non-molestation orders can be applied for even though no other proceedings have been begun and such orders do not just relate to spouses or former partners; they apply to anyone who is 'associated' with the respondent.

Under s 62, a person is 'associated' with another person if:

(3) ...

(a) they are or have been married to each other;

(b) they are cohabitants or former cohabitants;

(c) they live or have lived in the same household, otherwise than merely by reason of one of them being the other's employee, tenant, lodger or boarder;

(d) they are relatives;

(e) they have agreed to marry one another (whether or not that agreement has been terminated);

(f) in relation to any child, they are both persons falling within subsection (4); or

(g) they are parties to the same family proceedings (other than proceedings under this Part).

(4) A person falls within this subsection in relation to a child if—

(a) he is a parent of the child; or

(b) he has or has had parental responsibility for the child.

In deciding whether or not to make such an order, the court must consider all the circumstances including the need to secure the health, safety and well-being of the applicant or any relevant child (s 42(5)).

A person under 16 cannot apply for a non-molestation order without leave of the court (s 43(1)) but, if the person satisfies the court that he/she has sufficient understanding to make the application, he/she may be granted leave (s 43(2)).

---

Power of arrest for breach of the order

Section 47 of the 1996 Act states:

(2) If—

(a) the court makes a relevant order; and

(b) it appears to the court that the respondent has used or threatened violence against the applicant or a relevant child,

it shall attach a power of arrest to one or more provisions of the order unless satisfied that in all the circumstances of the case the applicant or child will be adequately protected without such a power of arrest.

...

(6) If, by virtue of subsection (2) or (3), a power of arrest is attached to certain provisions of an order, a constable may arrest without warrant a person whom he has reasonable cause for suspecting to be in breach of any such provision.

**KEYNOTE**

Under s 47(3), the ability to attach a power of arrest will also apply to a non-molestation order which has been made *ex parte*, that is, without telling the other person, but only if:

- the respondent has used or threatened violence against the applicant or a relevant child; or

- there is a risk of significant harm to the applicant or relevant child attributable to the conduct of the respondent if a power of arrest is not attached immediately.

Section 47(7) states:

(7) If a power of arrest is attached under subsection (2) or (3) to certain provisions of the order and the respondent is arrested under subsection (6)—

(a) he must be brought before the relevant judicial authority within the period of 24 hours beginning at the time of his arrest; and

(b) if the matter is not then disposed of forthwith, the relevant judicial authority before whom he is brought may remand him.

In reckoning for the purposes of this subsection any period of 24 hours, no account is to be taken of Christmas Day, Good Friday or any Sunday.

**KEYNOTE**

Where a judge makes a non-molestation order under s 47(2), he/she is obliged to attach a power of arrest unless there are exceptional circumstances. If the judge considers that to attach such a power would give the applicant an unacceptable amount of influence over the respondent, the appropriate course of action is to refuse to grant the order altogether (*Chechi* v *Bashir* [1999] 2 FLR 489).

If the court does not attach a power of arrest at the time of making an order, it may issue a warrant of arrest if the respondent fails to comply with the terms and conditions of the order (s 47(8)).

If it is not convenient to take the arrested person before the 'relevant judicial authority' (i.e. the court which made the order) in a courtroom within the 24-hour period, the judge or magistrate can sit at any convenient and suitably open place (*Practice Direction (Domestic Violence: Procedure on Arrest) (No. 2)* [1998] 1 WLR 476).

'Molesting' includes conduct which does not extend to actual physical violence and includes conduct which intentionally causes such a degree of harassment that the intervention of the courts is required (*Johnson* v *Walton* [1990] 1 FLR 350).

A person arrested under this section may be granted bail by the magistrates', county or High Court.

For harassment generally, see chapter 3.

For malicious communications, see chapter 3.

For the offence of 'actual bodily harm' and for powers in relation to the protection of children, see Crime, chapters 8 and 11.

## 7.3  Trade disputes

The law regulating trade disputes changed dramatically during the 1980s and 1990s. Over this period the workforce in the community became more disparate and fragmented; working practices changed and there was a general decline in the traditionally unionised industries.

Despite the best intentions of those involved, trade disputes will no doubt continue to arise but the occasions on which they require any significant police involvement will hopefully continue to be rare (see the Home Office Consolidated Circular on Crime and Kindred Matters).

In addition to the provisions discussed in this section you should also consider offences and powers under:

- offences against public order, **see chapter 4**;
- offences against the person, **see Crime, chapter 8**;
- offences involving weapons, **see chapter 6**;
- obstruction and danger to road users, **see Road Traffic, chapter 8**.

Most of the conditions regulating trade disputes can be found in the Trade Union and Labour Relations (Consolidation) Act 1992.

The areas which have historically created the greatest need for police involvement arise from the differences between those who wish to exercise their right to strike and those who wish to continue to work.

### 7.3.1 Picketing

Section 220 of the 1992 Act states:

(1) It is lawful for a person in contemplation or furtherance of a trade dispute to attend—
   (a) at or near his own place of work, or
   (b) if he is an official of a trade union, at or near the place of work of a member of the union whom he is accompanying and whom he represents,

   for the purpose only of peacefully obtaining or communicating information, or peacefully persuading any person to work or abstain from working.

(2) If a person works or normally works—
   (a) otherwise than at any one place, or
   (b) at a place the location of which is such that attendance there for a purpose mentioned in subsection (1) is impracticable,

   his place of work for the purposes of that subsection shall be any premises of his employer from which he works or from which his work is administered.

(3) In the case of a worker not in employment where—
   (a) his last employment was terminated in connection with a trade dispute, or
   (b) the termination of his employment was one of the circumstances giving rise to a trade dispute,

   in relation to that dispute his former place of work shall be treated for the purposes of subsection (1) as being his place of work.

(4) A person who is an official of a trade union by virtue only of having been elected or appointed to be a representative of some of the members of the union shall be regarded for the purposes of subsection (1) as representing only those members; but otherwise an official of a union shall be regarded for those purposes as representing all its members.

---

**KEYNOTE**

Section 220 effectively restricts lawful picketing to 'primary' picketing outside the person's own place of work.

If there is a real danger of any offence (such as a public order offence, **see chapter 4**) being committed, then pickets have no right to attend the place in question under s 220 (*Piddington v Bates* [1961] 1 WLR 162).

The power for police officers to give directions to people in the vicinity of someone's dwelling (under the Criminal Justice and Police Act 2001, s 42) does not apply to any conduct made lawful by s 220 above (**see chapter 4**). Given the restrictions on just what conduct s 220 allows, these may be occasions where the Criminal Justice and Police Act power could be used in connection with a trade dispute.

Although s 220 does not place any restriction on the numbers of pickets, if they gather in large enough numbers, there may be a presumption that the pickets intend to intimidate others (*Broome v DPP* [1974] AC 587).

Section 220 does not authorise pickets to enter onto private land (*British Airports Authority* v *Ashton* [1983] 1 WLR 1079).

A person's place of work does not include new premises of an employer who has moved since dismissing the people picketing (*News Group Newspapers Ltd* v *SOGAT'82 (No. 2)* [1987] ICR 181).

For the Code of Practice on Picketing, see the Code of Practice (Picketing) Order 1992 (SI 1992/476 made under Employment Act 1980 s3). The contents of this Order may now need to be reviewed in the light of the Human Rights Act 1998 and the incorporation of the European Convention into the law of England and Wales (**see chapter 2**). In particular, the recommended numbers for pickets may be an unreasonable infringement of Article 11.

---

7.3.2    ## Meaning of 'trade dispute'

Section 244(1) of the 1992 Act states:

(1) In this Part a 'trade dispute' means a dispute between workers and their employer which relates wholly or mainly to one or more of the following—
  (a) terms and conditions of employment, or the physical conditions in which any workers are required to work;
  (b) engagement or non-engagement, or termination or suspension of employment or the duties of employment, of one or more workers;
  (c) allocation of work or the duties of employment between workers or groups of workers;
  (d) matters of discipline;
  (e) a worker's membership or non-membership of a trade union;
  (f) facilities for officials of trade unions; and
  (g) machinery for negotiation or consultation, and other procedures, relating to any of the above matters, including the recognition by employers or employers' associations of the right of a trade union to represent workers in such negotiation or consultation or in the carrying out of such procedures.

---

**KEYNOTE**

If the dispute is between workers in a government department and the relevant minister, the dispute can still come within this section even though he/she is not the workers' 'employer' (s 244(2)).

---

OFFENCE:    **Intimidation or annoyance by violence or otherwise—*Trade Union and Labour Relations (Consolidation) Act 1992, s 241***
  • Triable summarily • Six months' imprisonment and/or a fine
  *(Statutory power of arrest)*

The Trade Union and Labour Relations (Consolidation) Act 1992, s 241 states:

(1) A person commits an offence who, with a view to compelling another person to abstain from doing or to do any act which that person has a legal right to do or abstain from doing, wrongfully and without legal authority—
  (a) uses violence to or intimidates that person or his wife or children, or injures his property,
  (b) persistently follows that person about from place to place,
  (c) hides any tools, clothes or other property owned or used by that person, or deprives him of or hinders him in the use thereof,
  (d) watches or besets the house or other place where that person resides, works, carries on business or happens to be, or the approach to any such house or place, or
  (e) follows that person with two or more other persons in a disorderly manner in or through any street or road.

(2) ...

(3) A constable may arrest without warrant anyone he reasonably suspects is committing an offence under this section.

---

**KEYNOTE**

'With a view to compelling' means with intent to compel. This is therefore an offence of 'specific intent' (**see Crime, chapter 1**).

'Wrongfully' means a civil wrong.

Although the breach of a contract is generally not a criminal offence, this section imposes a duty on some contracted personnel not to breach their contract under certain conditions.

For this offence you would have to show that the person acted wilfully and maliciously (**see Crime, chapter 1**); you would also have to show knowledge or reasonable cause to believe that the listed consequences would apply. This would clearly create practical difficulties and this offence is likely to be very rare.

---

# 8 Animals

## 8.1 Introduction

There is a considerable amount of legislation designed to protect animals or to restrict the way in which they are treated, ranging from the use of animals in public performances to the importation of destructive animals.

This chapter sets out some of the more relevant provisions, particularly those aimed at preventing and punishing acts of cruelty, and those designed to ensure community safety.

Some of the legislation is aimed at particular animals—such as dogs—but there will be times when an incident involving an animal falls under a number of different Acts.

It is worth remembering that, as animals can be considered as property for many purposes, any restrictions imposed by law on an individual's rights to possess them may be an unreasonable interference with Article 1, First Protocol of the European Convention on Human Rights (as to which, **see chapter 2**).

## 8.2 Dangerous dogs

### 8.2.1 Dangerous Dogs Act 1991

The Dangerous Dogs Act 1991 imposes a number of duties on dog owners and people who are in charge of dogs. The main aim of this part of the legislation is to make people responsible for their dogs in public and to avoid any dog presenting a danger to other people.

### 8.2.2 Failing to keep dogs under proper control

OFFENCE: **Failing to keep dogs under proper control—*Dangerous Dogs Act 1991, s 3(1)***
- Aggravated offence: triable either way • Two years' imprisonment and/or a fine on indictment; six months' imprisonment and/or a fine summarily
- Otherwise: triable summarily • Six months' imprisonment and/or a fine
*(No specific power of arrest)*

The Dangerous Dogs Act 1991, s 3 states:

(1) If a dog is dangerously out of control in a public place—
    (a) the owner; and
    (b) if different, the person for the time being in charge of the dog,
    is guilty of an offence, or, if the dog while so out of control injures any person, an aggravated offence, under this subsection.

(2) ...

(3) If the owner or, if different, the person for the time being in charge of a dog allows it to enter a place which is not a public place but where it is not permitted to be and while it is there—
  (a) it injures any person; or
  (b) there are grounds for reasonable apprehension that it will do so,
  he is guilty of an offence, or, if the dog injures any person, an aggravated offence, under this subsection.

---

**KEYNOTE**

For the definition of 'public place', see the Keynote to **para. 8.2.3** below.

The offence under s 3(1) can be committed by both the owner and the person in charge of the dog, the offence under s 3(3) applies to either the owner, or the person in charge.

Whether someone is 'in charge' of a dog is a question of fact for a court/jury to determine in each case.

For these offences under s 3 the type of dog is irrelevant.

---

Dangerously out of control

Under s. 10(3) of the 1991 Act, 'dangerously out of control' means:

... a dog shall be regarded as dangerously out of control on any occasion on which there are grounds for reasonable apprehension that it will injure any person, whether or not it actually does so, but references to a dog injuring a person or there being grounds for reasonable apprehension that it will do so do not include references to any case in which the dog is being used for a lawful purpose by a constable or a person in the service of the Crown.

---

**KEYNOTE**

'Grounds for reasonable apprehension' that a dog will injure someone may arise even where the dog's behaviour is sudden and unexpected (see *Rafiq* v *DPP* (1997) 161 JP 412); and, although the reasonable apprehension must be that the dog will injure any *person*, an attack on another dog may well give rise to that apprehension (see below). See also s 1 of the Dogs Act 1906, which extends the scope of the Dogs Act 1871 giving magistrates a power to make an order in relation to dangerous dogs to cover dogs that injure certain farm animals.

If an offence is committed under s 3 above and the person who owns the dog is under 16, the 'head of the household' also commits the offence (s 6 and **see para. 8.2.3**).

The offences are 'strict liability' offences, that is, there is no need to show any particular *mens rea* (state of mind) on the part of the defendant (**see Crime, chapter 1**) and there is no need to prove even an element of negligence by a defendant (*R* v *Bezzina* [1994] 1 WLR 1057).

The proviso relating to the use of police dogs or other dogs in the service of the Crown would appear to cover properly-conducted training exercises and displays if they could be shown to be 'lawful purposes'.

---

Defence

Section 3(2) of the 1991 Act states:

(2) In proceedings for an offence under subsection (1) above against a person who is the owner of a dog but was not at the material time in charge of it, it shall be a defence for the accused to prove that the dog was at the material time in the charge of a person whom he reasonably believed to be a fit and proper person to be in charge of it.

---

**KEYNOTE**

The statutory defence under s 3(2) does not call for a minute examination as to which member of a family had charge of a dog kept in the home at any one particular moment in time. Therefore, where the wife of an owner of a dog let it out and it bit someone, the owner could not claim that he had momentarily transferred charge of that dog to her (*R* v *Huddart*, 24 November 1998, unreported). The Court of Appeal held that, in order to avail himself/herself of that defence, there must be evidence to show that the owner had for the time being divested himself/herself of responsibility for the dog in favour of an identifiable person (see also *R* v *Harter* [1988] Crim LR 336 which was distinguished in this case).

8.2.3    **Possessing dogs under section 1**

OFFENCE:    **Possessing dogs of type controlled by section 1—*Dangerous Dogs Act 1991, s 1(3)***
• Triable summarily • Six months' imprisonment and/or a fine
*(No specific power of arrest)*

The Dangerous Dogs Act 1991, s 1 states:

(3)  After such day as the Secretary of State may by order appoint for the purposes of this subsection no person shall have any dog to which this section applies in his possession or custody except—
(a) in pursuance of the power of seizure conferred by the subsequent provisions of this Act; or
(b) in accordance with an order for its destruction made under those provisions;
but the Secretary of State shall by order make a scheme for the payment to the owners of such dogs who arrange for them to be destroyed before that day of sums specified in or determined under the scheme in respect of those dogs and the cost of their destruction.

OFFENCE:    **Breeding, selling, offering etc. dogs of type controlled by section 1—*Dangerous Dogs Act 1991, s 1(2)***
• Triable summarily • Six months' imprisonment and/or a fine
*(No specific power of arrest)*

The Dangerous Dogs Act 1991, s 1 states:

(2)  No person shall—
(a) breed, or breed from, a dog to which this section applies;
(b) sell or exchange such a dog or offer, advertise or expose such a dog for sale or exchange;
(c) make or offer to make a gift of such a dog or advertise or expose such a dog as a gift;
(d) allow such a dog of which he is the owner or of which he is for the time being in charge to be in a public place without being muzzled and kept on a lead; or
(e) abandon such a dog of which he is the owner or, being the owner or for the time being in charge of such a dog, allow it to stray.

**KEYNOTE**

The breeding of dogs generally is regulated by the Breeding of Dogs Act 1973. This piece of legislation has been amended in several respects by the Breeding and Sale of Dogs (Welfare) Act 1999. Between them the Acts provide for a system of licensing for breeding establishments and create a number of summary offences for breaching the relevant requirements. The 1999 Act creates a number of new summary offences in respect of the sale of dogs by keepers of licensed breeding establishments (s 8). The Act requires breeders to provide any dogs that they sell with a collar tag showing the date and place of birth of the animal (see the Sale of Dogs (Identification Tags) Regulations 1999 (SI 1999/3191)). The 1999 Act also allows a court to disqualify a person from keeping a licensed breeding establishment upon conviction for a relevant offence.

The above offence, however, relates solely to the breeding etc. of dogs that are of the 'types' specified below. For the law relating to dog fights, see para. 8.3.

The offence under s 1 is not committed if a person has a certificate of exemption in respect of the dog, or if the person has custody of the dog under the power of seizure provided by the 1991 Act (see para. 8.2.4).

The expression used in the legislation is dogs of the 'type' known as pit bull terriers etc. This expression is much wider than 'breed' and will include dogs which have a substantial number of the breed characteristics.

Therefore the Act will cover some cross-breeds (see *R v Knightsbridge Crown Court, ex parte Dunne* [1994] 1 WLR 296). The statutory controls also apply to the Japanese tosa, the dogo Argentino and the fila Braziliero.

The offences under s 1 are 'strict liability' offences (**see Crime, chapter 1**).

'Public place' includes any street, road or other place to which the public have access, whether for payment or otherwise and includes common parts of a building containing two or more separate dwellings (s 10(2)). Therefore a shared landing or garden within a residential complex could fall within the definition.

A dog locked in a car which is parked in a public place is itself 'in a public place' (*Bates* v *DPP* (1993) 157 JP 1004).

A private path or driveway is *not* necessarily a public place simply because certain people have an implied licence to come to the door (*Fellowes* v *DPP* (1993) 157 JP 936).

In showing that a place is a 'public place' for the purposes of the 1991 Act there is no need to prove *actual use* by the public. A court may infer that an area is a 'public place' from the fact that it is publicly owned (e.g. by the local council), even though the land has been fenced off and is not generally used by the public (*Cummings* v *DPP* [1999] COD 288).

'Muzzled' means having a muzzle *securely fitted* in a way which prevents the dog from biting anyone (s 7(1)(a)).

'Kept on a lead' means *securely* held on a lead by a *person who is not less than 16* (s 7(1)(b)).

'Advertisement' *includes* any means of bringing a matter to the attention of the public (s 10(2)); but this does necessarily *exclude* any private or restricted advertisement such as in a workplace or club.

If an offence is committed under s 1(2)(d) or (e) above and the person who owns the dog is under 16, the 'head of the household' also commits the offence (s. 6).

The Secretary of State may add other types of dog to this list (s 1(1)(c)) and may impose further conditions on any other types of dog (s 2).

---

Many cases have been brought where the characteristics of the dog's type are in dispute. Section 5 of the 1991 Act states:

> (5) If in any proceedings it is alleged by the prosecution that a dog is one to which section 1 or an order under section 2 above applies it shall be presumed that it is such a dog unless the contrary is shown by the accused by such evidence as the court considers sufficient; and the accused shall not be permitted to adduce such evidence unless he has given the prosecution notice of his intention to do so not later than the fourteenth day before that on which the evidence is to be adduced.

---

**KEYNOTE**

This statutory presumption does not apply in civil cases (*R v Walton Street Magistrates' Court, ex parte Crothers* (1996) 160 JP 427).

Some forces have officers who are specifically trained as expert witnesses in giving evidence of a dog's 'type'.

---

### Defence

Section 1(7) of the 1991 Act states:

> (7) Any person who contravenes this section is guilty of an offence . . . except that a person who publishes an advertisement in contravention of subsection (2)(b) or (c)—
> (a) shall not on being convicted be liable to imprisonment if he shows that he published the advertisement to the order of someone else and did not himself devise it; and
> (b) shall not be convicted if, in addition, he shows that he did not know and had no reasonable cause to suspect that it related to a dog to which this section applies.

8.2.4    **Enforcement**

Power of seizure

Section 5(1) of the Dangerous Dogs Act 1991 states:

(1)  A constable or an officer of a local authority authorised by it to exercise the powers conferred by this subsection may seize—
  (a)  any dog which appears to him to be a dog to which section 1 above applies and which is in a public place—
    (i)   after the time when possession or custody of it has become unlawful by virtue of that section; or
    (ii)  before that time, without being muzzled and kept on a lead;
  (b)  any dog in a public place which appears to him to be a dog to which an order under section 2 above applies and in respect of which an offence against the order has been or is being committed; and
  (c)  any dog in a public place (whether or not one to which that section or such an order applies) which appears to him to be dangerously out of control.

Entry and search

Section 5(2) and (4) provides for the issuing of a warrant to enter and search premises in connection with offences under the 1991 Act, and for the destruction of any dog lawfully seized.

8.2.5    **Courts' powers**

The powers of the courts to make orders in relation to dogs under the Dangerous Dogs Act 1991 were amended by the Dangerous Dogs (Amendment) Act 1997.

Those powers are now contained in ss 4 and 4A which state:

**4.**—(1)  Where a person is convicted of an offence under section 1 or 3(1) or (3) above or of an offence under an order made under section 2 above the court—
  (a)  may order the destruction of any dog in respect of which the offence was committed and shall do so in the case of an offence under section 1 or an aggravated offence under section 3(1) or (3) above; and
  (b)  may order the offender to be disqualified, for such period as the court thinks fit, for having custody of a dog.

**4A.**—(1)  Where—
  (a)  a person is convicted of an offence under section 1 above or an aggravated offence under section 3(1) or (3) above;
  (b)  the court does not order the destruction of the dog under section 4(1)(a) above; and
  (c)  in the case of an offence under section 1 above, the dog is subject to the prohibition in section 1(3) above,
  the court shall order that, unless the dog is exempted from that prohibition within the requisite period, the dog shall be destroyed.

S 4A added by Dangerous Dog (Amendment) Act 1997 s 2.

---

**KEYNOTE**

It is a summary offence to have custody of a dog in contravention of s 4(1)(b) above or to fail to comply with a requirement under s 4(4)(a) (s 4(8)).

The courts' powers to make control or destruction orders under s 2 of the Dogs Act 1871 still apply and it is a summary offence to fail to comply with such an order (s 1(3) of the Dangerous Dogs Act 1989). A magistrates' court has jurisdiction under the 1871 Act to make an order in relation to a dog within the court's area even though the relevant offence (e.g. biting someone) occurred outside the country (*Shufflebottom* v *Chief Constable of Greater Manchester Police* [2003] EWHC 246—Stockport Magistrates' Court able to make order in respect of a dog that had bitten a child while in Scotland). The courts may also order that a person be disqualified from keeping a dog and failure to comply with such an order is also a summary offence (s 1(6) of the Dangerous Dogs Act 1989).

In making an order under the Dangerous Dogs Act 1989 magistrates should consider the normal, everyday meaning of the word 'dangerous'. That term is not therefore limited to a dog that presents a threat to humans but could also extend to dogs that attack other dogs (*Briscoe* v *Shattock* [1999] 1 WLR 432). Although this decision was made in relation to the 1871 Act, it tends to support the assertion above that a dog's dangerous disposition towards people might be demonstrated, in part, by its behaviour towards other animals.

Section 13(1) of the Protection of Badgers Act 1992 empowers a court to order the destruction of dogs which have been present when certain offences involving badgers have been committed (see also para. 8.9).

---

### 8.2.6 Control of dogs on roads

Section 27 of the Road Traffic Act 1988 creates a summary offence for any person to cause or permit a dog to be on a designated road without being held on a lead. 'Designated' roads for this purpose are roads specified by the relevant local authority. Certain limitations may be imposed on the extent of such an order by the local authority, provided that they have consulted with the relevant chief officer of police (s 27(3) and (5)).

The provisions do not apply to dogs kept for driving or tending sheep or cattle in the course of a trade or business, nor do they apply to dogs held at the material time to have been in use under proper control for sporting purposes (s 27(4)).

For the general meaning of 'cause or permit', **see Road Traffic, chapter 1**.

### 8.3 Animal fighting

In addition to the offence of cruelty (**see para. 8.7**), there are specific offences relating to animal fighting.

OFFENCE: **Attendance at animal fights—*Protection of Animals Act 1911, s 5A***
> • Triable summarily • Fine
> *(No specific power of arrest)*

The Protection of Animals Act 1911, s 5A states:

> A person who, without reasonable excuse, is present when animals are placed together for the purpose of their fighting each other shall be liable . . .

S 5A added by Animals (Amendment) Act 1988 s 2.

OFFENCE: **Advertising animal fights—*Protection of Animals Act 1911, s 5B***
> • Triable summarily • Fine
> *(No specific power of arrest)*

The Protection of Animals Act 1911, s 5B states:

> If a person who publishes or causes to be published an advertisement for a fight between animals knows that it is such an advertisement he shall be liable . . .

S 5B added by Animals (Amendment) Act 1988 s 2.

The first offence (s 5A) requires no knowledge by the defendant, and very little in the way of *actus reus* (criminal conduct; **see Crime, chapter 2**). Simply being present is enough.

The second offence (s 5B) requires proof that the person knew of the nature of the advertisement. Knowledge here will include shutting your eyes to the obvious (*Westminster City Council* v *Croyalgrange Ltd* [1986] 1 WLR 674 HL).

It is also a summary offence to cause, procure or assist at the fighting or baiting of any animal or to keep premises for that purpose (s 1(1)(c) of the 1911 Act).

### 8.3.1    Cockfighting

The Cockfighting Act 1952 creates a summary offence of having any instruments for use in cockfighting, while s 36 of the Town Police Clauses Act 1847 and s 47 of the Metropolitan Police Act 1839 create offences of keeping places for the fighting or baiting of animals.

## 8.4    Guard dogs

Guard dogs will be covered by much of the legislation above but there is also special provision made for the proper control of such animals.

OFFENCE:    **Control of guard dogs—*Guard Dogs Act 1975, s 1***
- Triable summarily  • Fine
*(No specific power of arrest)*

The Guard Dogs Act 1975, s 1 states:

(1)  A person shall not use or permit the use of a guard dog at any premises unless a person ('the handler') who is capable of controlling the dog is present on the premises and the dog is under the control of the handler at all times while it is being so used except while it is secured so that it is not at liberty to go freely about the premises.

(2)  The handler of a guard dog shall keep the dog under his control at all times while it is being used as a guard dog at any premises except—
(a)  while another handler has control over the dog; or
(b)  while the dog is secured so that it is not at liberty to go freely about the premises.

(3)  A person shall not use or permit the use of a guard dog at any premises unless a notice containing a warning that a guard dog is present is clearly exhibited at each entrance to the premises.

'Permitting' implies some form of unconditional 'allowing' or condoning of the use (**see Road Traffic, chapter 1**).

If a dog is tied up securely there is no need for the handler to be present (*Hobson* v *Gledhill* [1978] 1 WLR 215).

Under s 7, a 'guard dog' means a dog which is being used to protect:

- premises,

- property kept on the premises, or

- people guarding the premises or such property.

'Premises' are land (other than agricultural land and land around a dwelling house) and buildings, including parts of buildings, other than dwelling houses (s 7). Therefore the 1975 Act does not apply to dogs being used to protect houses or agricultural land (which includes fields, pig and poultry farms, allotments, nurseries and orchards).

## 8.5 Dogs and livestock

### 8.5.1 Worrying livestock

The activities of dogs around livestock is regulated by the Dogs (Protection of Livestock) Act 1953.

OFFENCE: **Worrying livestock—*Dogs (Protection of Livestock) Act 1953, s 1(1)***
• Triable summarily • Fine
*(No specific power of arrest)*

The Dogs (Protection of Livestock) Act 1953, s 1 states:

(1) Subject to the provisions of this section, if a dog worries livestock on any agricultural land, the owner of the dog, and if it is in the charge of a person other than its owner, that person also, shall be guilty of an offence...

---

**KEYNOTE**

For the purposes of s 1(2) of the 1953 Act, 'worrying livestock' means:

• attacking livestock, or

• chasing livestock in such a way as may reasonably be expected to cause injury or suffering to the livestock or, in the case of females, abortion, or loss of or diminution in their produce (s 1(1)(b) ), or

• not being on a lead or under close control in a field or enclosure in which there are sheep (s 1(1)(c) ).

The offence under s 1(1)(c) involving sheep does not apply in relation to:

• a dog owned by, or in the charge of, the occupier of the field or enclosure or the owner of the sheep or a person authorised by either of those people, or

• a police dog, a guide dog, a trained sheep dog, a working gun dog or a pack of hounds (s 1(2A) ).

---

Defence

Section 1(3) and (4) of the 1953 Act states:

(3) A person shall not be guilty of an offence under this Act by reason of anything done by a dog, if at the material time the livestock are trespassing on the land in question and the dog is owned by, or in the charge of, the occupier of that land or a person authorised by him, except in a case where the said person causes the dog to attack the livestock.

(4) The owner of a dog shall not be convicted of an offence under this Act in respect of the worrying of livestock by the dog if he proves that at the time when the dog worried the livestock it was in the charge of some other person, whom he reasonably believed to be a fit and proper person to be in charge of the dog.

Police powers

Section 2(2) of the 1953 Act states:

(2) Where in the case of a dog found on any land—
    (a) a police officer has reasonable cause to believe that the dog has been worrying livestock on that land, and the land appears to him to be agricultural land, and
    (b) no person is present who admits to being the owner of the dog or in charge of it,
    then for the purpose of ascertaining who is the owner of the dog the police officer may seize it and may detain it until the owner has claimed it and paid all expenses incurred by reason of its detention.

**KEYNOTE**

There is a difference between 'reasonable grounds to suspect' and 'reasonable cause to *believe*' (**see chapter 2**). The latter requirement needs more evidence than mere suspicion on the part of the officer concerned.

This power only applies to land which appears to the officer to be agricultural land.

Section 2A provides for the issue of search warrants in connection with dogs suspected of being involved in the worrying of livestock.

A prosecution for an offence involving a dog on agricultural land cannot be brought without the consent of the chief officer of police for that area, the occupier of the land or the owner of the relevant livestock (s 2(1)).

---

8.5.2    **Killing of or injury to dogs worrying livestock**

It is not uncommon for dogs found to be worrying livestock to be shot by farmers or landowners. Section 9 of the Animals Act 1971 states:

(1) In any civil proceedings against a person (in this section referred to as the defendant) for killing or causing injury to a dog it shall be a defence to prove—

    (a) that the defendant acted for the protection of any livestock and was a person entitled to act for the protection of that livestock; and

    (b) that within forty-eight hours of the killing or injury notice thereof was given by the defendant to the officer in charge of a police station.

(2) For the purposes of this section a person is entitled to act for the protection of any livestock if, and only if—

    (a) the livestock or the land on which it is belongs to him or to any person under whose express or implied authority he is acting; and

    (b) the circumstances are not such that liability for killing or causing injury to the livestock would be excluded by section 5(4) of this Act.

(3) Subject to subsection (4) of this section, a person killing or causing injury to a dog shall be deemed for the purposes of this section to act for the protection of any livestock if, and only if, either—

    (a) the dog is worrying or is about to worry the livestock and there are no other reasonable means of ending or preventing the worrying; or

    (b) the dog has been worrying livestock, has not left the vicinity and is not under the control of any person and there are no practicable means of ascertaining to whom it belongs.

---

**KEYNOTE**

Notice may be given over the telephone, in writing or, presumably, by fax or e-mail. Its purpose is to provide a record of the incident so that the information can be made available to any court at a later date. This defence is not applicable to criminal proceedings (see *Isted* v *Crown Prosecution Service* [1998] Crim LR 194).

---

8.6    **Rabies and disease**

For many years the main threat posted by widespread disease among animals in the community was rabies and there was fairly robust legislation in place to deal with that threat. However, following the outbreak of foot and mouth disease in 2001, the potential for other disease-based chaos within the community was revealed. More worryingly, the potential for damage caused by deliberate infection of animals also became clear and further legislation was enacted to address some of these areas.

8.6.1    **Rabies**

The Animal Health Act 1981 creates a number of provisions for regulating the movement of animals in and around the UK; for controlling and containing outbreaks of diseases; and for the enforcement of powers in relation to rabies.

Police powers

The Animal Health Act 1981, s 61 states:

(1) . . . a constable may arrest without warrant any person whom he, with reasonable cause, suspects to be in the act of committing or to have committed an offence to which this section applies.
(2) The offences to which this section applies are offences against this Act consisting of—
   (a) the landing or attempted landing of any animal in contravention of an order made under this Act and expressed to be made for the purpose of preventing the introduction of rabies into Great Britain; or
   (b) the failure by the person having the charge or control of any vessel, or boat to discharge any obligation imposed on him in that capacity by such order; or
   (c) the movement, in contravention of an order under section 17 or 23 above, of any animal into, within or out of a place or area declared to be infected with rabies.

S 61 amended by s 1 1990/2371 art 2.

---

**KEYNOTE**

The power of arrest is a preserved power under sch. 2 to the Police and Criminal Evidence Act 1984 (**see chapter 2**).

For the purposes of arresting someone under the above provisions, s 62 provides a power of entry (if need be, by force) and search of any boat, vessel, aircraft or vehicle where the officer has reasonable cause to suspect that person to be. The section goes on to provide similar powers in order to seize animals under the law relating to the spread of rabies.

The power of entry and search is governed by code B of the Police and Criminal Evidence Act 1984 codes of practice (**see chapter 2**).

Sections 72 and 73 create offences of doing or failing to do anything in contravention of the provisions of the 1981 Act.

For details of a pilot scheme to reduce the need for extended quarantine of some pets, see the Pet Travel Scheme (Pilot Arrangements) (England) Order 1999 (SI 1999/3443).

S 1 1999/3443 made under Animal Health Act 1981 s 10.

---

8.6.2    **Other diseases**

The Animal Health Act 2002 was passed in response to some of the concerns above. Amending the Animal Health Act 1981, the 2002 legislation extends the provisions for slaughtering animals in order to prevent spread of diseases including foot and mouth. Under the amended legislation, the Secretary of State can extend the relevant powers to other diseases besides foot and mouth. The 2002 Act also makes new provisions in order to control scrapie in sheep and creates a new power of entry for constables and animal health inspectors in order to carry out their functions (see the Animal Health Act 1981, s 36G).

The Animal Health Act 2002 creates further authorities to allow the enforcement of the legislative measures including powers for animal health inspectors to enter premises and, if accompanied by a uniformed police constable, to stop, detain and inspect vehicles in designated areas under certain circumstances (see Animal Health Act 1981, s 65A).

OFFENCE: **Deliberate infection of animals—*The Animal Health Act 1981, s. 28A***
- Triable either way • Two years' imprisonment on indictment;
  six months and or fine summarily
*(No specific power of arrest)*

The Animal Health Act 1981 s. 28A states:

(1) A person commits an offence if without lawful authority or excuse (proof of which shall lie on him) he knowingly does anything which causes or is intended to cause an animal to be infected with a disease specified in Schedule 2A.

---

**KEYNOTE**

The standard of proof required of a defendant here is on the balance of probabilities (**see Evidence and Procedure, chapter...**). Note the requirement for 'knowingly' to be proved here. It is not yet clear whether this offence would extend to omissions accompanied by the right state of mind.

Schedule 2A diseases include foot and mouth, Newcastle disease and classical swine fever. If a person is convicted of the above offence the court may disqualify them from keeping or dealing with *any* animals for such period as it thinks fit (see s 28B). The defendant has a right to apply for removal or variation of any such order.

Clearly if the deliberate infection of animals is carried out for some wider political purpose, the relevant offences under the Terrorism Act 2000 may be committed (**see chapter 4**). As animals are 'property', relevant offences of criminal damage could be considered (**see Crime, chapter 14**).

---

## 8.7 Cruelty

OFFENCE: **Cruelty—*Protection of Animals Act 1911, s. 1(1)***
- Triable summarily • Six months' imprisonment
*(Statutory power of arrest)*

The Protection of Animals Act 1911, s. 1 (amended by Protection against Cruel Tethering Act 1988, s. 1) states:

(1) If any person—
   (a) shall cruelly beat, kick, ill-treat, over-ride, over-drive, over-load, torture, infuriate, or terrify any animal, or shall cause or procure, or, being the owner, permit any animal to be so used, or shall, by wantonly or unreasonably doing or omitting to do any act, or causing or procuring the commission or omission of any act, cause any unnecessary suffering, or, being the owner, permit any unnecessary suffering to be so caused to any animal; or
   (b) shall convey or carry, or cause or procure, or, being the owner, permit to be conveyed or carried, any animal in such manner or position as to cause that animal any unnecessary suffering; or
   (c) shall cause, procure, or assist at the fighting or baiting of any animal; or shall keep, use, manage, or act or assist in the management of, any premises or place for the purpose, or partly for the purpose of fighting or baiting any animal, or shall permit any premises or place to be so kept, managed, or used, or shall receive, or cause or procure any person to receive, money for the admission of any person to such premises or place; or
   (d) shall wilfully, without any reasonable cause or excuse, administer, or cause or procure, or being the owner permit, such administration of, any poisonous or injurious drug or substance to any animal, or shall wilfully, without any reasonable cause or excuse, cause any such substance to be taken by any animal; or
   (e) shall subject, or cause or procure, or being the owner permit, to be subjected, any animal to any operation which is performed without due care and humanity; or

(f)  shall tether any horse, ass or mule under such conditions or in such manner as to cause that
     animal unnecessary suffering;

such person shall be guilty of an offence of cruelty within the meaning of this Act . . .

---

**KEYNOTE**

As can be seen, the legislation anticipates virtually every conceivable example of cruelty which might be inflicted on animals. This offence can be committed by omission as well as by a positive 'action' (**see Crime, chapter 2**). Where an owner of the relevant animal is shown to have failed to have exercised reasonable care for it, he/she will be deemed to have 'permitted' cruelty (s. 1(2)).

The archaic language of this section has caused some difficulties in practice and has been criticised by the courts (see *Isted* v *Crown Prosecution Service* [1998] Crim LR 194). In *Isted* the Divisional Court held that the test to be applied to the reasonableness or otherwise of the defendant's actions was an objective one, to be judged in the light of the facts and circumstances of the case. That case involved the shooting of a dog that was disturbing a farmer's pigs, whereupon the farmer shot it, injuring—but not killing—the dog. For the specific offence for owners or others in charge of dogs that worry livestock, **see para. 8.5.1**.

Where defendants put dogs into a badger sett with all means of exit sealed off and the badger caused significant injuries to one of the dogs, they were properly convicted of an offence under s. 1(1)(a) above (*Bandeira and Brannigan* v *RSPCA* (2000) 164 JP 307).

Animals are also property under many circumstances and can therefore be 'stolen' or 'damaged' by some of the acts described above (**see Crime, chapters 12 and 14**).

An 'animal' for the purposes of this offence means any domestic or captive animal, which will include most forms of farm animal and domestic pets but not invertebrates (s. 15). Animals which are wild but which have become temporarily trapped are not necessarily 'captive' and each case will have to be determined on its own facts.

Unnecessary suffering has been held to be suffering which could have been avoided and the test as to whether an animal has suffered 'unnecessarily' is an objective one; that is, it will depend on the view of a reasonable bystander and not the actual state of mind of the defendant (*RSPCA* v *Isaacs* [1994] Crim LR 517).

---

## 8.7.1   Police powers

A police officer may arrest without warrant anyone who he/she has reasonable cause to believe is guilty of an offence of cruelty which is punishable by imprisonment without the option of a fine. This expression would appear to mean that the power is available in respect of any act of cruelty covered under s. 1(1) except the offence of an owner permitting cruelty s. 1(2) (which is addressed by *Halsbury's Laws of England*, vol. 2, para. 459). The power applies if the officer witnesses the offence himself/herself or if a third person gives his/her name and address and provides information to the effect that such an offence was committed (s. 12(1)).

Section 12(2) of the 1911 Act goes on to provide a power of seizure in respect of any animal or vehicle stopped in connection with an offence of cruelty. Such powers would be governed by the Police and Criminal Evidence Act 1984 (**see chapter 2**).

Where a person has been proceeded against for an offence under s. 1 and the relevant animal was kept by them for commercial purposes, additional powers are available. In these circumstances the Protection of Animals (Amendment) Act 2000 allows the prosecutor to apply to the court for an order authorising the taking charge of, caring for, selling or slaughtering of the animal(s). Such an order may include a power to enter the relevant premises (though not a dwelling house) to mark the animals and to carry out the terms of the order (s. 3 of the 2000 Act). Any application for such an order must be supported by evidence from a veterinary surgeon that it is necessary in the interests of the animal's welfare to do the things set out in the order (s. 2). Obstruction of someone authorised by such an order is a summary offence punishable by a fine (s. 3(3)).

These court orders are likely to be of use in situations such as those arising out of the foot and mouth crisis. In a similar vein, the Animal Health Act 1981 gives the Secretary of State wide powers to make orders in relation to diseases such as foot and mouth (see e.g. the Foot and Mouth Disease (Amendment) (England) (No. 4) Order 2001 (SI 2001 No. 1078)). Those orders may provide for the closure of footpaths and restrict the movement of animals within certain areas. Breach of these orders will amount to a summary offence (under s. 73) punishable by a fine. The 1981 Act gives police officers powers to stop and detain vehicles and animals and also to require (and enforce) their return to the place they came from (s. 60). Authorised animal health inspectors have additional powers to arrest people who obstruct them in the exercise of these powers (this is a 'preserved' power of arrest under sch. 2 to the Police and Criminal Evidence Act 1984, **see chapter 2**).

It is worth remembering that some animals are capable of being damaged or stolen under the Theft Act 1968 and the Criminal Damage Act 1971 (**see Crime, chapters 12 and 14**), both of which create arrestable offences.

8.7.2     **Police powers: injured animals**

Section 11 of the 1911 Act states:

(1) If a police constable finds any animal so diseased or so severely injured or in such a physical condition that, in his opinion, having regard to the means available for removing the animal, there is no possibility of removing it without cruelty, he shall, if the owner is absent or refuses to consent to the destruction of the animal, at once summon a duly registered veterinary surgeon, if any such veterinary surgeon resides within a reasonable distance, and, if it appears by the certificate of such veterinary surgeon that the animal is mortally injured, or so severely, or so diseased, or in such physical condition, that it is cruel to keep it alive, it shall be lawful for the police constable, without the consent of the owner, to slaughter the animal, or cause or procure it to be slaughtered, with such instruments or appliances, and with such precautions, and in such manner, as to inflict as little suffering as practicable, and, if the slaughter takes place on any public highway, to remove the carcase or cause or procure it to be removed therefrom.

(2) If any veterinary surgeon summoned under this section certifies that the injured animal can without cruelty be removed, it shall be the duty of the person in charge of the animal to cause it forthwith to be removed with as little suffering as possible, and, if that person fails so to do, the police constable may, without the consent of that person, cause the animal forthwith to be so removed.

(3) Any expense which may be reasonably incurred by any constable in carrying out the provisions of this section (including the expenses of any veterinary surgeon summoned by the constable, and whether the animal is slaughtered under this section or not) may be recovered from the owner summarily as a civil debt, and, subject thereto, any such expense shall be defrayed out of the fund from which the expenses of the police are payable in the area in which the animal is found.

---

**KEYNOTE**

These very broad powers are of limited practical effect as they do not apply to the most frequently-encountered 'injured animals'—cats and dogs. 'Animals' for this purpose are confined to horses, mules, asses, bulls, sheep, goats and pigs (s. 11(4)).

Charitable organisations such as the RSPCA or the PDSA may assist in providing for injured animals.

---

## 8.8    Wild animals

Just as some types of dog are subject to special legislative control, so too are some species of wild animal. Although much of the legislation relating to animals is outside the scope of this Manual, there are several areas that are of direct relevance to police officers. The first area that has become of increasing importance is that affecting wildlife preservation generally. Although legislation such as the Wildlife Protection Act 1981 has been around for several decades, there has been a growing view that there is a need for more extensive powers and punishments to be made available for the protection of the environment. This is particularly the case where the activities of some people interfere—whether intentionally or incidentally—with wild animals and their habitat. As a result, the Countryside and Rights of Way Act 2000 introduced a range of measures designed to reinforce some of the offences and powers contained in the 1981 Act. The 2000 Act:

- introduces powers for police officers (and wildlife inspectors under certain circumstances) to require blood or tissue samples to be taken from animals for DNA analysis to determine their identity or ancestry;

- introduces custodial penalties for some offences under Pt I of the 1981 Act and makes several such offences 'arrestable' (**see chapter 2**);

- extends the powers of authorised wildlife inspectors (see s. 19ZA of the 1981 Act) and also increases the powers of magistrates' courts to issue entry and seizure warrants to the police in relation to certain suspected offences involving listed species.

Other legislation exists to prevent trading in certain species of animal (see the Control of Trade in Endangered Species (Enforcement) Regulations 1997 (SI 1997 No. 1372)).

This is simply a summary of some of the provisions regulating and protecting wildlife. Owing to their local policing conditions, some police services in England and Wales have their own wildlife officers who can provide detailed advice and guidance on the relevant legislation. Further information and advice is more generally available from the RSPCA and the DEFRA.

### 8.8.1    Dangerous wild animals

Another area of animal legislation that is of relevance to the police is that which relates to wild animals deemed to be 'dangerous'. The Dangerous Wild Animals Act 1976 regulates the keeping of those wild animals which are listed in its schedule. That schedule (which reads like Noah's passenger list) contains many exotic and rare wild animals including old-world monkeys, reptiles and birds.

Under s. 1 of the 1976 Act it is necessary to obtain a licence from a local authority before keeping any wild animal. Any such licence will contain details of which specific animals are covered and where they are to be kept. Certain exemptions are made for some zoos, scientific establishments, circuses and some licensed pet shops (s. 5). Local authorities are given powers to seize animals which are kept in contravention of the Act (s. 4).

### 8.8.2    Wild mammals

Given the restrictions on the applicability of the cruelty offence (**see para. 8.7**), further protection was provided by the Wild Mammals (Protection) Act 1996.

OFFENCE:    **Cruelty to wild mammals—*Wild Mammals (Protection) Act 1996, s. 1***
- Triable summarily • Six months' imprisonment and/or fine
*(No specific power of arrest)*

The Wild Mammals (Protection) Act 1996, s. 1 states:

> If, save as permitted by this Act, any person mutilates, kicks, beats, nails or otherwise impales, stabs, burns, stones, crushes, drowns, drags or asphyxiates any wild mammal with intent to inflict unnecessary suffering he shall be guilty of an offence.

## KEYNOTE

As its title suggests, this Act only applies to wild mammals which are defined as any mammal which is not a domestic or captive animal within the meaning of the Protection of Animals Act 1911 (or the Protection of Animals (Scotland) Act 1912) (s. 3 of the 1996 Act).

### Exceptions

Section 2 of the 1996 Act (amended by Protection of Wild Mammals (Scotland) Act 2002, sch. 1 para. 6) states:

> A person shall not be guilty of an offence under this Act by reason of—
>
> (a) the attempted killing of any such wild mammal as an act of mercy if he shows that the mammal had been so seriously disabled otherwise than by his unlawful act that there was no reasonable chance of its recovering;
>
> (b) the killing in a reasonably swift and humane manner of any such wild mammal if he shows that the wild mammal had been injured or taken in the course of either lawful shooting, hunting, coursing or pest control activity;
>
> (c) doing anything which is authorised by or under any enactment;
>
> (d) any act made unlawful by section 1 if the act was done by means of any snare, trap, dog, or bird lawfully used for the purpose of killing or taking any wild mammal; or
>
> (e) the lawful use of any poisonous or noxious substance on any wild mammal.

## KEYNOTE

These exceptions are fairly wide and allow some acts which might be regarded as 'cruel' by many people to go unchecked. Section 2(a) also provides an opportunity for a defendant to claim that he/she was simply 'putting an animal out of its misery' caused by injuries inflicted by someone else.

### Police powers

Section 4 of the 1996 Act states:

> Where a constable has reasonable grounds for suspecting that a person has committed an offence under the provisions of this Act and that evidence of the commission of the offence may be found on that person or in or on any vehicle he may have with him, the constable may—
>
> (a) without warrant, stop and search that person and any vehicle or article he may have with him; and
>
> (b) seize and detain for the purposes of proceedings under any of those provisions anything which may be evidence of the commission of the offence or may be liable to be confiscated under section 6 of this Act.

## KEYNOTE

Unlike the Protection of Animals Act 1911, the 1996 Act does not provide a power of arrest.

Section 6 empowers a court to order the confiscation of any vehicle or equipment used in the commission of the relevant offence.

8.9 **Badgers**

Because of the particular risk which faces badgers, both as a threatened species, and as a target of certain 'blood sports', there is specific legislation designed to protect them.

OFFENCE: **Taking, injuring or killing badgers—*Protection of Badgers Act 1992, s. 1(1)***

> • Triable summarily • Six months' imprisonment and/or a fine
> *(No specific power of arrest)*

The Protection of Badgers Act 1992, s. 1 states:

> A person is guilty of an offence if, except as permitted by or under this Act, he wilfully kills, injures or takes, or attempts to kill, injure or take, a badger.

---

**KEYNOTE**

Section 1(2) creates a statutory presumption that a defendant was trying to kill, injure or take a badger if there is evidence from which that fact might reasonably be concluded. Such evidence might include any equipment which the defendant had with him/her or the presence of blood, hair etc. in a vehicle.

Sections 2 and 3 go on to create summary offences (punishable as for s. 1) of cruelty to badgers, digging for badgers and of interfering with badger setts. The Divisional Court has held that the definition of a badger sett does not include the surface area above the system of tunnels and chambers. Therefore, if people are caught digging within this area, the proper charge ought to be the general one (under s. 2) and not the specific offence of interfering with a badger sett under s. 3A (*DPP* v *Green* [2001] 1 WLR 505). Where dogs are put into badger setts and are subsequently injured, an offence of cruelty under s. 1 of the Protection of Animals Act 1911 may also be committed (see para. 8.7).

---

OFFENCE: **Selling or possessing a live badger—*Protection of Badgers Act 1992, s. 4***

> • Triable summarily • Fine
> *(No specific power of arrest)*

The Protection of Badgers Act 1992, s. 4 states:

> A person is guilty of an offence if, except as permitted by or under this Act, he sells a live badger or offers one for sale or has a live badger in his possession or under his control.

8.9.1 **Police powers**

Section 11 of the 1992 Act states:

> Where a constable has reasonable grounds for suspecting that a person is committing an offence under the foregoing provisions of this Act, or has committed an offence under those provisions or those of the Badgers Act 1973 and that evidence of the commission of the offence is to be found on that person or any vehicle or article he may have with him, the constable may—
>
> (a) without warrant stop and search that person and any vehicle or article he may have with him;
> (b) seize and detain for the purposes of proceedings under any of those provisions anything which may be evidence of the commission of the offence . . .

**KEYNOTE**

These powers are governed by the Police and Criminal Evidence Act 1984 codes of practice (**see chapter 2**).

The Badgers Act 1973 referred to has been repealed but presumably the inclusion of it in this section is to deal with any offences committed during the transitional period of the two Acts.

### 8.9.2    Defence

Section 7 of the 1992 Act states:

(1) Subject to subsection (2) below, a person is not guilty of an offence under section 1(1) above by reason of—

(a) killing or taking, or attempting to kill or take, a badger; or

(b) injuring a badger in the course of taking it or attempting to kill or take it,

if he shows that his action was necessary for the purpose of preventing serious damage to land, crops, poultry or any other form of property.

(2) The defence provided by subsection (1) above does not apply in relation to any action taken at any time if it had become apparent, before that time, that the action would prove necessary for the purpose there mentioned and either—

(a) a licence under section 10 below authorising that action had not been applied for as soon as reasonably practicable after that fact had become apparent; or

(b) an application for such a licence had been determined.

Sections 8 and 9 create further exceptions from the provisions of the 1992 Act for people such as carriers or people taking injured badgers for treatment, while s. 10 provides for a system of licensing in relation to the possession etc. of badgers.

## 8.10    Pet shops

Under the Pet Animals Act 1951 pet shops must be licensed by a local authority (s. 1(1)). The local authority will need to be satisfied about the cleanliness and suitability of any premises, together with the applicants' precautions for preventing the spread of disease (s. 1(2)).

It is a summary offence to sell pet animals in the street (s. 2) and it is also an offence to sell an animal as a pet to a person where there is reasonable cause to believe that the person is under 12 (s. 3).

# 9 Offences relating to premises

## 9.1 Introduction

The law regulating the relationship between landlord and occupier falls largely within the province of 'civil' law. There are, however, a number of occasions and circumstances where the interests of landowners and occupiers conflict. Under some such circumstances the threat to public order, property or proprietary rights is considered to need the protection of the criminal law.

In addition, the rights given to individuals by the European Convention on Human Rights (**see chapter 2**) will be relevant in many of the circumstances dealt with in this chapter, in particular Articles 8 (respect for private life), 9 (freedom of thought, conscience and religion), 10 (freedom of expression), 11 (freedom of assembly and association) and Article 1, First Protocol (protection of property).

## 9.2 Criminal trespass

The law of trespass, as with that of landlord and tenant, is generally dealt with as civil law and, contrary to the many notices that appear on premises, trespass is not usually a matter for prosecution. However, there are an increasing number of occasions where trespass to property can attract criminal liability. Some examples considered elsewhere would include:

- burglary (**see Crime, chapter 12**)
- trespassing with a firearm (**see chapter 5**)
- trespassing with a weapon (**see chapter 6**).

These occasions can apply to most types of premises and usually depend on the actions or intentions of the trespasser. Other examples can be found in relation to poaching (e.g. under the Game Act 1831 or the Night Poaching Acts).

Some offences of criminal trespass only apply to certain types of premises such as railways (**see chapter 13**) or areas of special protection under the Wildlife and Countryside Act 1981 and in such cases there is usually no need to prove any intention or specific behaviour on the part of the trespasser.

Whatever the remedy, whether it be civil or criminal, trespass involves an interference with someone's occupation of land or premises. This chapter is concerned with four main aspects of such interference, namely:

- aggravated trespass (which can include common as well as private land)
- interfering with the rights of occupiers/intending occupiers
- trespassing during court order
- nuisances on educational premises.

## 9.3 Aggravated trespass

In the wake of several well-publicised encounters between police officers and groups of people who either had trespassed, or intended to trespass on someone else's land, Parliament created a number of criminal offences (in the Criminal Justice and Public Order Act 1994). It also created specific police powers to deal with such occasions.

The types of trespass addressed by the 1994 Act can be categorised into four main groups:

- trespassing with the intention of disrupting or obstructing a lawful activity, or intimidating those engaged in it;
- two or more people trespassing with the purpose of residing on the land;
- 100 or more people attending a 'rave';
- residing in vehicles on land.

### 9.3.1 Trespass intending to obstruct, disrupt or intimidate

OFFENCE: **Trespass intending to obstruct, disrupt or intimidate—*Criminal Justice and Public Order Act 1994, s. 68***

- Triable summarily • Three months' imprisonment and/or a fine
*(Statutory power of arrest)*

The Criminal Justice and Public Order Act 1994, s. 68 states:

(1) A person commits the offence of aggravated trespass if he trespasses on land in the open air and, in relation to any lawful activity which persons are engaging in or are about to engage in on that or adjoining land in the open air, does there anything which is intended by him to have the effect—
  (a) of intimidating those persons or any of them so as to deter them or any of them from engaging in that activity,
  (b) of obstructing that activity, or
  (c) of disrupting that activity.

(2) Activity on any occasion on the part of a person or persons on land is 'lawful' for the purposes of this section if he or they may engage in the activity on the land on that occasion without committing an offence or trespassing on the land.

---

**KEYNOTE**

Examples of the sort of conduct envisaged would be 'eco-warriors' disrupting a building programme or saboteurs disrupting a fox hunt (see *Winder* v *DPP* (1996) 160 JP 713).

This is an offence of specific intent (**see Crime, chapter 1**) rather than consequence. Therefore what must be shown is the defendant's intention to bring about the effects set out at s. 68(1)(a)–(c). There is no need to specify which of the intended activities (i.e. deterring, obstructing or disrupting) in any charge and use of all three expressions is not bad for duplicity (*Nelder* v *DPP*, The Times, 11 June 1988). However, proof is required of both the trespassing on land in the open air *and* of some overt act, other than the trespassing, which was intended to have the effects set out at s. 68(1)(a)–(c) (see *DPP* v *Barnard* [2000] Crim LR 371).

The activity of the defendant can include 'anything' provided it was accompanied by the relevant intention.

In order to establish the offence of aggravated trespass under s. 68, you must prove that the defendant had committed the act(s) complained of in the physical presence of a person engaged or about to engage in the lawful activity with which the defendant wished to interfere (*DPP* v *Tilly*, The Times, 27 November 2001).

The lawful activity that people are engaging in (or are about to engage in) must also take place (be proposed to take place) on the same land in the open air or on adjoining land in the open air.

Land does not include land forming part of a highway unless it is:

- a footpath, bridleway or byway open to all traffic or road used as a public path (as defined by s. 54 of the Wildlife and Countryside Act 1981) or

- a cycle track under the Highways Act 1980 or the Cycle Tracks Act 1984

(s. 68(5) ).

Lawful activity is defined at s. 68(2) and is a very wide concept. Arguments as to the lawfulness of activities such as protesting or canvassing support for a given cause are strengthened with the advent of the Human Rights Act 1998 (as to which, **see chapter 2**).

For a discussion of the offence of obstructing highways and the effect of the Human Rights Act 1998, **see Road Traffic**.

### Power of arrest

The Criminal Justice and Public Order Act 1994, s. 68 states:

> (4) A constable in uniform who reasonably suspects that a person is committing an offence under this section may arrest him without a warrant.

**KEYNOTE**

This power of arrest is restricted to officers in uniform and only applies where the person is reasonably suspected of being in the act of committing the offence. It is not a pre-requisite that the person *is* actually committing the offence, only that the officer reasonably suspects him/her of doing so (see *Capon v DPP*, The Independent, 23 March 1998).

For a discussion of 'reasonable suspicion', **see chapter 2**.

### Police powers

The Criminal Justice and Public Order Act 1994, s. 69 states:

> (1) If the senior police officer present at the scene reasonably believes—
>     (a) that a person is committing, has committed or intends to commit the offence of aggravated trespass on land in the open air; or
>     (b) that two or more persons are trespassing on land in the open air and are present there with the common purpose of intimidating persons so as to deter them from engaging in a lawful activity or of obstructing or disrupting a lawful activity,
>     he may direct that person or (as the case may be) those persons (or any of them) to leave the land.
> (2) A direction under subsection (1) above, if not communicated to the persons referred to in subsection (1) by the police officer giving the direction, may be communicated to them by any constable at the scene.

**KEYNOTE**

Although this power requires the senior officer present at the scene to have a reasonable *belief* (a narrower concept than mere suspicion) as to the circumstances set out at s. 69(1)(a) or (b), the power is available as a preventive measure and as a means of dealing with the incident after it has happened. In this respect it is far wider than the power of arrest above.

The direction to leave the land may be communicated to the relevant people by any police officer at the scene and there is no requirement for either officer to be in uniform.

OFFENCE:    **Failure to leave or re-entry when directed to leave—*Criminal Justice and Public Order Act 1994, s. 69(3)***

　　　　　　• Triable summarily • Three months' imprisonment and/or a fine

*(Statutory power of arrest)*

The Criminal Justice and Public Order Act 1994, s. 69 states:

(3) If a person knowing that a direction under subsection (1) above has been given which applies to him—

(a) fails to leave the land as soon as practicable, or

(b) having left again enters the land as a trespasser within the period of three months beginning with the day on which the direction was given,

he commits an offence . . .

### KEYNOTE

In order to prove this offence it must be shown that the person knew of the direction and that it applied to him/her. Clearly the easiest way of ensuring both elements would be to serve a written notice on the person at the same time as communicating the direction to leave and to record any response.

### Defence

The Criminal Justice and Public Order Act 1994, s. 69 states:

(4) In proceedings for an offence under subsection (3) it is a defence for the accused to show—

(a) that he was not trespassing on the land, or

(b) that he had a reasonable excuse for failing to leave the land as soon as practicable or, as the case may be, for again entering the land as a trespasser.

### Power of arrest

The Criminal Justice and Public Order Act 1994, s. 69 states:

(5) A constable in uniform who reasonably suspects that a person is committing an offence under this section may arrest him without a warrant.

### KEYNOTE

Although the direction to leave may be communicated by any police officer at the scene, the power of arrest is limited to officers in uniform. This power is subject to the same conditions as that at s. 68(4) above.

### 9.3.2    Two or more people trespassing for purpose of residence

OFFENCE:    **Two or more people trespassing for purpose of residence—*Criminal Justice and Public Order Act 1994, s. 61***

　　　　　　• Triable summarily • Three months' imprisonment and/or a fine

*(Statutory power of arrest)*

The Criminal Justice and Public Order Act 1994, s. 61 states:

(1) If the senior police officer present at the scene reasonably believes that two or more persons are trespassing on land and are present there with the common purpose of residing there for any period, that reasonable steps have been taken by or on behalf of the occupier to ask them to leave and—

(a) that any of those persons has caused damage to the land or to property on the land or used threatening, abusive or insulting words or behaviour towards the occupier, a member of his family or an employee or agent of his, or

(b) that those persons have between them six or more vehicles on the land,

he may direct those persons, or any of them, to leave the land and to remove any vehicles or other property they have with them on the land.

(2) Where the persons in question are reasonably believed by the senior police officer to be persons who were not originally trespassers but have become trespassers on the land, the officer must reasonably believe that the other conditions specified in subsection (1) are satisfied after those persons became trespassers before he can exercise the power conferred by that subsection.

(3) A direction under subsection (1) above, if not communicated to the persons referred to in subsection (1) by the police officer giving the direction, may be communicated to them by any constable at the scene.

---

**KEYNOTE**

The key features of this section can be broken down into two parts. First, the senior officer present at the scene must have a reasonable belief that:

- at least two people *are trespassing* on land *and*
- that they are there with the common purpose of residing there *and*
- that reasonable (though not *all* reasonable) steps have been taken by/on behalf of the occupier to ask them to leave.

If this is the case, the senior officer must also have a reasonable belief that:

- *any* of those people have caused damage to the land or to property on the land *or*
- *any* of those people have used threatening, abusive or insulting words or behaviour towards the occupier or a member of the occupier's family or staff or one of his/her agents *or*
- those people have between them six or more vehicles on the land.

If all the conditions under the first heading, together with any of the conditions under the second are met, the officer may direct the people to leave the land and to take their vehicles and other property with them.

Most of the terms used in this section are defined under s. 61(9). 'Land' does not include buildings other than agricultural buildings or scheduled monuments. It also has the same restrictions in relation to highways as those set out under s. 68 above.

The damaging of property includes the deposit of any substance capable of polluting the land and property for the purposes of damage has the same meaning as under the Criminal Damage Act 1971 (**see Crime, chapter 14**).

'Vehicles' do not have to be in a fit state for use on a road and can include a chassis or body (with or without wheels) appearing to have formed part of a vehicle. They also include caravans (as defined under the Caravan Sites and Control of Development Act 1960).

A person may be regarded as having a purpose of residing on land even though he/she has a home elsewhere.

Where the land concerned is 'common land', any references to trespassing will be construed as acts that are an infringement of the rights of the occupier or 'commoners' rights'. Where the public has access to that common land, references to the occupier will include the local authority (s. 61(7)).

If the people concerned were not originally trespassers (e.g. because they were given limited permission to be there), the senior officer present must have a reasonable belief that the relevant conditions above came about after the people became trespassers.

Again, the direction to leave the land may be communicated to the relevant parties by any police officer at the scene and there is no requirement for either officer to be in uniform.

---

OFFENCE: **Failure to leave when directed—*Criminal Justice and Public Order Act 1994, s. 61(4)***

- Triable summarily  • Three months' imprisonment and/or a fine

*(Statutory power of arrest)*

The Criminal Justice and Public Order Act 1994, s. 61 states:

(4) If a person knowing that a direction under subsection (1) above has been given which applies to him—
(a) fails to leave the land as soon as reasonably practicable, or
(b) having left again enters the land as a trespasser within the period of three months beginning with the day on which the direction was given,
he commits an offence . . .

---

**KEYNOTE**

The requirements as to proof of knowledge here are the same as those under s. 69 above. This offence is the same as that under s. 69 with the exception of the word *reasonably* before practicable. This suggests that the law provides more latitude to people directed to leave the land under s. 61 than under s. 69, a suggestion that is also borne out by the wording of the respective defences.

In a case involving travellers trespassing on local authority land, the Administrative Court has had the opportunity to review the compatibility of a s. 61 direction with the European Convention on Human Rights and to set out some views which will be of use to operational officers considering making s. 61 directions. The Court held as follows:

- Section 61 has to be construed narrowly because it creates a criminal offence (see below). As the fear of arrest can induce compliance with the direction even in someone who has an arguable justification for remaining on the land, it has to be construed all the more narrowly.
- Parliament could not have intended to impose criminal sanctions on trespassers who *complied* with requests to leave.
- The natural reading of s. 61(1) and (4) (see below) is that a direction amounts to an order to trespassers to leave—with their vehicles—as soon as reasonably practicable after the giving of the direction.
- When taking the operational decision to give a s 61 direction, the police officer in this case was entitled to assume that the local authority had not, by its decision to evict trespassers, breached the Convention.
- Article 3 (subjecting person to inhuman or degrading treatment—**see para. 2.4.2**) has no application to a s. 61 direction.
- Similarly, Article 6 (right to a fair trial—**see para. 2.4.5**) is concerned with procedure, not substantive law and is therefore not infringed by the 'criminalisation of trespass' in this way.
- The financial charges that could be made for the removal, retention, disposal or destruction of vehicles (under s. 67 of the Act) are not a 'penalty' making it a 'criminal process' but a civil debt.
- The exercise of power under s. 61 of the Act does not necessarily infringe Article 8 (right to private life—**see para. 2.4.7**) (see also *South Buckinghamshire District Council* v *Porter* The Times, 9 November 2001).
- The concept of 'home' in Article 8 involves a continuity that had been absent in the traveller's claim in this particular case.
- A trespasser is still free to enjoy his/her property—just not on the trespassed land. Therefore Protocol 1, Article 1 (**see para. 2.4.17**) is not necessarily infringed by s. 61.

Therefore, s. 61 was not shown to be incompatible with the Convention *per se*. However, the *actual* direction given *was* held to be unlawful because:

- insufficient opportunity was given to ensure compliance with the local authority's request that the land be vacated, and

- the direction did not require departure immediately or as soon as reasonably practicable, but simply gave a date for vacant possession

(*R (on the application of Fuller & Secretary of State for the Home Department)* v *Chief Constable of Dorset Police* [2001] EWHC Admin 105).

Defence

The Criminal Justice and Public Order Act 1994, s. 61 states:

> (6) In proceedings for an offence under this section it is a defence for the accused to show—
>     (a) that he was not trespassing on the land, or
>     (b) that he had a reasonable excuse for failing to leave the land as soon as reasonably practicable or, as the case may be, for again entering the land as a trespasser.

Power of arrest

The Criminal Justice and Public Order Act 1994, s. 61 states:

> (5) A constable in uniform who reasonably suspects that a person is committing an offence under this section may arrest him without a warrant.

---

**KEYNOTE**

Although the direction to leave may be communicated by any police officer at the scene, the power of arrest is limited to officers in uniform. This power is subject to the same conditions as those at s. 68(4) and s. 69(5) above.

---

Power of seizure

If a direction has been given under s. 61 and a police officer reasonably suspects that any person to whom it applies has, without reasonable excuse:

- failed to remove any vehicle on the land which appears to the officer to belong to him/her or to be in his/her possession or under his/her control; or

- entered the land as a trespasser with a vehicle within the period of three months beginning with the day when the direction was given

the officer may seize and remove the vehicle (s. 62).

### 9.3.3    One hundred or more people attending a rave

OFFENCE:    **Failing to leave land when directed: 'raves'—*Criminal Justice and Public Order Act 1994, s. 63***
- Triable summarily • Three months' imprisonment and/or a fine
*(Statutory power of arrest)*

The Criminal Justice and Public Order Act 1994, s. 63 states:

> (2) If, as respects any land in the open air, a police officer of at least the rank of superintendent reasonably believes that—
>     (a) two or more persons are making preparations for the holding there of a gathering to which this section applies,
>     (b) ten or more persons are waiting for such a gathering to begin there, or
>     (c) ten or more persons are attending such a gathering which is in progress,
>     he may give a direction that those persons and any other persons who come to prepare or wait for or to attend the gathering are to leave the land and remove any vehicles or other property which they have with them on the land.
>
> (3) A direction under subsection (2) above, if not communicated to the persons referred to in subsection (2) by the police officer giving the direction, may be communicated to them by any constable at the scene.
>
> (4) Persons shall be treated as having had a direction under subsection (2) above communicated to them if reasonable steps have been taken to bring it to their attention.

(5) ...

(6) If a person knowing that a direction has been given which applies to him—

    (a) fails to leave the land as soon as reasonably practicable, or

    (b) having left again enters the land within the period of 7 days beginning with the day on which the direction was given,

he commits an offence ...

---

## KEYNOTE

Whereas the powers to direct people to leave land above can be exercised by the senior police officer present at the scene, the power under s. 63 is restricted to an officer of at least superintendent rank.

Again, the officer must have a reasonable belief that one of the circumstances set out in s. 63(2) applies in respect of any land in the open air. Those circumstances are that:

- at least two people are making preparations for the holding of a relevant gathering; *or*

- at least ten people are waiting for such a gathering to begin or are attending such a gathering which is in progress.

Where this is the case, the officer may direct those people, together with any others who come to prepare, wait for or attend the gathering, to leave the land and to take their property with them.

Given the practical constraints on communicating with people at an open air 'rave', s. 63 makes provision for the communication of a direction to leave. If reasonable steps have been taken to bring the direction to the attention of the people concerned, s. 63(4) provides that the relevant person will be taken to have received it. Therefore a person cannot later argue that he/she had not been able to hear or understand the direction when it was given.

In common with the other sections above, the direction to leave the land may be communicated to the relevant people by any police officer at the scene and there is no requirement for either officer to be in uniform.

---

The elements of the type of gathering to which s. 63 applies are set out at s. 63(1):

(1) This section applies to a gathering on land in the open air of 100 or more persons (whether or not trespassers) at which amplified music is played during the night (with or without intermissions) and is such as, by reason of its loudness and duration and the time at which it is played, is likely to cause serious distress to the inhabitants of the locality; and for this purpose—

    (a) such a gathering continues during intermissions in the music and, where the gathering extends over several days, throughout the period during which amplified music is played at night (with or without intermissions); and

    (b) 'music' includes sounds wholly or predominantly characterised by the emission of a succession of repetitive beats.

---

## KEYNOTE

This offence does not apply to gatherings licensed by an entertainment licence (s. 63(9)). 'Land in the open air' includes a place partly open to the air (s. 63(10)).

---

### Defence

The Criminal Justice and Public Order Act 1994, s. 63 states:

(7) In proceedings for an offence under this section it is a defence for the accused to show that he had a reasonable excuse for failing to leave the land as soon as reasonably practicable or, as the case may be, for again entering the land.

### Powers of arrest

The Criminal Justice and Public Order Act 1994, s. 63 states:

(8) A constable in uniform who reasonably suspects that a person is committing an offence under this section may arrest him without a warrant.

---

**KEYNOTE**

In common with the other powers of arrest above, this power is limited to officers in uniform. It is also drafted in the present tense and is subject to the same conditions as those under ss. 61, 68 and 69 above.

In addition to these powers, raves have been held to amount to a public nuisance at common law and therefore the powers applicable to arrestable offences may be available (see chapter 3).

---

Power of entry

If a superintendent or above reasonably believes that circumstances justifying the giving of a direction under s. 63 above exist, he/she may authorise any police officer to enter the relevant land for the purposes of:

- ascertaining whether such circumstances exist and
- to exercise any power conferred by s. 63 or
- to exercise the power of seizure below

(s. 64).

The power of seizure arises if a direction has been given under s. 63 and a police officer reasonably suspects that any person to whom it applies has, without reasonable excuse:

- failed to remove any vehicle or sound equipment on the land which appears to the officer to belong to him/her or to be in his/her possession or under his/her control; or
- entered the land as a trespasser with a vehicle within the period of seven days beginning with the day when the direction was given

the officer may seize and remove the vehicle or equipment (provided it does not belong to an exempt person) (s. 64(4) and (5)).

Exemptions

The directions will not apply to 'exempt persons' (s. 63(5) of the 1994 Act). Such people include the occupier of the land, any member of his/her family or his/her employees/agents, or anyone whose home is situated on the land (s. 63(10)).

The directions will not apply to a gathering covered by an entertainment licence (s. 63(9)(a)).

Powers to stop people from proceeding to 'raves'

Under s. 65 of the 1994 Act, if a police officer in uniform reasonably believes that a person is on his/her way to a relevant gathering (as defined above) in relation to which a direction under s. 63(2) is in force, the officer may stop that person and direct him/her not to proceed in the direction of the gathering.

OFFENCE: **Failing to comply with direction not to proceed—*Criminal Justice and Public Order Act 1994, s. 65(4)***
- Triable summarily • Fine
*(Statutory power of arrest)*

The Criminal Justice and Public Order Act 1994, s. 65 states:

(4) If a person knowing that a direction under [s. 65(1)] has been given to him fails to comply with that direction, he commits an offence.

**KEYNOTE**

This power may only be exercised at a place within five miles of the boundary of the site of the gathering (s. 65(2)).

Unlike the other directions discussed above, this one must be given by a police officer in uniform. The power does not appear to authorise the stopping of vehicles and therefore the general power under the Road Traffic Act 1988 would need to be used (see Road Traffic, chapter 10).

For the general provisions in relation to the stopping of people and vehicles, see chapter 2.

### Power of arrest

The Criminal Justice and Public Order Act 1994, s. 65 states:

> (5) A constable in uniform who reasonably suspects that a person is committing an offence under this section may arrest him without warrant.

### 9.3.4   Residing in vehicles on land

In addition to the powers set out above, the Criminal Justice and Public Order Act 1994 gives local authorities powers to deal with people living in vehicles on certain land.

> OFFENCE:   **Failure to leave land when directed: residing in vehicles—*Criminal Justice and Public Order Act 1994, s. 77***
> - Triable summarily • Fine
> *(No specific power of arrest)*

The Criminal Justice and Public Order Act 1994, s. 77 states:

> (1) If it appears to a local authority that persons are for the time being residing in a vehicle or vehicles within that authority's area—
>   (a) on any land forming part of a highway;
>   (b) on any other unoccupied land; or
>   (c) on any occupied land without the consent of the occupier,
>   the authority may give a direction that those persons and any others with them are to leave the land and remove the vehicle or vehicles and any other property they have with them on the land.
>
> (2) Notice of a direction under subsection (1) must be served on the persons to whom the direction applies, but it shall be sufficient for this purpose for the direction to specify the land and (except where the direction applies to only one person) to be addressed to all occupants of the vehicles on the land, without naming them.
>
> (3) If a person knowing that a direction under subsection (1) above has been given which applies to him—
>   (a) fails, as soon as practicable, to leave the land or remove from the land any vehicle or other property which is the subject of the direction, or
>   (b) having removed any such vehicle or property again enters the land with a vehicle within the period of three months beginning with the day on which the direction was given,
>   he commits an offence...

**KEYNOTE**

This offence is committed after notice has been served by a local authority. Sections 77 to 79 make provision for the manner in which the notices are to be served. A direction in the notice is operative in relation to people who return to the land with their vehicles within three months of the serving of the notice (s. 77(4)).

A person can be regarded as 'residing' on land notwithstanding that he/she has a home elsewhere (s. 77(6)).

### Defence

The Criminal Justice and Public Order Act 1994, s. 77 states:

(5) In proceedings for an offence under this section it is a defence for the accused to show that his failure to leave or to remove the vehicle or other property as soon as practicable or his re-entry with a vehicle was due to illness, mechanical breakdown or other immediate emergency.

### Removal order

A local authority may apply to a magistrates' court for a removal order if people continue to reside in their vehicles on land in contravention of a notice under s. 77 of the 1994 Act (s. 78(1)).

The local authority can enforce the order by entering onto the land in question and taking such steps as are mentioned in the order. Before doing so, however, the local authority must give the owner of the land, and the occupiers 24 hours' notice of its intention (unless the names and addresses cannot be ascertained after reasonable enquiries) (s. 78(3)).

### Interim possession orders

Wilful obstruction of anyone executing such an order is a summary offence, punishable by a fine.

Under certain circumstances, a court may make an interim possession order when land is occupied by trespassers. Any person who is in occupation of those premises at the time such an order is served is, by the Criminal Justice and Public Order Act 1994, s. 76(6), to be treated for the purposes of the following offences as 'trespassers'.

OFFENCE: **Trespassing during interim possession order—*Criminal Justice and Public Order Act 1994, s. 76***
• Triable summarily • Six months' imprisonment and/or a fine
*(Statutory power of arrest)*

The Criminal Justice and Public Order Act 1994, s. 76 states:

(1) This section applies where an interim possession order has been made in respect of any premises and served in accordance with rules of court; and references to 'the order' and 'the premises' shall be construed accordingly.

(2) Subject to subsection (3), a person who is present on the premises as a trespasser at any time during the currency of the order commits an offence.

(3) No offence under subsection (2) is committed by a person if—
(a) he leaves the premises within 24 hours of the time of service of the order and does not return; or
(b) a copy of the order was not fixed to the premises in accordance with rules of court.

(4) A person who was in occupation of the premises at the time of service of the order but leaves them commits an offence if he re-enters the premises as a trespasser or attempts to do so after the expiry of the order but within the period of one year beginning with the day on which it was served.

---

**KEYNOTE**

For the power of entry without warrant for this offence, see chapter 2.

This offence is complete when the person is present as a trespasser during the currency of the order. There is no need to prove any further *actus reus* and there is no requirement for any *mens rea* (see Crime, chapter 1). Therefore, in practice, the person has got 24 hours from the time of service of the order to get out and stay out to avoid committing this offence. If the copy of the notice was not fixed to the premises as required, there will be no offence.

---

Power of arrest

(7) A constable in uniform may arrest without a warrant anyone who is, or whom he reasonably suspects to be, guilty of an offence under this section.

---

**KEYNOTE**

This power of arrest is not restricted to someone who is reasonably suspected of being in the act of committing an offence, but applies to anyone who has, or who is reasonably suspected to have, committed the offence.

Section 75 creates several either way offences in relation to the making of false or misleading statements in order to obtain or resist the making of an interim possession order.

---

OFFENCE:   **Making false statement to obtain interim possession order—*Criminal Justice and Public Order Act 1994, s. 75***
  - Triable either way  -  Two years' imprisonment and/or a fine on indictment;
    six months' imprisonment and/or a fine summarily
  *(No specific power of arrest)*

The Criminal Justice and Public Order Act 1994, s. 75 states:

(1) A person commits an offence if, for the purpose of obtaining an interim possession order, he—
  (a) makes a statement which he knows to be false or misleading in a material particular; or
  (b) recklessly makes a statement which is false or misleading in a material particular.

(2) A person commits an offence if, for the purpose of resisting the making of an interim possession order, he—
  (a) makes a statement which he knows to be false or misleading in a material particular; or
  (b) recklessly makes a statement which is false or misleading in a material particular.

## 9.4  **Other offences involving premises**

### 9.4.1  Depriving residential occupier

OFFENCE:   **Depriving residential occupier—*Protection from Eviction Act 1977, s. 1***
  - Triable either way  -  Two years' imprisonment and/or a fine on indictment;
    six months' imprisonment and/or a fine summarily
  *(No specific power of arrest)*

The Protection from Eviction Act 1977, s. 1 (amended by the Housing Act 1988, s. 9) states:

(2) If any person unlawfully deprives the residential occupier of any premises of his occupation of the premises or any part thereof, or attempts to do so, he shall be guilty of an offence unless he proves that he believed, and had reasonable cause to believe, that the residential occupier had ceased to reside in the premises.

(3) If any person with intent to cause the residential occupier of any premises—
  (a) to give up the occupation of the premises or any part thereof; or
  (b) to refrain from exercising any right or pursuing any remedy in respect of the premises or part thereof;
  does acts likely to interfere with the peace or comfort of the residential occupier or members of his household, or persistently withdraws or withholds services reasonably required for the occupation of the premises as a residence, he shall be guilty of an offence.

(3A) Subject to subsection (3B) below, the landlord of a residential occupier or an agent of the landlord shall be guilty of an offence if—
  (a) he does acts likely to interfere with the peace or comfort of the residential occupier or members of his household, or

(b) he persistently withdraws or withholds services reasonably required for the occupation of the premises in question as a residence,

and (in either case) he knows, or has reasonable cause to believe, that that conduct is likely to cause the residential occupier to give up the occupation of the whole or part of the premises or to refrain from exercising any right or pursuing any remedy in respect of the whole or part of the premises.

---

**KEYNOTE**

The first two offences can be committed by 'any person', whereas the offence under s. 1(3A) can only be committed by a landlord or his/her agent.

Where these offences are committed by a 'body corporate' (e.g. a company), then the company's officers may be guilty as well as the company itself (s. 1(6)).

Thankfully—from a police perspective—the Court of Appeal has refused to find that a duty of care is owed by the police to an assured tenant to prevent that tenant's eviction without the necessary court order in breach of the Protection from Eviction Act 1977 (*Cowan* v *Chief Constable of Avon & Somerset* [2002] HLR 44).

The actions envisaged by s. 1(2) are those which amount to an eviction for any length of time (*R* v *Yuthiwattana* (1984) 80 Cr App R 55), while anything less (e.g. changing the locks of an entrance door while the residential occupier is out) would amount to an offence under s. 1(3) (*Costelloe* v *London Borough of Camden* [1986] Crim LR 249).

A caravan may amount to 'premises' for these offences (*Norton* v *Knowles* [1969] 1 QB 572).

---

Under s. 1 of the 1977 Act 'residential occupier' means:

(1) . . . in relation to any premises, . . . a person occupying the premises as a residence, whether under a contract or by virtue of any enactment or rule of law giving him the right to remain in occupation or restricting the right of any other person to recover possession of the premises.

### Defence

In addition to the defence provided by s. 1(2) above, there is a specific defence to an offence under s. 1(3A):

(3B) A person shall not be guilty of an offence under subsection (3A) above if he proves that he had reasonable grounds for doing the acts or withdrawing or withholding the services in question.

## 9.4.2 Using or threatening violence to secure entry

OFFENCE: **Using or threatening violence to secure entry to premises—*Criminal Law Act 1977, s. 6(1)***
• Triable summarily • Six months' imprisonment and/or a fine
*(Preserved power of arrest)*

The Criminal Law Act 1977, s. 6 states:

(1) Subject to the following provisions of this section, any person who, without lawful authority, uses or threatens violence for the purpose of securing entry into any premises for himself or for any other person is guilty of an offence, provided that—

(a) there is someone present on those premises at the time who is opposed to the entry which the violence is intended to secure; and

(b) the person using or threatening the violence knows that that is the case.

**KEYNOTE**

This offence is not restricted to occasions involving 'residential occupiers'.

It is immaterial whether the violence used/threatened is against a person or property, or whether the purpose of the entry is to gain possession of the premises or any other purpose (s. 6(4)).

The fact that a person has any right or interest in premises will not constitute 'lawful authority' to use violence to secure entry into those premises (s. 6(2)).

For the power of entry for this offence, see chapter 2.

For police powers in relation to intimidation and harassment of individuals within their homes, see chapter 4.

### Defence

The Criminal Law Act 1977, s. 6(1A) states:

(1A) Subsection (1) above does not apply to a person who is a displaced residential occupier or a protected intending occupier of the premises in question or who is acting on behalf of such an occupier; and if the accused adduces sufficient evidence that he was, or was acting on behalf of, such an occupier he shall be presumed to be, or to be acting on behalf of, such an occupier unless the contrary is proved by the prosecution.

(2) Subject to subsection (1A) above, the fact that a person has any interest in or right to possession or occupation of any premises shall not for the purposes of subsection (1) above constitute lawful authority for the use or threat of violence by him or anyone else for the purpose of securing his entry into those premises.

A 'displaced residential occupier' is defined at s. 12(3), which states:

(3) Subject to subsection (4) below, any person who was occupying any premises as a residence immediately before being excluded from occupation by anyone who entered those premises, or any access to those premises, as a trespasser is a displaced residential occupier of the premises for the purposes of this Part of this Act so long as he continues to be excluded from occupation of the premises by the original trespasser or by any subsequent trespasser.

(4) A person who was himself occupying the premises in question as a trespasser immediately before being excluded from occupation shall not by virtue of subsection (3) above be a displaced residential occupier of the premises for the purposes of this Part of this Act.

**KEYNOTE**

The definition of a 'protected intending occupier' (s. 12A) must be one of the longest definitions in criminal law (if not criminal history) and takes up an entire page of the Act! The gist of it is that it will include someone with a freehold or leasehold interest in the premises which has at least two years left to run; where the person needs the premises for his/her own occupation as a residence; where he/she is excluded from those premises by a trespasser and where he/she has documentation to prove his/her right to occupy the premises. (For a full discussion, see *Blackstone's Criminal Practice*, 2003, section B13.27.)

### Power of arrest

The Criminal Law Act 1977, s. 6 states:

(6) A constable in uniform may arrest without warrant anyone who is, or whom he, with reasonable cause, suspects to be, guilty of an offence under this section.

**KEYNOTE**

The power of arrest above is a preserved power under Schedule 2 to the Police and Criminal Evidence Act 1984 (see chapter 2).

### 9.4.3 Failing to leave

OFFENCE: **Failing to leave premises—*Criminal Law Act 1977, s. 7***
• Triable summarily • Six  months' imprisonment and/or a fine
*(Preserved power of arrest)*

The Criminal Law Act 1977, s. 7 states:

(1) Subject to the following provisions of this section and to section 12A(9) below, any person who is on any premises as a trespasser after having entered as such is guilty of an offence if he fails to leave those premises on being required to do so by or on behalf of—
  (a) a displaced residential occupier of the premises; or
  (b) an individual who is a protected intending occupier of the premises.

Power of arrest

(6) A constable in uniform may arrest without warrant anyone who is, or whom he, with reasonable cause, suspects to be, guilty of an offence under this section.

---

**KEYNOTE**

The power of arrest above is a preserved power under Schedule 2 to the Police and Criminal Evidence Act 1984 (see chapter 2).

---

Defence

Section 7 of the 1977 Act provides the following defences:

(2) In any proceedings for an offence under this section it shall be a defence for the accused to prove that he believed that the person requiring him to leave the premises was not a displaced residential occupier or protected intending occupier of the premises or a person acting on behalf of a displaced residential occupier or protected intending occupier.

(3) In any proceedings for an offence under this section it shall be a defence for the accused to prove—
  (a) that the premises in question are or form part of premises used mainly for non-residential purposes; and
  (b) that he was not on any part of the premises used wholly or mainly for residential purposes.

Section 12A(9) of the 1977 Act states:

(9) In any proceedings for an offence under section 7 of this Act where the accused was requested to leave the premises by a person claiming to be or to act on behalf of a protected intending occupier of the premises—
  (a) it shall be a defence for the accused to prove that, although asked to do so by the accused at the time the accused was requested to leave, that person failed at that time to produce to the accused such a statement as is referred to in subsection (2)(d) or (4)(d) above or such a certificate as is referred to in subsection (6)(d) above; and
  (b) any document purporting to be a certificate under subsection (6)(d) above shall be received in evidence and, unless the contrary is proved, shall be deemed to have been issued by or on behalf of the authority stated in the certificate.

### 9.4.4 Found on enclosed premises

It is a summary offence under s. 4 of the Vagrancy Act 1824 for any person to be found in or upon any dwelling house, warehouse, coach house, stable or outhouse or in any inclosed yard, garden or area for *any unlawful purpose*. The unlawful purpose must be to commit some specific criminal offence as opposed to simply trespassing and a purely immoral purpose, and without more will not suffice (*Hayes* v *Stevenson* (1860) 3 LT 296).

Where the defendant is found on the relevant premises, he/she can be arrested elsewhere (*R* v *Lumsden* [1951] 2 KB 513). Where a defendant was found in the garden of a house peering through the window at a woman inside intending to frighten her, his conduct was held to amount to an 'unlawful purpose' (*Smith* v *Chief Superintendent of Woking Police Station* (1983) 76 Cr App R 234). Had there not been any intention to frighten, the 'unlawful' purpose would probably not have been made out.

An area may still be 'inclosed' even though there are spaces left in between buildings, arches etc. for access (*Goodhew* v *Morton* [1962] 1 WLR 210). Railway sidings have been held not to amount to 'inclosed' premises and the essential feature of yards and similar enclosed areas for the purposes of this offence would appear to be that they are small pieces of land ancillary to a building (see *Quatromini* v *Peck* [1972] 1 WLR 1318). However, a room within an office building has been held not to amount to an inclosed area for the purposes of this offence (*Talbot* v *Oxford City Justices* [2000] 1 WLR 1102). It appears from the findings of the Divisional Court in *Talbot* that the expression 'inclosed' relates only to yards, gardens and areas in the open air. If the defendant is found in a *building* then that building must be a 'dwelling house, warehouse, coach house, stable or outhouse' before the offence under s. 4 can be applied.

There is no need to show that the person intended to carry out the relevant criminal offence at the time or at that particular place. If the person is found in a building and either intends to commit certain offences there or had that intention when entering, the relevant offences of burglary may well apply (**see Crime, chapter 12**).

### Power of arrest

Section 6 of the 1824 Act provides any person with a power to apprehend any other person found committing an offence against the Act and to take them to a justice of the peace or to deliver them to a constable.

There was some confusion as to the extent of this power in relation to police officers. This has now been clarified by the decision in *Gapper* v *Chief Constable of Avon & Somerset Constabulary* [2000] QB 29 where it was held that the general power of arrest under s. 6 did apply to police officers.

### 9.4.5 Housing Act 1996

Under the Housing Act 1996 the High Court or a county court can grant an injunction to a local authority. Such an injunction, made under s. 152, can prohibit the respondent from:

- engaging in or threatening
- conduct that causes/is likely to cause
- nuisance or annoyance to
- a person residing in, visiting or otherwise engaged in lawful activity in
- 'residential premises' or their locality.

The injunction can also prevent a person from entering residential premises or from using such premises for an immoral or illegal purpose.

The injunction is only available in relation to dwelling houses held under tenancies from a local authority or accommodation provided by such a local authority.

The court cannot grant an injunction unless it is of the opinion that:

- the respondent has used/threatened violence against someone residing in, visiting or otherwise engaged in lawful activity in relevant premises; and

- there is a significant risk of harm to that person or to a person of a similar description if the injunction is not granted.

Under s. 155(1) of the 1996 Act, the court may attach a power for a constable to arrest without warrant a person whom he/she has reasonable cause to suspect to be in breach of any of the provisions of the injunction.

Further, more limited, powers to apply for an injunction are available to local housing authorities, housing action trusts and charitable housing trusts under s. 153.

Although the availability of all such injunctions is restricted to the relevant local or housing authority, liaison between the police and such agencies now has a firm statutory basis (under ss. 5 and 6 of the Crime and Disorder Act 1998) and the Housing Act 1996 may provide a further option to police and local authorities in tackling crime and the fear of it. (For other measures to restrain anti-social or disturbing behaviour, **see chapters 3 and 7**.)

9.4.6     **Nuisance on educational premises**

There has been increasing concern over recent years that schools and their premises are particularly vulnerable to crime and the fear of crime. There are two main areas of behaviour in relation to school premises which the law seeks to regulate; the carrying of certain weapons and the creation of nuisance or disturbance.

For the law relating to the carrying of weapons on school premises, **see chapter 6**.

There are virtually identical provisions made by two Acts in relation to nuisances on educational premises. The first Act, the Local Government (Miscellaneous Provisions) Act 1982, applies to premises that provide further or higher education and which are maintained by a local education authority. The second Act, the Education Act 1996, applies to premises that provide primary or secondary education (or both) and which are maintained by a local education authority or are grant-maintained.

OFFENCE:    **Causing or permitting nuisance—*Local Government (Miscellaneous Provisions) Act 1982, s. 40(1) and Education Act 1996, s. 547(1)***
- Triable summarily • Fine
*(No specific power of arrest. Statutory power of removal)*

The Local Government (Miscellaneous Provisions) Act 1982, s. 40 and the Education Act 1996, s. 547 state:

(1) Any person who without lawful authority is present on premises to which this section applies and causes or permits nuisance or disturbance to the annoyance of persons who lawfully use those premises (whether or not any such persons are present at the time) [shall be guilty of an offence].

---

**KEYNOTE**

These offences are designed to deal with many types of nuisance, from using school playing fields inappropriately to interrupting lessons and lectures.

To be guilty of the above offences the defendant must be on the relevant premises without lawful authority and have caused (been directly responsible for bringing about) or permitted a nuisance or disturbance.

Both sections apply to playing fields and other premises for outdoor recreation of the relevant institution. In the case of schools, the Education Act 1996 provisions extend to playgrounds as well (s. 547(2)).

Compare this with the definition in relation to carrying weapons on school premises (**see chapter 6**).

---

Police powers

Subsection (3) of each Act states:

(3) If—
   (a) a police constable or
   (b) [subject to subsection (5)]..., a person whom a local education authority have authorised to exercise the power conferred by this subsection,

has reasonable cause to suspect that any person is committing or has committed an offence under this section, he may remove him from the premises in question.

---

**KEYNOTE**

The nuisance or disturbance may have finished by the time the police officer gets to the premises but the wording of the subsection allows for the removal of the offender provided there is reasonable cause to suspect that he/she committed the offence.

The reference to subsection (5) is to a limitation on the appointment of such 'authorised' people in the case of certain types of school/establishment.

---

# 10 Licensed premises

## 10.1 Introduction

This chapter deals with the main provisions of the Licensing Act 1964 now repealed and replaced by the Licencing Act 2003, which comes into force in 2004, together with several related pieces of legislation. There are many other offences and powers which, though they involve intoxicating liquor and the behaviour of those who either wish to drink (or, as the 1964 Act terms it, 'consume') it or who have done so, are dealt with in other chapters (**see particularly chapter 4**). Conversely, this chapter includes some offences which do not have to be on 'premises' as such but involve the control of alcohol and so seem logically to fit here.

Many other offences are committed by people who are drunk at the time; for the effects of this on culpability, **see Crime, chapter 4**.

The licensing laws have already undergone some significant changes over the last few years. At the time of writing, the Licensing Act 2003 had just received Royal Assent. Only a few very specific sections had been brought into effect but, as and when the rest of the Act takes hold, the law in the rest of this chapter will be radically altered. One important change will be that the jurisdiction of licensing justices will go, being replaced instead by local authorities who will make all first instance licensing decisions. There will also be four licensing objectives, namely the prevention of crime and disorder, public safety, the prevention of public nuisance and the protection of children from harm. The Act provides for the current convoluted system of different types of licence to be replaced by authorisation for the four licensable activities: personal licences, premises licences, club premises certificates and temporary event notices. The Act will allow further removal of restrictions on children entering licensed premises but the introduction of new offences in relation to under-age sales and consumption. Finally, the powers of the police are to be increased. The Licensing Act 2003 received Royal Assent on 10 July 2003 (see www.lawsoc.org.uk), and comes into force next year.

## 10.2 Definitions

### 10.2.1 Intoxicating liquor

Section 201 of the Licensing Act 1964 defines intoxicating liquor as: 'spirits, wine, beer, cider and any fermented, distilled or spirituous liquor'.

Excluded from this definition are:

- any liquor which is of a strength not exceeding 0.5 per cent at the time of the sale or other relevant conduct;
- flavouring essences recognised as not being intended for consumption as, or with alcoholic liquor;
- spirits or wine intended for use as a medicine and not as a drink;
- perfumes.

In determining the status of flavouring essences or medicinal wine, the opinion of HM Customs and Excise may be sought.

### 10.2.2 Low alcohol drinks and shandy

The definition above was amended because of the problems in relation to low alcohol drinks which, at the time of their original manufacture, exceeded the permitted alcohol content and so attracted all the relevant provisions of the Licensing Act 1964. The amended definition was added by the Licensing (Low Alcohol Drinks) Act 1990.

Clearly drinks which have been *alcohol-free* throughout their manufacture are not included.

Another problematic area is whether or not the mixture of lemonade and beer is intoxicating liquor. It has been held that shandy is 'intoxicating liquor' if mixed by barstaff at the time of the sale, even if its overall strength is below that of proprietary shandy sold by retailers (*Hall* v *Hyder* [1966] 1 WLR 410). Such a sale is treated as two separate sales of the different constituents. Shandy sold in cans or bottles will be below the prescribed strength at the time of sale and will not therefore count as intoxicating liquor.

### 10.2.3 Licensed premises

Section 200 of the Licensing Act 1964 (as amended by Theatres Act 1968, sch. 2 and Finance Act 1967, sch. 7 para. 21) defines any reference to licensed premises as being:

> A reference to premises for which a justices' licence [or occasional licence . . .] is in force and including a reference to any premises in respect of which a notice under section 199(c) of this Act is for the time being in force.

This definition clearly includes both on and off-licences together with other premises such as theatres which enjoy a notice under s. 199(c) of the 1964 Act.

### 10.2.4 Bars

The Licensing Act 1964, s. 201(1) defines a bar as including any place exclusively or mainly used for the *sale and consumption* of intoxicating liquor.

Certain places become excluded from this definition (by s. 171) when they are set apart for the service of table meals which are accompanied by intoxicating liquor. As long as the sale of such liquor is confined to people having those table meals, the definition will not apply provided also that:

- those parts of the premises are usually set aside for the service of table meals; and
- the intoxicating liquor is *ancillary* to the meals being served, i.e. the food, and not the drink, is the primary purpose of that particular part of the premises.

The second requirement does *not* mean that drink can only be served to people who are seated at a table.

For these purposes a table meal will be a meal eaten by someone seated at a table (or at a counter or other structure which serves the purpose of a table) which is not used for the service of refreshments for consumption by other people.

The type of meal envisaged will include a substantial sandwich or ploughman's lunch but each case will be decided by the relevant court as a question of fact.

A 'bar counter' will always be 'a bar' (*Carter* v *Bradbeer* [1975] 1 WLR 1204).

Whether a place is exclusively or mainly used for the sale *and* consumption of intoxicating liquor is a question of fact and you will need to prove both elements in any offence involving bars.

## 10.3 Justices' licences

A licence issued by the licensing justices authorises the retail sale of intoxicating liquor. It also authorises the supply of intoxicating liquor to, or to the order of members of a club otherwise than by way of sale.

### 10.3.1    On-licence

An on-licence is a justices' licence authorising sale for consumption either on or off the relevant premises (s. 1(2)(a) of the Licensing Act 1964).

Under s. 1(3), it may authorise the sale of:

- intoxicating liquor of all descriptions; or
- beer, cider and wine only; or
- beer and cider only; or
- cider only; or
- wine only.

### 10.3.2    Off-licence

An off-licence is a justices' licence authorising sale for consumption off the relevant premises (s. 1(2)(b) of the 1964 Act).

Under s. 1(3)(b), it may authorise the sale of:

- intoxicating liquor of all descriptions; or
- beer, cider and wine only.

## 10.4    Other types of licence

### 10.4.1    Occasional permissions

The Licensing (Occasional Permissions) Act 1983 allows licensing justices to grant 'occasional permissions'—that is, temporary authorities for the sale of intoxicating liquor—to organisations not operating for profit or private gain.

An example would be a church committee wishing to hold a fund-raising event for the rebuilding of a community centre.

Application and the granting of such occasional permissions is regulated in the 1983 Act, which also sets out in its schedule offences such as the making of false statements in connection with an application, breaching any conditions imposed, the illegal sale of intoxicating liquor and failing to allow a constable admission to premises where the permission is in force. (See particularly para. 9 of the schedule for the power of entry by a constable for the purpose of preventing or detecting these offences.)

### 10.4.2    Occasional licences

The holder of an on-licence may apply for an occasional licence which allows the sale of intoxicants at a place other than the licensee's usual premises (s. 180 of the Licensing Act 1964).

Occasional licences are issued by a magistrates' court as opposed to licensing justices. They authorise the sale of intoxicants by the licensee at places such as dance halls, fêtes and exhibitions.

An occasional licence sets out the hours during which sale is permitted and runs for a period not exceeding three weeks. These licences will not apply on Christmas Day or Good Friday (s. 180(1)(b) of the 1964 Act).

The application procedure is set out under s. 180 of the 1964 Act. If applying in person an applicant must:

- give at least 24 hours' notice to his/her chief officer of police of his/her intention to apply;
- provide his/her name and address;
- provide details of the place and the occasion(s) for which the licence is required;

- state the period for which the licence is required; and

- specify the hours during which the licence is required.

Justices may grant an occasional licence without having a hearing.

In order to apply, an applicant must submit to the justices' clerk two copies of his/her written application within a period which is not less than one month before the licence is required. On receipt of the application the clerk will ordinarily send a copy to the chief officer of police. The police—or indeed anyone else—may object in writing within seven days of the justices' clerk sending that copy. In the event that someone does lodge an objection, the justices must hold a hearing.

If such a licence is granted and intoxicants are then sold outside the specified hours *but during the period when the occasional licence is still valid*, there is no offence of selling intoxicating liquor without a justices' licence contrary to s. 160 of the Licensing Act 1964 (*Southall* v *Haime* [1979] Crim LR 249).

The offence of selling liquor without a licence (s. 160(1)(b)) would be committed where intoxicating liquor is sold after the occasional licence has expired as the defendant would no longer be the holder of a licence in respect of those premises.

In practice, as most occasional licences are for one short function, e.g. dinners, dances, fêtes, etc., s. 160 will still apply to most cases where a sale takes place after the licence has expired.

The drinking of intoxicants outside permitted hours is dealt with under s. 59 of the 1964 Act. Section 59(3), however, states that the provisions preventing the sale of intoxicants outside permitted hours will not apply to intoxicants sold under an occasional licence.

### Occasional licences and 'licensed premises'

Although premises for which an occasional licence is in force will be classed as 'licensed premises' during the currency of that licence, they cease to be such when the licence expires. Therefore, drinking intoxicants after the hours specified in the occasional licence, even when the licence has expired, will not amount to an offence under s. 59 of the 1964 Act which only applies to 'licensed premises'.

In the case of a licensee permitting such behaviour, the police could object to any future application by that person (or for those premises), using evidence of non-conformity with the licensing conditions to support their objection.

### Occasional licences and children under 14

Section 168 of the 1964 Act prohibits anyone under 14 years from being in bars of 'licensed premises' during permitted hours.

Because there are no 'permitted hours' for occasional licences, it would seem that there is no restriction in respect of children under 14 on premises which are the subject of such a licence.

Again, any evidence of the presence of children on such premises could be used by the police—or others—in opposing any future application for an occasional licence in respect of those premises or that applicant.

Note that the offence of selling intoxicating liquor to a person under 18 years (**see para. 10.6.3**), and the drinking of intoxicating liquor by such a person can be committed at premises licensed under an occasional licence.

## 10.5    **Permitted hours**

'Permitted hours' are the general licensing hours for a district. These hours can be increased by a general order of exemption, a special order of exemption, a restaurant certificate (or 'supper hour extension'), a special hours certificate, and an extended hours order.

### 10.5.1 Permitted hours in licensed premises

The Licensing Act 1964, s. 60(1) (as amended by s. 1 of the Licensing Act 1988 and the Licensing (Sunday Hours) Act 1995) states:

(1) Subject to the following provisions of this Part of this Act and the Regulatory Reform (Special Occasions licensing) Order 2001, the permitted hours in licensed premises shall be—

    (a) on weekdays, other than Christmas Day, Good Friday or New year's Eve, the hours from 11 am to 11 pm, and

    (b) on Sundays, other than Christmas Day, Good Friday or New year's Eve, the hours from 12 noon to 10.30 pm,

    (c) on Christmas Day, the hours from 12 noon to 10.30 pm, with a break of four hours beginning at 3 pm.

Section 60(4) of the 1964 Act states:

(4) The licensing justices for any licensing district, if satisfied that the requirements of the district make it desirable, may by order modify for the district the hours specified in subsection (1)(a) of this section [so that the permitted hours begin at a time earlier than 11 am, but not earlier than 10 am].

---

**KEYNOTE**

Permitted hours for licensed premises generally will be 11 am to 11 pm on weekdays; 12 noon to 10.30 pm on Sundays and Good Fridays; and 12 noon to 3 pm and 7 pm to 10.30 pm on Christmas Day.

These hours may be modified in accordance with s. 60(4) above.

The permitted hours for registered clubs are the same as the general licensing hours with the exception that, on Christmas Day, the hours are determined by the rules of the club in accordance with the conditions set out in s. 62(1).

'General licensing hours' means, in relation to any licensing district, the hours specified in s. 60(1)(a) to (b), with any modification applying in the district by virtue of s. 60(4) (s. 60(5) ).

---

### 10.5.2 Off-licences

In premises licensed for the sale of intoxicating liquor for consumption off the premises only, the permitted hours on weekdays, other than Christmas Day shall begin at 8 am, and the permitted hours on Sundays, other than Christmas Day, shall begin at 10 am (s. 60(6) of the 1964 Act).

References to permitted hours shall (except in so far as the context otherwise requires) be construed, in relation to any licensed premises where the permitted hours are restricted by any conditions attached to the licence, as referring to the hours as so restricted (s. 60(7) ).

### 10.5.3 Offences

OFFENCE: **Selling intoxicating liquor outside permitted hours—*Licensing Act 1964, s. 59(1)***

    • Triable summarily • Fine

    *(No specific power of arrest)*

The Licensing Act 1964, s. 59 states:

(1) Subject to the provision of this Act, no person shall, except during the permitted hours—

    (a) himself or by his servant or agent sell or supply to any person in licensed premises or in premises in respect of which a club is registered any intoxicating liquor, whether to be consumed on or off the premises; or

    (b) consume in or take from such premises any intoxicating liquor.

**KEYNOTE**

The exceptions to s. 59 are shown below.

Section 59 does not apply in relation to intoxicating liquor sold under an occasional licence (s. 59(3)).

Exceptions

Section 63 of the Licensing Act 1964 (as amended by s. 2 of the Licensing Act 1988) states:

(1) Where any intoxicating liquor is supplied in any premises during the permitted hours, section 59 of this Act does not prohibit or restrict—
  (a) during the first 20 minutes after the end of any period forming part of those hours, the consumption of the liquor on the premises, nor, unless the liquor was supplied or is taken away in an open vessel, the taking of the liquor from the premises;
  (b) during the first half hour after the end of such a period, the consumption of the liquor on the premises by persons taking meals there, if the liquor was supplied for consumption as an ancillary to their meals.

(2) Section 59 of this Act does not prohibit or restrict—
  (a) the sale or supply to, or consumption by, any person of intoxicating liquor in any premises where he is residing;
  (b) the ordering of intoxicating liquor to be consumed off the premises, or the despatch by the vendor of liquor so ordered;
  (c) the sale of intoxicating liquor to a trader for the purposes of his trade, or to a registered club for the purposes of the club; or
  (d) the sale or supply of intoxicating liquor to any canteen or mess.

(3) Section 59 of this Act does not prohibit or restrict as regard licensed premises—
  (a) the taking of intoxicating liquor from the premises by a person residing there; or
  (b) the supply of intoxicating liquor for consumption on the premises to any private friends of a person residing there who are bona fide entertained by him at his own expense, or the consumption of intoxicating liquor by persons so supplied; or
  (c) the supply of intoxicating liquor for consumption on the premises to persons employed there for the purposes of the business carried on by the holder of the licence, or the consumption of liquor so supplied, if the liquor is supplied at the expense of their employer or of the person carrying on or in charge of the business on the premises.

(4) In subsection (2) of this section, as it applies to licensed premises, and in subsection (3) of this section, references to a person residing in the premises shall be construed as including a person not residing there but carrying on or in charge of the business on the premises.

**KEYNOTE**

The exceptions involving 'drinking-up' time under s. 63(1)(a) and (b) are those most commonly encountered.

Where the licensee takes advantage of this exception and *bona fide* entertains private friends, he/she must not do so with his/her ordinary customers. A licensee cannot transform regular customers into private friends to evade the effects of s. 59(1).

Whether a person is a private friend is a question of fact for the justices in each case. The onus is on the defendant to prove that the people concerned were friends (*Atkins* v *Agar* [1914] 1 KB 26). These exemptions do not extend to other offences and if the friends are drunk on licensed premises they still commit an offence.

OFFENCE:    **Failing to abide by terms of off-licence—*Licensing Act 1964, s. 164(1)***
            • Triable summarily • Fine
            *(No specific power of arrest)*

The Licensing Act 1964, s. 164 states:

(1) Where a person, having purchased intoxicating liquor from the holder of a justices' licence which does not cover the sale of that liquor for consumption on the premises, drinks the liquor—
  (a) in the licensed premises, or

(b) in premises which adjoin or are near the licensed premises and which belong to the holder of the licence or are under his control or used by his permission, or

(c) on a highway adjoining or near those premises,

then, if the drinking is with the privity or consent of the holder of the licence, the holder of the licence shall be liable ...

---

**KEYNOTE**

This offence can be committed in the off-licence premises, in premises adjoining them or on the highway near the premises. In all cases the privity or consent of the licensee must be proved.

To prove this offence you will also need to show more than mere knowledge by the licensee of the drinking. Evidence that the licensee provided glasses for drinking or set aside tables and chairs would support such proof.

---

## 10.6 Under age drinking

### 10.6.1 Children's certificates

Under s. 168A(1) of the Licensing Act 1964 the holder of a justices' licence may apply to the licensing justices for a certificate in relation to any area of his/her premises which consists of, or includes a bar.

Under s. 168A(2), the licensing justices may grant an application for a certificate if it appears to them to be appropriate to do so, but shall not do so unless they are satisfied:

- that the area to which the application relates constitutes an environment in which it is suitable for people under 14 to be present; and

- that meals and drinks other than intoxicating liquor will be available for sale for consumption in that area.

Under s. 168A(3), where a children's certificate is in force, the holder of the justices' licence must keep posted, in some conspicuous place in the area to which the certificate relates, a notice which both:

- states that a children's certificate is in force in relation to the area; and

- explains the effect of the certificate and of any conditions attached to it.

OFFENCE: **Failing to conform to conditions of children's certificate—*Licensing Act 1964, s. 168A(4)***
- Triable summarily • Fine
*(No specific power of arrest)*

The Licensing Act 1964, s. 168A states:

(4) A person who fails to perform the duty imposed on him by subsection (3) of this section shall be guilty of an offence.

---

**KEYNOTE**

Under s. 168(8), where it is alleged that a person was under 14 years, and he/she appears to the court to have been under that age, he/she shall be deemed to have been under that age, unless the contrary is shown.

---

Defence

Section 168A(5) of the 1964 Act states:

(5) In any proceedings for an offence under subsection (4) of this section it shall be a defence for the accused to prove that he took all reasonable precautions, and exercised all due diligence, to avoid the commission of the offence.

10.6.2    **Person under 14 in bar**

OFFENCE:    **Holder of justices' licence allowing person under 14 in bar—*Licensing Act 1964, s. 168(3)***

• Triable summarily • Fine

*(No specific power of arrest)*

The Licensing Act 1964, s. 168 states:

(1) The holder of a justices' licence shall not allow a person under fourteen to be in the bar of the licensed premises during the permitted hours.

(2) No person shall cause or procure, or attempt to cause or procure, any person under fourteen to be in the bar of licensed premises during the permitted hours.

(3) Where it is shown that a person under fourteen was in the bar of any licensed premises during the permitted hours, the holder of the justices' licence shall be guilty of an offence under this section unless he proves either—
   (a) that he exercised all due diligence to prevent the person under fourteen from being admitted to the bar, or
   (b) that the person under fourteen had apparently attained that age.

---

**KEYNOTE**

To avoid liability under this section the licensee must prove that he/she exercised *all* due diligence to prevent the commission of the offence *or* that the person had apparently reached the age of 14.

---

Defence

Section 168(3A) of the 1964 Act states:

(3A) No offence shall be committed under subsection (1) of this section if—
   (a) the person under fourteen is in the bar in the company of a person who is eighteen or over,
   (b) there is in force a certificate under section 168A(1) of this Act relating to the bar, and
   (c) the certificate is operational or subsection (3B) of this section applies.

Section 168(3C) states:

(3C) No offence shall be committed under subsection (2) of this section if the person causes or procures, or attempts to cause or procure, the person under fourteen to be in the bar in the circumstances mentioned in paragraphs (a) to (c) of subsection (3A) of this section.

---

**KEYNOTE**

Section 168(4) provides a defence if the person under 14:

• is the licence holder's child;

• resides in the premises, but is not employed there; or

- is in the bar solely for the purpose of passing to or from some part of the premises which is not a bar and to or from which there is no other convenient means of access (or exit).

Section 168 (3B) applies where:

- the person under 14, or a person in whose company he/she is, is eating a meal bought before the certificate ceased to be operational; and

- no more than 30 minutes have elapsed since the certificate ceased to be operational.

---

Section 168(5) states:

> (5) No offence shall be committed under this section if the bar is in any railway refreshment-rooms or other premises constructed, fitted and intended to be used bona fide for any purpose to which the holding of a justices' licence is merely ancillary.

### 10.6.3 Offences involving a person under 18

OFFENCE: **Providing intoxicating liquor in licensed premises for person under 18—*Licensing Act 1964, s. 169A(1)***

- Triable summarily • Fine • Discretionary forfeiture of licence on second offence
*(No specific power of arrest)*

The Licensing Act 1964, s. 169A states:

> (1) A person shall be guilty of an offence if, in licensed premises, he sells intoxicating liquor to a person under eighteen.

---

**KEYNOTE**

This amended offence is wider than its predecessor which required proof of certain knowledge if the defendant was the licensee (see the next offence below) and which was also limited to 'bars' (as to which, **see para. 10.2.4**). Section 169A creates a simplified offence in that the prosecution need only show that the relevant person sold intoxicating liquor to someone who, as a matter of fact, was under 18 at the time. Thereafter, the defendant may be able to avail himself/herself of one of the specific defences set out below.

**Exception**

If the person under 18 is at least 16 years old and the drink involved

- is beer, porter or cider

- for consumption with a meal

- in a part of the licensed premises that is not a 'bar' and which

- is set apart for the service of meals

this offence does not apply (s. 169D). This statutory exception also applies to several other offences (see below).

---

**Defence**

Section 169A (amended by Criminal Justice and Police Act 2001, s. 30) states:

> (2) It is a defence for a person charged with an offence under subsection (1) of this section, where he is charged by reason of his own act, to prove—
> (a) that he believed that the person was not under eighteen; and
> (b) either that he had taken all reasonable steps to establish the person's age or that nobody could reasonably have suspected from his appearance that the person was under eighteen.

(2A) For the purposes of subsection (2) of this section a person shall be treated as having taken all reasonable steps to establish another person's age if he asks the other person for evidence of his age unless it is shown that the evidence was such that no reasonable person would have been convinced by it.

(3) It is a defence for a person charged with an offence under subsection (1) of this section, where he is charged by reason of the act or default of some other person, to prove that he exercised all due diligence to avoid the commission of an offence under that subsection.

---

### KEYNOTE

The defence above was amended by the Criminal Justice and Police Act 2001. The requirement under s 169A(2)(b)—to show that the defendant had taken all reasonable steps to establish the person's age—is straightforward enough and will probably not be satisfied by simply asking the person their age. However, the alternative, to show that *nobody* could reasonably have suspected etc., not only seems to be a unique piece of statutory wording in criminal law, it is arguably a very difficult test to satisfy. Why the more conventional—and far easier—test of 'no reasonable person' that is used in the next subsection was not adopted here is unclear. The wording of s 169A(2A) encourages the use of such things as 'proof of age cards' or other genuine and convincing documentation.

---

OFFENCE: **Allowing the sale of intoxicating liquor in licensed premises to a person under 18—*Licensing Act 1964, s. 169B***
  - Triable summarily • Fine • Discretionary forfeiture of licence on second offence
  *(No specific power of arrest)*

The Licensing Act 1964, s. 169B states:

(1) A person to whom this subsection applies shall be guilty of an offence if, in licensed premises, he knowingly allows any person to sell intoxicating liquor to a person under eighteen.

(2) Subsection (1) of this section applies to a person who works in the licensed premises in a capacity, whether paid or unpaid, which gives him authority to prevent the sale.

---

### KEYNOTE

This offence replicates part of the old (s. 169(1)) offence governing licensees. It requires proof of knowledge of the selling on the part of the licensee (which can include turning a 'blind eye', see e.g. *Buxton* v *Chief Constable of Northumbria* (1983) 148 JP 9).

The re-worded offence is far wider than the previous one, however, and extends to any person who works in the particular licensed premises whether as a paid employee or as an unpaid helper, provided it can be shown that the person had authority to prevent that sale.

The statutory exception in relation to people aged 16 years or more taking a drink with their meal (see above) applies to this offence.

---

OFFENCE: **Buying or drinking intoxicating liquor in licensed premises—*Licensing Act 1964, s. 169C***
  - Triable summarily • Fine • Discretionary forfeiture of licence on second offence
  *(No specific power of arrest)*

The Licensing Act 1964, s. 169C states:

(1) A person under eighteen shall be guilty of an offence if, in licensed premises, he buys or attempts to buy intoxicating liquor.

(1A) Subsection (1) of this section does not apply where the person under eighteen buys or attempts to buy the intoxicating liquor at the request of—

(a) a constable, or

(b) an inspector of weights and measures appointed under section 72(1) of the Weights and Measures Act 1985,who is acting in the course of his duty.

(2) A person shall be guilty of an offence if in licensed premises, he buys or attempts to buy intoxicating liquor on behalf of a person under eighteen.

(3) A person shall be guilty of an offence if he buys or attempts to buy intoxicating liquor for consumption in a bar in licensed premises by a person under eighteen.

---

**KEYNOTE**

Section 169C creates three offences. The first two apply to licensed premises generally, while the third applies to intended consumption in a 'bar'.

The added defence at s. 169C(1A) specifically allows for test purchases under the control of a police officer or an inspector of weights and measures when acting as such. It is worth noting that s. 169I now imposes a positive duty on weights and measures authorities to enforce the provisions of ss. 169A and B. For the general considerations when carrying out test purchases and other covert operations, see Crime, chapter 3.

It is a defence for a person charged with an offence under s. 169C(2) or (3) to prove that he/she had no reason to suspect that the person was under 18 (s. 169C(4)).

This offence is a 'penalty offence' for the purposes of s. 1 of the Criminal Justice and Police Act 2001 (see para. 2.5.1).

---

OFFENCE: **Consumption of intoxicating liquor in a bar by a person under 18—** ***Licensing Act 1964, s. 169E***
 • Triable summarily • Fine • Discretionary forfeiture of licence on second offence
 *(No specific power of arrest)*

The Licensing Act 1964, s. 169E states:

(1) A person under eighteen shall be guilty of an offence if in a bar in licensed premises, he consumes intoxicating liquor.

(2) A person to whom this subsection applies shall be guilty of an offence if in licensed premises, he knowingly allows a person under eighteen to consume intoxicating liquor in a bar.

---

**KEYNOTE**

These offences specifically relate to conduct within a 'bar' (see para. 10.2.4).

As with the offence under s. 169B (above), the offence of allowing another to consume intoxicants in a bar extends to any person who works in the particular licensed premises whether as a paid employee or as an unpaid helper, provided it can be shown that the person had authority to prevent that sale (s. 169E(3)).

---

OFFENCE: **Delivery of intoxicating liquor to a person under 18—***Licensing Act 1964, s. 169F*
 • Triable summarily • Fine • Discretionary forfeiture of licence on second offence
 *(No specific power of arrest)*

The Licensing Act 1964, s. 169F states:

(1) A person who works in licensed premises, whether paid or unpaid, shall be guilty of an offence if he knowingly delivers to a person under eighteen intoxicating liquor sold in those premises for consumption off the premises.

(2) A person to whom this subsection applies shall be guilty of an offence if he knowingly allows any person to deliver to a person under eighteen intoxicating liquor sold in licensed premises for consumption off the premises.

**KEYNOTE**

These offences require specific proof of the defendant's knowledge, either in delivering the intoxicating liquor or in allowing another to do so.

In the case of subsection (2), the offence extends to any person who works in the particular licensed premises whether as a paid employee or as an unpaid helper, provided it can be shown that the person had authority to prevent that sale (s. 169F(3)).

Neither offence applies if:

- the delivery is made at the residence or working place of the purchaser, or

- the person under eighteen works in those licensed premises in a capacity (whether paid or unpaid) which involves delivering intoxicating liquor

(s. 169F(4)).

---

OFFENCE: **Sending a person under 18 for intoxicating liquor—*Licensing Act 1964, s. 169G***

- Triable summarily • Fine • Discretionary forfeiture of licence on second offence
*(No specific power of arrest)*

The Licensing Act 1964, s. 169G states:

(1) A person shall be guilty of an offence if he knowingly sends a person under eighteen for the purpose of obtaining intoxicating liquor sold or to be sold in licensed premises for consumption off the premises.

---

**KEYNOTE**

This offence, which requires proof of knowledge by the defendant, applies regardless of whether the drink is to be obtained from the licensed premises themselves, or from some other premises from which it is delivered (s. 169G(2)).

The offence does not apply where the person under 18 works in the relevant licensed premises in a capacity (whether paid or unpaid) which involves the delivery of intoxicating liquor (s. 169G(3)).

As with the defence under s. 169C, there is a defence where the person under 18 is sent by:

- a constable, or

- an inspector of weights and measures appointed under s. 72(1) of the Weights and Measures Act 1985

who is acting in the course of his/her duty (s. 169G(4)).

---

Approved Training Schemes

Section 170A of the Licensing Act 1964 allows the Secretary of State to make regulations for approval of training schemes. Under such a scheme, a person under 18 may be permitted to work behind a bar provided certain conditions in relation to his/her training and supervision are met. For information relating to such training schemes for the purpose of employing 16 and 17 year olds in bars, see Home Office Circular 16/99.

10.6.4 **Confiscation of alcohol**

The Confiscation of Alcohol (Young Persons) Act 1997, s. 1(1) states:

(1) Where a constable reasonably suspects that a person in a relevant place is in possession of intoxicating liquor and that either—
   (a) he is under the age of 18; or

(b) he intends that any of the liquor should be consumed by a person under the age of 18 in that or any other relevant place; or

(c) a person under the age of 18 who is, or has recently been, with him has recently consumed intoxicating liquor in that or any other relevant place,

the constable may require him to surrender anything in his possession which is, or which the constable reasonably believes to be, intoxicating liquor or a container for such liquor and to state his name and address.

(1A) But a constable may not under subsection (1) require a person to surrender any sealed container unless the constable reasonably believes that the person is, or has been, consuming, or intends to consume alcohol in any relevant place.

---

**KEYNOTE**

This is a discretionary power for police officers to exercise as they deem fit in accordance with general human rights principles and, in particular, Article 1 of the First Protocol (**see** chapter 2).

It is unusual that the wording of the section says 'either', then goes on to give *three* instances where the power will be available. However, if one of the instances at s. 1(1)(a)–(c) applies the police officer may require the person concerned to:

- surrender anything that is, or that the officer reasonably *believes* (a narrower expression than 'suspects') to be intoxicating liquor or a container for such liquor; and

- state his/her name and address.

The wording of this section is similar to that relating to powers to confiscate items in a designated public place (**see** para. 10.7.2). The former exclusion of sealed containers from the power to seize was removed from 10 September 2003. There is no requirement for the officer to be in uniform.

The requirement for the person to state his/her name and *his/her own address* appears to be quite specific. A similar provision under s. 170 of the Road Traffic Act 1988 (duty to give details after an accident; **see Road Traffic, chapter 4**) has been satisfied where the person concerned gave the name and address of his solicitor (*DPP* v *McCarthy* [1999] RTR 323). However, as the above power will affect mostly young people, it would seem unlikely that anything less than their own personal details would satisfy the requirements of this section. It is an important point, because failure to comply with either requirement under s. 1(1) triggers the power of arrest under s. 1(5) (see below).

Under s. 1(2), the officer may dispose of *anything* surrendered to him/her in answer to the making of such a requirement. This wide discretionary power is not limited to intoxicating liquor and the officer could dispose of any other drink surrendered under this section (see HC Official Report SC C, 12 February 1997).

This power (but *not* the power of arrest below) can be conferred on a Police Community Support Officer designated under sch. 4 to the Police Reform Act 2002 and a person accredited under sch. 5 to that (**see** chapter 2).

For policing powers to regulate drinking in public places and to confiscate bottles, glasses, etc., **see** para. 10.7.2.

---

OFFENCE: **Failing to surrender intoxicating liquor—*Confiscation of Alcohol (Young Persons) Act 1997, s 1(3)***

- Triable summarily • Fine

*(Statutory power of arrest)*

The Confiscation of Alcohol (Young Persons) Act 1997, s 1 states:

(3) A person who fails without reasonable excuse to comply with a requirement imposed on him under subsection (1) commits an offence.

**KEYNOTE**

Where a constable imposes a requirement on a person under s 1(1) above, he/she must inform that person of his/her suspicion and that to fail without reasonable excuse to comply with such a requirement is an offence (s. 1(4)).

Under s. 1(6), a 'relevant place' is:

* any public place, other than licensed premises; or

* any place, other than a public place, to which that person has unlawfully gained access;

and for this purpose a place is a public place if, at the material time, the public or any section of the public has access to it—on payment or otherwise—as of right or by virtue of express or implied permission. Therefore the power may be exercised in any public place (as defined above) not being 'licensed premises', an expression that includes off-licences (see para. 10.2.3). It may also be exercised in any other place that is not a public place to which the person has gained access unlawfully. This second expression suggests that the person must, as a matter of fact, have gained access to the place unlawfully—as opposed to the officer simply 'suspecting' or 'believing' that to be the case. It also suggests that, if the person was originally in the place lawfully but was later asked to leave, the power would not apply as the person's access would not have been 'unlawfully gained'. The section does not provide the police officer with a power of entry, nor a power to search.

The 1997 Act provides a useful power which might be considered in relation to events such as parties and 'raves' (see chapter 9).

Intoxicating liquor and licensed premises have the same meaning as in the Licensing Act 1964 (s. 1(7) of the 1997 Act).

---

### Power of arrest

Under s. 1(5) of the 1997 Act a constable may arrest without warrant a person who fails to comply with a requirement imposed on him/her under s. 1(1).

Perhaps unusually, this power is not restricted to police officers in uniform. It is triggered when the person fails to comply with either of the requirements under s. 1(1). Although the *offence* states that the failure must be without reasonable excuse, there is no such restriction on the power of arrest which becomes available once the person fails to comply with the requirement apparently whether that failure is supported by a reasonable excuse or not.

## 10.7  Drunkenness

OFFENCE:  **Permitting drunkenness—*Licensing Act 1964, ss. 172(1) and 172A(1) and (2)***
* Triable summarily • Fine
*(No specific power of arrest)*

The Licensing Act 1964, ss. 172 and 172A state:

172—(1)   The holder of a justices' licence shall not permit drunkenness or any violent, quarrelsome or riotous conduct to take place in the licensed premises.

172A—(1)   A relevant person shall not permit drunkenness or any violent, quarrelsome or riotous conduct to take place in licensed premises.

(2)   If a relevant person is charged under subsection (1) of this section with permitting drunkenness, and it is proved that any person was drunk in the licensed premises, the burden of proving that the relevant person and any persons employed by him took all reasonable steps for preventing drunkenness in the premises shall lie upon him.

**KEYNOTE**

The first offence above applies to the licensee, while the second offence applies to a 'relevant person'. A relevant person for these purposes is any person (other than the licensee) who works in the licensed premises in a capacity, whether paid or unpaid, which gives him/her authority to prevent the drunkenness or conduct concerned (s. 172A(6)). This offence was previously only capable of commission by the licensee, although he/she could also be vicariously liable for the acts of those working for them. However, although there is now this specific offence extending primary liability to bar staff and others, that offence does not remove the licensee's general vicarious liability under s. 172 (see s. 172A(5)).

If a relevant person is charged under subsection (1) with permitting drunkenness, and it is proved that any person was drunk in the licensed premises, the burden of proving that the relevant person (and anyone employed by him/her) took all reasonable steps for preventing drunkenness in the premises lies upon that relevant person or employee (s. 172A(2)).

OFFENCE: **Selling intoxicating liquor to a drunk person—*Licensing Act 1964, ss. 172(3) and 172A(3)***

- Triable summarily • Fine
*(No specific power of arrest)*

The Licensing Act 1964, ss. 172 and 172A state:

172—(3)   The holder of a justices' licence shall not sell intoxicating liquor to a drunken person.

172A—(3) A relevant person shall not, in licensed premises, sell intoxicating liquor to a drunken person.

OFFENCE: **Procuring intoxicating liquor for a drunk person—*Licensing Act 1964, s. 173(1)***

- Triable summarily • Fine
*(No specific power of arrest)*

The Licensing Act 1964, s. 173 states:

(1) If any person in licensed premises procures or attempts to procure any intoxicating liquor for consumption by a drunken person he shall be guilty of an offence ...

OFFENCE: **Aiding a drunk person to obtain intoxicating liquor—*Licensing Act 1964, s. 173(2)***

- Triable summarily • Fine
*(No specific power of arrest)*

The Licensing Act 1964, s. 173 states:

(2) If any person aids a drunken person in obtaining or consuming intoxicating liquor in licensed premises he shall be guilty of an offence ...

**KEYNOTE**

Where a licensee sells drink to someone who is drunk (s. 172(3)), it is an offence of absolute liability (**see Crime, chapter 1**). Therefore it is no defence to show that the licensee or his/her servants did not in fact know that the person was drunk. There is no requirement that the relevant liquor must be consumed for this offence to be complete.

As with the offences of permitting drunkenness etc. under s. 172, the first offence above applies to the licensee, while the second applies to a 'relevant person'. A relevant person for these purposes is any person (other than the licensee) who works in the licensed premises in a capacity, whether paid or unpaid, which gives him/her authority to sell the intoxicating liquor concerned (s. 172A(6)). Similarly, this does not remove the licensee's general vicarious liability under s. 172 (see s. 172A(5)).

The offence under s. 173 (procuring etc. for a person who is drunk) will apply to all licensed premises, including theatre bars and premises for which there is an occasional licence in force (see para. 10.4.2).

### 10.7.1    Power to exclude drunks

Section 174 of the Licensing Act 1964 states:

> (1) Without prejudice to any other right to refuse a person admission to premises or to expel a person from premises, the holder of a justices' licence or a relevant person may refuse to admit to, or may expel from the licensed premises any person who is drunken, violent, quarrelsome or disorderly, and the holder of a justices' licence may refuse to admit to, or may expel from, the licensed premises any person whose presence in the licensed premises would subject the licence holder to a penalty under this Act.

### KEYNOTE

The wording of the above power means that the licensee or a relevant person can refuse to admit or can expel anyone on the grounds that the person is drunk, violent, quarrelsome or disorderly but *only the licensee* may refuse to admit or may expel a person whose presence would subject the licensee to a penalty under the Act. This may be a fine distinction but no doubt someone will fall foul of its subtleties.

'Relevant person' for these purposes is any person who works in licensed premises in a capacity, whether paid or unpaid, which gives him/her authority to prevent drunkenness or conduct as is mentioned in s. 172A(1) (see s. 174(3) and (4)).

Other rights to refuse admission would include a person's common law right to revoke an otherwise open invitation or 'licence' to enter his/her premises.

Examples of situations where the presence of someone would make the licensee liable to a penalty would include people who were drunk or children under 14 (subject to the exceptions above).

OFFENCE:    **Failing to leave premises when required—*Licensing Act 1964, s. 174(2)***
   • Triable summarily • Fine
   *(No specific power of arrest)*

The Licensing Act 1964, s. 174 states:

> (2) If any person liable to be expelled from licensed premises under this section, when requested by the holder of the justices' licence or his agent or servant or (as the case may be) the relevant person or any agent or servant of his or by any constable to leave the premises, fails without reasonable excuse to do so, he shall be liable . . .

> (3) Any constable shall, on the demand of the holder of a justices' licence or his agent or servant or (as the case may be) a relevant person or any agent or servant of his, help to expel from the licensed premises any person liable to be expelled from them under this section, and may use such force as may be required for the purpose.

### KEYNOTE

In proving the offence under s. 174(2) you must show:

- that the defendant was drunk, violent, quarrelsome or disorderly; and

- that a request to leave had been made by the licensee, servant, relevant person or constable; and

- that the defendant failed to leave.

Note that the constable is there to help the licensee, servant or relevant person, not to expel the person of his/her own volition but, in doing so, may use reasonable necessary force.

Relevant person for these purposes is any person who works in licensed premises in a capacity, whether paid or unpaid, which gives him/her authority to prevent such drunkenness or such conduct as is mentioned in s. 172A(1) (see s. 174(4)). Because of the wording of s. 174(2) you must show that any person failing to leave the premises when required did so *without reasonable excuse*.

---

### 10.7.2 Alcohol consumption in designated public places

The Criminal Justice and Police Act 2001 introduces a statutory framework to regulate the drinking of alcohol in certain public places and to reinforce existing licensing laws.

In a number of areas, the police and local authorities have been using local by-laws to control alcohol-related disorder very successfully. The 2001 Act builds on these initiatives and makes provision to replace existing by-laws where they overlap with the new legislation below (see s. 15).

Under s. 13 of the 2001 Act, local authorities may identify public places within their area if they are satisfied that:

- nuisance or annoyance to members of the public (or section of the public), or

- disorder

has been associated with the consumption of intoxicating liquor in that place. This expression '*has been associated*' is a fairly loose one which does not appear to impose a particularly heavy burden on the local authority, who will clearly rely on evidence from the police in establishing whether such a situation exists. 'Public place' here means any place to which the public (or a section of the public) has access, on payment or otherwise, as of right or by virtue of any express or implied permission (s. 16(1)).

Once it is satisfied that one of the relevant conditions applies to a public place, the local authority may make an order (under s. 13(2)) designating that place. The procedure for making these orders is set out in regulations.

Although the 2001 Act allows places to be designated either by specific reference (e.g. to their street name), or by description, the following places cannot be 'designated public places':

- licensed premises or registered clubs (or places in their immediate boundaries)

- places covered by an occasional permission or occasional licence (**see para. 10.4**) or where such a permission/licence had been in force within the last 20 minutes

- places covered by a permission under s. 115E of the Highways Act 1980

(s. 14).

### Police powers

Where a constable reasonably believes that a person:

- is, or has been consuming

- or intends to consume

- intoxicating liquor

- in a designated public place

the constable may require the person

- not to consume in that place anything which is, or *which the constable reasonably believes to be* intoxicating liquor;
- to surrender anything in his/her possession which is, *or which the constable reasonably believes to be* intoxicating liquor or a container for such

and the constable may dispose of anything so surrendered in such a manner as he/she considers appropriate (s. 12).

This power is among those that can be conferred on a Police Community Support Officer designated under sch. 4 to the Police Reform Act 2002 and a person accredited under sch. 5 to that Act (**see chapter** 2).

Although there is nothing to prevent the use of this power when dealing with people under 18 years of age, there is a power designed specifically in relation to young people (**see para. 10.6.4**).

Any offence under s. 12 (see below) is a 'penalty offence' for the purposes of s. 1 of the Criminal Justice and Police Act 2001 (**see para. 2.5.1**).

OFFENCE:    **Failing to comply with requirement—*Criminal Justice and Police Act 2001, s. 12(4)***
- Triable summarily • Fine
*(Arrestable offence)*

The Criminal Justice and Police Act 2001, s. 12(4) states:

> A person who fails without reasonable excuse to comply with a requirement imposed on him under subsection (2) commits an offence.

---

**KEYNOTE**

This offence will not be made out if the person has a 'reasonable excuse' for not complying. Although there is no requirement for the officer to be in uniform, *the officer imposing the requirement* must tell the person that the above behaviour will amount to an offence. Failure to do so will almost certainly provide the person with a defence; it may also affect the lawfulness of any arrest. It seems a little odd that, although these powers are designed to deal with on the spot issues to avoid alcohol-related disorder, the power of arrest is for an arrestable offence under s. 24(2) of the Police and Criminal Evidence Act 1984 which allows for a person to be arrested some considerable time after the offence has been committed (or is suspected to have been committed)—see chapter 2.

---

## 10.8    Licensed premises

### 10.8.1    Failing to produce a licence

OFFENCE:    **Failing to produce a licence—*Licensing Act 1964, s. 185***
- Triable summarily • Fine
*(No specific power of arrest)*

The Licensing Act 1964, s. 185 states:

> If the holder of a justices' licence, an occasional licence, a canteen licence, an order under section 87A of this Act or a general or special order of exemption, on being ordered by a justice of the peace or constable to produce it for examination, fails to do so within a reasonable time he shall be liable . . .

---

**KEYNOTE**

Section 87A is unlikely to be relevant on many occasions—it relates to on-licences at vineyards. There appears to be no restriction on the time or place when such a demand can be made. However, for a power of entry onto licensed premises, see below.

---

### 10.8.2 Power of constable to enter licensed premises

The Licensing Act 1964, s. 186(1) states:

> (1) For the purpose of preventing or detecting the commission of any offence against this Act, a constable may enter licensed premises, a licensed canteen or premises for which or any part of which a special hours certificate is in force under section 78 or 78ZA of this Act—
>
> (a) at any time within the hours specified in relation to the premises in subsection (1A) of this section, and
>
> (b) in the case of premises for which a justices' licence is in force or a licensed canteen, at any time outside those hours when he suspects, with some reasonable cause, that such an offence is being or is about to be committed there.

---

**KEYNOTE**

The power to enter under the circumstances in s. 186(1)(b) has a preventive element and may be exercised where the officer has reasonable cause to suspect that an offence is about to be committed.

The order under s. 78ZA is another rare one—it relates to special hours certificates to registered clubs undergoing alteration.

Under s. 186(1A), the hours referred to above are:

- in the case of licensed premises (other than premises which are licensed premises by virtue only of an occasional licence) or a licensed canteen, the permitted hours and the first half hour after the end of any period forming part of those hours;

- in the case of premises for which an occasional licence is in force, the hours specified in the licence;

- in the case of premises for which (or for any part of which), a special hours certificate is in force under s. 78 (or s. 78ZA) of the 1964 Act, the hours beginning at 11 pm and ending 30 minutes after the end of the permitted hours fixed by s. 76 of the Act.

---

OFFENCE: **Failing to admit a constable—*Licensing Act 1964, s. 186(2)***
- Triable summarily • Fine
*(No specific power of arrest)*

The Licensing Act 1964, s. 186 states:

> (2) If any person, himself or by any person in his employ or acting with his consent, fails to admit a constable who demands entry to premises in pursuance of this section he shall be liable.

**KEYNOTE**

The effect of the above is that a constable may enter:

- Licensed premises (other than premises covered only by an occasional licence)—including licensed canteens—at any time during permitted hours and during the first half hour following the end of any period forming part of those hours.
- Premises for which an occasional licence is in force —during the hours specified in that licence.
- Premises for which (or for any part of which) a special hours certificate is in force—during the hours beginning at 11 pm and ending 30 minutes after the end of the permitted hours.
- Any licensed premises for which a justices' licence is in force (including a licensed canteen)—at any time outside the permitted hours where the constable reasonably suspects that an offence against the Licensing Act 1964 is being, or is about to be committed.

A constable seeking admission must identify himself/herself and demand admission (*Alexander* v *Rankin* [1899] 1 F 58).

The power to enter licensed premises during and immediately after permitted hours does not require any suspicion of an offence being committed. Although the offence under s. 186(2) carries no power of arrest, there is a power of arrest in relation to the obstruction of a police officer under circumstances where a breach of the peace is likely to be occasioned (see Crime, chapter 8).

Section 187 makes provision for a warrant to enter and search licensed premises to be issued by a magistrate.

10.8.3    **Exclusion of people from licensed premises**

Under the Licensed Premises (Exclusion of Certain Persons) Act 1980, courts may exclude people from licensed premises.

The power applies where any offence involving violence, or the threat of violence is committed on licensed premises. In such cases, a court may make an order that the offender cannot enter those licensed premises (or any other licensed premises specified) without the express consent of the licensee or his/her agent. Such an order may remain in force for any period between three months and two years.

Power to expel

The Licensed Premises (Exclusion of Certain Persons) Act 1980, s. 3 states:

> Without prejudice to any other right to expel a person from premises, the licensee of licensed premises or his servant or agent may expel from those premises any person who has entered or whom he reasonably suspects of having entered the premises in breach of an exclusion order; and a constable shall on the demand of the licensee or his servant or agent help to expel from licensed premises any person whom the constable reasonably suspects of having entered in breach of an exclusion order.

**KEYNOTE**

This power is similar to that above (see para. 10.7.1) in that the constable is obliged to help the licensee etc. to expel the person.

OFFENCE:    **Entering licensed premises in breach of exclusion order—*Licensed Premises (Exclusion of Certain Persons) Act 1980, s. 2(1)***
- Triable summarily • One month's imprisonment and/or fine
*(No specific power of arrest)*

The Licensed Premises (Exclusion of Certain Persons) Act 1980, s. 2 states:

> (1) A person who enters any premises in breach of an exclusion order shall be guilty of an offence.

---

**KEYNOTE**

In addition to exclusion, a person who has been charged with an offence may be subject to certain bail conditions which also prevent him/her from entering particular premises (for bail generally, see **Evidence and Procedure, chapter 5**).

---

10.8.4 ### Closure orders

The Criminal Justice and Police Act 2001 has introduced further police powers to tackle disorder and disturbance connected with certain licensed premises. Although these powers are relatively straightforward, the legislation is complicated by the fact that there are two separate types of closure order, one for some (though not all) licensed premises and the other for *unlicensed* premises. Strictly speaking, the latter orders should not qualify for inclusion in a chapter called 'licensed premises'. However, to include them anywhere else would be daft.

The following provisions amount to a significant interference with a number of key individual European Convention rights (**see chapter 2**) and, as such, the Human Rights Act considerations should be borne firmly in mind at each stage.

#### Closure orders: licensed premises

Like some powers under the Police and Criminal Evidence Act 1984, these powers are 'rank specific'. They apply to licensed premises other than off-licences (**see para. 10.3.2**), premises where an occasional licence is in force (**see para 10.4.2**) or premises such as theatres which have a 'notice' under s. 199(c) of the Licensing Act 1964.

Closure orders are basically orders that can be made in 'blocks' of up to 24 hours; breaching such orders is, as you would expect, an offence.

Again as you would expect, the legislation sets out who can make closure orders, when and how they can do it and what procedures must be followed; it also sets out the sanctions for breaching them and the consequences for licensees if they have such an order made.

As with any such powers, the application of the Human Rights Act 1998 is critical here, not only because of the Act's general importance on the activities of the police, but also because the general exemption from damages that applies to police officers and their chief officers in making closure orders does not apply if those damages are awarded for a breach of the 1998 Act (see below).

#### Police powers to make closure orders

A police officer of the rank of inspector or above may make an order requiring relevant licensed premises to be closed for a period not exceeding 24 hours if he/she reasonably believes that:

- there *is* disorder on, or in the vicinity of and related to the premises or

- there is *likely* to be disorder on, or in the vicinity of and related to the premises

and, in either case, he/she reasonably believes that the order is *necessary* in the interests of public safety; or

- a disturbance is being caused to the public by excessive noise emitted from the premises and the closure of the premises is *necessary* to prevent the disturbance

(s. 179A of the Licensing Act 1964).

Clearly the officer will have to be prepared to justify and provide evidence of his/her belief.

In determining whether to make a closure order the officer must consider the conduct of the licensee or the manager in relation to any disorder or disturbance (s. 179A(3)). The wording of the section does not specify that any such conduct being considered need be conduct *on that occasion* and it may be that past conduct by the licensee or manager needs to be considered. In any event, record keeping by the police in relation to such conduct is advisable.

### The order

A closure order comes into force as soon as *written* notice of it is given by a constable (i.e. a police officer and not necessarily the inspector or above who makes it) to the licensee or the manager (s. 179A(5)). Because another police officer of any rank may give the written notice bringing the order into effect, the inspector (or above) who makes the order need not be present at the premises. This does not mean that the power can be delegated to an officer below the rank of inspector.

A closure order must state:

- which premises are to be closed
- the period for which they must be closed
- the grounds for making the order

(s. 179A(4)).

In addition, the order must state the procedural matters that have to be followed once an order is made (see below), namely the consideration of the order by the relevant justices, the powers to extend, revoke, cancel or alter the order and the possible effect on any licence.

Once an order is made, the premises must be closed immediately for the period specified, unless it is cancelled (see below).

### Procedure following an order being made

Either the officer making the order or an officer of the rank of inspector or above designated for this purpose by the chief officer for that area (e.g. a designated licensing inspector) must apply to the relevant justices for them to consider the closure order *as soon as reasonably practicable* after the order has come into force (s. 179B(1)). He/she must also give a statutory notice to the relevant chief executive to the licensing justices (s. 179F).

The relevant justices must, *as soon as reasonably practicable*, consider whether to exercise their powers to revoke the order (and any extension), order the premises to remain or to be closed until the next licensing sessions or make any other order as they think fit in relation to the premises (s. 179B(2) and (3)).

In considering whether to order the premises to be or stay closed, the justices must consider whether the closure is necessary:

- in the interests of either public safety because of disorder/likely disorder on or in the vicinity of the premises, or
- to ensure that no disturbance is/is likely to be caused to the public by excessive noise from the premises

depending on the reason for the police officer making the closure order in the first place.

### Extension of a closure order

If, before the end of the closure order (or any extension to it), the officer making the order or an officer of the rank of inspector or above designated for this purpose by the chief officer reasonably believes that the relevant justices will not have considered the matter *and* that closure is necessary:

* in the interests of either public safety because of disorder/likely disorder on or in the vicinity of the premises, or
* to ensure that no disturbance is/is likely to be caused to the public by excessive noise from the premises

as appropriate, he/she may extend the closure order for a further period not exceeding 24 hours from the end of the previous closure period (see s. 179C). As with the original closure order, any extension comes into force as soon as a police officer has given written notice of it to the licensee or manager.

Although the wording of s. 179C allows more than one extension to be made provided the relevant conditions above are met, an extension cannot come into force unless the written notice of it was given *before the end* of the previous closure period (s. 179C(4)).

### Cancellation

The officer who made the closure order or, if there is one, the designated officer (see above) *must* cancel the order and any extension if he/she does not reasonably believe that closure is *necessary*:

* in the interests of either public safety because of disorder/likely disorder on or in the vicinity of the premises, or
* to ensure that no disturbance is/is likely to be caused to the public by excessive noise from the premises

as appropriate and such an officer *may* cancel the order and any extension at any time after it has been made but before it has been considered by the relevant justices (see s. 179D).

Where an order or extension is cancelled, as you would expect, written notice must be given to the licensee or the manager. However, although the officer who made the order (or the designated officer if there is one) has to ensure that such a notice is given, there is no requirement that the person giving it must be a police officer—unlike the notice of closure or extension (see s. 179D(3)).

### Consequences of closure orders

Where a closure order has been made the relevant justices have to consider the matter at the next licensing sessions. In doing so, the justices may revoke the licensee's licence altogether or attach conditions to it. There is an appeal procedure allowing application to the Crown Court (see s. 179G). There are several offences involved with breaching any closure order and, given the consequences for any licensee, it is likely that the threat of a closure order will often be sufficient to achieve the appropriate outcome.

Police officers are not liable for any relevant damages resulting from the proper exercise of their functions in good faith in relation to closure orders or extensions, nor is the chief officer of police (s. 179I). Both police officers and their chief officers may be liable in damages for an unlawful act or omission under s. 6(1) of the Human Rights Act 1998 (as to which, **see chapter** 2).

OFFENCE: **Contravening closure order—*Licensing Act 1964, ss. 179A(6) and 179B(5)***

> • Triable summarily • Three months' imprisonment and/or fine up to £20,000
> *(No specific power of arrest)*

The Licensing Act 1964, ss. 179A(6) and 179B(5) state:

179A—(6) A person who, without reasonable excuse, permits relevant licensed premises to be open in contravention of a closure order or any extension of it shall be guilty of an offence . . .

197B—(5) A person who, without reasonable excuse, permits relevant licensed premises to be open in contravention of an order made under subsection (3)(b) of this section shall be guilty of an offence...

---

**KEYNOTE**

The first of the above offences relates to the contravention of an order made by a police officer while the second refers to contravention of a further order made by justices after they have been notified by the police of an order having been made.

There is also a summary offence of failing to comply with, or contravening any other order that the justices may make after being notified of a closure order.

There is also a specific offence for permitting premises to be open in contravention of an order by justices to consider the revocation of a licensee's licence (see s. 179E(8)).

Premises will be 'open' if any person other than the licensee, the manager or their families enter the premises *and* purchase or is supplied with *any item of food, drink or any item usually sold on the premises.* This is clearly a very wide provision going well beyond the sale of intoxicating liquor to paying customers.

All of these offences can also be committed by a body corporate (e.g. a brewery) where it is proved that the offence was committed with the consent, connivance or neglect of a director, manager or company officer (see s. 179J).

---

OFFENCE: **Failing to leave premises—*Licensing Act 1964, s. 179H(2)***
- Triable summarily • Fine

*(No specific power of arrest)*

The Licensing Act 1964, s. 179H(2) states:

(2) Any person who without reasonable excuse fails to leave the premises when asked to do so, for the purposes of ensuring compliance with the order concerned (or with any extension of a closure order or with section 179E(7) of this Act), by the holder of the justices' licence for the premises or any manager of the premises shall be guilty of an offence.

---

**KEYNOTE**

The request to leave the premises must be made by the licensee of those premises or the manager.

A police officer is under a duty, on the request of the licensee or manager, or any agent or servant of either of them, to help them remove anyone who is requested to leave under the above provision from the premises. This duty is the same as that relating to drunken and quarrelsome people (see para. 10.7.1).

---

Closure orders: unlicensed premises

The key distinction between these orders and the ones relating to licensed premises is that, in the latter case, the police can make the order while, in the circumstances below, the police simply issue a notice which may lead to a magistrate's order being made.

Where a constable is satisfied that any premises (including land or any place whether covered or not):

- *are being* used or
- *have been* used within the last 24 hours
- for the unlicensed sale/exposure for sale
- of intoxicating liquor
- for consumption on or in the vicinity of the premises

he/she may serve a closure notice (s. 19 of the Criminal Justice and Police Act 2001). Note that the above power is available to any police officer of any rank. These powers may also be exercised by the relevant local authority.

The closure notice must specify the alleged use of the premises, the grounds on which it has been issued and the steps that are required to be taken; it must also state the consequences of the notice (as set out in s. 20 of the Criminal Justice and Police Act 2001).

The closure notice must be served by the officer making it (compare the procedure for closure orders above). The notice *must* be served on the person having control of, or responsibility for the activities carried on at the premises; it must also be served on any person occupying another part of any building or other structure of which the premises form part *if* the constable reasonably believes that, at the time of serving the notice, that person's access would be impeded by the making of a closure order resulting from the notice (s. 19(3) and (4)). This is to alert neighbours and adjoining occupiers of the possibility that an order may be made which restricts access to their property.

The notice *may* also be served on anyone else having such control or responsibility or an interest (i.e. a leaseholder, owner or occupier) in the premises (s. 19(5)). The closure notice can be cancelled by serving a cancellation notice and any cancellation will take effect as soon as the cancellation notice is served on at least one of the above people.

'Serving' of notices for all these purposes will include leaving them at, or posting them to the person's proper address (s. 27 of the 2001 Act).

Where a closure notice has been served, any police officer or local authority may make a complaint to a magistrate no less than seven days after service of the notice (but within six months) seeking a closure order. This effectively gives the owner or person in control etc. of the premises seven days to cease selling intoxicating liquor. If the officer (or local authority) is satisfied that this has ceased and there is no reasonable likelihood of the premises being so used again in the future, no complaint can be made to a magistrate (s. 20(3)).

On receiving a complaint under s. 20, a magistrate may summons anyone served with a closure notice to answer the complaint. Thereafter, the court may make an order requiring the premises to be closed immediately to the public and to remain closed until the police or local authority issue a certificate that the need for the order has ceased. The court can also make other conditions within the order, including a requirement that any defendant pay money into court (see generally s. 21). Sections 23 and 24 of the 2001 Act make provision for applications and complaints against closure orders.

### Enforcement

Where a closure order has been made, a constable or authorised person may (if necessary using reasonable force) enter the premises concerned at any reasonable time and, having so entered, do anything reasonably necessary to secure compliance with the order (s. 25(1)). If required by or on behalf of the owner or occupier, or person in charge of the premises, the constable or authorised person must produce evidence of their identity and authority before entering the premises (s. 25(2)).

Intentionally obstructing a constable or authorised person in the exercise of these— very wide—powers is, as you would expect, a summary offence (s. 25(3)). Similarly, permitting premises to be open in contravention of an order is an offence in the same way as the offence under s. 179E of the Licensing Act 1964 above, as is failing to comply with a closure order generally (see s. 25). The provisions for corporate liability set out in relation to the closure order for licensed premises above also apply to orders relating to unlicensed premises (see s. 26).

## 10.9    **Betting and gaming on premises**

The legislation regulating betting and gaming can be found in:

- the Betting, Gaming and Lotteries Act 1963; and
- the Gaming Act 1968.

### 10.9.1    **Betting**

Betting is not defined in the Betting, Gaming and Lotteries Act 1963 but is usually taken to mean the staking of money or something of value on the forecast outcome of an event which is in doubt at the time the stake is made.

Generally betting is not prohibited but it does become unlawful under certain circumstances:

- If it takes place on premises other than authorised premises, such as licensed dog-tracks and betting offices (s. 1). If everyone involved in the betting either lives or works on the premises concerned, the provisions of the 1963 Act do not apply.
- If it takes place in a street or public place (other than places such as licensed racetracks on race days) (s. 8).
- If it involves a person under 18 (s. 21).

#### Bookmakers and betting offices

A bookmaker is a person who receives or negotiates bets, whether on his/her own account or as a servant or agent to another (s. 55 of the 1963 Act). Bookmakers working for themselves or for others require a permit (unless they are registered pools promoters) (s. 2). Carrying on a business as a bookmaker without a permit to do so is a summary offence (s. 21).

Betting offices must be licensed and s. 10 and sch. 4 to the 1963 Act set out the conditions which must be adhered to by betting offices. These conditions include the opening hours (between 7 am and 6.30 pm), the posting of certain notices in betting offices and the provision of entertainment and refreshment. They also include strict regulation of any advertising of or in a betting office. At the time of writing, betting offices must remain closed on Christmas Day, Good Friday and Sundays.

#### Enforcement

Under s. 10(2) of the 1963 Act the licensee (or servant) may refuse to admit or may expel anyone who is drunk, quarrelsome or violent or whose presence on the premises is likely to attract a penalty for the licensee (e.g. children). These provisions are similar to those relating to bars and pubs under the Licensing Act 1964 (**see para. 10.7**).

#### Police powers

Section 10 of the 1963 Act states:

(3) Any constable may, on the request of the licensee or any servant or agent of the licensee, help to expel from a licensed betting office any person whom the constable has reasonable cause to believe to be liable to be expelled therefrom under subsection (2) of this section; and the constable may use such force as may be required for that purpose.

(4) Any constable may enter any licensed betting office for the purpose of ascertaining whether the provisions of subsection (1) of this section are being complied with, and any person who obstructs any constable in the exercise of his powers under this subsection shall be liable on summary conviction to a fine.

---

**KEYNOTE**

As with the corresponding provisions for licensed premises, the power given to police officers is to assist the licensee (or servant) to remove people from the relevant premises, although in the above case it is not a duty to do so (see para. 10.7.1).

A person convicted of an ofence under s 10(1) (failing to manage the premises in accordance with the provisions of sch. 4) may have his/her betting office licence cancelled by the court (s. 10A).

---

10.9.2 **Gaming**

The main piece of legislation regulating gaming is the Gaming Act 1968. Divided into four parts, the Act regulates:

- gaming elsewhere other than on licensed or registered premises (part I);
- gaming on premises which are licensed or registered (part II);
- gaming machines (part III);
- gaming at functions and parties (part IV).

Unlike betting, 'gaming' is defined and means the playing of a game of chance for winnings in money (or money's worth) whether anyone playing the game is at risk of losing any such money/money's worth or not (s. 52(1) of the Gaming Act 1968).

This definition means that even 'rigged' games or purely social games where there is no risk of losing money/money's worth are covered.

'Games of chance' do not include athletic games or sports; they do, however, include hybrid games of mixed chance and skill (such as many card games).

At the time of writing there was great excitement at the prospect of the relaxation of this legislation and the introduction of Las Vegas style venues. Until then, the law remains as summarised below.

Gaming other than on authorised premises

As with betting, there are restrictions on gaming in some premises and public places. Where the people playing the game are all residents in a private dwelling or a similar place which is not used as a place of business, gaming may be permitted under certain conditions (see s. 2 of the 1968 Act). For such games to be permitted, no charges must be levied, either on people taking part in such games or on their stakes/winnings (ss. 3 and 4).

It is a summary offence to take part in gaming in a street or public place (s. 5). It is, however, permissible to play games of cribbage and dominoes and other games approved by the licensing justices on licensed premises (see above) (s. 6). Under s. 6(4) justices may impose restrictions on the playing of those games as far as they consider it necessary to ensure that such gaming does not involve high stakes or does not become an inducement to people to come to the premises.

Gaming using some types of gaming machines with limited payouts may also be approved by the licensing justices in respect of licensed premises (see s. 34 and sch. 9).

Gaming on authorised premises

Gaming on premises which are licensed or registered is subject to strict regulations under the 1968 Act. The most important of those regulations relate to the age and status of the people taking part (i.e. they must be at least 18 years old and club members/guests).

Section 43 provides a power for police officers to enter premises licensed under the 1968 Act at any reasonable time to ascertain whether the Act has been contravened (see below).

The use of gaming machines is regulated by the 1968 Act which generally creates two main types of machine:

- Jackpot machines which:
  - have a charge limit for playing;
  - cannot be used when the relevant premises are open to the public;
  - must only have prizes in coins from that machine; and
  - for which premises must have a licence or be registered (under sch. 7).

- Amusements with prize machines which:
  - have a charge limit for playing;
  - have restrictions on prize money/tokens;
  - have restrictions on non-money prizes; and
  - for which premises must: have a permit (under sch. 9); have a licence or be registered and have no jackpot machines; form part of a travelling showman's 'pleasure fair'.

The respective amounts that can be charged and won by machine owners and players change frequently and the most recent regulations should be referred to when dealing with gaming offences under the Act.

There are, however, general exemptions for all gaming machines when they are used in connection with non-commercial entertainment on unlicensed or unregistered premises where all proceeds after expenses have been deducted are used other than for private gain (e.g. dinner-dances, garden fêtes, etc.) (s. 33).

Further concessions are made for gaming (by machines or otherwise) at charitable and not-for-profit events (Pt. IV). The 1968 Act imposes certain restrictions on admission charges, the type of gaming which may take place and the total value of any prizes. As might be expected, all proceeds after the deduction of reasonable costs must be used other than for private gain.

### Casinos

Casinos must have a gaming licence. Such licences are only issued after a very thorough process which includes an examination of the suitability of both the applicant and the location of the premises. Applicants must specify which of the permitted games (see sch. 2 of the 1968 Act) will be played at the club; they must also obtain a Certificate of Consent from the Gaming Board of Great Britain to support their application. The certificate will specify the period for which the licence may be requested. Applicants will then have to appear before a hearing held by the justices four times a year. The Gaming Board are very influential in the process of licensing and renewal and should be consulted in any cases involving impropriety by a licence holder or on premises licensed for gaming.

The law in this area has been modified by the Deregulation (Casinos) Order 1999 (SI 1999 No. 2136), the contents of which are explained in Home Office Circular 39/99.

### Police powers

Section 43 of the 1968 Act states:

(2) Any...constable may at any reasonable time enter any premises in respect of which a licence under this Act is for the time being in force, and while on the premises may—
  (a) inspect the premises and any machine or other equipment on the premises, and any book or document on the premises, which he reasonably requires to inspect for the purpose of ascertaining whether a contravention of this Act or of any regulations made under it is being or has been committed;
  (b) take copies of any such book or document or of any entry in it; and

(c) if any information reasonably required by him for that purpose is contained in a computer and is accessible from the premises, require it to be produced in a form in which it can be taken away and in which it is visible and legible.

(3) If any person, being the holder of a licence under this Act in respect of any premises or a person acting on behalf of the holder of such a licence—

(a) fails without reasonable excuse to admit...[a] constable who demands admission to the premises in pursuance of subsection (2) of this section, or

(b) on being required by...[a] constable to do so, fails without reasonable excuse to permit the... constable to inspect the premises or any machine or other equipment on the premises, or

(c) on being required by...[a] constable to produce any book or document in his possession or under his control which relates to those premises and which the...constable reasonably requires to inspect for the purpose specified in subsection (2) of this section, fails without reasonable excuse to produce it to the...constable and to permit the...constable (if he so desires) to take copies of it or of an entry in it, or

(ca) fails without reasonable excuse to comply with a requirement imposed in relation to those premises under subsection (2)(c) of this section; or

(d) ...

the holder of the licence shall be guilty of an offence.

---

### KEYNOTE

These powers also apply to Gaming Board inspectors. Section 43(5) provides a power for magistrates to issue a search warrant in respect of premises licensed for gaming; it also creates offences of failing to comply with requirements made under such a warrant.

For a full discussion of the law relating to betting, gaming and lotteries, together with the functions of the Gaming Board of Great Britain, see *Paterson's Licensing Acts* published annually by LexisNexis UK.

For general police powers of entry, search and seizure, **see chapter 2**.

---

# 11 Offences and powers relating to information

## 11.1 Introduction

This chapter considers the offences and powers concerned with accessing computer programs and also the handling of personal data held on such programs. In considering what follows in this chapter, it is worth noting the specific police powers in relation to gaining access to stored data, particularly where the data is encrypted in some form (**see chapter 2**).

Although not capable of being 'stolen' or 'damaged' (*Oxford* v *Moss* (1978) 68 Cr App Rep 183) (**see Crime, chapters 12 and 14**), information can be both extremely valuable and damaging. The Official Secrets Acts cover many of the situations involving information relating to the State (see *Blackstone's Criminal Practice*, 2003, section B9). Similarly, the Terrorism Act 2000 creates arrestable offences covering the unlawful collection of information likely to be useful to those planning acts of terrorism and failing to disclose information relating to terrorism or its investigation (**see chapter 4** and also *Blackstone's Criminal Practice*, 2003, section B10); it also broadens the definition of terrorism to encompass, among other things, interference with computer networks.

### 11.1.1 Access to information

Government departments and some other public authorities are required to make certain information available to the public and to provide responses to specific requests seeking certain types of information. This requirement arose principally from the Code of Practice on Access to Government Information which is a non-statutory scheme. However, the government clearly signalled its intention to extend these requirements to many other public authorities (including the police) and set up a new statutory system under the control of a specially appointed Commissioner. Those proposals now appear in the Freedom of Information Act 2000.

### 11.1.2 Freedom of Information Act 2000

The 2000 Act gives people a general right to access information that is being held by public authorities and will be phased in over five years. Introducing the general right of access to information held by public authorities (subject to a number of exceptions and conditions), the Act also imposes a duty on those public authorities to disclose certain types of information. The Act also creates the office of Information Commissioner whose remit also extends to the provisions of the Data Protection Act 1998 (as to which, **see para. 11.3**). Public authorities such as the police, the Crown Prosecution Service and government departments, along with National Health Service bodies, schools and colleges are required to draw up a publication scheme setting out their specific plans for making certain types of information available. Under proposed timetables for implementation the police had to set out their publication schemes by June 2003.

## 11.2 Offences under the Computer Misuse Act 1990

OFFENCE: **Unauthorised access to computer ('hacking')—***Computer Misuse Act 1990, s. 1*
- Triable summarily • Six months' imprisonment and/or a fine
*(No specific power of arrest)*

The Computer Misuse Act 1990, s. 1 states:

(1) A person is guilty of an offence if—
 (a) he causes a computer to perform any function with intent to secure access to any program or data held in any computer;
 (b) the access he intends to secure is unauthorised; and
 (c) he knows at the time when he causes the computer to perform the function that that is the case.

(2) The intent a person has to have to commit an offence under this section need not be directed at—
 (a) any particular program or data;
 (b) a program or data of any particular kind; or
 (c) a program or data held in any particular computer.

---

### KEYNOTE

This offence involves 'causing a computer to perform any function', which means more than simply looking at material on a screen or having any physical contact with computer hardware. In the latter case an offence of criminal damage may be appropriate. Any attempt to log on would involve getting the computer to perform a function (even if the function is to deny you access!). 'Computer' is not defined and therefore must be given its ordinary meaning. Given the multiple functions of many electronic devices such as mobile phones, this could arguably bring them within the ambit of the Act.

As this is a summary offence it cannot be 'attempted' in the sense of the Criminal Attempts Act 1981 (**see Crime, chapter 3**). However, the wording of the substantive offence covers virtually every activity from the switching on of the computer, including many activities which would ordinarily be classed as 'merely preparatory'.

Any access must be 'unauthorised'. If the defendant is authorised to *access* a computer, albeit for restricted purposes, then it was originally held that he/she did not commit this offence if he/she then *used* any information for some other unauthorised purpose (e.g. police officers using data from the Police National Computer for private gain (*DPP* v *Bignell* [1998] 1 Cr App R 1)). However, this case was overruled by the House of Lords where an employee of American Express accessed accounts that fell outside her normal scope of work and passed on the information to credit card forgers. Their lordships held that, although she was authorised to access certain data generally, she was not authorised to access the specific data involved—*R* v *Bow Street Metropolitan Stipendiary Magistrate, ex parte Government of the USA* [2000] 2 AC 216. This case still illustrates that the purpose of the Act is to address unauthorised access as opposed to unauthorised use of data and behaviour such as looking over a computer operator's shoulder to read what is on their screen would not be covered (for offences covering the protection of data, **see para. 11.3**).

In order to prove the offence under s. 1 you must show that the defendant intended to secure access to the program or data. This is therefore an offence of 'specific intent' (**see Crime, chapter 1**) and lesser forms of *mens rea* such as recklessness will not do.

You must also show that the defendant knew the access was unauthorised.

Section 11(2) of the 1990 Act states that proceedings for an offence under s. 1 must be brought within a period of six months from the date on which evidence sufficient in the opinion of the prosecutor to warrant the proceedings comes to his/her knowledge. It has been held that anyone actively involved in the making or prosecuting of a charge (e.g. the officer in charge of the investigation) can be 'the prosecutor' for this purpose and that the expression is not restricted to the Crown Prosecution Service (*Morgans* v *DPP* [1999] 1 WLR 968). It was also held that the time limit began from the date when sufficient evidence to warrant a prosecution had actually come to the knowledge of the prosecutor, i.e. when the evidence was assembled by the officer in charge of the case. It did not mean the point at which the prosecutor *formed the opinion* that the evidence was sufficient. This meant that, where the papers from the case had been assembled but the officer in charge had gone sick, leaving a long delay before the Crown Prosecution Service were able to form the opinion that there was sufficient evidence to warrant proceedings, the proceedings were 'out of time' and the defendant's conviction was quashed.

---

The 1990 Act defines a number of its terms at s. 17 which states:

(2) A person secures access to any program or data held in a computer if by causing a computer to perform any function he—
   (a) alters or erases the program or data;
   (b) copies or moves it to any storage medium other than that in which it is held or to a different location in the storage medium in which it is held;
   (c) uses it; or
   (d) has it output from the computer in which it is held (whether by having it displayed or in any other manner);

and references to access to a program or data (and to an intent to secure such access) shall be read accordingly.

(3) For the purposes of subsection (2)(c) above a person uses a program if the function he causes the computer to perform—
   (a) causes the program to be executed; or
   (b) is itself a function of the program.

(4) For the purposes of subsection (2)(d) above—
   (a) a program is output if the instructions of which it consists are output; and
   (b) the form in which any such instructions or any other data is output (and in particular whether or not it represents a form in which, in the case of instructions, they are capable of being executed or, in the case of data, it is capable of being processed by a computer) is immaterial.

(5) Access of any kind by any person to any program or data held in a computer is unauthorised if—
   (a) he is not himself entitled to control access of the kind in question to the program or data; and
   (b) he does not have consent to access by him of the kind in question to the program or data from any person who is so entitled

but this subsection is subject to section 10.

(6) References to any program or data held in a computer include references to any program or data held in any removable storage medium which is for the time being in the computer; and a computer is to be regarded as containing any program or data held in any such medium.

(7) A modification of the contents of any computer takes place if, by the operation of any function of the computer concerned or any other computer—
   (a) any program or data held in the computer concerned is altered or erased; or
   (b) any program or data is added to its contents;
and any act which contributes towards causing such a modification shall be regarded as causing it.

(8) Such a modification is unauthorised if—
   (a) the person whose act causes it is not himself entitled to determine whether the modification should be made; and
   (b) he does not have consent to the modification from any person who is so entitled.

S 17 Amended by Criminal Justice and Public Order Act 1994 s 162

---

## KEYNOTE

Securing access will therefore include:

- altering or erasing a program or data;

- copying or moving a program or data to a new storage medium;

- using data or having it displayed or 'output' in any form from the computer in which it is held.

Under s. 17(5) access is 'unauthorised' if the person is neither entitled to control that type of access to a program or data, nor does he/she have the consent of any person who is so entitled. The provision under s. 17(5)(a) was the basis for the decision in *Bow Street* above. This definition does not affect the powers available to any 'enforcement officers', i.e. police officers or other people charged with a duty of investigating offences (s. 10).

For the powers of a police officer to seize data contained on a computer, **see** chapter 2.

A modification will also take place if, by the operation of *any* computer (not just the one being 'misused') any program or data in the computer concerned is altered, erased or added. A modification is 'unauthorised' if the person whose act causes it is neither entitled to determine whether that modification should be made, nor has the consent of anyone who is so entitled.

---

OFFENCE: **Unauthorised access with intent to commit arrestable offence—** ***Computer Misuse Act 1990, s. 2***

  • Triable either way  • Five years' imprisonment and/or a fine on indictment;
    six months' imprisonment and/or a fine summarily
  *(Arrestable offence)*

The Computer Misuse Act 1990, s. 2 states:

(1) A person is guilty of an offence under this section if he commits an offence under section 1 above ('the unauthorised access offence') with intent—
   (a) to commit an offence to which this section applies; or
   (b) to facilitate the commission of such an offence (whether by himself or by any other person); and the offence he intends to commit or facilitate is referred to below in this section as the further offence.

(2) This section applies to offences—
   (a) for which the sentence is fixed by law; or
   (b) for which a person who has attained the age of twenty-one years [eighteen in relation to England and Wales] and has no previous convictions may be sentenced to imprisonment for a term of five years (or, in England and Wales, might be so sentenced but for the restrictions imposed by section 33 of the Magistrates' Courts Act 1980).

(3) It is immaterial for the purposes of this section whether the further offence is to be committed on the same occasion as the unauthorised access offence or on any future occasion.

(4) A person may be guilty of an offence under this section even though the facts are such that the commission of the further offence is impossible.

---

**KEYNOTE**

The defendant must be shown to have had the required intent at the time of the access or other *actus reus* (see Crime, chapter 2).

The 'further' offences must come under the particular classes of arrestable offence set out under s. 24 of the Police and Criminal Evidence Act 1984. This does not include offences that are made 'arrestable' by virtue only of their inclusion in the list under s. 24(2) of the 1984 Act (**see** chapter 2). The intended further offence does not have to be committed at the same time, but may be committed in the future (e.g. where the data is used to commit an offence of blackmail or to secure the transfer of funds from a bank account).

The provision as to impossibility (s. 2(4)) means that a person would still commit the offence if he/she tried, say, to access the bank account of a person who did not in fact exist (for impossibility generally, **see** Crime, chapter 3).

---

OFFENCE: **Unauthorised modification of computer material—***Computer Misuse Act 1990, s. 3***

  • Triable either way  • Five years' imprisonment and/or a fine on indictment;
    six months' imprisonment and/or a fine summarily
  *(Arrestable offence)*

The Computer Misuse Act 1990, s. 3 states:

(1) A person is guilty of an offence if—
   (a) he does any act which causes an unauthorised modification of the contents of any computer; and
   (b) at the time when he does the act he has the requisite intent and the requisite knowledge.

(2) For the purposes of subsection (1)(b) above the requisite intent is an intent to cause a modification of the contents of any computer and by so doing—
   (a) to impair the operation of any computer;
   (b) to prevent or hinder access to any program or data held in any computer; or
   (c) to impair the operation of any such program or the reliability of any such data.

(3) The intent need not be directed at—
   (a) any particular computer;
   (b) any particular program or data or a program or data of any particular kind; or
   (c) any particular modification or a modification of any particular kind.

(4) For the purposes of subsection (1)(b) above the requisite knowledge is knowledge that any modification he intends to cause is unauthorised.

(5) It is immaterial for the purposes of this section whether an unauthorised modification or any intended effect of it of a kind mentioned in subsection (2) above is, or is intended to be, permanent or merely temporary.

(6) For the purposes of the Criminal Damage Act 1971 a modification of the contents of a computer shall not be regarded as damaging any computer or computer storage medium unless its effect on that computer or computer storage medium impairs its physical condition.

---

**KEYNOTE**

This offence covers a whole range of behaviour provided that the defendant is shown to have had the required intent *and* knowledge at the time.

Causing a computer to record that information came from one source when it in fact came from another clearly affects the reliability of that information for the purposes of s. 3. This was made clear by the Divisional Court in a case involving the unauthorised use of international e-mails from within the computer network of a New York-based company which provided financial information (*Zezev* v *USA; Yarimaka* v *Governor of HM Prison Brixton* [2002] EWHC 589).

Implanting viruses would be caught by s. 3.

The purpose of s. 3(6) was to avoid future convictions such as that in *Cox* v *Riley* (1986) 83 Cr App R 54 where the defendant deleted information from a computer card and was convicted of criminal damage (as to which, see Crime, chapter 14).

For the general powers of seizure (including powers to 'sift' under the Criminal Justice and Police Act 2001) see chapter 2.

---

## 11.3    The Data Protection Act 1998

The Data Protection Act 1984 restricted the use made of some data stored in computer programs. The new Data Protection Act 1998 is intended to implement Council Directive 95/46 in relation to the protection of individuals with regard to the processing and free movement of personal data (see [1995] OJ L281/31).

Most of the 1998 Act came into force on 1 March 2000 but was accompanied by two 'transitional periods'. The first of these periods ended in October 2001 and the second runs until 2007. However, because the second period only affects a very small class of personal data, the Act to all practical intents and purposes came into effect in October 2001.

In essence the Act imposes three key obligations on 'data controllers' (**see para. 11.3.2**), namely notification, abiding by the rights of the data subject and observing the data protection principles (as to which, **see para. 11.3.1**).

One of the key changes brought about by the 1998 Act was the extension of restrictions on the storage of, and access to certain data to 'relevant filing systems'. This means that structured sets of information filed manually—as opposed to being stored on a computer—will also potentially fall within the provisions of the Act.

The 1998 Act provides for Regulations to be made in relation to a number of its sections. Part II of the 1998 Act provides a number of fundamental rights for individuals relating to records containing personal data about them. Section 7 entitles the individual to be given information and explanation by the relevant 'data controller' (see below) about some of that data, to identify the source of it and, under certain circumstances, to be informed as to some decision-making processes involved in its use. Part II makes specific provisions in relation to credit reference agencies and the use of personal data in direct marketing. Provision is made for the compensation of individuals where the requirements of the Act have not been complied with and there is now an Information Tribunal to which people can apply for remedy.

The person having overall responsibility for the implementation and observance of the Act is the Information Commissioner. The Commissioner may issue Codes of Practice; the first of these was issued in March 2002 and covers recruitment and selection. Other parts of the Code that have been published are employment records and monitoring at work.

The 1998 Act places many duties on data users who have to register their systems and the use for which data are held. Most police organisations have Data Protection Officers whose advice should be sought in every case and particularly in relation to the commencement dates and application of the Act's provisions.

Section 1 of the 1998 Act states:

(1) In this Act, unless the context otherwise requires—
'data' means information which—
  (a) is being processed by means of equipment operating automatically in response to instructions given for that purpose,
  (b) is recorded with the intention that it should be processed by means of such equipment,
  (c) is recorded as part of a relevant filing system or with the intention that it should form part of a relevant filing system, or
  (d) does not fall within paragraph (a), (b) or (c) but forms part of an accessible record as defined by section 68.

Accessible records as defined by s. 68(1) include a health record, an educational record and an accessible public record.

'Relevant filing system' means any set of information relating to individuals to the extent that, although the information is not processed by means of equipment operating automatically in response to instructions given for that purpose, the set is structured, either by reference to individuals or by reference to criteria relating to individuals, in such a way that specific information relating to a particular individual is readily accessible (s. 1(1)).

The Data Protection Act 1998 seeks to protect 'personal data', that is,

'data which relate to a living individual who can be identified—(a) from those data, or (b) from those data and other information which is in the possession of, or is likely to come into the possession of, the data controller, and includes any expression of opinion about the individual and any indication of the intentions of the data controller or any other person in respect of the individual' (s. 1(1)).

---

**KEYNOTE**

One of the effects of this legislation, combined with Article 8 of the European Convention on Human Rights (**see chapter 2**), has been to create what might be called a 'law of privacy' previously unrecognised in English and Welsh law.

The development of this area of law can be seen in the 'celeb' cases involving intrusive photographers and journalists (e.g. *Campbell v Mirror Group Newspapers* [2002] EWCA Civ 1373).

The individual must be capable of being identified from the data that the data controller has or is likely to get. This does not mean that the person's name and/or address must be known. If it is possible to distinguish the individual from other people (e.g. by e-mail addresses which contain the person's name or from CCTV film of them) then it may be that the above test is satisfied.

The definition of personal data would apply to data held on police computers about suspected and convicted offenders and may well apply to other similar paper records. Personal data held on the PNC clearly fall within this category (see *R v Rees* [2000] LTL 20 October).

---

The 1998 Act makes special provision in relation to 'sensitive personal data' which it defines (at s. 2) as:

> ... personal data consisting of information as to—
>> (a) the racial or ethnic origin of the data subject,
>> (b) his political opinions,
>> (c) his religious beliefs or other beliefs of a similar nature,
>> (d) whether he is a member of a trade union (within the meaning of the Trade Union and Labour Relations (Consolidation) Act 1992),
>> (e) his physical or mental health or condition,
>> (f) his sexual life,
>> (g) the commission or alleged commission by him of any offence, or
>> (h) any proceedings for any offence committed or alleged to have been committed by him, the disposal of such proceedings or the sentence of any court in such proceedings.

### 11.3.1   Data protection principles and schedules

A crucial element in the 1998 Act is the data protection principles set out at sch. 1. As well as introducing the principles, s. 4 makes it clear that it is the duty of the relevant 'data controller' (see para. 11.3.2) to comply with those principles wherever they apply. Part I of sch. 1 sets out the principles as being:

1. Personal data shall be processed fairly and lawfully and, in particular, shall not be processed unless—
   (a) at least one of the conditions in Schedule 2 is met, and
   (b) in the case of sensitive personal data, at least one of the conditions in Schedule 3 is also met.

2. Personal data shall be obtained only for one or more specified and lawful purposes, and shall not be further processed in any manner incompatible with that purpose or those purposes.

3. Personal data shall be adequate, relevant and not excessive in relation to the purpose or purposes for which they are processed.

4. Personal data shall be accurate and, where necessary, kept up to date.

5. Personal data processed for any purpose or purposes shall not be kept for longer than is necessary for that purpose or those purposes.

6. Personal data shall be processed in accordance with the rights of data subjects under this Act.

7. Appropriate technical and organisational measures shall be taken against unauthorised or unlawful processing of personal data and against accidental loss or destruction of, or damage to, personal data.

8. Personal data shall not be transferred to a country or territory outside the European Economic Area unless that country or territory ensures an adequate level of protection for the rights and freedoms of data subjects in relation to the processing of personal data.

Part II of sch. 1 contains further detail on the interpretation of these principles.

Schedule 2 sets out further conditions that apply to the first principle above, while sch. 3 deals specifically with sensitive personal data. Schedule 4 sets out occasions where the eighth principle above will not apply.

Schedules 5 and 6 make provision for the Data Protection Commissioner and the Data Protection Tribunal, together with a system for hearing appeals.

Schedule 7 makes a number of exemptions from some of the Act's provisions (**see para. 11.3.2**) while Sch. 8 sets out a number of transitional exemptions—especially in relation to manual data—between various dates up to 24 October 2007.

Schedule 9 gives powers and directions for the issuing and executing of search warrants.

Schedule 10 provides for the giving of assistance by the Commissioner in relation to someone bringing an action in connection with 'the special purposes', that is journalistic, artistic or literary purposes.

Schedule 11 deals with educational records, while sch. 12 sets out the authorities in relation to accessible public records.

The other schedules make transitional savings, modifications and repeals.

## 11.3.2 Other duties and responsibilities

Part III of the 1998 Act sets out the responsibilities of data controllers, defined as the people who (alone or jointly) determine the purposes for which and the manner in which any personal data are, or are to be processed (see s. 1(1)).

Personal data must not be processed unless and until the relevant data controller has registered the details ('registrable particulars') set out at s. 16.

Part II imposes responsibility on data controllers to register with the Commissioner and to notify him/her of any changes in the registrable particulars above.

Processing personal data without registration and failing to notify the Commissioner of any relevant changes are offences, triable either way and punishable on indictment with unlimited fines.

If an organisation fails to renew its registration under the Act despite reminders to do so, a court can reasonably infer that the organisation was aware of its omission and that its continued holding and use of personal data 'knowingly' or 'recklessly' is in breach of the relevant provisions (*Information Commissioner* v *Islington London Borough Council* [2002] EWHC Admin 1036).

Part III of the 1998 Act makes certain limited exemptions from the first data protection principle and from the provisions of s. 7 (see above). These exemptions apply to some occasions where personal data are processed for:

- the prevention or detection of crime

- the apprehension or prosecution of offenders

- the assessment or collection of tax or duty.

There is also an exemption from complying with the data protection principles and some other parts of the Act where that exemption is required for the purposes of safeguarding national security.

Regulatory activity (i.e. lawful activities that exist to protect people and organisations from fraud, malpractice or incompetence or to regulate some public bodies) is also exempt from many of the Act's provisions.

Further specific exemptions are made in relation to:

- journalism, literature and art (s. 32);

- research, history and statistics (s. 33);

- information that the data controller is obliged to make available to the public (s. 34);

- personal data processed by an individual for the purposes of his/her personal, family or household affairs (s. 36); and
- matters included in sch. 7 (examination marks and papers, armed forces, judicial appointments, employment by the Crown, corporate finance and forecasts, legal professional privilege and self-incrimination).

Offences under the 1998 Act may not be prosecuted by anyone other than the Commissioner or with the consent of the Director of Public Prosecutions.

# 12 Discrimination and equality

## 12.1 Introduction

This chapter sets out in brief summary the key features of the law relating to equality and discrimination in the workplace. This area of employment law is very specialised and, on occasions, very sensitive. Most police organisations have employee relations or human resources departments to help both managers and employees in these fields. The police staff associations, together with other groups such as the National Black Police Association will also provide help in ensuring that the spirit of this legislation is observed at work.

Most police organisations also have grievance procedures to deal with issues of equality in an informal setting. Although there is a growing array of legislative provisions to protect the rights of various groups within the workplace, recourse to the law is not the only—or even the best—solution to issues of diversity. The government has introduced further legislation aimed at averting litigation through the courts and employment tribunals and encouraging local resolution.

In most circumstances, a chief officer will now be liable for most of the actions of his/her staff in the course of their duties (**see chapter 1**). Generally, this concept of 'vicarious liability' for acts committed by people in the course of their work is passed up the chain to their employer. As *public office-holders* police officers are not 'employees' of their chief officers and therefore there are occasions where chief officers have not been held vicariously liable for wrongful acts committed by their police staff (for further discussion, see *Police Conduct, Complaints and Efficiency*, published by Blackstone Press (OUP)). This situation has attracted some criticism, particularly in the area of race relations. Under the Race Relations Act 1976 as it originally stood, chief officers had been held not to be vicariously liable for the discriminatory behaviour of their officers (see *R v Farah*, The Times, 17 October 1996). Similarly, there has been a lack of clarity as to which public authorities are covered by the provisions of the 1976 Act. As a result of these anomalies, highlighted in a number of cases, not least the inquiry into the death of Stephen Lawrence, the government introduced the Race Relations (Amendment) Act 2000 (see below). Increasingly, employment legislation is being drafted in a way that applies its provisions to police officers and their chief constables/police authorities *as if* they were in an employer–employee relationship. The Police Reform Act 2002 also broadened the vicarious liability of chief officers for the conduct of their officers (**see chapter 1**).

While these issues may now have been resolved, there was, until recently, still uncertainty as to the extent of a chief officer's liability under the Sex Discrimination Act 1975 for the individual acts 361 of his/her officers and the same arguments that preceded the Race Relations (Amendment) Act 2000 could be raised (for these arguments, see *Chief Constable of Bedfordshire v Liversidge* [2002] EWCA Civ 894). However, the introduction of secondary legislation (see below) has now placed the whole area of discrimination on a much clearer footing.

It is worth noting that discrimination and victimisation are included in the Code of Conduct for police officers (**see chapter 1**). Where acts amounting to discrimination take place outside the workplace, the employer and employees may still be caught within the framework of the legislation. So, for instance, where police officers engage in inappropriate sexual behaviour towards a colleague at a work-related social function, a tribunal may be entitled to hold that the function was an extension of the workplace and so hold the chief officer liable for the acts of his/her officers at that function (see *Chief Constable of Lincolnshire* v *Stubbs* [1999] IRLR 81). Similarly, the actions (or inaction) of a fellow officer or supervisor are capable of attracting personal liability to that individual under a claim for discrimination in addition to any claim that the victim might have against the relevant chief officer (see *AM* v *WC* [1999] ICR 1218) though this is an area that is still far from clear.

## 12.2 The law

There are four main sources of primary legislation which deal with equality and discrimination:

- Race Relations Act 1976
- Sex Discrimination Act 1975
- Equal Pay Act 1970
- Disability Discrimination Act 1995.

All of these Acts deal with matters which fall under the heading of employment law as that is the main area of their concern. It should be noted that, other than the 1995 Act, these Acts have been around for over 20 years.

Part-time workers now enjoy generally the right not to be treated less favourably than full-time workers (see the Part-time Workers (Prevention of Less Favourable Treatment) Regulations 2000 (SI 2000 No. 1551 made under Employment Relations Act 1991, s. 42)).

In addition to this legislation, the role of European law in this area is of considerable significance—and is growing all the time. Most important among the various pieces of European legislation are:

- the Equal Treatment Directive (76/207)
- the Equal Pay Directive (75/117)
- case law from the European Court of Justice.

The European Framework Equal Treatment Directive 2000/78 requires Member States to introduce legislation prohibiting discrimination on grounds of sexual orientation and religion by 2 December 2003 and legislation prohibiting discrimination on grounds of age by 2 December 2006.

In response to this and other requirements of the Directive, the government has introduced a series of statutory instruments under the Acts above which now standardise and clarify many of the anomalies in our discrimination law.

There are other pieces of legislation, such as those specific offences under the Public Order Acts (**see chapter 4**) which are aimed at discriminatory behaviour by anyone under certain circumstances. There are also offences under the Code of Conduct (**see chapter 1**) which deal with other forms of discriminatory behaviour by police officers in the course of their duties.

Generally, however, there is no overall legal restriction on discriminatory behaviour. There is no 'Equal Opportunities Act' and the UK has no written constitution protecting the individual from being discriminated against other than in the circumstances described in this·chapter and the specific provisions made under the European Convention on Human Rights (**see chapter 2**). It is worth noting that although Article 14 of the Convention gives individuals a right not to be discriminated against on certain grounds, this right exists alongside the other Convention rights and applies to the way in which *those rights* are protected; it does not grant a free-standing right not to be discriminated against. One of the cornerstones of the European Community, however, is the achievement of equality of treatment for individuals of each Member State within the Community and European law has had a significant influence on the impact of equal opportunities and discrimination (at least on the grounds of sex) in England and Wales.

The purpose of the two main Acts, the Race Relations Act 1976 and the Sex Discrimination Act 1975, was summed up by Waite LJ in *Jones* v *Tower Boot Company Ltd* [1997] 2 All ER 406:

> The legislation . . . broke new ground in seeking to work upon the minds of men and women and thus affect their attitude to the social consequences of differences between the sexes or the distinction of skin colour. Its general thrust was educative, persuasive, and where necessary coercive . . .

His Lordship went to on to say how, against this background, the courts would not adopt a technical or restrictive approach when interpreting the law in this area.

### 12.2.1 Procedure

The procedure relating to claims made against employers was significantly altered by the Employment Rights (Dispute Resolution) Act 1998. The 1998 Act re-named industrial tribunals 'employment tribunals' to convey their function more clearly. The Act went on to make provision for regulations permitting tribunals to determine cases without a full hearing or, at times, without a hearing at all under certain circumstances. It also made provisions for 'compromise agreements' made by relevant independent advisers—as opposed to just qualified lawyers—and set out a new class of individuals, to be known as 'legal officers' who may carry out some of the more straightforward functions currently carried out by tribunal chair people.

## 12.3 The Race Relations Act 1976

The Race Relations Act 1976 deals with racial discrimination, the first type of discrimination to be prohibited in England and Wales. It follows the same definitions as those used in the Sex Discrimination Act 1975 and has a Code of Practice to support it. Matters falling within its parameters are overseen by the Commission for Racial Equality.

Under s. 3, the 1976 Act aims to control discrimination (**see para. 12.10**) on grounds of:

- colour

- race

- nationality

- ethnic or national origins.

The meaning of 'nationality' here is wider than the normal 'legal' meaning and has been held by the Scottish Court of Session to include citizenship acquired at birth (*Souster* v *BBC Scotland* [2001] IRLR 150). As such, an English applicant can be discriminated against by a Scottish employer on the grounds of his/her nationality as occurred in the *Souster* case where the BBC replaced the applicant as a commentator on its 'Rugby Special' with someone of Scottish origin.

Ethnic group is a broad definition which may include any group with a shared culture or history (**see chapter 3**). It does not include Rastafarians (*Crown Suppliers* v *Dawkins* [1993] ICR 517). Speakers of a particular language (e.g. Welsh) are not an 'ethnic' group *per se* (*Gwynedd County Council* v *Jones* [1986] ICR 833); it would need to be shown that such people belonged to a group with a shared culture or history before they come under the provisions of the 1976 Act.

The classifications may need to be revised in the light of the Human Rights Act 1998.

The Act has been amended in two main ways since its inception. The first is by the amending Act set out in the next paragraph; the second is by the Race Relations Act 1976 (Amendment) Regulations 2003 (SI 2003 No. 1626). The Regulations came into force in July 2003 and make several extensions to the Act in a number of areas including the meaning of indirect discrimination (as to which **see para. 12.10.2**), the inclusion of harassment as a specific category of unlawful treatment (as to which **see para. 12.10.3**) and the broadening of the Act's ambit to cover organisations and people that were formerly excluded.

## 12.4    The Race Relations (Amendment) Act 2000

As discussed above, the Race Relations Act 1976 made it unlawful to discriminate against others on the grounds of race in relation to certain areas, namely employment, training and education, the provision of goods, facilities and services and some other specific activities. The 1976 Act did not extend to all functions of public authorities. In addition, the Act made employers vicariously liable for some discriminatory actions of their employees but, as police officers are not *employees*, this extended liability did not apply to chief officers in relation to the actions of their police staff (see *R* v *Farah,* The Times, 17 October 1996). These were two principal reasons why the 1976 Act was felt to be in need of amendment. The latter reason was given increased impetus by the recommendations of the Report of the Inquiry into the death of Stephen Lawrence (Cm 4262-1). The Race Relations (Amendment) Act 2000 addresses both of these issues.

Interestingly, the Employment Appeal Tribunal was not persuaded that the concept of 'institutional racism' as levelled against the Metropolitan Police Service (MPS) in the Stephen Lawrence Report was related to the statutory definition of race discrimination and refused to accept that the MPS could generally be regarded in this context as having been racist at the time covered by the Report for the purposes of bringing discrimination claims against it—*Commissioner of Police for the Metropolis* v *Hendricks* (2001) EAT case no. 614/01. However, the Court of Appeal has allowed a claim in negligence (brought under s. 20 of the Race Relations Act 1976) by Duwayne Brooks against the Metropolitan Police for the way in which he was alleged to have been treated during the course of the Stephen Lawrence murder investigation—*Brooks* v *Metropolitan Police Commissioner* [2002] EWCA Civ 407. At the time of writing, permission for appeal to the House of Lords by both parties had been granted.

### 12.4.1    Public authorities

First, the Race Relations (Amendment) Act 2000 inserts several new provisions into s. 19 of the 1976 Act. These provisions together with the 2003 Regulations above generally make it unlawful for a public authority to discriminate against or harass a person on grounds of race in carrying out any of its functions. 'Public authority' here follows the definition used in the Human Rights Act 1998 (**see chapter 2**) and clearly includes the police. The Act allows for some exemptions and these include (controversially) a limited exemption where the person discriminates on grounds of nationality or ethnic/national origins and, in doing so, is properly acting on behalf of a Minister of the Crown in relation to immigration or nationality functions (see s. 19D).

Under s. 71 of the 1976 Act, specific public authorities are now under a general duty to have due regard to the need to eliminate unlawful discrimination and to promote equality of opportunity and good relations between people of different racial groups. Police Authorities (including the Metropolitan Police Authority) established under ss. 3 and 5B of the Police Act 1996 are specified public authorities for this purpose, as are the National Crime Squad and the National Criminal Intelligence Service (see sch. 1A to the 1976 Act). Others included on the list of specified public authorities include local government bodies, educational and housing organisations. The Secretary of State may (after consulting the Commission for Racial Equality) make an order imposing specific duties on a public authority to ensure that they perform this general statutory duty. Police forces (Home Office and others), chief officers and police authorities are under a statutory duty to publish Race Equality Schemes setting out how they intend to fulfil their duties under s. 71(1) of the Act. These Schemes must include details of those functions and policies that they have assessed as being relevant to the performance of their duties under s. 71(1) and their arrangements for:

- assessing and consulting on the likely impact of those proposed policies on the promotion of race equality
- monitoring policies for adverse impact on the promotion of race equality
- publishing the results of such assessments and consultation
- ensuring public access to information and services and
- training staff

(see the Race Relations Act 1976 (Statutory Duties) Order 2001 (S1 2001 No. 3458 made under Race Relations Act 1976 s. 71)). In addition, those bodies must, within a period of three years from 31 May 2002, review their assessments of their relevant functions and policies and carry out further review every three years thereafter.

Section 71 also empowers the Commission to issue Codes of Practice to help public authorities in carrying out their duties in this area. As with many such codes, a breach of the Code would not be actionable on its own but it would certainly provide significant evidence in support of a claim against a public authority. The Commission for Racial Equality is also given the power to issue and enforce compliance notices to public authorities in respect of this statutory duty.

### 12.4.2   Extension of police liability

Secondly, the Race Relations (Amendment) Act 2000 inserts new ss. 76A and 76B into the original 1976 Act. This addition makes a police authority and chief officers liable for acts *done by them* to a police constable (which includes special constables and cadets); it also makes chief officers vicariously liable for racially discriminatory acts by such constables under his/her direction or control. This largely puts the police service on the same footing as other 'employers' and 'employees'. As a result, the statutory defence provided by the 1976 Act (under s. 32) that an employer took reasonable steps to prevent the acts of discrimination complained of will also be available to chief officers.

## 12.5    **The Sex Discrimination Act 1975**

The Sex Discrimination Act 1975 is aimed at preventing discrimination on the grounds of sex or marital status.

This Act also has a Code of Practice to support it and matters falling within its parameters are overseen by the Equal Opportunities Commission.

The 1975 Act makes it unlawful to discriminate on the grounds of a person's sex (s. 1) or marital status (s. 3). The provisions apply in favour of both men and women equally (s. 2); they do not, however, operate equally in respect of married and single people and an employer may provide greater benefits for employees who are married.

The Act has been extended by the Sex Discrimination Act 1975 (Amendment) Regulations 2003 (SI 2003 No. 1657). One effect of the Regulations is to clarify the applicability of the Act's provisions to police officers. The legislation now treats constables as being in the employ of their chief officer for the purposes of making that chief officer liable for unlawful acts done in the performance (or purported performance) of the constable's functions. This amendment to the law was necessary as a result of some common law decisions involving police officers and their chief officers' liability (see *Liversidge* above).

The Regulations also generally prohibit sex discrimination after the end of an employment-type relationship in line with the Equal Treatment Directive.

## 12.6    **The Equal Pay Act 1970**

The Equal Pay Act 1970 requires that men and women who do the same type of work receive the same rewards. Originally enacted to come into force with the Sex Discrimination Act 1975, the first Act failed to satisfy the requirements of the relevant European directive and had to be amended.

Unlike the 1975 and 1976 Acts, this Act only relates to issues within the field of employment.

## 12.7    **The Disability Discrimination Act 1995**

The Disability Discrimination Act 1995, which also goes beyond the field of employment, introduced a relatively new area of discrimination, that of disability. The 1995 Act is supported by a Code of Practice, together with other materials and regulations to help with the complexity of its application. The Act makes it unlawful to discriminate against people on grounds of disability.

A person is 'disabled' for the purposes of the Act if they have a physical or mental impairment which has a substantial and long-term adverse effect on their ability to carry out normal day-to-day functions (s. 1).

Again there are exceptions which may be justified. However, under the 1995 Act employers and others are required to make 'reasonable adjustments' to prevent disabled people from being put at a substantial disadvantage when compared with others (s. 6). This means for example that entry and exit points to certain buildings and public vehicles will need to be adapted for wheelchairs, and provisions made for those who are visually or aurally disadvantaged.

The Act is extended by the Disability Discrimination Act 1995 (Amendment) Regulations 2003 (SI 2003 No. 1673).

Although exempt from the provisions of the 1995 Act at the time of writing, the police service is to lose that exemption by 2004.

## 12.8    **Recently extended areas of discrimination**

Areas which were not directly covered by the original legislation in the context of discrimination included:

- religious belief
- sexual orientation
- age.

Taking these in order, there have been many attempts to extend legal protection to religious beliefs. Outside a purely employment context, the Anti-terrorism, Crime and Security Act 2001 has introduced statutory measures to protect groups with reference to their religious beliefs (**see chapter 3**).

In the context of employment, discrimination on grounds of religion or belief is now covered by the Employment Equality (Religion or Belief) Regulations 2003 (SI 2003 No. 1660). The Regulations, which come into force in December 2003, implement Council Directive 2000/78/EC and make it unlawful to discriminate on the grounds of religion or belief in the field of employment or vocational training.

Religion or belief means any religion, religious belief or similar philosophical belief (reg. 2) and specific provision is made for police constables (reg. 11). Both direct and indirect discrimination are covered, as are victimisation and harassment. All of these generic areas are addressed in more detail below.

The issue of discrimination on grounds of sexual orientation kept the courts busy for many years until the latest decision of the House of Lords in *Pearce* v *Governors of Mayfield School* [2003] IRLR 512. One of the main legal difficulties created by this controversial subject was that applicants were forced to bring their claims under the general heads of sex discrimination. As with religion and belief, however, this area has now been provided for in specific legislation passed to implement the same Council Directive above in the form of the Employment Equality (sexual Orientation) Regulations 2003 (SI 2003 No. 1661) which also come into force in December 2003. The Regulations make it unlawful to discriminate on grounds of sexual orientation in employment and vocational training and apply to direct and indirect discrimination and also victimisation and harassment.

Sexual orientation means a sexual orientation towards people of the same sex, people of the opposite sex or to both people of the same sex and the opposite sex (reg. 2). Again, specific provision is made for police constables (reg. 11).

The issue of age remains unaddressed at the time of writing.

While there are now broad similarities across many of the protected categories, the specific definitions, qualifications and exemptions under the relevant regulations must be considered in each case.

## 12.9    **Gender reassignment**

Many of the provisions of the Sex Discrimination Act 1975 have been extended to cover discrimination on the grounds of gender reassignment in employment and vocational training. These extensions were made by the Sex Discrimination (Gender Reassignment) Regulations 1999 (SI 1999 No. 1102 made under European Communities Act, s. 2) in response to a case in the European Court of Justice (*P* v *S and Cornwall County Council* (case C-13/94) [1996] All ER (EC) 397). Gender reassignment means a process which is undertaken under medical supervision for the purpose of reassigning a person's sex by changing physiological or other characteristics of sex (reg. 2(3)). The Regulations only extend the provisions of some sections of the 1975 Act and include a number of concessions and exemptions.

Taking time off work in order to undergo reassignment surgery attracts the protection of the Act and is to be treated as a special category of absence.

The employment of transsexuals as police officers has caused the police service some difficulties. In a case arising before the Sex Discrimination (Gender Reassignment) Regulations 1999 (SI 1999 No. 1102 made under European Communities Act, s. 2), a transsexual applicant was turned down by a police force on the basis that she would not be able to perform all the duties of a constable—in particular the searching of prisoners. The force claimed a genuine occupational qualification for discriminating against transsexuals in this way and the Employment Appeal Tribunal (EAT) upheld its appeal against a finding of unlawful discrimination (*Chief Constable of West Yorkshire Police* v *A* [2002] IRLR 103).

In *A* above, the EAT referred to the established legal principle that gender in law is set at birth—if you are born a man, you remain a man and vice versa (see *Corbett* v *Corbett* [1970] 2 WLR 1306). The EAT went on to find that a police force could not condone a police officer searching someone of the opposite sex in contravention of the PACE Codes of Practice (**see chapter 2**) even if that officer's true 'legal' gender could be concealed by their general appearance and dress. Although the number of occasions when such an officer might be called upon to carry out a search in this way were few and far between, the EAT did not accept that they were 'minimal' or 'negligible' considerations. The EAT also held that the Regulations did not amount to an absolute bar on a transsexual ever being a police constable and therefore they were not incompatible with the Equal Treatment Directive (No. 76/207).

However, following the decision of the European Court of Human Rights in *Goodwin* v *United Kingdom* [2002] IRLR 664, the Court of Appeal held that it was no longer possible in the context of employment to regard a transsexual in these circumstances as being anything other than female. Although there might be public interest considerations that outweighed the interests of an individual applicant to the police service and a chief officer might decide on the balance of those interests not to appoint such a person, such circumstances were held not to exist in the case of *A* and the decision of the EAT was eventually overturned— *A* v *Chief Constable of West Yorkshire and the Secretary of State for Work and Pensions* [2002] EWCA Civ 1584.

## 12.10 Discrimination

Discrimination in the context of this chapter may come about in four main ways:

- directly
- indirectly
- harassment
- by victimisation.

### 12.10.1 Direct discrimination

This type of discrimination generally happens when one person is treated less favourably than another on the protected grounds (e.g. his/her racial origin, marital status, sex, religion or belief etc.). The key elements here are the 'treatment' of the person and the fact that such treatment was 'less favourable' than it would have been had the person not fallen into that particular group. Treatment will generally involve dealing with or behaving towards someone—as opposed to simply talking in a derogatory fashion *about* them (see e.g. *De Souza* v *Automobile Association* [1986] ICR 514). Treatment can be shown by a continuing state of affairs as well as a particular act (*Owusu* v *London Fire & Civil Defence Authority* [1995] IRLR 574—employer continually failing to re-grade appellant's post).

It must be shown that the treatment was made *on the grounds* of or *by reason* of the person's belonging to a protected group or having the protected characteristics. Like the test of 'causation' in criminal law (as to which, **see Crime, chapter 2**), the 'but for' test is helpful here, i.e. asking whether the person would have received the same treatment as others *but for* their sex, race, etc. In determining whether a person has been so treated the courts will not look at the motive of an employer or individual, only at the cause of the treatment (see *R* v *Birmingham City Council, ex parte Equal Opportunities Commission* [1989] AC 1155—more boys than girls allocated places at a school).

It can be seen that these elements of discrimination (so-called 'positive discrimination', e.g. deliberately favouring applications for jobs from one sex over the other) would generally be unlawful because treating people of one sex *more* favourably necessarily involves treating people from the other sex *less* favourably. A notable exception to the general principle that 'positive discrimination' is unlawful can be found in the Sex Discrimination (Election Candidates) Act 2002 which allows political parties (if they wish to do so) to adopt selection measures in order to reduce inequality in the numbers of men and women elected as candidates. Positive discrimination as described here should be contrasted with positive action (as to which, **see para. 12.11.2**).

Claims in the courts and tribunals for direct discrimination are rare. Examples of such have included:

- getting someone to carry out unpleasant tasks or duties (*Ministry of Defence* v *Jeremiah* [1980] QB 87)

- rescinding an officer's posting on the grounds of force policy that spouses should not work in the same Division because neither officer would be competent or compellable as witnesses against each other (*Graham* v *Chief Constable of Bedfordshire Constabulary* [2002] IRLR 239)

- treating a police officer of one racial group, who was under investigation for disciplinary matters, differently from another officer under such investigation belonging to a different racial group (*Virdi* v *Commissioner of Police for the Metropolis* (2000) LTL 5 February)

- acceding to a request by a customer not to be served by someone of a particular colour (*Eldridge & Barbican Car Hire Ltd* v *Zhang* (2001) LTL 10 May),

in each case as a result of their membership of a protected group.

Legislation that treats same-sex couples differently from unmarried heterosexual couples is open to challenge under Article 14 of the European Convention on Human Rights (**see chapter 2**), either by requiring the relevant court or tribunal to interpret the law in a way that is compatible with the Convention or by seeking a declaration of incompatibility. Discrimination between same-sex couples and *married* heterosexual couples is more difficult, largely because the courts have accepted differences in treatment between married and unmarried couples generally. The government's proposals allowing same-sex couples to register their relationships formally may go some way to alleviating the disparities in treatment in this area.

## 12.10.2 Indirect discrimination

Broadly speaking, indirect discrimination involves applying the same conditions to all relevant people (e.g. job applicants or employees), but in circumstances where a person belonging to the protected group is disadvantaged. For instance, if an employer imposes a requirement on all employees to work on certain days and at certain times, it may be that this requirement puts people of a certain nationality, sex or religious belief at a disadvantage when compared with other employees (for an earlier example see *Walker (J.H.) Ltd v Hussain* [1996] IRLR 11). This would raise an initial inference of indirect discrimination. This inference is not the end of the matter and in some cases the legislation allows an employer or other respondent to demonstrate justification of their actions.

This concept was first altered by the introduction of the Sex Discrimination (Indirect Discrimination and Burden of Proof) Regulations 2001 (SI 2001 No. 2660) and then was followed by the regulations relating to race, sexual orientation and religion referred to above.

While there are some differences in specific aspects of discrimination law, as a very general rule indirect discrimination will now occur if:

- a person or organisation (R) in the relevant context applies a provision, criterion or practice equally and

- that provision, criterion or practice puts people in the protected group at a disadvantage when compared to others and

- it puts a person (A) at that disadvantage and

- the R cannot show their actions to be a proportionate means of achieving a legitimate aim.

The practical effect of this in a sex discrimination context was recently summarised by the Employment Appeal Tribunal in *Barton* v *Investec Henderson Crosthwaite Securities Ltd* [2003] IRLR 332. Following the reasoning of the Tribunal in that case, in order to discharge the burden of proof, an employer must prove on the balance of probabilities that the treatment of the applicant was 'in no sense whatsoever' on the grounds of sex, race or other protected category.

Earlier decisions of the courts based on the disproportionate effect of generally-applied requirements serve to illustrate the nature of indirect discrimination. So, for instance, the fact that someone can *physically* comply with a criterion (e.g. a woman could decide not to have children in order to comply with an age requirement in a promotion system) does not mean that it falls outside the legislation. What the courts have looked at is the person's *practical* ability to comply. In *Mandla* v *Dowell Lee* [1983] 2 AC 548, the fact that the complainant could physically remove his turban and cut his hair in order to comply with his chosen school's admission policy did not prevent that policy from being indirectly discriminatory. The House of Lords said that the test of whether someone could comply with a condition would be taken to mean could he/she comply in practice or in a way that was consistent with the customs and cultural conditions of the group.

A further example of indirect discrimination can be seen in the case of *London Underground Ltd* v *Edwards (No. 2)* [1998] IRLR 364. Despite the fact that a managerial policy only had an adverse effect on one woman train driver among a total of 24, the fact that *all* 2,023 male drivers could comply with it made the policy discriminatory. While 100 per cent of males could comply with the policy, which related to rostering of duties, only 95.2 per cent of females were able to do so. Accordingly, the Court of Appeal held that the policy discriminated indirectly against the applicant who was unable to continue in her job as a result.

Even where the difference between the number of female police officers unable to comply with a practice (e.g. a shift system) compared with male police officers is only a few per cent (or vice versa), an employment tribunal can find that a disparate effect has been established and that indirect sex discrimination has occurred (*Chief Constable of Avon & Somerset Constabulary* v *Chew* [2002] Emp LR 370).

Other examples of indirect discrimination would include:

- requiring all employees to work within 'normal office hours' (*Bhudi* v *IMI Refiners* [1994] IRLR 204)
- requiring all workers to have short hair—thereby making it more difficult for some groups such as Sikhs to comply (*Mandla* v *Dowell Lee*)
- denying a police officer access to operational duties as a result of a colour vision deficiency where the condition was not objectively justifiable in relation to those duties but where the condition *was* shown to affect a greater percentage of males than females (*Webster* v *Chief Constable of Hertfordshire Constabulary*, 2000, unreported).

Note that Article 14 of the European Convention on Human Rights does not make express provision for *indirect* discrimination (**see chapter 2** and *R (on the application of Barber)* v *Secretary of State for Work and Pensions* [2002] EWHC 1915 (Admin.)).

### 12.10.3 Harassment

The Race Relations Act 1976 now contains a specific definition of harassment which outlaws unwanted conduct on the grounds of race or ethnic or national origins which violates the person's dignity or which creates an intimidating, hostile, degrading, humiliating or offensive environment (see ss. 3A and 4). The specific legislation addressing other areas of discrimination (e.g. disability, sexual orientation and religious belief) contains similar provisions.

Harassment was not a separate category of discrimination until recently and came under the general heading of sex discrimination. Sexual harassment is basically unwanted conduct of a sexual nature, or other conduct based on sex affecting the dignity of women and men at work (see *Wadman* v *Carpenter Farrer Partnership* [1993] IRLR 374). This can include verbal remarks, written comments and physical contact. Most equal opportunities policies include some reference to this type of behaviour and grievance procedures take account of sexual harassment as if it were a separate heading; there are plans within the European Union legislative programme to make this a separate category of less favourable treatment.

Harassment is also a criminal offence (**see chapter 3**) and, if anxiety or shock caused to another person is sufficiently serious, a charge of assault may be brought (**see Crime, chapter 8**).

Guidance is provided in the Code of Practice on Sexual Harassment (1992 OJ L49/1). This Code sets out guidelines for dealing with allegations of sexual harassment and can be used in assessing whether an employer has been in breach of the Sex Discrimination Act 1975 by allowing practices to go unchecked (see *Wadman* above).

### 12.10.4 Victimisation

Victimisation is a type of discrimination and therefore only attracts protection in the same circumstances as the other discrimination provisions of the various Acts.

People often refer to having been 'victimised' at work in the sense that they have been singled out or persecuted in some way. While this treatment may contain elements of discrimination and other unlawful conduct, it is not the same as victimisation in the statutory sense used here.

In other words, it will not be enough for an employee to claim that he/she has been 'picked on' in some way; they will have to show that they belong to a protected group of people and have thereby been discriminated against.

A person is discriminated against by way of 'victimisation' under s. 2 of the Race Relations Act 1976, s. 3 of the Sex Discrimination Act 1975 and s. 55 of the Disability Discrimination Act 1995, if they are treated less favourably than another person is (or would be) treated in the same circumstances with regard to any action covered by any of those Acts because the person:

- brought proceedings against any person under any of those Acts;
- has given evidence or information in connection with proceedings brought by any person under any of those Acts;
- otherwise did anything under or by reference to the Acts with regard to any person (e.g. provided advice to someone as to his/her rights);
- has alleged that any person has done anything which would amount to a contravention of those Acts (whether or not the allegation specifically so states); or
- because the discriminator knows or suspects that the person victimised has done or intends to do any of the things set out above.

These listed actions above are generally referred to above as 'protected acts'. The test to be applied in assessing whether or not victimisation has taken place is 'was the real reason for the victim's treatment the fact that he/she had carried out a protected act?' (see the House of Lords' decision in *Chief Constable of West Yorkshire Police* v *Khan* [2001] UKHL 48).

The legislation relating to other specific types of discrimination such as religious belief and sexual orientation contain their own elements of protection from victimisation on a similar basis and reference should be made to them as appropriate.

The protection from victimisation does not extend to treatment of a person by reason of any allegation that the person makes falsely and not in good faith.

Where the person victimised has (or had) a disability, that disability is to be disregarded when deciding whether or not he/she has been treated 'less favourably' than another person in the same circumstances.

In proving victimisation, the person must show that less favourable treatment occurred as a result of his/her involvement in the protected action described that is, applying the 'but for' test (see *Aziz* v *Trinity Street Taxis Ltd* [1989] QB 463).

## 12.11 Exceptions and defences

There are a number of exceptions and defences to the provisions of the various Acts and Regulations discussed above. As with other defences and exceptions, not all of them apply to all types of behaviour and it is necessary to refer to the relevant legislation in each case. Below are some of the more common exceptions and defences.

### 12.11.1 Genuine occupational qualification

The most frequently encountered defence to acts made unlawful by the Race Relations Act 1976 and the Sex Discrimination Act 1975 is that of 'genuine occupational qualification' (GOQ).

In each case the GOQ defence only applies to:

- recruitment
- refusing employment, and
- affording access to promotion, training, etc.

The principle behind the GOQ defence is that, in certain jobs and roles, there may well be a legitimate reason demanded by that job/role for the relevant person to be a particular sex or to belong to a particular racial group. Such occasions are generally concerned with:

- preserving decency and privacy (e.g. public lavatory attendants),
- authenticity (e.g. actors/actresses in plays), or
- the provision of personal services.

Exceptions to unlawful discrimination can be found in a number of areas under the relevant Acts and statutory instruments, though there are far more potential exceptions to discrimination on the grounds of sex and sexual orientation than for reasons of race.

12.11.2    **Positive action**

In order to encourage members of particular groups to follow training courses, employers and other bodies may discriminate in their provision of training opportunities under certain circumstances.

Positive action may in some circumstances be permitted where there is a legitimate need within a particular area of work or where it is necessary to train people from specified protected groups to fill certain jobs. These areas are provided for in the specific legislation and are beyond the general scope of this Manual.

Efforts made under these circumstances are positive *action* and should not be confused with positive *discrimination* or *affirmative* action as used in the United States and elsewhere. Affirmative action in that sense (whereby people are selected in preference to others solely on the basis of their membership of a certain minority group) is unlawful in England and Wales. Consequently, an attempt to recruit female police officers into a specialist department by excluding male applicants was held to be unlawful in *Jones* v *Chief Constable of Northamptonshire Police* The Times, 1 November 1999.

12.12    **Maternity and parental leave**

In addition to the protection which appears in the above enactments, women have other statutory protection in relation to pregnancy and childbirth. These include:

- rights to unpaid time off work
- protection against dismissal
- rights to maternity pay
- rights to maternity leave
- rights to return to work.

These and other protections are contained in the Employment Rights Act 1996 (as amended). Similarly there are many regulations setting out parental entitlements to time off, including paternity leave and leave for adoptive parents. Most of this legislation is driven by European law and is outside the scope of this Manual. For guidance on the agreed policies to such leave within the police service, see Home Office Circular 12/2002.

# 13 Railways

## 13.1 Introduction

Responsibility for providing police services to the railway network—including the London underground—in England and Wales (and Scotland) lies primarily with the British Transport Police (BTP). Owing to geographical factors, however, there are occasions where the assistance of other police forces may be required or requested. There is a considerable amount of legislation that relates to the railway network, together with many operational policies. These are properly the concern of the BTP and, where officers from other forces are called upon to deal with incidents involving railways, it is suggested that they confer with their colleagues at BTP.

This chapter sets out some of the legislation that is relevant to police officers in general.

## 13.2 Powers of entry

Although much railway property is now owned by private commercial companies, railway stations and platforms are generally public places for most purposes. Where there is any doubt as to the existence of a power of entry or an implied permission to enter (as to which, **see chapter 2**), the guidance of the BTP should be sought.

There are some specific offences concerned with trespassing on railway property—including the running lines—and this is one of the few areas of criminal law where there is a direct sanction imposed for a simple trespassory act (see s. 23 of the Regulation of Railways Act 1868, as amended). For trespass generally, **see chapter 9**.

### 13.2.1 Railway Safety Accreditation Schemes

The Police Reform Act 2002 gives chief officers powers to set up Community Safety Accreditation Schemes (CSASs) and to accredit employees of participating organisations with certain policing powers (**see chapter 2**). The Act also gives the Secretary of State powers to make regulations allowing the chief constable of the BTP to establish and maintain Railway Safety Accreditation Schemes (RSASs). RSASs are schemes within the jurisdiction of the BTP by which people may be accredited with some limited policing powers. The Act leaves some of the detail in any such scheme to the regulations but provides that an accredited person may be given powers of a constable in uniform to issue a fixed penalty notice under the Criminal Justice and Police Act 2001 in relation to ss. 55 and 56 of the British Transport Commission Act 1949 (trespass and stone throwing—**see para. 13.3.**) The regulations cannot permit wider powers than those allowed under a CSAS (s. 43(6)). Before making any such regulations, the Secretary of State must consult with a number of people and organisations including bodies representing the interests of chief officers, police authorities, the British Transport Police Committee and the Mayor of London.

## 13.3 | Offences

There are many offences that relate specifically to railways; in particular those set out under the relevant by-laws. Many of these are summary offences and often require proof of certain facts or circumstances that existed at the time.

Among the more serious offences are:

OFFENCE: **Obstruction with intent to cause damage etc.—*Malicious Damage Act 1861, s. 35***
- Triable on indictment • Life imprisonment
*(Arrestable offence)*

The Malicious Damage Act 1861, s. 35 states:

> Whosoever shall unlawfully and maliciously put, place, cast, or throw upon or across any railway any wood, stone, or other matter or thing, or shall unlawfully and maliciously take up, remove, or displace any rail, sleeper, or other matter or thing belonging to any railway, or shall unlawfully and maliciously turn, move, or divert any points or other machinery belonging to any railway, or shall unlawfully and maliciously make or show, hide or remove, any signal or light upon or near to any railway, or shall unlawfully and maliciously do or cause to be done any matter or thing, with intent, in any of the cases aforesaid, to obstruct, upset, overthrow, injure, or destroy any engine, tender, carriage, or truck using such railway, shall be guilty of an offence...

**KEYNOTE**

For the meaning of 'maliciously' here, **see Crime, chapter 2.**

This offence extends to privately-owned railways that are not constructed under statute. This offence requires proof of 'specific intent' (**see Crime, chapter 2**). Where there is no such intent, the lesser offence under s. 36 (triable either way and carrying two years' imprisonment) may be charged.

OFFENCE: **Obstruction with intent to endanger safety—*Offences Against the Person Act 1861, s. 32***
- Triable on indictment • Life imprisonment
*(Arrestable offence)*

The Offences Against the Person Act 1861, s. 32 states:

> Whosoever shall unlawfully and maliciously put or throw upon or across any railway any wood, stone, or other matter or thing, or shall unlawfully and maliciously take up, remove, or displace any rail, sleeper, or other matter or thing belonging to any railway, or shall unlawfully and maliciously turn, move or divert any points or other machinery belonging to any railway, or shall unlawfully and maliciously make or show, hide or remove, any signal or light upon or near to any railway, or shall unlawfully and maliciously do or cause to be done any other matter or thing, with intent, in any of the cases aforesaid, to endanger the safety of any person travelling or being upon such railway, shall be guilty of an offence...

**KEYNOTE**

This is also an offence of 'specific intent' and has a lesser alternative charge where no such intent was present (under s. 33).

The intention necessary is an intention to endanger the safety (not necessarily the *life*) of any person travelling or being upon the railway concerned.

It is an either way offence for any person, by any unlawful act or wilful omission, to endanger the safety of any person on the railway (s. 34). An offence is committed where there is a potential danger caused, even though the threat is removed by the intervention of a third party (*R* v *Pearce* [1967] 1 QB 150).

---

Other relevant offences include:

OFFENCE: **Trespass on railways etc.—*British Transport Commission Act 1949, s. 55 (as amended)***
- Triable summarily • One month's imprisonment or fine (s. 55(1) offence); fine (s. 55(2) offence)
*(No specific power of arrest)*

The British Transport Commission Act 1949, s. 55 states:

(1) If any person wilfully trespasses on any railway or on any of the stations or other works or premises connected with it and refuses to quit it on request by any officer or agent of the railway company, that person and anyone aiding or assisting him will [commit an offence].

(2) Any person who trespasses on any railway lines, sidings, railway embankments, tunnels, cuttings or similar works belonging to, leased to or worked by the British Railways Board or London Regional Transport or on other land of the Board or London Regional Transport, in dangerous proximity to such lines or other works or to any electrical apparatus used in connection with the railway, is liable . . .

OFFENCE: **Stone throwing on railways etc.—*British Transport Commission Act 1949, s. 56 (as amended)***
- Triable summarily • Fine
*(No specific power of arrest)*

The British Transport Commission Act 1949, s. 56 states:

(1) It is an offence, subject to a penalty, unlawfully to throw at any rolling stock or apparatus on any railway belonging to, leased to, or worked by the British Railways Board or London Regional Transport any stone or thing likely to damage or injure persons or property.

---

**KEYNOTE**

It is a condition of the above section that a notice warning people not to trespass on the railway is displayed at the nearest station and a statement to that effect should be included in any prosecution evidence.

References to the 'Boards' and to any wholly owned subsidiary have effect as if they were references to any successor of the British Railways Board (see e.g. sch. 27 to the Transport Act 2000).

The offences under ss. 55 and 56 are 'penalty offences' for the purposes of s. 1 of the Criminal Justice and Police Act 2001 (see para. 2.5.1).

---

## 13.4 Offences involving drink and drugs

Given the potential safety risks presented by railway operations, there are a number of legislative provisions aimed at regulating the behaviour of people on railway or similar transport systems where those people have taken drink or drugs. In addition to these provisions, which are set out below, many if not all employment contracts for people working on railway systems will contain some clauses dealing with the effects of drink/drugs when 'on duty'. Again, in cases of doubt, the guidance of the BTP should be sought.

### 13.4.1 The Transport and Works Act 1992

Modelled largely on the provisions of the Road Traffic Act 1988 (**see Road Traffic, chapter 5**), the Transport and Works Act 1992 gives the police certain powers in relation to suspected offences involving drink or drugs by staff on railway or similar transport systems. The provisions of the 1992 Act are not restricted to railways but also extend to tramways and systems using a mode of guided transport that have been designated by the Secretary of State (e.g. the 'people movers' operated at Gatwick airport).

The 1992 Act will not apply unless the transport system concerned is used or intended to be used wholly or partly for the carriage of members of the public. It need not be shown that a particular part of the system or an individual carriage was so used or intended; it is the use/intended use of the system as a whole that will be considered in determining whether or not the Act applies.

### 13.4.2 Staff

Unlike the road traffic legislation, the Transport and Works Act 1992 is not only concerned with those people who are driving, attempting to drive or in charge of vehicles. The 1992 Act will apply to any relevant worker whose duties or job description bring him/her into the categories set out under s. 27. These relevant workers will include:

- train drivers
- guards
- signalmen/women
- any other worker who can, in their capacity as such, control or affect the movement of a vehicle
- maintenance workers employed to work on the tracks and lines, signalling equipment or the electricity supply to the vehicles or their guidance systems
- supervisors and look-outs for such maintenance workers.

OFFENCE: **Relevant worker unfit through drink or drugs—*Transport and Works Act 1992, s. 27(1)***
- Triable summarily • Six months' imprisonment and/or fine
*(Statutory power of arrest)*

The Transport and Works Act 1992, s. 27(1) states:

(1) If a person works on a transport system to which this Chapter applies—
    (a) as a driver, guard, conductor or signalman or in any other capacity in which he can control or affect the movement of a vehicle, or
    (b) in a maintenance capacity or as a supervisor of, or look-out for, persons working in a maintenance capacity,

when he is unfit to carry out that work through drink or drugs, he shall be guilty of an offence.

OFFENCE: **Relevant worker over the prescribed limit—*Transport and Works Act 1992, s. 27(2)***
- Triable summarily • Six months' imprisonment and/or fine
*(No specific power of arrest)*

The Transport and Works Act 1992, s. 27(2) states:

(2) If a person works on a transport system to which this Chapter applies—

    (a) as a driver, guard, conductor or signalman or in any other capacity in which he can control or affect the movement of a vehicle, or

    (b) in a maintenance capacity or as a supervisor of, or look-out for, persons working in a maintenance capacity,

after consuming so much alcohol that the proportion of it in his breath, blood or urine exceeds the prescribed limit, he shall be guilty of an offence.

---

### KEYNOTE

The prescribed limits are the same as those set out in relation to road traffic offences; so too are the relevant provisions in relation to approved breath test devices and police station procedure (see Road Traffic, chapter 5).

'Drug' includes intoxicants other than alcohol.

A constable may arrest a person without warrant if he/she has reasonable cause to suspect that the person is, or has been committing an offence under s. 27(1) (s. 30). For a discussion of the requirements for 'reasonable cause to suspect', see chapter 2. In order to arrest a person under this section a constable may enter (if need be by force) any place where that person is or where the constable, with reasonable cause, suspects him/her to be (s. 30(3)).

Under s. 29 a constable in uniform may require a person to provide a specimen of breath for a breath test where the constable has reasonable cause to suspect that:

- the person is working on a transport system in any capacity mentioned under s. 27 (i.e. a relevant worker) and that he/she has alcohol in his/her body; or

- the person has been working in such a capacity with alcohol in his/her body and that he/she still has alcohol in his/her body.

In addition, where an accident or an incident which *in the constable's opinion* involved a danger of death or personal injury (to anyone) occurs on a relevant transport system, a constable in uniform may also require a specimen of breath if he/she has reasonable cause to suspect that:

- at the time of the accident or dangerous incident, the person was working on the transport system in the capacity of a 'relevant worker'; and

- that an act or omission of that person while so working *may have been a cause* of the accident/dangerous incident.

It is not necessary that the person's act/omission may have been the *only*, or even a substantial cause of the accident/dangerous incident.

For the purposes of:

- requiring a person to provide a specimen of breath under s. 29(2) where the constable reasonably suspects that the accident/dangerous incident involved the death of or personal injury to another person, or

- arresting a person in such a case

the constable may enter (if need be by force) any place where that person is or where the constable, with reasonable cause, suspects him/her to be (s. 30(4)).

The requirement for the provision of the breath specimen may be made at or near the place where the requirement is made or, if it is made under s. 27(2) and the constable thinks fit, at a police station (s. 29(4)).

Failing or refusing to provide a specimen under s. 29 is a summary offence (s. 29(5)).

If, as a result of a breath test under s. 29, a constable has reasonable cause to suspect that the proportion of alcohol in the person's breath or blood exceeds the prescribed limit, he/she may arrest the person without warrant (s. 30(2)(a)).

If the person fails or refuses to provide a specimen under s. 29 and the constable has reasonable cause to suspect that that person has alcohol in his/her body, he/she may arrest them without warrant (s. 30(2)(b)).

A person arrested under this provision will have been 'arrested for an offence' for the purposes of the Police and Criminal Evidence Act 1984 (see s. 34(6) ).

Further offences are committed by the operator of the transport system if a person working on that system commits an offence under s. 27 (s. 28). There is, however, a general defence open to the 'responsible operators' if they can show that they exercised all due diligence to prevent the commission of a s. 27 offence on their system.

# Appendix 1

# PACE Code of Practice for the Exercise by Police Officers of Statutory Powers of Stop and Search (Code A)

**Commencement—Transitional Arrangements**

This code applies to any search by a police officer which commences after midnight on 31 March 2003.

## General

This code of practice must be readily available at all police stations for consultation by police officers, detained persons and members of the public.

The notes for guidance included are not provisions of this code, but are guidance to police officers and others about its application and interpretation. Provisions in the annexes to the code are provisions of this code.

This code governs the exercise by police officers of statutory powers to search a person or a vehicle without first making an arrest. The main stop and search powers to which this code applies are set out in Annex A, but that list should not be regarded as definitive. [See *Note 1*]

This code does not apply to:

(a) the powers of stop and search under:
   (i) Aviation Security Act 1982, section 27(2);
   (ii) Police and Criminal Evidence Act 1984, section 6(1) (which relates specifically to powers of constables employed by statutory undertakers on the premises of the statutory undertakers);

(b) searches carried out for the purposes of examination under Schedule 7 to the Terrorism Act 2000 and to which the Code of Practice issued under paragraph 6 of Schedule 14 to the Terrorism Act 2000 applies.

## 1 Principles governing stop and search

1.1 Powers to stop and search must be used fairly, responsibly, with respect for people being searched and without unlawful discrimination. The Race Relations (Amendment) Act 2000 makes it unlawful for police officers to discriminate on the grounds of race, colour, ethnic origin, nationality or national origins when using their powers.

1.2 The intrusion on the liberty of the person stopped or searched must be brief and detention for the purposes of a search must take place at or near the location of the stop.

1.3 If these fundamental principles are not observed the use of powers to stop and search may be drawn into question. Failure to use the powers in the proper manner reduces their effectiveness. Stop and search can play an important role in the detection and prevention of crime, and using the powers fairly makes them more effective.

1.4   The primary purpose of stop and search powers is to enable officers to allay or confirm suspicions about individuals without exercising their power of arrest. Officers may be required to justify the use or authorisation of such powers, in relation both to individual searches and the overall pattern of their activity in this regard, to their supervisory officers or in court. Any misuse of the powers is likely to be harmful to policing and lead to mistrust of the police. Officers must also be able to explain their actions to the member of the public searched. The misuse of these powers can lead to disciplinary action.

1.5   An officer must not search a person, even with his or her consent, where no power to search is applicable. Even where a person is prepared to submit to a search voluntarily, the person must not be searched unless the necessary legal power exists, and the search must be in accordance with the relevant power and the provisions of this Code. The only exception, where an officer does not require a specific power, applies to searches of persons entering sports grounds or other premises carried out with their consent given as a condition of entry.

## 2   Explanation of powers to stop and search

2.1   This code applies to powers of stop and search as follows:

(a) powers which require reasonable grounds for suspicion, before they may be exercised; that articles unlawfully obtained or possessed are being carried, or under Section 43 of the Terrorism Act 2000 that a person is a terrorist;

(b) authorised under section 60 of the Criminal Justice and Public Order Act 1994, based upon a reasonable belief that incidents involving serious violence may take place or that people are carrying dangerous instruments or offensive weapons within any locality in the police area;

(c) authorised under section 44(1) and (2) of the Terrorism Act 2000 based upon a consideration that the exercise of one or both powers is expedient for the prevention of acts of terrorism;

(d) powers to search a person who has not been arrested in the exercise of a power to search premises (see Code B paragraph 2.3a).

## Searches requiring reasonable grounds for suspicion

2.2   Reasonable grounds for suspicion depend on the circumstances in each case. There must be an objective basis for that suspicion based on facts, information, and/or intelligence which are relevant to the likelihood of finding an article of a certain kind or, in the case of searches under section 43 of the Terrorism Act 2000, to the likelihood that the person is a terrorist. Reasonable suspicion can never be supported on the basis of personal factors alone without reliable supporting intelligence or information or some specific behaviour by the person concerned. For example, a person's race, age, appearance, or the fact that the person is known to have a previous conviction, cannot be used alone or in combination with each other as the reason for searching that person. Reasonable suspicion cannot be based on generalisations or stereotypical images of certain groups or categories of people as more likely to be involved in criminal activity.

2.3   Reasonable suspicion can sometimes exist without specific information or intelligence and on the basis of some level of generalisation stemming from the behaviour of a person. For example, if an officer encounters someone on the street at night who is obviously trying to hide something, the officer may (depending on the other surrounding circumstances) base such suspicion on the fact that this kind of behaviour is often linked to stolen or prohibited articles being carried. Similarly, for the purposes of section 43 of the Terrorism Act 2000, suspicion that a person is a terrorist may arise from the person's behaviour at or near a location which has been identified as a potential target for terrorists.

2.4   However, reasonable suspicion should normally be linked to accurate and current intelligence or information, such as information describing an article being carried, a suspected offender, or a person who has been seen carrying a type of article known to have been stolen recently from premises in the area. Searches based on accurate and current intelligence or information are more likely to be effective. Targeting searches in a particular area at specified crime problems increases their effectiveness and minimises inconvenience to law-abiding members of the public. It also helps in justifying the use of searches both to those who are searched and to the general public. This does not however prevent stop and search powers being exercised in other locations where such powers may be exercised and reasonable suspicion exists.

2.5   Searches are more likely to be effective, legitimate, and secure public confidence when reasonable suspicion is based on a range of factors. The overall use of these powers is more likely to be effective when up to date and accurate intelligence or information is communicated to officers and they are well-informed about local crime patterns.

2.6   Where there is reliable information or intelligence that members of a group or gang habitually carry knives unlawfully or weapons or controlled drugs, and wear a distinctive item of clothing or other means of identification to indicate their membership of the group or gang, that distinctive item of clothing or other means of identification may provide reasonable grounds to stop and search a person. [See *Note 9*]

2.7   A police officer may have reasonable grounds to suspect that a person is in innocent possession of a stolen or prohibited article or other item for which he or she is empowered to search. In that case the officer may stop and search the person even though there would be no power of arrest.

2.8   Under section 43(1) of the Terrorism Act 2000 a constable may stop and search a person whom the officer reasonably suspects to be a terrorist to discover whether the person is in possession of anything which may constitute evidence that the person is a terrorist. These searches may only be carried out by an officer of the same sex as the person searched.

2.9   An officer who has reasonable grounds for suspicion may detain the person concerned in order to carry out a search. Before carrying out a search the officer may ask questions about the person's behaviour or presence in circumstances which gave rise to the suspicion. As a result of questioning the detained person, the reasonable grounds for suspicion necessary to detain that person may be confirmed or, because of a satisfactory explanation, be eliminated. [See *Notes 2* and *3*] Questioning may also reveal reasonable grounds to suspect the possession of a different kind of unlawful article from that originally suspected. Reasonable grounds for suspicion however cannot be provided retrospectively by such questioning during a person's detention or by refusal to answer any questions put.

2.10   If, as a result of questioning before a search, or other circumstances which come to the attention of the officer, there cease to be reasonable grounds for suspecting that an article is being carried of a kind for which there is a power to stop and search, no search may take place. [See *Note 3*] In the absence of any other lawful power to detain, the person is free to leave at will and must be so informed.

2.11   There is no power to stop or detain a person in order to find grounds for a search. Police officers have many encounters with members of the public which do not involve detaining people against their will. If reasonable grounds for suspicion emerge during such an encounter, the officer may search the person, even though no grounds existed when the encounter began. If an officer is detaining someone for the purpose of a search, he or she should inform the person as soon as detention begins.

## Searches authorised under section 60 of the Criminal Justice and Public Order Act 1994

2.12   Authority for a constable in uniform to stop and search under section 60 of the Criminal Justice and Public Order Act 1994 may be given if the authorising officer reasonably believes:

- (a) that incidents involving serious violence may take place in any locality in the officer's police area, and it is expedient to use these powers to prevent their occurrence, or
- (b) that persons are carrying dangerous instruments or offensive weapons without good reason in any locality in the officer's police area.

2.13   An authorisation under section 60 may only be given by an officer of the rank of inspector or above, in writing, specifying the grounds on which it was given, the locality in which the powers may be exercised and the period of time for which they are in force. The period authorised shall be no longer than appears reasonably necessary to prevent, or seek to prevent incidents of serious violence, or to deal with the problem of carrying dangerous instruments or offensive weapons. It may not exceed 24 hours. [See *Notes 10–13*]

2.14   If an inspector gives an authorisation, he or she must, as soon as practicable, inform an officer of or above the rank of superintendent. This officer may direct that the authorisation shall be extended for a further 24 hours, if violence or the carrying of dangerous instruments or offensive weapons has occurred, or is suspected to have occurred, and the continued use of the powers is considered necessary to prevent or deal with further such activity. That direction must also be given in writing at the time or as soon as practicable afterwards. [See *Note 12*]

## Powers to require removal of face coverings

2.15   Section 60AA of the Criminal Justice and Public Order Act 1994 also provides a power to demand the removal of disguises. The officer exercising the power must reasonably believe that someone is wearing an item wholly or mainly for the purpose of concealing identity. There is also a power to seize such items where the officer believes that a person intends to wear them for this purpose. There is no power to stop and search for disguises. An officer may seize any such item which is discovered when exercising a power of search for something else, or which is being carried, and which the officer reasonably believes is intended to be used for concealing anyone's identity. This power can only be used if an authorisation under section 60 or an authorisation under section 60AA is in force.

2.16   Authority for a constable in uniform to require the removal of disguises and to seize them under section 60AA may be given if the authorising officer reasonably believes that activities may take place in any locality in the officer's police area that are likely to involve the commission of offences and it is expedient to use these powers to prevent or control these activities.

2.17   An authorisation under section 60AA may only be given by an officer of the rank of inspector or above, in writing, specifying the grounds on which it was given, the locality in which the powers may be exercised and the period of time for which they are in force. The period authorised shall be no longer than appears reasonably necessary to prevent, or seek to prevent the commission of offences. It may not exceed 24 hours. [See *Notes 10–13*]

2.18   If an inspector gives an authorisation, he or she must, as soon as practicable, inform an officer of or above the rank of superintendent. This officer may direct that the authorisation shall be extended for a further 24 hours, if crimes have been committed, or are suspected to have been committed, and the continued use of the powers is considered necessary to prevent or deal with further such activity. This direction must also be given in writing at the time or as soon as practicable afterwards. [See *Note 12*]

## Searches authorised under section 44 of the Terrorism Act 2000

2.19   An officer of the rank of assistant chief constable (or equivalent) or above, may give authority for the following powers of stop and search under section 44 of the Terrorism Act 2000 to be exercised in the whole or part of his or her police area if the officer considers it is expedient for the prevention of acts of terrorism:

(a) under section 44(1) of the Terrorism Act 2000, to give a constable in uniform power to stop and search any vehicle, its driver, any passenger in the vehicle and anything in or on the vehicle or carried by the driver or any passenger; and

(b) under section 44(2) of the Terrorism Act 2000, to give a constable in uniform power to stop and search any pedestrian and anything carried by the pedestrian.

An authorisation under section 44(1) may be combined with one under section 44(2).

2.20   If an authorisation is given orally at first, it must be confirmed in writing by the officer who gave it as soon as reasonably practicable.

2.21   When giving an authorisation, the officer must specify the geographical area in which the power may be used, and the time and date that the authorisation ends (up to a maximum of 28 days from the time the authorisation was given). [See *Notes 12 and 13*]

2.22   The officer giving an authorisation under section 44(1) or (2) must cause the Secretary of State to be informed, as soon as reasonably practicable, that such an authorisation has been given. An authorisation which is not confirmed by the Secretary of State within 48 hours of its having been given, shall have effect up until the end of that 48 hour period or the end of the period specified in the authorisation (whichever is the earlier). [See *Note 14*]

2.23   Following notification of the authorisation, the Secretary of State may:

   (i)   cancel the authorisation with immediate effect or with effect from such other time as he or she may direct;

   (ii)   confirm it but for a shorter period than that specified in the authorisation; or

   (iii)   confirm the authorisation as given.

2.24   When an authorisation under section 44 is given, a constable in uniform may exercise the powers:

   (a)   only for the purpose of searching for articles of a kind which could be used in connection with terrorism (see paragraph 2.25);

   (b)   whether or not there are any grounds for suspecting the presence of such articles.

2.25   The selection of persons stopped under section 44 of the Terrorism Act 2000 should reflect an objective assessment of the threat posed by the various terrorist groups active in Great Britain. The powers must not be used to stop and search for reasons unconnected with terrorism. Officers must take particular care not to discriminate against members of minority ethnic groups in the exercise of these powers. There may be circumstances, however, where it is appropriate for officers to take account of a person's ethnic origin in selecting persons to be stopped in response to a specific terrorist threat (for example, some international terrorist groups are associated with particular ethnic identities). [See *Notes 12 and 13*]

2.26   The powers under sections 43 and 44 of the Terrorism Act 2000 allow a constable to search only for articles which could be used for terrorist purposes. However, this would not prevent a search being carried out under other powers if, in the course of exercising these powers, the officer formed reasonable grounds for suspicion.

## Powers to search in the exercise of a power to search premises

2.27   The following powers to search premises also authorise the search of a person, not under arrest, who is found on the premises during the course of the search:

   (a)   section 139B of the Criminal Justice Act 1988 under which a constable may enter school premises and search the premises and any person on those premises for any bladed or pointed article or offensive weapon; and

   (b)   under a warrant issued under section s. 23(3) of the Misuse of Drugs Act 1971 to search premises for drugs or documents but only if the warrant specifically authorises the search of persons found on the premises.

2.28   Before the power under section 139B of the Criminal Justice Act 1988 may be exercised, the constable must have reasonable grounds to believe that an offence under section 139A of the Criminal Justice Act 1988 (having a bladed or pointed article or offensive weapon on school premises) has been or is being committed. A warrant to search premises and persons found therein may be issued under section s. 23(3) of the Misuse of Drugs Act 1971 if there are reasonable grounds to suspect that controlled drugs or certain documents are in the possession of a person on the premises.

2.29   The powers in paragraph 2.27(a) or (b) do not require prior specific grounds to suspect that the person to be searched is in possession of an item for which there is an existing power to search. However, it is still necessary to ensure that the selection and treatment of those searched under these powers is based upon objective factors connected with the search of the premises, and not upon personal prejudice.

## 3   Conduct of searches

3.1   All stops and searches must be carried out with courtesy, consideration and respect for the person concerned. This has a significant impact on public confidence in the police. Every reasonable effort must be made to minimise the embarrassment that a person being searched may experience. [See *Note 4*]

3.2   The co-operation of the person to be searched must be sought in every case, even if the person initially objects to the search. A forcible search may be made only if it has been established that the person is unwilling to co-operate or resists. Reasonable force may be used as a last resort if necessary to conduct a search or to detain a person or vehicle for the purposes of a search.

3.3   The length of time for which a person or vehicle may be detained must be reasonable and kept to a minimum. Where the exercise of the power requires reasonable suspicion, the thoroughness and extent of a search must depend on what is suspected of being carried, and by whom. If the suspicion relates to a particular article which is seen to be slipped into a person's pocket, then, in the absence of other grounds for suspicion or an opportunity for the article to be moved elsewhere, the search must be confined to that pocket. In the case of a small article which can readily be concealed, such as a drug, and which might be concealed anywhere on the person, a more extensive search may be necessary. In the case of searches mentioned in paragraph 2.1(b), (c), and (d), which do not require reasonable grounds for suspicion, officers may make any reasonable search to look for items for which they are empowered to search. [See *Note 5*]

3.4   The search must be carried out at or near the place where the person or vehicle was first detained. [See *Note 6*]

3.5   There is no power to require a person to remove any clothing in public other than an outer coat, jacket or gloves except under section 45(3) of the Terrorism Act 2000 (which empowers a constable conducting a search under section 44(1) or 44(2) of that Act to require a person to remove headgear and footwear in public) and under section 60AA of the Criminal Justice and Public Order Act 1994 (which empowers a constable to require a person to remove any item worn to conceal identity). [See *Notes 4* and *6*] A search in public of a person's clothing which has not been removed must be restricted to superficial examination of outer garments. This does not, however, prevent an officer from placing his or her hand inside the pockets of the outer clothing, or feeling round the inside of collars, socks and shoes if this is reasonably necessary in the circumstances to look for the object of the search or to remove and examine any item reasonably suspected to be the object of the search. For the same reasons, subject to the restrictions on the removal of headgear, a person's hair may also be searched in public (see paragraphs 3.1 and 3.3).

3.6   Where on reasonable grounds it is considered necessary to conduct a more thorough search (e.g. by requiring a person to take off a T-shirt), this must be done out of public view, for example, in a police van unless paragraph 3.7 applies, or police station if there is one nearby. [See *Note 6*] Any search involving the removal of more than an outer coat, jacket, gloves, headgear or footwear, or any other item concealing identity, may only be made by an officer of the same sex as the person searched and may not be made in the presence of anyone of the opposite sex unless the person being searched specifically requests it. [See *Notes 4, 7* and *8*]

3.7   Searches involving exposure of intimate parts of the body must not be conducted as a routine extension of a less thorough search, simply because nothing is found in the course of the initial search. Searches involving exposure of intimate parts of the body may be carried out only at a nearby police station or other nearby location which is out of public view (but not a police vehicle). These searches must be conducted in accordance with paragraph 11 of Annex A to Code C except that an intimate search mentioned in paragraph 11 (f) of Annex A to Code C may not be authorised or carried out under any stop and search powers. The other provisions of Code C do not apply to the conduct and recording of searches of persons detained at police stations in the exercise of stop and search powers. [See *Note 7*]

## Steps to be taken prior to a search

3.8   Before any search of a detained person or attended vehicle takes place the officer must take reasonable steps to give the person to be searched or in charge of the vehicle the following information:

(a) that they are being detained for the purposes of a search;

(b) the officer's name (except in the case of enquiries linked to the investigation of terrorism, or otherwise where the officer reasonably believes that giving his or her name might put him or her in danger, in which case a warrant or other identification number shall be given) and the name of the police station to which the officer is attached;

(c) the legal search power which is being exercised; and

(d) a clear explanation of:
   (i)   the purpose of the search in terms of the article or articles for which there is a power to search; and
   (ii)  in the case of powers requiring reasonable suspicion (see paragraph 2.1(a)) the grounds for that suspicion; or
   (iii) in the case of powers which do not require reasonable suspicion (see paragraph 2.1 (b), and (c)), the nature of the power and of any necessary authorisation and the fact that it has been given.

3.9   Officers not in uniform must show their warrant cards. Stops and searches under the powers mentioned in paragraphs 2.1 (b), and (c) may be undertaken only by a constable in uniform.

3.10   Before the search takes place the officer must inform the person (or the owner or person in charge of the vehicle that is to be searched) of his or her entitlement to a copy of the record of the search, including his entitlement to a record of the search if an application is made within 12 months, if it is wholly impracticable to make a record at the time. If a record is not made at the time the person should also be told how a copy can be obtained (see section 4). The person should also be given information about police powers to stop and search and the individual's rights in these circumstances.

3.11   If the person to be searched, or in charge of a vehicle to be searched, does not appear to understand what is being said, or there is any doubt about the person's ability to understand English, the officer must take reasonable steps to bring information regarding the person's rights and any relevant provisions of this Code to his or her attention. If the person is deaf or cannot understand English and is accompanied by someone, then the officer must try to establish whether that person can interpret or otherwise help the officer to give the required information.

## 4   Recording requirements

4.1   An officer who has carried out a search in the exercise of any power to which this Code applies, must make a record of it at the time, unless there are exceptional circumstances which would make this wholly impracticable (e.g. in situations involving public disorder or when the officer's presence is urgently required elsewhere). If a record is not made at the time, the officer must do so as soon as practicable afterwards. There may be situations in which it is not practicable to obtain the information necessary to complete a record, but the officer should make every reasonable effort to do so.

4.2   A copy of a record made at the time must be given immediately to the person who has been searched. The officer must ask for the name, address and date of birth of the person searched, but there is no obligation on a person to provide these details and no power of detention if the person is unwilling to do so.

4.3   The following information must always be included in the record of a search even if the person does not wish to provide any personal details:

(i)    the name of the person searched, or (if it is withheld) a description;

(ii)   a note of the person's self-defined ethnic background; [See *Note 18*]

(iii)  when a vehicle is searched, its registration number; [See *Note 17*]

(iv)   the date, time, and place that the person or vehicle was first detained;

(v)    the date, time and place the person or vehicle was searched (if different from (iv));

(vi)   the purpose of the search;

(vii)  the grounds for making it, or in the case of those searches mentioned in paragraph 2.1(b) and (c), the nature of the power and of any necessary authorisation and the fact that it has been given; [See *Note 17*]

(viii) its outcome (e.g. arrest or no further action);

(ix)   a note of any injury or damage to property resulting from it;

(x)    subject to paragraph 3.8(a), the identity of the officer making the search. [See *Note 15*]

4.4   Nothing in paragraph 4.3 (x) requires the names of police officers to be shown on the search record or any other record required to be made under this code in the case of enquiries linked to the investigation of terrorism or otherwise where an officer reasonably believes that recording names might endanger the officers. In such cases the record must show the officers' warrant or other identification number and duty station.

4.5   A record is required for each person and each vehicle searched. However, if a person is in a vehicle and both are searched, and the object and grounds of the search are the same, only one record need be completed. If more than one person in a vehicle is searched, separate records for each search of a person must be made. If only a vehicle is searched, the name of the driver and his or her self-defined ethnic background must be recorded, unless the vehicle is unattended.

4.6   The record of the grounds for making a search must, briefly but informatively, explain the reason for suspecting the person concerned, by reference to the person's behaviour and/or other circumstances.

4.7   Where officers detain an individual with a view to performing a search, but the search is not carried out due to the grounds for suspicion being eliminated as a result of questioning the person detained, a record must still be made in accordance with the procedure outlined above.

4.8   After searching an unattended vehicle, or anything in or on it, an officer must leave a notice in it (or on it, if things on it have been searched without opening it) recording the fact that it has been searched.

4.9   The notice must include the name of the police station to which the officer concerned is attached and state where a copy of the record of the search may be obtained and where any application for compensation should be directed.

4.10   The vehicle must if practicable be left secure.

## 5   Monitoring and supervising the use of stop and search powers

5.1   Supervising officers must monitor the use of stop and search powers and should consider in particular whether there is any evidence that they are being exercised on the basis of stereotyped images or inappropriate generalisations. Supervising officers should satisfy themselves that the practice of officers under their supervision in stopping, searching and recording is fully in accordance with this Code. Supervisors must also examine whether the records reveal any trends or patterns which give cause for concern, and if so take appropriate action to address this.

5.2   Senior officers with area or force-wide responsibilities must also monitor the broader use of stop and search powers and, where necessary, take action at the relevant level.

5.3   Supervision and monitoring must be supported by the compilation of comprehensive statistical records of stops and searches at force, area and local level. Any apparently disproportionate use of the powers by particular officers or groups of officers or in relation to specific sections of the community should be identified and investigated.

5.4   In order to promote public confidence in the use of the powers, forces in consultation with police authorities must make arrangements for the records to be scrutinised by representatives of the community, and to explain the use of the powers at a local level. [See *Note 19*]

## *Notes for Guidance*

### *Officers exercising stop and search powers*

*1   This code does not affect the ability of an officer to speak to or question a person in the ordinary course of the officer's duties without detaining the person or exercising any element of compulsion. It is not the purpose of the code to prohibit such encounters between the police and the community with the co-operation of the person concerned and neither does it affect the principle that all citizens have a duty to help police officers to prevent crime and discover offenders. This is a civic rather than a legal duty; but when a police officer is trying to discover whether, or by whom, an offence has been committed he or she may question any person from whom useful information might be obtained, subject to the restrictions imposed by Code C. A person's unwillingness to reply does not alter this entitlement, but in the absence of a power to arrest, or to detain in order to search, the person is free to leave at will and cannot be compelled to remain with the officer.*

*2   In some circumstances preparatory questioning may be unnecessary, but in general a brief conversation or exchange will be desirable not only as a means of avoiding unsuccessful searches, but to explain the grounds for the stop/search, to gain co-operation and reduce any tension there might be surrounding the stop/search.*

*3   Where a person is lawfully detained for the purpose of a search, but no search in the event takes place, the detention will not thereby have been rendered unlawful.*

*4   Many people customarily cover their heads or faces for religious reasons—for example, Muslim women, Sikh men, Sikh or Hindu women, or Rastafarian men or women. A police officer cannot order the removal of a head or face covering except where there is reason to believe that the item is being worn by the individual wholly or mainly for the purpose of disguising identity, not simply because it disguises identity. Where there may be religious sensitivities about ordering the removal of such an item, the officer should permit the item to be removed out of public view. Where practicable, the item should be removed in the presence of an officer of the same sex as the person and out of sight of anyone of the opposite sex.*

*5   A search of a person in public should be completed as soon as possible.*

*6   A person may be detained under a stop and search power at a place other than where the person was first detained, only if that place, be it a police station or elsewhere, is nearby. Such a place should be located within a reasonable travelling distance using whatever mode of travel (on foot or by car) is appropriate. This applies to all searches under stop and search powers, whether or not they involve the removal of clothing or exposure of intimate parts of the body (see paragraphs 3.6 and 3.7) or take place in or out of public view. It means, for example, that a search under the stop and search power in section 23 of the Misuse of Drugs Act 1971 which involves the compulsory removal of more than a person's outer coat, jacket or gloves cannot be carried out unless a place which is both nearby the place they were first detained and out of public view, is available. If a search involves exposure of intimate parts of the body and a police station is not nearby, particular care must be taken to ensure that the location is suitable in that it enables the search to be conducted in accordance with the requirements of paragraph 11 of Annex A to Code C.*

*7   A search in the street itself should be regarded as being in public for the purposes of paragraphs 3.6 and 3.7 above, even though it may be empty at the time a search begins. Although there is no power to require a person to do so, there is nothing to prevent an officer from asking a person voluntarily to remove more than an outer coat, jacket or gloves (and headgear or footwear under section 45(3) of the Terrorism Act 2000) in public.*

*8   Where there may be religious sensitivities about asking someone to remove headgear using a power under section 45(3) of the Terrorism Act 2000, the police officer should offer to carry out the search out of public view (for example, in a police van or police station if there is one nearby).*

*9   Other means of identification might include jewellery, insignias, tattoos or other features which are known to identify members of the particular gang or group.*

## *Authorising officers*

*10   The powers under section 60 are separate from and additional to the normal stop and search powers which require reasonable grounds to suspect an individual of carrying an offensive weapon (or other article). Their overall purpose is to prevent serious violence and the widespread carrying of weapons which might lead to persons being seriously injured by disarming potential offenders in circumstances where other powers would not be sufficient. They should not therefore be used to replace or circumvent the normal powers for dealing with routine crime problems. The purpose of the powers under section 60AA is to prevent those involved in intimidatory or violent protests using face coverings to disguise identity.*

*11   Authorisations under section 60 require a reasonable belief on the part of the authorising officer. This must have an objective basis, for example: intelligence or relevant information such as a history of antagonism and violence between particular groups; previous incidents of violence at, or connected with, particular events or locations; a significant increase in knife-point robberies in a limited area; reports that individuals are regularly carrying weapons in a particular locality; or in the case of section 60AA previous incidents of crimes being committed while wearing face coverings to conceal identity.*

*12   It is for the authorising officer to determine the period of time during which the powers mentioned in paragraph 2.1 (b) and (c) may be exercised. The officer should set the minimum period he or she considers necessary to deal with the risk of violence, the carrying of knives or offensive weapons, or terrorism. A direction to extend the period authorised under the powers mentioned in paragraph 2.1 (b) may be given only once. Thereafter further use of the powers requires a new authorisation. There is no provision to extend an authorisation of the powers mentioned in paragraph 2.1(c); further use of the powers requires a new authorisation.*

*13   It is for the authorising officer to determine the geographical area in which the use of the powers is to be authorised. In doing so the officer may wish to take into account factors such as the nature and venue of the anticipated incident, the number of people who may be in the immediate area of any possible incident, their access to surrounding areas and the anticipated level of violence. The officer should not set a geographical area which is wider than that he or she believes necessary for the purpose of preventing anticipated violence, the carrying of knives or offensive weapons, acts of terrorism, or, in the case of section 60AA, the prevention of commission of offences. It is particularly important to ensure that constables exercising such powers are fully aware of where they may be used. If the area specified is smaller than the whole force area, the officer giving the authorisation should specify either the streets which form the boundary of the area or a divisional boundary within the force area. If the power is to be used in response to a threat or incident that straddles police force areas, an officer from each of the forces concerned will need to give an authorisation.*

*14   An officer who has authorised the use of powers under section 44 of the Terrorism Act 2000 must take immediate steps to send a copy of the authorisation to the National Joint Unit, Metropolitan Police Special Branch, who will forward it to the Secretary of State. The Secretary of State should be informed of the reasons for the authorisation. The National Joint Unit will inform the force concerned, within 48 hours of the authorisation being made, whether the Secretary of State has confirmed or cancelled or altered the authorisation.*

## *Recording*

15   *Where a stop and search is conducted by more than one officer the identity of all the officers engaged in the search must be recorded on the record. Nothing prevents an officer who is present but not directly involved in searching from completing the record during the course of the encounter.*

16   *Where a vehicle has not been allocated a registration number (e.g. a rally car or a trials motorbike) that part of the requirement under 4.3(iii) does not apply.*

17   *It is important for monitoring purposes to specify whether the authority for exercising a stop and search power was given under section 60 of the Criminal Justice and Public Order Act 1994, or under section 44(1) or 44(2) of the Terrorism Act 2000.*

18   *Officers should record the self-defined ethnicity of every person stopped according to the categories used in the 2001 census question listed in Annex B. Respondents should be asked to select one of the five main categories representing broad ethnic groups and then a more specific cultural background from within this group. The ethnic classification should be coded for recording purposes using the coding system in Annex B. An additional 'Not stated' box is available but should not be offered to respondents explicitly. Officers should be aware and explain to members of the public, especially where concerns are raised, that this information is required to obtain a true picture of stop and search activity and to help improve ethnic monitoring, tackle discriminatory practice, and promote effective use of the powers. If the person gives what appears to the officer to be an 'incorrect' answer (e.g. a person who appears to be white states that they are black), the officer should record the response that has been given. Officers should also record their own perception of the ethnic background of every person stopped and this must be done by using the PNC/Phoenix classification system. If the 'Not stated' category is used the reason for this must be recorded on the form.*

19   *Arrangements for public scrutiny of records should take account of the right to confidentiality of those stopped and searched. Anonymised forms and/or statistics generated from records should be the focus of the examinations by members of the public.*

## ANNEX A   SUMMARY OF MAIN STOP AND SEARCH POWERS

| Power | Object of Search | Extent of Search | Where Exercisable |
| --- | --- | --- | --- |
| **Unlawful articles general** | | | |
| 1. Public Stores Act 1875, s. 6 | HM Stores stolen or unlawfully obtained | Persons, vehicles and vessels | Anywhere where the constabulary powers are exercisable |
| 2. Firearms Act 1968, s. 47 | Firearms | Persons and vehicles | A public place, or anywhere in the case of reasonable suspicion of offences of carrying firearms with criminal intent or trespassing with firearms |
| 3. Misuse of Drugs Act 1971, s. 23 | Controlled drugs | Persons and vehicles | Anywhere |
| 4. Customs and Excise Management Act 1979, s. 163 | Goods: (a) on which duty has not been paid; (b) being unlawfully removed, imported or exported; (c) otherwise liable to forfeiture to HM Customs and Excise | Vehicles and vessels only | Anywhere |
| 5. Aviation Security Act 1982, s. 27(1) | Stolen or unlawfully obtained goods | Airport employees and vehicles carrying airport employees or aircraft or any vehicle in a cargo area whether or not carrying an employee | Any designated airport |

Annex A    (Continued)

| Power | Object of Search | Extent of Search | Where Exercisable |
|---|---|---|---|
| 6. Police and Criminal Evidence Act 1984, s. 1 | Stolen goods; articles for use in certain Theft Act offences; offensive weapons, including bladed or sharply-pointed articles (except folding pocket knives with a bladed cutting edge not exceeding 3 inches) | Persons and vehicles | Where there is public access |
| Police and Criminal Evidence Act 1984, s. 6(3) (by a constable of the United Kingdom Atomic Energy Authority Constabulary in respect of property owned or controlled by British Nuclear Fuels plc) | HM Stores (in the form of goods and chattels belonging to British Nuclear Fuels plc) | Persons, vehicles and vessels | Anywhere where the constabulary powers are exercisable |
| 7. Sporting events (Control of Alcohol etc.) Act 1985, s. 7 | Intoxicating liquor | Persons, coaches and trains | Designated sports grounds or coaches and trains travelling to or from a designated sporting event |
| 8. Crossbows Act 1987, s. 4 | Crossbows or parts of crossbows (except crossbows with a draw weight of less than 1.4 kilograms) | Persons and vehicles | Anywhere except dwellings |
| 9. Criminal Justice Act 1988, s. 139B | Offensive weapons, bladed or sharply pointed article | Persons | School premises |

**Evidence of game and wildlife offences**

| Power | Object of Search | Extent of Search | Where Exercisable |
|---|---|---|---|
| 10. Poaching Prevention Act 1862, s. 2 | Game or poaching equipment | Persons and vehicles | A public place |
| 11. Deer Act 1991, s. 12 | Evidence of offences under the Act | Persons and vehicles | Anywhere except dwellings |
| 12. Conservation of Seals Act 1970, s. 4 | Seals or hunting equipment | Vehicles only | Anywhere |
| 13. Protection of Badgers Act 1992 s. 11 | Evidence of offences under the Act | Persons and vehicles | Anywhere |
| 14. Wildlife and Countryside Act 1981, s. 19 | Evidence of wildlife offences | Persons and vehicles | Anywhere except dwellings |

**Other**

| Power | Object of Search | Extent of Search | Where Exercisable |
|---|---|---|---|
| 15. Terrorism Act 2000, s. 43 | Evidence of liability to arrest under section 14 of the Act | Persons | Anywhere |
| 16. Terrorism Act 2000, s. 44(1) | Articles which could be used for a purpose connected with the commission, preparation or instigation of acts of terrorism | Vehicles, driver and passengers | Anywhere within the area or locality authorised under subsection (1) |
| 17. Terrorism Act 2000, s. 44(2) | Articles which could be used for a purpose connected with the commission, preparation or instigation of acts of terrorism | Pedestrians | Anywhere within the area of locality authorised |

Annex A    (Continued)

| Power | Object of Search | Extent of Search | Where Exercisable |
|---|---|---|---|
| 18.  Paragraphs 7 and 8 of Schedule 7 to the Terrorism Act 2000 | Anything relevant to determining if a person being examined falls within paragraph 2(1)(a) to (c) of Schedule 5 | Persons, vehicles, vessels etc. | Ports and airports |
| 19.  Section 60 Criminal Justice and Public Order Act 1994, as amended by s. 8 of the Knives Act 1997 | Offensive weapons or dangerous instruments to prevent incidents of serious violence or to deal with the carrying of such items | Persons and vehicles | Anywhere within a locality authorised under subsection (1) |

## ANNEX B    SELF-DEFINED ETHNIC CLASSIFICATION CATEGORIES

| | |
|---|---|
| *White* | **W** |
| A.  *White—British* | *W1* |
| B.  *White—Irish* | *W2* |
| C.  *Any other White background* | *W9* |
| *Mixed* | **M** |
| D.  *White and Black Caribbean* | *M1* |
| E.  *White and Black African* | *M2* |
| F.  *White and Asian* | *M3* |
| G.  *Any other Mixed Background* | *M9* |
| *Asian/Asian—British* | **A** |
| H.  *Asian—Indian* | *A1* |
| I.  *Asian—Pakistani* | *A2* |
| J.  *Asian—Bangladeshi* | *A3* |
| K.  *Any other Asian background* | *A9* |
| *Black/Black—British* | **B** |
| L.  *Black—Caribbean* | *B1* |
| M.  *Black African* | *B2* |
| N.  *Any other Black background* | *B9* |
| *Other* | **O** |
| O.  *Chinese* | *O1* |
| P.  *Any other* | *O9* |
| **Not Stated** | **NS** |

# Appendix 2

# PACE Code of Practice for Searches of Premises by Police Officers and the Seizure of Property found by Police Officers on Persons or Premises (Code B)

**Commencement—Transitional Arrangements**

This Code applies to applications for warrants made after 31 March 2003 and to searches and seizures taking place after midnight on 31 March 2003.

## 1 Introduction

1.1   This Code of Practice deals with police powers to:

- search premises
- seize and retain property found on premises and persons

1.1A   These powers may be used to find:

- property and material relating to a crime
- wanted persons
- children who abscond from local authority accommodation where they have been remanded or committed by a court

1.2   A justice of the peace may issue a search warrant granting powers of entry, search and seizure, e.g. warrants to search for stolen property, drugs, firearms and evidence of serious offences. Police also have powers without a search warrant. The main ones provided by the Police and Criminal Evidence Act 1984 (PACE) include powers to search premises:

- to make an arrest
- after an arrest

1.3   The right to privacy and respect for personal property are key principles of the Human Rights Act 1998. Powers of entry, search and seizure should be fully and clearly justified before use because they may significantly interfere with the occupier's privacy. Officers should consider if the necessary objectives can be met by less intrusive means.

1.4   In all cases, police should:

- exercise their powers courteously and with respect for persons and property
- only use reasonable force when this is considered necessary and proportionate to the circumstances

1.5   If the provisions of PACE and this Code are not observed, evidence obtained from a search may be open to question.

## 2   **General**

2.1   This Code must be readily available at all police stations for consultation by:

- police officers
- detained persons
- members of the public

2.2   The *Notes for Guidance* included are not provisions of this Code.

2.3   This Code applies to searches of premises:

   (a) by police for the purposes of an investigation into an alleged offence, with the occupier's consent, other than:

   - routine scene of crime searches;
   - calls to a fire or burglary made by or on behalf of an occupier or searches following the activation of fire or burglar alarms or discovery of insecure premises;
   - searches when *paragraph 5.4* applies;
   - bomb threat calls;

   (b) under powers conferred on police officers by PACE, sections 17,18 and 32;

   (c) undertaken in pursuance of search warrants issued to and executed by constables in accordance with PACE, sections 15 and 16. See *Note 2A*;

   (d) subject to *paragraph 2.6*, under any other power given to police to enter premises with or without a search warrant for any purpose connected with the investigation into an alleged or suspected offence. See *Note 2B*.

For the purposes of this Code, 'premises' as defined in PACE, section 23, includes any place, vehicle, vessel, aircraft, hovercraft, tent or movable structure and any offshore installation as defined in the Mineral Workings (Offshore Installations) Act 1971, section 1. See *Note 2D*

2.4   A person who has not been arrested but is searched during a search of premises should be searched in accordance with Code A. See *Note 2C*

2.5   This Code does not apply to the exercise of a statutory power to enter premises or to inspect goods, equipment or procedures if the exercise of that power is not dependent on the existence of grounds for suspecting that an offence may have been committed and the person exercising the power has no reasonable grounds for such suspicion.

2.6   This Code does not affect any directions of a search warrant or order, lawfully executed in England or Wales that any item or evidence seized under that warrant or order be handed over to a police force, court, tribunal, or other authority outside England or Wales. For example, warrants and orders issued in Scotland or Northern Ireland, see *Note 2B(f)* and search warrants issued under the Criminal Justice (International Co-operation) Act 1990, section 7.

2.7   When this Code requires the prior authority or agreement of an officer of at least inspector or superintendent rank, that authority may be given by a sergeant or chief inspector authorised to perform the functions of the higher rank under PACE, section 107.

2.8   Written records required under this Code not made in the search record shall, unless otherwise specified, be made:

- in the recording officer's pocket book ('pocket book' includes any official report book issued to police officers) or
- on forms provided for the purpose

2.9   Nothing in this Code requires the identity of officers (or anyone accompanying them during a search of premises) to be recorded or disclosed:

   (a) in the case of enquiries linked to the investigation of terrorism; or

   (b) if officers reasonably believe recording or disclosing their names might put them in danger.

In these cases officers should use warrant or other identification numbers and the name of their police station. See *Note 2E*

2.10 The 'officer in charge of the search' means the officer assigned specific duties and responsibilities under this Code. Whenever there is a search of premises to which this Code applies one officer must act as the officer in charge of the search. See *Note 2F*

2.11 In this Code:

(a) 'designated person' means a person other than a police officer, designated under the Police Reform Act 2002, Part 4 who has specified powers and duties of police officers conferred or imposed on them;

(b) any reference to a police officer includes a designated person acting in the exercise or performance of the powers and duties conferred or imposed on them by their designation.

2.12 If a power conferred on a designated person:

(a) allows reasonable force to be used when exercised by a police officer, a designated person exercising that power has the same entitlement to use force;

(b) includes power to use force to enter any premises, that power is not exercisable by that designated person except:

(i) in the company and under the supervision of a police officer; or
(ii) for the purpose of:
- saving life or limb; or
- preventing serious damage to property.

2.13 Designated persons must have regard to any relevant provisions of the Codes of Practice.

## Notes for guidance

*2A   PACE sections 15 and 16 apply to all search warrants issued to and executed by constables under any enactment, e.g. search warrants issued by a:*

*(a) justice of the peace under the:*

- *Theft Act 1968, section 26—stolen property;*
- *Misuse of Drugs Act 1971, section 23—controlled drugs;*
- *PACE, section 8—evidence of serious arrestable offence*
- *Terrorism Act 2000, Schedule 5, paragraph 1;*

*(b) circuit judge under the:*

- *PACE, Schedule 1;*
- *Terrorism Act 2000, Schedule 5, paragraph 11.*

*2B   Examples of the other powers in paragraph 2.3(d) include:*

*(a) Road Traffic Act 1988 giving police power to enter premises:*

*(i) under section 4(7) to:*
- *arrest a person for driving or being in charge of a vehicle when unfit;*

*(ii) under section 6(6) to:*
- *require a person to provide a specimen of breath; or*
- *arrest a person following:*
  - *~ a positive breath test;*
  - *~ failure to provide a specimen of breath;*

*(b) Transport and Works Act 1992, sections 30(3) and 30(4) giving police powers to enter premises mirroring the powers in (a) in relation to specified persons working on transport systems to which the Act applies;*

*(c) Criminal Justice Act 1988, section 139B giving police power to enter and search school premises for offensive weapons, bladed or pointed articles;*

(d) *Terrorism Act 2000, Schedule 5, paragraphs 3 and 15 empowering a superintendent in urgent cases to give written authority for police to enter and search premises for the purposes of a terrorist investigation;*

(e) *Explosives Act 1875, section 73(b) empowering a superintendent to give written authority for police to enter premises, examine and search them for explosives;*

(f) *search warrants and production orders or the equivalent issued in Scotland or Northern Ireland endorsed under the Summary Jurisdiction (Process) Act 1881 or the Petty Sessions (Ireland) Act 1851 respectively for execution in England and Wales.*

*2C The Criminal Justice Act 1988, section 139B provides that a constable who has reasonable grounds to believe an offence under the Criminal Justice Act 1988, section 139A has or is being committed may enter school premises and search the premises and any persons on the premises for any bladed or pointed article or offensive weapon. Persons may be searched under a warrant issued under the Misuse of Drugs Act 1971, section 23(3) to search premises for drugs or documents only if the warrant specifically authorises the search of persons on the premises.*

*2D The Immigration Act 1971, Part III and Schedule 2 gives immigration officers powers to enter and search premises, seize and retain property, with and without a search warrant. These are similar to the powers available to police under search warrants issued by a justice of the peace and without a warrant under PACE, sections 17, 18, 19 and 32 except they only apply to specified offences under the Immigration Act 1971 and immigration control powers. For certain types of investigations and enquiries these powers avoid the need for the Immigration Service to rely on police officers becoming directly involved. When exercising these powers, immigration officers are required by the Immigration and Asylum Act 1999, section 145 to have regard to this Code's corresponding provisions. When immigration officers are dealing with persons or property at police stations, police officers should give appropriate assistance to help them discharge their specific duties and responsibilities.*

*2E The purpose of paragraph 2.9(b) is to protect those involved in serious organised crime investigations or arrests of particularly violent suspects when there is reliable information that those arrested or their associates may threaten or cause harm to the officers. In cases of doubt, an officer of inspector rank or above should be consulted.*

*2F For the purposes of paragraph 2.10, the officer in charge of the search should normally be the most senior officer present. Some exceptions are:*

(a) *a supervising officer who attends or assists at the scene of a premises search may appoint an officer of lower rank as officer in charge of the search if that officer is:*

- *more conversant with the facts;*
- *a more appropriate officer to be in charge of the search;*

(b) *when all officers in a premises search are the same rank. The supervising officer if available must make sure one of them is appointed officer in charge of the search, otherwise the officers themselves must nominate one of their number as the officer in charge;*

(c) *a senior officer assisting in a specialist role. This officer need not be regarded as having a general supervisory role over the conduct of the search or be appointed or expected to act as the officer in charge of the search.*

*Except in (c), nothing in this Note diminishes the role and responsibilities of a supervisory officer who is present at the search or knows of a search taking place.*

## 3 Search warrants and production orders

### (a) Before making an application

3.1 When information appears to justify an application, the officer must take reasonable steps to check the information is accurate, recent and not provided maliciously or irresponsibly. An application may not be made on the basis of information from an anonymous source if corroboration has not been sought. See *Note 3A*

3.2  The officer shall ascertain as specifically as possible the nature of the articles concerned and their location.

3.3  The officer shall make reasonable enquiries to:

(i)  establish if:

- anything is known about the likely occupier of the premises and the nature of the premises themselves;
- the premises have been searched previously and how recently;

(ii)  obtain any other relevant information.

3.4  An application:

(a)  to a justice of the peace for a search warrant or to a circuit judge for a search warrant or production order under PACE, Schedule 1

must be supported by a signed written authority from an officer of inspector rank or above:

Note: If the case is an urgent application to a justice of the peace and an inspector or above is not readily available, the next most senior officer on duty can give the written authority.

(b)  to a circuit judge under the Terrorism Act 2000, Schedule 5 for

- a production order;
- search warrant; or
- an order requiring an explanation of material seized or produced under such a warrant or production order

must be supported by a signed written authority from an officer of superintendent rank or above.

3.5  Except in a case of urgency, if there is reason to believe a search might have an adverse effect on relations between the police and the community, the officer in charge shall consult the local police/community liaison officer:

- before the search; or
- in urgent cases, as soon as practicable after the search

### (b)  Making an application

3.6  A search warrant application must be supported in writing, specifying:

(a)  the enactment under which the application is made, see *Note 2A*;

(b)  the premises to be searched;

(c)  the object of the search, see *Note 3B*;

(d)  the grounds for the application, including, when the purpose of the proposed search is to find evidence of an alleged offence, an indication of how the evidence relates to the investigation;

(e)  there are no reasonable grounds to believe the material to be sought, when making application to a:

(i)  justice of the peace or a circuit judge, consists of or includes items subject to legal privilege;

(ii)  justice of the peace, consists of or includes excluded material or special procedure material;

Note: this does not affect the additional powers of seizure in the Criminal Justice and Police Act 2001, Part 2 covered in paragraph 7.7, see *Note 3B*;

(f)  if applicable, a request for the warrant to authorise a person or persons to accompany the officer who executes the warrant, see *Note 3C*.

3.7  A search warrant application under PACE, Schedule 1, paragraph 12(a), shall if appropriate indicate why it is believed service of notice of an application for a production order may seriously prejudice the investigation. Applications for search warrants under the Terrorism Act 2000, Schedule 5, paragraph 11 must indicate why a production order would not be appropriate.

3.8  If a search warrant application is refused, a further application may not be made for those premises unless supported by additional grounds.

# Notes for guidance

*3A    The identity of an informant need not be disclosed when making an application, but the officer should be prepared to answer any questions the magistrate or judge may have about:*

- *the accuracy of previous information from that source*

- *any other related matters*

*3B    The information supporting a search warrant application should be as specific as possible, particularly in relation to the articles or persons being sought and where in the premises it is suspected they may be found. The meaning of 'items subject to legal privilege', 'special procedure material' and 'excluded material' are defined by PACE, sections 10, 11 and 14 respectively.*

*3C    Under PACE, section 16(2), a search warrant may authorise persons other than police officers to accompany the constable who executes the warrant. This includes, e.g. any suitably qualified or skilled person or an expert in a particular field whose presence is needed to help accurately identify the material sought or to advise where certain evidence is most likely to be found and how it should be dealt with. It does not give them any right to force entry, to search for or seize property but it gives them the right to be on the premises during the search without the occupier's permission.*

## 4    Entry without warrant—particular powers

*(a)    Making an arrest etc*

4.1    The conditions under which an officer may enter and search premises without a warrant are set out in PACE, section 17. It should be noted that this section does not create or confer any powers of arrest. See other powers in *Note 2B(a)*.

*(b)    Search of premises where arrest takes place or the arrested person was immediately before arrest*

4.2    The powers of an officer to search premises where that officer arrested a person or where the person was immediately before being arrested are set out in PACE, section 32.

*(c)    Search of premises occupied or controlled by the arrested person*

4.3    The specific powers to search premises occupied or controlled by an arrested person are set out in PACE, section 18. They may not be exercised, except if section 18 (5) applies, unless an officer of inspector rank or above has given written authority. That authority should only be given when the authorising officer is satisfied the necessary grounds exist. If possible the authorising officer should record the authority on the Notice of Powers and Rights and, subject to *paragraph 2.9*, sign the Notice. The record of the grounds for the search and the nature of the evidence sought as required by section 18(7) of the Act should be made in:

- the custody record if there is one, otherwise

- the officer's pocket book, or

- the search record

## 5    Search with consent

5.1    Subject to *paragraph 5.4*, if it is proposed to search premises with the consent of a person entitled to grant entry the consent must, if practicable, be given in writing on the Notice of Powers and Rights before the search. The officer must make any necessary enquiries to be satisfied the person is in a position to give such consent. See *Notes 5A* and *5B*

5.2    Before seeking consent the officer in charge of the search shall state the purpose of the proposed search and its extent. This information must be as specific as possible, particularly regarding the articles or persons being sought and the parts of the premises to be searched. The person concerned must be clearly informed they are not obliged to consent and anything seized may be produced in evidence. If at the time the person is not suspected of an offence, the officer shall say this when stating the purpose of the search.

5.3   An officer cannot enter and search or continue to search premises under *paragraph 5.1* if consent is given under duress or withdrawn before the search is completed.

5.4   It is unnecessary to seek consent under *paragraphs 5.1* and *5.2* if this would cause disproportionate inconvenience to the person concerned. See *Note 5C*

## *Notes for guidance*

5A   *In a lodging house or similar accommodation, every reasonable effort should be made to obtain the consent of the tenant, lodger or occupier. A search should not be made solely on the basis of the landlord's consent unless the tenant, lodger or occupier is unavailable and the matter is urgent.*

5B   *If the intention is to search premises under the authority of a warrant or a power of entry and search without warrant, and the occupier of the premises co-operates in accordance with paragraph 6.4, there is no need to obtain written consent.*

5C   *Paragraph 5.4 is intended to apply when it is reasonable to assume innocent occupiers would agree to, and expect, police to take the proposed action, e.g. if:*

- *a suspect has fled the scene of a crime or to evade arrest and it is necessary quickly to check surrounding gardens and readily accessible places to see if the suspect is hiding*

- *police have arrested someone in the night after a pursuit and it is necessary to make a brief check of gardens along the pursuit route to see if stolen or incriminating articles have been discarded*

## 6   Searching premises—general considerations

### (a)   Time of searches

6.1   Searches made under warrant must be made within one calendar month of the date of the warrant's issue.

6.2   Searches must be made at a reasonable hour unless this might frustrate the purpose of the search.

6.3   A warrant authorises an entry on one occasion only. When the extent or complexity of a search mean it is likely to take a long time, the officer in charge of the search may consider using the seize and sift powers referred to in *section 7*.

### (b)   Entry other than with consent

6.4   The officer in charge of the search shall first try to communicate with the occupier, or any other person entitled to grant access to the premises, explain the authority under which entry is sought and ask the occupier to allow entry, unless:

(i)   the search premises are unoccupied;

(ii)   the occupier and any other person entitled to grant access are absent;

(iii) there are reasonable grounds for believing that alerting the occupier or any other person entitled to grant access would frustrate the object of the search or endanger officers or other people.

6.5   Unless *sub-paragraph 6.4(iii)* applies, if the premises are occupied the officer, subject to *paragraph 2.9*, shall, before the search begins:

(i)   identify him or herself, show their warrant card (if not in uniform) and state the purpose of and grounds for the search;

(ii)   identify and introduce any person accompanying the officer on the search (such persons should carry identification for production on request) and briefly describe that person's role in the process.

6.6   Reasonable and proportionate force may be used if necessary to enter premises if the officer in charge of the search is satisfied the premises are those specified in any warrant, or in exercise of the powers described in *paragraphs 4.1* to *4.3*, and if:

(i)   the occupier or any other person entitled to grant access has refused entry;

(ii)  it is impossible to communicate with the occupier or any other person entitled to grant access; or

(iii) any of the provisions of *paragraph 6.4* apply.

*(c)   Notice of Powers and Rights*

6.7   If an officer conducts a search to which this Code applies the officer shall, unless it is impracticable to do so, provide the occupier with a copy of a Notice in a standard format:

(i)   specifying if the search is made under warrant, with consent, or in the exercise of the powers described in *paragraphs 4.1* to *4.3*. Note: the notice format shall provide for authority or consent to be indicated, see *paragraphs 4.3* and *5.1*;

(ii)  summarising the extent of the powers of search and seizure conferred by PACE;

(iii) explaining the rights of the occupier, and the owner of the property seized;

(iv)  explaining compensation may be payable in appropriate cases for damages caused entering and searching premises, and giving the address to send a compensation application, see *Note 6A*;

(v)   stating this Code is available at any police station.

6.8   If the occupier is:

- present, copies of the Notice and warrant shall, if practicable, be given to them before the search begins, unless the officer in charge of the search reasonably believes this would frustrate the object of the search or endanger officers or other people

- not present, copies of the Notice and warrant shall be left in a prominent place on the premises or appropriate part of the premises and endorsed, subject to *paragraph 2.9* with the name of the officer in charge of the search, the date and time of the search

The warrant shall be endorsed to show this has been done.

*(d)   Conduct of searches*

6.9   Premises may be searched only to the extent necessary to achieve the object of the search, having regard to the size and nature of whatever is sought.

6.9A  A search may not continue under:

- a warrant's authority once all the things specified in that warrant have been found

- any other power once the object of that search has been achieved

6.9B  No search may continue once the officer in charge of the search is satisfied whatever is being sought is not on the premises. See *Note 6B*. This does not prevent a further search of the same premises if additional grounds come to light supporting a further application for a search warrant or exercise or further exercise of another power. For example, when, as a result of new information, it is believed articles previously not found or additional articles are on the premises.

6.10  Searches must be conducted with due consideration for the property and privacy of the occupier and with no more disturbance than necessary. Reasonable force may be used only when necessary and proportionate because the co-operation of the occupier cannot be obtained or is insufficient for the purpose. See *Note 6C*

6.11  A friend, neighbour or other person must be allowed to witness the search if the occupier wishes unless the officer in charge of the search has reasonable grounds for believing the presence of the person asked for would seriously hinder the investigation or endanger officers or other people. A search need not be unreasonably delayed for this purpose. A record of the action taken should be made on the premises search record including the grounds for refusing the occupier's request.

6.12   A person is not required to be cautioned prior to being asked questions that are solely necessary for the purpose of furthering the proper and effective conduct of a search, see Code C, *paragraph 10.1(c)*. For example, questions to discover the occupier of specified premises, to find a key to open a locked drawer or cupboard or to otherwise seek co-operation during the search or to determine if a particular item is liable to be seized.

6.12A   If questioning goes beyond what is necessary for the purpose of the exemption in Code C, the exchange is likely to constitute an interview as defined by Code C, *paragraph 11.1A* and would require the associated safeguards included in Code C, *section 10*.

(e)   Leaving premises

6.13 If premises have been entered by force, before leaving the officer in charge of the search must make sure they are secure by:

- arranging for the occupier or their agent to be present
- any other appropriate means

(f)   Searches under PACE Schedule 1 or the Terrorism Act 2000, Schedule 5

6.14   An officer of inspector rank or above shall be the officer in charge of the search, see *paragraph 2.10*, in respect of any search made under a warrant issued under PACE Act 1984, Schedule 1 or the Terrorism Act 2000, Schedule 5. They are responsible for making sure the search is conducted with discretion and in a manner that causes the least possible disruption to any business or other activities carried out on the premises.

6.15   Once the officer in charge of the search is satisfied material may not be taken from the premises without their knowledge, they shall ask for the documents or other records concerned. The officer in charge of the search may also ask to see the index to files held on the premises, and the officers conducting the search may inspect any files which, according to the index, appear to contain the material sought. A more extensive search of the premises may be made only if:

- the person responsible for them refuses to:
  - ~ produce the material sought, or
  - ~ allow access to the index
- it appears the index is:
  - ~ inaccurate, or
  - ~ incomplete
- for any other reason the officer in charge of the search has reasonable grounds for believing such a search is necessary in order to find the material sought

## *Notes for guidance*

*6A   Whether compensation is appropriate depends on the circumstances in each case. Compensation for damage caused when effecting entry is unlikely to be appropriate if the search was lawful, and the force used can be shown to be reasonable, proportionate and necessary to effect entry. If the wrong premises are searched by mistake everything possible should be done at the earliest opportunity to allay any sense of grievance and there should normally be a strong presumption in favour of paying compensation.*

*6B   It is important that, when possible, all those involved in a search are fully briefed about any powers to be exercised and the extent and limits within which it should be conducted.*

*6C   In all cases the number of officers and other persons involved in executing the warrant should be determined by what is reasonable and necessary according to the particular circumstances.*

## 7  Seizure and retention of property

*(a)  Seizure*

7.1  Subject to *paragraph 7.2*, an officer who is searching any person or premises under any statutory power or with the consent of the occupier may seize anything:

(a)  covered by a warrant

(b)  the officer has reasonable grounds for believing is evidence of an offence or has been obtained in consequence of the commission of an offence but only if seizure is necessary to prevent the items being concealed, lost, disposed of, altered, damaged, destroyed or tampered with

(c)  covered by the powers in the Criminal Justice and Police Act 2001, Part 2 allowing an officer to seize property from persons or premises and retain it for sifting or examination elsewhere

See *Note 7B*

7.2  No item may be seized which an officer has reasonable grounds for believing to be subject to legal privilege, as defined in PACE, section 10, other than under the Criminal Justice and Police Act 2001, Part 2.

7.3  Officers must be aware of the provisions in the Criminal Justice and Police Act 2001, section 59, allowing for applications to a judicial authority for the return of property seized and the subsequent duty to secure in section 60, see *paragraph 7.12(iii)*.

7.4  An officer may decide it is not appropriate to seize property because of an explanation from the person holding it but may nevertheless have reasonable grounds for believing it was obtained in consequence of an offence by some person. In these circumstances, the officer should identify the property to the holder, inform the holder of their suspicions and explain the holder may be liable to civil or criminal proceedings if they dispose of, alter or destroy the property.

7.5  An officer may arrange to photograph, image or copy, any document or other article they have the power to seize in accordance with *paragraph 7.1*. This is subject to specific restrictions on the examination, imaging or copying of certain property seized under the Criminal Justice and Police Act 2001, Part 2. An officer must have regard to their statutory obligation to retain an original document or other article only when a photograph or copy is not sufficient.

7.6  If an officer considers information stored in any electronic form and accessible from the premises could be used in evidence, they may require the information to be produced in a form:

- which can be taken away and in which it is visible and legible; or

- from which it can readily be produced in a visible and legible form

*(b)  Criminal Justice and Police Act 2001: Specific procedures for seize and sift powers*

7.7  The Criminal Justice and Police Act 2001, Part 2 gives officers limited powers to seize property from premises or persons so they can sift or examine it elsewhere. Officers must be careful they only exercise these powers when it is essential and they do not remove any more material than necessary. The removal of large volumes of material, much of which may not ultimately be retainable, may have serious implications for the owners, particularly when they are involved in business or activities such as journalism or the provision of medical services. Officers must carefully consider if removing copies or images of relevant material or data would be a satisfactory alternative to removing originals. When originals are taken, officers must be prepared to facilitate the provision of copies or images for the owners when reasonably practicable. See *Note 7C*

7.8  Property seized under the Criminal Justice and Police Act 2001, sections 50 or 51 must be kept securely and separately from any material seized under other powers. An examination under section 53 to determine which elements may be retained must be carried out at the earliest practicable time, having due regard to the desirability of allowing the person from whom the property was seized, or a person with an interest in the property, an opportunity of being present or represented at the examination.

7.8A   All reasonable steps should be taken to accommodate an interested person's request to be present, provided the request is reasonable and subject to the need to prevent harm to, interference with, or unreasonable delay to the investigatory process. If an examination proceeds in the absence of an interested person who asked to attend or their representative, the officer who exercised the relevant seizure power must give that person a written notice of why the examination was carried out in those circumstances. If it is necessary for security reasons or to maintain confidentiality officers may exclude interested persons from decryption or other processes which facilitate the examination but do not form part of it. See *Note 7D*

7.9   It is the responsibility of the officer in charge of the investigation to make sure property is returned in accordance with sections 53 to 55. Material which there is no power to retain must be:

- separated from the rest of the seized property

- returned as soon as reasonably practicable after examination of all the seized property

7.9A   Delay is only warranted if very clear and compelling reasons exist, e.g. the:

- unavailability of the person to whom the material is to be returned

- need to agree a convenient time to return a large volume of material

7.9B   Legally privileged, excluded or special procedure material which cannot be retained must be returned:

- as soon as reasonably practicable

- without waiting for the whole examination

7.9C   As set out in section 58, material must be returned to the person from whom it was seized, except when it is clear some other person has a better right to it. See *Note 7E*

7.10   When an officer involved in the investigation has reasonable grounds to believe a person with a relevant interest in property seized under section 50 or 51 intends to make an application under section 59 for the return of any legally privileged, special procedure or excluded material, the officer in charge of the investigation should be informed as soon as practicable and the material seized should be kept secure in accordance with section 61. See *Note 7C*

7.11   The officer in charge of the investigation is responsible for making sure property is properly secured. Securing involves making sure the property is not examined, copied, imaged or put to any other use except at the request, or with the consent, of the applicant or in accordance with the directions of the appropriate judicial authority. Any request, consent or directions must be recorded in writing and signed by both the initiator and the officer in charge of the investigation. See *Notes 7F* and *7G*

7.12   When an officer exercises a power of seizure conferred by sections 50 or 51 they shall provide the occupier of the premises or the person from whom the property is being seized with a written notice:

(i)   specifying what has been seized under the powers conferred by that section;

(ii)   specifying the grounds for those powers;

(iii)   setting out the effect of sections 59 to 61 covering the grounds for a person with a relevant interest in seized property to apply to a judicial authority for its return and the duty of officers to secure property in certain circumstances when an application is made;

(iv)   specifying the name and address of the person to whom:

- notice of an application to the appropriate judicial authority in respect of any of the seized property must be given;

- an application may be made to allow attendance at the initial examination of the property.

7.13   If the occupier is not present but there is someone in charge of the premises, the notice shall be given to them. If no suitable person is available, so the notice will easily be found it should either be:

- left in a prominent place on the premises

- attached to the exterior of the premises

*(c)*    *Retention*

7.14    Subject to *paragraph 7.15*, anything seized in accordance with the above provisions may be retained only for as long as is necessary. It may be retained, among other purposes:

    (i)    for use as evidence at a trial for an offence;

    (ii)   to facilitate the use in any investigation or proceedings of anything to which it is inextricably linked, see *Note 7H*;

    (iii)  for forensic examination or other investigation in connection with an offence;

    (iv)   in order to establish its lawful owner when there are reasonable grounds for believing it has been stolen or obtained by the commission of an offence.

7.15    Property shall not be retained under *paragraph 7.14(i)*, *(ii)* or *(iii)* if a copy or image would be sufficient.

*(d)*    *Rights of owners etc*

7.16    If property is retained, the person who had custody or control of it immediately before seizure must, on request, be provided with a list or description of the property within a reasonable time.

7.17    That person or their representative must be allowed supervised access to the property to examine it or have it photographed or copied, or must be provided with a photograph or copy, in either case within a reasonable time of any request and at their own expense, unless the officer in charge of an investigation has reasonable grounds for believing this would:

    (i)    prejudice the investigation of any offence or criminal proceedings; or

    (ii)   lead to the commission of an offence by providing access to unlawful material such as pornography.

A record of the grounds shall be made when access is denied.

## Notes for guidance

*7A    Any person claiming property seized by the police may apply to a magistrates' court under the Police (Property) Act 1897 for its possession and should, if appropriate, be advised of this procedure.*

*7B    The powers of seizure conferred by PACE, sections 18(2) and 19(3) extend to the seizure of the whole premises when it is physically possible to seize and retain the premises in their totality and practical considerations make seizure desirable. For example, police may remove premises such as tents, vehicles or caravans to a police station for the purpose of preserving evidence.*

*7C    Officers should consider reaching agreement with owners and/or other interested parties on the procedures for examining a specific set of property, rather than awaiting the judicial authority's determination. Agreement can sometimes give a quicker and more satisfactory route for all concerned and minimise costs and legal complexities.*

*7D    What constitutes a relevant interest in specific material may depend on the nature of that material and the circumstances in which it is seized. Anyone with a reasonable claim to ownership of the material and anyone entrusted with its safe keeping by the owner should be considered.*

*7E    Requirements to secure and return property apply equally to all copies, images or other material created because of seizure of the original property.*

*7F    The mechanics of securing property vary according to the circumstances; 'bagging up', i.e. placing material in sealed bags or containers and strict subsequent control of access is the appropriate procedure in many cases.*

*7G    When material is seized under the powers of seizure conferred by PACE, the duty to retain it under the Code of Practice issued under the Criminal Procedure and Investigations Act 1996 is subject to the provisions on retention of seized material in PACE, section 22.*

*7H Paragraph 7.14 (ii) applies if inextricably linked material is seized under the Criminal Justice and Police Act 2001, sections 50 or 51. Inextricably linked material is material it is not reasonably practicable to separate from other linked material without prejudicing the use of that other material in any investigation or proceedings. For example, it may not be possible to separate items of data held on computer disk without damaging their evidential integrity. Inextricably linked material must not be examined, imaged, copied or used for any purpose other than for proving the source and/or integrity of the linked material.*

## 8 Action after searches

8.1 If premises are searched in circumstances where this Code applies, unless the exceptions in *paragraph 2.3(a)* apply, on arrival at a police station the officer in charge of the search shall make or have made a record of the search, to include:

(i) the address of the searched premises;

(ii) the date, time and duration of the search;

(iii) the authority used for the search:

- if the search was made in exercise of a statutory power to search premises without warrant, the power which was used for the search:
- if the search was made under a warrant or with written consent;
    ~ a copy of the warrant and the written authority to apply for it, see *paragraph 3.4*; or
    ~ the written consent;

shall be appended to the record or the record shall show the location of the copy warrant or consent.

(iv) subject to *paragraph 2.9*, the names of:

- the officer(s) in charge of the search;
- all other officers who conducted the search;

(v) the names of any people on the premises if they are known;

(vi) any grounds for refusing the occupier's request to have someone present during the search, see *paragraph 6.11*;

(vii) a list of any articles seized or the location of a list and, if not covered by a warrant, the grounds for their seizure;

(viii) whether force was used, and the reason;

(ix) details of any damage caused during the search, and the circumstances;

(x) if applicable, the reason it was not practicable;

(a) to give the occupier a copy of the Notice of Powers and Rights, see *paragraph 6.7*;
(b) before the search to give the occupier a copy of the Notice, see *paragraph 6.8*;

(xi) when the occupier was not present, the place where copies of the Notice of Powers and Rights and search warrant were left on the premises, see *paragraph 6.8*.

8.2 When premises are searched under warrant, the warrant shall be endorsed to show:

(i) if any articles specified in the warrant were found;

(ii) if any other articles were seized;

(iii) the date and time it was executed;

(iv) subject to *paragraph 2.9*, the names of the officers who executed it;

(v) if a copy, together with a copy of the Notice of Powers and Rights was:

- handed to the occupier; or
- endorsed as required by *paragraph 6.8*; and left on the premises and where.

8.3 Any warrant shall be returned within one calendar month of its issue, if it was issued by a:

- justice of the peace, to the clerk to the justices for the petty sessions area concerned
- judge, to the appropriate officer of the court concerned

## 9    *Search registers*

9.1 A search register will be maintained at each sub-divisional or equivalent police station. All search records required under *paragraph 8.1* shall be made, copied, or referred to in the register. See *Note 9A*

## *Note for guidance*

9A *Paragraph 9.1 also applies to search records made by immigration officers. In these cases, a search register must also be maintained at an immigration office. See also Note 2D*

# Appendix 3

# CPS Public Order Offences Charging Standard

**AGREE BY THE POLICE AND
THE CROWN PROSECUTION SERVICE**

**PUBLIC ORDER OFFENCES CHARGING STANDARD**

**INDEX**

## PUBLIC ORDER OFFENCES CHARGING STANDARD AGREED BY THE POLICE AND CROWN PROSECUTION SERVICE

### 1 Charging Standard—Purpose

1.1 The purpose of joint charging standards is to make sure that the most appropriate charge is selected, in the light of the evidence which can be proved, at the earliest possible opportunity. This will help the police and Crown Prosecutors in preparing the case. Adoption of this joint standard should lead to a reduction in the number of times charges have to be amended which in turn should lead to an increase in efficiency and a reduction in avoidable extra work for the police and the Crown Prosecution Service.

1.2 This joint charging standard offers guidance to police officers who have responsibility for charging and to Crown Prosecutors on the most appropriate charge to be preferred in cases relating to public order offences. The guidance:

- **should not be used** in the determination of any **pre-charge** decision, such as the decision to arrest;

- **does not** override any guidance issued on the use of appropriate alternative forms of disposal **short of charge**, such as cautioning;

- **does not** override the principles set out in the Code for Crown Prosecutors;

- **does not** override the need for consideration to be given in every case as to whether a charge/prosecution is in the public interest;

- **does not** remove the need for each case to be considered on its individual merits or fetter the discretion of the police to charge and the CPS to prosecute the most appropriate offence depending on the particular facts of the case in question.

### 2 Introduction

2.1 The criminal law in respect of public order offences is intended to penalise the use of violence and/or intimidation by individuals or groups. The principal public order offences are contained in Part I of the Public Order Act 1986 ('the Act'). Further offences are found in Part III of the Act which deals with public disorder designed to stir up racial hatred. Other public order offences are set out in the Football Offences Act 1991, and reference is also made to the offence of drunk and disorderly behaviour. This joint standard gives guidance about the charge which should be preferred if the criteria set out in the Code for Crown Prosecutors are met.

2.2 This standard covers the following offences:

- using threatening, abusive or insulting words or behaviour, or disorderly behaviour likely to cause harassment, alarm or distress—**section 5 of the Act**;

- using threatening, abusive or insulting words or behaviour, or disorderly behaviour **intending to and causing** harassment, alarm or distress—**section 4A of the Act**;

- using threatening, abusive or insulting words or behaviour causing fear of or provoking violence—**section 4 of the Act**;

- using threatening, abusive or insulting words or behaviour **intended or likely to stir up racial hatred—section 18 of the Act**;

- publishing or distributing material which is threatening, abusive or insulting and **intended or likely to stir up racial hatred—section 19 of the Act**;

- possessing racially inflammatory material—**section 23 of the Act**;

- affray—**section 3 of the Act**;

- violent disorder—**section 2 of the Act**;

- riot—**section 1 of the Act**;

- drunk and disorderly behaviour—**section 91 Criminal Justice Act 1967**;
- offences contrary to **sections 2, 3, and 4 of the Football (Offences) Act 1991**.

2.3   Offences involving public disorder are often a precursor to, or part of, the commission of other offences. An offence under the Act may, for example, also lead to or involve an assault, unlawful possession of a weapon or the causing of criminal damage. Paragraph 10 below gives guidance on the selection of the appropriate number and type of charges in such cases.

### 3   General Principles: Charging Practice

3.1   You should always have in mind the following general principles when selecting the appropriate charge(s):

(i)   the charge(s) should accurately reflect the extent of the defendant's alleged involvement and responsibility, thereby allowing the courts the discretion to sentence appropriately;

(ii)   the choice of charges should ensure the clear and simple presentation of the case, particularly where there is more than one defendant;

(iii)   it is wrong to encourage a defendant to plead guilty to a few charges by selecting more charges than are necessary;

(iv)   it is wrong to select a more serious charge which is not supported by the evidence in order to encourage a plea of guilty to a lesser allegation.

### 4   General Principle: Public Order Act offences

4.1   The purpose of public order law is to ensure that individual rights to freedom of speech and freedom of assembly are balanced against the rights of others to go about their daily lives unhindered.

### 5   Offences contrary to sections 5, 4A, 4, 18, 19 and 23 of the Act and section 9 Criminal Justice Act 1967

5.1   There is an overlap in the conduct required to commit any one of these offences.

5.2   To use this section of the Charging Standard you should:

- consider which category the behaviour complained of falls into; and
- refer to the relevant paragraphs to identify which offence may be appropriate to charge and prosecute.

5.3   The categories of conduct are:

- disorderly behaviour (paragraph 5.5–5.18);
- using threatening, abusive or insulting words or behaviour (paragraph 5.19–5.28); and
- publishing, distributing or displaying any writing, sign or other visible representation which is threatening, abusive or insulting (paragraph 5.29–5.33).

5.4   Not all the offences cover each type of behaviour.

## Disorderly Behaviour

5.5   Whether behaviour can be properly categorised as disorderly is a question of fact. Disorderly behaviour does not require any element of violence, actual or threatened; and it includes conduct that is not necessarily threatening, abusive or insulting. It is not necessary to prove any feeling of insecurity, in an apprehensive sense, on the part of a member of the public: *Chambers and Edwards v DPP* [1995] Crim LR 896. The following types of conduct are examples which may at least be capable of amounting to disorderly behaviour:

- causing a disturbance in a residential area or common part of a block of flats by, for example:
  - persistently shouting;
  - knocking over dustbins;
  - putting refuse through letter-boxes;
  - banging on doors;
  - blockading entrances;
  - throwing things down the stairs;
  - peering in windows;
- persistently shouting abuse or obscenities at passers-by;
- pestering people waiting to catch public transport or otherwise waiting lawfully in a queue;
- rowdy behaviour in a street late at night which might alarm residents or passers-by, especially those who may be vulnerable, such as the elderly or members of an ethnic minority group;
- causing a disturbance in a shopping precinct or other area to which the public have access or might otherwise gather;
- the use of placards, slogans or language aimed at causing distress.

5.6   Where you are satisfied that you are dealing with an offence amounting to disorderly behaviour, the choice of charge is between the following:

- drunk and disorderly behaviour—**section 91 of the Criminal Justice Act 1967**;
- **section 5 of the Act**;
- **section 4A of the Act**.

5.7   The following table sets out what has to be proved in respect of each offence:

**TABLE I: ELEMENTS REQUIRED TO PROVE OFFENCES CONTRARY TO S. 91 CJA 1967, S. 5 AND S. 4A OF THE PUBLIC ORDER ACT—DISORDERLY BEHAVIOUR.**

| Drunk and Disorderly contrary to Section 91 CJA 1967 | Section 5 of the Act | Section 4A of the Act |
|---|---|---|
| disorderly behaviour | disorderly behaviour | disorderly behaviour |
| in any public place | in a public or private place (but not when confined to a dwelling house—see paragraph 5.11) | in a public or private place (but not when confined to a dwelling house—see paragraph 5.11) |
| while drunk | | |
| | with intention or awareness that behaviour may be disorderly; **or** with intention or awareness that such behaviour may be threatening, abusive or insulting | with intent to cause and thereby causing |
| | within the hearing or sight of a person likely to be caused | |
| | harassment, alarm or distress | harassment, alarm or distress |

5.8   An offence under **section 5** should be charged where there is **disorderly behaviour**, together with evidence that:

- the suspect intended his behaviour to be or was aware that it may be disorderly;
- and it was likely that harassment, alarm or distress would occur as a result: section 6 of the Act.

5.9   There must be a person within the sight or hearing of the suspect who is likely to be caused harassment, alarm or distress by the conduct in question. A police officer may be such a person, but remember that this is a question of fact to be decided in each case by the magistrates. In determining this, the magistrates may take into account the familiarity which police officers have with the words and conduct typically seen in incidents of disorderly conduct. (*DPP v Orum* [1988] Crim LR 848.)

5.10   Although the existence of a person who is caused harassment alarm and distress must be proved, there is no requirement that they actually give evidence. In appropriate cases, the offence may be proved on a police officer's evidence alone.

5.11   The conduct may take place in a public or private place. No offence is committed under this section, however, if such conduct takes place inside a dwelling and the other person is also inside that or another dwelling.

5.12   Police officers are aware of the difficult balance to be struck in dealing with those whose behaviour may be perceived by some as exuberant high spirits but by others as disorderly. In such cases informal methods of disposal may be appropriate and effective; but if this approach fails and the disorderly conduct continues then criminal proceedings may be necessary. Section 5 should be used in cases which amount to less serious incidents of anti-social behaviour. Where violence has been used, it is not normally appropriate to charge an offence under section 5.

5.13   In deciding whether a charge under section 5 is appropriate, the nature of the conduct must be considered in light of the penalty that the suspect is likely to receive on conviction.

5.14   As a prerequisite to the execution of a lawful arrest for an offence under section 5, the accused must have been warned by the arresting police officer to refrain from continuing with the disorderly behaviour: *DPP v Hancock and Tuttle* [1995] Crim LR 139. (**NB** Any officer may exercise the power of arrest so long as the warning has been given by a police officer on or after 17 October 1996—Public Order (Amendment) Act 1996.)

5.15   Where there is reliable evidence that the accused was drunk in a public place at the time of the alleged offence to the extent that the accused had lost the power of self control, a charge of drunk and disorderly behaviour should be preferred where otherwise a section 5 charge would be appropriate.

5.16   A charge under section 4A will **only** be appropriate if:

(i) the accused **intended** to cause harassment alarm or distress

**and**

(ii) the accused actually **caused** harassment alarm or distress.

If **either** one or both of these additional features is **not** present, a charge under section 5 or, if appropriate, a charge of drunk and disorderly will be the only alternatives available.

5.17   Section 4A may be appropriate where there is evidence of a persistent course of conduct causing harassment, alarm and distress; for example, in cases of racial harassment or 'stalking' behaviour.

5.18   The offence may take place in a public or private place. No offence under this section is committed, however, if such conduct takes place inside a dwelling and the person to whom it is directed is inside that or another dwelling.

## Using threatening, abusive or insulting words or behaviour

5.19   The following types of conduct are examples which may at least be capable of amounting to threatening, abusive or insulting words or behaviour:

- threats made or abuse directed towards individuals carrying out public service duties or jobs, such as ambulance workers, fire fighters or bus or train drivers;
- the throwing of missiles by a person taking part in a demonstration or other public gathering where no injury is caused;

- scuffles or incidents of minor violence or threats of violence committed in the context of a brawl (such as in or in the vicinity of a public house);
- incidents between neighbours or within domestic relationships which do not justify a charge of assault;
- incidents which do not justify a charge of assault where an individual is picked on by a gang.

5.20   Where you are satisfied that you are dealing with an offence of using threatening, abusive or insulting words or behaviour, the choice of charge is between the following:

- **section 5**;
- **section 4A**;
- **section 4**;
- **section 18**.

5.21   The following table sets out what has to be proved in respect of each offence:

**TABLE II: ELEMENTS REQUIRED TO PROVE OFFENCES CONTRARY TO S. 5, S. 4A, S. 4(1)(a) OR S. 18 OF THE PUBLIC ORDER ACT—THREATENING, ABUSIVE OR INSULTING WORDS OR BEHAVIOUR.**

| Section 5 | Section 4A | Section 4(1)(a) | Section 18* |
|---|---|---|---|
| threatening, abusive or insulting words or behaviour | threatening, abusive or insulting words or behaviour | threatening, abusive or insulting words or behaviour | uses threatening, abusive or insulting words or behaviour |
| | | towards another person | |
| within the hearing or sight of person likely to be caused | with intent to cause and thereby causing | *either:* with intent to cause that person to believe that immediate unlawful violence will be used against him or another by any person | with intent to stir up racial hatred or by which racial hatred is likely to be stirred up |
| | | *or:* with intent to provoke the immediate use of unlawful violence by that person or another | |
| harassment, alarm or distress | harassment, alarm or distress | *or:* whereby that person is likely to believe that such violence will be used | |
| | | *or:* it is likely that such violence will be provoked | |
| with intention or awareness that such behaviour may be threatening, abusive or insulting | | | *requires AG's consent. |

5.22   Conduct which may be capable of amounting to threatening, abusive or insulting words or behaviour for the purposes of an offence under section 4 will be more serious than that required under section 5 or section 4A.

5.23   A charge under section 4 will only be appropriate where there is evidence that the accused **intended** or was aware that his words or behaviour—**being directed towards another person**—were or may have been threatening, abusive or insulting **and** either:

- the accused intended the person against whom the conduct was directed to believe that immediate unlawful violence would be used against him or another by any person; **or**
- the accused intended to provoke the immediate use of unlawful violence by that person or another; **or**

- the person against whom the conduct was directed was likely to believe that violence would be used; **or**

- it was likely that such violence would be provoked.

5.24 The offence may take place in a public or private place. No offence under this section is committed, however, if such conduct takes place inside a dwelling and the other person is also inside that or another dwelling.

5.25 Where there is insufficient evidence to establish any of the elements specified in paragraph 5.23:

*either:*

a charge under *section 4A* may be appropriate if:

— the suspect had an **intent** to cause harassment alarm or distress **and**

— actually **caused** harassment alarm or distress;

*or:*

a charge under *section 5* may be appropriate if:

— the prohibited conduct took place within the hearing or sight of a person **likely** to be caused harassment alarm or distress.

5.26 In deciding upon the correct charge as between section 5, section 4A and section 4, it will be necessary to consider the nature of the conduct and the likely penalty that the suspect would receive on conviction.

5.27 If you think that a charge under section 18 may be appropriate, you must refer to the guidance given in paragraphs 5.34–5.48. Please note in particular that a prosecution may not be instituted for an offence under section 18 of the Act, without the consent of the Attorney General.

5.28 The offence under section 18 may be committed in a public or private place. No offence is committed, however, if such conduct takes place inside a dwelling and the person to whom it is directed is inside that or another dwelling.

## Publishing, distributing or displaying any writing, sign or other visible representation

5.29 Where you are satisfied that you are dealing with an offence amounting to the publishing, distributing or displaying of any writing, sign or other visible representation, the choice of charge is between the following:

- section 5;
- section 4A;
- section 4;
- section 18;
- section 19.

5.30 The following table sets out what has to be proved in respect of each offence:

TABLE III: ELEMENTS REQUIRED TO PROVE OFFENCES CONTRARY TO S. 5, S. 4A, S. 4, S. 18 OR S. 19 OF THE PUBLIC ORDER ACT—PUBLISHING, DISTRIBUTING OR DISPLAYING ANY WRITING, SIGN ETC.

| Section 5 | Section 4A | Section 4 | Section 18* | Section 19* |
|---|---|---|---|---|
|  |  | distributes or |  | publishes/ distributes |
| displays | displays | displays | displays |  |

**Table III** (Continued)

| Section 5 | Section 4A | Section 4 | | Section 18* | Section 19* |
|---|---|---|---|---|---|
| any writing sign or other visible repres. | any writing sign or other visible representation | any writing sign or other visible representation | | | |
| which is threatening, abusive or insulting | which is threatening, abusive or insulting | which is threatening, abusive or insulting | | which is threatening, abusive or insulting | which is threatening, abusive or insulting |
| within the hearing or sight of a person likely to be caused | with intent to cause and thereby causing | *either:* | with intent to cause that person to believe that immediate unlawful violence will be used against him or another by any person; | with intent to stir up racial hatred or racial hatred is likely to be stirred up | with intent to stir up racial hatred or racial hatred is likely to be stirred up |
| | | *or:* | with intent to provoke the immediate use of unlawful violence by that person or another; | | |
| harassment, alarm or distress thereby | harassment, alarm or distress thereby | *or:* | whereby that person is likely to believe that such violence will be used; | | |
| | | *or:* | it is likely that such violence will be provoked | | |
| with intention or awareness | | | | * requires AG's consent. | * requires AG's consent |

5.31   If you think that a charge under section 18 or 19 may be appropriate, **you must refer to the guidance given in paragraphs 5.34–5.48.** Please note in particular that a prosecution may not be instituted for an offence under section 18 or 19 of the Act, without the consent of the Attorney General.

5.32   Section 1 of the Malicious Communications Act 1988 may be a useful charge if a letter or other article has been sent to a person or persons to cause distress or anxiety. In particular, you may use it as an alternative to section 18 where the material in question is sent to a selected individual or individuals with a hostile intent which is racially motivated but the more general intention to stir up racial hatred required by section 18 is not present.

5.33   For the purposes of section 19, it must be proved that there was a publication or distribution to the public or to a section of the public. Written matter includes any sign or other visible representation.

## Racially motivated crimes: Relationship between offences contrary to Part I of the Act and Part III of the Act

5.34   Part III Public Order Act 1986 (sections 17 to 29) creates a number of offences concerned with inciting racial hatred. The offences involve:

- conduct (using words or behaviour, publishing, displaying etc);
- which is threatening, abusive or insulting; and

which is either intended or likely to stir up racial hatred.

Part III offences involve **incitement to racial hatred**. Conduct which is contrary to offences set out in Part I of the Act (sections 1 to 5) may be racially motivated but may not involve incitement to racial hatred. If that is the case, you should charge the appropriate Part I offence. Remember that racial motivation, whether a Part I or Part III offence is involved, is recognised as a public interest factor weighing in favour of prosecution in the Code for Crown Prosecutors. Thus, the public interest will always tend to favour a prosecution in these cases when there is sufficient evidence.

5.35 'Racial hatred' is defined as 'hatred against a group of persons in Great Britain defined by reference to colour, race, nationality ... or ethnic or national origins': section 17.

5.36 'Hatred' is not defined by the Act. It is much stronger than ridicule or contempt; it is not enough to cause offence or to mock a racial group. 'Hatred' connotes an element of hostility.

5.37 It is an offence to use words or behaviour, or display any written material, which is threatening, abusive or insulting and either intended or likely in all the circumstances to stir up racial hatred: section 18.

5.38 **Part III offences require the consent of the Attorney General to be prosecuted**: section 27. Consent need not be obtained pre-charge (section 25 Prosecution of Offences Act 1985) but must be obtained before the case proceeds to mode of trial proceedings. Generally, however, you should submit the case for consent prior to charging. Police should therefore submit such cases to the CPS for pre-charge advice, with a view to seeking consent if that it appropriate.

5.39 The Attorney General's consent must be sought by the CPS Area through CPS Central Casework (Prosecutions). CPS Central Casework will be responsible for reviewing the evidence and applying for consent in appropriate cases. Whenever there is sufficient evidence to support a Part III charge the case must be referred by the CPS Area to CPS Central Casework (Prosecutions).

5.40 It is important to distinguish between conduct which amounts to an offence under Part I of the Act (particularly sections 5, 4A and 4) and conduct which amounts to an offence under Part III (particularly section 18). The distinction is in the effect the conduct has on the audience (person or persons) who sees/hears the conduct.

5.41 The effect of Part I conduct is to cause offence to the audience of that conduct, by being threatening, abusive or insulting towards the audience. The effect, likely or intended, of Part III conduct is not to offend the audience but to incite them to hatred of a racial group other than that of the audience.

5.42 The general guide is that a charge under Part I should be considered when the conduct is motivated by the audience's race; and a charge under Part III should be considered when the conduct is motivated by the race of a group other than that of the audience.

5.43 A practical example may help: a person uses language which is abusive of a racial group.

- If the audience is exclusively made up of that racial group then it is unlikely that the speaker either intends or is likely to stir up the audience to hatred of the audience's own racial group: a Part III charge will be inappropriate; a Part I charge may be appropriate, aggravated by the racial motivation.

- If the audience is exclusively made up of some other racial group (for example, the same racial group as the speaker) then it may be that there is an intention or likelihood of the speaker stirring up racial hatred in the audience, in which instance a charge under Part III may be appropriate.

5.44 There may be instances when the defendant's conduct does amount to an offence under Part I and Part III of the Act. This is likely to occur when the audience is not exclusively made up of one racial group but is made up of individuals of more than one racial group, each affected by the conduct in different ways, such as in the following circumstances:

- when members of the abused racial group and the defendant's supporters (of a different racial group) are both present and the defendant's conduct, or individual parts of the conduct, is aimed at both groups;

- when there are two or more defendants acting together in a racially motivated attack (verbal and/or physical) upon a victim; as well as the conduct towards the victim of the attack, there may be some conduct, either express or implied, between the defendants amounting to mutual encouragement; and

- when bystanders unconnected with either the defendant or the victim witness the defendant racially attacking (verbally and/or physically) a victim.

5.45   In each instance the conduct must be considered both as a whole and by its constituent parts. The appropriate charge(s) must reflect the seriousness of the conduct. The following should be in mind:

- when there are two or more defendants acting together in a racially motivated attack, as equal partners, it will be more appropriate to pursue a non-Part III offence and to emphasise the racial motivation as an aggravating feature;

- when there are two or more defendants acting together in a racially motivated attack, and one defendant takes a lead role, encouraging and directing others to commit a racially motivated crime while standing apart from the actual attack on the victim, a Part III charge should be considered: such a Part III charge will attach to the conduct of the defendant towards others within his group, not to the conduct of the defendant towards the victim of the racially motivated crime;

- when there are bystanders, unconnected with either the defendant(s) or the victim of a racially motivated attack, a Part III charge may follow if there is some explicit act on the part of the defendant, intended or likely to incite the bystanders. Otherwise, a Part I offence, aggravated by the racial motivation, should be charged. In cases where bystanders make statements expressing sympathy for the victim it will be difficult to support a Part III offence.

5.46   When the evidence supports an offence contrary to sections 5, 4A or 4 of the Act and section 18 of the Act, the section 18 offence should be preferred.

5.47   When the evidence supports an offence contrary to sections 1, 2 or 3 of the Act and section 18, both the Part I and Part III offence should be charged.

5.48   When there is evidence of any other offence linked to the section 18 offence, you should refer to paragraph 10 for further guidance.

## Possessing Racially Inflammatory Material

5.49   A charge under section 23 of the Act may be appropriate where there is evidence that a person:

- was in possession of written material
- which is threatening, abusive or insulting
- with a view to its being displayed, published, distributed broadcast or included in a cable programme service
- intending racial hatred to be stirred up thereby; or where,
- having regard to all the circumstances, racial hatred is likely to be stirred up thereby.

5.50   A prosecution may not be instituted for an offence under section 23 of the Act without the consent of the Attorney General.

5.51   For the purposes of section 23, it is not necessary to prove that the accused had physical custody of the material, provided it can be established that he exercised control over it.

5.52   It is a defence for the accused to prove that he was not aware of the content of the material and neither suspected nor had reason to suspect that it was threatening, abusive or insulting.

## Penalties and Venue for all offences in paragraph 5

5.53   Table IV sets out details of the mode of prosecution and the penalties for all offences referred to in paragraph 5.

**TABLE IV: PROSECUTION AND PUNISHMENT OF OFFENCES REFERRED TO IN PARAGRAPH 5**

| Offence | General Nature of Offence | Mode of Prosecution | Punishment | Additional Provisions |
|---|---|---|---|---|
| S. 91 CJA 1967 | Drunk and disorderly | Summary | Level 3 fine | |
| S. 5 POA 1986 | Harassment, alarm or distress | Summary | Level 3 fine | |
| S. 4A POA 1986 | Intentional harassment, alarm or distress | Summary | 6 months and/or level 5 fine | |
| S. 4 POA 1986 | Fear or provocation of violence | Summary | 6 months and/or level 5 fine | |
| S. 18 POA 1986 | Acts intended or likely to stir up racial hatred—use of words or behaviour or display of written material | Either way | (a) Summary: 6 months and/or level 5 fine (b) On indictment: 2 years and/or a fine | Requires AG's consent |
| S. 19 POA 1986 | Acts likely to stir up racial hatred—publishing or distributing written material | Either way | (a) Summary: 6 months and/or level 5 fine (b) On indictment: 2 years and/or a fine | Requires AG's consent |
| S. 23 POA 1986 | Possession of racially inflammatory material | Either way | (a) Summary: 6 months and/or level 5 fine (b) On indictment: 2 years and/or a fine | Requires AG's consent |
| S. 1 Malicious Communications Act 1988 | Offence of sending letters etc. with intent to cause distress or anxiety | Summary | Level 4 fine | |

## 6   Affray

6.1   Under section 3 of the Act, it must be proved that a person has used or threatened:

— unlawful violence

— towards another

— and his conduct is such as would cause

— a person of reasonable firmness

— present at the scene

— to fear for his personal safety.

6.2   The seriousness of the offence lies in the effect that the behaviour of the accused has on members of the public who may have been put in **fear**. There must be some conduct, **beyond the use of words**, which is threatening and directed towards a person or persons. Mere words are not enough. Violent conduct towards property alone is not sufficient for the purposes of an offence under section 3. The offence is **not** confined to group disorder.

6.3   An offence under section 3 is triable either way. The maximum penalty on conviction on indictment is three years' imprisonment and/or a fine of unlimited amount. On summary conviction the maximum penalty is six months' imprisonment and/or a fine not exceeding level 5.

6.4   The offence may be committed in a **public or private place**.

6.5   Examples of the type of conduct appropriate for a section 3 offence include:

• a fight between two people in a place where members of the general public are present (for example, in a public house, discotheque, restaurant or street) and are put in fear for their safety (although the fighting is not directed towards them);

- a person who, on being refused entry to a nightclub, throws objects at the staff whilst at the same time issuing threats towards them;
- a person armed with a knife or other weapon who, when approached by police officers, brandishes the weapon and threatens to use it against them;
- a person who brandishes a knife or other weapon and issues threats of violence towards another while both are on private property (for example inside a dwelling).

6.6   Affray should be charged where there is relevant conduct and it can be proved that the accused:

- used or threatened unlawful violence **towards another; and**
- his conduct was such that it would cause a person of reasonable firmness present at the scene **to fear for his personal safety**. No person of reasonable firmness need actually be, or be likely to be, present at the scene however: **section 3(4)**.

R v *Sanchez* (1996) *The Times*, 3 March, makes it clear that the two persons—the 'victim' of the affray and the 'person of reasonable firmness present at the scene'—must be distinguished. It was necessary to show that a notional third person at the scene would have feared for his personal safety, not that the victim was put in fear. Were it otherwise, the definition of affray would be extended to include every common assault.

6.7   The accused must have **intended** to use or threaten violence; or have been **aware** that his conduct may be violent or may threaten violence.

6.8   In cases where an offence under section 3 is a precursor to, or part of, the commission of an offence of **assault**, the question of selecting the number and type of appropriate charge arises. Generally, the more serious the injury, the less likely the need to charge a section 3 offence. For further guidance on charge selection see paragraph 10 below.


## 7   Violent disorder

7.1   Under section 2 of the Act, it must be proved that:

— three or more persons

— present together

— used or threatened

— unlawful violence

— so that the conduct of them (taken together) would cause

— a person of reasonable firmness

— present at the scene

— to fear for his or her personal safety.

7.2   This offence should only be charged in relation to instances of serious disorder. It will be an especially appropriate charge where such disorder has been planned, although the violence does not have to be premeditated. The offence should **not** be charged simply because three or more persons are involved in minor disorder.

7.3   An offence under section 2 is triable either way. The maximum penalty on conviction on indictment is five years' imprisonment and/or a fine of unlimited amount. On summary conviction the maximum penalty is six months' imprisonment and/or a fine not exceeding level 5.

7.4   The offence may be committed in a **public or private place**. The relevant conduct may be directed against a person or persons or against property.

7.5   Examples of the type of conduct appropriate for a section 2 offence include:

- fighting, involving the use of weapons, between large groups of rival football supporters in a street or town centre;
- fighting, including the use of weapons, between rival groups in a place to which members of the public have access (for example a restaurant, discotheque, public house, street or town centre);

- disorder causing major disruption at a public demonstration where missiles are thrown and other violence is used against and directed towards the police.

7.6   There must be evidence which shows that:

- three or more people (including the accused), while present together, used or threatened unlawful violence; **and**

- their conduct (taken together) was such that it would have caused a person of reasonable firmness present at the scene to fear for his personal safety.

7.7   There must also be evidence which shows that the accused intended to use or threaten violence, or was aware that his conduct may be violent or threaten violence.

7.8   Whilst three or more persons must have been present and used or threatened unlawful violence, it is not necessary that three or more persons should actually be charged and prosecuted: *R v Mahroof* (1988) 88 Cr App R 317. The charge must make clear, however, that the defendant was one of the three or more involved in the commission of the offence.

7.9   A charge under section 2 will reflect the potential danger that existed to innocent members of the public. Accordingly, an offence under section 2 should almost always be charged (where there is sufficient evidence) **in addition** to any offence(s) which may also be made out under section 20 or 18 of the Offences Against the Person Act 1861. For further guidance on charge selection see paragraph 10 below.

## 8   Riot

8.1   Under section 1 of the Act, it must be proved that

- twelve or more persons
- present together
- used or threatened unlawful violence
- for a common purpose; and that
- the conduct of them (taken together)
- was such as to cause
- a person of reasonable firmness
- present at the scene
- to fear for his personal safety.

8.2   An offence under section 1 will be an appropriate charge **only** in wholly exceptional circumstances, where the most serious outbreaks of violence have occurred. Such circumstances will be **rare**.

8.3   A prosecution for riot or incitement to riot may be commenced **only** by, or with the consent of, the Director of Public Prosecutions.

8.4   An offence under section 1 is triable on indictment only. The maximum penalty on conviction is ten years' imprisonment and/or a fine of unlimited amount.

8.5   A charge of riot should be confined to the most serious outbreaks of public disorder. These can be distinguished from other examples of group disorder by virtue of:

- the **scale** of the disruption;
- the **violence** used;
- the **number** of individuals involved;
- the element of **common purpose**.

8.6   Conduct which falls within the scope of this offence includes:

- exceptionally serious acts of violence against public order committed in furtherance of industrial disputes;
- public disturbance on a wide scale involving serious acts of violence, serious damage to property and looting;

- organised attacks on people and property in the context of marches and demonstrations;
- large scale acts of football violence which have an element of organisation;
- serious and organised violent attacks on the police or other public servants.

8.7  The defendant must intend to use violence, or be aware that his conduct may be violent.

8.8  Where there is sufficient evidence for a charge under section 1 of the Act, and an offence under section 20 or 18 of the Offences Against the Person Act 1861 can also be made out, it will almost always be appropriate to continue with the section 1 offence, **in addition** to the assault charge. For further guidance on charge selection see paragraph 10 below.

## 9  Alternative Verdicts

9.1  The Act recognises that there may be some overlap between some public disorder offences by providing for the return of an alternative verdict where the offences of **affray** or **violent disorder** have been tried on indictment. In these circumstances, the jury may, in finding the defendant not guilty as charged, find him guilty of an offence under section 4. It is important to emphasise, however, that the offence which is most appropriate to the circumstances of the case should **always** be charged. An offence of affray or violent disorder should **never** be charged with a view to obtaining a guilty verdict under section 4.

9.2  The operation of **section 6(3) Criminal Law Act 1967** is not affected by the Act. Hence, a jury may on an indictment for riot, return an alternative verdict of guilty of violent disorder or guilty of affray: *R v Fleming* (1989) 153 JP 517. Section 6(3) may also be used where a defendant faced with an indictment charging either violent disorder or affray wishes to plead not guilty as charged, but guilty to an offence contrary to section 4: *R v O'Brien* (1992) 156 JP 925.

9.3  Similar provisions do not exist for the return of alternative verdicts in the magistrates' courts.

## 10  Additional Charges and Charge Selection

10.1  It is a common feature of public order incidents that sufficient evidence exists to charge the accused with offences other than those under the Act, for example, unlawful possession of an offensive weapon, assault and/or criminal damage.

10.2  It is difficult to give general guidance in this area, because each course of conduct should be considered in the light of the facts of the particular case. However, the following general factors may help in deciding which combination of offences should be charged where more than one is possible.

- Is the offence basically one of public disorder in which there has been some minor assault; or vice versa? If the former, concentrate on the public disorder aspect.
- Where there are aggravating features to an assault, such as the use of a weapon, it is likely that an assault charge should be preferred.
- Where there is an allied assault or act of criminal damage, is it one in which compensation is an issue? If so, an assault charge or criminal damage charge may **also** be appropriate. But remember compensation may be payable to a victim in respect of offences of affray and violent disorder. This will be so, if the loss, damage or personal injury arose from the group activity in which the offender took part, and there is sufficient connection between his participation in the offence and the injury to support the making of a compensation order.

10.3  A charge under the Football (Offences) Act 1991 ('F(O)A') will be more suitable where the following types of conduct have occurred at a designated football match:

- throwing missiles onto the playing area, or any area adjacent to the playing area to which spectators are not usually admitted: section 2, F(O)A;
- racialist or indecent chanting: section 3, F(O)A;
- going onto the playing area or any area adjacent to the playing area to which spectators are not usually admitted without lawful authority or lawful excuse: section 4, F(O)A.

10.4   The choice of charge will ultimately be made on the facts of individual cases and in accordance with paragraphs 1.2 and 3.1 above. Paragraph 3.1 (ii) has particular relevance to public order offences. Where the additional factors listed in paragraph 10.2 are not present, the following paragraphs offer **general guidance** about the correct combination of offences to charge where there is sufficient evidence to proceed on each of them.

## Assaults

10.5   If there is sufficient evidence to justify a charge under section 1 of the Public Order Act and an assault contrary to:

- section 18 of the Offences Against the Person Act 1861 (OAPA); or
- section 20 OAPA

it will usually be appropriate to **charge both**. It will not normally be appropriate to charge section 47 or common assault contrary to section 39 of the Criminal Justice Act 1988 together with an offence contrary to section 1 of the Act.

10.6   If there is sufficient evidence to justify a charge under sections 2 or 3 of the Public Order Act and an assault contrary to

- section 18 OAPA; or
- section 20 OAPA; or
- section 47 OAPA

it will usually be appropriate to **charge both**. It will not normally be appropriate to charge common assault (section 39 of the CJA 1988) together with an offence contrary to sections 2 or 3 of the Act.

10.7   If there is sufficient evidence to justify a charge under section 4, 4A, or 5 of the Act and an assault contrary to

- section 18 OAPA; or
- section 20 OAPA; or
- section 47 OAPA

it will usually be appropriate to **charge the assault alone**. In cases of section 4 conduct, if other victims have not been assaulted, it will usually be appropriate to charge section 4 **in addition to the assault**.

10.8   Where you have evidence to prove conduct contrary to section 4, 4A or 5, together with a common assault (section 39 of the CJA 1988), it will usually be appropriate to proceed on the common assault alone. But if the conduct contrary to section 4, 4A or 5 was directed at others who were not victims of common assault, **consider charging both**.

## Section 18—conduct intended to or likely to stir up racial hatred

10.9   Where the evidence supports a charge under section 18 of the Act and there is evidence of an assault, and/or criminal damage, and/or unlawful possession of an offensive weapon, the section 18 offence should always be charged in addition to the other offence(s). Refer to paragraph 5.34–5.48, especially 5.38.

## Offensive Weapons

10.10   Generally, the more serious the outbreak of public disorder—when the defendant is also in possession of an offensive or bladed weapon—the more likely it will be to add a further charge to reflect that fact.

10.11   Where any type of weapon is carried by those involved in public disorder, this is an aggravating factor to be taken into account in the presentation of the case. The approach to be taken will depend on the following factors:

- the type of weapon concerned;
- whether the weapon was used or its use threatened;
- how the weapon was used;
- the potential for serious injury;
- the time when the weapon was discovered or produced (i.e. was it produced during the incident or found on arrest).

10.12   Where a summary only public order offence is appropriate, but where the defendant is in unlawful possession of an offensive weapon, police officers and prosecutors should consider carefully whether it might be more appropriate to focus on the possession of the offensive weapon (which is an offence triable either way) and recount the circumstances of the disorder in presenting the case to the relevant tribunal. If, however, the summary public order offence is itself serious, such as, for example, racially motivated harassment or 'stalking', consider charging **both** offences.

10.13   You should reflect the possession of a bladed weapon in a separate charge when the appropriate public disorder offence is summary only.

10.14   You should reflect the unlawful possession of an offensive weapon in a separate charge when the appropriate public order offence is triable either way or only triable on indictment.

## Criminal Damage

10.15 Acts of criminal damage are frequently committed during public disorder. Where there is sufficient evidence to support both offences, consider charging both. If, however, offences contrary to section 1 or 2 of the Public Order Act are being charged and the criminal damage is minor, charge the section 1 or 2 offence alone. (Paragraph 10.2—last bullet point deals with the issue of compensation.) If the criminal damage is serious and the public order act offence is minor, then you should consider charging the criminal damage alone.

### 11   Alternative Disposal—Bind Over

11.1   Both the Crown Court and magistrates' courts may make an order binding over an individual to keep the peace. An application for a bind over should never be made as a matter of convenience and should not be made in the Crown Court except in exceptional circumstances. A court may be asked to exercise its power to bind over where:

- there has been an outbreak of bad behaviour which is not sufficiently serious to prefer a charge under the Act but which amounts to a **breach of the peace**; and
- there is a danger that the conduct complained of will be **repeated**; and
- the accused **consents** to the proposed course of action.

11.2   For conduct to constitute a breach of the peace, the conduct must involve violence or the threat of violence. The violence need not be perpetrated by the defendant, provided that the natural consequence of his conduct was that others would be provoked to violence (*Percy* v *DPP* [1995] Crim LR 714).

11.3   It will be appropriate to seek a bind over where conduct falling short of that required for a substantive offence under the Act has been committed. If you have identified the case as one which should proceed by way of bind over, then you should pursue the case on the basis of a complaint rather than charge for an offence.

11.4   Where a decision has been made to prosecute in accordance with the Code for Crown Prosecutors, the circumstances in which it will be appropriate to dispose of the case by way of a bind over will be rare. There must have been a significant change in circumstances; for example, where a witness refuses to give evidence against the defendant, but there remains sufficient evidence that the defendant was involved in a disturbance.

# Appendix 4

# Football Spectators Act 1989, Schedule 1

## SCHEDULE 1

### OFFENCES

Sch. 1 para 1 amended by Football (Disorder) Act 2000 sch.1 para 5

1. This Schedule applies to the following offences:

   (a) any offence under section 2(1), 5(7), 14J(1) or 21C(2) of this Act,

   (b) any offence under section 2 or 2A of the Sporting Events (Control of Alcohol etc.) Act 1985 (alcohol, containers and fireworks) committed by the accused at any football match to which this Schedule applies or while entering or trying to enter the ground,

   (c) any offence under section 5 of the Public Order Act 1986 (harassment, alarm or distress) or any provision of Part III of that Act (racial hatred) committed during a period relevant to a football match to which this Schedule applies at any premises while the accused was at, or was entering or leaving or trying to enter or leave, the premises,

   (d) any offence involving the use or threat of violence by the accused towards another person committed during a period relevant to a football match to which this Schedule applies at any premises while the accused was at, or was entering or leaving or trying to enter or leave, the premises,

   (e) any offence involving the use or threat of violence towards property committed during a period relevant to a football match to which this Schedule applies at any premises while the accused was at, or was entering or leaving or trying to enter or leave, the premises,

   (f) any offence involving the use, carrying or possession of an offensive weapon or a firearm committed during a period relevant to a football match to which this Schedule applies at any premises while the accused was at, or was entering or leaving or trying to enter or leave, the premises,

   (g) any offence under section 12 of the Licensing Act 1872 (persons found drunk in public places, etc.) of being found drunk in a highway or other public place committed while the accused was on a journey to or from a football match to which this Schedule applies being an offence as respects which the court makes a declaration that the offence related to football matches,

   (h) any offence under section 91(1) of the Criminal Justice Act 1967 (disorderly behaviour while drunk in a public place) committed in a highway or other public place while the accused was on a journey to or from a football match to which this Schedule applies being an offence as respects which the court makes a declaration that the offence related to football matches,

   (j) any offence under section 1 of the Sporting Events (Control of Alcohol etc.) Act 1985 (alcohol on coaches or trains to or from sporting events) committed while the accused was on a journey to or from a football match to which this Schedule applies being an offence as respects which the court makes a declaration that the offence related to football matches,

(k)  any offence under section 5 of the Public Order Act 1986 (harassment, alarm or distress) or any provision of Part III of that Act (racial hatred) committed while the accused was on a journey to or from a football match to which this Schedule applies being an offence as respects which the court makes a declaration that the offence related to football matches,

(l)  any offence under section 4 or 5 of the Road Traffic Act 1988 (driving etc. when under the influence of drink or drugs or with an alcohol concentration above the prescribed limit) committed while the accused was on a journey to or from a football match to which this Schedule applies being an offence as respects which the court makes a declaration that the offence related to football matches,

(m)  any offence involving the use or threat of violence by the accused towards another person committed while one or each of them was on a journey to or from a football match to which this Schedule applies being an offence as respects which the court makes a declaration that the offence related to football matches,

(n)  any offence involving the use or threat of violence towards property committed while the accused was on a journey to or from a football match to which this Schedule applies being an offence as respects which the court makes a declaration that the offence related to football matches,

(o)  any offence involving the use, carrying or possession of an offensive weapon or a firearm committed while the accused was on a journey to or from a football match to which this Schedule applies being an offence as respects which the court makes a declaration that the offence related to football matches,

(p)  any offence under the Football (Offences) Act 1991,

(q)  any offence under section 5 of the Public Order Act 1986 (harassment, alarm or distress) or any provision of Part III of that Act (racial hatred)—
  (i)  which does not fall within paragraph (c) or (k) above,
  (ii)  which was committed during a period relevant to a football match to which this Schedule applies, and
  (iii)  as respects which the court makes a declaration that the offence related to that match or to that match and any other football match which took place during that period,

(r)  any offence involving the use or threat of violence by the accused towards another person—
  (i)  which does not fall within paragraph (d) or (m) above,
  (ii)  which was committed during a period relevant to a football match to which this Schedule applies, and
  (iii)  as respects which the court makes a declaration that the offence related to that match or to that match and any other football match which took place during that period,

(s)  any offence involving the use or threat of violence towards property—
  (i)  which does not fall within paragraph (e) or (n) above,
  (ii)  which was committed during a period relevant to a football match to which this Schedule applies, and
  (iii)  as respects which the court makes a declaration that the offence related to that match or to that match and any other football match which took place during that period,

(t)  any offence involving the use, carrying or possession of an offensive weapon or a firearm—
  (i)  which does not fall within paragraph (f) or (o) above,
  (ii)  which was committed during a period relevant to a football match to which this Schedule applies, and
  (iii)  as respects which the court makes a declaration that the offence related to that match or to that match and any other football match which took place during that period,

(u)  any offence under section 166 of the Criminal Justice and Public Order Act 1994 (sale of tickets by unauthorised persons) which relates to tickets for a football match.

2.  Any reference to an offence in paragraph 1 above includes—

(a) a reference to any attempt, conspiracy or incitement to commit that offence, and

(b) a reference to aiding and abetting, counselling or procuring the commission of that offence.

3.  For the purposes of paragraphs 1(g) to (o) above—

    (a) a person may be regarded as having been on a journey to or from a football match to which this Schedule applies whether or not he attended or intended to attend the match, and

    (b) a person's journey includes breaks (including overnight breaks).

4(1)  In this Schedule, 'football match' means a match which is a regulated football match for the purposes of Part II of this Act.

  (2)  Section 1(8) and (8A) above apply for the interpretation of references to periods relevant to football matches.

# Appendix 5

# Firearms Act 1968, Schedule 6

## PART I   TABLE OF PUNISHMENTS

| Section of this Act creating offence | General nature of offence | Mode of prosecution | Punishment | Additional provisions |
|---|---|---|---|---|
| Section 1(1) | Possessing etc. firearm or ammunition without certificate. | (a) Summary | 6 months or a fine of the prescribed sum; or both. | |
| | | (b) On indictment | (i) where the offence is committed in an aggravated form within the meaning of section 4(4) of this Act, 7 years, or a fine; or both. (ii) in any other case, 5 years or a fine; or both. | Paragraph 1 of Part II of this Schedule applies |
| Section 1(2) | Non-compliance with condition of firearm certificate. | Summary | 6 months or a fine of level 5 on the standard scale; or both. | Paragraph 1 of Part II of this Schedule applies |
| Section 2(1) | Possessing, etc. shot gun without shot gun certificate. | (a) Summary | 6 months or the statutory maximum; or both. | as above |
| | | (b) On indictment | 5 years or a fine; or both. | |
| Section 2(2) | Non-compliance with condition of shot gun certificate. | Summary | 6 months or a fine of level 5 on the standard scale; or both. | as above |
| Section 3(1) | Trading in firearms without being registered as firearms dealer. | (a) Summary | 6 months or a fine of the prescribed sum; or both. | |
| | | (b) On indictment | 5 years or a fine; or both. | |
| Section 3(2) | Selling firearm to person without a certificate. | (a) Summary | 6 months or a fine of the prescribed sum; or both. | |
| | | (b) On indictment | 5 years or a fine; or both. | |
| Section 3(3) | Repairing, testing etc. firearm for person without a certificate. | (a) Summary | 6 months or a fine of the prescribed sum; or both. | |
| | | (b) On indictment | 5 years or a fine; or both. | |
| Section 3(5) | Falsifying certificate, etc. with view to acquisition of firearm. | (a) Summary | 6 months or a fine of the prescribed sum; or both. | |
| | | (b) On indictment | 5 years or a fine; or both. | |
| Section 3(6) | Pawnbroker taking firearm in pawn. | Summary | 3 months or a fine of level 3 on the standard scale; or both. | |
| Section 4(1) (3) | Shortening a shot gun; conversion of firearms. | (a) Summary | 6 months or a fine of the prescribed sum; or both. | |
| | | (b) On indictment | 7 years or a fine; or both. | |

**Part I Table**  (continued)

| Section of this Act creating offence | General nature of offence | Mode of prosecution | Punishment | Additional provisions |
|---|---|---|---|---|
| *Section 5(1)* | *Possessing or distributing prohibited weapons or ammunition.* | *(a) Summary* | *6 months or a fine of the prescribed sum; or both.* | |
| | | *(b) On indictment* | *10 years or a fine; or both.* | |
| *Section 5(1A)* | *Possessing or distributing other prohibited weapons or ammunition.* | *(a) Summary* | *6 months or a fine of the statutory maximum; or both.* | |
| | | *(b) On indictment* | *10 years or a fine; or both.* | |
| *Section 5(5)* | *Non-compliance with condition of Defence Council authority.* | *Summary* | *6 months or a fine of level 5 on the standard scale; or both.* | |
| *Section 5(6)* | *Non-compliance with requirement to surrender authority to possess, etc. prohibited weapon or ammunition.* | *Summary* | *A fine of level 3 on the standard scale.* | |
| *Section 6(3)* | *Contravention of order under s. 6 (or corresponding Northern Irish order) restricting removal of arms.* | *Summary* | *3 months or, for each firearm or parcel of ammunition in respect of which the offence is committed, a fine of level 3 on the standard scale; or both.* | *Para. 2 of Part II of this Schedule applies.* |
| *Section 7(2)* | *Making false statement in order to obtain police permit.* | *Summary* | *6 months or a fine of level 5 on the standard scale; or both.* | |
| *Section 9(3)* | *Making false statement in order to obtain permit for auction of firearms etc.* | *Summary* | *6 months or a fine not exceeding level 5 on the standard scale; or both.* | |
| *Section 13(2)* | *Making false statement in order to obtain permit for removal of signalling apparatus.* | *Summary* | *6 months or a fine of level 5 on the standard scale; or both.* | |
| *Section 16* | *Possession of firearm with intent to endanger life or injure property.* | *On indictment* | *Life imprisonment or a fine; or both.* | |
| *Section 16A* | *Possession of firearm or imitation firearm with intent to cause fear of violence.* | *On indictment* | *10 years or a fine, or both.* | |
| *Section 17(1)* | *Use of firearm or imitation firearm to resist arrest.* | *On indictment* | *Life imprisonment or a fine; or both.* | *Paras 3 to 5 of Part II of this Schedule apply.* |
| *Section 17(2)* | *Possessing firearm or imitation firearm while committing offence in schedule an 1 or, in Scotland, an offence specified in schedule 2.* | *On indictment* | *Life imprisonment or a fine; or both.* | *Paras 3 and 6 of Part II of this Schedule apply.* |
| *Section 18(1)* | *Carrying firearm or imitation firearm with intent to commit indictable offence (or, in Scotland, an offence specified in schedule 2) or to resist arrest.* | *On indictment* | *Life imprisonment or a fine; or both.* | |

**Part I Table**   (continued)

| Section of this Act creating offence | General nature of offence | Mode of prosecution | Punishment | Additional provisions |
|---|---|---|---|---|
| Section 19 | Carrying loaded firearm in public place. | (a) Summary | 6 months or a fine of the prescribed sum; or both. | |
| | | (b) On indictment (but not if the firearm is an air weapon) | 7 years or a fine; or both. | |
| Section 20(1) | Trespassing with firearm or imitation firearm in a building. | (a) Summary | 6 months or a fine of the prescribed sum; or both. | |
| | | (b) On indictment (but not in the case of an imitation firearm or if the firearm is an air weapon) | 7 years or a fine; or both. | |
| Section 20(2) | Trespassing with firearm or imitation firearm on land. | Summary | 3 months or a fine of level 4 on the standard scale; or both. | |
| Section 21(4) | Contravention of provisions denying firearms to ex-prisoners and the like. | (a) Summary | 6 months or a fine of the prescribed sum; or both. | |
| | | (b) On indictment | 5 years or a fine; or both. | |
| Section 21(5) | Supplying firearms to person denied them under section 21. | (a) Summary | 6 months or a fine of the prescribed sum; or both. | |
| | | (b) On indictment | 5 years or a fine; or both. | |
| Section 22(1) | Person under 17 acquiring firearm. | Summary | 6 months or a fine of level 5 on the standard scale; or both. | |
| Section 22(1A) | Person under 18 using certificated firearm for unauthorised purpose. | Summary | 3 months or a fine of level 5 on the standard scale; or both. | |
| Section 22(2) | Person under 14 having firearm in his possession without lawful authority. | Summary | 6 months or a fine of level 5 on the standard scale; or both. | |
| Section 22(3) | Person under 15 having with him a shot gun without adult supervision. | Summary | A fine of level 3 on the standard scale. | Para. 8 of Part II of this Schedule applies. |
| Section 22(4) | Person under 14 having with him an air weapon or ammunition therefor. | Summary | A fine of level 3 on the standard scale. | Paras 7 and 8 of Part II of this Schedule apply. |
| Section 22(5) | Person under 17 having with him an air weapon in a public place. | Summary | A fine of level 3 on the standard scale. | Paras 7 and 8 of Part II of this Schedule apply. |
| Section 23(1) | Person under 14 making improper use of air weapon when under supervision; person supervising him permitting such use. | Summary | A fine of level 3 on the standard scale. | Paras 7 and 8 of Part II of this Schedule apply. |
| Section 24(1) | Selling or letting on hire a firearm to person under 17. | Summary | 6 months or a fine of level 5 on the standard scale; or both. | |

**Part I Table**   (continued)

| Section of this Act creating offence | General nature of offence | Mode of prosecution | Punishment | Additional provisions |
|---|---|---|---|---|
| *Section 24(2)* | *Supplying firearm or ammunition (being of a kind to which section 1 of this Act applies) to person under 14.* | *Summary* | *6 months or a fine of level 5 on the standard scale; or both.* | |
| *Section 24(3)* | *Making gift of shot gun to person under 15.* | *Summary* | *A fine of level 3 on the standard scale.* | *Para. 9 of Part II of this Schedule applies.* |
| *Section 24(4)* | *Supplying air weapon to person under 14.* | *Summary* | *A fine of level 3 on the standard scale.* | *Paras 7 and 8 of Part II of this Schedule apply.* |
| *Section 25* | *Supplying firearm to person drunk or insane.* | *Summary* | *3 months or a fine of level 3 on the standard scale; or both.* | |
| *Section 26(5)* | *Making false statement in order to procure grant or renewal of a firearm or shot gun certificate.* | *Summary* | *6 months or a fine of level 5 on the standard scale; or both.* | |
| *Section 29(3)* | *Making false statement in order to procure variation of a firearm certificate.* | *Summary* | *6 months or a fine of level 5 on the standard scale; or both.* | |
| *Section 30D(3)* | *Failing to surrender certificate on revocation.* | *Summary* | *A fine of level 3 on the standard scale.* | |
| *Section 32B(5)* | *Failure to surrender expired European firearms pass.* | *Summary* | *A fine of level 3 on the standard scale.* | |
| *Section 32C(6)* | *Failure to produce European firearms pass or Article 7 authority for variation or cancellation etc.; failure to notify loss or theft of firearm identified in pass or to produce pass for endorsement.* | *Summary* | *3 months or a fine of level 5 on the standard scale; or both.* | |
| *Section 38(8)* | *Failure to surrender certificate of registration [or register of transactions] on removal of firearms dealer's name from register.* | *Summary* | *A fine of level 3 on the standard scale.* | |
| *Section 39(1)* | *Making false statement in order to secure registration or entry in register of a place of business.* | *Summary* | *6 months or a fine of level 5 on the standard scale; or both.* | |
| *Section 39(2)* | *Registered firearms dealer having place of business not entered in the register.* | *Summary* | *6 months or a fine of level 5 on the standard scale; or both.* | |
| *Section 39(3)* | *Non-compliance with condition of registration.* | *Summary* | *6 months or a fine of level 5 on the standard scale; or both.* | |
| *Section 40(5)* | *Non-compliance by firearms dealer with provisions as to register of transactions; making false entry in register.* | *Summary* | *6 months or a fine of level 5 on the standard scale; or both.* | |
| *Section 42A* | *Failure to report transaction authorised by visitor's shot gun permit.* | *Summary* | *3 months or a fine of level 5 on the standard scale; or both.* | |

**Part I Table**   (continued)

| Section of this Act creating offence | General nature of offence | Mode of prosecution | Punishment | Additional provisions |
|---|---|---|---|---|
| *Section 46* | *Obstructing constable or civilian officer in exercise of search powers.* | *Summary* | *6 months or a fine of level 5 on the standard scale; or both.* | |
| *Section 47(2)* | *Failure to hand over firearm or ammunition on demand by constable.* | *Summary* | *3 months, or a fine of level 4 on the standard scale; or both.* | |
| *Section 48(3)* | *Failure to comply with requirement of a constable that a person shall declare his name and address.* | *Summary* | *A fine of level 3 on the standard scale.* | |
| *Section 48A(4)* | *Failure to produce firearms pass issued in another Member State.* | *Summary* | *A fine of level 3 on the standard scale.* | |
| *Section 49(3)* | *Failure to give constable facilities for examination of firearms in transit, or to produce papers.* | *Summary* | *3 months or, for each firearm or parcel of ammunition in respect of which the offence is committed, a fine of level 3 on the standard scale; or both.* | *Para. 2 of Part II of this Schedule applies.* |
| *Section 52(2)(c)* | *Failure to surrender firearm or shot gun certificate cancelled by court on conviction.* | *Summary* | *A fine of level 3 on the standard scale.* | |

# Appendix 6

# The Human Rights Act 1998

## CHAPTER 42

### ARRANGEMENT OF SECTIONS

*Supplemental*

20. Orders etc. under this Act.

21. Interpretation, etc.

22. Short title, commencement, application and extent.

SCHEDULES:

# Human Rights Act 1998

## 1998 CHAPTER 42

An Act to give further effect to rights and freedoms guaranteed under the European Convention on Human Rights; to make provision with respect to holders of certain judicial offices who become judges of the European Court of Human Rights; and for connected purposes. [9th November 1998]

BE IT ENACTED by the Queen's most Excellent Majesty, by and with the advice and consent of the Lords Spiritual and Temporal, and Commons, in this present Parliament assembled, and by the authority of the same, as follows:—

*Introduction*

### 1. The Convention Rights

(1) In this Act 'the Convention rights' means the rights and fundamental freedoms set out in—
   (a) Articles 2 to 12 and 14 of the Convention,
   (b) Articles 1 to 3 of the First Protocol, and
   (c) Articles 1 and 2 of the Sixth Protocol,
   as read with Articles 16 to 18 of the Convention.

(2) Those Articles are to have effect for the purposes of this Act subject to any designated derogation or reservation (as to which see sections 14 and 15).

(3) The Articles are set out in Schedule 1.

(4) The Lord Chancellor may by order make such amendments to this Act as he considers appropriate to reflect the effect, in relation to the United Kingdom, of a protocol.

(5) In subsection (4) 'protocol' means a protocol to the Convention—
   (a) which the United Kingdom has ratified; or
   (b) which the United Kingdom has signed with a view to ratification.

(6) No amendment may be made by an order under subsection (4) so as to come into force before the protocol concerned is in force in relation to the United Kingdom.

S1 Amended by Transfer of Functions (Miscellaneous) Order (SI 2001/3500) Sch. 2

### 2.   Interpretation of Convention rights

(1) A court or tribunal determining a question which has arisen in connection with a Convention right must take into account any—

   (a) judgment, decision, declaration or advisory opinion of the European Court of Human Rights,

(b) opinion of the Commission given in a report adopted under Article 31 of the Convention,

(c) decision of the Commission in connection with Article 26 or 27(2) of the Convention, or

(d) decision of the Committee of Ministers taken under Article 46 of the Convention,

whenever made or given, so far as, in the opinion of the court or tribunal, it is relevant to the proceedings in which that question has arisen.

(2) Evidence of any judgment, decision, declaration or opinion of which account may have to be taken under this section is to be given in proceedings before any court or tribunal in such manner as may be provided by rules.

(3) In this section 'rules' means rules of court or, in the case of proceedings before a tribunal, rules made for the purposes of this section—

(a) by the Lord Chancellor or the Secretary of State, in relation to any proceedings outside Scotland;

(b) by the Secretary of State, in relation to proceedings in Scotland; or

(c) by a Northern Ireland department, in relation to proceedings before a tribunal in Northern Ireland—

(i) which deals with transferred matters; and

(ii) for which no rules made under paragraph (a) are in force.

*Legislation*

### 3. Interpretation of legislation

(1) So far as it is possible to do so, primary legislation and subordinate legislation must be read and given effect in a way which is compatible with the Convention rights.

(2) This section—

(a) applies to primary legislation and subordinate legislation whenever enacted;

(b) does not affect the validity, continuing operation or enforcement of any incompatible primary legislation; and

(c) does not affect the validity, continuing operation or enforcement of any incompatible subordinate legislation if (disregarding any possibility of revocation) primary legislation prevents removal of the incompatibility.

### 4. Declaration of incompatibility

(1) Subsection (2) applies in any proceedings in which a court determines whether a provision of primary legislation is compatible with a Convention right.

(2) If the court is satisfied that the provision is incompatible with a Convention right, it may make a declaration of that incompatibility.

(3) Subsection (4) applies in any proceedings in which a court determines whether a provision of subordinate legislation, made in the exercise of a power conferred by primary legislation, is compatible with a Convention right.

(4) If the court is satisfied—

(a) that the provision is incompatible with a Convention right, and

(b) that (disregarding any possibility of revocation) the primary legislation concerned prevents removal of the incompatibility,

it may make a declaration of that incompatibility.

(5) In this section 'court' means—

(a) the House of Lords;

(b) the Judicial Committee of the Privy Council;

(c) the Courts-Martial Appeal Court;

(d) in Scotland, the High Court of Justiciary sitting otherwise than as a trial court or the Court of Session;

(e) in England and Wales or Northern Ireland, the High Court or the Court of Appeal.

(6) A declaration under this section ('a declaration of incompatibility')—

(a) does not affect the validity, continuing operation or enforcement of the provision in respect of which it is given; and

(b) is not binding on the parties to the proceedings in which it is made.

### 5.  Right of Crown to intervene

(1)  Where a court is considering whether to make a declaration of incompatibility, the Crown is entitled to notice in accordance with rules of court.

(2)  In any case to which subsection (1) applies—

(a)  a Minister of the Crown (or a person nominated by him),

(b)  a member of the Scottish Executive,

(c)  a Northern Ireland Minister,

(d)  a Northern Ireland department,

is entitled, on giving notice in accordance with rules of court, to be joined as a party to the proceedings.

(3)  Notice under subsection (2) may be given at any time during the proceedings.

(4)  A person who has been made a party to criminal proceedings (other than in Scotland) as the result of a notice under subsection (2) may, with leave, appeal to the House of Lords against any declaration of incompatibility made in the proceedings.

(5)  In subsection (4)—

'criminal proceedings' includes all proceedings before the Courts-Martial Appeal Court; and 'leave' means leave granted by the court making the declaration of incompatibility or by the House of Lords.

*Public authorities*

### 6.  Acts of public authorities

(1)  It is unlawful for a public authority to act in a way which is incompatible with a Convention right.

(2)  Subsection (1) does not apply to an act if—

(a)  as the result of one or more provisions of primary legislation, the authority could not have acted differently; or

(b)  in the case of one or more provisions of, or made under, primary legislation which cannot be read or given effect in a way which is compatible with the Convention rights, the authority was acting so as to give effect to or enforce those provisions.

(3)  In this section 'public authority' includes—

(a)  a court or tribunal, and

(b)  any person certain of whose functions are functions of a public nature,

but does not include either House of Parliament or a person exercising functions in connection with proceedings in Parliament.

(4)  In subsection (3) 'Parliament' does not include the House of Lords in its judicial capacity.

(5)  In relation to a particular act, a person is not a public authority by virtue only of subsection (3)(b) if the nature of the act is private.

(6)  'An act' includes a failure to act but does not include a failure to—

(a)  introduce in, or lay before, Parliament a proposal for legislation; or

(b)  make any primary legislation or remedial order.

### 7.  Proceedings

(1)  A person who claims that a public authority has acted (or proposes to act) in a way which is made unlawful by section 6(1) may—

(a)  bring proceedings against the authority under this Act in the appropriate court or tribunal, or

(b)  rely on the Convention right or rights concerned in any legal proceedings,

but only if he is (or would be) a victim of the unlawful act.

(2)  In subsection (1)(a) 'appropriate court or tribunal' means such court or tribunal as may be determined in accordance with rules; and proceedings against an authority include a counterclaim or similar proceeding.

(3)  If the proceedings are brought on an application for judicial review, the applicant is to be taken to have a sufficient interest in relation to the unlawful act only if he is, or would be, a victim of that act.

(4) If the proceedings are made by way of a petition for judicial review in Scotland, the applicant shall be taken to have title and interest to sue in relation to the unlawful act only if he is, or would be, a victim of that act.

(5) Proceedings under subsection (1)(a) must be brought before the end of—

(a) the period of one year beginning with the date on which the act complained of took place; or

(b) such longer period as the court or tribunal considers equitable having regard to all the circumstances,

but that is subject to any rule imposing a stricter time limit in relation to the procedure in question.

(6) In subsection (1)(b) 'legal proceedings' includes—

(a) proceedings brought by or at the instigation of a public authority; and

(b) an appeal against the decision of a court or tribunal.

(7) For the purposes of this section, a person is a victim of an unlawful act only if he would be a victim for the purposes of Article 34 of the Convention if proceedings were brought in the European Court of Human Rights in respect of that act.

(8) Nothing in this Act creates a criminal offence.

(9) In this section 'rules' means—

(a) in relation to proceedings before a court or tribunal outside Scotland, rules made by the Lord Chancellor or the Secretary of State for the purposes of this section or rules of court,

(b) in relation to proceedings before a court or tribunal in Scotland, rules made by the Secretary of State for those purposes,

(c) in relation to proceedings before a tribunal in Northern Ireland—

(i) which deals with transferred matters; and

(ii) for which no rules made under paragraph (a) are in force,

rules made by a Northern Ireland department for those purposes,

and includes provision made by order under section 1 of the Courts and Legal Services Act 1990.

(10) In making rules, regard must be had to section 9.

(11) The Minister who has power to make rules in relation to a particular tribunal may, to the extent he considers it necessary to ensure that the tribunal can provide an appropriate remedy in relation to an act (or proposed act) of a public authority which is (or would be) unlawful as a result of section 6(1), by order add to—

(a) the relief or remedies which the tribunal may grant; or

(b) the grounds on which it may grant any of them.

(12) An order made under subsection (11) may contain such incidental, supplemental, consequential or transitional provision as the Minister making it considers appropriate.

(13) 'The Minister' includes the Northern Ireland department concerned.

## 8. Judicial remedies

(1) In relation to any act (or proposed act) of a public authority which the court finds is (or would be) unlawful, it may grant such relief or remedy, or make such order, within its powers as it considers just and appropriate.

(2) But damages may be awarded only by a court which has power to award damages, or to order the payment of compensation, in civil proceedings.

(3) No award of damages is to be made unless, taking account of all the circumstances of the case, including—

(a) any other relief or remedy granted, or order made, in relation to the act in question (by that or any other court), and

(b) the consequences of any decision (of that or any other court) in respect of that act,

the court is satisfied that the award is necessary to afford just satisfaction to the person in whose favour it is made.

(4) In determining—

(a) whether to award damages, or

(b) the amount of an award,

the court must take into account the principles applied by the European Court of Human Rights in relation to the award of compensation under Article 41 of the Convention.

(5) A public authority against which damages are awarded is to be treated—

(a) in Scotland, for the purposes of section 3 of the Law Reform (Miscellaneous Provisions) (Scotland) Act 1940 as if the award were made in an action of damages in which the authority has been found liable in respect of loss or damage to the person to whom the award is made;

(b) for the purposes of the Civil Liability (Contribution) Act 1978 as liable in respect of damage suffered by the person to whom the award is made.

(6) In this section—

'court' includes a tribunal;

'damages' means damages for an unlawful act of a public authority; and

'unlawful' means unlawful under section 6(1).

## 9. Judicial acts

(1) Proceedings under section 7(1)(a) in respect of a judicial act may be brought only—

(a) by exercising a right of appeal;

(b) on an application (in Scotland a petition) for judicial review; or

(c) in such other forum as may be prescribed by rules.

(2) That does not affect any rule of law which prevents a court from being the subject of judicial review.

(3) In proceedings under this Act in respect of a judicial act done in good faith, damages may not be awarded otherwise than to compensate a person to the extent required by Article 5(5) of the Convention.

(4) An award of damages permitted by subsection (3) is to be made against the Crown; but no award may be made unless the appropriate person, if not a party to the proceedings, is joined.

(5) In this section—

'appropriate person' means the Minister responsible for the court concerned, or a person or government department nominated by him;

'court' includes a tribunal;

'judge' includes a member of a tribunal, a justice of the peace and a clerk or other officer entitled to exercise the jurisdiction of a court;

'judicial act' means a judicial act of a court and includes an act done on the instructions, or on behalf, of a judge; and

'rules' has the same meaning as in section 7(9).

*Remedial action*

## 10. Power to take remedial action

(1) This section applies if—

(a) a provision of legislation has been declared under section 4 to be incompatible with a Convention right and, if an appeal lies—

(i) all persons who may appeal have stated in writing that they do not intend to do so;

(ii) the time for bringing an appeal has expired and no appeal has been brought within that time; or

(iii) an appeal brought within that time has been determined or abandoned; or

(b) it appears to a Minister of the Crown or Her Majesty in Council that, having regard to a finding of the European Court of Human Rights made after the coming into force of this section in proceedings against the United Kingdom, a provision of legislation is incompatible with an obligation of the United Kingdom arising from the Convention.

(2) If a Minister of the Crown considers that there are compelling reasons for proceeding under this section, he may by order make such amendments to the legislation as he considers necessary to remove the incompatibility.

(3) If, in the case of subordinate legislation, a Minister of the Crown considers—

(a) that it is necessary to amend the primary legislation under which the subordinate legislation in question was made, in order to enable the incompatibility to be removed, and

(b) that there are compelling reasons for proceeding under this section,

he may by order make such amendments to the primary legislation as he considers necessary.

(4) This section also applies where the provision in question is in subordinate legislation and has been quashed, or declared invalid, by reason of incompatibility with a Convention right and the Minister proposes to proceed under paragraph 2(b) of Schedule 2.

(5) If the legislation is an Order in Council, the power conferred by subsection (2) or (3) is exercisable by Her Majesty in Council.

(6) In this section 'legislation' does not include a Measure of the Church Assembly or of the General Synod of the Church of England.

(7) Schedule 2 makes further provision about remedial orders.

*Other rights and proceedings*

## 11.  Safeguard for existing human rights

A person's reliance on a Convention right does not restrict—

(a) any other right or freedom conferred on him by or under any law having effect in any part of the United Kingdom; or

(b) his right to make any claim or bring any proceedings which he could make or bring apart from sections 7 to 9.

## 12.  Freedom of expression

(1) This section applies if a court is considering whether to grant any relief which, if granted, might affect the exercise of the Convention right to freedom of expression.

(2) If the person against whom the application for relief is made ('the respondent') is neither present nor represented, no such relief is to be granted unless the court is satisfied—

(a) that the applicant has taken all practicable steps to notify the respondent; or

(b) that there are compelling reasons why the respondent should not be notified.

(3) No such relief is to be granted so as to restrain publication before trial unless the court is satisfied that the applicant is likely to establish that publication should not be allowed.

(4) The court must have particular regard to the importance of the Convention right to freedom of expression and, where the proceedings relate to material which the respondent claims, or which appears to the court, to be journalistic, literary or artistic material (or to conduct connected with such material), to—

(a) the extent to which—

(i) the material has, or is about to, become available to the public; or

(ii) it is, or would be, in the public interest for the material to be published;

(b) any relevant privacy code.

(5) In this section—

'court' includes a tribunal; and

'relief' includes any remedy or order (other than in criminal proceedings).

## 13.  Freedom of thought, conscience and religion

(1) If a court's determination of any question arising under this Act might affect the exercise by a religious organisation (itself or its members collectively) of the Convention right to freedom of thought, conscience and religion, it must have particular regard to the importance of that right.

(2) In this section 'court' includes a tribunal.

*Derogations and reservations*

## 14.  Derogations

(1) In this Act 'designated derogation' means any derogation by the United Kingdom from an Article of the Convention, or of any protocol to the Convention, which is designated for the purposes of this Act in an order made by the Lord Chancellor.

(2) [repealed]

(3) If a designated derogation is amended or replaced it ceases to be a designated derogation.

(4) But subsection (3) does not prevent the Lord Chancellor from exercising his power under subsection (1) to make a fresh designation order in respect of the Article concerned.

(5) The Lord Chancellor must by order make such amendments to Schedule 3 as he considers appropriate to reflect—
   (a) any designation order; or
   (b) the effect of subsection (3).

(6) A designation order may be made in anticipation of the making by the United Kingdom of a proposed derogation.

S14 Amended by Transfer of Functions (Miscellaneous) Order (SI 2001/3500) Sch. 2

## 15. Reservations

(1) In this Act 'designated reservation' means—
   (a) the United Kingdom's reservation to Article 2 of the First Protocol to the Convention; and
   (b) any other reservation by the United Kingdom to an Article of the Convention, or of any protocol to the Convention, which is designated for the purposes of this Act in an order made by the Lord Chancellor.

(2) The text of the reservation referred to in subsection (1)(a) is set out in Part II of Schedule 3.

(3) If a designated reservation is withdrawn wholly or in part it ceases to be a designated reservation.

(4) But subsection (3) does not prevent the Lord Chancellor from exercising his power under subsection (1)(b) to make a fresh designation order in respect of the Article concerned.

(5) The Secretary of State must by order make such amendments to this Act as he considers appropriate to reflect—
   (a) any designation order; or
   (b) the effect of subsection (3).

S15 Amended by Transfer of Functions (Miscellaneous) Order (SI 2001/3500) Sch. 2

## 16. Period for which designated derogations have effect

(1) If it has not already been withdrawn by the United Kingdom, a designated derogation ceases to have effect for the purposes of this Act at the end of the period of five years beginning with the date on which the order designating it was made.

(2) At any time before the period—
   (a) fixed by subsection (1), or
   (b) extended by an order under this subsection,
   comes to an end, the Lord Chancellor may by order extend it by a further period of five years.

(3) An order under section 14(1) ceases to have effect at the end of the period for consideration, unless a resolution has been passed by each House approving the order.

(4) Subsection (3) does not affect—
   (a) anything done in reliance on the order; or
   (b) the power to make a fresh order under section 14(1).

(5) In subsection (3) 'period for consideration' means the period of forty days beginning with the day on which the order was made.

(6) In calculating the period for consideration, no account is to be taken of any time during which—
   (a) Parliament is dissolved or prorogued; or
   (b) both Houses are adjourned for more than four days.

(7) If a designated derogation is withdrawn by the United Kingdom, the Lord Chancellor must by order make such amendments to this Act as he considers are required to reflect that withdrawal.

S16 Amended by Transfer of Functions (Miscellaneous) Order (SI 2001/3500) Sch. 2

## 17. Periodic review of designated reservations

(1) The appropriate Minister must review the designated reservation referred to in section 15(1)(a)—
   (a) before the end of the period of five years beginning with the date on which section 1(2) came into force; and

    (b) if that designation is still in force, before the end of the period of five years beginning with the date on which the last report relating to it was laid under subsection (3).

(2) The appropriate Minister must review each of the other designated reservations (if any)—

    (a) before the end of the period of five years beginning with the date on which the order designating the reservation first came into force; and

    (b) if the designation is still in force, before the end of the period of five years beginning with the date on which the last report relating to it was laid under subsection (3).

(3) The Minister conducting a review under this section must prepare a report on the result of the review and lay a copy of it before each House of Parliament.

*Judges of the European Court of Human Rights*

## 18. Appointment to European Court of Human Rights

(1) In this section 'judicial office' means the office of—

    (a) Lord Justice of Appeal, Justice of the High Court or Circuit judge, in England and Wales;

    (b) judge of the Court of Session or sheriff, in Scotland;

    (c) Lord Justice of Appeal, judge of the High Court or county court judge, in Northern Ireland.

(2) The holder of a judicial office may become a judge of the European Court of Human Rights ('the Court') without being required to relinquish his office.

(3) But he is not required to perform the duties of his judicial office while he is a judge of the Court.

(4) In respect of any period during which he is a judge of the Court—

    (a) a Lord Justice of Appeal or Justice of the High Court is not to count as a judge of the relevant court for the purposes of section 2(1) or 4(1) of the Supreme Court Act 1981 (maximum number of judges) nor as a judge of the Supreme Court for the purposes of section 12(1) to (6) of that Act (salaries etc.);

    (b) a judge of the Court of Session is not to count as a judge of that court for the purposes of section 1(1) of the Court of Session Act 1988 (maximum number of judges) or of section 9(1)(c) of the Administration of Justice Act 1973 ('the 1973 Act') (salaries etc.);

    (c) a Lord Justice of Appeal or judge of the High Court in Northern Ireland is not to count as a judge of the relevant court for the purposes of section 2(1) or 3(1) of the Judicature (Northern Ireland) Act 1978 (maximum number of judges) nor as a judge of the Supreme Court of Northern Ireland for the purposes of section 9(1)(d) of the 1973 Act (salaries etc.);

    (d) a Circuit judge is not to count as such for the purposes of section 18 of the Courts Act 1971 (salaries etc.);

    (e) a sheriff is not to count as such for the purposes of section 14 of the Sheriff Courts (Scotland) Act 1907 (salaries etc.);

    (f) a county court judge of Northern Ireland is not to count as such for the purposes of section 106 of the County Courts Act (Northern Ireland) 1959 (salaries etc.).

(5) If a sheriff principal is appointed a judge of the Court, section 11(1) of the Sheriff Courts (Scotland) Act 1971 (temporary appointment of sheriff principal) applies, while he holds that appointment, as if his office is vacant.

(6) Schedule 4 makes provision about judicial pensions in relation to the holder of a judicial office who serves as a judge of the Court.

(7) The Lord Chancellor or the Secretary of State may by order make such transitional provision (including, in particular, provision for a temporary increase in the maximum number of judges) as he considers appropriate in relation to any holder of a judicial office who has completed his service as a judge of the Court.

*Parliamentary procedure*

## 19. Statements of compatibility

(1) A Minister of the Crown in charge of a Bill in either House of Parliament must, before Second Reading of the Bill—

    (a) make a statement to the effect that in his view the provisions of the Bill are compatible with the Convention rights ('a statement of compatibility'); or

(b) make a statement to the effect that although he is unable to make a statement of compatibility the government nevertheless wishes the House to proceed with the Bill.

(2) The statement must be in writing and be published in such manner as the Minister making it considers appropriate.

*Supplemental*

## 20. Orders etc. under this Act

(1) Any power of a Minister of the Crown to make an order under this Act is exercisable by statutory instrument.

(2) The power of the Lord Chancellor or the Secretary of State to make rules (other than rules of court) under section 2(3) or 7(9) is exercisable by statutory instrument.

(3) Any statutory instrument made under section 14, 15 or 16(7) must be laid before Parliament.

(4) No order may be made by the Lord Chancellor or the Secretary of State under section 1(4), 7(11) or 16(2) unless a draft of the order has been laid before, and approved by, each House of Parliament.

(5) Any statutory instrument made under section 18(7) or Schedule 4, or to which subsection (2) applies, shall be subject to annulment in pursuance of a resolution of either House of Parliament.

(6) The power of a Northern Ireland department to make—
　(a) rules under section 2(3)(c) or 7(9)(c), or
　(b) an order under section 7(11), is exercisable by statutory rule for the purposes of the Statutory Rules (Northern Ireland) Order 1979.

(7) Any rules made under section 2(3)(c) or 7(9)(c) shall be subject to negative resolution; and section 41(6) of the Interpretation Act (Northern Ireland) 1954 (meaning of 'subject to negative resolution') shall apply as if the power to make the rules were conferred by an Act of the Northern Ireland Assembly.

(8) No order may be made by a Northern Ireland department under section 7(11) unless a draft of the order has been laid before, and approved by, the Northern Ireland Assembly.

## 21. Interpretation etc.

(1) In this Act—
'amend' includes repeal and apply (with or without modifications);
'the appropriate Minister' means the Minister of the Crown having charge of the appropriate authorised government department (within the meaning of the Crown Proceedings Act 1947);
'the Commission' means the European Commission of Human Rights;
'the Convention' means the Convention for the Protection of Human Rights and Fundamental Freedoms, agreed by the Council of Europe at Rome on 4th November 1950 as it has effect for the time being in relation to the United Kingdom;
'declaration of incompatibility' means a declaration under section 4;
'Minister of the Crown' has the same meaning as in the Ministers of the Crown Act 1975;
'Northern Ireland Minister' includes the First Minister and the deputy First Minister in Northern Ireland;
'primary legislation' means any—
　(a) public general Act;
　(b) local and personal Act;
　(c) private Act;
　(d) Measure of the Church Assembly;
　(e) Measure of the General Synod of the Church of England;
　(f) Order in Council—
　　(i) made in exercise of Her Majesty's Royal Prerogative;
　　(ii) made under section 38(1)(a) of the Northern Ireland Constitution Act 1973 or the corresponding provision of the Northern Ireland Act 1998; or
　　(iii) amending an Act of a kind mentioned in paragraph (a), (b) or (c);
and includes an order or other instrument made under primary legislation (otherwise than by the National Assembly for Wales, a member of the Scottish Executive, a Northern Ireland Minister or

a Northern Ireland department) to the extent to which it operates to bring one or more provisions of that legislation into force or amends any primary legislation;

'the First Protocol' means the protocol to the Convention agreed at Paris on 20th March 1952;

'the Sixth Protocol' means the protocol to the Convention agreed at Strasbourg on 28th April 1983;

'the Eleventh Protocol' means the protocol to the Convention (restructuring the control machinery established by the Convention) agreed at Strasbourg on 11th May 1994;

'remedial order' means an order under section 10;

'subordinate legislation' means any—

- (a) Order in Council other than one—
    - (i) made in exercise of Her Majesty's Royal Prerogative;
    - (ii) made under section 38(1)(a) of the Northern Ireland Constitution Act 1973 or the corresponding provision of the Northern Ireland Act 1998; or
    - (iii) amending an Act of a kind mentioned in the definition of primary legislation;

- (b) Act of the Scottish Parliament;
- (c) Act of the Parliament of Northern Ireland;
- (d) Measure of the Assembly established under section 1 of the Northern Ireland Assembly Act 1973;
- (e) Act of the Northern Ireland Assembly;
- (f) order, rules, regulations, scheme, warrant, byelaw or other instrument made under primary legislation (except to the extent to which it operates to bring one or more provisions of that legislation into force or amends any primary legislation);
- (g) order, rules, regulations, scheme, warrant, byelaw or other instrument made under legislation mentioned in paragraph (b), (c), (d) or (e) or made under an Order in Council applying only to Northern Ireland;
- (h) order, rules, regulations, scheme, warrant, byelaw or other instrument made by a member of the Scottish Executive, a Northern Ireland Minister or a Northern Ireland department in exercise of prerogative or other executive functions of Her Majesty which are exercisable by such a person on behalf of Her Majesty;

'transferred matters' has the same meaning as in the Northern Ireland Act 1998; and

'tribunal' means any tribunal in which legal proceedings may be brought.

(2) The references in paragraphs (b) and (c) of section 2(1) to Articles are to Articles of the Convention as they had effect immediately before the coming into force of the Eleventh Protocol.

(3) The reference in paragraph (d) of section 2(1) to Article 46 includes a reference to Articles 32 and 54 of the Convention as they had effect immediately before the coming into force of the Eleventh Protocol.

(4) The references in section 2(1) to a report or decision of the Commission or a decision of the Committee of Ministers include references to a report or decision made as provided by paragraphs 3, 4 and 6 of Article 5 of the Eleventh Protocol (transitional provisions).

(5) Any liability under the Army Act 1955, the Air Force Act 1955 or the Naval Discipline Act 1957 to suffer death for an offence is replaced by a liability to imprisonment for life or any less punishment authorised by those Acts; and those Acts shall accordingly have effect with the necessary modifications.

### 22. Short title, commencement, application and extent

(1) This Act may be cited as the Human Rights Act 1998.

(2) Sections 18, 20 and 21(5) and this section come into force on the passing of this Act.

(3) The other provisions of this Act come into force on such day as the Secretary of State may by order appoint; and different days may be appointed for different purposes.

(4) Paragraph (b) of subsection (1) of section 7 applies to proceedings brought by or at the instigation of a public authority whenever the act in question took place; but otherwise that subsection does not apply to an act taking place before the coming into force of that section.

(5) This Act binds the Crown.

(6) This Act extends to Northern Ireland.

(7) Section 21(5), so far as it relates to any provision contained in the Army Act 1955, the Air Force Act 1955 or the Naval Discipline Act 1957, extends to any place to which that provision extends.

SCHEDULES

Section 1(3)                         SCHEDULE 1

THE ARTICLES

PART I

THE CONVENTION

RIGHTS AND FREEDOMS

## Article 2
### Right to life

1. Everyone's right to life shall be protected by law. No one shall be deprived of his life intentionally save in the execution of a sentence of a court following his conviction of a crime for which this penalty is provided by law.

2. Deprivation of life shall not be regarded as inflicted in contravention of this Article when it results from the use of force which is no more than absolutely necessary:
   (a) in defence of any person from unlawful violence;
   (b) in order to effect a lawful arrest or to prevent the escape of a person lawfully detained;
   (c) in action lawfully taken for the purpose of quelling a riot or insurrection.

## Article 3
### Prohibition of torture

No one shall be subjected to torture or to inhuman or degrading treatment or punishment.

## Article 4
### Prohibition of slavery and forced labour

1. No one shall be held in slavery or servitude.

2. No one shall be required to perform forced or compulsory labour.

3. For the purpose of this Article the term 'forced or compulsory labour' shall not include:
   (a) any work required to be done in the ordinary course of detention imposed according to the provisions of Article 5 of this Convention or during conditional release from such detention;
   (b) any service of a military character or, in case of conscientious objectors in countries where they are recognised, service exacted instead of compulsory military service;
   (c) any service exacted in case of an emergency or calamity threatening the life or well-being of the community;
   (d) any work or service which forms part of normal civic obligations.

## Article 5
### Right to liberty and security

1. Everyone has the right to liberty and security of person. No one shall be deprived of his liberty save in the following cases and in accordance with a procedure prescribed by law:
   (a) the lawful detention of a person after conviction by a competent court;
   (b) the lawful arrest or detention of a person for non-compliance with the lawful order of a court or in order to secure the fulfilment of any obligation prescribed by law;
   (c) the lawful arrest or detention of a person effected for the purpose of bringing him before the competent legal authority on reasonable suspicion of having committed an offence or when it is reasonably considered necessary to prevent his committing an offence or fleeing after having done so;
   (d) the detention of a minor by lawful order for the purpose of educational supervision or his lawful detention for the purpose of bringing him before the competent legal authority;
   (e) the lawful detention of persons for the prevention of the spreading of infectious diseases, of persons of unsound mind, alcoholics or drug addicts or vagrants;

(f) the lawful arrest or detention of a person to prevent his effecting an unauthorised entry into the country or of a person against whom action is being taken with a view to deportation or extradition.

2. Everyone who is arrested shall be informed promptly, in a language which he understands, of the reasons for his arrest and of any charge against him.

3. Everyone arrested or detained in accordance with the provisions of paragraph 1(c) of this Article shall be brought promptly before a judge or other officer authorised by law to exercise judicial power and shall be entitled to trial within a reasonable time or to release pending trial. Release may be conditioned by guarantees to appear for trial.

4. Everyone who is deprived of his liberty by arrest or detention shall be entitled to take proceedings by which the lawfulness of his detention shall be decided speedily by a court and his release ordered if the detention is not lawful.

5. Everyone who has been the victim of arrest or detention in contravention of the provisions of this Article shall have an enforceable right to compensation.

### Article 6
#### Right to a fair trial

1. In the determination of his civil rights and obligations or of any criminal charge against him, everyone is entitled to a fair and public hearing within a reasonable time by an independent and impartial tribunal established by law. Judgment shall be pronounced publicly but the press and public may be excluded from all or part of the trial in the interest of morals, public order or national security in a democratic society, where the interests of juveniles or the protection of the private life of the parties so require, or to the extent strictly necessary in the opinion of the court in special circumstances where publicity would prejudice the interests of justice.

2. Everyone charged with a criminal offence shall be presumed innocent until proved guilty according to law.

3. Everyone charged with a criminal offence has the following minimum rights:
   (a) to be informed promptly, in a language which he understands and in detail, of the nature and cause of the accusation against him;
   (b) to have adequate time and facilities for the preparation of his defence;
   (c) to defend himself in person or through legal assistance of his own choosing or, if he has not sufficient means to pay for legal assistance, to be given it free when the interests of justice so require;
   (d) to examine or have examined witnesses against him and to obtain the attendance and examination of witnesses on his behalf under the same conditions as witnesses against him;
   (e) to have the free assistance of an interpreter if he cannot understand or speak the language used in court.

### Article 7
#### No punishment without law

1. No one shall be held guilty of any criminal offence on account of any act or omission which did not constitute a criminal offence under national or international law at the time when it was committed. Nor shall a heavier penalty be imposed than the one that was applicable at the time the criminal offence was committed.

2. This Article shall not prejudice the trial and punishment of any person for any act or omission which, at the time when it was committed, was criminal according to the general principles of law recognised by civilised nations.

### Article 8
#### Right to respect for private and family life

1. Everyone has the right to respect for his private and family life, his home and his correspondence.

2. There shall be no interference by a public authority with the exercise of this right except such as is in accordance with the law and is necessary in a democratic society in the interests of national security, public safety or the economic well being of the country, for the prevention of disorder or crime, for the protection of health or morals, or for the protection of the rights and freedoms of others.

## Article 9
### Freedom of thought, conscience and religion

1. Everyone has the right to freedom of thought, conscience and religion; this right includes freedom to change his religion or belief and freedom, either alone or in community with others and in public or private, to manifest his religion or belief, in worship, teaching, practice and observance.

2. Freedom to manifest one's religion or beliefs shall be subject only to such limitations as are prescribed by law and are necessary in a democratic society in the interests of public safety, for the protection of public order, health or morals, or for the protection of the rights and freedoms of others.

## Article 10
### Freedom of expression

1. Everyone has the right to freedom of expression. This right shall include freedom to hold opinions and to receive and impart information and ideas without interference by public authority and regardless of frontiers. This Article shall not prevent States from requiring the licensing of broadcasting, television or cinema enterprises.

2. The exercise of these freedoms, since it carries with it duties and responsibilities, may be subject to such formalities, conditions, restrictions or penalties as are prescribed by law and are necessary in a democratic society, in the interests of national security, territorial integrity or public safety, for the prevention of disorder or crime, for the protection of health or morals, for the protection of the reputation or rights of others, for preventing the disclosure of information received in confidence, or for maintaining the authority and impartiality of the judiciary.

## Article 11
### Freedom of assembly and association

1. Everyone has the right to freedom of peaceful assembly and to freedom of association with others, including the right to form and to join trade unions for the protection of his interests.

2. No restrictions shall be placed on the exercise of these rights other than such as are prescribed by law and are necessary in a democratic society in the interests of national security or public safety, for the prevention of disorder or crime, for the protection of health or morals or for the protection of the rights and freedoms of others. This Article shall not prevent the imposition of lawful restrictions on the exercise of these rights by members of the armed forces, of the police or of the administration of the State.

## Article 12
### Right to marry

Men and women of marriageable age have the right to marry and to found a family, according to the national laws governing the exercise of this right.

## Article 14
### Prohibition of discrimination

The enjoyment of the rights and freedoms set forth in this Convention shall be secured without discrimination on any ground such as sex, race, colour, language, religion, political or other opinion, national or social origin, association with a national minority, property, birth or other status.

*Article 16*

*Restrictions on political activity of aliens*

Nothing in Articles 10, 11 and 14 shall be regarded as preventing the High Contracting Parties from imposing restrictions on the political activity of aliens.

*Article 17*

*Prohibition of abuse of rights*

Nothing in this Convention may be interpreted as implying for any State, group or person any right to engage in any activity or perform any act aimed at the destruction of any of the rights and freedoms set forth herein or at their limitation to a greater extent than is provided for in the Convention.

*Article 18*

*Limitation on use of restrictions on rights*

The restrictions permitted under this Convention to the said rights and freedoms shall not be applied for any purpose other than those for which they have been prescribed.

PART II

THE FIRST PROTOCOL

*Article 1*

*Protection of property*

Every natural or legal person is entitled to the peaceful enjoyment of his possessions. No one shall be deprived of his possessions except in the public interest and subject to the conditions provided for by law and by the general principles of international law.

The preceding provisions shall not, however, in any way impair the right of a State to enforce such laws as it deems necessary to control the use of property in accordance with the general interest or to secure the payment of taxes or other contributions or penalties.

*Article 2*

*Right to education*

No person shall be denied the right to education. In the exercise of any functions which it assumes in relation to education and to teaching, the State shall respect the right of parents to ensure such education and teaching in conformity with their own religious and philosophical convictions.

*Article 3*

*Right to free elections*

The High Contracting Parties undertake to hold free elections at reasonable intervals by secret ballot, under conditions which will ensure the free expression of the opinion of the people in the choice of the legislature.

PART III

THE SIXTH PROTOCOL

*Article 1*

*Abolition of the death penalty*

The death penalty shall be abolished. No one shall be condemned to such penalty or executed.

*Article 2*

*Death penalty in time of war*

A State may make provision in its law for the death penalty in respect of acts committed in time of war or of imminent threat of war; such penalty shall be applied only in the instances laid down in the law and in accordance with its provisions. The State shall communicate to the Secretary General of the Council of Europe the relevant provisions of that law.

SCHEDULE 2

REMEDIAL ORDERS

*Orders*

1.—(1)　A remedial order may—

   (a)　contain such incidental, supplemental, consequential or transitional provision as the person making it considers appropriate;

   (b)　be made so as to have effect from a date earlier than that on which it is made;

   (c)　make provision for the delegation of specific functions;

   (d)　make different provision for different cases.

   (2)　The power conferred by sub-paragraph (1)(a) includes—

   (a)　power to amend primary legislation (including primary legislation other than that which contains the incompatible provision); and

   (b)　power to amend or revoke subordinate legislation (including subordinate legislation other than that which contains the incompatible provision).

   (3)　A remedial order may be made so as to have the same extent as the legislation which it affects.

   (4)　No person is to be guilty of an offence solely as a result of the retrospective effect of a remedial order.

*Procedure*

2.　No remedial order may be made unless—

   (a)　a draft of the order has been approved by a resolution of each House of Parliament made after the end of the period of 60 days beginning with the day on which the draft was laid; or

   (b)　it is declared in the order that it appears to the person making it that, because of the urgency of the matter, it is necessary to make the order without a draft being so approved.

*Orders laid in draft*

3.—(1)　No draft may be laid under paragraph 2(a) unless—

   (a)　the person proposing to make the order has laid before Parliament a document which contains a draft of the proposed order and the required information; and

   (b)　the period of 60 days, beginning with the day on which the document required by this sub-paragraph was laid, has ended.

   (2)　If representations have been made during that period, the draft laid under paragraph 2(a) must be accompanied by a statement containing—

   (a)　a summary of the representations; and

   (b)　if, as a result of the representations, the proposed order has been changed, details of the changes.

*Urgent cases*

4.—(1)　If a remedial order ('the original order') is made without being approved in draft, the person making it must lay it before Parliament, accompanied by the required information, after it is made.

   (2)　If representations have been made during the period of 60 days beginning with the day on which the original order was made, the person making it must (after the end of that period) lay before Parliament a statement containing—

   (a)　a summary of the representations; and

   (b)　if, as a result of the representations, he considers it appropriate to make changes to the original order, details of the changes.

   (3)　If sub-paragraph (2)(b) applies, the person making the statement must—

   (a)　make a further remedial order replacing the original order; and

   (b)　lay the replacement order before Parliament.

   (4)　If, at the end of the period of 120 days beginning with the day on which the original order was made, a resolution has not been passed by each House approving the original or replacement order, the order ceases to have effect (but without that affecting anything previously done under either order or the power to make a fresh remedial order).

*Definitions*

5. In this Schedule—

'representations' means representations about a remedial order (or proposed remedial order) made to the person making (or proposing to make) it and includes any relevant Parliamentary report or resolution; and 'required information' means—

   (a) an explanation of the incompatibility which the order (or proposed order) seeks to remove, including particulars of the relevant declaration, finding or order; and

   (b) a statement of the reasons for proceeding under section 10 and for making an order in those terms.

*Calculating periods*

6. In calculating any period for the purposes of this Schedule, no account is to be taken of any time during which—

   (a) Parliament is dissolved or prorogued; or

   (b) both Houses are adjourned for more than four days.

7.—(1) This paragraph applies in relation to—

   (a) any remedial order made, and any draft of such an order proposed to be made,—

      (i) by the Scottish Ministers; or

      (ii) within devolved competence (within the meaning of the Scotland Act 1998) by Her Majesty in Council; and

   (b) any document or statement to be laid in connection with such an order (or proposed order).

   (2) This Schedule has effect in relation to any such order (or proposed order), document or statement subject to the following modifications.

   (3) Any reference to Parliament, each House of Parliament or both Houses of Parliament shall be construed as a reference to the Scottish Parliament.

   (4) Paragraph 6 does not apply and instead, in calculating any period for the purposes of this Schedule, no account is to be taken of any time during which the Scottish Parliament is dissolved or is in recess for more than four days.

Part 7 added by Scotland Act 1998 (Consequential Modifications) Order SI 2000/2040, Sch 1

In relation to Scotland only

SCHEDULE 3
DEROGATION AND RESERVATION

PART I
DEROGATION

*United Kingdom's derogation from Article 5(1)*

The United Kingdom Permanent Representative to the Council of Europe presents his compliments to the Secretary General of the Council, and has the honour to convey the following information in order to ensure compliance with the obligations of Her Majesty's Government in the United Kingdom under Article 15(3) of the Convention for the Protection of Human Rights and Fundamental Freedoms signed at Rome on 4 November 1950.

Part I added by Human Rights Act 1998 (Amendment No. 2) Order (SI 2001/4032) Sch 1

*Public emergency in the United Kingdom*

The terrorist attacks in New York, Washington, D.C. and Pennsylvania on 11th September 2001 resulted in several thousand deaths, including many British victims and others from 70 different countries. In its resolutions 1368 (2001) and 1373 (2001), the United Nations Security Council recognised the attacks as a threat to international peace and security.

The threat from international terrorism is a continuing one. In its resolution 1373 (2001), the Security Council, acting under Chapter VII of the United Nations Charter, required all States to take measures to prevent the commission of terrorist attacks, including by denying safe haven to those who finance, plan, support or commit terrorist attacks.

There exists a terrorist threat to the United Kingdom from persons suspected of involvement in international terrorism. In particular, there are foreign nationals present in the United Kingdom who are suspected of being concerned in the commission, preparation or instigation of acts of international terrorism, of being members of organisations or groups which are so concerned or of having links with members of such organisations or groups, and who are a threat to the national security of the United Kingdom.

As a result, a public emergency, within the meaning of Article 15(1) of the Convention, exists in the United Kingdom.

### The Anti-terrorism, Crime and Security Act 2001

As a result of the public emergency, provision is made in the Anti-terrorism, Crime and Security Act 2001, inter alia, for an extended power to arrest and detain a foreign national which will apply where it is intended to remove or deport the person from the United Kingdom but where removal or deportation is not for the time being possible, with the consequence that the detention would be unlawful under existing domestic law powers. The extended power to arrest and detain will apply where the Secretary of State issues a certificate indicating his belief that the person's presence in the United Kingdom is a risk to national security and that he suspects the person of being an international terrorist. That certificate will be subject to an appeal to the Special Immigration Appeals Commission ('SIAC'), established under the Special Immigration Appeals Commission Act 1997, which will have power to cancel it if it considers that the certificate should not have been issued. There will be an appeal on a point of law from a ruling by SIAC. In addition, the certificate will be reviewed by SIAC at regular intervals. SIAC will also be able to grant bail, where appropriate, subject to conditions. It will be open to a detainee to end his detention at any time by agreeing to leave the United Kingdom.

The extended power of arrest and detention in the Anti-terrorism, Crime and Security Act 2001 is a measure which is strictly required by the exigencies of the situation. It is a temporary provision which comes into force for an initial period of 15 months and then expires unless renewed by Parliament. Thereafter, it is subject to annual renewal by Parliament. If, at any time, in the Government's assessment, the public emergency no longer exists or the extended power is no longer strictly required by the exigencies of the situation, then the Secretary of State will, by Order, repeal the provision.

### Domestic law powers of detention (other than under the Anti-terrorism, Crime and Security Act 2001)

The Government has powers under the Immigration Act 1971 ('the 1971 Act') to remove or deport persons on the ground that their presence in the United Kingdom is not conducive to the public good on national security grounds. Persons can also be arrested and detained under Schedules 2 and 3 to the 1971 Act pending their removal or deportation. The courts in the United Kingdom have ruled that this power of detention can only be exercised during the period necessary, in all the circumstances of the particular case, to effect removal and that, if it becomes clear that removal is not going to be possible within a reasonable time, detention will be unlawful (R v *Governor of Durham Prison, ex parte Singh* [1984] 1 All ER 983).

### Article 5(1)(f) of the Convention

It is well established that Article 5(1)(f) permits the detention of a person with a view to deportation only in circumstance where 'action is being taken with a view to deportation' (*Chahal* v *United Kingdom* (1996) 23 EHRR 413 at paragraph 112). In that case the European Court of Human Rights indicated that detention will cease to be permissible under Article 5(1)(f) if deportation proceedings are not prosecuted with due diligence and that it was necessary in such cases to determine whether the duration of the deportation proceedings was excessive (paragraph 113).

In some cases, where the intention remains to remove or deport a person on national security grounds, continued detention may not be consistent with Article 5(1)(f) as interpreted by the Court in the *Chahal* case. This may be the case, for example, if the person has established that removal to their own country might result in treatment contrary to Article 3 of the Convention. In such circumstances, irrespective of the gravity of the threat to national security posed by the person concerned, it is well established that Article 3 prevents removal or deportation to a place where there is a real risk that the person will suffer treatment contrary to that article. If no alternative destination is immediately available then removal or deportation may not, for the time being, be possible even though the ultimate intention remains to remove or deport the person once satisfactory arrangements can be made. In addition, it may not be possible to prosecute the person for a criminal offence given the strict rules on the admissibility of evidence in the criminal justice system of the United Kingdom and the high standard of proof required.

### *Derogation under Article 15 of the Convention*

The Government has considered whether the exercise of the extended power to detain contained in the Anti-terrorism, Crime and Security Act 2001 may be inconsistent with the obligations under Article 5(1) of the Convention. As indicated above, there may be cases where, notwithstanding a continuing intention to remove or deport a person who is being detained, it is not possible to say that 'action is being taken with a view to deportation' within the meaning of Article 5(1)(f) as interpreted by the Court in the *Chahal* case. To the extent, therefore, that the exercise of the extended power may be inconsistent with the United Kingdom's obligations under Article 5(1), the Government has decided to avail itself of the right of derogation conferred by Article 15(1) of the Convention and will continue to do so until further notice.

Strasbourg, 18 December 2001

### PART II
### RESERVATION

At the time of signing the present (First) Protocol, I declare that, in view of certain provisions of the Education Acts in the United Kingdom, the principle affirmed in the second sentence of Article 2 is accepted by the United Kingdom only so far as it is compatible with the provision of efficient instruction and training, and the avoidance of unreasonable public expenditure.

Dated 20 March 1952. Made by the United Kingdom Permanent Representative to the Council of Europe.

### SCHEDULE 4
### JUDICIAL PENSIONS

#### *Duty to make orders about pensions*

1.—(1)  The appropriate Minister must by order make provision with respect to pensions payable to or in respect of any holder of a judicial office who serves as an ECHR judge.

(2)  A pensions order must include such provision as the Minister making it considers is necessary to secure that—

(a)  an ECHR judge who was, immediately before his appointment as an ECHR judge, a member of a judicial pension scheme is entitled to remain as a member of that scheme;

(b)  the terms on which he remains a member of the scheme are those which would have been applicable had he not been appointed as an ECHR judge; and

(c)  entitlement to benefits payable in accordance with the scheme continues to be determined as if, while serving as an ECHR judge, his salary was that which would (but for section 18(4)) have been payable to him in respect of his continuing service as the holder of his judicial office.

#### *Contributions*

2.  A pensions order may, in particular, make provision—

(a)  for any contributions which are payable by a person who remains a member of a scheme as a result of the order, and which would otherwise be payable by deduction from his salary, to be made otherwise than by deduction from his salary as an ECHR judge; and

(b)  for such contributions to be collected in such manner as may be determined by the administrators of the scheme.

#### *Amendments of other enactments*

3.  A pensions order may amend any provision of, or made under, a pensions Act in such manner and to such extent as the Minister making the order considers necessary or expedient to ensure the proper administration of any scheme to which it relates.

*Definitions*

4.  In this Schedule—

    'appropriate Minister' means—

    (a) in relation to any judicial office whose jurisdiction is exercisable exclusively in relation to Scotland, the Secretary of State; and

    (b) otherwise, the Lord Chancellor;

    'ECHR judge' means the holder of a judicial office who is serving as a judge of the Court;

    'judicial pension scheme' means a scheme established by and in accordance with a pensions Act;

    'pensions Act means—

    (a) the County Courts Act (Northern Ireland) 1959;

    (b) the Sheriffs' Pensions (Scotland) Act 1961;

    (c) the Judicial Pensions Act 1981; or

    (d) the Judicial Pensions and Retirement Act 1993; and

    'pensions order' means an order made under paragraph 1.

# Appendix 7

# Best value performance indicators

## SCHEDULE 1

### CITIZEN FOCUS

| Indicator Number | Description of Indicator |
|---|---|
| PBV 1 | Quality of service surveys showing—<br>(a) percentage of the public satisfied with the time taken to answer a 999 call from a member of the public,<br>(b) percentage of the public satisfied with the arrival time of an officer dealing with an immediate response incident,<br>(c) percentage of the public satisfied with police action in response to 999 calls,<br>(d) percentage of victims satisfied with police initial response to a report of violent crime,<br>(e) percentage of victims satisfied with police initial response to a report of burglary to a dwelling,<br>(f) percentage of victims of road traffic collisions satisfied with the police service at the scene of the collision, and<br>(g) percentage of victims of racist incidents satisfied with the police service when dealing with the incident. |
| PBV 2 | Public reassurance and quality of life as identified by—<br>(a) percentage of residents surveyed who said that they feel 'fairly safe' or 'very safe' after dark whilst outside in the local authority area, and<br>(b) percentage of residents surveyed who said that they feel 'fairly safe' or 'very safe' during the day whilst outside in the local authority area. |

## SCHEDULE 2

### REDUCING CRIME

| Indicator number | Description of Indicator |
|---|---|
| PBV 3 | Using the British Crime Survey, the level of crime. |
| PBV 4 | (a) Percentage of domestic violence incidents where there was a power of arrest, in which an arrest was made relating to the incident, and<br>(b) of these, what percentage involved partner-on-partner violence. |

# SCHEDULE 3

## INVESTIGATING CRIME

| Indicator number | Description of Indicator |
|---|---|
| PBV 5 | (a) Number of Police and Criminal Evidence Act 1984 (PACE) stop/searches of minority ethnic persons per 1,000 population compared with the number of PACE stop/searches of white persons per 1,000 population; and<br>(b) percentage of PACE stop/searches of minority ethnic persons leading to arrest compared with the percentage of PACE stop/searches on white people leading to arrest. |
| PBV 6 | Percentage of recorded racially-aggravated crimes detected. |
| PBV 7 | (a) Number of offenders charged, reported for summons or cautioned for supply offences in respect of Class A drugs per 1,000 population; and<br>(b) of the overall figure of (a) above, the number which related to cocaine, and<br>(c) of the overall figure of (a) above, the number which related to heroin. |
| PBV 8 | (a) Working with CPS and the courts to narrow the justice gap by increasing the number of notifiable/recorded offences that result in a caution/conviction or taken into consideration by a court (TIC), and<br>(b) percentage of notifiable offences for which a person has been charged, reported for summons, cautioned or the offence has been TIC. |

# SCHEDULE 4

## PROMOTING SAFETY AND SECURITY

| Indicator number | Description of Indicator |
|---|---|
| PBV 9 | Using the British Crime Survey, the fear of crime. |
| PBV 10 | Using the British Crime Survey, feelings of public safety. |
| PBV 11 | Number of road traffic collisions involving death or serious injury per 1,000 population. |

# SCHEDULE 5

## HELPING THE PUBLIC

| Indicator number | Description of Indicator |
|---|---|
| PBV 12 | Percentage of occasions on which the police meet immigration service requests for assistance in the removal of immigration offenders. |
| PBV 13 | Percentage of police officers in operational posts. |

# SCHEDULE 6

## RESOURCE USAGE

| Indicator number | Description of Indicator |
|---|---|
| PBV 14 | Percentage of minority ethnic police officers in the force compared with the percentage of minority ethnic population of working age. |
| PBV 15 | Number of working days lost through sickness by (a) police officers and (b) civilian employees. |
| PBV 16 | Number of medical retirements of (a) police officers per 1,000 officers and (b) civilian employees per 1,000 employees. |

THE LOCAL GOVERNMENT (BEST VALUE) PERFORMANCE INDICATORS
AND PERFORMANCE STANDARDS ORDER 2003
(SI 2003 No. 530)

## SCHEDULE 2

## COMMUNITY SAFETY PERFORMANCE INDICATORS

| Indicator number | Description of Indicator |
| --- | --- |
| 1 | Domestic burglaries per 1,000 households and percentage detected. |
| 2 | Violent crimes per 1,000 population and percentage detected, broken down to show—<br>(i)   violent offences committed by a stranger per 1,000 population;<br>(ii)  violent offences committed in a public place per 1,000 population;<br>(iii) violent offences committed in connection with licensed premises per 1,000 population;<br>(iv) violent offences committed under the influence of an intoxicating substance per 1,000 population; and<br>(v)  in respect of local authorities and police authorities in Greater Manchester, Merseyside, Metropolitan, West Midlands and West Yorkshire, robberies per 1,000 population and percentages of these that are detected. |
| 3 | Vehicle crimes per 1,000 population and percentage detected. |
| 4 | The number of racial incidents recorded by the authority per 100,000 population. |
| 5 | The percentage of recorded racial incidents that resulted in further action |
| 6 | The number of domestic violence refuge places per 10,000 population which are provided or supported by the authority. |

THE LOCAL GOVERNMENT (BEST VALUE PERFORMANCE INDICATORS) (WALES)
ORDER 2002
(SI 2002 No. 757 W.80)

## SCHEDULE 12

## CROSS CUTTING COMMUNITY SAFETY INDICATORS

| Indicator number | Description of Indicator |
| --- | --- |
| NAWPI 12.1/BV 126 | Domestic burglaries per 1,000 households in the best value authority area. |
| NAWPI 12.2/BV 127 | Violent crimes per 1,000 population, of the best value authority:<br>(a) violent offences committed by a stranger;<br>(b) violent offences committed in a public place;<br>(c) violent offences committed in connection with licensed premises;<br>(d) violent offences committed under the influence. |
| NAWPI 12.3/BV 128 | Vehicles crimes per 1,000 population of the best value authority. |
| NAWPI 12.4/BV 173 | Has the best value authority established a corporate strategy to reduce crime and disorder in their area? If it hasn't, has the best value authority established a timetable for doing so? |

# Index